W9-CSR-032

MORE PRAISE FOR *ROOSEVELT SWEEPS NATION*

"It is a testament to David Pietrusza's mastery of storytelling—and his historian's knack for finding all the good quotes—that the reader goes through *Roosevelt Sweeps Nation* wondering if FDR is going to pull off an election victory that happened almost a century ago. What seems in hindsight to have been inevitable was anything but at the time, and the forces against the New Deal ran the gamut from the rarefied to the ridiculous."

—MICHAEL MALICE, author of *The New Right: A Journey to the Fringe of American Politics*; *Dear Reader: The Unauthorized Biography of Kim Jong Il*; and *The Anarchist Handbook*

"With eye-popping detail and a breezy, relatable style, David Pietrusza sweeps through the political dynamics and quirky personalities pressing on FDR's first re-election campaign in 1936. *Roosevelt Sweeps Nation* shows that victory was no guarantee against the 'isms' of socialism, fascism, and communism and the Great Depression's devastation when the American people were still hungry for happier days. Pietrusza not only captures a pivotal campaign, but he also captures an era."

—JANE HAMPTON COOK, author of *The Burning of the White House: James and Dolley Madison and the War of 1812*

"*Roosevelt Sweeps Nation* is a remarkable book! David Pietrusza is America's preeminent presidential historian, providing history lovers with a thoughtful, highly-entertaining portrait of Roosevelt's thrilling 1936 campaign and victory. Readers will enjoy Pietrusza's engaging narrative and crisp, thoughtful writing style. He does what all the great historians do—bring critical moments in history to life for a new generation of readers!"

—BOB BATCHELOR, cultural historian, and author of *The Bourbon King: The Life and Crimes of George Remus, Prohibition's Evil Genius*

"David Pietrusza is my favorite historian, and *Roosevelt Sweeps Nation* is Pietrusza at his best. Nobody can tell a better story than Pietrusza, who always shows you there's more to the story than you thought—that there is juicy stuff hidden in our history that nobody has bothered to suss out or that has long been forgotten. This is another page-turner you won't want to put down. At a time when Americans can use a reprieve from today's news, *Roosevelt Sweeps Nation* is just what the doctor ordered. And David Pietrusza is a national treasure."

—MATT LEWIS, Senior Columnist, *The Daily Beast*

"Who could spin an interesting tale out of an election in which one candidate gets 62 percent of the vote and carries all but two states? David Pietrusza, the author of some of the best campaign books ever written, renders FDR's 1936 landslide over Alf Landon into a page turner with an operatic cast of characters. Like his volumes on 1920, 1932, 1948, and 1960, Pietrusza has produced another masterpiece."

—JOHN BICKNELL, author of *America 1844: Religious Fervor, Westward Expansion and the Presidential Election That Transformed the Nation* and *Lincoln's Pathfinder: John C. Fremont and the Violent Election of 1856*

"The 1936 election was not just another FDR victory, but an important turning point in the nation's history. The story David Pietrusza tells is riveting and the cast of characters is fascinating. Franklin Roosevelt was the most skillful American politician of the 20th century, and this election was a decisive affirmation of his power and appeal."

—RON FAUCHEUX, political analyst

"I am always stoked when I learn that a new book will soon be released by David Pietrusza, who has written the best accounts of presidential elections. The former baseball writer turned top tier historian has hit home runs in his wonderful accounts of the elections of 1920, 1932, 1948, and 1960. His upcoming account of FDR's landslide victory of Kansas Governor Alf Landon (sorry for the spoiler) in the Depression era contest promises to explore an undiscovered gem of presidential election history."

—POTUSGeeks Blog

"Many of us think we know the 1936 election. Not so! In this gripping, rip-roaring tale, David Pietrusza shows just how varied and deeply divisive was the Roosevelt-Landon race in all its demagogic, demographic diversity. Readers will find the author's portrayal of his characters, well-known ones like Father Charles Coughlin, Jesse Owens, William Randolph Hearst, and Alice Roosevelt Longworth—but also less familiar people like the feather-wielding asylum escapee, Frank 'Woody' Hockaday—to add hugely to our understanding of the time and its divisions over the nascent New Deal. In this exhaustive but always energizing treatment, the parallels with today's polarizing politics, especially around issues related to race, elections, polling, the media, and the role of government, are all telling. Those who think our time's challenges are unprecedented will find this deep dive a bracing corrective."

—Katherine A. S. Sibley, Professor of History and Director of American Studies, Saint Joseph's University

"A superb addition to our understanding of presidential elections, written by one of our most gifted historians."

—Professor J. Edward Lee, Past President South Carolina Historical Association

Roosevelt Sweeps Nation

ALSO BY DAVID PIETRUSZA

Too Long Ago: A Childhood Memory. A Vanished World.

TR's Last War: Theodore Roosevelt, the Great War, and a Journey of Triumph and Tragedy

1932: The Rise of Hitler and FDR—Two Tales of Politics, Betrayal, and Unlikely Destiny

1948: Harry Truman's Improbable Victory and the Year that Transformed America

1960: LBJ vs JFK vs Nixon: The Epic Campaign That Forged Three Presidencies

1920: The Year of the Six Presidents

Rothstein: The Life, Times and Murder of the Criminal Genius Who Fixed the 1919 World Series

Judge and Jury: The Life and Times of Judge Kenesaw Mountain Landis

Silent Cal's Almanack: The Homespun Wit and Wisdom of Vermont's Calvin Coolidge

Calvin Coolidge: A Documentary Biography

Calvin Coolidge on the Founders: Reflections on the American Revolution & the Founding Fathers

Roosevelt Sweeps Nation

FDR's 1936 Landslide
&
the Triumph of the Liberal Ideal

DAVID PIETRUSZA

DIVERSION
BOOKS

Copyright © 2022 by David Pietrusza
All rights reserved, including the right to reproduce this book
or portions thereof in any form whatsoever.

For more information, email info@diversionbooks.com

Diversion Books
A division of Diversion Publishing Corp.
www.diversionbooks.com

First Diversion Books edition, September 2022

Hardcover ISBN: 978-1-635767-77-3
eBook ISBN: 978-1-635767-78-0

Printed in The United States of America

1 3 5 7 9 10 8 6 4 2

Library of Congress cataloging-in-publication data is available on file

CONTENTS

Cast of Characters vii

1 "Franklin is on his own now" 1
2 "Try something" 9
3 "One bullet" 33
4 "Five negroes on my place . . ." 51
5 "A great pity" 63
6 "Common, ignorant, and half-tight" 81
7 "Methodist picnic people" 103
8 "A voice made for promises" 122
9 "Shirt Mania" 142
10 "Heil Hearst" 161
11 "The Old Deal" 184
12 "Anno Domini Father Divine" 205
13 "Dumb-bells, freaks, rubes and hicks" 226
14 "It's myself" 247
15 "20,000 morons" 271
16 "Innocuous as a watermelon . . . boiled in a bathtub" 294
17 "Keep on running" 320
18 "The very essence of un-Americanism" 336
19 "I welcome their hatred" 349
20 "Send for a priest" 387

Acknowledgments 427
Bibliography 429
Sources 453
Index 509
About the Author 520

CAST OF CHARACTERS

Charles Jasper Bell (1885–1978)—Kansas City Democratic congressman. Chair of the special committee probing the Townsend Plan.

Mary Jane McLeod Bethune (1875–1955)—Director of the National Youth Administration's Division of Negro Affairs. Friend of Eleanor Roosevelt. A key member of FDR's "Black Cabinet."

William Edgar "The Lion of Idaho" Borah (1865–1940)—Maverick GOP Idaho US senator. An isolationist progressive. Running for 1936's GOP presidential nomination. "Borah is, first and foremost, a prima donna," maintains columnist Nicholas Roosevelt; "he has all of the independence of spirit of a leading lady—and most of her inconsistencies and unreasonableness."

Heywood Campbell Broun Jr. (1888–1939)—Left-wing Scripps-Howard syndicated columnist. Former Socialist Party congressional nominee. Founder of the newly formed Newspaper Guild. Broun, says H. L. Mencken, is "by nature a portly, amiable, and somewhat frumpy fellow, and if the messianic delusion had not fetched him he would have spent his old age going to baseball games, mooning over his fan mail, and quietly scratching himself."

Earl Russell "The Bookkeeper" Browder (1891–1973)—Kansas-born Communist Party presidential nominee. Stalin's servile mouthpiece as head of the CPUSA. "If one is not interested in directives from Moscow," Browder scolds party leadership, "that only means that he is not interested in building socialism at all."

William Christian "Bill Buddha" Bullitt Jr. (1891–1967)—FDR's once-radical, now increasingly anti-Communist ambassador to Moscow. Briefly a reelection campaign speechwriter.

Robert Earl Clements (1894–1979)—Amarillo-born, Long Beach, California real estate man. Co-founder and organizing mastermind of the Townsend plan. "Many of our critics," Clements admits, "seek to dismiss our proposal with a wave of the hand as being impossible and preposterous."

Edmond David Coblentz (1882–1959)—Longtime Hearst editor. Publisher of Hearst's *New York American.* "Never a day passes that the Radicals do not hold a meeting," Coblentz warns his boss; "not [only] in Union Square, but in school houses, meeting halls, etc., and ask for a boycott of our papers. They are working among the young, the Jews and the parent teachers' organizations."

Thomas Gardiner "Tommy the Cork" Corcoran (1900–1981)—Youthful New Deal attorney. Felix Frankfurter protégé. FDR speechwriter. A recent and rising member of his inner circle. Author of FDR's ringing phrase "rendezvous with destiny." Arthur Krock describes Corcoran as "an able, brilliant young Harvard man, who thinks along the same lines as another Harvard man [FDR]." Henry Morgenthau derides him as "an intellectual crook . . . I would not trust him as far as I could see him."

Father Charles Edward "The Radio Priest" Coughlin (1891–1979)—Canadian-born Royal Oak, Michigan Catholic priest. Wildly popular radical radio commentator. Pro-FDR in 1932; now virulently opposed to him. "We were supposed to be partners," moans Coughlin. "He said he would rely on me. . . . But he was a liar. He just used me."

James Michael "The Mayor of the Poor" Curley (1874–1958)—Controversial Democratic Massachusetts governor; former Boston mayor. Angling for VP in 1936. US Senate candidate.

Marion Cecilia Davies (née Marion Cecilia Elizabeth Douras) (1897–1961)—Brooklyn-born showgirl and actress. William Randolph Hearst's longtime mistress. Disappointed in her hopes to meet Hitler. "He looked like Chaplin," she writes, "I imagined. Possibly worse."

Lester Jesse "L. J." or "Dick" Dickinson (1873–1968)—Nebraska US senator. The very darkest of 1936's GOP dark horses.

Reverend Major Jealous Divine ("Father Divine") (real name, perhaps, George Baker) (c. 1876–1965)—Diminutive Harlem-based cult leader who modestly claims to be God. Pro-Hoover in 1932. Working with the Communists in 1936. "I give everything," he boasts to his devotees, "because I am omnipotent. I give you plenty of good food, clothes, shelter, work. And you are fat and merry."

Thomas Frederick Dixon Jr. (1864–1946)—Best-selling author of *The Clansman*, the basis for D. W. Griffith's *The Birth of a Nation*. For FDR in 1932. A speaker at Gene Talmadge's 1936 anti-FDR Macon convention. Eventually for Landon. "I think this New Deal is all wrong," Dixon admits; "I am full of fire and pizen."

Lewis Williams Douglas (1894–1974)—FDR's disgruntled first budget director. To Douglas, Roosevelt's 1933 junking of the gold standard marks "the end of western civilization."

David Dubinsky (née David Isaac Dobnievski) (1892–1982)—Diminutive Russian-born leader of the International Ladies Garment Union. In 1936, he bolts the Socialist Party to help found New York State's pro-FDR American Labor Party. Says Dubinsky: "I can no longer be identified with a party which is making alliances with Communists."

Irénée (1876–1963), Lammot II (1880–1952), and Pierre Samuel (1870–1954) du Pont—The du Pont brothers. Leading lights of E. I. du Pont de Nemours and Company—and of the anti-FDR American Liberty League.

Stephen Tyree "Steve the Earl" Early (1889–1951)—FDR's Virginia-born press secretary. A veteran of his 1920 campaign. Former Paramount newsreel head.

James Aloysius "Big Jim" Farley (1888–1976)—Democratic National Chairman. FDR's patronage-dispensing postmaster general. "President Roosevelt," Farley dares forecast, "will carry every state except Maine and Vermont."

Hamilton Stuyvesant Fish (aka Hamilton Fish III or Hamilton Fish Jr.) (1888–1991)—FDR's GOP congressman. Bill Borah campaign manager.

James William "Rabbit" Ford (1893–1957)—Harlem Communist leader and his party's three-time vice presidential nominee. African American. If Ford speaks at Uniontown, Pennsylvania, the local Ku Klux Klan supposedly warns, its streets will "ooze with nigger blood."

Wilfred John Funk (1883–1965)—Editor of the *Literary Digest.* "We make no claim to infallibility," Funk sheepishly admits of the magazine's once-vaunted presidential straw poll.

Archbishop Michael James Gallagher (1866–1937)—Catholic Archbishop of Detroit. Father Coughlin's ardent defender. "It's the voice of God that comes to you from the great orator from Royal Oak," exclaims Gallagher, "Rally round it."

Dr. George Horace Gallup (1901–1984)—Unlike the rival *Literary Digest* poll, Gallup's "scientific" American Institute of Public Opinion ultimately predicts FDR's victory. "The essential requirement," Gallup explains, "is not how many people are polled, but what kind of people—what classes, what ages, what economic groups."

John Nance "Cactus Jack" Garner III (1868–1967)—Former Speaker of the House of Representatives. FDR's conservative vice president. He was, as one journalist noted, "as out of place in the New Deal as a dead mouse in a mince pie."

Sufi Abdul ("The Black Hitler of Harlem") Hamid (né Eugene Brown) (1903–1938)—Openly anti-Semitic leader of Harlem commercial boycotts.

John Daniel Miller Hamilton (1892–1973)—A youthful conservative veteran of Kansas GOP politics. Alf Landon's campaign manager and choice for Republican national chairman. Hamilton publicly predicts: "The absolute minimum is 310 [electoral] votes for [Landon] and anything in excess of that would be in no way surprising." He doesn't believe it.

William Randolph "The Chief" Hearst (1863–1951)—Powerful—but widely hated—newspaper and magazine baron. He blasts FDR's "Raw Deal." "Professionally, Hearst is a form of poison," concludes progressive journalist William Allen White. "Politically, he has degenerated into a form of suicide. Whoever ties up with him begins to smell of lilies and attract the undertaker."

Dr. Stanley Hoflund High (1895–1961)—Congregationalist minister. NBC commentator on religious news. Head of FDR's vote-getting "Good Neighbor League."

Frank "Woody" Hockaday (aka "Chief Pow-Wow") (1884–1947)—Deranged distributor of feathers for peace. Assailant of Father Coughlin. "People think I'm a nut," admits Hockaday. "That's why I get away with this stuff."

Herbert Clark "The Chief" Hoover (1874–1964)—Former commerce secretary and president. Even in 1932, publisher Roy Howard viewed him as "a pitiable spectacle—a man hopelessly miscast for his job yet giving his life to it and eating his heart out with malice toward all and charity toward none—except himself." Angling for revenge—and to run again—in 1936.

Harry Lloyd "Harry the Hop" Hopkins (1890–1946)—Former New York social worker. Controversial head of the New Deal's Federal Emergency Relief Administration (FERA) and Works Progress Administration (WPA). Among FDR's most intimate confidants. "The trouble with Harry," assessed pro–New Deal *Collier's* Washington staff writer George Creel, ". . . was that he had never spent his own money."

Perry Wilbon Howard II (1877–1961)—Veteran African-American GOP committeeman from Mississippi.

Louis McHenry "Felix the Cat" Howe (1871–1936)—FDR's longtime top political aide. Long ailing, he expires just as 1936's campaign commences. Howe's death, recalls Eleanor, "was one of the greatest losses my husband sustained."

Emil Edward Hurja (1892–1953)—Chief pollster and executive director for the Democratic National Committee. Dispenser of Democratic patronage. Inventor of the "tracking poll."

Harold LeClair "The Old Curmudgeon" Ickes (1874–1952)—FDR's acerbic Secretary of the Interior. Former Bull Moose Republican. Ickes, H. L. Mencken avers, "was a professional public nuisance in Chicago."

Hugh Samuel "Old Iron Pants" Johnson (1882–1942)—Controversial former head of FDR's National Recovery Administration. "If present trends continue," Johnson predicts in June 1936, "the election is lost to the New Deal."

Joseph Patrick Kennedy Sr. (1888–1969)—Wall Street speculator. Womanizing Hollywood mogul. First head of FDR's Securities and Exchange Commission. The Catholic Kennedy unsuccessfully toils to soften Father Coughlin's growing anti–New Deal animus. In his ghost-written pro-FDR tome, *I'm for Roosevelt*, Joe declares, "I have no political ambitions for myself or for my children."

Frank Richardson Kent (1877–1958)—*Baltimore Sun* syndicated columnist. A conservative.

John Henry "The Prince of the Pines" Kirby (1860–1940)—Once-wealthy Texas lumberman. Chairman of the anti–New Deal Southern Committee to Uphold the Constitution. Kirby boosts Georgia governor Gene Talmadge as "a plumed knight on an errand for the republic, refusing to bend his knee . . . for Federal Gold."

Col. William Franklin "Frank" Knox (1874–1944)—Publisher of the *Chicago Daily News*. A candidate for the 1936 GOP nod. Landon's frenzied and far-too-voluble running-mate. "Knox," complains Henry Ford, "won't keep his mouth shut."

Arthur Bernard Krock (1886–1974)—Influential *New York Times* Washington correspondent and columnist. Joe Kennedy's ghostwriter. Kennedy "was amoral . . ," recalled Krock. "He probably never liked me at all but found me useful."

Fritz Julius Kuhn (1896–1951)—Munich-born Führer of the newly formed German-American Bund. His goal: to "combat the Moscow-directed madness of the Red world menace and its Jewish bacillus-carriers."

Fiorello Henry "The Little Flower" La Guardia (1882–1947)—Republican-Fusion mayor of New York. A progressive FDR ally. "He comes to Washington and tells me a sad story," FDR recalls. "The tears run down my cheeks and the tears run down his cheeks and the first thing I know, he has wangled another fifty million dollars."

Alfred Mossman "The Kansas Coolidge" Landon (1887–1987)—Kansas oilman and GOP governor. A former "Bull Moose" progressive. The party's 1936 standard-bearer. He blandly offers such wisdom as "Wherever I have gone in this country, I have found Americans."

Theo Cobb Landon (1898–1996)—Alf Landon's second wife. "I thought," she recalls of meeting her future husband, "he was an insurance salesman when he first telephoned."

Marguerite Alice "Missy" LeHand (1898–1944)—FDR's statuesque blue-eyed, silver-haired, intensely devoted, and well-liked private secretary.

William Frederick "Liberty Bill" Lemke (1878–1950)—Yale-educated populist Republican North Dakota congressman. Presidential nominee of the National Union Party. "A complete composite of a hayseed," sneers Gerald L. K. Smith. "He wore a cap. He was not eloquent and all he could talk about was money and agriculture."

John Llewellyn Lewis (1880–1969)—Combative United Mine Workers (UMW) president. Nominally a Republican. FDR's major source of campaign funds in 1936. "The interests supporting the Republican Party seek a centralized control in the hands of a few, . . ." Lewis asserts. "Their plans are equivalent to setting up a Fascist state."

Walter William Liggett (1886–1935)—Crusading Minnesota journalist. Critic of Governor Floyd Olson ("a damned sight more of a racketeer than he is a radical"). Rubbed out gangland-style.

Walter Lippmann (1889–1974)—Influential syndicated columnist. Wary of Roosevelt's "unreal and unnecessary divisions . . . at a time when solidarity and union are of the utmost importance."

Huey Pierce "The Kingfish" Long Jr. (1893–1935)—Rabble-rousing Democratic US senator and former governor from Louisiana. Founder of a huge national network of "Share Our Wealth" clubs, he plots to challenge FDR in 1936. Accused of widespread graft in his highway program, he responds, "We got the roads in Louisiana, haven't we? In some states they only have the graft." Assassinated in 1935.

Alice Lee "Princess Alice" Roosevelt Longworth (1884–1980)—Theodore Roosevelt's very independent firstborn child. Eleanor's first cousin. The mother of Senator Borah's illegitimate daughter, Paulina. Widow of Speaker of the House Nick Longworth. She derides FDR as "one-third mush and two-thirds Eleanor."

Joe "The Brown Bomber" Louis (née Joseph Louis Barrow) (1914–1981)—World heavyweight boxing champion. Campaigning for FDR.

Edward John "Pirate Jack" Margett (aka Edward John Marquette) (1889–1954)—French-born former Seattle police officer, nightclub owner, and San Francisco furniture dealer. Former bootlegger and alleged "dope peddler." Dr. Townsend praises Margett as among his "chief right hand men."

Louis Burt Mayer (née Lazar Meir) (1884–1957)—Head of Hollywood's Metro-Goldwyn-Mayer studios. Friend of Hearst and Hoover. A staunch Republican—up to a point.

Elizabeth "Lizzie" Stanfield McDuffie (1881–1960)—The Roosevelts' loyal maid—and energetic African-American campaign surrogate. "Lizzie," Eleanor informs her, "I believe the Negro race has many things to contribute to our nation. Certain things, such as song and rhythm, come to them naturally, whereas we have to work for those accomplishments."

Marvin Hunter McIntyre (1878–1943)—FDR's Kentucky-born chief of presidential appointments. A veteran of FDR's Navy Department and 1920 campaign days.

Henry Louis "The Sage of Baltimore" Mencken (1880–1956)—Iconoclastic *Baltimore Sun* columnist. An unlikely Landon supporter. "There was a time when the Republicans were scouring the country for a behemoth to pit against [Roosevelt]," opines Mencken. "Now they begin to grasp the fact that, if they can beat him at all, which seems most likely, they can best him with a Chinaman, or even a Republican."

Charles "Charlie the Mike" Michelson (1869–1948)—Highly skilled Democratic National Committee publicity director. In June, he nervously predicts the loss of "nearly, if not quite, one hundred [House] seats."

Robert Berkeley "Fighting Bob" Minor (1884–1952)—CPUSA candidate for New York governor. Formerly among the most prominent political cartoonists in America. Now merely "a political hack."

Raymond Charles Moley (1886–1975)—Former Columbia University law professor. Charter member of FDR's famed "Brain Trust." Now distrustful of Franklin's anti-business sentiment. Roosevelt "was turning into a demagogue," recalled Moley, ". . . out-Huey Longing Huey Long."

Henry "Henny-Penny" or "Henry the Morgue" Morgenthau Jr. (1891–1967)—FDR's Hyde Park neighbor, friend, and Secretary of the Treasury. "Never let your left hand," FDR informs Morgenthau regarding his tactics, "know what your right hand is doing."

Robert Moses (1888–1981)—New York City Triborough Bridge and Tunnel Authority chairman and its parks commissioner. Hated by FDR—and the feeling is mutual. "I don't trust him," says Moses of FDR; "I don't like him."

Vance Muse (1890–1950)—Pioneer of Right-to-Work legislation. General manager of John Henry Kirby's Southern Committee to Uphold the Constitution. "I am a Southerner," Muse informs Hugo Black's senate committee, "and I am for white supremacy."

Thomas Charles "Hamburger Tom" O'Brien (1887–1951)—Former Boston district attorney. Dual vice presidential and US Senate nominee of the National Union Party. Of his new party's efforts, he vows: "A ruthless autocracy nourished by greed and controlled by wealth will be wiped out forever."

John Joseph O'Connor (1885–1960)—Tammany Democratic congressman and chairman of the powerful House Rules Committee. Brother of FDR's former law partner Basil "Doc" O'Connor. "If you will please come to Washington," he threatens Father Coughlin, "I shall guarantee to kick you all the way from the capitol to the White House."

Floyd Bjørnstjerne Olson (1891–1936)—Minnesota's radical Farmer-Labor Party governor. Did stomach cancer prevent his left-wing third-party challenge? "I am what I want to be—" he exclaims; "I am a radical."

James Cleveland "Jesse" Owens (1913–1980)—Four-time 1936 Olympic gold-medal winner. "The World's Fastest Human." Snubbed by FDR. Says Owens: "After seeing the oppression [of] dictatorship in Europe, I welcome the opportunity to work for Governor Landon [who] will save us from a dictatorship here."

Eleanor Josephine Medill "Cissy" Patterson, Countess Gizycki (1881–1948)—Editor of Hearst's *Washington Herald*. Sister of the *New York Daily News*'s publisher Joseph Medill Patterson. Cousin of the *Chicago Tribune*'s Robert McCormick. "Fear is depressing industry," she openly chides FDR. "With due respect, you should concede the obvious. This fear is fear of you."

Francis James Westbrook Pegler (1894–1969)—Left-leaning Scripps-Howard chain syndicated columnist. "Mr. Landon," Pegler advises, "ought to get hot."

Fannie Coralie "Frances" Perkins (1880–1965)—FDR's Secretary of Labor. Troubled by FDR's increasingly combative rhetoric.

John Jakob "Raskal" Raskob (1879–1950)—Wealthy former Democratic national chairman. Close friend to Al Smith. A founder of the well-heeled anti-FDR Liberty League—a "very definite organization . . . for educating the people to the value of encouraging people to work; encouraging people to get rich."

Milo Reno (1866–1936)—Tousle-haired septuagenarian Iowa populist. Briefly a Church of Christ minister. For FDR in 1932. Spellbinding leader of the radical Farmers' Holiday Association opposing farm foreclosures—often by violent means. Anti-AAA (Agricultural Adjustment Agency).

Joseph Taylor Robinson (1872–1937)—Arkansas Democrat. Al Smith's 1928 running mate. Effective US Senate Majority Leader. Conservative by nature but loyal to FDR: "So long as they [The New Dealers] fought the money power and the big industries—so long as they were pro-farmer and did not stir up the niggers—he was with them."

Anna Eleanor Roosevelt Roosevelt (1884–1962)—First Lady of the United States. Author of the Scripps-Howard syndicated newspaper column "My Day." Champion of the underprivileged. "I realize more & more that F.D.R. is a great man, & he is nice to me but as a person," she confides, "I'm a stranger & I don't want to be anything else."

Elliott Roosevelt (1910–1990)—FDR's freewheeling son. His father's son but W. R. Hearst's employee. Elliott's shady business dealings with the Soviets emerge only in October 1936.

Franklin Delano Roosevelt (1882–1945)—Patrician president of the United States. "There's one issue in this campaign," FDR lectures apostate Brain Truster Ray Moley. "It's myself, and people must be either for me or against me."

James "Jay the Rose" Roosevelt II (1907–1991)—FDR's oldest son. A close associate of James M. Curley and Joseph P. Kennedy. His father's literal strong right arm in assisting his polio-hobbled public appearances.

Nicholas Roosevelt (1893–1982)—Syndicated columnist. A cousin to both Franklin and Eleanor Roosevelt. Republican.

Sara Ann Delano Roosevelt (1854–1941)—FDR's doting mother. "She was," evaluates one newsman, "even more of a snob than her son."

Samuel Irving "Sammy the Rose" Rosenman (1896–1973)—FDR's veteran speechwriter. New York State Supreme Court justice. Jumpy about FDR's 1936 chances. "Lots of things can happen before November," Franklin soothes him. "Tides turn in politics; the sentiment of the voters changes very quickly."

Albert Cabell Ritchie (1876–1936)—Former long-serving Democratic Maryland governor. A Liberty League conservative. Will he challenge FDR in 1936? "I for one," he states, "do not believe in fundamental or revolutionary changes."

Jouett Shouse (1879–1968)—Former Kansas congressman and chairman of the executive committee of the Democratic National Committee.

President of the American Liberty League. The League "certainly isn't anti-New Deal." he initially protests. Few believe him.

Alfred Emanuel "The Happy Warrior" Smith (1873–1944)—Former governor of New York and 1928's Democratic presidential nominee. Opposed to FDR. "There can be only one Capital—Washington or Moscow," Smith warns, ". . . only one atmosphere of government, the clear, pure, fresh air of free America, or the foul breath of Communistic Russia."

Gerald Lyman Kenneth Smith (1898–1976)—Former Shreveport Disciples of Christ minister. Fanatical acolyte of Huey Long. A powerful orator in his own right—"the greatest rabble-rouser since Peter the Hermit," says H. L. Mencken. Ally of Dr. Townsend. A key to Father Coughlin's new National Union Party. "I am a symbol," Smith boasts, ". . . of a state of mind. When politicians and practitioners on the gullibility of the population overplay their hand, certain nerve centers in the national population begin to scream—and I am one of the yellers."

Gomer Griffith Smith (1896–1953)—Townsend movement vice president and a failed US Oklahoma Senate hopeful. Opposed to the Lemke candidacy. FDR, proclaims the partially Cherokee Smith, is a "church-going, Bible-reading, God-fearing, golden-hearted man who has saved the country from Communism."

Margaret Lynch "Daisy" or "Cousin Daisy" Suckley (1891–1991)—Eleanor's Hudson Valley "prim spinster" fourth cousin. FDR's sixth cousin—and, perhaps, his most trusted confidante. "The President is a man—*mentally, physically & spiritually,*" Daisy writes to her diary. "What more can I say."

Mark Sullivan (1874–1952)—*New York Herald Tribune* syndicated columnist. A Republican.

Eugene "The Wild Man from Sugar Creek" Talmadge (1884–1946)—Democratic governor of Georgia. Mulling a challenge to FDR. Talmadge, sneers Harold Ickes, looks "more like a rat than any other human being that I know . . . with all of the mean, poisonous and treacherous characteristics of that rodent."

Norman Mattoon Thomas (1884–1968)—Former Presbyterian minister. Perennial—almost obsessive—Socialist Party candidate for office. Reluctantly running for president again in 1936. "Mr. Roosevelt," jibes Thomas, "did not carry out the Socialist platform, unless he carried it out on a stretcher."

Dr. Francis Everett "Old Doc" Townsend (1867–1960)—Long Beach, California, physician. Promoter of California's old-age pension scheme, the "Townsend Plan." Uncertain supporter of the National Union Party. "Just think," he marvels after viewing the Lincoln Monument. "They built that . . . because he freed four million slaves. Wonder what they will do for me after I've liberated all mankind."

Rexford Guy "The Sweetheart of the Regimenters" Tugwell (1891–1979)—Columbia University agricultural expert. Among the more radical "Brain Trusters." "It has already been suggested that business will logically be required to disappear," he has written. "This is not an overstatement for the sake of emphasis; it is literally meant."

Arthur Hendrick Vandenberg (1884–1951)—Former Grand Rapids, Michigan, newspaper editor. US senator. Dark-horse GOP presidential aspirant. Widely mocked as "the only Senator who can strut sitting down." Described as looking and acting "more like a strutting, orating Claghornesque caricature than any Northerner in history."

Robert Lee Vann (1879–1940)—Editor of the African-American *Pittsburgh Courier*. "My friends," Vann advised fellow Blacks in 1932, "go turn Lincoln's picture to the wall. That debt has been paid in full."

James Wolcott Wadsworth Jr. (1877–1952)—Upstate New York GOP congressman. Former US senator. A "wet." Target of the Black Committee. Active Liberty Leaguer.

Robert Ferdinand Wagner Sr. (1877–1953)—Prussian-born New York US senator. Like Al Smith, a product of Tammany. Author of the Social Security Act, the Wagner Labor Relations Act, and the ill-fated Costigan-Wagner Anti-Lynching Act.

Henry Agard Wallace (1888–1965)—FDR's Secretary of Agriculture. Originally a progressive Republican. Wallace, thought Louis McHenry Howe, was "crazy but he gets his way."

Earl Warren (1891–1974)—Alameda County, California, district attorney and California Republican chairman. His state's favorite son.

Dr. Carl Austin Weiss Sr. (1906–1935)—Baton Rouge eye specialist. Huey Long's assassin. "Weiss, Dr. Weiss," the wounded Long mutters. "What did he want to shoot me for?"

Burton Kendall Wheeler (1882–1975)—Montana US senator. A progressive Democrat. Co-sponsor of 1935's Public Utility Holding Company Act. An early Roosevelt booster but still friendly with Huey Long. "If [Long] is a crook," Wheeler counsels FDR, "he's too smart for you to catch him."

Walter Francis White (1893–1955)—Light-skinned, blue-eyed African-American executive secretary of the NAACP. Lobbying FDR for a federal anti-lynching bill.

William Allen "The Sage of Emporia" White (1868–1944)—Nationally famed Emporia, Kansas, newspaper editor. Old-time TR progressive. Early—but unfaithful—ally of Landon. White, jibes FDR, "is a very old friend of mine . . . a good friend of mine three and a half years out of every four."

Rev. Clinton L. "The Liberal Voice of Los Angeles" Wunder (1892–1975)—Former Baptist minister. Townsend Plan organizer and speaker. "[A] converted pocketbook," he writes, "is the most certain proof of a converted soul. The use of money is the acid test of religion. We have a right to judge a man's Christianity by his gifts. . . . Ten percent of one's income is a good beginning."

· 1 ·

"Franklin is on his own now"

Franklin Roosevelt was alone at a very bad time.

Yes, there was Eleanor. There was, despite everything, *always* Eleanor. But their personal relationship had long lain in tatters—still wounded and bleeding from Franklin's Great War tryst with her too-charming former social secretary Lucy Mercer.

Mr. and Mrs. Franklin Delano Roosevelt remained a *political* team—but just barely. In 1928, when Franklin had narrowly stormed into New York's governor's mansion, Eleanor coldly *and publicly* proclaimed her decided indifference to his triumph—"I don't care"—and that hostility never fully vanished. "[W]hen Eleanor was around you could always feel tension of a certain kind," recalled FDR speechwriter Sam Rosenman. The Roosevelts' eldest son, James, phrased it more harshly, labeling their marriage "an armed truce that endured until the day [Franklin] died" and recalling several instances when his father literally "held out his arms to mother and she flatly refused to enter his embrace."

One evening, at the White House, in late April 1935, Eleanor casually confessed—to James Roosevelt and to her mother-in-law, Sara Delano Roosevelt—that her wifely heart would *not* fall to pieces if defeat visited her husband in 1936. When Eleanor departed the room, Sara painfully queried James: "Do you think [your] Mother would do anything to defeat Father? Is that why she stays in politics, just to hurt his chances of re-election?"

Decades later, Eleanor's devoted radio and television agent, Thomas Stix, sheepishly confessed to his client that he had voted for Socialist Norman Thomas in 1932—and not for her deceased spouse. "So would I," she answered Stix, "if I had not been married to Franklin."

Mother Sara, of course, was different. She remained ever-loyal, ever-doting. But arch-aristocrat and arch-reactionary that she was (not the sort at all to vote Socialist), she was hardly of value as her son's increasingly liberal New Deal tottered on the brink.

Brain Trusters like Rex Tugwell and Democratic Party operatives like Jim Farley and functionaries like Harry Hopkins all stood by, eager to abet Franklin's reelection. Yet, might they storm away as had so many other old "friends"? Like Al Smith? Father Coughlin? William Randolph Hearst? Huey Long?

Beyond the brains and bosses and bigwigs still supporting Franklin were hosts of supporters spanning the political spectrum—from old-line Republican progressives like cabinet members Harold Ickes and Henry Wallace to Democratic moneymen like Joe Kennedy, Bernard Baruch, and Hugh Johnson. But, again, might they, too, desert if fate—and public opinion—spurned Franklin?

Politics can be cruel.

Even for a Roosevelt.

There remained one man whose dog-like loyalty Roosevelt never questioned—Louis McHenry Howe. Longtime adviser. Close friend. Brutally frank confidant. The churlish little man so many said had "*made*" Franklin Delano Roosevelt. Louis had fought alongside FDR almost from the start, from Franklin's 1912 typhoid-plagued state senate reelection campaign, to their years together at Woodrow Wilson's Navy Department, to FDR's ill-fated 1920 vice presidential run, to his valiant fight against polio. Howe proved invaluable when Franklin squeaked into the Governor's Mansion. Four years later, Louis finally anointed his idol as president—slaving sixteen-hour days in the bargain, his spindly, barely five-foot-tall frame plummeting from 130 to 98 pounds.

Yes, even in what passed for good health, this gnome-like, hard-bitten ex-newspaperman looked mummified. In January 1934, the now-sixty-four-year-old Howe fell seriously ill. By March 1935, bronchitis had weakened him further. Relying on an oxygen tent in his filthy, littered, liquor-bottle-strewn, Eleanor-portrait-festooned third-floor White House suite, he nonetheless demanded to be rolled around White House corridors in one of Franklin's makeshift wheelchairs—gasping for breath but still furiously chain-smoking on his beloved Sweet Caporals.

In April 1935, FDR summoned *Liberty* magazine editor Fulton Oursler to the White House for an overnight stay. "I had never seen such a face outside of a grave, . . ." a shocked Oursler wrote of Howe. "Nothing could have prepared me for this sight. . . . His face looked like a mask molded in yellow clay by a child with clumsy fingers. There were lumps and protuberances in unlikely places where part of the skin seemed to have been peeled away. The little man's eyelids seem too heavy to lift, but underneath those weary sheaths his eyes were bright and gleaming. There was a brown spot under one eye and a red spot under the other. He looked like a gargoyle on its last day alive."

Soon, Howe lapsed into a coma. Doctors prepared FDR for the worst. Franklin canceled events. He readied plans for Howe's White House funeral and for his funeral train back to Massachusetts.

Miraculously, Howe awoke, growling, "Why in Hell doesn't somebody give me a cigarette?"

Another downturn struck. As they often do. In late August 1935, Howe was transferred to Bethesda Naval Hospital. At Bethesda, Howe remained abed, still struggling to breathe, still puffing like a chimney upon his Sweet Caporals. He demanded a telephone—to pepper FDR (and everyone else) with ideas. Franklin said no—then capitulated, but only if Louis stuck to phoning him during business hours. To the obsessive Howe, the middle of the night was business hours.

Howe was never much to look at. At Bethesda, he looked worse, sporting an unkempt Vandyke beard, in rough imitation of his late bewhiskered father. Lying abed in normal fashion only aggravated his painful heart condition, so Howe balanced himself upon his knees and elbows, reminding FDR of a goat and causing Franklin to "Baa" at him. The most partisan Republican could never have imagined this scene.

But while Louis Howe was neither handsome nor healthy, it must also be admitted that he was also . . . neither normally pleasant nor particularly hygienic. *But* he was brilliant and canny and loyal; and, as much as the Sphinx-like, calculating FDR might become a real friend to anyone, he became one to Louis.

Which he rarely showed.

Even now.

"The way we understood it in the servants' quarters," recollected mixed-race White House maid Lillian Rogers Parks (herself a crutch-bound polio victim), "FDR could not stand the pain of seeing people close to him slipping away and hid from them, letting Eleanor handle whatever needed handling. But it didn't mean he cared less. He cared too much."

As Eleanor herself once observed, her husband was "not one to express his feelings very much," surprisingly adding, "I think it is a form of shyness."

Others saw it far differently—saw a much darker, essentially emptier side. By July 1941, Harold Ickes had reached a far different conclusion, writing in his diary that "despite his very pleasant and friendly personality, [FDR] is cold as ice inside. He has certain conventional family affections for his children and probably for Missy LeHand and Harry Hopkins, but nothing else. Missy, who has been desperately ill for several weeks [since June 27, when she suffered what turned out to be a permanently debilitating stroke], might pass out of his life and he would miss her. The same might be true as to Harry, but I doubt whether he would miss either of them greatly or for a long period." Decades later, Franklin's economic adviser, Eliot Janeway, mused to historian Doris Kearns Goodwin that "Roosevelt had absolutely no moral reaction to Missy's tragedy. It seemed only that he resented her for getting sick and leaving him in the lurch. This was proof that he had ceased to be a person; he was simply the president. If something was good for him as president, it was good; if it had no function for him as president, it didn't exist."

Which was *not*, of course, the way Louis McHenry Howe felt about Franklin. His banter toward his boss might be blunt, his advice blunter, yet *everyone* knew Louis McHenry Howe *adored* Franklin Delano Roosevelt. "I have been as close to Franklin as a valet," he gushed in 1935, "and he is still a hero to me."

As for Eleanor, well, Louis was *her* hero. When few—including Franklin—paid much attention to her, Louis Howe was the singular exception, shaping her political thought, shepherding a wounded ugly duckling's public persona. Louis McHenry Howe not only "made" Franklin Roosevelt; he created Eleanor as well. Now, she watched over her counselor's sickbed, monitored his doctors' visits and his diet; and when it was time to transport him to Bethesda, it was she who drove him there in her private limousine. Virtually each day the peripatetic E. R. remained in Washington, she visited her friend's bedside. It was Eleanor—not Louis's short, dowdy, and often absent widow—who finally planned each detail of his White House funeral.

"He always wanted to 'make' me President," Eleanor once privately confided in a letter, "when F.D.R. was thro' & insisted he could do it. You see he was interested in his power to create personages more than in a person, tho' *I think he probably cared for me as a person as much as he cared for anyone & more than anyone else has!*" (Emphasis added)

That Eleanor wrote this to Lorena Hickok says much.

On Easter Sunday afternoon, April 12, 1936, Franklin and Eleanor visited Howe for the last time. Six days later, FDR took a late afternoon White House meeting with Joe Kennedy before traveling to the nearby Willard Hotel for that spring's Gridiron Club dinner. He received the news on returning home: Louis McHenry Howe was dead. "I think," Eleanor wrote, "it was one of the greatest losses my husband sustained."

Franklin needed Louis Howe. The fabric of his New Deal was fast unraveling. A hostile Supreme Court had already dismantled its two most controversial linchpins—the National Recovery Administration (NRA), and the Agricultural Adjustment Agency (AAA). The Court's narrow conservative majority stood poised to demolish still more. The Democratic-dominated US Senate had rejected his bid for World Court membership. It vetoed his plan for a cross-Florida barge canal, a $200 million boondoggle.

Republicans, massively repudiated in both 1932 and 1934, plotted their grand comeback. Franklin's most potent press ally four years previously—press baron William Randolph Hearst—now flayed him with a vengeance. The Democratic Party's sullen anti–New Deal wing—Al Smith and friends—angrily jumped ship. "The young brain trusters," jibed Smith, "caught the Socialists in swimming and ran away with their clothes."

Radicalism raged on every street corner—unsatisfied by any New Deal measure or promise. Not by its farm program. Nor its array of public-works and relief efforts. Not by the Tennessee Valley Authority or rural electrification. Nor by unemployment insurance, nor even by Social Security or even through soaking the rich or the corporations.

Franklin's New Deal had stolen some of these critics' ideas.

It had not stolen their hearts.

Radicals emerged in all shapes and sizes, all ideological hues. A handful were unapologetic fascists like the diminutive former screenwriter William Dudley Pelley's Silver Shirt movement or Fritz Kuhn's outright Nazi German-American Bund. In Harlem, a 5'2" preacher called himself "Father Divine" and proclaimed himself God. A surprising number of people—both Black and white—actually believed him.

More "mainstream" radicalism ranged from the late Sen. Huey "the Kingfish" Long's "Share the Wealth" scheme, to Father Charles Coughlin's pungently anti-Semitic "National Union for Social Justice" radio screeds, to the septuagenarian Dr. Francis Townsend's unsound old-age pension "Townsend Plan." In the Midwest, Milo Reno's National Farmers' Holiday Association and North Dakota Rep. William Lemke demanded canceling farm debt. Reno's angry devotees staged farmers' strikes (euphemistically labeled "holidays") to drive up agricultural prices. Armed farmers barricaded highways, dumping milk shipments on roadsides. They menaced foreclosure procedures and even kidnapped an Iowa judge.

Long, Coughlin, Townsend, Reno, Lemke, and others all comprised the *populist* Left. To the left of *their* Left lay the *Marxist* Left. Trotskyites fomented huge strikes in Minneapolis and Akron; Earl Browder's Moscow-dominated Communist Party enjoyed unprecedented popularity and could jam Madison Square Garden at the drop of a ukase from Moscow. Socialists were led by Norman Thomas—like Coughlin, Father Divine, Milo Reno, and Huey Long's fanatical henchman, the Rev. Gerald L. K. Smith—all clergymen now pursuing other goals. Thomas had polled 884,885 votes in 1932 and might easily deprive the Democrats of

New York's 1936 electoral votes, where labor occasionally manifested a distinct ingratitude to New Deal largesse, including shutting down work on several key WPA projects. In August 1935, the city's Central Trades and Labor Council's George Meany called for a citywide strike of skilled WPA labor to protest its wage scales—a stoppage threatening to go nationwide. "No one has to work that does not want to," Harry Hopkins shot back, sounding very much like a top-hatted Liberty League capitalist. "Those declining to work will go off our rolls and what happens to them after that is not our business. . . . [W]hat, if any, relief they receive thereafter [will be] from local funds. They will receive none from the Federal Government." At his weekly press conference, FDR backed up Hopkins, and Meany's strike collapsed.

And so, to men like Browder and Thomas, Franklin Roosevelt remained, at best, a mere hapless tool of Wall Street; at worst, a Machiavellian, warmongering fascist. Or, as the brilliant young Trotskyite James Burnham bluntly charged in March 1935, "the consolidation of bourgeois rule . . . under Roosevelt, is preparing the United States for the comparatively smooth transition to Fascism."

The Depression hung on. Even with millions of persons on relief and hundreds of thousands more drawing checks from New Deal "alphabet agencies," ten million workers remained jobless. Unemployment in 1935 remained stalled at 20.1 percent. Inflation—hitherto long unknown—slithered upward to a relatively disquieting 3.0 percent. Spending and deficits exploded. In 1932, Franklin had promised that they would not. His enemies—even many of his friends—remembered that.

Abroad, Hitler remilitarized the Rhineland. Mussolini invaded Ethiopia. Republican Spain tottered on the brink of civil war. Japan, having occupied Manchuria in 1931, coveted the rest of China—the remainder of East Asia, really. In October 1935, FDR promised anxious Americans a "great and earnest effort to keep this country free and unentangled from any great war . . . across the seas." Americans weren't sure if they believed him or not. He wasn't sure if they believed him either.

In January 1936, *The Literary Digest* asked, "Do you now approve the acts and policies of the Roosevelt New Deal to date?" A whopping 62 percent of its 1,907,681 respondents suddenly thundered "no." Dr. George

Gallup's more scientific and generally more pro-FDR Institute of American Politics poll revealed that the loss of a mere three of four battleground states such as New York or Michigan could spell FDR's doom. The liberal *New Republic* warned, "Roosevelt's strength has been waning rapidly."

In 1934, a quick-witted, hard-drinking recent Dartmouth grad by the name of John Keller had arrived in Washington, seeking fame and fortune (or, at least, a paycheck) in the New Deal. Tipped off that the White House needed someone to read to Louis Howe each evening, Keller got the job—one that included watering Louis's assorted hospital-room house plants. Howe playfully dubbed Keller chairman of his "Plant Protection Administration."

Keller's grandiose new title was pretty fanciful, but no more so than Howe's oft-stated illusion that he would soon depart Bethesda for lodging at Manhattan's Biltmore Hotel (headquarters of the Democratic National Committee) and, from a hotel-room sickbed, again peerlessly command his chief's election efforts.

One evening, Keller was, however, indulging Louis's fantasy. "Of course," Keller assured him, "you'll get better. Why, you have to. They'll be needing you to run the campaign."

But, for at least this one moment, reality intruded into Howe's battered psyche. "No," he responded, "I will not be there." He paused, slowly taking another drag on his Sweet Caporal before sorrowfully concluding, "Franklin is on his own now."

Yes, he was.

· 2 ·

"Try something"

When Louis Howe arrived in Washington in March 1933, he could not cash a check.

Nobody could.

Not Eleanor Roosevelt. Not even Franklin Roosevelt, about to raise his hand and take the oath as president of the United States.

It wasn't Louis, Eleanor, or Franklin who were busted.

The country was.

Its slide had commenced well before the stock market's horrendous 1929 flameout, with a less spectacular but still pernicious agricultural downturn. Farmers had overplanted, overinvested, and overborrowed during the Great War. They soon paid the price.

When the market did collapse, it carried everything else with it. From its September 1929 plateau of 381.17, the Dow Jones Industrial Average dissolved to a minuscule 59.29 on New Year's Eve 1932. By Inauguration Day 1933—March 4—it had skidded another 6.01 percent to just 53.28.

A full quarter of the Gross National Product simply vanished. In 1933, Michigan's unemployment rate reached 35.9 percent. "Hoovervilles" of desperate homeless men dotted the landscape. Mortgages went unpaid. Bank solvency tottered. Depositors feared for their savings. Bank runs, whether justified or not, became commonplace. The country was terrified; and starting with the collapse of Michigan's system, twenty states—including New York at four thirty in the morning of Franklin's inauguration—ordered their banks shuttered.

Thus, as the Roosevelt entourage entered Washington to take power, the city's Hotel Association jolted prospective guests with the following warning: "Due to unsettled banking conditions throughout the country, checks on out-of-town banks cannot be accepted." Eleanor fretted over how she and Franklin might pay for their own Mayflower Hotel suite.

Of course, they would soon enjoy larger accommodations on Pennsylvania Avenue.

Of course, others were *not* so lucky.

The New York Stock Exchange suspended trading. So did Chicago's Board of Trade. In the White House, Herbert Hoover nervously awaited Franklin Roosevelt's arrival and mourned to his press secretary, Ted Joslin, "We are at the end of our string. There is nothing more we can do."

The country had, however, *already* done something: it had dumped Hoover. And whether or not it believed that Franklin Roosevelt—or anyone else, for that matter—could fix the colossal mess it was in, it now gave its new president his chance to succeed—or fail.

If he failed, after all, more radical men—and measures—lurked offstage.

Was Roosevelt himself a radical? That remained the thing about Franklin: you never fully grasped *what* he might think, exactly what he believed.

Or even what he found amusing. One day, a Warm Springs employee chatted to Marguerite "Missy" LeHand regarding FDR's trademark uproarious laugh. For once, the faithful and oh-so-discreet Missy ("No secret of the Roosevelt family or affairs of state has ever escaped her") slipped up, revealing, "That's his *political* laugh" (emphasis added). Later reminded of her remark, her temper flared "madder than hell." Yes, even laughter was a weapon in her boss's already formidable arsenal of charm, a political ruse to be detonated as needed.

Of what Franklin knew, he knew a lot. His biographer James MacGregor Burns assessed him as "voracious . . . in his quest for information [, possessing] a startling capacity to soak up notions and facts like a sponge, and to keep this material ready for instant use. He could overwhelm miners with a vast array of facts about the dismal coal situation; he could impress businessmen with a detailed description of the intricacies of their enterprises. He had, observed [Brain Truster Rexford] Tugwell, a flypaper mind."

And a complex, calculating one too.

"His character was not only multiplex," observed Franklin's eventual speechwriter, the Pulitzer Prize–winning playwright Robert Sherwood, "it was contradictory to a bewildering degree. He was hard and he was soft. . . . He could appear to be utterly cynical, worldly, illusionless, and yet his religious faith was the strongest and most mysterious force that was in him. . . . He loved peace and harmony in his surroundings and (like many others) greatly preferred to be agreed with, and yet most of his major appointments to the Cabinet and to the various New Deal and War Agencies were peculiarly violent, quarrelsome, recalcitrant men."

Yes, he *did* prefer to be agreed with. It was said that following Louis Howe's passing, nary a one of his advisers dared contradict him. *Collier's* Washington staff writer George Creel once queried a member of FDR's inner circle as to whether anything but "yes" men then remained among them. He answered "no," quickly qualifying that answer to indicate that he might be as close to a "no" man as Franklin now possessed. "You see," he explained, "I'm a super-yes man. When the Boss comes out with one of his big ideas, everybody gives a gasp of awed admiration except me. I come back with a violent dissent, saying that the idea is no good and won't work. Then suddenly I stop short and beg him to go over it again. When he does, I gasp, throw up my hands, and exclaim, 'God! It's so tremendous I didn't get it at first!'"

When polio had struck Franklin, his Hyde Park neighbor (and fellow tree farmer) Henry Morgenthau Jr. took care to look in on him. In January 1934, FDR installed Henry as Secretary of the Treasury, and in May 1935 they discussed Roosevelt's anticipated veto of the controversial veterans' bonus legislation. Morgenthau grew uneasy as to where FDR actually stood on the issue (or, even, with him). FDR was more than willing to keep "Henry the Morgue" in the dark, cynically adding, "Never let your left hand know what your right hand is doing."

"Which hand am I, Mr. President?"

"My right hand," Franklin first reassured Morgenthau—before instantly unnerving him: "but I keep my left hand under the table."

"This," concluded Morgenthau, "is the most frank expression of the real FDR that I ever listened to and that is the real way he works."

Some may term the Roosevelt Method sleight-of-hand. Others were less generous. As his disgruntled economy-minded first budget director, Lewis Douglas, fumed, he is both "a consummate actor and an unmitigated liar." *Chicago Tribune* White House correspondent Walter Trohan recalled the *New York Times*'s Turner Catledge saying "that FDR's first instinct was to lie when asked a probing question at a news conference, but often the President would realize he could tell the truth and so he would execute a 180-degree turn in mid-paragraph and come up with the truth or a good bit of it."

One day, on the Senate floor, Huey Long flat-out accused Franklin of lying. Interior Secretary Harold Ickes heard about it and recorded in his diary: "A fellow Congressman remarked to [New Mexico Congressman John J. Dempsey] that Long ought to be impeached. Dempsey cautioned him that an impeachment meant a trial and that at a trial it might not be possible to prove the case against Long."

"It is pretty tough," a depressed Ickes pondered, "when things like this can be said about the President . . . and when members of his own official family and of his own party in Congress feel that his word cannot be relied upon. It hurts me to set down such a fact, but it is the fact as I have had occasion to know more than once. For a long time I refused to admit even to myself that it was the fact, but there is no use fooling myself any longer."

And so, on the Saturday morning in March 1933, as Franklin Roosevelt took the oath of office, reassuring the nation that all it need "fear was fear itself," it was not sure which Roosevelt hand was on the Bible and which lay under the table. Was he the dangerous radical Herbert Hoover claimed he was? Or the Hyde Park aristocrat elected on a platform pledging economies and restraint far to the right of Hoover? Once in office, Roosevelt proposed cutting federal salaries (including his own) 15 percent (a $100 million savings) and trimming the military from $752 million to $531 million (slashing Army spending by half).

He demanded the power to unilaterally decrease veterans' pensions by another $400 million.

As late as January 1935, in his State of the Union Address, he promised (to deafening applause), "The federal government must and shall quit this business of relief. I am not willing that the vitality of our people be further sapped by the giving of cash, of market baskets, of a few hours of weekly work cutting grass, raking leaves or picking up papers in the public parks. We must preserve not only the bodies of the unemployed from destitution but also their self-respect, their self-reliance and courage and determination."

"Before long," wrote FDR biographer H. W. Brands, "the image of Roosevelt as budget slasher would appear quaintly ironic, even ludicrous. But at the outset of his administration he was deadly earnest, and perfectly plausible."

He was also a star performer. Following the leaden Herbert Hoover, anyone might have looked like a star. But FDR did possess formidable powers to inspire a nation. What his words may not have accomplished in radio "Fireside Chats"—and they achieved plenty—his beaming, jaunty smile and upturned cigarette holder delivered in the newsreels. Roosevelt was the first genuine celebrity president—the sort of celebrity that "visited" millions of ordinary homes and comforted a nervous and battered populace into believing that everything was going to be all right. Beyond that, he was a whirlwind, acting fast and acting often. "Take a method and try it," he proclaimed at Oglethorpe University in May 1932. "If it fails, admit it frankly, and try another. But by all means, try something."

He got off to a good start—again, not so very hard to do following Herbert Hoover. Rarely if ever does one hear the phrase "Roosevelt Boom," but Franklin's March–July 1933 economic uptick certainly qualified for the title as much as any boom attributed to a Coolidge or a Reagan.

He declared a national "bank holiday," and it worked pretty well. Once the banks had their books examined and their doors reopened, "fear itself" may not have vanished, but it receded mightily. Money poured out of buried tin cans and from underneath lumpy mattresses and into bank vaults, propping up businesses, creating jobs, and further buttressing a growing national optimism. By July 1933, manufacturing had increased by 78 percent. The Dow Jones Average climbed by 71 percent. Manufacturing production rose 78 percent. Durable-goods production soared by a phenomenal 199 percent. Auto production increased from 97,000 units to 191,000. Daily steel production surged from 33 tons to 116.4 tons. The nation's manufacturing workforce increased from 5,029,000 to 6,155,000. The average workweek rose from 32.1 hours per week in March to 42.9 in July.

Not a bad day's work.

And not very radical work at all. "People don't realize," assessed Raymond Moley, an early Brain Truster, "that Roosevelt chose a conservative [Republican] banker as Secretary of Treasury [William Woodin] and a conservative from Tennessee as Secretary of State [Cordell Hull]. Most of the reforms . . . put through might have been agreeable to Hoover, if he had the political power to put them over. They were all latent in Hoover's thinking, especially the bank rescue. The rescue was not done by Roosevelt—he signed the papers—but by Hoover leftovers in the administration. They knew what to do.

"The bank rescue of 1933 was probably the turning point of the Depression. When people were able to survive the shock of having all the banks closed, and then see the banks open up, with their money protected[,] there began to be confidence. Good times were coming. Most of the legislation that came after didn't really help the public. The public helped itself, after it got confidence. . . .

"The guarantee of bank deposits was put through by Vice President [John Nance] Garner, Jesse Jones (a Texas banker), and Senator [Arthur] Vandenberg—three conservatives. They rammed it down Roosevelt's throat, and he took credit for it ever after. . . . You didn't have any bank trouble after that."

Thanks to massive New Deal relief efforts, the unemployment rate continued its decline, to "just" 16.64 percent in April 1934—its lowest number since September 1931. But that number only masked what might easily be called a "Roosevelt Bust." From July 1933 through that November, industrial production declined by 19 percent, the Index of Business Activity by 20 percent, and manufacturing production collapsed by 31 percent. Steel production fell by half, to just 57.7 tons per day. Auto production tumbled even below March levels (to just 42,000 units). The total number of manufacturing hours worked slipped from 264 million to 221.6 million; the average weekly number of hours worked in manufacturing stumbled backward from 42.9 to 33.8 hours.

Among the earliest and most popular of New Deal initiatives was profoundly libertarian: Repeal of the Eighteenth Amendment (Prohibition), often marketed by its advocates as an economic and fiscal panacea. Legalize booze, "wets" claimed, and hundreds of thousands of jobs would suddenly blossom. Moreover, tax money would flow into the Treasury to simultaneously balance the budget and provide more cash for relief. Such estimates proved rosier than an imbiber's complexion, but who cared? Legal booze was back.

The New Deal advanced from the staid certainty of solvent banking and the unstaid reverie of Repeal to the uncertainty of "bold experimentation." The nation—and certainly Roosevelt's New Dealers—had largely soured on unbridled capitalism. If capitalism was to be retained at all, it would have to be reined in, its excesses controlled. Its peaks and valleys of boom and bust, surpluses and shortages, overproduction and under-consumption would have to go—sent packing by the fine hand of expert, dispassionate bureaucratic, technocratic planning. Even many conservatives and businesspeople jumped on board.

In Roosevelt's Oglethorpe University "by all means, try something" speech, he unveiled much of the New Deal's forthcoming agenda: the "vital necessity of planning," an attack on "an insufficient distribution of buying power" (the *New York Times* used that phrase to describe what he still only hinted at: "the redistribution of income"), and the construction of a social safety net:

> The reward for a day's work will have to be greater, on the average, than it has been, and the reward to capital, especially capital which is speculative, will have to be less. But I believe that after the experience of the last three years, the average citizen would rather receive a smaller return upon his savings in return for greater security for the principal, than experience for a moment the thrill or the prospect of

> being a millionaire only to find the next moment that his fortune, actual or expected, has withered in his hand because the economic machine has again broken down.

"[T]he Oglethorpe speech," calculated Rexford Tugwell approvingly, "represented the high tide of collectivism."

In 1933, Roosevelt, still tacking to the right on economy in government, nonetheless swerved away from laissez-faire by proposing an ambitious and massive "National Industrial Recovery Act"—"a great cooperative movement," as he pitched it, "throughout all industry . . . to obtain wide reemployment, to shorten the working week, to pay a decent wage for the shorter week and to prevent unfair competition and disastrous overproduction."

The nation's business community, battered and unsure of itself, leaped on board. The *Wall Street Journal* proclaimed, "To plan or not to plan no longer seems to be the question," its enthusiasm stemming in part from the resultant National Recovery Administration's guarantee of a "large measure of [industry] self-regulation—with necessary exemptions from anti-trust law prosecutions." In other words, business would be cartelized through the implementation of 557 basic industry codes and 208 supplementary codes, regulating everything from automobile and steel production to lightning rods and corncob pipes, and impacting roughly 22 million workers.

Under the symbol of the "Blue Eagle" and the slogan "We Do Our Part," the new "National Recovery Administration," under its blustery administrator, former US Army Brigadier General and Bernard Baruch adviser Hugh "Iron Pants" Johnson, promised an end to "the murderous doctrine of savage and wolfish individualism, looking to dog-eat-dog and devil take the hindmost." That was the promise: the reality was a confusing tangle of government regulation and the resultant harassment of businesses that failed to submit to its "voluntary" regulations. In April 1934, Jersey City tailor Jacob Maged dared press a suit of clothes for 25 cents. The NRA code mandated 40 cents, and Maged received a $100 fine plus a thirty-day sentence.

Beyond such idiocy, the NRA exhibited the penumbra of fascism. No, the NRA wasn't about to proclaim a "Mare Nostrum" or force castor oil down opponents' throats (even Maged's), but it nonetheless bore an uncanny resemblance to Mussolini's corporate state. And unreconstructed advocates of laissez-faire were not the only ones who noticed it. From the Left, *The Nation*'s Raymond Gram Swing warned, "Unless labor is given equal power with management, . . . ours will be a fascism of the European brand. There is no escape from it."

Not helping matters were Hugh Johnson's often-alcohol-induced tirades, nor his handing to Labor Secretary Frances Perkins of a copy of the pro-fascist tract *The Corporate State*, nor the authoritarian, propagandistic omnipresence of the "Blue Eagle." And it wasn't just Johnson. Something was in the air. It was ephemeral, but there it was, and for a brief while it exhibited itself in the most unlikely quarters. Eleanor's boon companion Lorena Hickok proclaimed, "If I were 20 years younger and weighed 75 pounds less, I think I'd start out to be the Joan of Arc of the Fascist Movement in the United States." Even FDR expressed admiration for Mussolini's experiment. "I am," he confessed, "much interested and deeply impressed by what he has accomplished and by his evidenced honest purpose of restoring Italy."

In his 1933 inaugural address, Franklin had, in fact, hinted at requesting essentially dictatorial powers:

> In the event that the Congress shall fail to [act], and in the event that the national emergency is still critical, I shall not evade the clear course of duty that will then confront me. I shall ask the Congress for the one remaining instrument to meet the crisis—broad Executive power to wage a war against the emergency, as great as the power that would be given to me if we were in fact invaded by a foreign foe.

Barely a day later, Roosevelt took to the airwaves, delivering a remarkably brief and bland talk to the American Legion. An early draft of the speech, however, contained these ominous words: "As new commander-in-chief under the oath to which you are still bound I reserve to myself the right to command you in any phase of the situation which now confronts us."

"This was dictator talk—," noted historian Jonathan Alter, "an explicit power grab."

Yet . . . Roosevelt held back.

By September 1934, the erratic, hard-drinking Hugh Johnson (also beset by widespread—and true—rumors of an affair with his ubiquitous secretary, the redheaded, twenty-something Frances "Robbie" Robinson) had worn out his welcome. Then, in May 1935, the Supreme Court heard a case involving the four Schechter brothers, Brooklyn poultry dealers, who had dared to allow customers to select their own chickens, rather than sell the first chicken that randomly blundered into a customer's hands—as NRA rules mandated. In *Schechter Poultry Corporation v. United States*, the Court cried "fowl," unanimously declaring the NIRA unconstitutional, and putting FDR's experiment out of business. Even liberal justice Louis Brandeis had had enough, immediately summoning FDR aide Tommy Corcoran after the decision to lecture him: "This is the end of this business of centralization, and I want you to go back and tell the President that we're not going to let this government centralize everything. It's come to an end. As for your young men, you call them together and tell them to get out of Washington—tell them to go home, back to the states. That is where they must do their work."

FDR publicly fumed that "We have been relegated to the horse-and-buggy definition of interstate commerce," but the Court had actually rendered Franklin a marvelous favor. "You know the whole thing has been a mess," Roosevelt privately confided to Frances Perkins. "It has been an awful headache. Some of the things they have done in NRA are pretty wrong. . . . I don't want to impose a system on this country that will set aside the anti-trust laws on any permanent basis. So let's give the NRA a certain amount of time to liquidate. Have a history of it written, and then it will be over."

Also key to Roosevelt's monumental "First 100 Days" was his Agricultural Adjustment Act, dealing with farm prices, most significantly with crop and commodity surpluses. "Normal" farm prices (based on a 1914 standard of "100") had plummeted to a mere "65" in 1932. By 1936 they had achieved a remarkable upswing, ascending to "114." Corn rose from $0.25 a bushel to $1.08; barley from a wretched $0.16 to $0.67, and so on.

Good farm prices were good politics—at least in the farm belt—which FDR well knew. "Henry," he scolded Secretary of Agriculture Henry Wallace in February 1936, "through July, August, September, October and up to the fifth of November, I want cotton to sell at 12 cents. I do not care how you do it. That is your problem. It can't go below 12 cents. Is that clear?"

Such boons to farmers translated into higher food and commodity prices for unemployed or underemployed city dwellers. But New Deal planning planned only so far and so wisely. Sometimes only until the fifth of November.

Implementing Roosevelt's Agricultural Adjustment Act was the new Agricultural Adjustment Administration (AAA)—a decidedly left-wing operation, inspired by the radical Brain Truster Rexford Tugwell and overseen by the equally left-leaning Agriculture Secretary Henry Wallace. Its policies—in the midst of widespread hunger and deprivation—of paying farmers not to grow crops and to slaughter "surplus" animals generated enormous controversy, even in Midwestern agricultural states. The administration limited farm production, plowing under ten million acres of cotton and slaughtering (but not eating) six million small pigs. An outraged *Chicago Tribune* dubbed Wallace "The Greatest Butcher in Christendom."

Moreover, reducing surplus crops or livestock translated into reducing surplus *people*, because if you eliminated, say, cotton acreage by a third, you similarly eliminated at least a third of the sharecroppers. "By some means or other," pondered Lorena Hickok, "these [now superfluous] people have to be removed from the labor market. . . . The only way out is to remove from the labor market enough poor Whites and Blacks so that members of both races who are left will have some sort of chance."

A January 5, 1935, Gallup poll revealed that Americans rejected Roosevelt's AAA by a hefty 59–41 percent margin. Anti-AAA sentiment reigned in every region but the staunchly Democratic South. The following day, the Supreme Court—again acting unanimously—put it out of its misery.

The Supreme Court definitely had its doubts regarding Franklin Roosevelt. Tens of millions of Americans didn't, exhibiting an unshakeable faith they never possessed for any other leader. "He is at once God and their intimate friend," wrote the twenty-something journalist and New

Deal functionary Martha Gellhorn (the future third Mrs. Ernest Hemingway); "he knows them all by name, knows their little town and mill, their little lives and problems. And, though everything else fails, he is there, and will not let them down."

Such a personality might overshadow even a Depression. *Fortune* magazine praised him as both "the best actor in motion pictures and the best voice in radio." People trusted him—they had to. Who else was there? "Roosevelt is the only President we have, . . ." conceded columnist Mark Sullivan, a Republican and a close friend of Herbert Hoover, "the only symbol through which the country can think and act and feel. . . . The only one in whom the people now have faith. And it would be much too dangerous to destroy that faith."

They *trusted* him a great deal.

No . . . they *loved* him.

They loved him even when things went not quite right. "[T]he braintrust is denounced; the professors indicted; the NRA and the AAA ridiculed, and the 'Administration' scored," observed *Baltimore Sun* columnist Frank Kent, among the earliest of the New Deal's critics, "but the one man who creates, continues and controls all these things is treated by those who disagree with him with a self-conscious tenderness unprecedented in public affairs."

The personality that so charmed tens of millions also repulsed many. Not just his policies, his deficits, or his alphabet agencies infuriated his critics—so did *he*.

To his detractors, "That Man in the White House" seemed . . . well . . . he seemed a bit too full of himself. With his chin jutting out like a weapon, his head tilted back and weaving like a prizefighter's, his nicotine-stained teeth bared in a perpetual smile, his oily greeting of "My Friends," he was just a tad *too* confident in himself, too cocky, too sneering, too much in love with . . . Franklin Delano Roosevelt.

As a clearly annoyed *Detroit Free Press* managing editor Malcolm W. Bingay grumbled:

> Roosevelt laughs and smiles all the time. . . . When Roosevelt smokes a cigarette it is an act. He waves his arms above his head

> as though the thing were a conductor's baton. He puffs out his cheek; throws back his head and blows the smoke toward the ceiling; laughs and smirks and winks; waves his arms and blows again. One moment he has a cigarette holder and the next his cigarette is held in his fingers. The ashes are constantly being flicked even when there is no ash.

"I felt that he was enjoying what he was doing as a show," Mark Sullivan privately complained after enduring another bravura FDR press conference performance; "that he was getting pleasure and delight out of proving to the newspaperman how clever he is and how able."

To many voters he seemed at best a middling lightweight controlled by dangerous radicals like Rex Tugwell ("My plans are fashioned and practical," Tugwell wrote in his youth; "I shall roll up my sleeves—make America over!"); Harry Hopkins (formerly a social worker once enrolled in New York's Socialist Party and, according to FDR's remote cousin/close confidante Daisy Suckley, "one of the most unattractive people I've ever met. . . . A strange, weak-looking face, thin, slouching, untidy—impossible socially"); the mystical (i.e., rather strange) Henry Wallace; the acerbic Harold Ickes ("forever putting chips on his shoulder for others to knock off"); and so on.

Or even guided from afar by Harvard Law professor Felix Frankfurter, who salted the administration with such protégés as Ben Cohen and Tommy "The Cork" Corcoran, along with Undersecretary of the Treasury Dean Acheson, the FTC and SEC's James Landis, the TVA's David Lilienthal, Interior Department Solicitor Nathan Margold, and, last, and certainly unfortunately, the Hiss brothers, Donald and Alger. By October 1935, even Hugh Johnson was publicly slamming Frankfurter for having artfully "insinuated" his "boys" (the "happy hot dogs") into "obscure but key positions in every vital [New Deal] department."

Many decried the left-wing activism of Tugwell, et al. Even FDR had his doubts. "[H]e had," wrote Rex, "been half-persuaded—and Eleanor even more than he—that I had totalitarian leanings."

Other critics derided the dominance of patronage-dispensing party functionaries like Jim Farley. Since he hailed from New York and was

Irish, Catholic, and Democratic, observers often tagged "Big Jim" as part and parcel of Manhattan's infamous Tammany Hall. True, Farley crossed himself at Mass on Sunday and literally signed his name in green ink, but he was no Tammanyite nor even from the city, being, like Franklin, a rare successful upstate Democrat. He did not even drink.

Still others (well, actually, they may have been all the same people) suspected Franklin—and, particularly, wife, Eleanor—of being a little too sympathetic to hitherto downtrodden minorities. One ditty outlined alleged Roosevelt family strategies and preferences:

You kiss the negroes,
I'll kiss the Jews;
We'll stay in the White House
As long as we choose.

Private whispers turned into very public shouts when Michigan's septuagenarian former progressive Republican governor Chase S. Osborn theorized that the Roosevelt clan was, in fact, originally Jewish. "The Rosenvelts in north Holland finally became Roosevelt," he contended in February 1934. In March 1935, *Detroit Jewish Chronicle* editor Philip Slomovitz finally queried FDR on the subject, adding, "This is not the first time that we have seen your name coupled with the Jews, especially in the efforts of anti-Semites to label you as a tool of Jews and Catholics." Terming Osborn an "old friend," Franklin skillfully pled ignorance to Osborn's allegations, concluding, "In the dim distant past [my ancestors] may have been Jews or Catholics or Protestants. What I am more interested in is whether they were good citizens and believers in God. I hope they were both."

Such public hostilities, while irksome, were hardly fatal, though July 1933 levels of industrial production were not again achieved until August 1935. By then, deflation had been eliminated, assisting those least able to repay loans and mortgage payments. The stock market inched up. Unemployment inched downward, though only to 20.1 percent by December 1935. The Gross Domestic Product increased by 10.8 percent in 1934, by another 8.9 percent in 1935, and then again by

12.9 percent in 1936. Most importantly, FDR's relief and public works programs fashioned bridges, canals, tunnels, post offices, parks, sewage systems, and armories, even theatres and golf courses—not to mention the Tennessee Valley Authority. Many survive to this day. It cannot be said they built poorly back then.

Aggressively adept at soliciting New Deal funding was New York's recently installed Fusion mayor Fiorello La Guardia, who (when he wasn't banning burlesque houses, pushcarts, or slot machines, speeding to oversee firemen battling street fires, or reading the funny papers over the radio) devoted so much time to personally lobbying FDR that he soon maintained a Washington apartment. "He . . . tells me a sad story," FDR recalled of La Guardia. "The tears run down my cheeks and the tears run down his cheeks and the first thing I know, he has wangled another fifty million dollars." Franklin wasn't joking—or even exaggerating. The New Deal's Public Works Administration (PWA) ultimately built what became LaGuardia Airport, the Lincoln Tunnel, the Triborough Bridge, and housing projects in Williamsburg and on the Lower East Side; refurbished beaches and hospitals; repaired streets and highways; screened 400,000 children for tuberculosis; transformed an old city garbage dump into the site of the 1939 World's Fair; built 255 playgrounds and 17 municipal swimming pools; and funded the Federal Arts Project—and, if that were not enough, also funded the New York Negro Theatre Project, which, surprisingly, engaged both John Houseman and the very, very young Orson Welles to helm its April 1936 hit production nicknamed the "Voodoo Macbeth." At any one time, the WPA employed between 100,000 and 245,000 Gothamites—ultimately 700,000 New Yorkers in all. Very soon, the city received one-seventh of all WPA funding nationwide.

City slickers benefited. Country folk cashed in too. Arkansas's Joe Robinson, Roosevelt's conservative but loyal Senate Majority Leader, moaned to Virginia's even-more-conservative Carter Glass of his angst in kowtowing to the administration: "You can't imagine the hell I have to go through."

"In your case, Joe," an unsympathetic Glass shot back, "the road seems to be lined with post offices."

But dispensing billions of dollars of public works and outright relief projects was not as easy as it looked. Critics derided many a New Deal project as hopeless boondoggles—particularly one that involved a study of ancient safety pins. Harry Hopkins simply stonewalled such criticism, seething to reporters: "Dumb people criticize something they do not understand . . . G-d damn it! . . . We are not backing down on any of those projects. . . . We don't need any apologies!"

Once, while speaking at the University of Iowa, Hopkins was extolling all things WPA, which was all well and good until he completed his laundry list, and a voice boomed out, "Who's going to pay for all that?" He boldly shot back: "You are. And who better? Who can better afford to pay for it? Look at this great university. Look at these fields, these forests and rivers. This is America, the richest country in the world. We can afford to pay for anything we want. And we want a decent life for all the people in this country. And we are going to pay for it."

The "put-men-to-work-now" Hopkins and the "get-the-most-long-term-value-for-your-money" Ickes feuded violently over their respective roles (and FDR's favor). Ickes believed that Hopkins's WPA (Works Progress Administration; to critics, "We Poke Along") had created "thousands of inconsequential make-believe projects in all parts of the country." He seethed that Hopkins was "a lawless individual bent on building up a reputation for himself as a great builder, even at the expense of the President and the country." Worse, he judged his rival as "the greatest threat today to the President's re-election."

Hopkins retaliated not only by milking his special relationship with FDR, but by leaking tales of Ickes's love life to sympathetic reporters: sympathetic to good gossip—not to Ickes.

Exactly what Hopkins leaked, we know not, but we know this: during Roosevelt's First 100 Days, a divorcée (discreetly known to history as "Mrs. X") sidled up to Ickes at his temporary Mayflower Hotel residence. Her mission: to secure a job for her fiancé (Ickes described said beau as "one of the most unattractive men I have ever met"). Ickes accommodated "X" but also took up with her, gave her a job in the Interior Department (hers was near his office, her fiancé's in "the far middlewest"), and even escorted her on passionate rides in his government limousine under the discreet eye of his "quiet, loyal, and devoted" Black chauffeur.

Less quiet (and increasingly suspicious) was Ickes's paramour's fiancé. He requested a transfer back to Washington—which the arrogantly clueless Ickes granted. Returned to the scene of the crime, Mr. Fiancé's apprehensions hardened into unpleasant (but highly accurate) theories. He dispatched anonymous letters regarding "Mrs. X" and Ickes—to Harold's absent wife, Anna (conveniently away in New Mexico), to the *Washington Post,* and to the *Chicago Tribune*. The flustered Ickes protested to Louis Howe, who ordered Secret Service chief William Moran to investigate. Moran found nothing, so Ickes hatched a scheme involving the Interior Department's Division of Investigation chief, Louis Russell Glavis.

Decades earlier, Glavis had been at the heart of the Ballinger–Pinchot affair that helped sunder TR's friendship with William Howard Taft. As Ickes's investigations chief, Glavis now played rough, running what columnists Drew Pearson and Robert S. Allen termed "a virtual OGPU . . . at one time employing 1,000 detectives." Former director of the National Park Service Horace Albright recalled:

> Glavis became a super-detective, one of the best we had there and built up quite a force, and it got to be a situation in the Interior Department, I'm sorry to say, where for . . . some years—men couldn't be sure they weren't being followed and spotted as if they were in Russia. There were recorders put on telephones, downstairs. There were bugs . . . put in rooms, particularly of bureau chiefs and assistant bureau chiefs. I can recall going into the office of one bureau chief one morning, sticking my head in there—to talk with an old friend that I knew—and he put his finger up to his mouth, indicating for me not to say anything. He got up and came out and we went down and got in his car and had our conversation in the car, because he said he was afraid to say anything in his office, because he was quite sure it was wired.

Ickes's new strategy was this: he would send Mr. Fiancé south on a business trip—and dispatch Glavis to burglarize the man's apartment.

Glavis returned with carbon copies of the incriminating letters, and Ickes (now shamelessly as well as cluelessly) grilled Mr. Fiancé. Mr. Fiancé denied all; Ickes fired him anyway, and patted himself on the back for his genius.

Yes, "Honest Harold" Ickes was nowhere near wonderful. Behind his acerbic, unpleasant façade lay a not very admirable person at all. In reviewing Ickes's voluminous diaries, the *New Yorker*'s Richard Rovere noted "the character we encounter here is so contemptible that one is forced to conclude he couldn't possibly have been as bad as he seems. . . . He was, by the testimony of [his own words], selfish, vindictive, suspicious, servile, and disloyal. Lust for power ruled him. He loved no one and admired only those who regularly bathed him in flattery or conferred on him some portion of their authority. . . . In his apparent innocence of the nature of corruption, Ickes calmly bequeathed us a self-portrait of a man corrupt in the deepest sense. . . . Ickes was the embodiment of a stunning paradox. He was corrupt on the inside and pure as the driven snow on the outside."

To broker peace between the sparring Ickes and Hopkins, in October 1935 Franklin dragooned both onto a two-week ocean fishing vacation aboard the heavy cruiser USS *Houston*. At one point, FDR sent the pair off alone (save for FDR's trusted military aide "Pa" Watson) on a whaleboat for the day. They ended up rain-soaked on a deserted island and somehow patched things over. Remarkably, the patches held.

•••

Despite such contretemps, the New Deal got things done. Big things. Rural electrification programs extended the benefits of modern life to the hitherto most remote and backward areas. The Civilian Conservation Corps (actually FDR's first big relief measure) ultimately dispatched three million young unmarried men to work on such countryside projects as reforestation, flood control, erosion, forest-fire control, swamp drainage, dam-building, and park maintenance—and also, very importantly, to send money home. Though Eleanor thought little of the program ("I'm not criticizing your CCC camps, Frank, but I know there is nothing really being done there. . . . My dear, forestry is a joke."), it remained remarkably popular throughout its existence, recording an 82–18 percent favorability rating in July 1936. Even 67 percent of Republicans approved of CCC efforts.

New Deal programs put people on the payroll—people who would look upon FDR as their savior and their friend, who would vote not just for him but for the entire Democratic ticket. And so would their families. In 1936, New Deal agencies such as the WPA, PWA, CCC, and NYA employed over 4 million persons—2,628,373 in the WPA alone.

"[T]he elections would have been much closer," admitted Virginia Democrat Carter Glass, "had my party not had a four billion, eight hundred million dollar relief bill as campaign fodder."

It didn't take a Jim Farley to figure that part out.

Civil-service reform reversed itself under the New Deal. Patronage swelled. In 1884, only 10.5 percent of federal positions were "merit"-based, the remainder being filled through traditional patronage mills. TR increased merit-based positions to 51.2 percent; Wilson to 67.2 percent; Hoover to 80.8 percent. By 1936, FDR and Farley had reduced them to 60.7 percent. In the first six and a half months of the New Deal, Farley canned 661 incumbent postmasters. The "F.R.B.C."—"For Roosevelt Before Chicago"—held pride of place, among all New Deal "alphabet agencies."

Many—if not most—of FDR's major initiatives arrived in apparent reaction to other more radical legislation or events. This wasn't always the case—nobody had to push him into the CCC or the Tennessee Valley Authority. But soon that would change. "The vast maneuver [of] changing the whole tenor of the New Deal in 1935 was made necessary, . . ." theorized Rexford Tugwell, by Franklin's having "to put himself in the main stream of progressivism before trying to harness and transform it."

Roosevelt unveiled the AAA hot on the heels of Milo Reno's threatened national farmers' strike. Abandoning the gold standard closely followed a failed silver-coinage bill by Montana Democrat Burton K. Wheeler (an old ally) and another inflationary measure offered by Oklahoma Democratic senator Elmer Thomas. Unlike Wheeler's bill, Thomas's proposal was unstoppable. FDR grudgingly signed on to it, with the caveat that its provisions be discretionary on his part rather than mandatory.

The NIRA was partially a reaction to Alabama senator Hugo Black's "Thirty Hour Bill," a clearly unconstitutional (and insane) measure barring products manufactured by workers toiling more than five days a week or six hours a day from interstate or international commerce. Regarding the NIRA's massive public-works component, FDR again played follower rather than leader. First arguing that there wasn't more than a billion dollars of public-works measures worth doing, he soon reversed course and signed on for three billions' worth.

In early 1934, a curious story broke of a Georgetown dinner party held the previous September. A group of young radical (perhaps Communist) New Dealers had supposedly boasted of having "Mr. Roosevelt in the middle of a swift stream and the current is so strong he cannot turn back or escape from it." Perhaps the incident occurred. Perhaps it didn't. In any case, the braggarts in question overstated their own powers—but did not necessarily exaggerate the very real currents Franklin Roosevelt faced: of politics, of national turmoil, of the need to short-circuit opposition, of the swift stream of history itself—and, not necessarily last—of the need to demonstrate that he, the jaunty, smiling aristocrat who reassured you and your family on the radio, led, rather than followed, so many of those tides. Roosevelt may have masterly piloted his political boat through those raging tides, but he mastered them, very often in their direction, not his.

A direction in which he wished to sail—though he never quite reached port—was this: the realignment of Republicans and Democrats along sounder ideological lines. "We'll have eight years in Washington," Roosevelt once confided to Rex Tugwell, Harry Hopkins, and Wisconsin's progressive Republican senator Robert La Follette Jr. "By that time there may not be a Democratic Party, but there will be a progressive one." FDR's funneling of New York City patronage through the Republican-Fusionist mayor La Guardia was one hint of that. His willingness to funnel California WPA appointments through Hiram Johnson was another. As was his hiring on of such GOP progressives as Ickes, Henry Wallace, and Hugh Johnson's successor at the NRA, Donald R. Richberg. AAA administrator George Peek had also once been a Republican.

Franklin's admiration for Senate Republican progressives, like Nebraska's septuagenarian George W. Norris (cosponsor of the TVA) or Idaho's

William Borah, was well known. It was, after all, five Republican votes that had slid the NIRA through the Senate. And while FDR wasn't quite ready to jettison Democratic conservatives like Virginia's brilliant but inflexible Carter Glass or his brutally tough Senate Majority Leader Joe Robinson, if, and when, that time ever came, he would shed few tears. Tugwell viewed FDR as "a Democrat of convenience" and theorized that Roosevelt "saw no alternative, in the long run, to creating a new [political] force. . . . The campaign of 1936 was not so much an election contest as an appeal for ratification of progressivism quite as much Republican as Democratic."

The midterm elections of 1934 augured well for Franklin Roosevelt's survival two years hence. For only the second instance since the Civil War, the party in power actually gained congressional seats—from 313 to 322 seats in the House; from 60 to 69 seats in the Senate. In monolithically Republican Maine, Frederick Hale held on to his Senate seat with just 50.1 percent of the vote. Michigan's rising star Arthur Vandenberg survived with only 51.32 percent. Wisconsin's Robert M. La Follette Jr. jumped the GOP ship to win reelection as a third-party Progressive.

Republicans retained a mere seven governorships. They forfeited Pennsylvania's for the first time since 1882. Nevada's incumbent GOP chief executive received just 34.52 percent of the vote. In New York—much to Roosevelt's joy—Robert Moses, running as a Republican, garnered a mere 36.57 percent against incumbent Democrat Herbert Lehman.

The year 1935 saw Roosevelt zigging left to counteract Louisiana senator Huey Long's "Share-the-Wealth" movement. On June 19, 1935, just two days following the Senate's defeat of Long's redistributionist measure, FDR introduced a tax package imposing hikes on upper-income taxpayers, increasing business taxes, and stiffening inheritance taxes. "The transmission from generation to generation of vast fortunes by will, inheritance, or gift is not consistent with the ideals and sentiments of the American people," trust-fund patrician FDR announced, and the gods of irony laughed. His fellow patricians sobbed.

So did Congress, having expected to recess soon rather than to remain roasting this newest hot potato in Washington's even hotter summer.

Oklahoma congressman Wilburn Cartwright spoke for many when he privately griped "it is disgusting to have to stay here and wrangle and the President keeps shooting new and more argumentative legislation at us. The Lord only knows when we will adjourn."

But if alienating Congress and soaking the rich was necessary to counteract the populist Long, then so be it. If such actions hobbled recovery, so be it. As historian David M. Kennedy conceded, "For the moment, Roosevelt seemed willing to slacken his pursuit of recovery . . . to consolidate his political gains."

Yet that "recovery" was not only fragile, it was by any historic standard decidedly anemic; as scholar Ellis Hawley summarized, it hardly justified "jubilation. Over ten and a half million workers were still unemployed; approximately twenty million people still dependent upon relief. Basic industries still ran at little more than half capacity, and the real income of the average family remained thirteen percent below that of 1929." That was good reason for resentment—not just at Hoover—but at FDR.

FDR had failed to calculate the cost—both economically and politically—of detonating business confidence. As Scripps-Howard newspaper chain publisher Roy Howard (Roosevelt's remaining major backer in the press) warned him that August:

> Any experienced reporter will tell you that throughout the country many business men who once gave you sincere support are now, not merely hostile, they are frightened. Many of these men whose patriotism and sense of public service will compare with that of any men in political life, have become convinced and sincerely believe: That you fathered a tax bill that aims at revenge rather than revenue—revenge on business; That the Administration has side-stepped broadening the tax base to the extent necessary to approximate the needs of the situation; That there can be no real recovery until the fears of business have been allayed through the granting of a breathing spell to industry, and a recess from further experimentation until the country can recover its losses.

A chastened FDR publicly backtracked, vowing that his administration's "very considerable legislative program . . . has now reached substantial completion" and promised a "breathing spell" in its often dizzying pace of trial and error. The business community—at least, its more liberal and moderate elements—seemed reassured.

But his other flanks still rumbled ominously. In California, muckraking author Upton Sinclair (an unrepentant former Socialist, who in 1932 proclaimed, "The Communist road is rough, dangerous and often confusing, but it happens to be the only road that leads into the new world") captured the state's Democratic gubernatorial nomination on an "End Poverty in California" (EPIC) program demanding a government takeover and operation of vacant factories and farms, a state income tax with a top rate of 30 percent, as well as California state pensions for the aged, the disabled, and widows. Sinclair ultimately lost to incumbent Republican Frank Merriam (no easy trick in Democratic-dominated 1934), but not before scaring the hell out of most Californians—and Americans. Nonetheless, Sinclair demonstrated how an unabashedly radical program could capture a sizable slice of the vote. If that vote detached itself from FDR's 1936 totals, otherwise dead-horse Republicans might inevitably transform 1936 into a real horse race.

Such data was hardly lost on Franklin Roosevelt, whose business was politics, whose hobby was politics, and whose dreams and nightmares were similarly political. He had not attained the apex of his occupation to have it snatched from him by characters like Upton Sinclair. They would not outflank him in 1936. As he had outflanked Milo Reno and legislative Democratic wildmen like Burton K. Wheeler, Elmer Thomas, and Hugo Black, he would outmaneuver them as well.

Unfortunately for Roosevelt, there were a lot of "them" out there. Communists and Socialists inhabited his extreme outer flanks, but they were too few in number and their respective brands too toxic to cause him much worry. As Upton Sinclair eventually perceived, "The American People will take Socialism, but they won't take the label."

Not peddling the Socialist label was Sinclair's fellow Californian, the aged Dr. Francis E. Townsend. Townsend seemed to be a Republican (he vaguely recalled voting for Hoover in 1932), but a big-spending one:

his "Townsend Plan" promised a generous $200-a-month pension to all native-born citizens sixty or older. Millions of desperate Americans flocked to "Townsend Clubs" supporting his scheme.

Detroit's Father Charles Coughlin had a less targeted aim but boasted a much louder voice, enjoying a nationwide radio network, a flair for the dramatic, and a mellifluous delivery second only to Franklin Roosevelt's. Millions joined Coughlin's new "National Union for Social Justice." Not long previously, Coughlin had waged war against Hoover and Prohibition and for Roosevelt and Repeal. Now he despised FDR more than he had ever loathed Hoover. But whatever his feelings about Roosevelt, he hated Wall Street and the bankers—"the money changers in the temple," as he damned them—more.

More and more, people said he also hated the Jews.

But neither Coughlin nor Townsend nor the Communists nor the Socialists had ever held public office or possessed any real concept of how to run a successful political campaign—let alone against so cunning an opponent as Franklin Roosevelt.

But one man filled that bill with talent and ambition and calculation to spare.

That man was Huey Long.

· 3 ·

"One bullet"

Death's bony finger cheated Franklin of Louis Howe. It reimbursed him by summoning Louisiana's Huey Pierce Long Jr.

Franklin Delano Roosevelt was well-born, aristocratic, Groton and Ivy League–educated, a Washington insider. He oozed reassurance.

Huey Long—His Excellency, "the Kingfish"—was none of these things. And, while he gave hope and free textbooks and good roads to the poor, he exuded more than a faint sense of menace. "Exuded" is actually too polite a word. He gloried in it.

He had elbowed himself up from high school dropout (actually, he was expelled) to traveling salesman to upstart Shreveport lawyer (having completed his legal studies in a single year) to the State Railroad Commission in 1918, and—after a failed 1924 gubernatorial race—storming into the governor's mansion in 1928. At thirty-five, he was the youngest chief executive in state history.

Early on, some people questioned Franklin Roosevelt's intelligence. They never questioned Huey's. His sanity, perhaps, but not his intelligence. He was plain whip-smart, surprisingly well read, and possessed a photographic memory. He might cajole voters with piney-woods banter; but when he argued before the United States Supreme Court, Chief Justice William Howard Taft marveled, "He is the most brilliant legal mind to appear before me."

He was brilliant and ruthless and, even in some sense, idealistic—but, most of all, ambitious.

Radicals were a dime a dozen in the Depression-savaged 1930s. Long was tempestuously radical throughout the prosperous, conservative '20s. Much of that attitude stemmed from his environment. Louisiana languished as a third-world, extractive economy. Seventy-five percent of state residents remained illiterate. Most Louisianans—Black and white—were too poor to pay the $1-per-year poll tax to vote.

Huey himself hailed from a family and an area, northeastern Louisiana's Winn Parish, marinated in the bitter residue of William Jennings Bryan populism. In 1892, the Populist Party's gubernatorial candidate had carried the parish, and by 1907 their sympathizers had purchased the local paper and renamed it *The Comrade*. Much of Long's program and persona was original. But not his slogan—"Every man a king but no man wears a crown"—swiped directly and unapologetically from "The Great Commoner" Bryan.

In 1912, Winn Parish cast 35.4 percent of its ballots (highest in the state) for Socialist presidential candidate Eugene V. Debs. That same year, Socialists elected a school-board member in the parish seat of Winnville plus their party's entire municipal slate. The county even boasted its own Socialist publication, *The Forum*.

As a fledgling attorney, Huey helped win acquittal for a state-senator friend indicted for violating World War I's Sedition Act. As a member and later chairman of the Railroad Commission (renamed the Public Service Commission in 1926), he established a solid reputation of fighting for the "little man" against the state's major financial interests, most notably Standard Oil. Long hated Standard Oil, and the feeling was mutual. As governor, he quickly enacted a bold program of social reform: free schoolbooks for children, night-school classes for the illiterate, and, above all, a supercharged ramping up of Louisiana's primitive system of roads and bridges. In 1928, Louisianans had enjoyed only 331 miles of paved roads. By 1932, he had built 2,301 miles of paved highway plus 2,816 more miles of graveled roads. Four years later, that aggregate total had reached 9,700 miles. He built 111 bridges. Widespread corruption accompanied said infrastructure. But so what? Huey snorted,

"We got the roads in Louisiana, haven't we? In some states they only have the graft."

Roads cost money, and Huey resolved that Standard Oil would foot their bill. He also determined that the state's growing ranks of public employees would support his political machine. If you were not a Long person, you were out. If you stayed, you paid—from 2 to 5 percent of your salary—into the Kingfish's political treasury, his infamous "deduct box."

Huey's opponents—a mix of business interests, good-government groups, and rival local Democratic machines (such as New Orleans's "Old Regulars")—counterattacked. In 1929, they filed impeachment charges—some frivolous, some serious—against him. Huey corralled fifteen friendly state senators into a "round robin," pledged to vote against conviction under any circumstances. Long thus escaped, but not without cost. "[I]mpeachment did something to him," one supporter recalled. "It made him vicious."

Huey ruthlessly ridiculed his opponents—tarring them with unflattering nicknames—"France-ass" Williams, New Orleans mayor "Turkey Head" Walmsley, the bearded US senator "Feather-Duster" Ransdell, wealthy attorney "Shinola" Phelps, and state legislator "Whistle Britches" Rightor. The anti-Long "Constitutional League" emerged as the "Constipational League." And, as for those men who still dared impeach him, well, as he calculated, he'd just "have to grow me a new crop of legislators."

He would become a legislator himself, though not in Baton Rouge. He had long grown far too big for *that*. He fancied himself a national figure—ultimately *the* national figure. Accordingly, he would first advance to Washington as a United States senator. Years before, when an absolute nobody, he would spontaneously write to various US senators. "I want to let them know I'm here," he confided to his wife, Rose; "I'm going to be there myself someday." First, as he informed her, he'd win a secondary state office, then the governorship, then his US Senate seat—and, finally, the presidency. "It almost gave you the cold chills to hear him tell it," Rose recalled decades later. "He was measuring it all."

Such calculations rested upon careful timing. Elected at just thirty-four, he was a young governor in a hurry, hurrying toward Washington.

In 1930, he won election to the Senate, easily ousting the veteran septuagenarian incumbent "Feather Duster" Ransdell.

But he did *not* go to Washington. At least, not then.

His problem was this: to retain his iron grip on state politics, he required a pliant, trusted successor. Originally that was to be his lieutenant governor, a wealthy dentist named Paul Cyr. But Cyr and Long soon quarreled. If Huey departed for Washington, his gubernatorial flank would now suddenly tumble into enemy hands. Accordingly, Long—ostentatiously leaving his newly won Senate seat vacant—refused to abandon his governorship.

In October 1931, Cyr, his patience exhausted, declared that Long had forfeited the governorship thanks to his Senate election and claimed the former for himself. Long's fine legal mind sprung into action. Maintaining that he was still governor, Huey accused Cyr not merely of illicitly claiming his office, but of having vacated his own. Thus, Cyr no longer held *any* office. Huey called out the militia and went to court. Cyr was out, and Huey installed the ultimate Long stooge—his boyhood friend Oscar "O. K." Allen—into the Executive Mansion. "Governor" Long finally moved north as "Senator" Long.

Arriving in Congress in January 1932, Huey immediately lambasted the Senate Democratic leadership, most particularly conservative Minority Leader Joe Robinson of Arkansas, emerging, as one journalist trenchantly observed, as "a nuisance without becoming a power." In May 1932, Long, however, swaggered into the race to reelect Arkansas's other senator, Hattie Caraway, named as a mere "placeholder" to succeed her late progressive husband, Sen. Thaddeus Caraway. Few besides Huey gave Hattie any chance. But he furiously invaded the Razorback State—and her campaign—armed with two four-speaker sound trucks, bales of campaign literature, and, most importantly, his unique self. Within eight days, he addressed an estimated two hundred thousand persons; and when he was done, Mrs. Caraway was overwhelmingly elected senator to complete her husband's unexpired term. No longer might anyone dismiss Huey Long as a mere Louisiana phenomenon. He had ripped apart Arkansas like a "circus hitched to a tornado," and might just as well demolish you as handily as he had bulldozed any of Hattie's opponents. He was no longer an entry-grade nuisance but really had become a power in his own right, ignored at one's own peril.

Nineteen thirty-two was, more significantly, a presidential year, and Long remained unimpressed by front-runner Franklin Roosevelt, assessing him as not merely mediocre but atrocious enough to lose to the pathetic Hoover. Nonetheless, he fell in behind FDR, informing Sen. Burton K. Wheeler, "I don't like your son of a bitch. But I'll be for him," providing key support at that year's Democratic National Convention, and later campaigning with surprising effectiveness for Franklin in four Midwestern states. "We never again underestimated him," conceded Jim Farley.

Prior to FDR's inauguration, the Kingfish conferred with him at Warm Springs, Georgia, a meeting only fueling his burgeoning mistrust of Roosevelt's magnetic smile and reassuring chatter. "When I talk to him," complained Long, "he says, 'Fine! Fine! Fine!' But Joe Robinson goes to see him the next day and again he says 'Fine! Fine! Fine!' Maybe he says 'Fine!' to everybody."

Long barely cast a majority of votes with the new administration. He was particularly unimpressed by FDR's National Industrial Recovery Administration. "Every fault of socialism is found in this bill without one of its virtues," he raged. "Every crime of monarchy is in here. . . . It is a combination of everything that is impractical and impossible. . . . I have cast my last blind vote."

Foreseeing revolution, he meant to profit from it. "Men," he warned his colleagues in early 1933, "it will not be long until there will be a mob assembling here to hang senators from the rafters. . . . I have to determine whether I will stay and be hung with you, or go out and lead the mob."

Few were sure he was kidding. He probably wasn't.

In late July 1933, FDR summoned Huey, hoping, perhaps, to beguile the Kingfish back into the fold; more likely merely trudging through the motions of amity. Huey had his own agenda: demanding assurances that he and not any administration flunky would control federal patronage down Louisiana way.

"It was a [late] morning appointment," recalled Jim Farley. "The day was hot, and Huey came charging into the White House in his usual breezy and jaunty manner. He was nattily dressed in light summer clothes and wore a sailor [boater] straw hat. . . .

"Huey had come in with a chip on his shoulder, and although his words were courteous enough, it was obvious . . . that he was there for the purpose of testing . . . the President."

Part of Long's analysis involved his snazzy straw boater, discourteously remaining atop his head as the meeting progressed. Such gaucheries, though common now, were simply taboo in more mannered days, triggering Farley's suspicion of deliberate disrespect.

"I glanced at Roosevelt," he recollected, "and saw that he was perfectly aware of what was taking place and, furthermore, was enjoying it immensely. . . . He had a broad smile on his face which never changed for a moment, not even when Huey leaned over to tap him on the knee or elbow with the straw hat to emphasize one of his finer points, a trick which Huey pulled not once but several times."

Farley had known Roosevelt long enough to recognize his boss's subtle hint to ignore Huey's lèse-majesté. Roosevelt's flinty Kentucky-born appointments secretary, Marvin McIntyre, with FDR off-and-on since his Navy days, proved less forgiving. "I saw McIntyre standing there with his teeth clenched," Farley recalled, "and I thought for a moment that he was going to walk over and pull the hat off Huey's head."

The Long–Roosevelt tête-à-tête lasted all of fifteen minutes—normal for FDR's helter-skelter schedule. Huey departed absent any guarantee. "What the hell is the use of coming down to see this fellow?" he groused to Farley. "I can't win any decision over him." Farley concluded that Long was admitting FDR's political mastery. Long biographer T. Harry Williams concluded differently: "What Huey was trying to say was that he could not get a straight answer out of Roosevelt."

Feuding continued over federal patronage, with Long and Harold Ickes trading public potshots. Finally, a frustrated Long urged reporters to "pay them my further respects up there in Washington. Tell them they can go to hell." The war was on.

In February 1934, Huey unveiled his own New Deal, a radical redistribution of income and assets, dubbed "Share-Our-Wealth." Had Roosevelt or the Depression never existed, some form of Long's scheme would have.

Consider his plea, campaigning in 1928's palmier times, to South Louisiana Acadians gathered around their famed Evangeline Oak:

> It is here under this oak where Evangeline waited for her lover, Gabriel, who never came. This oak is an immortal spot, made so by Longfellow's poem. But Evangeline is not the only one who has waited here in disappointment. Where are the schools that you have waited for your children to have, that have never come? Where are the roads and the highways that you send your money to build, that are no nearer now than ever before? Where are the institutions to care for the sick and disabled? Evangeline wept bitter tears in her disappointment, but it lasted through only one lifetime. Your tears in this country, around this oak, have lasted for generations. Give me the chance to dry the eyes of those who still weep here.

He would dry them in Louisiana with roads and schools and hospitals. He would dry them nationwide with cold, hard cash. As *The Nation*'s Ben Stolberg reckoned in September 1935, "The American people do not crave New Deals, which they cannot understand, or Epics or Utopias or technocracies. They just want more money."

Huey's "Share-Our-Wealth Plan" (or, as he often modestly called it, "the Long Plan") promised just that. More money than many had ever dreamt of, stacks of money just for being (and voting) and not for doing. Each deserving household (and they were *all* deserving) would receive $5,000, "enough for a home, an automobile, a radio, and the ordinary conveniences, and the opportunity to educate their children." And that was just for starters. These households were also to be made "debt free," and in each succeeding year, would receive anywhere between $2,000 and $2,500, a sum, Long proclaimed, big enough "to maintain a family in comfort."

Long further promised:

> Old Age Pensions of $30 per month to persons over 60 years of age who do not earn as much as $1,000 per year or who possess less than $10,000 in cash or property, thereby to remove from the field

> of labor, in times of unemployment, those who have contributed their share to the public service.
>
> To limit the hours of work to such an extent as to prevent over-production and to give the workers of America some share in the recreations, conveniences and luxuries of life.
>
> To balance agricultural production with what can be sold and consumed according to the laws of God, which have never failed.

Said mazuma would come from the rich, the super-rich, the Vanderbilts, the Mellons, the Baruchs, the Morgans—maybe even the Roosevelts. And why not? "God invited us all to come and eat and drink all we wanted," he orated over the radio in early 1935. "He smiled on our land and we grew crops of plenty to eat and wear. He showed us in the earth the iron and other things to make everything we wanted. He unfolded to us the secrets of science so that our work might be easy. God called: 'Come to my feast.'" But a greedy few had elbowed everyone else aside.

"Rockefeller, Morgan, and their crowd stepped up and took enough for 120 million people, and left only enough for 5 million [of] all the other 125 million to eat. And so many millions must go hungry and without these good things God gave us unless we call on them to put some of it back."

In Baton Rouge, in 1932, exhorting crowds to eject Louisiana's senior senator, Edwin Broussard, from office, he had essentially dared voters:

> They'll tell you that what you've got to do is tear up Longism in this state. All right, my friends—get you a bomb or some dynamite and blow up that building yonder [pointing to the new state capital]. That's a good place to start.
>
> Then go out and tear up the concrete roads I've built. Get your spades and your shovels and scrape the gravel off them roads we've graveled, and let a rain come on 'em. That'll put 'em back like they was before I come.
>
> Tear down the new buildings I built at the University. Take the money away from the school boards that I give 'em to run your school.

> And when your child starts out to school tomorrow morning, call him back and snatch the free school books out of his hand that Huey Long gave him.
>
> Then you'll be rid of Longism in this state, my friends, and not till then.

And so Huey would just lop off a little—or a lot—of what the rich didn't need. A graduated tax on wealth would commence at assets of $1 million and over—before grabbing every dime after $8 million. All income over $1 million per year was similarly 100 percent confiscated, as was every inheritance over $1 million. Whether Long's math all added up, or even whether he believed it did, was not exactly clear (one economist estimated that he would have had to confiscate all incomes above $4,000 to provide even a $1,400 payment to the needy), but millions of Americans believed it and joined their local "Share-Our-Wealth" club.

"It must be understood," Huey explained of these clubs, "that there are no dues or assessments are [*sic*] made on any member joining a [local chapter]. Most of the people have not the money to pay any dues, and when there is need for a little sum to defray a little item of expense (which should never be very much) it must come from voluntary contribution. Avoid creating any items of expense. Look about and get a free meeting place; get some members or some friends to do everything free that you can. . . . Let the men and women understand they are not expected to give anything."

Within a year, Long boasted 4.5 million Share-Our-Wealth Club members in 27,431 chapters nationwide. His "American Progress" newspaper enjoyed 275,000 subscribers. His mailing list totaled 7,682,768 persons. In March 1935, he lambasted FDR over the radio. Thirty-five million people listened.

Long's sharing the wealth, his roads and bridges and free schoolbooks, all his free largesse, aimed toward buying votes. Yet one group that he assisted never really voted for him, probably never would vote for him, and whose votes he never even wanted.

Blacks.

His Louisiana programs helped poor Blacks substantially, particularly his night-school efforts. Many noticed that he race-baited far less than the average Southern politician. "Long," contended his friend, Montana's Sen. Burton K. Wheeler, "had less racial prejudice than any other Southerner in the Senate." Yet Long invariably termed Blacks "niggers." To the NAACP's Roy Wilkins, he protested "I'm not working for equality or anything like that. I figger when you teach niggers to read and write and figger they can look out for themselves—you know, people can't cheat them like they did before. . . . That ain't right. I taught 'em to figger. They got to look out for themselves."

"Don't say I'm working for niggers," he continued. "I'm not. I'm for the poor man—all poor men. . . . 'Every Man a King'—that's my slogan. That means every man, niggers 'long with the rest, but not specially for niggers."

Yet, in his own rough way, he'd supply a spot at the Long table for them as well, even though that might *cost* him votes. "One of them newspapers, . . ." he told Wilkins, "tried to put me on the spot about niggers voting. You saw it? Why, say, I ain't going to get into that fight. They don't vote in the South . . . they don't vote down there, so why should I get into that? I have been able to do a hell of a lot down there because I am Huey Long—they know I'm square: a lot of guys would have been murdered politically for what I've been able to do quietly for the niggers. But do you think I could get away with niggers voting? No sirree!"

While Wheeler assessed the Kingfish as remarkably free of prejudice, he was, however, hardly blind to one of Huey's less admirable traits: his insufferable boasting. "Well, I don't care anything about society," he defended himself to Wheeler. "I don't care anything about golf. I don't care anything about cards. The only pleasure I get out of life is boasting, and you want to take that away from me! When you stop to think of where I've come from and what I've got to do—don't you think I've got a right to boast?"

Wheeler possessed no answer for that. But boasting was hardly the Kingfish's only bad habit. He was, in fact, very good at not being good—"a grown-up bad boy," as *The Nation*'s Raymond Gram Swing put it.

Or, as Gertrude Stein observed with understatement, the senator was "not boring."

"Huey Long had a [very fine] brain, . . ." recalled Raymond Moley, "only he abused his power. He was arrogant and he drank too much.

You'd go to see Huey after three o'clock in the afternoon, and he didn't make much sense. He made sense in the morning. He had a rather contemptuous attitude toward Roosevelt. He didn't think Roosevelt was very smart. . . . One of the things he destroyed was himself. He didn't need to go swaggering around. He was much too good for that. It was one of the great tragedies."

Long, noted the contemporary journalist John Franklin Carter, "is so high-strung emotionally that it is hard to tell when he has been drinking and when he is sober. Even though no drop of intoxicants has passed his lips for weeks, he will weave back and forth, and flail his arms about like an inebriate who has reached the 'fighting drunk' stage. . . . [H]e can become intoxicated by whatever he says."

"Every serious blunder that Mr. Long made during his lifetime," admitted his most loyal aide, Gerald L. K. Smith, "was made under the influence of liquor."

They called the Kingfish a clown, and his flamboyant wardrobe—his pastel-colored shirts and wild ties and white linen suits—hardly softened that image. He greeted dignitaries and granted interviews (even to the Black Roy Wilkins) in his pajamas. He paraded around his beloved Louisiana State University like a veritable drum major. Newsreels chronicled his musical rendition of "Every Man a King," featuring not just an ordinary band but an all-girl one and led by "The Blonde Bombshell of Rhythm," Miss Ina Ray Hutton (for good measure, a mixed-race performer passing for white).

In August 1933, he emerged from the men's room of Gold Coast Long Island's exclusive Sands Point Bath and Racquet Club sporting an embarrassing black eye. "It is not clear what precipitated the denouement—," wrote Arthur Schlesinger Jr., "whether [it was] his free comments to a woman at a neighboring table ["I'll eat this for you. You're too fat already"], or an ingenious but misguided effort to urinate between the legs of the man in front of him while waiting his turn in the men's room, but, someone, goaded beyond endurance, hit Long in the face and opened a cut over his left eye. There was considerable merriment over the Kingfish's humiliation; medals were offered to the assailant, lists printed of men who regretted they had not committed the assault themselves."

Huey was, however, widely reputed to be a physical coward. In World War I, he sought exemption from conscription as a public official. He was, he claimed, a notary public. His younger brother Earl famously damned him as the "yellowest physical coward that God had ever let live." Some said he was a crook. One day FDR alleged that to Senator Wheeler. "Well, I don't think so," Wheeler countered, "but if he is a crook, he's too smart for you to catch him."

Roosevelt certainly did try to catch him. As early as 1930, Herbert Hoover's Treasury Department had been peering into Long machine finances ("Long and his gang are stealing everything in the state . . . and they're not paying taxes on the loot"), but its probe went nowhere. In January 1934, just three days after being appointed Secretary of the Treasury, Henry Morgenthau demanded of Elmer L. Irey, the departmental tax expert who snared Al Capone, "Why have you stopped investigating Huey Long[?] . . . Get all your agents back on the Louisiana job." Irey dutifully reported back to Morgenthau each and every week. Once, having nothing new to convey, he skipped a week—quickly earning Morgenthau's ire. By 1935, the IRS had indicted eight of Long's top henchmen including the oily Seymour Weiss, head of the Hotel Roosevelt Corporation and the New Orleans Dock Board, and Abe "The Collector" Sushan, president of the Levee Board and Huey's prime bagman.

FDR, too, received direct reports from Irey. He squeezed Long on tax matters; he squeezed him mightily on patronage from his various relief efforts. "Don't put anybody in," he ordered underlings, "and don't help anybody that is working for Huey Long or his crowd. That is 100 percent. . . . Everybody and every agency."

He meant it. In late March 1935, Henry Morgenthau recorded in his diary: "The Vice-President said at Cabinet to-day: 'Don't give those people in New Orleans $1.00. Let them starve to death. If they get rid of Huey Long we will give them some money—otherwise we will not.' The President agreed with the Vice-President."

"Hell," Huey snapped later that year, "if Jim Farley and Ickes spent as much money getting rid of Republicans as they've spent against me in . . . Louisiana, there would not be a Republican left in the Senate."

Nineteen thirty-five was not Franklin's most restful year. Racked with headaches as its congressional session rumbled to a close, associates found him unusually irritable. To his "Cousin Daisy" Suckley, he confided that he would "need either to swear at somebody or to have a long-suffering ear like yours to tell it to quietly!" That June, in the wake of the Supreme Court's NRA decision, his longtime friend the multi-talented ambassador Claude G. Bowers (a noted popular historian, skilled Democratic speechwriter and orator, and former Hearst columnist) returned from Madrid and twice met his chief. FDR commenced their first session with his normal upbeat jauntiness but soon revealed his powerful bitterness ("the bankers have had the people by the throat") over business opposition to his programs. Ten days later, Bowers returned for an outdoor White House lunch. "Having been caught in a traffic jam, I was two or three minutes late," he recalled, "and I found [FDR] at the table with a rather cold expression on his face. He accepted my . . . apology rather grimly, I thought. The old gaiety was not apparent this time." He found his host's overall manner "cold," beset by worries that "scarcely . . . a single metropolitan paper" would back him in 1936. More ominously, Bowers could not help but notice how Franklin's hand shook as he lit his cigarette. That evening, Bowers shared his experiences with Secretary of Commerce Daniel Roper, inquiring if FDR's nervousness was a new development. "Yes," responded Roper, ". . . since the Supreme Court decision."

"I was so tired," Roosevelt later admitted to Henry Morgenthau of those days, "that I would have enjoyed seeing you cry or would have gotten pleasure out of sticking pins into people and hurting them."

Franklin had reason for alarm. As he pursued Huey, Huey pursued him.

The Kingfish would never wrest 1936's nomination from Roosevelt. That wasn't his game. But by hook or crook, he'd tip the election against FDR, turn the country over to the Republicans (who would botch things even worse than previously), and cakewalk into the White House four years later; "1940," he boasted, "will be my real year."

A story circulated on Capitol Hill that Huey propositioned Henry Ford's son Edsel into running on 1936's Republican ticket. Neither the elder nor the younger Ford was interested in the idea. Other prospective

Long stalking horses included Idaho Republican William E. Borah, Georgia governor Eugene Talmadge, and California radical Upton Sinclair. None panned out, and Huey settled on himself—as a third-party spoiler to toss the race to the GOP.

His conscience bothered him not at all regarding sabotaging the Democratic Party. Like FDR, he was, in essence, "a Democrat of convenience," possessing no real respect for either party. He had explained that back in 1932, while first proposing his plans to distribute wealth:

> So the Democratic leaders and the Republican leaders got together and they jumped on my little resolution with all four feet. . . . [T]hey killed it deader'n a doornail. Oh, I tell you, they've got a set of Republican waiters on one side and a set of Democratic waiters on the other side, but back in the kitchen is only Wall Street, and no matter which set of waiters brings you the dish, it's Wall Street that has cooked it up.
>
> It puts me in mind of the patent-medicine man that used to come around our part of the country with two bottles of medicine. One he called High Popalorum. The other he called Low Popahirum. We asked him what was the difference, and he said the High Popalorum was made by taking the bark off a tree from the ground up, and the Low Popahirum by taking off the bark from the top down. And these days the only difference between the two parties in Congress that I can see is that the Republican leaders are skinning the people from the ankle up, and the Democratic leaders are taking off the hide from the ear down. Skin 'em up or skin 'em down, but skin 'em!

He ultimately came to believe that Franklin Roosevelt was the best skinner of all.

Which was *not* a compliment.

Jim Farley estimated that Huey would draw votes not merely in the South (a situation not too harmful to Roosevelt, save in Louisiana), but by equal percentages in battleground areas. After all, Long's 1932 campaigning in the radical populist Upper Midwest had proven startlingly effective. "It was easy to conceive a situation," Farley later wrote, "whereby Long [with] more than 3,000,000 votes, might have the balance of power in the 1936 election. For example the poll indicated that he would command upward of 100,000 votes in New York State, a pivotal state . . . ; and a vote of that size . . . mostly from our side . . . might spell disaster."

For his part, Long calculated that "Hoover is the logical nominee of the Republican Party after the Roosevelt raw deal. But it's bad logic. Everything that I believe to be crazy in the Roosevelt Administration was initiated by Herbert Hoover. The only difference between Roosevelt and Hoover is that Hoover was sincere and frightened. Roosevelt is a natural gambler: he'll take a chance on anything."

Huey penned a little book, *My First Days in the White House*, semi-jokingly outlining his new administration and tweaking opponents (and even friends) by naming them to various posts, including:

Secretary of Commerce—Herbert Hoover
Secretary of State—William E. Borah
Director of the Budget—Al Smith

The biggest and best tweak of all was for Secretary of the Navy—Lord of the Seas Franklin Delano Roosevelt.

Huey depicted the defeated Roosevelt protesting, "What in the world do you mean by offering me a Cabinet post, after all the things you have said about me as President?"

Answered Huey's imaginary self: "I only offered you a position which I thought you were qualified to fill."

Less pixieish and charming was Huey's growing reputation as the first American dictator, running Louisiana as his own private fiefdom, buying, selling, and threatening legislators and local officials at will—all but abolishing local government in New Orleans, Baton Rouge, and Alexandria. In 1930, before besting Lt. Governor Cyr in court, he ringed the state capitol with state militiamen. New Orleans's 1934 mayoral race witnessed both Long and his rival Mayor "Turkey Head" Walmsley stampede toward outright civil war. Huey's puppet governor, O. K. Allen, mobilized 2,500 state National Guardsmen; Walmsley deputized 400 special police armed with machine guns and tear gas.

Violence choked the air in Louisiana. An inordinate amount of talk concentrated on simply murdering Huey Long. In April 1935, as Huey rammed yet another oppressive measure through the legislature, anti-Longite state representative Mason Spencer vowed, "I am not gifted with second sight. Nor did I see a spot of blood on the moon last night. But I can see blood on the polished floor of the Capitol. For if you [Long] ride this thing through, you will travel with the white horse of death. White men have ever made poor slaves."

"There is no doubt his life is in danger," John Franklin Carter recorded in early 1935, "or that his assassination would be secretly applauded by the 'better element' in New Orleans. His armed bodyguard is not just showmanship." The *New York Times*'s Arthur Krock spotted Long tooling about Washington with not one, but two shotgun-toting bodyguards.

On Friday, August 9, 1935, Huey informed a stone-faced US Senate that during a July 22, 1935, meeting at Room 506 of New Orleans's De Soto Hotel, an anti-Long cabal schemed his assassination. "This," alleged Long, "is a great meeting of the higher element that is sent from Washington, D.C. with assurance that they had a right to indict anybody they wanted to, to hire anybody they wanted to, to fire anybody they wanted to, with all the money they needed."

The conspiracy, alleged Long, had been recorded on a dictagraph from an adjoining room, and one man proposed, "I would draw in a lottery to go out and kill Long. It would only take one man, one gun, and one bullet. . . . I haven't the slightest doubt that Roosevelt would pardon any man who killed Long."

Huey's charges were promptly denied. "As far as I am concerned," scoffed Mayor Walmsley, "the Senator is drunk again."

But no one dared deny the level of outright hatred festering among Long's enemies. "I attended the meeting, . . ." admitted former Shreveport mayor George W. Hardy, "but no such plan was suggested. However, since he has suggested it, I don't think it would be such a bad idea. And I, for one, should certainly make no objection."

Within a week, Long traveled to Manhattan, touting a third-party presidential campaign. "Mr. Long," noted the *New York Herald Tribune,* "was magnificent in a double-breasted tan suit of tropical worsted, violet shirt and yellow figured cravat. His smile flashed recurrently and his nose glistened in the glare of flashlight batteries."

He still predicted a race between Hoover and FDR: the "twin bed mates of disaster." "The country," he charged, "can't afford . . . a campaign . . . with no choice between Hoover, that we know what is, and Roosevelt, that we don't know what is and hope we never find out."

"If either Hoover or Roosevelt is elected," he informed a press gaggle of nearly two dozen reporters and cameramen, "there won't be any more millionaires in this country. If I'm elected, the country will have more millionaires than you ever dreamed of, and everyone else will be well-to-do in the bargain."

He nonetheless still proclaimed his unwillingness to run, naming eight senators he'd step aside for: Republicans William E. Borah (his first choice—"Borah would carry forty-eight states"), George W. Norris, Arthur Capper, Gerald Nye, and Lynn Frazier, or Democrats Burton Wheeler, Elmer Thomas, Kansas's George McGill, and South Dakota's William J. Bulow. The latter two could not be picked out of a police lineup by their mothers.

Thus, not all (if any) of his proposed "candidates" were quite genuine. Entirely real was a cool $1 million tucked away in the Kingfish's "deduct box," for his own presidential run. Nonetheless, work remained back home. In early September 1935, he roamed the state capitol, hectoring legislators to support his latest passel of vindictive, power-grabbing laws. One would gerrymander a special target of his ire, Opelousas District Court Judge Benjamin H. Pavy. Two of Pavy's relations had already been dropped from state payrolls, and, it was rumored, Long was prepared to play an even rougher game: a whispering campaign touting Mrs. Pavy's alleged "coffee blood"—i.e., African-American ancestry.

Huey definitely had race on his mind. Departing the House chamber, he spied Rep. Mason Spencer, he who back in April had dared predict "blood on the polished floor of the Capitol."

"You," Long snarled at Spencer, "remind me of an old nigger woman."

At 9:20 on Sunday night, September 8, 1935, Huey Pierce Long Jr. raced down a marble state capitol corridor. His omnipresent squad of bodyguards encircled him. A bespectacled white-suited young man darted out from behind a pillar, aimed his .32 caliber Browning pistol, and fired. Long wailed "I've been shot" and bolted away "like a hit deer" as his men pumped sixty-one bullets into his assailant, literally cutting him to pieces. Their victim was twenty-nine-year-old Dr. Carl Austin Weiss Sr., son-in-law of Judge Pavy. Some say Weiss had been at New Orleans's DeSoto Hotel that July, and it was he who had drawn the short straw. "He wanted it," it was alleged, but never proven, of Weiss. "He hated Huey because of the nigger business."

Thirty hours later, Long, suffering from massive internal bleeding, was dead. His last words were a plea, as genuine as anything he ever said: "God, don't let me die. I have so much to do."

What needed doing was demolishing Franklin Delano Roosevelt.

Among the nominees for the job was one Alfred Emanuel Smith.

· 4 ·

"Five negroes on my place . . ."

A very old friend of Franklin's was also dead—not anywhere deceased literally. Just personally and politically stone-cold departed.

Meet Alfred E. Smith.

Both Smith and Roosevelt hailed from New York. Both were Democrats. They had served alongside each other as state legislators. Both won election and reelection as governor of New York. Both served as their party's presidential standard-bearers.

Yet, as Long and Roosevelt were dissimilar, Smith and Roosevelt were as well. Smith was born poor; FDR rich. Smith hailed from a Lower East Side tenement; FDR from a Hudson Valley mansion. FDR graduated from Harvard; Smith from what he termed "FFM"—a $12-a-week, twelve-hour-per-day, six-day-per-week job at the Fulton Fish Market. Smith was Roman Catholic; FDR Protestant Episcopal. Smith was a loyal product of Manhattan's notoriously corrupt Tammany machine; FDR made his first mark spitting in Tammany's eye. Most recently, an explosive shift had emerged: FDR grew more liberal (or, at least, maintained his liberalism); Smith lurched rightward.

But the greatest disparity, the most profound spark of hatred—as it is so often politically—was this: FDR was "in." Al Smith was "out."

In 1918, both had coveted the same job: governor of New York. FDR, however, drew back from the contest, remaining assistant secretary of the

Navy. Smith abandoned his berth as president of New York City's Board of Aldermen and, in a generally Republican year, narrowly defeated a GOP incumbent. By 1920, Al had established a national reputation as a solid, efficient, progressive chief executive. He got things done, and, if it were not for the three strikes against him—his Tammany links, his Catholicism, and his too-vocal opposition to national Prohibition—he might well have someday reached the White House.

By 1920, Franklin Roosevelt had also decided on the very same destination, though his path seemed less certain. He might seek a US Senate seat or maybe even land on a national ticket. But frankly, there was at first no great reason to wager on either scenario. Tammany remained wary of his skills, his character, and his inclinations. They had crushed him in 1914's US senatorial primary—and, if he gave them the chance, would shed no tears thrashing him once more.

Both FDR and Smith had traveled to San Francisco for 1920's Democratic National Convention: Smith as a very dark horse favorite-son presidential candidate; FDR as a mere delegate with shifting loyalties. Sometimes he voted for Smith, sometimes for front-runner William Gibbs McAdoo, once even for the conservative ultra-long-shot John W. Davis. Smith departed the convention's forty-four ballots as a quickly discarded candidate. FDR emerged as nominee James M. Cox's running mate. By then, however, the patrician Roosevelt and the plebian Smith had hit it off, with Assistant Secretary Roosevelt plying fellow delegates with booze aboard his quarters on the battleship *New York*. FDR and Smith were pals—"Frank" and "Al."

Both lost in 1920's Republican landslide, but nonetheless acquitted themselves with grace. By 1922, Smith had easily recaptured the Governor's Mansion. By 1924, he was a serious presidential candidate—but with a new problem. His choice to provide his convention nominating address—the spellbinding veteran Tammanyite Congressman Bourke Cockran—was dead, and Smith turned instead to the squeaky-clean upstater Franklin Roosevelt.

Franklin faced far grimmer problems. Polio had paralyzed him in August 1921. Simply hobbling toward the Madison Square Garden speaker's podium was torture. Yet he did it, and the very sight of his valiant crutch-ridden walk—and the force of his manner and his words—galvanized a deeply divided convention.

Al Smith lost the nomination—to John W. Davis—but Franklin Roosevelt was back.

FDR nominated Smith—"The Happy Warrior"—yet again in 1928, this time successfully. Smith's nomination, however, created a huge hole on the statewide Democratic slate. Smith begged FDR to fill it. Franklin said no—1928 was too early for him, both in terms of his own muted White House plans and his rather fanciful plans for physical recovery. Smith wore him down. In November, Franklin squeaked to victory. Al—too Tammany, too Catholic, too "wet"—lost by historic margins to Herbert Hoover.

Yet Smith would soldier on. Suspicious of Franklin's competence and political will, he planned on serving as the power behind the wheelchair. FDR thought otherwise, not only ignoring Smith's offer of advice, but also jettisoning Smith's two most trusted—and capable—aides: Secretary of State Robert Moses (who had once refused a patronage job to Louis Howe; neither Howe nor Roosevelt ever forgave Moses for that) and, more hurtful to Smith, secretary to the Governor ("his strong right hand") Belle Moskowitz.

The bloom was off the Smith–Roosevelt rose.

The more Smith saw of Roosevelt (and increasingly that was from afar), the less he admired. As Al's close friend Judge Joseph Proskauer perceived, "Smith felt that there was [in FDR a] lack of sober judgment, of painstaking investigation and a propensity to play . . . hunches to a dangerous degree, particularly in [formulating] the domestic policies of the nation," and that Smith had grown to distrust Roosevelt's "approach to problems—not . . . the laborious study which Smith always gave, but . . . an intuitive process that no doubt at times produced brilliant results, but which Smith had always feared would end in disaster. We older lawyers sometimes admonish our juniors not to practice law 'by ear.' Smith believed that Roosevelt did practice statecraft by ear."

By 1932, FDR was not only the Democratic front-runner—he was someone who Smith regarded first and foremost as a tremendous ingrate. Smith also detected signals of FDR's emerging leftward tilt and a dangerous tendency toward fomenting class resentment and outright class warfare. FDR's famed April 1932 "Forgotten Man" address simply infuriated Smith. "This is no time for demagogues, . . ." he fumed. "[W]hen millions . . . are starving throughout the land, there is always a temptation . . . to stir up class prejudice, to stir up the bitterness of the rich against the poor, and the poor against the rich. . . . I will take off my coat and vest and fight to the end against any candidate who persists in any demagogic appeal to the masses of the working people of this country, to destroy themselves by setting class against class and rich against poor."

Smith belatedly entered 1932's presidential race. He fared well in the late primaries, but never possessed any genuine chance. His real game remained sabotaging Franklin's chances, to dispatch him to history's ash heap of discarded front-runners. Smith slowed FDR down but failed to stop him, and while Smith grudgingly endorsed his old pal, he never again loved him.

Smith's never-quite-mollified resentments ignited once more in 1933, as FDR again studiously avoided seeking Al's counsel on anything. Rumors had once swirled that he would appoint Al to head the federal government's then-most powerful recovery agency, the Reconstruction Finance Corporation. That went to Houston lumberman Jesse Jones, as FDR loaded his cabinet with Southerners and Westerners, the very antithesis of city-slicker Smith's version of the party. Adding insult to injury, Franklin's cabinet included South Carolinian Daniel Roper at Commerce. Roper was a McAdoo man, opposed to Smith in 1924 and, worse, who jumped ship to boost Hoover in 1928. When FDR's seventy-three-year-old choice for attorney general, Montana senator Thomas J. Walsh (for whom FDR had double-crossed Jouett Shouse at the 1932 convention), quickly keeled over following his appointment to the cabinet (and even more quickly following his marriage to a wealthy, much younger Cuban widow, Mina Nieves Perez Chaumont de Truffin), FDR replaced him with yet another McAdoo loyalist, Connecticut's Homer Cummings.

It was not exactly a "Team of Rivals" cabinet. "Scurrying through *Who's Who*, the *World Almanac*, and the United States Fingerprint Department trying to find out who they were, I can say the forgotten man has been found," joshed Will Rogers. "There's nine of 'em and a woman." To benefit such nonentities, Al Smith had once again been passed over.

In November 1933, the uneasy Smith–FDR cease-fire exploded. Smith fired the first shot: targeting FDR's abolition of the national gold standard. "I am for gold dollars as against baloney dollars," he snapped. "I am for experience as against experiment."

Other Democrats shared Smith's unease over FDR's leftward, big-spending, big-deficit drift. Under Secretary of the Treasury Dean Acheson resigned in protest of Roosevelt's gold-standard move. Budget Director Lewis Douglas, administration financial adviser James Warburg, and Treasury Under Secretary T. Jefferson Coolidge, all infuriated by New Deal spending, also exited. The distraught Douglas fretted that FDR's decision to outlaw gold foreshadowed "the end of western civilization."

Literally seated alongside "The Happy Warrior," in 1932, when he had unhappily denounced Roosevelt's "Forgotten Man" speech, were two more disgruntled Democrats: Maryland's long-serving governor Albert Ritchie and former Democratic National Chairman John Jakob Raskob. By mid-1934, Smith, Raskob, and Ritchie had allied themselves in opposition to Roosevelt in an entirely new venture: the American Liberty League.

The Liberty League was new. The Smith–Raskob–Ritchie alliance was not. While presidential wannabe Franklin Roosevelt dodged and weaved on repealing the Eighteenth Amendment, Smith, Raskob, and Ritchie led the way. If possible, Ritchie was even "wetter" than Smith. He was, certainly, more conservative, more Jeffersonian-small-government. Smith's fellow Catholic, Raskob, had grown rich from his dealings with the du Pont family and later as vice president of General Motors. Alongside the du Ponts, he helped found the Association Against the Prohibition Amendment (AAPA), providing Prohibition with a final hefty push into oblivion. In 1928, Smith appointed Raskob (a former independent who had donated to Coolidge in 1924) as Democratic national chairman. Raskob not only helped fund threadbare Democratic coffers, he provided $100,000 to keep FDR's beloved Warm Springs polio treatment center afloat as Franklin sought New York's governorship. Four years later, FDR fired Raskob and replaced him with Jim Farley.

When Smith retired from politics and needed something to do (not to mention something to live on), Raskob installed him as the $50,000-per-year president of his newest venture, Manhattan's towering Empire State Building. The Depression, however, took its toll, leaving Smith in charge of what many wisenheimers now mocked as the "Empty State Building."

In March 1934, R. R. M. "Ruly" Carpenter, brother-in-law to the three du Pont brothers—Pierre, Irénée, and Lammot—wrote Raskob, grousing about certain New Deal consequences:

> Five negroes on my place in South Carolina refused work this spring . . . saying they had easy jobs with the government. A cook on my houseboat at Fort Myers quit because the government was paying him a dollar an hour as a painter.

Raskob, equally skittish regarding New Deal largesse, responded: "You haven't much to do, and I know of no one that could better . . . induce the du Pont and General Motors groups, followed by other big industries, to definitely organize to protect society from the sufferings which it is bound to endure if we allow communistic elements to lead the people to believe that all businessmen are crooks." Raskob pointed to the need for "some very definite organization [to] come out openly with some plan for educating the people to the value of encouraging people to work; encouraging people to get rich."

Carpenter wasn't all that interested. He was already rich. But Raskob soldiered on, dubbing his brainchild "The Union Asserting the Integrity of Persons and Property." John W. Davis, arguing for economy of language, as well as government, countered with "Liberty League." He won.

To oversee this new "American Liberty League," Raskob hired a former Kansas Democratic congressman named Jouett Shouse. Like Franklin Roosevelt, Shouse sported a pince-nez, served in his state senate, and also in Woodrow Wilson's sub-cabinet. Like Ruly Carpenter, Shouse married into money—in Shouse's case, the daughter of Boston department store owner Edward Filene (a staunch FDR supporter). More to the point, Shouse had served as DNC executive director under Raskob.

Like Raskob, he had been canned by the new Roosevelt–Farley combine. Like Smith, he needed a job.

A *lot* of people still needed a job in 1934.

FDR had seriously double-crossed Shouse in the run-up to 1932's Democratic Convention. It went like this. Smith and Roosevelt forces negotiated a compromise on convention leadership: FDR's man, the stentorian and mesmerizing Kentucky senator Alben Barkley, would keynote the event; Shouse would chair it. That lasted as long as it was convenient for Franklin—i.e., not long at all, with FDR arguing that he had merely "commended" the deal, rather than having agreed to it. Roosevelt, noted historian Jonathan Alter, had "double-crossed his rival in a way that would sound familiar to his New Deal critics of later years. His move was cunning, shameless, and effective."

In forming their American Liberty League, Raskob and Shouse quickly recruited a seemingly impressive membership roster. For glamour, there was Mrs. Pauline Sabin, the aristocratic star of the women's Repeal movement—and veteran Hollywood slapstick producer Hal Roach. Montgomery Ward's Sewell Avery, and stockbroker E. F. Hutton (another active "wet"), and Woodrow Wilson's last secretary of state, Bainbridge Colby, all signed on. So did Al Smith's former speechwriter, Judge Joseph Proskauer. Republican recruits included ex-New York governor Nathan Miller and western New York congressman (and former US senator) James W. Wadsworth Jr., yet another ardent AAPA "wet." Some foresaw the brilliant Wadsworth as 1936's GOP nominee. John W. Davis recruited TR's ninety-year-old former Secretary of State Elihu Root.

It was a coalition of old adversaries, bound by new antipathies. Nathan Miller had defeated Smith for the governorship in 1920. Smith swamped Miller two years later. Wadsworth and Colby (then a Bull Moose Progressive) had battled each other in 1914's US Senate race.

Shouse optimistically predicted two or three million members—perhaps, yes, even four million. The *New York Times* naively editorialized that Raskob's new organization would enjoy "the blessing of all save the Socialists, the Communists and the wilder radicals of the two great parties. . . . The Administration and the League start out with an identic profession of aims."

Which was about the last good publicity the League ever got. It was no mere coincidence that each prominent Liberty Leaguer seemed to have the same first name: "*Former*." Current office holders fled its entreaties like the plague. Conservative Democratic senators like Virginia's Harry Flood Byrd and Carter Glass, Maryland's Millard Tydings, Oklahoma's sightless Thomas Gore, and North Carolina's Josiah Bailey all possessed significant anti–New Deal qualms but far more regarding the Liberty League. All quickly dashed for cover.

They retreated. FDR's legions attacked. "I've been hoping ever since 1912 that we'd have political parties divided on the real issues, . . ." Harold Ickes asserted. "[I]t's working out that way at last . . . all the progressives together and all the conservatives together. Then you'd always be facing your enemy and not wondering about what is happening behind your back."

Harry Hopkins taunted Liberty Leaguers as "right-thinking people . . . so far over to the right that no one would ever find them."

"All the big guns have started shooting," FDR confided to his newly-minted Moscow ambassador, Bill Bullitt. "Al Smith, John W. Davis, James W. Wadsworth, du Pont, Shouse, etc. Their organization has already been labeled the 'I can't take it club.'"

FDR soon unleashed his own blast. At his August 24, 1934 press conference, he revealed that an unidentified friend had humorously opined that the League only obeyed two of its own Ten Commandments ("Love thy God and hate thy neighbor"). He ratcheted it up to sneer that League members believed "property is God."

The *New York Times*, stripping gears, suddenly projected "rough going" for the League.

The League had debuted politely, though hardly honestly, with Shouse denying any anti-administration hostility. "It certainly isn't anti-New Deal, . . ." he alibied. "Suppose there were a tendency to extreme radicalism that the president sought to check. This organization would be helpful." Irénée du Pont also protested his loyalty to Roosevelt ("I am most desirous of being of use to the administration, having voted for Mr. Roosevelt")—but nonetheless demanded that FDR "in due course" dismantle his National Recovery Administration.

But not all the hypocrisy resided with Shouse and company. Hardly. Before publicly debuting the League, Shouse privately briefed FDR on its formal agenda. "I can subscribe to that one hundred percent," Roosevelt reassured him. "And so can you. I think it is fine." Franklin thought—or said he thought—it so fine that, before Shouse departed, he instructed his press secretary, Marvin McIntyre:

> Mac, Jouett has just told me of an Association which is being formed. . . . If I should be away, or for any reason I'm unavailable at the time this Association is made public, I want you to call in the newspaper men and tell them that the aims and purposes of the Association have been presented to me; that I approve of that most heartily; that I approve . . . of such an Association and think it is a valuable thing for the country and that I am delighted that Jouett is to head the Association.

He didn't mean a word of it.

The League filled two voids. First, as a coherent vehicle for anti–New Deal opposition. The shell-shocked Republican Party no longer seemed capable of that—or of much of anything else. What remained of it was an ideological mess. Many of its most prominent members, such as Senators Borah, Johnson, Norris, McNary, Capper, and the recently deceased Bronson Cutting, were definitely progressive. North Dakota's Republican congressional delegation was outright radical: Senators Gerald Nye and Lynn Frazier and Representatives Quentin Burdick and William Lemke. East Harlem Republican Vito Marcantonio (a protégé of ultra-progressive New York City mayor La Guardia) went them all one better, essentially operating as an outright Communist fellow traveler.

Johnson, Nye, Norris, Cutting, and Lemke had endorsed FDR in 1932. The obstreperous Borah had pointedly sat on his hands. Harding-Coolidge-Mellon-style conservatism was dead (or hibernating so soundly no one could tell the difference). Formerly progressive, big-spending Herbert Hoover had finally moved rightward. But the widely reviled former "Great Engineer" was nobody's idea of a Republican or conservative poster boy, save in a negative sense.

Nor was the Liberty League Hoover's idea of a swell time. Unable to now carry any election, he could still carry a grudge. In September 1934, when a friend solicited his advice on joining the League, Hoover seethed:

> This is the group that financed the Democratic smearing campaign. . . . Also, this is the group who supported the election of the New Deal. If this group had told the truth, either during the Republican Administration or during the campaign, as they . . . now acknowledge it to be, the country would not be in this situation. They are, therefore, hardly the type of men to lead the cause of Liberty.

The Liberty League failed to quell Herbert Hoover's smoldering anger. It marvelously fulfilled Franklin Roosevelt's desire for a convenient punching bag. His Democrats now virtually won elections almost by just showing up. Yet, even wildly popular movements require a bogeyman. Love is a great motivator in politics, but not as much as hate; and the American Liberty League—loaded with moneybag du Ponts—instantly became the organization that New Deal Democrats, liberals, progressives, and assorted radicals loved to hate. Its more agitated critics loathed them not merely as greedy, heartless capitalists but fantasized them into outright fascists, excitedly mistaking stuffed shirts for brown shirts.

The League's wheels fell off far too suddenly. Its engine wouldn't even start. Nowhere near to four million or three million or even two million members ever appeared on its rosters. After eleven months, membership stalled at 36,055. By January 1936, it had advanced to a mere 70,000. Even the frenzy of 1936's election only heightened "membership" to 124,856. But, in fact, as the League officially reported to the House that March, just 22,433 persons were "contributing members," making those larger figures less a galloping membership roster than a limping mailing list. Many rich donors pulled away. Raskob's friends at General Motors, led by its president William Knudsen and its chairman Alfred P. Sloan, retreated. E. F. Hutton—an anti–New Deal hard-liner—privately complained that he had no idea what the League actually stood for.

Raskob entreated Jim Farley for a meeting with FDR. In May 1935, he got one—flavored with a healthy dose of Roosevelt charm—and departed convinced that Franklin was not such a bad egg after all and really innocent of the anti-business animus Raskob's crowd now feared.

Franklin Roosevelt, however, was extremely proficient at leaving visitors with positive impressions, most importantly with the warm feeling that he agreed with you. He, of course, did *not* agree with John Jakob Raskob, who essentially remained as a critic had described him in 1932, "a naive amateur with an inaccurate idea of the importance his money . . . [still hobbled by] an amazing awkwardness at the political game."

In October 1935, Raskob learned the truth: Franklin had mocked his recent advice as that of "the long-time, privileged crowd [that has] failed to understand the social crisis of America." Worse still, FDR had crowed that he had no fear of any "rightist third party." In fact, he calculated, any such challenge "in truth, might even help" his reelection odds.

Such brickbats from Franklin Delano Roosevelt—*son* of wealth, *grandson* of wealth, *great-grandson* of wealth, and the cousin of a United States president—infuriated the up-from-his-bootstraps Raskob. Injury had already accompanied insult. In December 1934, the IRS probed a joint securities account he held with Shouse. In August 1935, Joe Kennedy's Securities and Exchange Commission accused Raskob of insider-trading 16,000 shares of GM stock. Those charges weren't true. In January 1936, the IRS announced an investigation of suspicious post–crash-stock transfers between Raskob and Pierre du Pont. Eventually, du Pont and Raskob ponied up an extra $586,369 and $1,473,202 in taxes, respectively, as a result.

The Liberty League stumbled forward—but stumbled elegantly. Its million-dollar budget supported fifty well-paid staff in thirty-one rooms, versus seventeen staff in twelve rooms for the Republican National Committee. Twenty-six college and university chapters dotted the map. It published a monthly newsletter and sponsored numerous radio broadcasts. Cigar-chomping Raoul E. Desvernine (Nathan Miller's law partner before becoming president of Crucible Steel) chaired its very active National Lawyers' Committee. Pauline Sabin helmed a far less active women's division.

The League specialized, however, in issuing pamphlets, almost invariably criticizing New Deal initiatives. In 1935–36, it published 135 such tracts, some with snappy titles like *Is the Constitution for Sale?*; *Americanism at the Crossroads*; and *What Is the Constitution between Friends?* But also others—with such less-snappy titles as *The Bituminous Coal Bill: An Analysis of a Proposed Step Toward Socialization of Industry;* and *The AAA Amendments: An Analysis of Proposals Illustrating a Trend toward a Fascist Control Not Only of Agriculture but Also of a Major Sector of Manufacturing and Distributing Industries.* The latter subtitle was clearly put together by a committee. A very large committee.

The Liberty League published. The general public shut its eyes. Few receiving a government check cared whether that check was constitutional or not. Many more resented hearing that it wasn't from folks they suspected of having crashed the economy in the first place.

As Bill Borah pointed out, "You can't eat the Constitution."

Authoritarian fascism swept Europe—and Americans were warned that it *could* happen here; and that if it did, it would come from these gentlemen, arguing for less government and less governmental power. The argument made no great sense but made for great headlines.

Two factors abetted anti-League hysteria. Most persistent was the era's widespread isolationism. America marched to war in 1917, convinced (or at least hoping) its blood and treasure would "Make the World Safe for Democracy." By 1934, many—perhaps most—suspected that we'd intruded upon Europe's squabbles to augment the fortunes of Wall Street moneylenders or to enrich "Merchants of Death" munition-makers—primarily the du Ponts, who had sold 1.5 billion pounds of explosives to the various Allied powers and grown fabulously rich as American doughboys died.

Du Pont money was now dirty money. Blood money.

· 5 ·

"A great pity"

Al Smith was always central to the American Liberty League. "The Happy Warrior" may not have supplied its bankroll or subtitled its pamphlets, but he starred as the League's leading man. If anyone could sway the Democratic masses—or at least enough of them—to capsize "That Man in the White House," it was Al Smith. The nation's Catholics still loved him. So did Tammany's bosses and ward heelers, aggrieved as they were by FDR's funneling of patronage and projects through their latest rival, the city's newly elected reform mayor, Fiorello La Guardia.

Smith towered over the League's other marquee names. John W. Davis was brilliant—but colorless and far too connected to Wall Street. Maryland's Albert Ritchie had been offered the vice presidential nomination at 1932's Democratic Convention by Jim Farley, but had his limitations, looking, as Scripps-Howard columnist Thomas Stokes noted, "somehow like a wax figure in a show window." Ritchie's limitations caught up with him in 1934—when he somehow managed to lose his governorship in an otherwise landslide Democratic year. Massachusetts governor Joseph Ely always found himself in the role of "leading man's best friend" to Al Smith's "leading man" bravura performances. Bainbridge Colby served as Woodrow Wilson's least-remembered Secretary of State. Never much of a public figure, he was now suspect for hiring out as legal counsel for the controversial William Randolph Hearst.

Yes, if anyone were to finally bell the New Deal cat and not just harmlessly tug at its tail, it would have to be Franklin Roosevelt's old pal Alfred Emanuel Smith.

Yet, as FDR's New Deal took shape throughout mid-1933, Smith gritted his teeth and remained publicly on board, even expressing support for the NIRA. This was doubly surprising: first, because of his never-quelled resentments against FDR; but, perhaps even more so, from his own increasing conservatism. In so many ways, Al was still fighting the last war. His national career had always revolved around opposition to Prohibition, and the longer he thought about national issues, the more he saw them through the prism of a beer glass—i.e., the more he resisted federal power. For, if the federal government had stupidly run roughshod over states' rights with the Eighteenth Amendment, well, then, perchance a federal constitutional amendment to (say) ban child labor might lead to another distasteful run of noble intentions and ignoble unintended consequences run amok. Better, Al now thought, to leave matters in local hands.

In October 1932, the once-progressive Smith wrote:

> [F]reedom of persons under 18 from labor is not an absolute, basic human right. It is a relative matter of age, race, climate, family, and economic conditions, and local sentiment. In other words, it is a matter to be settled by the conscience and common-sense of each community and not by Federal mandate.

Smith, noted his biographer Christopher Finan, "began to believe that the danger of giving new power to the federal government outweighed any good it might do. He was . . . on a collision course with the New Deal."

And, as Smith had already reasoned, if votes in party primaries had once assisted the Anti-Saloon League and the Methodist Board of Temperance to corral "dry" legislative votes, well, then, maybe direct primaries weren't so hot either. In March 1931, he announced his opposition to them as well.

Yet he hung back from fully assaulting the administration. True, he had signed on with the Liberty League's August 1934 launch, but the League swore—and continued to swear—that it bore no particular grudge versus FDR, insisting that it only stood against radicalism and for the Constitution. In the early summer of 1935, Raskob and Irénée du Pont hectored Smith to speak out publicly against Roosevelt. E. F. Hutton, too, groused about his inaction. Yet Smith still hesitated. Perhaps out of respect for Roosevelt. Perhaps because he had a new book out, a textbook on government called *The Citizen and His Government.* Perhaps because of talk he might reclaim the governorship in 1936.

He would not waver forever.

As Election Year 1936 swung open, his assault commenced.

The League, which held very few public events, hosted a gala dinner on Saturday evening, January 25, 1936, at Washington's swank Mayflower Hotel. A fortnight previously, the same hotel had showcased FDR addressing a $50-a-plate Democratic Jackson Day fundraiser—his remarks broadcast nationwide to 250,000 Democrats at 2,000 similar affairs. Ominously (to Smith, at least), FDR framed the upcoming election as "the retention of popular government" in the face of "reactionaries" and "the minority in business and finance who would 'gang up' against the people's liberties."

"We will," FDR thunderously concluded, "not retreat."

Retreat, however, might well have been in the air.

On Wednesday, January 22, 1936, *New York Times* editorialists commented on the ill feelings dividing New Dealers and old Tammanyites, positing that in cities like New York, Chicago, St. Louis, and San Francisco:

> the Democratic organization [is] not satisfactory to the party authorities at national headquarters. Evidence of dissension and . . . disloyalty trickles out from large centers of population. The rural heart is said still to be true to the Administration but the urban pulse is not so steady. . . .
>
> Democratic majorities have largely been won in the cities. If their votes drop off, the presidential election may be closer than any Democratic prophet had hitherto admitted. Federal patronage is mighty, but cannot be expected to prevail after it has been so nearly exhausted.

Jim Farley's mailbag contained too many letters echoing one loyal (but nervous) Democrat: "If the boys want to keep their feet in the hog trough they better be looking around to find another Democratic candidate for use in next July."

The *Literary Digest* reported an abrupt drop in New Deal popularity. For twenty years, the *Digest* had mailed out millions of straw ballots to ascertain public opinion. It was, by later standards, a highly unscientific exercise; but with so huge a sample, it usually proved correct, forecasting presidential contests accurately from 1916 through 1932.

In October 1934, an astounding 69.03 percent of those polled by the *Digest* had endorsed New Deal policies, presaging solid Democratic gains in that November's midterms. In January 1936, however, the *Digest* asked: "Do you NOW approve the acts and policies of the Roosevelt New Deal to date?" Only 38.11 percent of its 1.7 million respondents answered yes. In crucial New York, New Deal support languished at 32.09 percent. It cratered in Massachusetts at just 19.70 percent—a figure that might, however, have aroused some suspicion as to the poll's overall veracity.

As Al Smith prepared to depart for Washington in January 1936, he received an invitation—from Eleanor Roosevelt. E.R. had always exhibited a particular enthusiasm, even a fondness, for Al. In 1924, she broke family ranks, not only to campaign against her first cousin Ted Roosevelt in his ill-fated gubernatorial run against Al, but to also install a huge vapor-belching white canvas "teapot" upon her campaign touring car. It was a pointed—and unfair—dig at Ted's alleged role in the Teapot Dome oil scandal and forever soured relations between Hyde Park and Oyster Bay Roosevelts.

In September 1928, Smith entreated Eleanor to intervene with her reluctant husband on a potential FDR gubernatorial run. That November, she answered press queries regarding her husband's upset triumph thusly: "If the rest of the ticket [Smith] didn't get in, what does it matter? No, I am not excited about my husband's election. I don't care. What difference does it make to me?" She conveyed the same sentiment to her friend and neighbor, Henry Morgenthau's wife, Elinor: "I felt Gov. Smith's election meant something, but whether Franklin spends two years in Albany or not matters as you know comparatively little."

And so, in December 1935, as the press trumpeted Al's appearance at 1936's Liberty Lobby gala, Eleanor innocently (or not) wrote to the Happy Warrior: "I see by the papers that you will be down here to speak on the 25th of January. Franklin and I hope very much that you and any of your family will stay with us at least for the night. You can feel as free as you wish to come and go."

Eleanor's missive may have triggered an unpleasant déjà vu within Al. In 1932, on the very verge of announcing his own candidacy, he had received another invitation—from Franklin—enjoining him to a personal tête-à-tête. Smith, of course, had other things to do.

And so he also did now, answering Eleanor on that December 26: "It is a matter of regret that I will be unable to avail myself of it. No member of my family is to accompany me and I have made arrangements with a party of men and it looks like I will have to stay with them." His "party of men" included John Jakob Raskob.

Things were heating up. In Boston, on Monday, December 30, 1935, Joseph L. Kaplan, general counsel of the National Support Roosevelt League, urged a Senate investigation of the Liberty League. At Massachusetts's far end, at Lenox in the Berkshires, Joseph Ely declared that should Smith seek that year's Democratic nomination, he would "back him to the sky."

In New York, Al Smith *was* in the sky, at his thirty-second-floor Empire State Building offices, celebrating his sixty-second birthday. He posed in funny paper party hats with reporters. But not all was unalloyed merriment.

The Happy Warrior was not happy.

By now, word of his response to Eleanor had leaked out to the papers—displeasing him even further. "I notice by the public press," Smith told reporters, "that a spokesman for the President is responsible for the following statement: 'This is not the first time that Mr. Smith has been invited to be an overnight guest of the White House. At least once a year Mr. Smith has been invited to pass either a night or a week-end there, but he never saw fit to accept even one of these invitations.' This statement is false.

"Since the Inauguration of President Roosevelt I received one invitation, through Secretary [Marvin] McIntyre, when it was known that

I was to attend a meeting of the trustees of Catholic University at Washington.

"That invitation was to tea at 5 o'clock in the afternoon [of November 14, 1933] in the company of Mr. Raskob and [my doctor] Dr. [Francis] Sullivan, and that invitation I accepted.

"It is the only one I ever received up to the one that came last week from Mrs. Roosevelt, which was promptly acknowledged.

"We might just as well have the record straight."

Smith's blast set off alarm bells. The Roosevelt press office frantically responded:

> The only statement made by anyone within the White House was that which Mrs. Roosevelt made today, in answer to questions at a press conference. The statement was spoken by Mrs. Roosevelt. . . . Transcribed from the stenographic reports, . . . the statement, complete and literal, follows in full:
>
> > I cannot imagine how anyone got hold of that (the invitation extended to Mr. Smith). I worked with Governor Smith in every state campaign and when he ran for president. I have always asked him here. I asked if he and his family were coming down for the 25th and if they would care to come and stay, just as I would have asked any other friend.

"There is no change in my statement," Smith rebutted. "My statement is the facts about the matter. Mrs. Smith never was in Washington. She doesn't know what it looks like—that's No. 1. No. 2—I have not been in Washington since October [sic] of '33."

Events had deteriorated beyond what either Al or Eleanor would have wished—either politically or personally. She now wrote him: "The newspapers seem to have managed to involve us in a rather foolish and extremely disagreeable controversy." At her conciliatory best, she commented on how both she and Al recognized "only too well how untrue quotes often are" and gently refreshed Smith's memory regarding an invitation from the previous summer—not accepted as Mrs. Smith was still recuperating from a seriously fractured right arm.

She continued: "I feel sure that you have the same desire that I have, not to let political differences injure a personal relationship. I have never felt anything but friendship for you and your family. . . . I think it is a great pity for people who have had respect and admiration for each other to be prodded into antagonistic personal feelings, and so, in this new year, I wish to assure you and all your family of our good wishes for the future, and that always . . . our home is open to you, with or without an invitation."

On Sunday, January 5, 1936, a more docile Al responded: "Personal and Confidential—Like you, [I know] it would be a great pity if political differences were permitted to grow into personal animosities and I deprecate the efforts being made to that end. . . . Throughout my political life I have had honest differences with many men but have never allowed them to interfere with personal friendship. I earnestly supported Frank in 1928, 1930 and 1932 and if I take issue now with some of the policies of the administration it is not with any personal animosity towards him or you. Please accept the assurance of my regard for you both and my best wishes for the new year."

Their spat receded from public view. Even Governor Ely's hints of a possible Smith candidacy vaporized, and he now joked about what role he might play in the upcoming presidential contest: "Probably that of a fellow who talks too much."

Franklin delivered his latest State of the Union Address on Friday, January 3. Originally, he had doubts on how to proceed. The ailing Louis Howe had none. "Franklin," he rasped, "get in there and fight. Give them the old 'Roosevelt Dutch' in this speech. Remind them of the conditions in the country when you took over. Tell them what you have done. Ask them if the country is not infinitely better off than when you came on the scene. Give them a resume of the laws passed for the benefit of the people. You have a lot to brag about, nothing to apologize for. Let 'em have it. They'll lap it up!"

Franklin agreed.

Both his message and his medium broke new ground. At the last moment, FDR surprised observers by announcing that he'd speak not during Congress's normal business hours, but at 9:00 p.m. Eastern Time. Many a congressman was flummoxed, unsure of what to wear at such an hour. Full formal dress? Dinner jackets? Morning coats? An exasperated Roosevelt fumed that he was ready to tell 'em: wear your pajamas!

Such unprecedented scheduling vastly augmented his audience, essentially transforming the event into a spin-off of his famed Fireside Chats. *The Nation* observed that the new time slot had converted the affair into "a political rally," with congressmen, senators, and the galleries reduced to mere props, essentially to his "studio audience."

It was great box office. But reviews of its artistic quality proved mixed. The left-leaning *New Republic* observed that FDR "cannot hope to hold the masses . . . by expressions of sympathy which . . . give hardly an inkling of what, after nearly three years of office, he proposes to do for them."

The Nation's Paul Ward accused FDR of junking the role of "statesman" for that of a "pure politico" who subverted

> a thoughtful discussion of the nation's ills and ways of treating them into a political diatribe. It was received as such by his partisans, the Democrats . . . whooping, hollering, and stamping their feet as Roosevelt hurled barb after barb at the helpless Republicans present and thundered defiance at unnamed and unseen forces of darkness. Soon he had whipped his followers into that senseless ecstasy that overtakes political conventions when a leading contender has just been placed in nomination, and for such unprecedented behavior the Republicans at last retaliated in a fashion that promptly wiped the grin from Roosevelt's face and made it grim. They broke into raucous laughter at his expense when he referred to his address as "this message on the state of the union."

FDR delivered a two-pronged message. He commenced by addressing Europe's increasingly ominous affairs (the "growing ill-will, of marked trends toward aggression, of increasing armaments, of shortening tempers . . . the elements that lead to the tragedy of general war"). He concluded by declaring war on his own Right flank—throwing huge chunks of red meat to his critics on the Left. For, as Harold Ickes warned him in early December, "the general sentiment of the country is much more radical than that of the Administration."

"[W]e have invited battle," FDR declared without apology:

> we have earned the hatred of entrenched greed. The very nature of the problem that we faced made it necessary to drive some people from power and strictly to regulate others. . . . I spoke of the practices of the unscrupulous money-changers who stood indicted in the court of public opinion. I spoke of the rulers of the exchanges of mankind's goods, who failed through their own stubbornness and their own incompetence. I said that they had admitted their failure and had abdicated. . . .
>
> They seek the restoration of their selfish power. They offer to lead us back round the same old corner into the same old dreary street. . . . They seek—this minority in business and industry—to control and often do control and use for their own purposes legitimate and highly honored business associations; they engage in vast propaganda to spread fear and discord among the people—they would "gang up" against the people's liberties. . . .
>
> Shall we say to the several millions of unemployed citizens who face the very problem of existence, of getting enough to eat, "We will withdraw from giving you work. We will turn you back to the charity of your communities and those men of selfish power who tell you that perhaps they will employ you if the Government leaves them strictly alone?"
>
> Shall we say to the needy unemployed, "Your problem is a local one except that perhaps the Federal Government, as an act of mere generosity, will be willing to pay to your city or to your county a few grudging dollars to help maintain your soup kitchens?" Shall we say to the children who have worked all day in the factories, "Child labor is a local issue and so are your starvation wages; something to be solved or left unsolved by the jurisdiction of forty-eight States?"

Shall we say to the laborer, "Your right to organize, your relations with your employer have nothing to do with the public interest; if your employer will not even meet with you to discuss your problems and his, that is none of our affair?"

Shall we say to the unemployed and the aged, "Social security lies not within the province of the Federal Government; you must seek relief elsewhere?"

Shall we say to the men and women who live in conditions of squalor in country and in city, "The health and the happiness of you and your children are no concern of ours?"

Shall we expose our population once more by the repeal of laws which protect them against the loss of their honest investments and against the manipulations of dishonest speculators?

Shall we abandon the splendid efforts of the Federal Government to raise the health standards of the Nation and to give youth a decent opportunity through such means as the Civilian Conservation Corps? . . .

If this is what these gentlemen want, let them say so. . . . Let them no longer hide their dissent in a cowardly cloak of generality. Let them define the issue. We have been specific in our affirmative action. Let them be specific in their negative attack.

But the challenge . . . is more menacing than merely a return to the past—bad as that would be. Our resplendent economic autocracy does not want to return to that individualism of which they prate, even though the advantages under that system went to the ruthless and the strong. They realize that in thirty-four months we have built up new instruments of public power. In the hands of a people's Government this power is wholesome and proper. But in the hands of political puppets of an economic autocracy such power would provide shackles for the liberties of the people. Give them their way and they will take the course of every autocracy of the past—power for themselves, enslavement for the public.

A new FDR was emerging, objected the clearly uneasy editorialists of the *New York Herald Tribune*. The Roosevelt message, it charged, was now tainted by a "strain of manner and a bitterness [and] its incitement to hatred at home . . . for the first time [he] made the fomenting of hatred among Americans his open goal. . . . A smiling president has been replaced by a bitter one who will omit no appeal to prejudice or selfishness or passion in his effort to stave off defeat."

If Franklin was not then bitter, he surely was just two days later—when the Supreme Court invalidated the AAA.

Everyone was getting nervous, making wild charges, ascribing ever more vicious motives to their opponents. Columnist Mark Sullivan mused:

> Much talk says that . . . Franklin D. Roosevelt [aims] to outdo his fifth cousin, Theodore. Such an urge might lead President Roosevelt to wish to choose the Democratic nominee in 1940. If so, some circumstances would lead him to prefer Hopkins. But if Franklin has an urge to outdo Theodore . . . let him get himself nominated by the Democrats for a third term, and get himself elected. That would be genuinely dramatic. . . .
>
> Limiting occupants of the presidency to two terms is a tradition. . . . [As] democracy everywhere is under attack, those who cherish democracy ought to be especially careful to respect its traditions. But I do not know if this would appeal to Mr. Roosevelt. He is not one who cherishes traditions.

Meanwhile, the political world breathlessly awaited Al Smith's own "State of the Union." Speculation continued to swirl regarding Smith challenging FDR for the nomination. Or, if not Smith, someone else. Perchance, Maryland's Albert Ritchie—though his fatal February 1936 heart attack soon obviously short-circuited that option. Much, much further down any list lay Woodrow Wilson's former Assistant Secretary of War Henry Breckinridge, a favorite of another anti-Roosevelt organization, the "Sentinels of the Republic." Breckinridge stirred the pot by requesting petitions for Ohio's May 12 Democratic primary for an unnamed mystery candidate, who some speculated was Charles Lindbergh. In the end, it was Breckinridge himself, and not even the Liberty League was interested in that goose chase.

By Thursday, January 23, 1936, capital gossip was abuzz, anticipating Smith's expected salvos. Washington State first-term Democrat Lewis B. Schwellenbach (a rising administration hatchetman) took to the Senate floor for a preemptive strike, lambasting Raskob and Pierre du Pont as tax-cheating "leeches and bloodsuckers . . . rascals and crooks."

The evening preceding Smith's blast, John W. Davis laid down his own barrage. At Manhattan's Waldorf Astoria, he addressed the New York Bar Association, excoriating both the bureaucracy ("the least responsible, the least intelligent and the most arrogant and tyrannical" portion of government) and the weakening of Congress ("it will become something worse than an occasional rubber stamp").

"The more favors and advantages government has to bestow," Davis argued, "the fiercer must become the strife to possess them; and out of this perpetual warfare of man against man, class against class, industry against industry, section against section, all striving to influence the agencies of government for their selfish desires, there must come legislative blocks, organized lobbies, pressure politics, and the ultimate degradation and pollution of our whole political life. We have such evils in our midst today. In God's name, why aggravate them by broadening the field in which they can operate?"

Assembling for Smith's Liberty Lobby address was the largest crowd in Mayflower Hotel history, and—despite its ominous absence of current office holders—one among the most glamorous in recent Washington memory.

The evening was indeed glittery, exciting. It was also remarkably affordable. Democrats had charged $50.00 for Jackson Day; the League a mere $5.00—definitely a deflationary policy.

"Unlike [the Democrats'] dinner, no raid was made on Government employes [sic]," jibed master of ceremonies Jouett Shouse, "no attempt was made to urge or compel them to be present. There has been no need to go into the highways and byways to try to get an audience. We have turned away 9,000 people tonight. We could have turned away 20,000."

"Unlike that other dinner," he continued, "there will be no recriminations. There will be no suggestion that those who do not agree with us are crooks."

Two thousand guests dined on the evening's elegant cuisine. It included:

Tomatoes Stuffed with Lobster and Crab Flakes
Mock Turtle with Old Sherry
Celery Olives Nuts
Filet Mignon with Paté de Foie Gras
Fresh Mushroom Sauce
Baked Broccoli with Sauce Roast Potato
Hearts of Romaine with Honeydew Melon and Alligator Pear
Bengal Dressing Cheese Wafers
Fresh Strawberries with Hazelnut Ice Cream
Macarons and Madelines
Coffee

A smattering of disgruntled former administration officials attended: Treasury's Dean Acheson, and James P. Warburg, along with former Assistant Postmaster General Silliman Evans. That was about it. Current members of Congress were also in short supply: aside from Rep. James Wadsworth and Pennsylvania's senator "Puddler Jim" Davis, only seven other congressmen (all Republicans) attended. A single Democratic senator sat in—Oklahoma's Elmer Thomas—but only to spy and scoff ("The Democrats can afford to hire Al Smith to make that speech everywhere. If he makes this often enough, Roosevelt is sure to be re-elected") and, perhaps, while present, to feast on filet mignon and macarons.

And, while the League's board of directors was dotted with many a "former" celebrity (Smith, Davis, Wadsworth, Ely, Ritchie, Nathan Miller), in a world now littered with Republican "formers," few bothered attending: two ex-senators, Pennsylvania's David A. Reed and Connecticut's Hiram Bingham, and two ex-representatives—Pennsylvania's James M. Beck (a dynamo on the League's lawyer's committee) and East St. Louis's long-retired William A. Rodenberg.

In a highly segregated city, this event was not. Present were James A. Cobb ("colored, former judge of the Municipal Court of the District") and Howard University's Dr. Emmett J. Scott, a Booker T. Washington protégé and a former Taft and Wilson appointee.

Distaff guests included *Washington Herald* publisher Eleanor Medill "Cissy" Patterson as well as a pair of Eleanor's paternal cousins: Corinne Robinson Alsop and Alice Roosevelt Longworth, widow of House Speaker Nicholas Longworth. Alsop, a former Connecticut Republican state representative, was herself lodging at the White House for the evening. Longworth (a Washington resident) was now an anti–New Deal newspaper columnist. Her column was fairly dull. Her barely private opinions (Franklin was "two-thirds mush and one-third Eleanor") weren't.

Alice Longworth wore white with a brown fur jacket. President Grant's granddaughter, Madame Julia Dent Cantacuzène, now a White Russian princess, chose "black silk with a draping of dotted lace about her shapely shoulders." The prize for elegance went, however, as usual, to the svelte and blonde Mrs. Pauline Sabin, Repeal's guiding feminine light, gracing the head table in an "evening jacket made of solid white sequins, overlapping and intertwining, over a gown of black crepe." Representing far more money but not nearly as much glamour were Wall Street banker Grayson Mallet-Prevost Murphy (recently publicly accused of plotting FDR's forcible overthrow), the Sun Oil Company's Howard Pew, Cornelius Vanderbilt Jr., steel magnate Ernest T. Weir, Chase National Bank President Winthrop W. Aldrich, Guggenheim copper fortune heir Col. M. Robert Guggenheim, publisher J. B. Lippincott, the *Washington Post*'s Eugene Meyer, and, of course, the evening's major-domo, John Jakob Raskob.

Overshadowing even their wealth, however, were the du Ponts. They numbered an even dozen—a delicious talking point for anti–Liberty League commentators and politicos: two of the famed du Pont brothers—Irénée and Pierre—and their wives; plus Felix A. du Pont Jr.; Mr. and Mrs. Alfred V. du Pont; Emile F. du Pont; Eugene E. du Pont; Mr. and Mrs. Henry B. du Pont; and Irénée's daughter Miss Octavia du Pont.

"Few of the diners wore tails and white ties," the *Chicago Tribune* reflected. "Dinner jackets predominated and a few even had on business suits and colored four-in-hands."

Conspicuously (nearly, incongruously), however, in gleaming white tie and tails, stood Alfred Emanuel Smith. The graphic transformation of the

Lower East Side's Happy Warrior into a stern habitué of Upper East Side salons would long haunt both him and the League itself. Clothes make the man. They *unmake* men as well.

From the side rooms and corridors of the Mayflower, hundreds of League sympathizers now poured into the ballroom as Smith grimly took the podium. His audience, however, flaunted a roaring good humor, striking up Smith's theme "The Sidewalks of New York." A good part of them seemed drunk (this was, after all, a Repeal crowd), including one Philadelphia matron who trailed her fur muff through her ice cream.

Jouett Shouse pounded his oversized gavel. "This is not a gavel," said Fulton Fish Market alumni Smith, with a laugh. "It's a lobster mallet." Shouse slammed it again—so hard, it splintered. Finally, Smith commenced:

> At the outset of my remarks, let me make one thing perfectly clear. I am not a candidate for any office of any party at any time. I have no ax to grind. There is nothing personal in what I have to say. I have no feeling against any man, woman or child in the United States. I represent no group, no man, and I speak for no man or group. But I do speak for what I believe is the best interests of the American people.

Like it or not, he *did* represent the Liberty League, and his words (ghosted in part, some said, by Robert Moses, though Moses refused Smith's entreaties to join the League) were soon hung around the League's gilded neck.

Unlike John W. Davis, Smith delivered no mere treatise on constitutional government or abstract bureaucracy. Rather, he unleashed a root-and-branch assault on the New Deal, commencing with a point-by-point contrast of 1932's Democratic platform and how FDR's administration actually ruled. "Regulation of the Stock Exchange and the repeal of the Eighteenth Amendment, plus one or two minor planks . . . have been carried out," was virtually all Smith would concede, "but the balance of the platform was thrown in the wastebasket. About that there can be no question."

He derided Roosevelt's promise to Scripps-Howard publisher Roy Howard of a business breathing spell, asking, "Did you read in the papers a short time ago where somebody said that business was going to get a breathing spell? What is the meaning of that? And where did that expression arise? I'll tell you where it comes from. It comes from the prize ring. When the aggressor is punching the head off the other fellow he suddenly takes compassion on him and he gives him a breathing spell before he delivers the knockout wallop."

He accused the White House not only of insincerity and of a failure to fulfill 1932 campaign promises, and he denounced his party's leftward pitch into literally foreign territory:

> Make a test for yourself. Just get the platform of the Democratic Party, and get the platform of the Socialist Party, and lay them down on your dining room table, side by side, and get a heavy lead pencil and scratch out the word "Democrat," and scratch out the word "Socialist," and let the two platforms lay there.
>
> Then study the record of the present Administration up to date. After you have done that, make your mind up to pick up the platform that more nearly squares with the record, and you will put your hand on the Socialist platform. . . .
>
> And, incidentally, let me say that it is not the first time in recorded history, that a group of men have stolen the livery of the church to do the work of the devil.
>
> If you study this whole situation, you will find that that is at the bottom of all our troubles. This country was organized on the principles of representative democracy, and you can't mix Socialism or Communism with that. They are like oil and water; they refuse to mix. And incidentally, let me say to you, that is the reason why the United States Supreme Court is working overtime throwing the alphabet out the window three letters at a time.
>
> Now I am going to let you in on something else. How do you suppose all this happened? Here is the way it happened: the young Brain Trusters caught the Socialists in swimming and they ran away with their clothes.

> It is all right with me. It is all right with me if they want to disguise themselves as Norman Thomas or Karl Marx, or Lenin, or any of the rest of that bunch, but what I won't stand for is to let them march under the banner of Jefferson, Jackson, or Cleveland. . . .
>
> There can be only one Capital—Washington or Moscow. There can be only one atmosphere of government, the clear, pure, fresh air of free America, or the foul breath of Communistic Russia. There can be only one flag, the Stars and Stripes, or the Red Flag of the godless union of the Soviet. There can be only one National Anthem. The Star Spangled Banner or the Internationale.

Smith challenged his listeners, his party, and his nation: "There is only one of two things we can do. We can either take on the mantle of hypocrisy or we can take a walk, and we will probably do the latter."

A walk.

An outraged bolt from the party. Democrats had been doing that for a while. Numerous party members had abandoned Smith in 1928. Others fled John W. Davis four years before that—including FDR's friend Burton K. Wheeler, the vice presidential candidate of that year's third-party Progressive ticket. Cleveland "Gold Democrats" (including Woodrow Wilson, Louis Brandeis, and Bourke Cockran) had deserted William Jennings Bryan back in 1896. Young Franklin Roosevelt voted for Republican cousin Theodore in 1900.

"It was perfect," said Pierre du Pont of Smith's peroration.

Others disagreed. Reporters covering the event—men who had idolized Al Smith in 1928—were disgusted. Smith, mourned *The Nation*'s Paul Ward, "did more than read himself out of the Democratic Party. He read himself out of the respect and affections of all men of good faith." Columnist Heywood Broun pronounced Smith's effort "a good technical performance—but otherwise lousy."

Smith long felt that FDR had betrayed him; Franklin's admirers now cast Smith as a "traitor" and a "Judas." In Washington State, a hundred men burned him in effigy.

Harold Ickes listened to Smith over the CBS network. He wrote to his diary: "I was struck with Al Smith's bad radio voice. His utterance is so thick that at times it is difficult to understand. . . . There were words and phrases that were unintelligible to me."

Smith's diction hadn't bothered Ickes when he endorsed him in 1928.

The following morning, Ickes and Kentucky senator Alben Barkley headlined a "Town Hall" breakfast forum at Washington's Shoreham Hotel. While dressing himself for the event, Ickes received a phone call informing him that when, in October 1928, Herbert Hoover had damned Smith's advocacy of public water power as "Socialist," Smith had shot back, "The cry of Socialism has been patented by the powerful interests that desire to put a damper on progressive legislation." At the Shoreham, Barkley served as Ickes's straight man, as Ickes gleefully recounted Smith's old defense.

Two evenings later, Smith's 1928 running mate, Senate Majority Leader Joe Robinson, poured it on. Following bandleader Fred Waring and his Pennsylvanians over CBS airwaves, Robinson recited numerous examples of Smith's previous progressivism—including his initial support of the NRA and even for an FDR dictatorship—concluding with what was already becoming a cliché: "The brown derby has been discarded for the high hat."

It had been a swell party at the Mayflower, but with a hangover the dozen du Ponts never hoped for. "From all of this preliminary ballyhoo," concluded the magazine *Contemporary Speeches*, "the country was led to expect something sensational, a bombshell which would blast the very foundations from under the administration and bring it crashing down. No man could live up to such advance notices. The bombshell was fated to be a dud."

Al Smith was indeed the du Ponts' most spectacular dud . . . but hardly their worst. That blow fell, within days, not in Washington . . . but way down South in Dixie, in Macon, Georgia.

· 6 ·

"Common, ignorant, and half-tight"

Huey Long lay moldering in his grave, leaving the ranks of current Democratic officeholders who were battling Franklin Roosevelt shriveled to a precious few.

One being the approximate number.

Georgia governor Eugene Talmadge was as Southern as Huey. More so. Like Huey, he had leapfrogged from small-town lawyer to minor statewide official to governor and was now aiming for the US Senate. Like Huey, he loathed FDR. Like Huey, he toyed with a presidential run.

The Kingfish defied FDR from the populist Left. The bespectacled Talmadge confronted the New Deal from distinctly conservative moorings. He had surprised observers by winning election as state agriculture commissioner in 1926, rapidly cementing a reputation as the friend of the small farmer. Handily winning reelection in 1928, he then faced impeachment charges for filching state funds. "Sure, I stole it!" he argued to his constituents. "But I stole it for you." And, so, formal charges were never brought.

As Talmadge fought his way to the top (of Georgia, anyway), he perfected a down-home manner, snapping his trademark red suspenders, and even personally plowing fields for his constituents. "[T]here is," observed the *Saturday Evening Post*, "one type of Georgian who loves Gene Talmadge with a deep and undying love—the small farmer, the tenant farmer and sharecropper, men with bearded, sun-scorched faces, who wear overalls and big black hats, stiff with the sweat and grease of 20 summers . . . the 'Wool-Hat Boys.'"

As Talmadge was once introduced at a rally: "You folks only got three friends who never let you down—God! Sears Roebuck! And Ol' Gene!"

Governor Richard Russell vacated his position in 1930 to enter the United States Senate. Talmadge sought the office, pledging fiscal economy, a balanced budget, lower utility rates and property taxes, a reformed highway board, and lower automobile tag fees. Neither a "Share-Our-Wealth" nor a "New Deal" platform, it was, instead, traditional Jeffersonian Democracy.

Talmadge's promise to reduce automobile tag (license plate) fees to three dollars elected him. A tag could cost up to $30, causing some poor farmers to share one; sometimes even entire rural communities shared one—with it left hanging at the general store, much like a washroom key. At Talmadge rallies, entertainers sang:

I gotta Eugene dog, I gotta Eugene cat.
I'm a Eugene man from ma shoes to ma hat.
Farmers in the cornfield hollerin' whoa gee haw.
Kain't put no thirty-dollar tag on a three-dollar car.

A majority of dogs and cats may have preferred Eugene. In 1932, only a plurality of actual voters did. Georgia Democrats nominated statewide officials not by direct popular vote, but instead through a "county unit system" that increased the power of the state's rural, sparsely populated counties—Talmadge's power base. Ol' Gene attracted just 116,000 of 292,000 popular votes (40.2 percent). He corralled a solid majority (252) of the state's 410 "unit" votes (61.46 percent).

Talmadge kept his auto-tag promise—and his vow to slash taxes. Though the Depression hit Georgia as hard as anywhere else, Talmadge provided almost no state funds for badly needed relief measures. The federal government did, supporting 500,000 (out of a total population of just 2,800,000) state relief recipients. Such largesse failed to impress Talmadge, who soon commenced an all-out war on Roosevelt's "mad course of socialism" and emerged as a national hero for disaffected conservative

Democrats (and, of course, amused Republicans). In 1934, despite Roosevelt's active opposition, Talmadge carried 65.95 percent of the popular vote, sweeping 156 of 159 counties.

Talmadge proved extraordinarily hostile (even by Southern standards) to organized labor—and not just rhetorically. In 1934, he ordered National Guardsmen to round up 200 strikers—and later, 130 more. Like Huey Long, he played rough with legislators. When they refused to lower auto tag fees, he did it by executive order. "I reckon," Ol' Gene would say a few years later, "I'm what you'd call a minor dictator. But did you ever see anybody who was much good who didn't have a little dictator in him?"

Talmadge grew bolder—and nastier—regarding FDR. In April 1935, he sneered, "The greatest calamity in this country is that President Roosevelt can't walk around and hunt up people to talk to. He can only talk to those [people] his secretaries and assistants allow to come in, . . . and 90 percent of the crowd is the gimme crowd. If I'd stayed in my office like that, never going out to meet and talk to people, I'd mildew. . . . The next President we have should be able to walk a two-by-four."

He possessed no use for Social Security either. "Listen, my countrymen," he enlightened one audience in 1936, "I been studyin' the pension act of the New Deal. I find they's mo' niggers in Jawjah that would git the pension than there are white folks. They's mo' niggers past sixty-five than there are white people. An' listen to this: eve'y nigger that got his pension would be suppo' un a passle of young niggers able to work. The white people wouldn't git the pension, but they'd be taxed to pay the niggers. An' listen to this—listen to this carefully. You wouldn't be able ta have a nigger plow-hand, a nigger washwoman or cook 'cause they'd all be livin' high on pensions."

In November 1935, Roosevelt visited Atlanta. Talmadge pointedly ducked out of town, saying he had gone hunting—"hunting something to plant that there's not any [AAA] processing tax on." At four o'clock that morning, on the state capitol grounds, a hundred pro-Roosevelt men hung Talmadge in effigy.

Talmadge sought anti–New Deal allies—or, perhaps, they sought him. Texas's John Henry Kirby had been, until recently, the South's biggest lumberman. Some said the portly, freckle-faced Kirby was the biggest harvester of pine ("The Prince of the Pines") in the world. He'd also grown rich in oil and natural gas (his gas company eventually became Enron). For good measure, he served as a director of the Dr. Pepper Corporation. His glory, however, eventually faded. By May 1933, he was bankrupt.

Kirby had long hated a big federal government, not just Franklin Roosevelt's New Deal but even Woodrow Wilson's "New Freedom." In July 1935, he formed the "Southern Committee to Uphold the Constitution" (SCUC), grandly claiming fifty thousand members—and the support of 70 percent of all Southerners.

As Democrats still required a two-third delegate vote to nominate a presidential candidate, Kirby dreamt of a deadlocked convention dumping the hated FDR and floated a number of alternate hopefuls: Maryland's Albert Ritchie, Virginia senators Byrd and Glass, Woodrow Wilson's former Secretary of War Newton D. Baker, or Reconstruction Finance Corporation Chairman Jesse H. Jones (his office landlord). Even Huey Long. Soon, Kirby settled on Talmadge. Frankly, hardly anyone, save for the forgettable Henry Breckinridge, remotely craved the assignment.

More significantly, a Huey Long–Eugene Talmadge alliance was forming. Ideologically, it made little sense. Their mutual antipathy remained wide open. In February 1935, Huey sneered, "That Talmadge ain't got the brains to suit his ambition." He derided the Talmadge operation as a "g-ddamn bush league outfit." That April, Talmadge complained that Long's "doctrine of 'share-the-wealth' is out[-]Roosevelting Roosevelt." Yet, as 1936 approached, the two inched toward rapprochement.

By September 1935, however, the Kingfish was gone.

The man who helped inter him now required something else to do—the Rev. Gerald L. K. Smith.

Huey's family had anointed Smith to eulogize the Kingfish at his massive Baton Rouge funeral. A hundred thousand mourners wept as the distraught Smith praised and mourned their—and *his*—hero:

> The blood which dropped upon this soil shall seal our hearts together. Take up the torch, complete the task, subdue selfish ambition, sacrifice for the sake of victory.

I was with him when he died. I said "amen" as he breathed his last. His final prayer was this: "Oh, God, don't let me die. I have a few things more to do." The work which he left undone, we must complete. As one with no political ambition, and who seeks no gratuities at the hand of the State, I challenge you, my comrades, to complete the task.

Oh, God, why did we have to lose him?

Championing the still-living Kingfish back in February 1935, Smith had gushingly pronounced:

> Huey Long is the greatest headline writer I have ever seen. His circulars attract, bite, sting and convince. It is difficult to imagine what would happen in America if every human being were to read one Huey Long circular on the same day. As a mass-meeting speaker, his equal has never been known in America. His knowledge of national and international affairs, as well as local affairs, is uncanny. He seems to be equally at home with all subjects. . . . Besides this, I am convinced that he is the greatest political strategist alive. Huey Long is a superman. I actually believe that he can do as much in one day as any ten men I know. He abstains from alcohol, he uses no tobacco; he is strong, youthful and enthusiastic. Hostile communities and individuals move toward him like an avalanche once they see him and hear him speak. His greatest recommendation is that we who know him best, love him most.

The Wisconsin-born Smith had always been a populist, a progressive. His father, L. Z. Smith, an admirer of Senator Robert La Follette Sr., toiled as an itinerant patent-medicine salesman but also as a part-time Disciples of Christ preacher. As a boy, Gerald won an oratorical gold medal for reciting Bryan's electrifying Cross of Gold speech. In 1916, he himself was ordained into the ministry, eventually serving congregations in both Wisconsin and Indiana. While at Gary, Indiana, in 1929, his wife, Elna, contracted tuberculosis from the city's coal-smoked atmosphere, and the Smiths headed south to presumably healthier Shreveport, Louisiana.

Smith's oratory was powerful. His message progressive. His work charitable. When the Depression struck, and his congregants faced foreclosure on their homes, Smith appealed to Huey Long for help. "Governor," Smith entreated, "some of these bloodsuckers, they are planning to put my people out on the street. Are you going to let them do it?" Long came through, and Smith enlisted in Huey's traveling entourage. When the *Washington Herald* mistakenly identified the stocky, powerfully built Smith as one of the Kingfish's bodyguards, church trustees demanded his resignation.

Smith sued the *Herald* for $150,000 and dramatically exited his congregation before a crowd of five thousand. "I am embracing Huey P. Long," he proclaimed, "and I am going to attempt to help make him President of the United States, but I want you to understand that I am not becoming a whiskey-drinking ex-preacher. I am standing with the people to whom this great man has given his life. I am resigning, not because I have less faith in God but because I refuse to be a servile puppet of people who would use the holy church to satisfy their greedy ambition."

Smith might indeed have enlisted elsewhere—with causes even less respectable. Some say he dabbled with the Klan. Many contend he joined William Dudley Pelley's outright fascist "Silver Shirt" movement. In January 1933, signing his name as "Schmidt," he wrote to a German-American publisher in San Antonio, imploring to be introduced to Adolf Hitler. "The Semitic propaganda in America," contended Smith, "is growing more serious every day . . . the Jews are trying to rob the American people just as they attempted to do in Germany[,] and Germany and America will be closer together than any two nations in the world."

In Smith, Huey Long obtained not merely a powerful, almost hypnotic orator, but an intensely loyal—indeed obsessive—disciple. He set Gerald to traveling around the country (largely through the South) to peddle Share-Our-Wealth Clubs, eventually addressing an estimated two million people in an eighteen-month period. Huey (a man of few compliments) appraised him as "the only man I ever saw who was a better rabble-rouser than I am."

"A steam locomotive is not a pretty object," contended Smith regarding the Kingfish. "It puffs, it belches soot and cinders, it curses, it blows off steam, and it lacks the gracious attributes of refinement. But the beautiful and refined parlor car is quite helpless without it. Huey Long, whose thinking is a correct representation of the mass mind, is the locomotive whose power moves the entire Share-the-Wealth train, and his ego is the fire that generates the motive force of steam pressure in the boiler. When he is absorbed in what outsiders may regard as sordid and petty political manipulations, . . . he is supplying the practical machinery to put a social philosophy into operation. . . . And he is likewise too busy to pass his weekends on some millionaire's yacht where he might be won away from our ideal."

"Wall Street and its newspapers, and the radio liars," Smith raged in February 1935, "say [Share-Our-Wealth] is a scheme to make money for your friend Huey Long. They'd kill him if they could, my brethren. And they're going to have to kill him to keep him from helping you. As God is my judge, the only way they will keep Huey Long from the White House is to kill him. But when they do, his great work will go marching on."

Smith's allegiance with Long represented an oddly debased, frenzied liberalism, concluded *The Nation*'s Raymond Gram Swing, who found Smith unusually helpful and eager in securing his interview with the Kingfish. "He assured me," recalled Swing, "that Huey Long would be found to be *The Nation*'s man. He himself, he said, had been brought up in Wisconsin on *La Follette's Weekly*. He promised me that I would find Louisiana under Long's domination all that *The Nation* could pray for in generous liberalism."

"I think," continued Swing, "that at the time [Smith] genuinely believed that Long was a liberal and that as an editor of *The Nation* I would recognize it. What convinces me of this is that he vouched for me without reservation to Senator Long, so that I was admitted to anything and everything I cared to attend." This included a session in which the green-pajama-clad, periodically urinating Kingfish discussed with his pliant henchmen all manner of nefarious dealings. "If I had printed the dialog I heard," Swing added, "it might well have convicted Huey Long of being a crooked politician. But this was not news in Louisiana."

Swing found much of Long's program admirable. His *Nation* article, nevertheless, proved critical enough ("The Menace of Mr. Long") to trigger Smith's bitter complaint. A few weeks later, Smith reconsidered. "He had changed his mind," recalled Swing. "My article had done Huey Long a great service. I had elevated him from being a clown into being a menace."

Smith ranked among Long's more idealistic henchmen. "If God was Governor of Louisiana," Huey supposedly once informed him, "He couldn't find enough honest men to make a chairman for each county. If anything happens to me, Gerald, you're the only one of this gang that shouldn't go to the federal penitentiary. These boys who were barefoot when I found them just can't keep their hands out of the public till."

It was true. Federal bloodhounds were already trailing Huey's less savory associates. When their chieftain permanently departed, they begged Washington for a truce. The administration calculated that without their fallen leader, his machine would soon be driven out of office and powerless. Accordingly, the New Deal said "No Deal" to Long's ex-minions.

They guessed very, very wrong. January 1936's Louisiana elections resoundingly endorsed anti-FDR Longism, and Roosevelt caved. His Justice Department dropped all criminal charges. His relief agencies opened the spigots of federal aid. Cynics dubbed it "The Second Louisiana Purchase." Nine outraged members of the grand jury investigating the machine protested in writing to Attorney General Homer Cummings. Cummings ignored them.

"Peace, it was wonderful!" noted one observer. "Buildings, bridges, hospitals, grade crossings, zoos, swimming pools, playgrounds. . . . Washington [DC] was the father of all good; a kindly, older friend who cut corners, snipped red tape, looked with a special altruism on projects marked Louisiana. Evidences of prosperity thrust themselves upward on all sides; parts of Louisiana became gardens of WPA and PWA goodwill."

Long's heirs not only ceased all anti–New Deal efforts, but in June 1936 descended to astonishingly abject obeisance as the Louisiana legislature pilgrimaged to Texas for an unprecedented out-of-state official session. Groveling before the visiting FDR, they praised "divine providence for providing a great leader, Franklin D. Roosevelt, who saved the nation from ruin and chaos." They entreated Republicans to "abandon [their] vain and useless effort to overcome the will of the people of the United States."

As part of their deal, Long's successors also pledged to shutter his "Share-Our-Wealth" clubs—rendering the Rev. Gerald L. K. Smith unemployed. He had earned his pink slip. Largely a political amateur, Smith had artlessly alienated all surviving Long factions, clumsily switching sides in 1936's gubernatorial primary, even attempting to extort $10,000 from one candidate. As early as the morning of the Kingfish's funeral, Smith propositioned Huey's former secretary Earle J. Christenberry to keep the old Share-Our-Wealth operation going as a racket, fleecing the faithful at the clip of a dime a week.

Despised by all factions ("get out of Louisiana under your own power or be carried out") and unwilling to resume his ministry, Smith desperately searched for new allies—and a new crusade.

Luckily, there were several to choose from. Conveniently, one lay in the South.

Gene Talmadge and John Henry Kirby had scheduled a massive anti–New Deal "Grass Roots" convention of "the Jeffersonian Democrats of Southern and border states" at Macon, Georgia, on January 25. Ten thousand patriots, they trumpeted, would attend. So would Smith, hankering to hitch his battered wagon to their new star.

There wasn't anything Jeffersonian about Smith. Nor Hamiltonian, come to think of it. But it was any port in a New Deal storm. From New York City, he boasted, "I've made 432 speeches and traveled 22,000 miles since Huey Long died. I've been into every bayou, swamp and cotton pickers' settlement in Louisiana. . . . [Governor Talmadge] is the leader of [Georgia], just as the ghost of Huey P. Long is the leader of all the South. Roosevelt's enemies are our friends. Louisiana is taking the lead in repudiating Roosevelt. Georgia will be next. We'll have at least five states from the Deep South before the [Democratic] convention."

Yet only about three thousand persons showed up at Macon—with few attending from outside Georgia—the latter group being dismissed by *Time* magazine as "about 150 professional soreheads." What attendees lacked in numbers, they possessed in genuine rebel flair. An immense

Confederate battle flag fluttered above the speaker's platform. Strains of "Dixie" punctuated the air. Delegates cussed out Yankees—at least one attendee declared that he wished his daddy had killed more of 'em. Kirby touted Talmadge as "a plumed knight on an errand for the republic, refusing to bend his knee . . . for Federal Gold." He solemnly vowed to "re-affirm the platform of 1932" and to "nominate a Democrat and not a Socialist" at their approaching national convention.

Talmadge, himself, delivered a fairly standard anti–New Deal address, enlivened by a graphic attack on farm policy, specifically on the now-defunct AAA's planned scarcity policies:

> Every true Democrat hangs his head in shame, when he realizes that under the name of a Democratic administration, boards and bureaus, and the President himself, say that the way to bring back prosperity in this country is through scarcity—have less to eat, and less to wear. To carry out this crazy, infamous plan, they ordered millions of hogs and cattle killed, and thrown into the rivers or buried. Millions more of little suckling pigs were shipped off to Chicago. On top of this, they paid a premium to get to cut a good brood sow's throat. It took a little time for this travesty but when they struck the sheep and goats, they drove them on top of the mountains, forcing them to jump off the cliffs and kill themselves in the valleys below. And when the starving people went there to retrieve some of these carcasses that were not too badly mangled by the rocks, the trained welfare workers ran them off, leaving them as food only for the coyotes and wolves. They burned up wheat and oats, and plowed under cotton here in the South.

The Rev. Smith had previously derided the politician he labeled "Franklin Lenin Roosevelt." "We're going to turn that cripple out of the White House, . . ." he now stormed. "He and his gang are in the death rattle. We have only to put the cloth of the ballot over his dead mouth." He derided Eleanor as "a Rasputin in the White House," denouncing her for fostering Communism among the nation's ten million Blacks.

It might, however, have been worse.

"Those who have heard the Rev. Smith . . . in Louisiana," observed Hearst's International News Service, "say his speech . . . was mild [compared] to what he has to say in his own bayous, among his own people."

Smith was also tame compared to the rest of the show. "Too many . . . political clip-joint keepers, bigot-buyers and stale-hokum slingers got into the picture," judged *Collier's Weekly*. "Somewhat to his chagrin, Gene found himself sharing the cheers with Kluxers, professional lilywhites, racketeering nigger-haters, lynch-mob promoters, Yankee-baiters, left-over Populists, something-for-nothing brethren, pension preachers and a wide assortment of free-lance hookworms who would howl like a full-moon dog for anything that omitted work."

Falling into at least one of those categories was seventy-two-year-old Thomas Dixon Jr. Like Gerald Smith, Dixon was also a former minister (in his case, a Baptist), but he was clearly much more than that, as a highly successful novelist and playwright, his most prominent opus being the 1905 novel *The Clansman: A Historical Romance of the Ku Klux Klan*—the basis for D. W. Griffith's 1915 blockbuster silent film, *Birth of a Nation.* Recent years had proven less kind to Dixon. Plagued by declining sales and heavy real estate and stock market losses, he was now essentially bankrupt.

He had campaigned for FDR in 1932, and he later went on the air to praise the NRA coal industry code as "a Magna Carta of human rights." But his liberalism had its limits, and it often stalled at the door marked racial equality. When the NAACP had telegraphed the Macon convention that "it would make itself a laughingstock" unless it guaranteed African Americans their constitutional rights, Dixon (attired, it was said, in a dressing gown rather than an actual suit) responded, "We do not lower ourselves to reply to the Association of Colored People, because it is the rottenest Communist organization in the United States."

The NAACP, he continued, "is the author of the Wagner-Costigan [anti-lynching] Act— . . . to place bayonets at our breasts." He charged that Eleanor Roosevelt supported such measures—which, come to think of it, was actually true.

Racial matters similarly obsessed Mrs. James Rogers (Jessie) Wakefield, the forty-three-year-old managing editor of an Atlanta-based eight-page semi-monthly broadsheet, the *Georgia Women's World,* which despite its innocuous title resembled neither the *Ladies' Home Journal* nor *Better Homes & Gardens*. At Macon, *The Nation*'s Benjamin Stolberg made Jessie Wakefield's acquaintance and found her "incredibly common, ignorant, and half-tight." Alluding to the Democratic Party's recent Jackson Day dinner, her broadsheet (proudly distributed to every attendee) pointed out:

> Andrew Jackson didn't appoint a Negro Assistant Attorney General of the United States.
>
> Andrew Jackson didn't have a negro confidential clerk in the White House.
>
> Andrew Jackson didn't try to ram an anti-lynching bill down the throats of the southern people through a Democratic Congress.
>
> Andrew Jackson said, "To the victor belong the spoils," and when Andrew Jackson got to be president he didn't put in Republicans, Socialists, Communists and Negroes to tell him how they run these good old United States.

Georgia Women's World's current issue also sported a series of photographs. Several, as *Collier's Weekly* sarcastically noted, showed "Mrs. Roosevelt being escorted into and out of [all-Black] Howard University by students and members of the faculty who, God help the White Race, are Negroes. Then there is a photograph of President Roosevelt talking to members of the Colored Elks—proof in itself that we are headed for racial social equality. Next a photograph of Miss Josephine Roche, Assistant Secretary of the Treasury, standing beside Mrs. Mary McLeod Bethune, president of Bethune-Cookman College (colored). Arise, proud men and noble mothers of the Southland! Do you know that this picture was taken at the meeting of the National Association for the Advancement of Colored People? Are we to permit the people who rule us to go truckin' around like that with niggers?"

Such sentiments did little to popularize the Southern Committee to Uphold the Constitution much beyond a three-block radius of the convention itself. Excuses were made. John Henry Kirby played dumb about the contents of the *Georgia Women's World* but, nonetheless, averred that "in Dixie" such practices were "not to be condemned." Gene Talmadge piously refused to censure a friend whose "heart is in the right place." A few months later, however, the *New York Times* could report that "an automobile owned and driven by [Talmadge's] stepson was wrecked in Atlanta. Police . . . reported officially that the car was filled with bundles of the paper."

The NAACP's monthly journal, *The Crisis,* dismissed the gathering as "Despicable and Stupid." The entire Northern press (and, probably, a significant portion of the Southern press) concurred.

Worse press soon arrived. Franklin Roosevelt had always been a proponent of public power utilities, and, not surprisingly, skeptical of many privately owned utilities, particularly those controlled by so-called "holding companies."

"[H]olding companies," noted historian John A. Riggs, "could provide good management advice, acquire capital on favorable terms, build larger and more efficient plants, and obtain better prices by purchasing in larger quantities." Infamous Chicago holding-company magnate Samuel Insull, for example, regularly lowered not just his costs but also customer rates.

But, as Riggs added, holding companies "could also apply more effective pressure on government, through campaign contributions or expert testimony before regulatory commissions, to keep rates from being cut as fast as technological advances might warrant. Another [feature] was to concentrate power in the hands of a small number of owners, who could regularly mark up the value of the securities of their subsidiaries, increases that were magnified as they moved up the pyramid. Not all holding company owners were driven by such motivations, but the reputations of all utility industry officials suffered from their actions"—as did such practices as padding engineering contracts and watering stocks.

Years previously, Harvard undergraduate Franklin Roosevelt had attended Prof. William Z. Ripley's course on corporate concentration. Ripley argued that a "serious defect of overdeveloped holding company organization is the temptation afforded to prestidigitation, double shuffling, honeyfugling, hornswoggling, and skullduggery. Sound and defensible management shades off almost imperceptibly under stress of self-interest, given such concentration of control . . . into all sorts of nefarious dealings." FDR never forgot Ripley's thesis.

In his January 1935 State of the Union Address, Franklin declared war on holding companies—employing a rhetorical twist. His prepared remarks included the phrase "abolition of the evil features of holding companies." Thanks to a slip of the tongue (perhaps), he instead demanded the "abolition of the evil of holding companies." And, following a contentious meeting with utility executive Wendell Willkie, he dispatched to Congress the Public Utility Holding Company Act of 1935 (the "Wheeler–Rayburn Bill") to regulate such entities.

Wheeler–Rayburn's most controversial aspect was its "death sentence" provision, eliminating any holding company not part of a geographically or economically integrated system, by January 1, 1938. Said "death sentence" proved so contentious that when proposed to the measure's sponsors, Senator Burton Wheeler and Rep. Sam Rayburn, by the rising young New Deal attorneys Ben Cohen and "Tommy the Cork" Corcoran (drafters not only of Wheeler–Rayburn but also of the TVA and, later, of the Rural Electrification Administration Act), both Wheeler and Rayburn initially resisted its inclusion within their bill.

Power companies—an unusually powerful and well-organized group—fought FDR's "death sentence" tooth and nail. Wendell Willkie (a delegate to both 1924 and 1932's Democratic Conventions) proved not only to be an effective advocate against the "death penalty" (supposedly even coining the term) but emerged as a media star—and, eventually, even what passed for a Republican. The industry inundated Washington with lobbyists, telegrams, letters, and phone calls. They pressured newspapers into favorable coverage, or, at least, to soft-peddle unfavorable coverage. Back home, as one scholar noted, "regulation of public utilities . . . affected directly or indirectly millions of Americans. Every hamlet . . . had its public utility and millions of Americans either owned stock in their local utility or worked for it. Any attempt to tamper with, or restrict the profitability of, these institutions . . . naturally [met] with a broad and hostile reception from people [with] a very personal financial interest in their welfare."

In July 1935, Wheeler–Rayburn squeaked through the Senate 45–44—but cratered 215–146 in the House. In retaliation, FDR commanded the Senate to empower a "Special Committee to Investigate Lobbying Activities"—essentially targeting holding companies' lobbying tactics, particularly how they had flooded congressional offices with thousands of telegrams, ostensibly from voters but in reality from industry operatives. Chairing the committee was Alabama's Hugo Black, who regarded holding companies as "a blood-sucking business, a vampire" and proceeded to subpoena telegraph-company records. But not just *any* telegraph records—but *every single telegram* sent in or out of Washington, DC from February 1, 1935, through September 1, 1935—five million telegrams in all, to be peered into by committee staffers and by personnel borrowed from the Federal Communications Commission. Subpoenas reached into the communications of law firms and newspapers, impinging on both attorney-client privilege and freedom of the press. Committee investigators rousted one witness from his Plainfield, New Jersey, bed at 1:00 a.m. to whisk him to Washington and to groggily testify before Black.

Black ("There is no constitutional right to lobby") also requested a "general blanket order" from the IRS for tax returns of suspected miscreants. "Most of the individuals on [the committee's] list," noted scholar David Beito, "had no conceivable role in fake telegrams. Black asked for returns from as early as 1925, predating the death sentence by a decade." His immense dragnet included columnist David Lawrence and even two anti–death sentence congressmen: Liberty Leaguer James Wadsworth Jr. and Alabama Democrat George Huddleston.

The committee's overbearing tactics triggered opposition. The *New York Times*'s Arthur Krock excoriated the administration's "vindictive spirit . . . towards its critics" as well as the "snooping of Congressional bodies more interested in getting political ammunition against the enemies of the party in power than in . . . the orderly consideration of legislation."

The American Society of Newspaper Editors warned against an impending "threat to liberty of individual action and particularly of the freedom of the press."

While evincing little sympathy for "the philosophies of those . . . involved," the American Civil Liberties Union nonetheless issued its own protest, citing its mission to "defend civil rights." Even "Death Penalty" clause co-author Ben Cohen eventually came to believe that Black "went too far."

When Chicago attorney Silas Hardy Strawn (not only the former national finance chair of the Republican Party, but also past president of both the American Bar Association and the US Chamber of Commerce) discovered that his own telegrams had been subpoenaed, he brought suit. In March 1936, the US District Court for the District of Columbia ruled that the Black Committee's "subpoena goes way beyond . . . legitimate use. . . . The plaintiffs . . . have the right to be protected."

Visiting the White House, former Brain Truster Raymond Moley, still an occasional FDR speechwriter, dared protest to the president. "I simply wanted to set in the record, . . ." he recalled, "that it would have been better to let the guilty go free than to establish the principle of dragnet investigations. I did not believe that the end justified the means. I did not believe . . . that the kettle of the newspapers was particularly blacker than the pot of the administration." Roosevelt wouldn't budge. "This nightmarish conversation," added Moley, "went on and on in circles for some two hours. It left me with the harrowing intimation that Roosevelt was looking forward to nothing more than having the opposition of his 'enemies'—the newspapers, the bankers, the businessmen—re-elect him."

Black's rough methods nonetheless got results, and the House reversed course to pass a revised form of Wheeler–Rayburn. Wendell Willkie was hardly mollified. "While a strait-jacket will keep a man out of trouble," he grumbled, "it is not a suitable garment in which to work."

Black now shifted his committee's focus from holding companies to the Liberty League. Avoiding a frontal assault, he attacked more obscure flanks: thirteen organizations that League members, such as Raskob and the du Ponts, had funded as individuals.

In May and June 1936, Black placed said organizations under his microscope: the American Federation of Utility Investors, the American Taxpayers League, The Crusaders (a youthful offshoot of Jouett Shouse's old Association Against the Prohibition Amendment), the National

Committee on Monetary Policy, the Farmers Independence Council, the League for Industrial Rights, the Minute Men and Women of Today, the National Economy League, the New York State Economic Council, Repeal Associates, the Sentinels of the Republic, the Women Investors of America, Inc.—and, hardly least, John Henry Kirby's Southern Committee to Uphold the Constitution.

"The American Liberty League was itself never called," noted historian George Wolfskill. "It did not have to be. Tried in absentia, it was declared guilty by association."

On June 20, 1936, the Black Committee released "without comment" the following listing of donors to these groups and to the Liberty League itself:

du Pont family	$204,045
du Pont associates	$152,622
Pitcairn family (Pittsburgh Plate Glass)	$100,250
J. P. Morgan associates	$68,226
Mellon associates	$60,752
Rockefeller associates	$49,852
Hutton (E. F.) associates	$40,671
Sun Oil associates	$37,260
Banks and brokers	$184,224
Utilities companies and associates	$27,069
	$929,974

As the *New York Times* noted, this was "an analysis . . . to show [that] the principal sources of revenue [of] these bodies draw their financial support almost exclusively from groups of wealthy individuals, banks and utility companies." Why the committee selected these organizations (as opposed to, say, the American Civil Liberties Union or the United Mine Workers) was no mystery.

As Hugo Black's adulatory biographer, David K. Newman, admitted, "Black's hatred of business interests caused him to trample over witness's rights protected by the Fourth Amendment. He used to the fullest the investigatory powers of Congress—few have used, or can use, them more so—but directed them only toward hard-core conservatives. If they had been aimed at the other end of the political spectrum, he would have been the first to howl at the infringement of constitutional rights."

Among the Black Committee's more interesting findings were that the "Farmers Independence Council" boasted few (if any) farmers among its benefactors ("Wall Street Farmers," as Black jeered). Particularly noxious was correspondence between the Boston banker (and chairman of the Massachusetts Board of Tax Appeals) Alexander Lincoln, president of the three-thousand-member Sentinels of the Republic, and New Jersey attorney W. Cleveland Runyon. "The fight for Western Christian civilization can be won," fumed Runyon, "but only if we recognize [that] the enemy is Jewish in origin."

"[T]he Jewish threat is a real one," Lincoln responded. "My hope is in the election next autumn, and I believe that our real opportunity lies in accomplishing the defeat of Roosevelt."

"The people are crying for leadership and not getting it," Runyon wrote again. "Our leaders are asleep. The Sentinels should lead on the outstanding issue. The old-line Americans of $1200 a year want a Hitler."

The damage to the Sentinels was immense. Donors Alfred P. Sloan and Robert McCormick quickly repudiated the organization. But an investigation by the Jewish War Veterans of the United States found that Lincoln, in fact, did not "entertain any antipathy against the Jewish people or any other racial minority. . . . My associates join me in expressing our regrets at the embarrassment caused you by this incident."

By that time, however, Bay State governor James M. Curley had forced Lincoln off the Tax Board, pointedly replacing him with the Jewish Abraham Webber.

Last, but hardly least, Black targeted John Henry Kirby's Southern Committee to Uphold the Constitution—and Kirby's longtime associate, the 6'4" scar-faced Houstonian Vance Muse.

Muse was a veteran hired gun, operating for a variety of causes, generally involving tax policy, though best remembered as the "father" of "Right-to-Work" legislation. In the 1920s, Vance and Kirby promoted the "Southern Tariff Association," a group advocating higher tariffs on agricultural products, as well as in movements to trim income and inheritance taxes.

In 1928, while with the Southern Tariff Association, Muse pondered how to retain that year's unprecedented Republican gains in the Solid South. He developed an incredibly shortsighted plan to entice whites into the Southern GOP by recruiting Blacks in such places as Harlem, St. Louis, and Chicago to run for Congress—*as Democrats*. That was in 1928–29. By late 1935, Muse was scurrying about, preparing John H. Kirby's big "Grass Roots" confab. To gin up anti-FDR sentiments, he contacted his fellow Houstonian Allen Sheppard, who honchoed the Election Managers Association of Texas, conveniently located down the hall at Houston's Kirby Building. Sheppard, like Muse, hated the idea of Black equality. ("I am fighting any step . . . toward social equality for Negroes. For 43 years I have been fighting this movement—ever since I was 19.") Eventually, through Muse and others, ten thousand copies of a "lithograph" of Eleanor Roosevelt alongside various Blacks circulated throughout the South.

In April 1936, Hugo Black summoned Kirby and Muse to the stand. Kirby's testimony provoked little public interest. Muse's proved too interesting. His manner seemed odd, nervous ("you are putting a strain on my feeble mind, and I can't answer"). He refused to sit, preferring to testify while standing ("I think I should stand in the presence of the Senate of the United States, in which I have implicit faith"). Black queried Muse regarding membership in something called the "Order of American Patriots." Muse declined to answer. "I decline to tell this committee what my fraternal affiliations are, . . ." he apprised the senator, "with the Masons, or the Ku Klux Klan, the Knights of Columbus, or anybody. . . . I am not going to talk when I have sworn on the flag and the Bible that I am not going to discuss these things."

Black asked about the Eleanor photographs. The testimony went like this:

BLACK: Can you describe the pictures . . . ?

MUSE: Yes, but it is nauseating for me to do it. . . . I am a Southerner and I am for white supremacy [here he beat his chest]. . . . It was a picture of Mrs. Roosevelt going to some nigger meeting with two escorts, niggers on each arm. And you force me to say that.

BLACK: At Howard University?

MUSE: Yes, I think so.

BLACK: You circulated them without anybody forcing you to circulate them?

MUSE: No, sir, except my conscience. . . . And my granddaddy, who wore this kind of uniform right here, forced me to do it [here, Muse pointed to his suit of Confederate gray].

How greatly these photos offended Senator Black, himself a former Klan member and more recently a leader of the filibuster against the Wagner–Costigan anti-lynching bill, remains questionable. Not open to question was his interest in unearthing the Southern Committee to Uphold the Constitution's funding sources. He confirmed the following contributions:

John Jakob Raskob	$5,000
Pierre du Pont	$5,000
Lammot du Pont	$2,500
Alfred P. Sloan (President of General Motors)	$1,000
Ogden Mills (former Treasury Secretary)	$100
Frank B. Kellogg (former Secretary of State)	$500

Raskob and Pierre du Pont provided their funding specifically for the Macon meeting—though, as Muse averred, they "didn't know anything about" the Roosevelt photos. Sloan provided his own donation well after the Macon fiasco.

The Raskob–du Pont connection to Talmadge's Macon circus spelled *finis* to what few pretensions of influence the Liberty League harbored. Raskob's brainchild, mused Robert Moses, was "God's gift to Franklin Roosevelt."

Yet what goes around comes around . . . and before the Black Committee completed its handiwork, its net swept too wide and too deep.

For, when you subpoena five million telegrams and paw through your political opponents' files, you never know what might show up.

If the stillborn Talmadge–Huey Long alliance had been illogical, only more so was Franklin Roosevelt's New Deal coalition, at one point or another including everyone from Talmadge, the Kingfish, and Tom Dixon to Al Smith and John Jakob Raskob to Rexford Tugwell and Harold Ickes. It seemed, in fact, to include every white person, save Herbert Clark Hoover and Robert Moses.

Among its more Right-leaning (and more prominent) members was Vice President John Nance "Cactus Jack" Garner. Despite his conservatism, however, Garner not only remained outwardly loyal to his boss, but proved remarkably efficient in guiding FDR's ever-shifting agenda through the Congress—both in the Senate, where he now served as presiding officer, and, more so, in the House, where he had served as Speaker, immediately succeeding his friend Alice Roosevelt Longworth's late husband, Nick Longworth.

Accepting his vice presidential nomination in August 1932, he sounded more like a Liberty League pamphlet of August 1935:

> In my opinion nearly all of our civic troubles are the consequences of government's departure from its legitimate functions. . . . Had it not been for the steady encroachment of federal government on the rights and duties reserved for the states, we perhaps would not have the present spectacle of the people rushing to Washington to set right whatever goes wrong. . . .
>
> The gravitation of power to Washington has builded [sic] a structure of administration vast beyond the imagination of the builders of the Constitution—complex, involved, and uncoordinated; a fabric of bureaus, commissions, boards and departments that overlap and interfere with one another—and all at the cost of the people.

In September 1934, Raymond Moley visited Cactus Jack's Uvalde, Texas, ranch, asking him in what direction he might wish the administration to proceed. Cut "spendin'" and "relief," Garner answered. By 1935, Garner had concluded that the time for New Deal experimentation was over—and, moreover, was leaking the contents of behind-closed-doors administration meetings to his old pals on Capitol Hill. He was, as one journalist noted, "as out of place in the New Deal as a dead mouse in a mince pie."

Texas being a big state but essentially still a small-town network of its rich and powerful, Garner, in fact, knew John Henry Kirby. In July 1935, Kirby wrote Garner:

> My Dear John:
> How long are you going to tolerate that apostasy of the Roosevelt administration to the cardinal principles of the Democratic party and its notorious contempt for the plain terms of the Constitution?
> Your friend,
> John Henry Kirby

Garner responded:

> Dear John Henry:
> Your favor just called to my attention. You can't do everything you want to, and I can't do half what I would like to do. You don't control everybody you would like to, and I am in a similar fix. I think that answers your question.
> Sincerely,
> Jno. N. Garner

On this uneasy note, the heyday of the Black Committee ended, but other committees and investigations marched on—one of them aimed straight at Dr. Francis E. Townsend, who had precious little affection for the New Deal.

Or it for him.

· 7 ·

"Methodist picnic people"

The oratorical landscape abounded with charmers—Huey Long, Gerald L. K. Smith, Herman Talmadge, Al Smith. And, of course, on a far higher and more fruitful plain, the most magnificent charmer of all, Franklin D. Roosevelt.

In California, however, a wizened old man, possessing little charisma (perhaps none whatsoever), mesmerized literally millions of faithful dues-paying adherents. H. L. Mencken, in fact, damned Dr. Francis E. Townsend as "one of the dullest speakers on earth."

Dr. Francis E. Townsend was old. His plan was new.

Dr. Francis E. Townsend was dull. His plan excited millions.

Many a man has sprung from obscurity to command vast followings or possess vast fortunes. A Lincoln or a Hitler. An Al Smith or a Herbert Hoover. A Benjamin Franklin or a Henry Ford. The story is familiar. Much, much rarer is to ascend from obscurity and near indigence to nationwide fame and power so rapidly—and at such an advanced age—as Townsend.

Not until his late sixties did Dr. Townsend bloom. Born in an Illinois log cabin in 1867, he was almost thirty (and his class's oldest member) when he graduated from medical school. Initially, practicing in South Dakota's remote Black Hills, he did not reach California to stay until 1920. And, while he was never quite a failure, neither was he ever a real success—even before the Great Depression knocked his finances sideways.

A modest appointment as assistant director of the City Health Office of Long Beach then rescued him from penury. Ill-paid, he moonlighted in a small real estate office. As the Depression deepened, he lost both jobs.

He was never a born salesman. Yet, he soon emerged as one of history's greatest pitchmen, his task complicated further by a product almost universally derided as among the most unworkable and impractical ideas of a century jammed with unworkable political and economic notions.

A solitary moment in time generated Townsend's grand notion. An early authorized biography gave this version of events, thusly:

> THE LAND FILLED WITH POOR
>
> "For a long, long while a bitterness had been growing in me. The land was filled with poor, and the scantiest of half-hearted measures were being taken to alleviate their distress. I knew, for example, what I should see if I looked into that alley below. I had seen such sights before.
>
> "Rubbish barrels and garbage cans, and tattered folk rummaging in them, scavenging for the castaway things that no man could give another without a sense of shame.
>
> "Still, when I did look out, it was something in the nature of a mild surprise. Call it the last straw that broke the camel's back. I saw three haggard, very old women, stooped with great age, bending over the barrels, clawing into the contents."
>
> "Dr. Townsend paused. I think it was more for personal contemplation than for dramatic effect. He is not, truth to tell, a dramatic person. Soft spoken always, easy spoken, and interesting, but never one to lift his voice, thump a table, or even give you a meaning[ful] glance to emphasize his point. Whatever may be said about the Townsend plan, and in spite of all that has been said by those who maintain that it is ridiculous and hair-brained, I think it must be acknowledged without reservation that Francis E. Townsend is a sincere man. His whole life points to earnest hard work and sincerity.
>
> "I've lived among mule-skinners and the toughest tough guys in the world," he said, "I've lived in towns wide open with drunks and

gamblers and prostitutes, and men who shot to kill and fought to maim. And so I know all the words.

"I used them all. A torrent of invectives tore out of me, the big blast of all the bitterness that had been building in me for years. I swore and I ranted, and I let my voice bellow with the wild hatred I had for things as they were.

"My wife came a-running.

"'Doctor! Doctor!' She's always called me doctor, having been my nurse—and the best one in the world—before our marriage and after. 'Doctor! Oh, you mustn't shout like that! All the neighbors will hear you!'

"I want all the neighbors to hear me!" I roared defiantly. "I want God almighty to hear me! I'm going to shout till all the country hears."

A mighty fine story. It might even be true—though most historians doubt it.

Townsend actually *didn't* shout. He just wrote a letter—to the editor of the local *Long Beach Press-Telegram*. Published on Saturday, September 30, 1933, it outlined a simple plan to not only eliminate old-age poverty but to heal the larger tragedy of the Depression itself: what soon became known as the "Townsend Recovery Plan."

In May 1936, he explained that his plan was:

> . . . not just an old-age-pension proposal:
>
> There are three objectives in the Townsend Plan: (1) stabilizing employment, (2) stimulating industrial and business activity, and (3) establishing social security for our elders. . . .
>
> [W]e propose . . . : (a) levying a tax on every business transaction, to be paid into a revolving Citizens' Retirement Annuity Fund in the U. S. Treasury; (b) paying each citizen over 60 years old, upon retiring from gainful occupation, $200 per month from this revolving fund; (c) providing that he or she spends this money, within the United States, in the channels of trade within 30 days after receiving it.

Originally, Townsend had proposed a $150-per-month pension, but he quickly upped the ante to $200, reasoning that the larger figure would "compel attention, and has great psychological value. Second, *with our figure set as high as $200 we can feel reasonably sure* that no one will bring out a pension plan with a higher amount."

There were some governmental pensions already in operation. By 1928, eleven states possessed state-run pensions; by 1933, there were twenty-eight, though none in the South. By 1932, 102,000 persons were receiving state pensions, totaling $22,000,000. Two years later, 231,000 recipients collected $32,186,000, seriously straining individual systems.

Nineteen thirty-two's Democratic platform had "advocated . . . old-age insurance under state laws," and 1933's Dill–Connolly bill provided some modest, though concrete, support for state plans—providing $100,000 in federal funds for each $300,000 an individual state expended, and moves were afoot to increase that to $100,000 for each $200,000. By 1934, Dill–Connery had cleared both the House Labor and Senate Pensions committees, though without help from the administration. In fact, FDR blocked it from a full House vote, before stalling for time and appointing a commission to study the larger issue. To journalist Fulton Oursler, in April 1935, he had, in fact, fussed: "Old age pensions! The states would have to carry the burden if the payments were to be increased; the government could only do so much and not go broke."

Townsend's initial emphasis lay with pensions for the elderly. Soon, however, he argued that his plan would boost employment for younger workers once older workers departed the workforce ("Age for leisure; youth for work"). He also contended that this monthly torrent of spending by the elderly would stimulate the economy—creating still more jobs for the young.

New Dealers termed FDR's version of stimulating the economy "pump priming." Townsendites dubbed theirs the "velocity of money," reasoning that their plan selected "people over 60 . . . to be the circulators of large sums of money because they have more buying experience" than their juniors. Eventually, Townsendites claimed that their "velocity of money" might generate such great prosperity that it would miraculously balance the federal budget.

A "velocity of money" indeed resulted. But not for the federal treasury. Townsend's September 1933 letter to the editor had ignited an immediate—and not just a local—response, as spellbound elderly readers mailed accounts of his message to far-off friends and relatives. By November, Townsend and his real estate agent friend Earl Clements had already opened a modest office to handle responses. By January 1934, they incorporated "Old-Age Revolving Pension, Ltd." (OARP). In August 1934, they also incorporated the "Prosperity Publishing Co., Ltd." and chartered the first "Townsend Club." By September 1934, they required ninety-five staffers to process the two thousand letters flooding their office each and every day.

November 1934 witnessed Townsend's electoral breakthrough, as Republican incumbent Frank Merriam defeated the radical Democrat nominee Upton Sinclair for California's governorship. Merriam had endorsed the Townsend Plan; Sinclair, though offering his own pension ideas, had not. In Long Beach, voters dumped their incumbent Republican congressman in favor of the Townsendite seventy-two-year-old poet laureate of California, John S. McGroarty.

Such portents not only failed to soften FDR's hostility to Townsendism; they seemingly hardened his opposition to any form of federal old-age pensions in the near future. When in mid-November Harry Hopkins publicly proclaimed that "now is the hour" for a national pension plan—within three hours and from the very same podium—Roosevelt publicly torpedoed him, basically arguing that his current social program boiled down to unemployment insurance (up until about that time the more fashionable issue)—and that pensions would have to wait their turn. "I do not know whether this is the time for any Federal legislation on old-age security," he argued, as he pilloried "organizations [obviously such as Townsend's] promoting fantastic schemes which cannot possibly be fulfilled."

Undaunted, Townsend marched on. By December, he claimed two thousand clubs nationwide. Soon afterward he reported three hundred thousand club members, each paying $0.25 in yearly dues. His movement soon exploded to three thousand clubs in February 1935 and then to approximately seven thousand clubs with between 1.5 and 2 million members. Somewhere between twenty and thirty million Americans petitioned Congress favoring the plan.

Dr. Townsend posed as the kindly, elderly, sincere face of the movement—albeit a cadaverous, quite spooky one, a Midwestern 1930s Nosferatu kind of face, more akin to a neighborhood mortician's than a national messiah's. Toiling behind the scenes was the much younger, more practical Earl Clements. The hustling Clements "left few stones unturned, . . ." one scholar noted. "He arranged card parties and quilting bees, raffles, and box suppers. He wrote a manual for OARP speakers . . . described as 'the last word in high-pressure salesmanship applied to an economic idea.' . . . He marketed Townsend license plates, tire covers, radiator emblems, pictures, pamphlets, songs, buttons, badges, and banners, all . . . sold at a handsome profit for the national headquarters. He set up a society known as the Townsend National Legion of Honor, [making] old folks who could afford more than regular dues 'special Townsendites.' For $12 per year, membership was offered in the 'National Legion's program of Proxy[,] a personification which substitutes the purse for the self.' He explained that 'thousands of the world's best people do not possess the qualifications for leadership in our cause, yet they can partake by 'letting their money become proxy for them in the Legion.'"

By late 1935, OARP income exceeded $300,000. Over a two-year period, Clements personally netted $79,000. As Townsend himself wrote Clements in January 1935, "You and I have the world by the tail, Earl, if we work it right."

The movement increasingly attracted less-savory characters. Former San Francisco nightclub owner Edward J. Margett oversaw Townsend's highly lucrative California operations, raking in between $1,800 and $2,000 per month in commissions. Margett had previously served as a Seattle police officer, linked to gambling and "dope" and indicted for grand larceny, bootlegging, and accepting the earnings of a prostitute.

The Rev. Clinton Wunder ranked as Townsend's star speaker. An accomplished, even charismatic, orator, he once debated Clarence Darrow on evolution and keynoted a dinner honoring Albert Einstein. Before Father Coughlin ruled national airwaves, Wunder broadcast over station WGOD.

In the 1920s, Wunder served as pastor of Rochester, New York's Baptist Temple, overseeing construction of a $7 million, fourteen-story church and office building complete with a 1,300-seat auditorium for worship plus a fully functioning, open-to-the-public cafeteria. Not shy about soliciting funds, his 1926 book, *Crowds of Souls*, argued that "a converted pocketbook is the most certain proof of a converted soul. The use of money is the acid test of religion. We have a right to judge a man's Christianity by his gifts. The amount is not so important as the proportion. Ten percent of one's income is a good beginning. As the income increases let the proportion increase."

Not long afterward, Wunder pulled up stakes to become a professional church fundraiser in Manhattan, and then, amazingly, to Hollywood, as executive vice president of the Academy of Motion Pictures Arts and Sciences. Wunder ("The Liberal Voice of Los Angeles") raked in $500 per pro–Townsend Plan speech, plus commissions as an eleven-state organizer.

Townsend and Clements earned more. From January 1935 onward, they derived huge personal profits from the organization's official publication, *Townsend Weekly.* In 1936, *Modern Monthly* reported that the *Townsend Weekly*'s 250,000-copy circulation helped Townsend and Clements clear "a fortune from advertisements. All sorts of quack remedies and fly-by-night swindlers were allowed the use of Townsend's organ. Occasionally in an advertisement would appear the line 'Used by Officials of the Townsend Clubs.' The fact that Townsend himself was a doctor facilitates the duping of the aged and ailing multitude to subscribe to the paper. There was 'Rattler liniment' to 'rouse fresh blood quickly' and 'Yogi Alpha' who volunteered to give an 'astrology reading' for twenty-five cents.

"Townsend made a deal with certain manufacturers and received a form of rebate on all products purchased by Townsendites."

In July 1935, *Townsend Weekly* even featured a half-page ad for the barely disguised Communist-front monthly magazine *Soviet Russia Today.*

Every dollar—and every ruble—counted.

One more exotic ad read:

MARRIED AT 120

Thomas _____ Parr married the second time at 120. We grow old solely because "age" is in our consciousness. Edwin J. Dingle,

> founder of this institute, taught in Tibet by masters of the Far East, offers you secret knowledge for you to enjoy unfading youth of body and mind.
>
> You need not grow old.
>
> Too good to be true? It is the truth! Learn the rationale of Pranic Power and Creative Intelligence . . . how to become healthy, happy in all conditions, solve your life problems—live by knowledge. Mental physics is the greatest teaching accessible to man. Book—free to you—tells you how.
>
> This sealed book is of priceless value to you if you have studied either astrology, psychology, mental science, correct living, new thought humanism, metaphysics, religion with science, health living, Christian Science, Yogi, or hermetic philosophy.

Yogis aside, Townsendites were very middle-American, largely Protestant, most likely Republican, and, despite their support for a massive government-run wealth-transfer program, not at all Socialistic. They were, as one member put it, "just folks . . . just Methodist picnic people."

There were a lot of "just folks" back then; and, as Townsend detected early in the game, *they voted.*

"We might be too old to work," he boasted, "but we were not too old to vote. And there were millions of others . . . too old to work but not too old to vote!"

In Southern California, they had, of course, elected Townsendite John McGroarty. Arriving in Washington in January 1935, the congressman promptly introduced legislation to implement the plan. Privately, the majority of his new colleagues simply loathed it. Publicly, they remained warily silent, unsure of just how many excited Townsendites populated their respective districts. Eleanor Roosevelt, however, spoke her mind, decrying the Plan as "utterly impractical. It is unfortunate that the impression should be given that such a plan can be accomplished. It cannot." Townsend shot back: "Roosevelt has raised a lot of false hopes, I have a real hope that this bill will pass the house this session."

That day, January 16, 1935, McGroarty unveiled Townsend's bill.

FDR introduced Social Security the following day.

Roosevelt considered OARP simply beyond irresponsible. In March 1935, his young relation James Davis wrote him for information on the plan for a class project. He quickly responded that it "would accomplish two very definite results: 1, it would bankrupt the Government, and 2, . . . cause such an inflationary rise in prices that $200 a month would not go any further in purchasing power for these old people than $30 or $40 a month goes at the present time." FDR, hardly the most deficit-conscious or inflation-conscious president, positively despised any form of a dole. Any able-bodied person receiving a New Deal check would, hopefully, work for it, building a dam or a courthouse or just raking leaves. As Rexford Tugwell explained (or, perhaps, complained), Franklin was "from the very first prejudiced against relief as such . . . just as much convinced as Hoover . . . that unearned income eroded character." And so, in Roosevelt's mind, a pension plan must, in some sense, be contributory. Otherwise, it simply remained another form of dole.

Thus Roosevelt headed off Townsend. Others unleashed their own potshots. Some lectured that OARP's estimated $20 billion annual cost totaled five times all federal revenues for 1935. Its revenue basis—a wide-ranging cumulative transaction tax—aroused particular scrutiny. Columnist Nicholas Roosevelt, first cousin once removed of Theodore, contended that "In the comparatively simple process of making a shirt there would be at least 17 Townsend taxes, covering production, transportation, ginning, weaving, tailoring, wholesaling, and merchandising. The pyramiding of these taxes . . . would inevitably result in an increase in prices ranging from 25 per cent to perhaps as much as 250 per cent."

Like any sales tax, Townsend's avalanche of taxes was completely regressive, falling on the poor—including the still-working younger poor—more so than upon the rich. Critiqued Missouri freshman Democrat Rep. C. Jasper Bell: "Even the man upon the dole must pay before he can eat his crust of bread."

As modern scholars have noted, "witnesses—Townsend especially—proved unequal to actually defending [the Plan] before Congress. Particularly damaging were Townsend's admission that $200 per month was more than the tax would bear, that 75 years of age was a more viable retirement age, and that the transactions tax was merely a sales tax by a different name."

In April 1935, Congress voted. Townsend calculated that he enjoyed roughly 160 House votes—and soon discovered that he couldn't calculate votes any better than he could calculate pensions. An amendment to convert FDR's rival Social Security plan into Townsend's flopped 266–56. A day later, Social Security itself passed 372–33, with even Republicans favoring it 81–15 (with four abstaining and two not voting). The Senate steamrolled it to passage 77–6 with twelve abstentions.

Townsendites weren't about to settle for half a pension loaf. October 1935 witnessed the movement's first annual national convention. Seven thousand "nondrinking, nonsmoking and Bible-reading" delegates from 4,552 chartered clubs gathered in Chicago to salute their "beloved leaders" Townsend and Clements, and, above all, to be reassured of their cause's—sooner, rather than later—triumph. Keynoter Clinton Wunder proclaimed that "God is on our side." Townsend declared that OARP's "sure thing" success would "end not only this depression but all depressions and save the country."

At a pre-convention banquet, his acolytes sang "Brothers, do your duty; make your ballots count" to the tune of "Onward Townsend Soldiers." Townsend jokingly babbled on, "We're all going crazy together. It is a tremendously surprising thing to see the avidity with which people grasp this idea. If we keep looking we'll find that every one is insane, which isn't surprising in view of our experience in the last six years. At last we're beginning to think, something we haven't been guilty of in many years."

Also in October 1935, West Michigan Republicans shocked national analysts by choosing a "dry" Townsendite, Verner W. Main, as their nominee over four other candidates in a special House election. That December—refusing help from either the national or state GOP—Main crushed his Democratic opponent to become the first avowed Townsendite House member east of the Mississippi. His triumph sent shock waves through both parties. "As Main goes, so goes the nation," went the joke. Few on Capitol Hill laughed.

Within a fortnight, Townsend's movement began registering massive gains in hitherto unresponsive Massachusetts. The *New York Times* reported:

> Townsend plan converts are multiplying more rapidly . . . than in any other state. In the five days ending Dec. 13 the certified gains were 2,535 bringing the total membership close to 30,000.
>
> Lynn has a Townsend Club of 2,000 and Melrose has 1,400. A young men's club in Brookline aims for 1,000. A year ago there were forty-five clubs in the Bay State. Now there are 154, including twenty-five in Boston with an average of 500 members.
>
> These are "official" figures. They may be subject to revision, but no politician in the Commonwealth discounts the significance of the Townsend phalanx especially the Republican leaders. . . . [F]our in every five of these converts are derived from the Republican Party.

Townsend now pondered whom he might catapult into the White House. It would *not* be Franklin D. Roosevelt. Townsend hated Roosevelt's Social Security Plan, and FDR certainly hated OARP. Compounding Townsend's animus was FDR's December 1934 refusal to meet with him ("an insult that the masses of people should resent"). Townsend never forgot or forgave the slight.

Townsend initially favored Idaho's obstreperous Republican senator William E. Borah, who had labeled his Plan "the most extraordinary social and political movement in recent years and perhaps in our entire history." But, the nearer Borah inched to a candidacy, the further he moved from Townsendism. By January 1936, Townsend was lambasting Borah, though still exhibiting Republican sympathies. By March, he had changed his registration from Independent to Republican, revealing that he had not voted for Roosevelt in 1932.

As Townsend aimed for the stars, more and more people aimed at him—even Winston Churchill.

"If twenty billion dollars a year are to be raised," Churchill wrote in June 1936:

> the people will have to find it. Merely concealing the fact by representing it as two per cent of every transaction will not alter the fact that the money has to be produced, nor that there is no increase in real wealth but merely a transference attendant with infinite friction and waste from one set of poor people to another. Even in the United States, with its vast resources, any attempt to put into practice such crazy theories will be productive of misery and impoverishment going far beyond the limits of the American continent.
>
> I believe that prosperity will return. I believe that the greatest days of that system of private enterprise which has done so much for the world during the last century lie in the future and not in the past. But the gains of tomorrow can be won only by thought and effort. Work and good will are still the keys that unlock the doors of wealth. The specious promises of the prophets of an unearned plenty are a mirage which beckons and lures us, not to the millennial city, but into the deserts of disillusion and ruin. And perhaps we shall even lose our liberties on the way.

Churchill took Townsend seriously. Oklahoma Democratic representative Percy Lee "The Cowboy Congressman" Gassaway did not. In January 1936, Gassaway (who liked Margaret Sanger, FDR, and riding his horse up the Capitol steps, albeit not necessarily in that order) debated Earl Clements over the CBS radio network. Gassaway unleashed a torrent of outright ridicule:

> Considering the fact that people from 50 to 60 years of age are more active than those who have passed 60, I propose to give them the sum of $5,000 a month. Now, all of you know that the most active business years of a person is from 40 to 50 years of age, and I would give those persons $10,000 a month.
>
> Those of us who have lived half a century or more realize that from 20 to 40 years are the years when we have to go to dances and parties and have a hilarious time, generally speaking, and for that class of people I would suggest $20,000 a month.

> I propose to raise taxes on people for crooning over the radio, or for playing a saxophone over the radio, or for going to church or not going to church, for running for office or for proposing plans for relief, or for naming Pullman cars.
>
> If we wreck the country by adopting some fool plan, let's do it in a big way. Adopt old Gassaway's plan and while it lasts we will have one grand big spree.

Internal dissension now wracked OARP as its leaders jostled for power—and cash. In February 1936, Townsend canned Clinton Wunder as his eastern director.

Meanwhile, Congressman McGroarty plotted to run a slate of delegates to June's Democratic convention, pledged to support him as the designated nominee. His real goal, however, was to force a pro–Townsend Plan plank into the platform. Clements gave his OK. Townsend, back to favoring a Borah candidacy and loath to even consider support for FDR and his Democrats, vetoed it. Moreover, when McGroarty's newest pension bill failed to include Townsend's patented full $200-per-month allotment, Townsend accused him of "private political ambitions." McGroarty shot back that Townsend was "talking just like a fool." He exited the Townsend crusade.

"Beloved leaders" Townsend and Clements drew apart. Townsend's head swelled from unremitting adulation. ("Just think. They built [the Lincoln Monument] because he freed four million slaves. Wonder what they will do for me after I've liberated all mankind.") His third-party fantasies accelerated. Clements, more cautious, drew back.

FDR—and Congress—were now gunning for Townsend and everyone and everything connected with him. Their weapon was by now highly familiar: a congressional investigation. Senator Gerald Nye attacked the du Ponts. Lower East Side congressman Samuel Dickstein had probed alleged Wall Street plots. Hugo Black pried into the utilities and John Henry Kirby. Now, the brand-new "Select Committee Investigating Old Age Pension Organizations"—mobilized to skewer Townsend. The committee's purpose, wrote one historian, was "almost wholly political in nature; its objective was the discrediting of the movement. . . . It aimed to destroy the Townsend organization's effectiveness as a political force in the 1936 elections."

House leadership moved carefully. This new special committee would be completely nonpartisan, equally apportioned between Democrats and Republicans. As chairman, they selected a legislator presumably safe from any Townsendite electoral pressure: the aforementioned C. Jasper Bell. Bell hailed from Kansas City, a city so under the thumb of Democratic boss Tom Pendergast (first-term senator Harry Truman's mentor) that Bell needn't fear any backlash. In 1934, after all, Bell had swamped his Republican opponent 82,995–18,368.

Bell and his counsel, former Kansas City police court prosecutor James R. Sullivan, mercilessly tore into both Townsend and Clements. Clements soon folded. Having already sold off his share of Prosperity Publishing Co., Ltd., in March 1936, he resigned his OARP national secretaryship. With (literally) little now invested in the movement, he essentially turned state's evidence on his old comrades. It was he who revealed Townsend's January 1935 comment "You and I have the world by the tail, Earl, if we work it right." Deflecting attention from his own substantial OARP income, he excoriated California organizer Edward Margett's hefty proceeds. Chief Counsel Sullivan exposed Margett's shady Seattle and San Francisco past, down to his early 1920s bank deposits. *Everything* got inserted into the record.

An OARP Western organizer purported that Townsend had tried shaking down California governor Frank Merriam for $12,000 in 1934. Investigators unearthed a Michigan organizer who had previously toiled for the Ku Klux Klan. Another organizer, Dr. Frank Dyer, attired himself in monk robes to fundraise as a "Brother Sylvester." Some alleged that Townsend and Clements derided their enthusiasts as "old fossils"—and that Clements bragged, "We don't give a damn about poor people."

By now the Rev. Wunder had rejoined the OARP fold, again ready to plead Townsend's cause: "We of the new management are not responsible for the old [Clements]. Dr. Townsend, a man of faith, trusted another man too much, and the other man failed him. Shall Dr. Townsend be crucified for the sins of another?" Speaking of sins, Bell and Sullivan delved into Wunder's own record, unearthing recent correspondence unbefitting either a Baptist minister or even just plain Methodist picnic folk.

To one damsel, Wunder wrote (and these were the unexpurgated parts):

> DEAR HELENE
> You are the unique honey—gosh! You've been everything but the bride—want to apply? Oh I forget you are to be a mother—
> . . . Am writing Loess [Lois?] under "sep." cover so she'll have fun opening her mail. You have to be a wife to me so I'll be a "hoosbun" to her—ain't we all polygamous? I'll say. . . .
> "You say you'll do anything for me—O Helen.
> "Of course you could pose as my bride if both had to apply—you look like a movie queen.
> "Hey! Ho! Hum! . . ."
>
> Your virginal pal,
> "Clint."

Wunder's letter, one disgruntled Townsend leader averred, "impresses me as having been written by a degenerate. I would not read those to my boys. I can't associate those letters with a minister of the Gospel."

A fifty-one-year-old Jackson, Michigan, volunteer, coincidentally named Mrs. Juanita H. Jackson, testified to committee member Rep. Clare Hoffman (R-MI) that "Dr. Wunder bore down harder than anyone I ever have seen, on getting the money. I have never seen anybody make such a plea, such a rampant, perspiring, raging plea for money, money, money."

Which was hardly the sum total of his faults:

> MRS. JACKSON: We had a meeting in the First Methodist Church in Jackson, Michigan, and had over 800 in attendance. Dr. Wunder spoke. He had his new bride with him.
> MR. HOFFMAN: His what?
> JACKSON: He had his new bride with him.
> MR. HOFFMAN: His what?

MRS. JACKSON: His new bride at that time, that is, the second edition.

MR. HOFFMAN: We want to be fair to Reverend Dr. Wunder. He is a doctor of divinity as I understand?

MRS. JACKSON: I think he graduated and once was that.

MR. HOFFMAN: There is some implication in your statement. What do you mean by "new edition"?

MRS. JACKSON: I mean that he left his wife in Rochester, N. Y. flat, and went out of the picture. Nobody could find him. Then he turned up with a brand new bride Easter Sunday, 1935.

MR. HOFFMAN: Where did he turn up with her?

MRS. JACKSON: He turned up with her in Jackson, Mich. She divorced him in 6 weeks.

MR. HOFFMAN: He is something of a go-getter by nature?

MRS. JACKSON: I understand he had the third edition at the convention at [OARP] Chicago in October.

MR. HOFFMAN: At a convention in Chicago in October; was it June or October?

MRS. JACKSON: October 1935.

MR. HOFFMAN: You say he had a third wife?

MRS. JACKSON: And I cannot say this of my own knowledge, but a friend introduced—

MR. HOFFMAN: Wait a minute; you did not see the third wife?

MRS. JACKSON: No, Mr. Hoffman; I did not see the first one either but I knew she existed.

MR. HOFFMAN: Did Dr. Wunder tell his life history to you?

MRS. JACKSON: His wife did.

MR. HOFFMAN: You mean the second wife?

MRS. JACKSON: The second edition.

If Dr. Wunder really had acquired a "third edition," it resulted by virtue of common law, not God's, as his "second edition," while almost instantly ready to call it quits, would not formally file for divorce until May 1937.

The instantly disgruntled "second edition" was Thelma Mills, a descendant of Robert E. Lee, and a dancer both onstage and with

Warner Brothers' brilliant Busby Berkeley, her most recent film being Fred Astaire's *The Gay Divorcee*. Thelma (just twenty-four on marrying the forty-two-year-old Wunder) was, to say the least, a trifle star-crossed in marriage. Her first fiancé committed suicide. Her second died in a car crash. A third trip to the altar was interrupted by both another car crash (hospitalizing her for a month) and a bout of ptomaine. It turned out that marriage to Dr. Wunder wasn't much better than ptomaine.

For such reasons (and more), Dr. Townsend ordered Dr. Wunder, Edward Margett, and Chicago-area organizer John B. "Jack" Kiefer to ignore any subpoenas Bell issued. "After reading the obscene, degrading and filthy language sent through the United States mails by a minister of God," commented committee member Scott Lucas (D-Illinois), "it is not difficult to understand why Doctor Townsend did not want Wunder and Kiefer—members of his board—to testify before this committee."

Townsend did testify. It did not go well. As historian David Bennett noted, the committee aimed not only to obliterate the Townsend movement, but also to effect "the humiliation of its leader." Faced with accusations that his panacea was simply pure hogwash, he blathered: "You can't argue this idea away with just figures. People have to buy or die. . . . If we can catch every person and tax him when he buys, the taxing would be harmless." As writer E. B. White observed, "When forced to deal with the fundamental problems, [Townsend] quietly came apart, like an inexpensive toy."

An inexpensive toy demolished by a hydrogen bomb. Yet, while the Bell Committee unearthed many an embarrassing detail, they failed to demonstrate any outright illegality. As historian Abraham Holtzman explained:

> Unable to uncover legal or fraudulent practices, the committee belabored the doctor with the accusations. . . . His letters were cited to prove his intent to reap millions from the movement, although it was apparent that their meaning differed from the one fashioned by the committee. His words were so misconstrued by his inquisitors that at times he despaired of answering, and he agreed with their wildest assertions. So confused did Dr. Townsend become under

this sledge-hammer questioning that he contradicted himself on the most simple terms.

At two thirty on Thursday afternoon, May 21, 1936, the Bell Committee reconvened. Townsend, on the stand since Tuesday, was mysteriously absent. His attorney, Sheridan Downey (Upton Sinclair's 1934 EPIC running mate), requested an hour's delay. Bell demanded to know if Townsend was ill. Downey answered no; he would return at three thirty. "Isn't that nice," Congressman Hoffman scoffed. To kill time, Bell interrogated two other witnesses, one being the garrulous Mrs. Juanita Jackson.

At three thirty, Townsend, flanked by his office manager, Harrison N. Hiles, and OARP's Scottish-born treasurer, Baxter G. Rankine, returned as promised. Clutching his brand-new straw boater, the doctor looked pale—ashen, even. He fidgeted as he waited. At 4:00 p.m., Juanita Jackson (having branded Townsend a "plagiarist" and an "atheist") finally concluded. Townsend stepped forward, requesting to read a prepared statement.

Bell barked, "No written statements here. Why have you kept us waiting?" Nonetheless, he demanded to see Townsend's statement. Townsend refused. Bell ordered him to the stand. Townsend crumpled his document in his hand, saying:

> In view of the apparent unfriendly attitude of this committee and the unfair attitude it has shown to me and the members of my organization I shall no longer attend these committee meetings. I am retiring from this sort of an inquisition, and I do not propose to come back again except under arrest. And I do refuse absolutely to make any further statement pertaining to this movement to this committee. Thank you, and good-bye, gentlemen.

Attorney Sheridan Downey stood there, his mouth agape. Townsend, accompanied by office manager Hiles, slowly struggled back through the hearing's stunned two-hundred-member audience comprised mostly of his shocked elderly supporters. Manhattan congressman Joseph Gavagan yelled, "Shut that door!" Congressman Hoffman shouted, "Stop him!" A confused Capitol police officer not only failed to halt Townsend's escape, he politely opened the door for him.

We now retreat ever so slightly backward in time. As Townsend reentered the room at three thirty, a stocky, powerfully built man greeted him and then followed him toward the witness stand. As Townsend and the sixty-year-old Hiles exited, this same man shoved aside anyone astride their path. "A hurrying reporter got in the way . . ." noted the *Chicago Tribune*, and Townsend's defender "swung a big fist," sweeping him back.

Townsend rushed down the Capitol steps as fast as his old body would carry him, barely ahead of the frenzied crowd. Occasionally he stumbled. His two companions propped him up. They forced him forward. A taxi cab, reserved by Townsend's fist-swinging protector, awaited them.

All three sped away: Harrison Hiles, Dr. Francis E. Townsend, and Dr. Townsend's new white knight—*the Rev. Gerald L. K. Smith.*

· 8 ·

"A voice made for promises"

Things hadn't been working out for Gerald L. K. Smith.

His Shreveport congregation had fired him. Huey Long lay dead. The Kingfish's old machine shunned him. Gene Talmadge's "Grass Roots" rally fell on its face—for good measure, taking the Liberty League down with it. In the process, Smith alienated not only Talmadge but every du Pont along the Eastern Seaboard.

One slim hope remained—Huey's "Share-Our-Wealth" clubs. The "Second Louisiana Purchase" mandated that Long's massive mailing list's metal printing plates be destroyed. Smith, however, heard rumors that another set resided with Long's youthful former secretary Earle J. Christenberry—now affiliated with Townsend. Smith tracked him down. There were no plates. One dream ended. Another began: enlisting with Townsend.

Smith timed it perfectly. The Bell Committee now assaulted Townsend. Smith angled to protect him. Earl Clements's recent departure left Townsend with a huge organizational and personal void. Smith knew *exactly* how to fill it.

Smith rendezvoused with Townsend on Monday, May 20, 1936, the day before the doctor commenced his testimony. "Doc," Smith warned, "they're going to destroy you. You treat them with courtesy. You should hold them in contempt. I would stand up, pronounce my contempt, walk out and *defy* them to come and get me."

"If I had a young man like you beside me," rejoined Townsend, "I'd do it."

"You've got him," Smith responded.

Thus, Townsend had Smith.

And Smith had Townsend.

Three days later, they raced away from the Capitol to Baltimore. Grilled by waiting reporters, Smith overshadowed the now-docile and drained Townsend, informing them that it was Bell's persecution that drew him to Townsend's side.

"Isn't that right?" he asked Townsend.

"That's right," Townsend meekly replied.

Smith proclaimed that "we" had a statement to make:

> Without reference to any plan for recovery we here and now join hands in what shall result in a nation-wide protest against this communistic dictatorship in Washington. The assassination of Huey Long plus the persecution of Dr. Townsend calls for action.

Smith was just full of news. He notified reporters—as the *New York Daily News* reported— "that he and Townsend would confer soon with Father Charles Coughlin, Detroit Radio Priest, but said it was too soon to discuss a possible union of the Townsend forces, the Share-the-Wealth movement and Coughlin's Union for Social Justice."

The *Daily News* reported that on page 56. Nonetheless, it was news indeed.

News indeed.

•••

Rarely have two words been used more often to describe a person than "Radio Priest" to define Father Charles E. Coughlin. And neither he—nor his ten million mesmerized listeners—could be safely ignored.

Born in Ontario, Canada, to an American father, in October 1891, Coughlin was formally incardinated in the Diocese of Detroit in February 1923. In June 1926, Detroit bishop Michael J. Gallagher assigned him to a newly formed parish in Royal Oak, Michigan, a Detroit suburb. Serving just twenty-eight families, the Shrine of the Little Flower wasn't exactly a plum assignment. Worse, local Klansmen are said to have burned a fiery cross on parish property. But Coughlin was a gifted speaker with a flair for the dramatic. One Sunday, he invited members of the Detroit Tigers and the visiting New York Yankees (including Babe Ruth) to attend Mass—and boost attendance. Also, in 1926, he took to the airwaves on Detroit radio station WJR. He commenced with a mixture of children's stories and religious orthodoxy, pledging to "avoid prejudicial subjects, all controversies, and especially bigotry," but quickly lurched into political commentary—and controversy.

Above all, above any content or controversy, was his extraordinary voice: "a voice of such mellow richness," marveled author Wallace Stegner, "such manly, heart-warming, confidential intimacy, such emotional and ingratiating charm, that anyone tuning past it almost automatically returned to hear it again . . . one of the great speaking voices of the twentieth century. Warmed by the touch of Irish brogue, it lingered over words and enriched their emotional content. It was a voice made for promises."

To support his work, in January 1928 Coughlin incorporated the "League of the Little Flower." Dues were steep: $1 per broadcast, but the money poured in. In just one week in the early 1930s, he deposited $21,000 in a local bank—all in $1 and $5 bills.

The year 1930 saw Father Coughlin update his act, attacking Bolshevism ("It is either the marriage feast of Cana or the brothel of Lenin!") and Socialism ("Only the soft-brained radical attempts to have the laboring man declare a war of sabotage against the millionaire").

In July 1930, he testified before Rep. Hamilton Fish's "Special Committee to Investigate Communist Activities in the United States," offering up a confused mélange of opinions, tracing Socialism back to 1776 and to "avowed atheist" Adam Weishaupt and the "Order of the Illuminati." He excoriated Henry Ford, an early investor in Soviet industry, as "instrumental in subsidizing what was known as the Russian country." Already, he could not help discussing Jews, though, in a surprisingly moderate manner: "It does happen that 90% of the Soviet government is Jewish;

but in this country the communists are not the Jews. I think that is a libel on the Jewish race to say only Jews are communists."

In October 1930, he went big-time, launching a 7:00 p.m. Sunday evening series ("The Golden Hour of the Little Flower") over the CBS radio network. Eighty thousand letters a week poured into Royal Oak, requiring ninety-six clerks to process them. Royal Oak required—and got—a new post office just to handle the avalanche of his correspondence.

Coughlin opposed divorce, birth control, Prohibition—and, yes, capitalism. "Modern capitalism as we know it," he concluded, "is not worth saving. In fact it is a detriment to civilization."

"Hoover," he sniped, "tried to cure this damnable depression by pouring in gold at the top while people starved at the bottom. He fed grain to pigs in Arkansas, but he wouldn't give a loaf of bread to the people of Michigan."

He leapt early and eagerly into Franklin Roosevelt's camp. November 1930 saw him prophesize, "Another Roosevelt shall have the courage to uncloak the hypocritical human factors who have debased our systems. . . . Another Roosevelt shall labor for the development of our country!"

Already, however, he exhibited a crackpot streak. In early January 1931, he collaborated with Pennsylvania's notoriously anti-Semitic congressman Louis McFadden to prepare an attack on the Treaty of Versailles. CBS objected (most likely at the behest of the Hoover White House). Coughlin yelled "censorship," and 350,000 letters flooded CBS supporting him.

CBS nonetheless booted Coughlin off the air at season's end. NBC similarly refused his services, so he jerry-rigged his own network, initially running from St. Louis to Maine, then from coast to coast. By now his admiration for rising-star Franklin Roosevelt rivaled Gerald Smith's ardor for Huey Long.

Detroit was coincidentally also home to Eleanor Roosevelt's youngest brother, G. Hall Roosevelt, city comptroller under Coughlin's close ally Mayor Frank Murphy (one of Coughlin's first altar servers). In May 1931, Hall wrote brother-in-law FDR:

> Father Coughlin is probably known to you by this time. . . . He would like to tender his services. From what I can make out his brethren in the Church tolerate him. He would be difficult to handle and might be full of dynamite, but I think you had better prepare to say "yes" or "no."

FDR *rarely* said either "yes" or "no." He would, however, accept helpful support when it was tendered and as long as it was tendered—and as long as it was helpful. Coughlin could, after all, be *very* helpful. He kept bashing Hoover ("the banker's friend, the Holy Ghost of the rich, the protective angel of Wall Street") and boosting FDR. Yet he ruffled feathers with his inflammatory anti–Wall Street, anti–international banker, populist rhetoric ("driving the money changers out of the temple").

"The Catholic Church is a tremendously serious organization," Boston's William Cardinal O'Connell publicly warned Coughlin in April 1932. "It deals in human souls. You can't begin speaking about the rich, or making sensational accusations against banks and bankers, or uttering demagogic stuff to the poor. You can't do it, for the Church is for all."

Coughlin poured it on. He advocated a World War veterans' bonus and put his money where his mouth was, donating a hefty $5,000 to the Bonus Marchers' food fund. He rushed to New York to support his embattled co-religionist, the flamboyantly corrupt mayor of New York, James J. Walker. FDR, agonizing over how to discipline Walker, hardly relished Coughlin's interference. It may have been then, however, when Coughlin first met Franklin—and, as Coughlin later claimed, when FDR first assured him that he would be his close adviser not only on the economy but on other social issues. Returning to Michigan, Coughlin continued lobbying for Walker. Absent any discernible proof, he smeared Walker's patrician prosecutor, Judge Samuel Seabury, as "a member of the Klan."

If FDR hadn't already been chary of Coughlin, he likely was by now. More probably, he never could stand him. The two possessed a few commonalities: a great radio presence, incredibly doting mothers, and a semblance of shared political goals. That was it. Franklin "disliked and distrusted him," Eleanor once recalled, adding that she "never liked or trusted him" either.

Yet, Coughlin remained a power to be appeased—and feared. Roosevelt's "Fireside Chats" had yet to commence, but Coughlin already boasted millions of loyal listeners. As FDR's battle for the nomination went down to the wire at June 1932's Democratic National Convention, Coughlin and Mayor Murphy testified before the platform committee regarding the unemployment issue. On June 29, 1932, Coughlin addressed the entire convention. Sharing the bill with Will Rogers, radio comics Amos and Andy, former heavyweight champion Gene Tunney, and attorney Clarence Darrow, he argued that the country required a "Carpenter from Nazareth" rather than "an engineer from Palo Alto." By all accounts (save Coughlin's), Rogers, not Coughlin, stole the show.

FDR secured his nomination. Coughlin wired his congratulations. FDR wired back: "I do hope if you come East you will stop off in Albany to see me. I want to talk with you about many things." Yet he remained distrustful of The Radio Priest. To Rexford Tugwell, he dismissed Coughlin as a demagogue akin to Huey Long. "We must tame these fellows," he advised Tugwell, "and make them useful to us."

Coughlin remained blissfully unaware that he was being played. In early September 1932, he wrote Franklin: "I have twenty-six of the most powerful stations in our network. The east is thoroughly covered as is the middle west and the west as far as Denver"—all ready, of course, to boost FDR's election. Ravenous for FDR's (and the nation's) praise, Coughlin entreated Roosevelt to tout him in an upcoming speech as a cleric "who spoke for the rights of the common man."

FDR wasn't touting.

Their first dustup erupted as Roosevelt assumed office. Michigan's banks ranked among the shakiest in the nation, and Coughlin queried Treasury Secretary William Woodin and presidential secretary Marvin McIntyre if he might speak for the new administration regarding its banking policy. Woodin and McIntyre mumbled their responses, which Coughlin interpreted as a mumbled "OK." It wasn't. Coughlin, nonetheless, went on the air announcing that he was sanctioned to speak for the administration and unleashing a particularly vituperative, personal, and probably slanderous tirade against Detroit's banking community ("the banksters"). An outraged White House avoided a public break, but in late 1933 FDR privately fumed to Jim Farley of being "angry as hell at Coughlin for getting the administration involved in that mess." The priest "should run for the presidency himself," FDR seethed. "Who the hell does he think he is?"

Coughlin remained obliviously loyal. In November 1933, Al Smith hammered FDR for abandoning the gold standard and printing "baloney dollars." Coughlin, a natural inflationist, falsely accused his fellow Catholic of being a tool of J. P. Morgan. Invading Smith's Manhattan turf (and introduced by Henry Morgenthau Sr., the seventy-seven-year-old father of FDR's new Treasury Secretary), he excoriated Smith before an overflow Hippodrome crowd of seven thousand. New Yorkers booed native-son Smith's name twice.

The year 1934 saw the priest thrice visit FDR at the White House—in January ("Mr. Roosevelt is about twenty years ahead of the thought that is current in this country today . . . the disease of unemployment will be relegated to the Dark Ages"), in late March, and that October. In January, Coughlin had also appeared before a House committee, declaring his own doctrine of New Deal infallibility: "President Roosevelt is not going to make a mistake, for God Almighty is guiding him. . . . I predict revolution in this country and a revolution that will make the French Revolution silly. It is either Roosevelt or ruin." In April 1934, he vowed, "I will never change my philosophy that the New Deal is Christ's deal."

Yet, truth be told, Coughlin already felt the chill from FDR's cold shoulder. In January 1934, he sullenly lamented to Frank Murphy (now FDR's High Commissioner to the Philippines): "Sometimes, I am of the opinion that while I certainly rebuilt the confidence of the people in him, a confidence which had been greatly impaired, I sometimes wonder whether or not he favors my being with him."

Monetary policy—banking, Wall Street, currency, credit, etc.—formed the heart of Coughlin's obsessions, and FDR's policies, no matter how bold, never quite matched Coughlin's unfounded expectations. On April 23, 1934, Coughlin attended a pro-silver meeting in Washington, and threatened, "Unless the Democrat or Republican party adopt a sound policy of currency expansion, I think it is time to start another party. Let us bury the philosophy of the Rothschilds and the Federal Reserve

System, the Brain Trusters, the Communists and Experimentalists and get back to the Constitution, where Congress has the right to coin money and regulate its value."

"Let us bury . . . the Brain Trusters . . ."

Three days later, the Brain Trusters' friends would bury him.

Treasury Secretary Henry Morgenthau now released to the Senate a list of persons holding long-term contracts for silver purchases. Notable names included Gene Tunney, Robert Sterling Clark (a supposed accessory to Grayson Murphy's alleged 1935 Wall Street plot to overthrow Roosevelt), Calvin Coolidge's former presidential secretary Everett Sanders, former Maryland Republican US senator Joseph I. France—and, a far less familiar name, "A. Collins, Royal Oak, Mich."

"A. Collins," in fact, held a $20,000 margin investment in 500,000 ounces of silver. "A. Collins" was more specifically Amy Collins, Father Coughlin's thirty-two-year-old Canadian-born secretary and also the treasurer for the "Radio League of the Little Flower." Miss Collins protested that she had made the investment of her own volition and that such ventures were quite commonplace for an operation as substantial as the League. They had only amounted to less than "one week's expenses" for it. Coughlin accused Morgenthau of acting to protect "the gold advocates, the Federal bankers, and the international bankers."

". . . the international bankers."

Anti-Semitism was in the air. And not just in Germany. In 1933, a New York African-American newspaper justified Hitler's persecution of Jews. Abdul "Harlem's Black Hitler" Hamid touted himself as the "only one fit to carry on the war against the Jews." The Rev. Gerald "The Jayhawk Nazi" Winrod published *The Truth about the Protocols*, a 1935 defense of the debunked *The Protocols of the Wise Men of Zion*. In January 1935, anti-Semites briefly got their own presidential candidate when Father Coughlin's old pal Louis McFadden announced his bid under the aegis of "the Independent Republican National Christian-Gentile Committee" and the slogan "keep the Jew out of control of the Republican Party!"

From offices in the National Press Club, the lean, white-maned, spats-wearing James True published a weekly newsletter entitled *Industrial Control Reports*—and fulminated about the growing influence of "'Karl Marx' Professor Frankfurter and his legal kikes." In 1935, True patented (#2,026,077) a heavy-duty three-foot-long nightstick he marketed as the "Kike-Killer," boasting it was powerful enough to split "even a Negro's skull wide open." A more petite edition sold as the "Kike-Killer, Lady's Size." In August 1936, the revolver-toting, probably psychopathic True promised a national Jewish pogrom within a month, vowing, "We're not going to drive the Jews from this country. We're going to bury 'em right here."

In Detroit, the Klan-like Black Legion plotted to kill Jews by injecting typhoid germs into their milk and cottage cheese. Another abortive Black Legion plan involved planting timed mustard-gas bombs in every synagogue in America during Yom Kippur. William Dudley Pelley's Christian Party pledged "to defranchise the Jew by constitutional amendment, to make it impossible for a Jew to own property in the United States excepting under the same licensing system successfully employed against Occidentals in Japan, and to limit Jews to the professions, trades, and sciences by license according to their quotas of representation in the population."

Between 1934 and 1936, veteran newspaperman Robert Edmondson disseminated an estimated five million pieces of anti-Semitic literature. A particularly unusual obsession gripped him: his unfounded assertion that Gentile Frances Perkins was Jewish. By 1936, an infuriated Fiorello La Guardia had Edmondson indicted for "criminal libel." Thanks in part to the American Civil Liberties Union and the American Jewish Congress, Edmondson eventually beat the wrap.

Even Communists caught the bug, occasionally running derogatory cartoons of stereotypically Semitic capitalists and Palestinian settlers. One cartoon, wrote Nathan Glazer, depicting "hook-nosed and bloated Jews sadistically attacking Arabs could have appeared in any German anti-Semitic newspaper."

In January 1936, *Fortune* magazine ran a poll, asking, "Do you believe that in the long run Germany will be better off if it drives out the Jews?" Fourteen percent answered yes. Thirty percent professed no opinion. Gerald Smith, while "naturally" denying his own anti-Semitism, estimated "there are 25,000,000 anti-Semites in America today."

Coughlin larded his secular sermons with such phrases as "money-changers," "the Hebrew, Karl Marx," "Jewish gold," "gentile silver," and numerous attacks upon the "Rothschilds." He protested (perhaps too much) that his intentions were pure. Launching his new radio season in November 1934, he affirmed that "if there is anti-Jewish propaganda being maliciously circulated it will never find support from a Catholic pulpit. And be it recorded for the benefit of the slanderers of the Jew that to my knowledge not many Jews of any importance held office in Washington during the period of the past twenty years which was recently characterized as 'the period of conspiracy against the poor.'"

All Americans, he continued, "must stand shoulder to shoulder undivided by the paid agents of those few Jews or few Gentiles who either through ignorance or malice hold us fast in financial servitude. Not all Jews are in this. Thanks be to God, the vast majority of them as well as the vast majority of gentiles are fellow sufferers and, if need be, fellow battlers for our independence."

Interviewed that same month by the New York–based *Jewish Daily Telegraph*, he averred that American anti-Semitism was "either dead or dying." He nonetheless opposed any boycott of German goods, arguing that it would merely punish the German people for the sins of Hitler and Göring. While opposing Jewish settlements of Palestine, he advocated their settlement in the "Mississippi Valley."

He went so far as to praise Treasury Secretary Morgenthau. "I know Mr. Morgenthau better than ninety-nine per cent of the Jewish people. He is the finest and ablest man in Washington. I honor him for his sincerity and his honesty."

"The priest," reported the *Jewish Daily Telegraph*, "declared he can not understand why Jews should have suspected him of bias."

Coughlin's answers, the paper editorialized, "will no doubt help to eradicate the suspicion which prevailed that the famed priest is biased against the Jews. No matter whether many will agree or disagree with his analysis of the Jewish situation, . . . none will continue to carry the impression that Father Coughlin is grinding the anti-Jewish axe."

Perhaps he just laid his axe aside momentarily—to better swing it at the New Deal. As he stated to an interviewer decades later:

> Listen. I was never stupid. I realized the President now considered me burdensome. But he owed me things. After all I helped make him President. Besides it wasn't him who was against me. It was the people around him. I was determined that I would win him back. . . . We were supposed to be partners. He said he would rely on me. That I would be an important advisor. But he was a liar. He just used me and when he was through with me he double-crossed me on that silver business.

Just days before his *Jewish Daily Telegraph* interview, Coughlin incorporated a new organization, a mass movement akin to either Huey Long's "Share-Our-Wealth" clubs or Dr. Townsend's OARP, and christened the "National Union for Social Justice" (NUSJ). Members pledged to support his program thusly:

> 1. I believe in liberty of conscience and liberty of education, not permitting the state to dictate either my worship to my God or my chosen avocation in life.
> 2. . . . every citizen willing to work shall receive a just, living, annual wage which will enable him both to maintain and educate his family according to the standards of American decency.
> 3. . . . nationalizing these public resources which by their very nature are too important to be held in the control of private individuals.
> 4. . . . private ownership of all other property.
> 5. . . . upholding the right to private property but in controlling it for the public good.
> 6. . . . the abolition of the privately owned Federal Reserve Banking system and the establishment of a government owned Central Bank.
> 7. . . . rescuing from the hands of private owners the right to coin and regulate the value of money, which right must be restored to Congress where it belongs.
> 8. . . . that one of the chief duties of this government-owned Central Bank is to maintain the cost of living on an even keel and arrange for the repayment of dollar debts with equal value dollars.
> 9. . . . the cost of production plus a fair profit for the farmer.

10. . . . the right of the laboring man to organize in unions but also in the duty of the Government, which that laboring man supports, to protect these organizations against the vested interests of wealth and intellect.
11. . . . the recall of all non-productive bonds and therefore in the alleviation of taxation.
12. . . . the abolition of tax exempt bonds.
13. . . . broadening the base of taxation according to the principles of ownership and the capacity to pay.
14. . . . the simplification of government and the further lifting of crushing taxation from the slender revenues of the laboring class.
15. . . . that in the event of a war for the defense of our nation and its liberties, there shall be a conscription of wealth as well as a conscription of men.
16. . . . the sanctity of property rights; for the chief concern of government shall be for the poor because, as it is witnessed, the rich have ample means of their own to care for themselves.

In December 1934, Coughlin clarified his position on capitalism. By and large, he remained "agin it"—or, at least, for controlling it at New Deal levels. Government, he argued, should "limit the amount of profits acquired by any industry," as "Capitalism produces for a profit to the individual owner. Social justice advocates the production for use at a profit for the national welfare as well as for the owner . . . there can be no lasting prosperity if free competition exists in any industry. Therefore, it is the business of government not only to legislate for a minimum annual wage and a maximum working schedule to be observed by industry, but also to curtail individualism that, if necessary, factories shall be licensed and their output shall be limited." That same month, he excoriated the American Liberty League and proposed an ambitious $10 billion public works funded not by borrowing but by simply inflating the currency.

He insisted that the NUSJ was not a political party. It was instead a lobby, fighting for "social justice." Yet he claimed that the "old parties are all but dead." Thus began (or at least accelerated) Coughlin's confused, contradictory, often halting—and ultimately stupidly disastrous—pathway toward the 1936 election.

In January 1935, FDR momentarily returned to his Wilsonian roots and proposed United States membership in the World Court. Isolationists sprang into opposition, led by William Randolph Hearst and senators like Hiram Johnson and Bill Borah and joined by Huey Long ("Rockefeller millions are keeping the League of Nations and the World Court alive") and Father Coughlin. Coughlin, trumpeting himself as "old-fashioned enough to prefer Washington . . . to Wilson and those who follow him with their crude internationalism and their unsound love of minorities," excitedly argued that the Court represented "an internationalism which is a greater menace to our prosperity than the type advocated by the Soviet Third International."

Coughlin generated forty thousand telegrams to Congress in opposition. The Court sunk like a rock, and Coughlin received much of the credit—or blame. An angry Roosevelt bluntly wrote Hoover's pro–World Court Secretary of State Henry Stimson:

> You are right that we know [who] the enemy [is]. In normal times, the radio and other appeals by them would not have been effective. However, these are not normal times; people are jumpy and very ready to run after strange gods. This is so in every other country as well as our own. I fear common sense dictates no new method for the time being—but I have an unfortunately long memory and I'm not forgetting either our enemies or our objectives.

Coughlin and Roosevelt now differed on virtually everything. FDR, like Hoover before him, opposed accelerating the soldiers' bonus. Coughlin still favored it. The morning following a Coughlin pro-bonus broadcast, 150 telegrams per minute flooded the Capitol. "Mr. Roosevelt," wrote columnist Ray Tucker, "now knows whom to fear most among the 'pied pipers.' . . . [I]t is Father Coughlin."

In May 1935, FDR fulminated regarding his former ally to Henry Morgenthau, confiding that he hoped to leverage his power to appoint (or not appoint) an ambassador to the new Vatican City State, in order to pressure Church hierarchy on Coughlin. FDR further threatened that "If Coughlin kept it up much longer . . . he was going to release the file he had on him and perhaps even send for the three [American] cardinals and Apostolic delegate and show them the attacks that Father Coughlin has made on the sovereign of the United States—namely the President—and ask them how that jibes with their theory that the Church should have an ambassador in each country."

In September 1935, Huey Long involuntarily bade our story adieu. He and Coughlin had long eyed a possible alliance—though their massive egos certainly hamstrung its fruition. At Des Moines's Iowa State Fairgrounds in April 1935, Long orated to an audience of ten thousand at Milo Reno's National Farm Holiday Association convention. Coughlin had addressed that same gathering in 1934; but on learning he'd now have to share a stage with the magnetic Long, declined and sullenly dispatched unofficial representatives as his proxies. Publicly, Long respectfully responded, "I like Coughlin. I think his ideas are sound." Privately, he informed *The Nation*'s Benjamin Stolberg, "Coughlin is just a political Kate Smith on the air. They'll get tired of him."

Roosevelt was certainly sick of both of them. "The nation," Franklin confided to his old friend (and current ambassador to Italy) Breckinridge Long in early March 1935, is "going through a bad case of Huey Long and Father Coughlin influenza—the whole country aching in every bone."

In early March 1935, Coughlin took to the airwaves to scorch the "first two years of the New Deal . . . as two years of compromise, two years of social planning, two years of endeavoring to mix bad with good, two years of surrender, two years of matching the puerile, puny brains of idealists against the virile viciousness of business and finance."

Coughlin's words infuriated former NRA chieftain Gen. Hugh Johnson. Fired by FDR in September 1934, Johnson nonetheless remained a loyal (though often vexatious) New Dealer. On March 4, 1935, he delivered his own radio tirade, ripping both Long and Coughlin. ("There comes burring over the air the dripping brogue of the Irish-Canadian priest.") Johnson's harangue supplied Coughlin with a wonderful opportunity for rebuttal (and forty-five minutes of precious free air time on NBC), taunting "Old Iron Pants" as "the chocolate soldier," the "New

Deal's greatest casualty," and, for good measure, a pawn of his old business partner, Wall Street financier par excellence Bernard Baruch.

In late April, Harold Ickes savaged Long, Townsend—and Coughlin. FDR had "no objections" to pounding on Townsend. But he judged attacking Coughlin unwise, still somehow counting on Frank Murphy to placate this meddlesome priest. Why Franklin possessed such faith in Murphy's mastery over Coughlin remains a mystery—with Murphy still stationed at Manila, 8,300 miles from Royal Oak. In August 1935, however, Murphy returned stateside. Coughlin whimpered to him that Roosevelt had "broken every promise that he has made . . . he seeks means and methods closely allied with socialism and communism. . . . For the most part I shall remain silent until Mr. Roosevelt will commit himself either to retain or reject the present advisers." A month later, Coughlin counseled Murphy, "Not one New England State will go for President Roosevelt. His cause is definitely lost there. . . . New York is quite hostile, of course. Pennsylvania is dubious and is swinging away from him. Huey Long can control at least three States, directing them away from Mr. Roosevelt. . . . Michigan and Illinois are practically lost to the cause of the Democrats."

Coughlin remained a powerhouse—on the airwaves and on the stump. On May 8, 1935, he addressed 25,000 in Cleveland. Two weeks later, he attracted 23,000 to Madison Square Garden (general admission: 50 cents; $2.00 for the better seats). Coughlin's acolytes now booed FDR's name.

Coughlin and Roosevelt each supported 1935's Wagner Act for organized labor, but again parted company on both the Nye–Sweeney amendment to the Omnibus Banking Act of 1935, and a Nye–Sweeney bill establishing a Bank of the United States. The former measure defanged the Federal Reserve System, creating a central bank with the exclusive power to issue currency and to control credit. Forty-eight directors—one from each state—would govern said bank, with detractors warning that the larger, richer states would be "snowed under" by the smaller, poorer ones. Roosevelt never gave the bill a second thought. Neither did the Senate, smothering it 59–10.

Nonetheless, Coughlin's pal SEC Chairman Joseph P. Kennedy (Coughlin on Kennedy: a "shining star among the dim 'knights' of the

Administration") stood ready to patch things up, stringing the priest along with tidbits on how he—Kennedy—supposedly really felt about Roosevelt. When Coughlin had fumed to Murphy that FDR was "allied with socialism and communism," his next sentence read, "Joseph Kennedy agrees with me in this analysis."

In September 1935, the phone rang at Royal Oak, and Joe Kennedy's voice asked where Coughlin had been keeping himself. "Home, I'm busy," the priest answered.

Kennedy cut to the chase: the "Boss"—Roosevelt—wanted to see him.

"Where are you calling from, Joe?"

"Up the river!" Kennedy boomed—"Up the river" being his code for Hyde Park.

Roosevelt cut in: "Hiya Padre! Where have you been all the time? I'm lonesome. I've got a couple of days off down here. Come on down and see me." Coughlin begged off. He had "an important funeral" to attend to. The dead had precedence over the living.

Unfazed, FDR persisted: "You get ready and come down the next night then."

And so, just five days after Coughlin conveyed to Frank Murphy his pessimistic assessment of FDR's 1936 chances, he detrained at 5:15 a.m. at Albany's Union Station. Joe Kennedy's Rolls-Royce awaited his arrival. Inside sat Kennedy, poised to personally transport him to Hyde Park.

Tuesday morning, September 10, 1935—and Huey Pierce Long was dead.

Under any circumstance, such news was a shock. More so since as late as 10:30 p.m., New York time, Long's physicians had gamely pronounced that he was "holding his own."

Hearing the news at Albany, Coughlin decried the shooting as "the most regrettable thing in modern history." To reporters, he revealed that in 1934 he'd warned Long of a conspiracy to ambush him somewhere between Baton Rouge and New Orleans: "My Washington office received the information and passed it on to me. There have been plots for the last two years . . . now his enemies have finally succeeded."

Coughlin kept his mission to Hyde Park hush-hush. He informed the press that he was headed to "Hilltop," the seventy-five-acre Berkshires estate of an old classmate, the wealthy New York silver broker Francis P. Keelon. Indeed, he often traveled to Hilltop and would today—but only after one long detour to meet with FDR.

Kennedy and Coughlin motored south for over an hour, arriving far too early to see the invariably late-rising Roosevelt. They let themselves in through the front door and prepared breakfast for themselves, before retreating to the library to await their host. Finally, as Coughlin recalled:

> The Boss [Roosevelt] was at the head of the stairs. He had the most powerful arms—he had to. He walked on his arms, the poor fellow. His legs weren't of much use to him: I ran up the stairs with the newspaper [headlining Long's death] under my arm . . . I was going to give him my shoulder. That was the custom in the house. . . . I said, "By the way your boyfriend is dead." That was the first he heard that the wounded Long had died. . . . He blanched white. It was a shock to him.

Roosevelt shooed Joe Kennedy away, dismissively ordering him to "go look at the pigs." FDR, now alone with Coughlin, commanded, "Cards on the table, Padre. Cards on the table. Why are you cooling off to me? Why are you criticizing the things I'm doing?"

"I told him," Coughlin recalled, "that I wasn't criticizing anything that he was doing, but only some of his administrators. He said, 'Come on, Padre, the truth.' I said, 'We have had bad news from Mexico. This is it.'"

As Coughlin told it, when he had cleared his visit with Bishop Gallagher, Gallagher produced a canceled check from Henry Morgenthau to the Mexican Communist Party. Coughlin, like many American Catholics, remained extremely sensitive to long-term Mexican persecution of the Church.

"I took the photostat of the check from my pocket," Coughlin's story continues, "and showed it to [FDR]. As he was looking at it, I told him that '[Bishop] Michael Gallagher's afraid we are going soft on communism.' After a pause the President asked, 'How in the name of God did this thing ever get into your hands?' So I told him."

It all resembles a fable from one of Coughlin's "Children's Hour" broadcasts. On another occasion, Coughlin recounted his Gallagher-Morgenthau tale as occurring in the "summer" of 1935, minus any connection to FDR. Absent contradiction, it's the version we present (though not necessarily believe). We know not what Coughlin and Roosevelt really discussed before Joe Kennedy's return from the pigs (i.e., swine before pols). Presidential records circumstantially verify the day's events, however, indicating that his meeting with "Joseph B. Kennedy & Father Coughlan" commenced at 11:00 a.m., and that his schedule remained clear until 6:00 p.m.

It was, indeed, all very hush-hush. Marvin McIntyre initially denied the meeting's occurrence. To curious reporters, however, FDR soon fessed up, sloughing it off as a purely "social visit." Coughlin kept his counsel. "I was there in the capacity of a guest, . . ." he informed reporters. "I consider it a simple matter of etiquette. It would be unethical for a private citizen to discuss . . . a visit with his President."

Asked if another chat was forthcoming, FDR blandly responded, "Not that I know of."

"I went down to see Mr. Roosevelt and spent eight hours talking with him, during which time I did most of the talking, . . ." Coughlin eventually reported to Frank Murphy. "I sincerely feel that Mr. Roosevelt is a socialist of the radical type . . . not for what he has done so much as what he has left undone and which he has no intention of doing as he told me."

Roosevelt asked Coughlin and Kennedy to stay for dinner. Coughlin again begged off, with the excuse that he had already accepted an invitation from "a friend in Great Barrington." That he nixed an invitation from a president of the United States clearly hints how far off the rails their meeting had really gone.

Yet whatever tension festered that day was outright harmony compared to what erupted in February 1936. The wildly inflationary $3 billion Frazier–Lemke Farm Refinance bill ("The Farmers' Relief Act") advanced through Congress, and Coughlin dispatched his rotund, cigar-puffing Washington lobbyist (and his early official biographer) Louis B. Ward to bludgeon Congress and the administration into action. It did not go well. Harold Ickes recorded in his diary:

> According to the President, [Ward] went in to see [Marvin] McIntyre recently. He told McIntyre that he had never blackmailed the

> administration but there was something that Father Coughlin wanted . . . the President [should] put on pressure to get the Frazier–Lemke bill through, failing which Father Coughlin would attack the president. McIntyre told the man that this savored very strongly of blackmail and that he wouldn't even put up such a proposition to the president.

Coughlin carried through on his threat. FDR maintained a discreet silence. Coughlin also blasted House Rules Committee Chair John J. O'Connor (the elder brother of FDR's former law partner Basil O'Connor) for blocking the bill in committee, castigating O'Connor as "a servant of the money changers." O'Connor did not maintain a discreet silence, irately wiring the priest:

> The truth is not in you. You are a disgrace to my church and any other church and especially to the citizenship of America which you recently embraced. You do not dare print what you said about me. If you will please come to Washington I shall guarantee to kick you all the way from the capitol to the White House with clerical garb and all the silver in your pockets which you got from speculating in Wall Street. . . . Come on!

Rep. Martin Sweeney of Cleveland—formerly national president of the Ancient Order of Hibernians and now Coughlin's premier congressional champion—read O'Connor's telegram to the House, triggering an uproar as he yelled, "He [Coughlin] accepts your challenge and will be here at 10 o'clock tomorrow morning."

O'Connor retorted:

> Every decent Catholic in America has been ashamed of [Coughlin] since he came to this country. There isn't a clergyman of the Catholic Church except one [Bishop Gallagher] that I know of who has approved of his desecration of the cloth by his intrusion into politics.

> I personally never heard a Catholic priest talk politics from the pulpit. In the old days of prohibition and the KKK the cry of many of us to Bishop [James] Cannon [head of the Anti-Saloon League] was "Back to the pulpit, Stay where you belong."
>
> Just because Father Coughlin is an egomaniac he thinks he can run the government. He stepped into the bonus and world court issues, but had as much to do with Congressional action on them as any elevator operator in the Capitol.

Veteran fight promoter Jimmy Johnston proposed to stage a Coughlin–O'Connor bout at Madison Square Garden, guaranteeing a sellout at $100 a ticket. From California, an offer arrived to stand in for Coughlin: from former middleweight champion "Kid" McCoy—sixty-one years old, married ten times, and out on parole after killing his wealthy (and hefty) married girlfriend.

The big fight never came off—though smart money might well have rested on the muscular former rugby, football, and baseball player Coughlin. Frazier–Lemke never came off either, being roundly defeated (235–142) in the House. It was, as Coughlin headlined in his magazine *Social Justice*, "The Last Straw."

Coughlin exited the Roosevelt bandwagon.

Others were just getting on board.

Franklin's raucous "these forces [ha
met their master" Madison Square
Garden rally on October 31, 1936.
Alongside are fellow New Yorkers,
Governor Herbert Lehman and
Senator Robert F. Wagner. (COURT
OF THE FRANKLIN D. ROOSEVELT
PRESIDENTIAL LIBRARY & MUSEU

Franklin Roosevelt addressing the Young Democrats at Baltimore, April 1935. That January he had declared "we have built up new instruments of public power. In the hands of a people's Government this power is wholesome and proper. But in the hands of political puppets of an economic autocracy such power would provide shackles for the liberties of the people. Give them their way and they will take the course of every autocracy of the past—power for themselves, enslavement for the public." (COURTESY OF THE LIBRARY OF CONGRESS)

FDR's Fireside Chats transpo
him into millions of homes.
Fortune magazine praised hi
as both "the best actor in mo
pictures and the best voice in
radio." (COURTESY OF THE
LIBRARY OF CONGRESS)

FDR's former friend and mentor, the Democratic Party's 1928 presidential candidate, Gov. Alfred E. Smith. By January 1936, he fumes, "There can be only one flag, the Stars and Stripes, or the Red Flag of the godless union of the Soviet. There can be only one National Anthem. The Star Spangled Banner or the Internationale." (COURTESY OF THE LIBRARY OF CONGRESS)

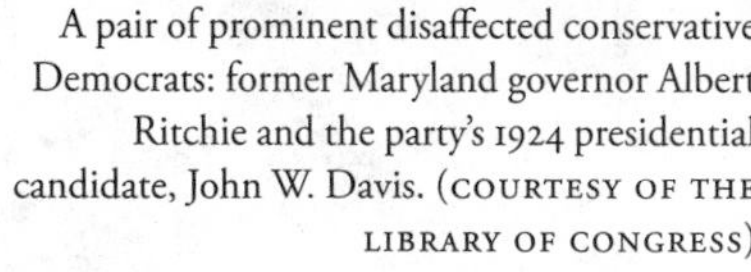

A pair of prominent disaffected conservative Democrats: former Maryland governor Albert Ritchie and the party's 1924 presidential candidate, John W. Davis. (COURTESY OF THE LIBRARY OF CONGRESS)

Liberty League powerhouse, the fabulously wealthy John Jakob Raskob. Said *Baltimore Sun* columnist Frank Kent of Raskob in 1932: "a naive amateur with an inaccurate idea of the importance his money . . . [that] gives him and an amazing awkwardness at the political game." (COURTESY OF THE LIBRARY OF CONGRESS)

Three movers and shakers behind the pro-FDR "Labor Non-Partisan League": its chairman of the board, the United Mine Workers' John L. Lewis, its secretary-treasurer, the Amalgamated Clothing Workers of America's Sidney Hillman and its president, the International Pressmen and Assistants' Union's Maj. George L. Berry. (COURTESY OF THE LIBRARY OF CONGRESS)

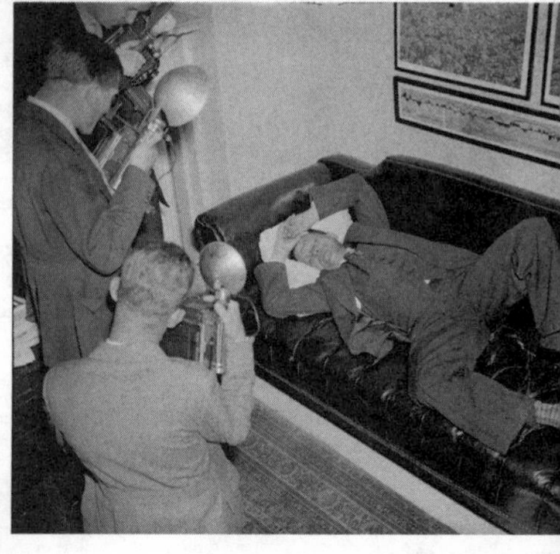

No, Louisiana Senator Huey Long isn't dead. He's just resting following his usual antics. (COURTESY OF THE LIBRARY OF CONGRESS)

Alf Landon's wife Theo Landon and their youngest child Jo Cobb Landon. "I thought," she recalls of first meeting her future husband, "he was an insurance salesman when he firs telephoned." (COURTESY OF THE LIBRARY OF CONGRESS)

BELOW: Eleanor Roosevelt at the all-Black Howard University. Distribution of this photo created a stir at Gene Talmadge's ill-fated anti-New Deal Macon convention. (COURTESY OF THE LIBRARY OF CONGRESS) BOTTOM LEFT: Eleanor Roosevelt with her friend Bethune-Cookman College President Mrs. Mary McLeod Bethune, as she addresses a National Youth Administration (N.Y.A.) meeting. BOTTOM RIGHT: The NAACP's Walter White. With Eleanor's support, he entreats Franklin to support federal anti-lynching legislation. FDR's response: he "just can't take that risk." (COURTESY OF THE LIBRARY OF CONGRESS)

Huey Long's former henchman, the spellbinding Gera
Smith, at Washington's National Press Club in August
Says Smith that day: "When politicians and practition
the gullibility of the population over play their hand, c
nerve centers in the national population begin to screa
I am one of the yellers." (COURTESY OF THE LIBRARY
CONGRESS)

Three of the four main pillars of 1936's ill-fated Union Party: Gerald L. K. Smith, Francis Townsend, and its nominee North Dakota Congressman William Lemke. "This Townsend show is really colossal," says H. L. Mencken, "Imagine 20,000 morons penned up in one hall . . ." (COURTESY OF THE LIBRARY OF CONGRESS)

The "Radio Priest," Father Charles
Coughlin testifying before Congre
in 1935—still on board with Roose
but soon jumping ship to organize
the ill-fated third party, Union Pa
(COURTESY OF THE LIBRARY OF
CONGRESS)

aristocratic—and ;—mother, Sara Delano velt. “Do you think [your] er would do anything to Father?” she queries James velt, “Is that why she stays in s, just to hurt his chances of ction?” (COURTESY OF THE RY OF CONGRESS)

Election Day, November 3, 1936: Eleanor arrives separately from FDR to cast her ballot at Hyde Park’s little wood-frame town hall. (COURTESY OF THE FRANKLIN D. ROOSEVELT PRESIDENTIAL LIBRARY & MUSEUM)

Eleanor and Franklin at Warm ngs. “I realize more & more that R. is a great man & he is nice to ,” she privately reveals, “but as a on I’m a stranger & I don’t want o be anything else.” (COURTESY OF THE NATIONAL ARCHIVES ID RECORDS ADMINISTRATION - #195635)

Former National Recovery Administration (NRA) Director Gen. Hugh "Iron Pants" Johnson. (COURTESY OF THE LIBRARY OF CONGRESS)

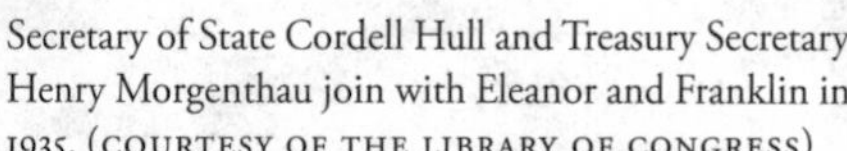

Secretary of State Cordell Hull and Treasury Secretary Henry Morgenthau join with Eleanor and Franklin in 1935. (COURTESY OF THE LIBRARY OF CONGRESS)

Postmaster General, Democratic National Chairman, and FDR camp manager James A. Farley. (COURTES THE LIBRARY OF CONGRESS))

The GOP's lackluster presidential nominee, Governor Alfred M. "The Kansas Coolidge" Landon. Eventually dismissed by columnist Walter Lippmann as "a dull and uninspired fellow, an ignorant man. . . . of no account." (COURTESY OF THE LIBRARY OF CONGRESS)

GOP Vice-Presidential nominee Col. Frank M. Knox, publisher of the Chicago Daily News and a former Theodore Roosevelt Rough Rider. "No life insurance policy is secure; no savings account is safe" under the New Deal, warns Knox. Few take him seriously. (COURTESY OF THE LIBRARY OF CONGRESS)

Republican National Chairman John D. M. Hamilton addressing Washington's National Press Club in September 1936. "We are going to break the Solid South;" predicts Hamilton, "it might happen that we will carry all 48 States. . . . Get that on record." He doesn't believe a word of it. (COURTESY OF THE LIBRARY OF CONGRESS)

· 9 ·

"Shirt Mania"

Charles Edward Coughlin and Gerald Lyman Kenneth Smith weren't the only clerics shaking things up.

So was Norman Mattoon Thomas, formerly the Socialist Party candidate for New York governor, US senator, and state senator; for New York City alderman and mayor; and, for good measure, United States president in both 1928 and 1932. And, because he was barely getting started, in 1936 as well.

Why the hell not?

Not every Socialist gets his start delivering papers for Warren G. Harding. Damned few, in fact. But Norman Thomas delivered Harding's *Marion Star* in his boyhood hometown of Marion, Ohio. Ordained a Presbyterian minister in 1911, he preached the increasingly fashionable Social Gospel. When war fever erupted in 1917, he dared preach unfashionable pacifism and conscientious objectionism. Pacifism led him into the anti-war Socialist Party. He left the ministry in 1931 but remained forever Socialist.

Progressive FDR might be, but he never quite measured up to Thomas's standards. Franklin regulated private utility companies. Thomas demanded public ownership. When Roosevelt addressed Tammany on July 4, 1928, Thomas was disgusted. Roosevelt vacillated on what to do about Mayor "Gentleman Jimmy" Walker. Thomas—who had run against "Beau James" in 1929 and wasn't about to stop saying "I told you so"—wanted Walker's head. That FDR cavalierly ignored Robert Moses's program of banking reforms—and bore grave responsibility for New York bank failures—infuriated Thomas. Thomas, concluded FDR biographer Kenneth S. Davis, considered Roosevelt to possess "an evil genius . . . for harnessing his ambition [to] halfway, hence, ineffectual measures."

Thomas was a new sort of Socialist, a new manner of radical. Protestant and Princeton-educated, he was neither of the Lower East Side type dominating New York's Socialist Party, nor a union-organizing workingman like Big Bill Haywood or Eugene Debs before him. Thomas was intellectual and sophisticated. On the party's left wing, he nonetheless provided it with a certain polish and respectability.

He could afford respectability. "[T]he least defensible feature of capitalism," mused columnist Jay Franklin, "—unearned income—was the means by which Norman Thomas was able to keep going as a Socialist leader. Mrs. Thomas had inherited a small but regular income. So that he did not need to worry or work for the necessities of his large family, although [living] in a simplicity [befitting] his Socialist beliefs."

"He is today," continued Franklin, "the hero of the timid college student and of the stenographer who has tried to read Spengler but has been discouraged by that awful task. He is the white-collar Socialist leader, the college professor of the proletarians, with the fluent pedantry of the professional teacher and pulpiteer, the rigid logic of the Wilsonian school of Presbyterian politics, and the heavy ironic humor of one who is bookish rather than realistic in his approach to life."

Huey Long and Father Coughlin were hot.

Norman Thomas was cool.

Even by 1928, Thomas was sufficiently eminent to draw Coughlin's broadcast ire. Running for president again in 1932, he excoriated Roosevelt for "running as a radical in the west, as a safe and sane friend of good business in the east." He warned that unless socialistic principles were adopted, humanity was "headed for hell or something worse." He performed well by Socialist standards, drawing 881,951 votes—the party's highest raw total since Gene Debs's 1920 high-water mark of 919,799.

His antipathy for the capitalist parties was a given. He loathed Coughlin and Huey Long. When Long died, he disdained the usual courtesies, deriding the Kingfish as "the ablest and most colorful forerunner of American Fascism."

In 1934, Thomas charged that FDR's AAA not only did little to assist Southern sharecroppers; it also ignored the often brutal tactics blocking their organizing efforts. Ignored by Henry Wallace, Rexford Tugwell, and even Eleanor Roosevelt, Thomas miraculously secured a meeting with the president himself, who (as was his habit) begged off from action for fear of alienating powerful Southern Democratic senators. "Norman," FDR lectured him, "I'm a damned sight better politician than you are."

"The President and his party," Thomas later raged, "knew of peonage, terrorism, the flogging of men and women . . . and they were silent."

Despite the 881,951 votes Thomas had garnered in 1932, the Socialist Party remained a fractured, shrinking, impoverished mess heading into 1936. Democrats like Woodrow Wilson and, now, Franklin Roosevelt, kept filching their program. In just one year, from 1932 to 1933, their party's vote in Gotham mayoral contests plummeted from 12.6 percent to 3.0 percent. Manhattan's 1935 municipal elections saw them outpolled by the hitherto moribund Communists. Actual party membership peaked at 125,826 way back in 1912—slipping to just over 100,000 in 1919; and wobbling to under 17,000 in 1932 and 11,922 in 1936. By 1935, Communist national membership had surpassed theirs.

Bitter factionalism divided its remaining membership. Socialists largely selected Thomas as their 1928 and 1932 standard-bearer because he was about their last remaining prominent American-born leader.

Now commanding the SP's younger, more pacifistic "Militant" wing, he battled its more conservative, anti-Communist, largely Jewish and New York–based "Old Guard." Thomas's "Militant" faction was, well, militant. Their June 1934 Declaration of Principles (largely Thomas's work) condemned the "bogus democracy of capitalist parliamentarism" and declared that if "general chaos and confusion" finally overtook the country, the Socialist Party, "whether or not . . . a majority, will not shrink from the responsibility of organizing and maintaining a government under the rule of the producing masses." Such talk struck the "Old Guard" as revolutionary, authoritarian, and quasi-Communist. It scared the hell out of them.

So did the general demeanor of these Militants. As Old Guard former New York State Socialist assemblyman Louis Waldman chronicled:

> Symptoms of a new and dangerous spirit among the Socialist youth began to become manifest on all sides. The youngsters appeared at meetings . . . in blue shirts and red ties. At first this attracted no special attention, for oddity in dress is no novelty among radicals. But gradually their number increased and we now could see that this was a uniform. The Socialist youth of America, like the fascist youth in Europe, had succumbed to the shirt mania.
>
> The shirt tendency was followed by the salute mania. In Europe, the Nazi salute was the outstretched arm; here [they adopted] the Communist clenched fist salute. This greeting, a raised arm at a slightly different angle from the Nazi or Communist salute, now became routine at all our meetings. . . . Some of the older members of the party were truly horrified, . . . but others couldn't resist the trend and fell into line. Among these, I painfully record, was Norman Thomas.
>
> Along with the blue shirts, the red ties, the clenched fists, the raised arm salute, came the banners, the slogans, the demonstrations; all the trappings that make for totalitarian, unthinking mass fervor. These now became regular features at party gatherings. I can still recall the howl of triumph that rose from these young people at one of our meetings when for the first time Norman Thomas returned the clenched fist salute to them. As I stood at his side, my arms deliberately folded to indicate that I would have no part of this, their cheers for Thomas rose to almost uncontrollable frenzy.

But Thomas had competition.

Occasionally, Socialists assumed power in cities like Milwaukee, Bridgeport, Schenectady, or Reading. They never remotely approached statewide power. Minnesota's radical Farmer-Labor Party (FLP) did. Both of the state's United States senators—Henrik Shipstead and Elmer Benson—were Farmer-Labor. So, too, was an earlier senator, Magnus Johnson. The party ultimately elected nine congressmen; two of whom may have been crypto-Communists. Sam Bernard, elected in 1936, eventually invoked the Fifth Amendment regarding Communist Party (CPUSA) membership. Rep. Ernest Lundeen later became dangerously pro-German. But in February 1934, he sponsored the Communist Party's "Worker's Unemployment Insurance Bill." Two-time Communist vice presidential candidate Benjamin Gitlow contended that Lundeen had been "a paid under cover agent of the Communist Party" since 1926.

By 1935, CPUSA leader Earl Browder and Farmer-Labor Governor Floyd B. Olson had secretly aligned their two parties. Previously, Communists had derided the controversial Olson as an "unscrupulous demagogue." Now the CPUSA swung around 180 degrees, devoting itself to "build[ing] the FLP." Olson provided numerous favors in return. "For two short years . . ." writes scholar Harvey Klehr, "the [Communist] Party enjoyed a status it had never attained in any American state. . . . [I]n no other state . . . did the Communists have so intimate a relationship with the executive branch and the political party that controlled it."

At Chicago, in May 1936, Olson convened a nationwide conference of radical organizations and state third parties to explore creation of a nationwide left-wing third party. He insisted on Communist participation. Wisconsin's Progressives—among others—walked out.

The hard-drinking son of Scandinavian immigrants, Olson had previously held office as a very corrupt Hennepin County (Minneapolis) county attorney. Elected governor in a 1930 landslide, his tenure proved radical—and violent. In September 1934, a scandal-mongering newsman named Howard A. Guilford publicly pledged to unveil "the truth about . . . Olson's connection with the underworld." Guilford was soon stone-cold dead thanks to a drive-by, gangland-style shooting. Farmer-Labor Party founder Arthur Townley accused Olson of advance knowledge of Guilford's rubout. Minnesota's Republican US senator Thomas D. Schall labeled the murder "press censorship by shotgun."

Olson won reelection by a substantially reduced margin, surviving, as one critic noted, thanks to "the Farmer-Labor press, large sums from businessmen, a war chest from liquor lobbyists and the underworld and an obligatory 3 percent donation from state employees—plus their unpaid labor." Also assisting was FDR, who sandbagged state Democrats. "In Minnesota," Franklin ordered Jim Farley, "*hands off*—don't encourage opposition to Shipstead and Oleson [sic]."

Howard Guilford wasn't the only reporter on Olson's trail. The *Midwest American*'s Walter W. Liggett had once been enthusiastically Farmer-Labor—until Olson took power and Liggett saw him as "a damned sight more of a racketeer than he is a radical."

"I don't think they will have me killed," Liggett reassured himself. "It wouldn't look good for one thing, and for another thing the whole damned cowardly crew know that they can't . . . besmirch my professional reputation in an attempt to justify a cold blooded murder as they did in poor Howard Guilford's case."

He was wrong on several counts—dead wrong. Romanian-born Minneapolis mob boss Isadore "Kid Cann" Blumenfeld offered Liggett a bribe to lay off. Liggett refused. Blumenfeld oversaw his beating. Next came a frame-up on a morals charge (sex with underage girls). Liggett won acquittal. The forty-nine-year-old Liggett spent most of Monday, December 9, 1935, crafting a speech urging Olson's impeachment. Night fell—and so did Liggett—shot dead in the alleyway outside his home. Five machine-gun bullets formed a bloody circle around his heart.

Liggett's wife, Edith, and ten-year-old daughter, Marda, witnessed his murder. Edith Liggett testified that she believed Olson was either behind the killing or permitted it. "Kid Cann" Blumenfeld stood trial for the slaying. The prosecution was, shall we say, lax, and he went free.

Meanwhile, Olson proclaimed, "You bet your life I'm a radical. You might say I'm radical as hell!" His party adopted a platform declaring that "capitalism has failed and that immediate steps must be taken . . . to abolish capitalism in a peaceful and lawful manner, and that a new, sane, and just society must be established; a system in which all the natural resources, machinery of production, transportation, and communication shall be owned by the government and operated democratically for the benefit of all and not for the benefit of the few."

"You can't have abundance with a capitalist system," he argued in November 1935. "You can't have profits and have abundance. There must be a third party."

Olson attracted all manner of left-wing ardor. Communists looked favorably upon his candidacy. Mysteriously, so, too, did such anti-Communist Old Guard Socialists as Louis Waldman and Rand School director Algernon Lee. Henry Morgenthau remarkably claimed to FDR that Rex Tugwell would jump ship to Olson in 1936.

Olson (like Huey Long), however, calculated that third-party success was more likely in 1940 than 1936—although he feared that, four years hence, he might not prove "radical enough."

His Farmer-Labor platform contained little that was unique, it being a virtual grab bag of radical and progressive nostrums—borrowings from Upton Sinclair's EPIC program; Kingfish-inspired free textbooks and a $4,000 homestead tax exemption; La Follette family-style tax increases; a state-run bank; public power plans à la Harold Ickes; and, of course, an "adequate old age pension."

Like Huey Long, Olson calculated that the jump from small-state governor to the presidency might prove too far a leap. Accordingly, he plotted to oust Thomas Schall from his Senate seat. That contest was, however, not to be. In December 1935—just thirteen days following Walter Liggett's gangland execution—the legally blind Schall was struck and killed while crossing the street near the US Capitol.

His death coincided with a national conference of traffic-safety experts.

In any case, Floyd Olson wasn't running for president in 1936.

Earl Browder was.

Sort of.

Like Floyd Olson and Norman Thomas, Browder hailed from the not-nearly-as-conservative-as-you-might-think Midwest. Once an active Socialist, he personally knew Gene Debs. Like Debs, his Great War anti-war activities had triggered a jail sentence. He served another stretch following the war—for conspiracy—before being recruited for the brand-new Communist Party. In an era that produced FDR, the Kingfish, and The Radio Priest, Browder ranged nearer Dr. Townsend on the charisma scale. His unflattering nickname was "the bookkeeper," but he was a plugger. By 1930, following the usual CPUSA inner-party bloodletting, he emerged as party general secretary. By 1934, he had risen even higher—to party chairman. Ben Gitlow (the party's 1924 and 1928 vice presidential candidate) recalled how it worked:

> Browder, a very gloomy figure in those days, confided to his friends that he had made many serious blunders [concerning the Bonus March], for which he was prepared to go into exile in Moscow for a number of years and do penance there. But Browder did not know Stalin. When [William] Weinstone's name was suggested [for general secretary], Stalin put his thumbs down. . . . He did not want a Jew to be General Secretary of the American Communist Party. Moreover, precisely because of Browder's numerous blunders and his repentant humility, Stalin looked with favor upon him. Stalin said that Browder could be trusted to carry out orders implicitly precisely because he lacked independence of both thought and spirit; and besides, he was by birth a Christian and a native American.

As author Eugene Lyons summarized: "In Browder, Stalin had found the perfect resident sales manager for one of the lesser of his foreign branches—too meek and ineffectual ever to set up in business on his own."

Depression-battered 1932 witnessed as great a "crisis of Capitalism" as Communists might have ever dreamt, yet their presidential candidate, William Z. Foster, received a mere 102,991 votes—in part due to the party's hard-line, dogmatic nature. As Foster himself vaingloriously vowed: "All the capitalist parties—Republican, Democratic, Progressive, Socialist—will be liquidated, the Communist Party [will be] functioning alone."

Thus, the party displayed little sympathy for either the Socialists ("the main social prop of the bourgeoisie [even] in the countries of open fascist dictatorship") or for the high-flying New Deal (a "step in the direction of fascism"). The new administration's goals, Browder alleged, were "to preserve the profits of the big capitalists at all costs, to establish fascism at home and to wage imperialist war abroad." He accused FDR of "carrying out more thoroughly and brutally than even Hoover the capitalist attack against the masses."

In August 1933, the CPUSA sponsored the "Opposition Labor Conference Against Industrial Recovery Bill," indicting the NIRA as "slave legislation"—"from beginning to end an enormous looting of the government treasury, a further robbery of the workers and toilers generally for the benefit . . . of Wall Street." In December 1934, the Communist-dominated *New Masses* magazine lashed out at the "Mussolini-schooled boys of the Administration."

Militant action paralleled militant words. Various left-wing factions fomented labor strife. From April 12 to June 3, 1934, the Marxist "American Workers Party" helped lead a massive strike versus Toledo's Auto-Lite plant. Late May witnessed the city's immense, five-day "Battle of Toledo" pitting 10,000 strikers versus 1,300 National Guardsmen. Two died. More than 200 were injured. That same month, Communist Harry Bridges launched an International Longshoreman's Association strike in San Francisco, eventually crippling every West Coast port. On May 16, 1934, Teamsters—led by the Trotskyite "Communist League of America"—struck in Minneapolis.

So the times demanded radicalism.

Or did they?

Communists did not play well with others. In 1930, when Communists busted up Socialist meetings in San Francisco, their newspaper, the *Daily Worker*, crowed, "Social-Fascist Enemies of Jobless Get Answer." In February 1934, five thousand of the comrades invaded a Socialist rally at Madison Square Garden, oblivious to the fact that its proceedings were being broadcast over the radio. "Socialist ushers, about five hundred in number, proved unable to control the situation," noted the *New York Times*. "Fifty policemen marched into the hall as the Communists were preparing to rush the platform. . . . They were stopped by the police and ushers as they sought to leap across a barrier of chairs occupied by Socialists. . . . [I]t seemed . . . as if the Communists would seize the platform and turn the meeting into a general battle."

Pre-1933 German Communists possessed one of the world's strongest parties outside Russia. Yet—aloof from all others, particularly the Weimar Republic's embattled Social Democrats (i.e., Socialists)—they stood idly by as Hitler seized power. Ideologically blinded, they regarded Hitler's rise sanguinely—even positively. Fascism in power, they reasoned, could only *accelerate* Germany's inevitable march toward Red Revolution. Hitler "won't last long," German Communist Party overlord Ernst Thälmann smirked. "The workers will rise. There will be civil war."

Thälmann wasn't alone in hideously miscalculating reality. In 1932, Comintern functionary D. Z. Manuilsky had asserted: "To deceive the masses, the Social Democrats deliberately proclaim that the chief enemy of the working class is Fascism. It is not true that Fascism of the Hitler type represents the chief enemy."

Such theories wilted as Hitler fomented the first real danger to Moscow since Russian Civil War days. Worse, France, too, looked like it might topple into the growing fascist camp. Moscow now jettisoned stiff-necked, dogmatic isolation for a happy-face, nationally patriotic "United Front" approach, even accepting membership in the hitherto "imperialist" League of Nations in 1934. At 1935's General Party Congress in Moscow, the Comintern's Bulgarian-born General Secretary Georgi Dimitroff unveiled a new official policy: a "broad people's anti-fascist front on the basis of the proletarian united front."

Said Dimitroff:

> Comrades: you remember the ancient tale of the capture of Troy. Troy was inaccessible to the armies attacking her, thanks to her impregnable walls. And the attacking army, after suffering many sacrifices, was unable to achieve victory until with the aid of the famous Trojan horse it managed to penetrate to the very heart of the enemy's camp.
>
> We revolutionary workers . . . should not be shy about using the same tactics with regard to our fascist foe, who is defending himself against the people with the help of a living wall of his cutthroats.

Gone were the rollicking good old days of pummeling Socialists at Madison Square Garden. Now Communists and Socialists and progressives—and even just plain Democrats—could work together: together, of course, under the iron discipline of the United Front's CPUSA operatives. Not every comrade grasped Stalin's latest brilliance, leaving Browder to lecture such laggards: "If one is not interested in directives from Moscow that only means that he is not interested in building socialism at all." Dimitroff put it more bluntly: anyone finding it "humiliating" to play this new game was "a windbag and not a revolutionary."

Thus, based merely on a speech delivered by a Bulgarian in Moscow (authorized, naturally, by a Georgian in the Kremlin), Communist attitudes from Paris to New York to Hollywood shifted seismically. The era of the United Front unleashed a dizzying myriad of Communist-front organizations—and what author Eugene Lyons ultimately dubbed "The Red Decade."

Communists, wrote historian Ted Morgan, could now "applaud democracy and the New Deal. FDR was no longer a fascist tool of Wall Street, but the protector of the working man. . . . The Communists suddenly seemed housebroken and socially acceptable. They were invited to parties. This was communism with a smile, benign and neighborly.

"Gone was the 'Crazy Red.' Here was the 'Lincoln Club,' celebrating Mother's Day. Instead of 'read Engels on housing,' it was 'we're just folks.' The Young Communist League celebrated Paul Revere's ride more noisily than it did the birth of Lenin."

Gone as well was the Communist image as a bunch of Greenwich Village bohemians and Lower East Side malcontents scoffing at conventional morality and patriotism. That *volte-face* had also similarly originated within the Great Soviet Motherland itself. Moscow banned male homosexuality in March 1934 and limited abortion in June 1936.

In America, the shift often manifested itself in terms of fashion. "Under Browder's leadership," observed Browder biographer James G. Ryan, "functionaries began to improve their public image. Business suits replaced leather jackets; Communist women began wearing high heels on formal occasions." Somehow, one cannot escape the image of Greta Garbo's new, haute-bourgeois (and more than slightly ridiculous) chapeau in the 1939 MGM film *Ninotchka*.

Patriotism became the vogue—almost an obsession. Comrade Dimitroff decreed that party members should not abandon "to the fascist falsifiers all that is valuable in the historical past of the nation, that the fascists may bamboozle the masses." The CPUSA obeyed.

"[B]y continuing the traditions of 1776 and 1861, . . ." Browder argued, the CPUSA "is really the only party entitled . . . to designate itself as 'sons and daughters of the American Revolution.'" Browder—not only a Kansan, but also a fifth-generation American—seemed perfectly cast to pitch the party's snappy new slogan, "Communism is Twentieth Century Americanism."

Most amazing of all was just how easy the new policy was, how well it worked, how eagerly non-Communists joined with party members in Communist-dominated groups (the "Innocents' Clubs," as the comrades termed them). Their causes were popular: the Scottsboro Boys, anti-war groups, anti-fascist coalitions, the West Side Mothers for Peace, the American Youth Congress, Friends of Ethiopia, the Abolish Peonage Committee, the National Congress for Unemployment and Social Insurance, and so on. The year 1936 witnessed a major boost for United Front efforts as Spain erupted into civil war, and leftists and liberals of all stripes rushed into such Communist front groups as the Theatre Committee for the Defense of the Spanish Republic, The Friends of the Abraham Lincoln Brigade, and the Spanish Children's Fund. "In the country's cultural world, in particular," as scholar Guenter Lewy would note, "the Communists were able to achieve a position of considerable influence and power."

In April 1935, the Communist-front League of American Writers convened at Manhattan's New School for Social Research. Party members Michael Gold, Granville Hicks, John Howard Lawson, and Samuel Ornitz (the latter two eventual members of the "Hollywood Ten") attended. But so did such literary heavyweights as novelists Theodore Dreiser, John Dos Passos, Nelson Algren, Erskine Caldwell, Nathaniel West, and Richard Wright; literary critic Malcolm Cowley; muckraker Lincoln Steffens; poet Langston Hughes; dance patron Lincoln Kirstein; and sociologist Lewis Mumford.

The year 1936 witnessed the birth of the particularly popular Communist-front Hollywood Anti-Nazi League. Party members Donald Ogden Stewart, Dorothy Parker, Alan Campbell, Marion Spitzer, Lillian Hellman, Ring Lardner Jr., and Herbert Biberman (all screenwriters) belonged, but so did many a well-meaning non-Communist such as Fredric March, Eddie Cantor, Oscar Hammerstein II, Ernst Lubitsch, Moss Hart, Melvyn Douglas, and Herman Mankiewicz. Ten thousand people attended their October 1936 rally at Los Angeles's Shrine Coliseum.

Big stars enlisted. So did still obscure starlets. Back in March, twenty-four-year-old RKO contract-player Lucille Ball had registered as a party member. "In those days," she later explained, "that was not a big, terrible thing to do. It was almost as terrible to be a Republican." That September, CPUSA bosses appointed Ball (perhaps without her knowledge) to their Central State Committee.

As young party member Budd Schulberg later put it, the CPUSA was "the only game in town."

If Communists were not under every bed, they were under enough of them. In December 1935, much to the chagrin of the SP's "Old Guard," their party's Socialist League for Industrial Democracy and the Communist Party's National Student League merged to form the American Student Union.

By 1938, *New Leader* literary critic Philip Rahv (formerly a party member) could state that "the Stalinists and their friends, under multiform disguises . . . managed to penetrate into the offices of publishing houses, the editorial staffs of magazines, and the book-review sections of conservative newspapers."

A big game for the party—it being officially a party, after all—remained political. The biggest "United Front" would involve the Democratic Party and reelecting Franklin Roosevelt. "[I]t was in [the party's] interest," Browder admitted decades later. "They needed Roosevelt then. They needed him as a counterweight to Hitler, . . . the greatest menace to . . . the Soviet Union at that time."

Browder, though amazingly pliant, wasn't entirely stupid. He realized a CPUSA endorsement would be the kiss of death (or, at least a case of syphilis) for FDR. Moscow, he recalled, "wanted [us] to endorse [FDR]. I opposed it. . . . An endorsement would lose [FDR] more votes than it would gain him. And so I became the [Communist] candidate for President upon the understanding that I was to campaign in such a way as to support Roosevelt in fact."

Which is exactly what happened.

A parallel (and perhaps contradictory) goal involved uniting Communists, "Militant" Socialists, North Dakota's Non-Partisan League, Floyd Olson's Minnesota's Farmer-Labor Party, Wisconsin's La Follette-led Progressives, left-wing unions, and even radical farmers such as belonged to the recently deceased Milo Reno's Farmers' Holiday

Association securely under one great Farmer-Labor banner, all ultimately under CPUSA sway.

Perhaps even Townsendites might fall in line. "In California," observed the monthly theoretical journal *The Communist* in July 1936, ". . . large numbers of [Townsend] clubs are swinging into joint struggles against reaction . . . and are moving in the direction of a Farmer-Labor Party. More intensive work among the Townsendites along the lines of Communist Party policy will produce such and even greater results." It was not to be. Townsend was no Communist. His new guru, Gerald Smith, was even less so.

As late as June 1936, however, such major journalistic figures as Scripps-Howard columnists Heywood Broun and Westbrook Pegler endorsed a Farmer-Labor united front. In 1930, Broun had run unsuccessfully as a Socialist for Congress on New York's Upper East Side—endorsed by every celebrity from George Gershwin and Irving Berlin to Walter Winchell and Theodore Dreiser to John Dewey and all four Marx Brothers. Facing Socialist Party expulsion for joining in an Al Smith demonstration at 1932's Democratic Convention, he quipped, a tad ominously, "in getting out of the Socialist Party one should leave by the door to the left."

"We've got to sink our differences—," Broun informed the *Daily Worker* that June of 1936. "Socialists, liberals, Communists and other progressives—faced with a very real threat of fascism, and I don't believe there can be any really important Farmer-Labor Party without Communists included."

"I'm not a Communist," Westbrook Pegler chimed in, "and I'm not for Communism but this idea of forming a Farmer-Labor party to put through real social legislation and Progressive policies and government is okay."

Such ideas, however, possessed diminishing fascination to the grab bag of non-Socialist Progressives the CPUSA hoped to co-opt. Winning an election with FDR was, after all, more to anyone's favor than losing one with Earl Browder or William Z. Foster.

But hope for a CPUSA–Militant Socialist alliance still fluttered within CPUSA hearts. Browder proposed to Norman Thomas that Socialists and

Communists gather together at Madison Square Garden—not to re-create the CPUSA blitzkrieg that rocked the joint back in February 1934—but in a fraternal debate between comrades Browder and Thomas—so fraternal that Browder ceded his share of gate receipts to the SP party newspaper, the *New York Call*. He possessed a two-pronged agenda: first to lure the SP into united action in the upcoming presidential election, but also to drive a deeper wedge between warring Old Guard and Militant SP factions. He certainly succeeded in the later goal. Old Guard chieftains, accusing Thomas of enrolling in a "United Front" with Moscow, demanded his expulsion from party ranks.

Thomas and Browder debated on Wednesday night, November 27, 1935, before a now remarkably amicable crowd of twenty thousand. Socialists and Communists harmonized in renditions of "The International," "Red Flag," and "Solidarity Forever." Thomas led them for a while, and conceded favoring "the maximum possible amount of joint action by all who are opposed to war and fascism." Nor would he exclude Communists from a Farmer-Labor Party, "provided they prove sincerity and good faith."

Browder reminded him of his previous statement that "to make Socialists swear that they could never conceive of any circumstances that will justify armed insurrection, or to compel Socialists to affirm a blind belief in a romantic parliamentarism is complete and unsocialist folly."

"Mr. Browder," observed the *New York Times*, "considered this good Communist doctrine."

Thomas did, however, toss a few jabs at Moscow ("Is Russia so weak that it cannot afford, eighteen years after the revolution, to grant civil liberties to its citizens? . . . It is by Russian oil that the defenseless Ethiopians are killed"), but Algernon Lee, an Old Guard New Yorker, still assessed the evening as "a love feast . . . there can be no doubt as to its services to the Communist party."

Yet Thomas had also protested that he "did not think the time has come for a formal united front." In January 1936, Browder would actually propose a joint Socialist-Communist presidential ticket—headed by Thomas. Thomas rejected it, soon writing:

> Under French conditions a united front has been found possible and so far useful. In America the question is different. By uniting Socialists and Communists in one political, nationwide front, we won't have enough strength to stop fascism. The question is, will such union help or hinder the education of workers toward socialism? A realistic view of the situation, in view of . . . the labor skepticism concerning communism, makes me believe such a united front would not be worth its cost.

All the while, Browder's minions maintained their guise as newly minted, super-wholesome patriots, disgusting not only capitalists and Socialists, but also their bitter Trotskyite rivals. In February 1936, the Trotskyite *New Militant* reported:

> SHADES OF LENIN!
>
> BOSTON.—Ushered in by a hysterical campaign in the Hearst *Boston American*, appealing to all patriotic Bostonians to prevent the meeting, the people of this city were astounded by a spectacle of patriotism and flag-waving under the guise of a Lenin memorial meeting held recently by the C. P. at Symphony Hall.
>
> In a truly American setting, without a single decoration of Communist origin, District Organizer [Philip] Frankfeld read a twenty-minute speech, whose theme was that throughout the land there were no better, more loyal Americans to be found than in the flock of Stalin.
>
> In introducing the following speaker, a C. P. member, he carefully addressed him as "Mr." Moore to the amusement of the audience.
>
> The high note of the meeting was a talk by that eminent American patriot, Earl Browder, who essayed the despicable and pathetic task of trying to justify the social-patriotism of the C. P. as sanctioned by Lenin! Among many other remarks of a similar stripe by this "revolutionist" is the following, delivered passionately and earnestly: "We Communists will never give up our American Flag to Al Smith's Liberty League, or the Hearsts, and we always have an

> American Flag at our meetings in remembrance of the Bill of Rights which assures life, liberty and happiness to all." (!)

The exclamation points are theirs.

In late May 1936, 250 delegates and 2,000 party faithful convened at the Socialists' national convention at Cleveland's Public Auditorium. Earl Browder barged in, unsuccessfully still hoping to forestall a separate SP presidential ticket. By voice vote, Socialists again nominated Norman Thomas ("America's foremost apostle of international socialism; a flaming symbol of hope to the oppressed of the land"). The Old Guard bolted, accusing their former party of being "honeycombed with Communists."

The CPUSA, hamstrung by its United Front two-step, delayed its own convention until late June. Convening at New York's Manhattan Opera House, its 710 delegates promptly (but only temporarily) abandoned their more-American-than-thou charade, electing an "Honorary Presiding Committee" featuring such sterling American patriots as Georgi Dimitrov, Ernst Thälmann, D. Z. Manuilsky—and Joseph Stalin.

Which proved to be mere prelude to a pretty wild show. The *Daily Worker* described it all in staccato fashion:

> The delegates from the shops keep marching in, bouquets in hand: Bronx hospital unit; dress shop after dress shop; restaurants, like the Gay Nineties now on strike; heavy industry like the New York Central.
>
> Blonde lad in shirt-sleeves, forearms tattooed, speaks for the seamen. Says the Party's prestige has gained greatly here on the Eastern seaboard since the recent [West Coast] strike. "Been reading about the French sailors taking over the ships, running up the red flag. That's the day I'm looking forward to."

Huge banners of Lenin, Stalin, Browder, and 1932 candidate William Z. Foster festooned the hall. Veteran party activist Ella Reeve "Mother" Bloor introduced Browder at the opening session. She appeared again—cradling a baby in her arms—when everyone reconvened for their final big show at Madison Square Garden. As Mother Bloor was now approaching seventy-four, said infant was, to be sure, not one of her own six children. One of her biological offspring, the recently deceased Harold Ware, had worked for FDR's ill-fated AAA, but, more importantly, also headed up a Communist cell within the New Deal informally known as the "Ware Group." Membership included Alger Hiss. Their clandestine contact with the party and actual Soviet espionage was, of course, Whittaker Chambers.

Communists jammed the Garden in a display worthy of major party conventions. As the *Herald Tribune* documented:

> Twenty-five thousand persons, packing every seat . . . and overflowing into the basement . . . and the streets around it, raised their clenched fists in the Communist salute and cheered what their leaders told them was the birth of a new mass revolutionary movement.

Delegates and supporters laughed and cheered. Ticker tape fluttered down. Horns blared. A trio of bands played. Mother Bloor nominated the Black party functionary James W. Ford for vice president. The *Daily Worker* portrayed Ford as the "Frederick Douglass of 1936." In reality, he was, as one scholar noted, a mere careerist, being the "Communist version of the man in the grey flannel suit"—a fitting running mate for a candidate dubbed the "bookkeeper."

The party also nominated the pockmarked, bald-headed, bushy-browed Robert "Fighting Bob" Minor for New York governor. Minor had once been the highest-paid editorial cartoonist in America—and an anti-Bolshevik anarchist. ("The dictatorship of the Proletariat is not liberty, nor an instrument of liberty. It is tyranny.") But Lenin's success turned his pockmarked head. "A truly gifted and powerful cartoonist, [Minor] renounced art for politics, . . ." noted historian Theodore Draper. "The wild man, tamed, became a political hack. If as an anarchist he had believed that politics was a filthy business, as a Communist he still seemed to believe it was—only now it was his business." Tonight, Minor also nominated Browder—"a true son of America. . . . His ancestors fought in the armies of George Washington but unlike some other sons of the American Revolution he is true to those traditions."

Browder droned on for two-and-a-quarter hours. Broadcast nationwide on NBC and CBS, his speech included this paean to Stalinism's imaginary glories:

> The Soviet Union has just proclaimed a Constitution, the most democratic in all history, which guarantees to every citizen a job, at union wages, with full social insurance, paid vacations, opportunity for education, leisure and education. When America, the richest country in the world, gives its workers half which Communism gives in the Soviet Union, it will be time enough to boast.

But like the Black Sox in 1919's World Series, Earl Browder wasn't playing to win. He was playing to reelect FDR—and, thus, to defeat the GOP. "At the head of . . . reaction stands the Republican Party—," stated his party's platform, "[its candidates] are supported by the barons of steel, oil, auto and munitions; by Morgan, the du Ponts; and by that arch enemy of all decency, William Randolph Hearst."

Communists hated no one in American life as they hated William Randolph Hearst.

And, for once, they were not alone.

· 10 ·
"Heil Hearst"

In 1920s' boom times, a Boston editorialist famously asked, "Who Made Coolidge?"

The same question might, of course, be posed of virtually any public figure—in 1936, most intriguingly regarding Franklin Roosevelt.

Was it Franklin's doting mother? The ever-loyal Louis Howe? The idealistic Eleanor? The now discarded, vengeful Al Smith? Campaign manager Jim Farley? Or Ray Moley, Rex Tugwell, and the rest of the gray matter comprising the Brain Trust?

Or, even—though, of course, highly unintentionally—Herbert Hoover?

Or was it William Randolph Hearst—that archenemy of all decency—who, after all, had pushed FDR over the top at 1932's Democratic National Convention and into the White House?

Few men held such sway over American life—and not just political life and for so long a time—as Hearst. Few had amassed so much wealth, wielded such power, lived so luxuriously, fomented as much scandal and controversy.

Or been so exquisitely hated.

•••

Hate possesses a certain logic. It makes far more sense to seethe against a powerful foe than to rail against a powerless, obscure one. The latter rage may work for the occasional deranged stalker but possesses little utility for political movements. Hearst—"The Chief" to his many employees, "W. R." to his friends—was not only big enough to hate—but, as a special bonus, to *enjoy* hating. In 1935, he owned twenty-eight major newspapers: three alone in New York City, two each in Washington and Chicago, as well as dailies in such other big cities as San Francisco, Los Angeles, Oakland, Boston, Detroit, Seattle, Milwaukee, Pittsburgh, and Baltimore. He controlled 13.6 percent of the nation's daily newspaper circulation and a whopping 24.2 percent of Sunday circulation. Moreover, he owned the International News Service and King Features Syndicate, eighteen magazines, the Cosmopolitan film studio, Hearst Metrotone newsreel service, plus a string of eight radio stations through his American Radio News Corporation.

In 1935, his newspapers generated $100 million a year in business—an immense sum. Only six state budgets exceeded that figure. Pegging Hearst as a prototype of Ted Turner or Rupert Murdoch would be mere understatement.

He was not shy about sharing his opinions. He certainly had a lot of them—often displayed in **IMMENSE CAPITAL LETTERS!** in personally signed editorials on his many front pages. He fought many a battle over the decades, scampering from radical progressive to hide-bound conservative, merrily burning many a bridge along the way. Luckily for him, he owned many bridges.

He had, after all, been *born* with several bridges—or at least with a ton of money, earned in Nevada's silver mines, not by him but by his father, California's nearly illiterate US senator George Hearst. Like FDR and Father Coughlin, W.R.'s mother doted on him (she bought him his first non–San Francisco paper, the *New York Morning Journal*). Like FDR, he attended Harvard. Unlike Franklin, he was expelled. Money goes only so far when you send chamber pots to the faculty with their images engraved inside.

He had printer's ink in his veins, an urge to reform the world, and overwhelming personal ambitions. If he did not create "Yellow Journalism," he made it yellower. He helped foist war with Spain in 1898, thus indirectly propelling his first Roosevelt—"Rough Rider" Theodore—into the White House. Some blamed his vitriolic editorials for William McKinley's assassination. He kept running for things. In 1902, he won election to Congress, though he barely bothered showing up in DC, having bigger fish to fry. Bankrolling a nationwide network of Democratic clubs, he hoped to ride them into 1904's Democratic presidential nomination and unseating TR. Alas, he was too radical, his personal life far too interesting for barely post-Victorian times. A year later, he fashioned his own "Municipal Ownership League" ticket to run for mayor of New York, barely losing to Tammany's George B. McClellan. In 1906, he lost the governorship to rising GOP reformer Charles Evans Hughes. In 1909, he launched another third-party bid for mayor. He finished third, and people ridiculed him as "William Also-Randolph Hearst."

Republicans, conservatives, and Tammany Hall, particularly Al Smith (whom he smeared in 1919 as "in league with the milk trust"—"babies in New York are dying for lack of milk"), despised him. But so did progressives and most Democrats. His newspapers were too sensational; his love life, as we alluded to, particularly with the talented but alcoholic showgirl and actress Marion Davies, too sordid; his lifestyle (including California's amazing Hearst castle, San Simeon), too opulent. As early as March 1904, the *New York Post* wrote regarding then-congressman Hearst's peccadilloes:

> An agitator we can endure; an honest radical we can respect; a fanatic we can tolerate; but a low voluptuary trying to sting his jaded senses to a fresh thrill by turning from private to public corruption is a new horror in American politics.

In the 1920s, he veered rightward, alienating Democrats more so, yet never fully soothing conservative mistrust. The year 1922 witnessed his last political hurrah, as he again sought New York's governorship, and, that having failed, a US-Senate-seat consolation prize. Tammany finally seemed on board—after all, Hearst controlled Gotham's bumbling mayor "Red Mike" Hylan and, thus, City Hall patronage. But, at the last minute, Al Smith quashed the deal—smothering the last flickering embers of Hearst's electoral ambitions. Six years later, Hearst repaid the favor, endorsing Hoover over Smith.

Among Hearst's fixed principles, however, were an intense patriotism and an insistence on American sovereignty. Not by chance were Hearst papers in New York, Chicago, Boston, Baltimore, Atlanta, Rochester, and Syracuse named "The American." Accordingly, he despised Woodrow Wilson and his internationalist League of Nations. In fact, he disliked all things Wilsonian, including Hoover (overlooking that fact only where Smith was involved) and Wilson's upstart Assistant Secretary of the Navy Franklin Roosevelt. Thus, as 1932 rolled around, and Smith and Roosevelt emerged as the leading Democratic contenders, Hearst faced a dilemma. He hated both of them (though only one yet very personally). Hearst's fellow businessman and movie magnate Joe Kennedy tried mightily to cajole the Lord of San Simeon into FDR's camp. Hearst resisted just as mightily.

As 1932 opened, Hearst took to the radio to slam both Smith and Roosevelt—and just about any other potential Democratic candidate. FDR conveniently and ignominiously jettisoned his support for the League of Nations, but Hearst remained unsuckered and basically invented a Stop-Roosevelt candidate out of whole cloth: the grizzled, hard-drinking Speaker of the House, John Nance Garner ("a loyal American citizen, a plain man of the plain people, a sound and sincere Democrat").

Smith's surge in the late Democratic primaries threatened to deadlock the convention and send Roosevelt into political oblivion. Kennedy and Boston mayor James M. Curley continued lobbying Hearst on FDR's behalf. Reluctantly, W. R. threw the California and Texas delegations to FDR, not only pushing Roosevelt over the top but also inserting Garner into the vice presidential slot as part of the deal. Best of all was slipping the harpoon once more into Al Smith's hide.

Hearst put his money where his printer's ink was. Through Kennedy, he donated $25,000 to FDR's 1932 radio efforts. But the Hearst–Roosevelt alliance frayed quickly. FDR never thought much of the publisher and never would. By now, Hearst had grown far too conservative to appreciate Roosevelt's New Deal. As early as FDR's inauguration, his Gotham tabloid, the *Daily Mirror*, headlined "ROOSEVELT ASKS DICTATOR'S ROLE."

Hearst hated internationalism and dictators (although, some ominously said, not *all* dictators), but also taxes, unions, and anyone telling him what to do with his prized newspapers. Thus, FDR's NRA seemed like a giant gun (or at least a big ice slush ball) aimed at his rather large head. In June 1933, Hearst commanded his longtime *New York American* editor Edmond Coblentz to "please tell the President that I consider his proposal to license the press under the NRA in direct violation of . . . the freedom of the press, . . . and that I will fight his proposal with every means at my command, even . . . taking it to the Supreme Court . . . even if it costs me every nickel I possess."

Coblentz conveyed Hearst's threat to Louis Howe. Howe instantly and nervously phoned FDR. "My proposal," FDR soft-soaped Coblentz, "is a regulatory measure and in no sense will it abridge the freedom of the press. It is similar, in a sense, to the fire department rules. When you violate the fire department regulations, the Chief steps in and compels you to conform, does he not?"

"Yes, Mr. President," Coblentz countered, "but he does not stop the presses."

FDR assured the wary Coblentz that the NRA wasn't about to mess with the First Amendment. Remarkably, Hearst calmed down, signed on to the NRA Code, and even placed the NRA logo upon his multiple front pages.

"Blue Eagles" were one thing. Unions were another. The NRA unleashed a torrent of industry unionizations—including of newspapers. When Heywood Broun announced plans for newspaper organizing (the "American Newspaper Guild"), Hearst panicked once more. Addressing a front-page open letter to American newspaper publishers in late October 1933, he resumed his war on the NRA, slamming it as

> a menace to political rights and constitutional liberties, a danger to American ideals and institutions, a handicap to industrial recovery, and a detriment to the public welfare. . . . [T]he publishers of a free press ought to tolerate it less and expose and oppose it

> more. . . . [T]hese publishers ought to be interested in every phase of NRA interference in business, whether or not it affects them personally, as long as it injuriously affects the public which the press and publishers are supposed to serve.

He soon jibed that "NRA" stood for "No Recovery Allowed." Ominously, he expanded his fire to include the entire administration:

> The people elected a Democratic Administration, not a socialistic dictatorship . . . not the theories of Karl Marx and the policies of Stalin. Why should recovery in America be made to recede by despotic interference with American industrial freedom and with resourceful individualism when progress in other countries is proceeding without such unjustifiable, not to say unconstitutional, interruption?

Yet he drew back from total war. In December 1933—hoping to secure administration cooperation in regard to trade policies (i.e., tariffs on imported newsprint)—he managed to assuage Roosevelt without sullying his own growing anti–New Deal reputation: by attacking Al Smith's "Baloney Dollars" salvo against FDR's gold devaluation. From San Simeon on NBC radio, Hearst (whose family fortune, after all, derived from silver) pounded the "all wet" Smith: "Mr. Roosevelt is striving to get the country away from the blood money of the Shylocks, away from the hard money of hard men."

May 1934 witnessed the last flowering of rapprochement. Hearst visited the White House—remaining overnight and presenting FDR with an antique silhouette of Andrew Jackson. His wife, Millicent, soon accompanied Roosevelt in reviewing the fleet in New York Harbor. All seemed, at least . . . adequate.

It wasn't. By late July 1934, Hearst was editorializing: "Much of the administration is more Communistic than the Communists themselves. . . . The fires of sedition . . . [are] lit by these visionary and voluble politicians. . . .

"The New Deal may be compared to the book which a critic reviewed, saying 'There are many good things and many new things in this book, but the good things are not new and the new things are not good.' There may be many new ideas and many good ideas in the New Deal, but certainly the idea of Communistic revolution is not good."

Franklin hoped for the best. He prepared for the worst. "I am told that when Hearst returns [from Europe] he is going to attack the administration," he confided to Henry Morgenthau. "Can't you look up his income tax and be prepared."

Morgenthau recalled that he "found . . . plenty there; also plenty on Marion Davies. I told the President . . . that . . . it would be much better to proceed at once on Hearst and Marion Davies' income tax before he attacked because if we started something after he attacked us he would say that we were doing it for revenge and spite. The President agreed."

And yet . . . no final rift emerged. One reason for, at least, FDR's patience was this: his second-oldest (and decidedly sketchiest) son, Elliott, had, in August 1933, landed a berth on Hearst's immense payroll, as aviation editor (some said for eventually $20,000 per year) and then, in 1935, with his radio division (for, as some speculated, even more).

And so FDR held off.

In late 1934, Hearst's pro-FDR Chicago editor Roy Keehn begged Roosevelt to invite Hearst once more to the White House. So did FDR's yachting buddy Vincent Astor, also chummy with Hearst. Thus, Joe Kennedy inveigled Hearst (ignorant of being under investigation) once more into the lion's den. Their October 8, 1934, summit proceeded swimmingly. Hearst departed the next morning, gushing that "a period of genuine recovery" lay at hand. "Genuine recovery" generated headlines. Less noticed was his pointed caveat that "government cannot continue forever spending the people's money in so wholesale a manner."

The year 1935 opened with Hearst joining Huey Long and Father Coughlin in bloodying Franklin's proposal to enter the World Court. Not until summer, however, would their final rupture arrive.

Franklin, nonetheless, still maintained considerable forbearance toward the press lord. To Harold Ickes, he shared details of an April 1935 talk with Hearst's white-maned confidant and star columnist, Arthur Brisbane. Brisbane, as Ickes recorded it, "told [FDR] that Hearst was pretty erratic these days but that he believed that if [FDR] kept sending him friendly messages and didn't do anything to disturb him unduly Hearst would support him next year. . . . The president remarked that, outside of Hearst and one or two other strings of newspapers, all the balance of the press . . . would be against him and naturally he wants all the support he can get. Therefore, he wants to watch his step on the Hearst matter."

In May 1935, Ed Coblentz returned to the White House. FDR played the gracious host, serving caviar supplied by his Moscow ambassador William Bullitt. Hoping to dampen hostilities, Franklin invited Vincent Astor and Raymond Moley.

It went pleasantly—until Coblentz queried Franklin about combating Communism. Franklin lectured Coblentz that he did more than fight Communism—he also tackled "Huey Longism, Coughlinism, Townsendism. I want to save our system, the capitalistic system; to save it is to give some heed to world thought of today. To combat ["Share-Our-Wealth"] and similar crackpot ideas, it may be necessary to throw the forty-six men who are reported to have incomes in excess of $1,000,000 a year to the wolves . . . limit incomes through taxation to $1,000,000 . . . see to it that vast estates bequeathed to one person are limited in size."

Coblentz knew the Chief wouldn't like *that*. And once he said it, FDR knew it too. For once, he had let slip too much of his true feelings. "The thinking men," he now stumbled to explain, "the young men, who are disciples of this new world idea of fairer distribution of wealth, they are demanding that something be done to equalize this distribution. . . . We do not want communism in this country, and the only way to fight communism is by—"

Here, his apologia got stuck. For once, the right words wouldn't come. Maybe there *weren't* right words.

Coblentz cut in: "Neocommunism."

Roosevelt laughed. Vincent Astor protested that Franklin's tax program might even bankrupt *his* sizable holdings. At which point, Coblentz picked up on something—something he relayed to his boss: "The attitude of the President . . . seemed to be 'well, that's just too bad.'"

•••

Hearst was a fellow you wanted on your side. Twenty million Americans, after all, read his newspapers. But powerful reasons compelled FDR to finally shun his embrace. There were, most certainly, the old rationales. The better people had long hated Hearst. As far back as 1911, presidential hopeful Woodrow Wilson had sneered, at Hearst's offer of support, "Tell Mr. Hearst to go to hell."

In 1918, Theodore Roosevelt excoriated W. R. as "the most sinister pro-German traitor in the country and much the ablest and most dangerous." In the early 1930s, people still pondered Hearst's loyalties. In 1928, he initiated a "March of Events" section for his Sunday papers, showcasing contributions by such world newsmakers as Lloyd George and Winston Churchill. Briefly, Benito Mussolini served as a Hearst columnist, but Il Duce proved to be an exceedingly dull, troublesome, and expensive pundit. Hearst gave him the old heave-ho.

When Adolf Hitler secured massive breakthroughs in September 1930's Reichstag elections, Hearst commissioned him to supply articles at $240 apiece—half Mussolini's rate. Hitler provided better copy than Mussolini—when he bothered to provide it—but often double-crossed Hearst on providing exclusive material. Nonetheless, W. R. kept communications open with Hitler.

In July 1934, the now seventy-one-year-old Hearst, the thirty-seven-year-old Miss Davies, and their respective dachshunds, Helena and Gandhi (ages unkown), sailed to Europe for a lengthy stay. The itinerary included a substantial excursion to Germany.

"Everybody is for Hitler," Hearst reported back to Julia Morgan, his architect at San Simeon. "We think he is a tyrant in America but his own people don't think so. They regard him as a savior. Nine-tenths of the people are for him. Even the Communists—that is, the working classes who were Communists—seem to be satisfied with him. His chief opposition is religious. The Catholics registered some objections in the recent elections, and of course the Jews hate him. Everything is very quiet and orderly here. There are no evidences of disturbance."

That August, W. R. sat for an interview with the official Nazi Party newspaper, the *Völkischer Beobachter,* conducted by Hitler's half-American foreign press chief, Ernst "Putzi" Hanfstaengl, an old Harvard Club associate of FDR. It was, to say the least, a mistake. On August 19, 1934, following the death of eighty-five-year-old Reich President Paul von Hindenburg, Germans had voted via plebiscite to combine the offices of president and chancellor. The move anointed the now forty-five-year-old Hitler as Führer, formalizing his dictatorship. Buttressed by widespread intimidation and fraud (not to mention by murdering a slew of opponents in June 1934's "Night of the Long Knives"), Hitler harvested a resoundingly suspicious 89.93 percent of the vote.

Hearst, nonetheless, supposedly gushed to Hanfstaengl:

> The results represent a unanimous expression of the popular will. Its overwhelming majority with which Hitler astonishes the world must, as we now learn, be accepted as self-evident and in a sense must open up a new chapter in modern history.
>
> If Hitler succeeds in pointing the way to peace and order in an ethical development which has been destroyed throughout the world by war, he will have accomplished a measure of good not only for his own people but for all humanity.
>
> Germany is battling for her liberation from the mischievous provisions of the Treaty of Versailles and for her redemption from the malicious suppression and encirclement to which she has been subjected by nations which in their avarice and short-sightedness, have only shown enmity and jealousy over her advancement.
>
> This battle, in fact, can only be viewed as a struggle which all liberty-loving people are bound to follow with understanding and sympathy.

Hearst claimed to have been egregiously misquoted, with Hanfstaengl outright inventing passages. Nonetheless, he did little to steer clear of Hanfstaengl and the Nazis. To his trusted confidential assistant, Col. Joseph Willicombe, W. R. placidly explained: "When you are interviewed in Germany, don't imagine that what you have to say matters in the least.

The interviewer looks you over, carefully listens indifferently, and then goes away and writes what he thinks will be pleasing to Hitler. I don't blame the interviewers. If they fail to do this they get their paper shut up for a week or so."

More trouble followed. In mid-September, the German press published Hearst's exchange of letters with the Nazis' chief "philosopher," the muddled Dr. Alfred Rosenberg. Britain's *Manchester Guardian* (now *The Guardian*) seemed surprised (and pleased) that Hearst "has not been captured by the Nazis. There are many frank comments in his letter. On the question of the freedom of the press he says, for example, that the dangers of a controlled press are a thousand times greater than the difficulties which may arise out of an occasional abuse of press freedom."

"'In our country,' he wrote, 'differences of opinion are not regarded as insulting. Discussion is desired. Criticism is tolerated. All official persons in our public life are subject to criticism.'"

The Nazi high command, however, seemed unperturbed by such democratic sentiments. Within days, W. R., Marion, Putzi, and forty-one-year-old *Los Angeles Examiner* columnist Harry Crocker hightailed it for Berlin via private plane to confer personally with Hitler.

The impetus had come largely from Hanfstaengl, who argued:

> Hitler is surrounded by provincial men; men who speak only German; men who have never traveled. There is no one who can or will point out to him that certain of his anti-Catholic, anti-Semitic programs may gain him domestic popularity, but that such popularity is overbalanced by world disapproval. If a man of Hearst's standing—and Hitler is fully aware that Hearst knows what he is talking about—would meet Hitler, and among other things point out the true world facts on certain subjects, I am sure the conference would have far-reaching results. I am risking my future by thinking in this fashion. Already there are whispers that Hanfstaengl is no longer a good party man. But I feel the council of these insular-minded idiots will lead Germany to a debacle. And I wish to do something to head off the catastrophe!

W. R. had first feared that meeting Hitler was a bad idea, alibiing to Hanfstaengl that taking the waters at Bad Nauheim took precedence. Via long-distance from America, Arthur Brisbane warned his boss: "No matter what you say or do, persons in America will not understand . . . they will hold it against you that you even talked to Hitler." But Marion Davies, disappointed not to have personally seen Mussolini orate in Rome, was eager to see Der Führer for herself, and despite her fear of flying to Berlin, deemed it a simply grand idea. "I'd heard [Hitler's] voice," she later reminisced, "and I wanted to see how he performed, to see what kind of character he was. . . . He looked like Chaplin, I imagined. Possibly worse."

"Have a heart," Miss Davies implored her paramour; "I want to see this mysterious person."

She never did. Landing in Berlin, Hearst, Davies, and Crocker—coincidentally Chaplin's close friend and former personal assistant—were met at the airport by a panic-stricken friend, Ruth Wilcox Selwyn, wife of producer/director Edgar Selwyn and sister-in-law to Nick Schenck, the Russian-born president of the Loew's Inc. theatre chain. "Marion!" the twenty-eight-year-old actress and former showgirl pled. "I can't get out of the hotel. Could you come over to the Statler?"

"Look," Davies nervously begged off, "I have a date."

But Crocker reassured Marion that she would not miss a thing. "We'll go on. And then you meet us."

Davies now accompanied Selwyn to her room at the Statler, where Selwyn complained that she had phoned her brother-in-law Schenk for assistance—only to be refused. "I haven't got a cent," she wailed. "The housemaids won't help me pack my things, and I can't get out." By now, Marion smelled a rat. Finally, the front desk rang for Marion: her party awaited her downstairs in the lobby.

And there they were, Hearst and Crocker, sheepishly bearing the unwanted news that they had already been to see Hitler. Angrily grousing that her Statler detour had been a setup, Marion "didn't talk to anyone for two days."

What adventures transpired while Selwyn had sidetracked Marion? Well, Hitler had dispatched his old party comrade and former personal chauffeur, SS-Standartenführer Julius Schreck, to ferry Hearst and

Crocker to the Chancellery. Crocker described Schreck as "a stout, red-faced, gay fellow," which was odd. Everyone else thought he looked eerily like Hitler himself, right down to his own little Chaplinesque/Hitleresque mustache. "Germany is much better now," Schreck reassured his passengers. "No communism—no socialism—order—no unemployment!"

At Hitler's Chancellery, Hearst commenced with flattery. "Hanfstaengl," he buttered up Hitler, "has been telling us that this was once Bismarck's study. One day, future generations may call it Hitler's study!"

Hitler, no fool (except, for example, when it came to invading Russia), responded with false modesty. "No, no," he protested, "Germany is too young a country to lose even one little tradition. Even Berlin is only three hundred years old. No, this must always be Bismarck's study!"

W. R. continued making small talk. Hanfstaengl reported that Hearst, possessor of a thirteenth-century castle in Wales, "asked Hitler whether he could borrow me for his trip [there], and Hitler laughingly replied, 'I envy Hanfstaengl—wish I could go with you.'"

One suspects that Hearst also congratulated Hitler on his recent plebiscite landslide. Yet their session quickly—and understandably—fizzled. Hitler possessed little patience for any meeting he could not dominate. Hearst had a habit of being Hearst.

Exiting, Hearst kept his counsel, explaining to waiting reporters, "Visiting Hitler is like calling on the President of the United States—one doesn't talk about it for publication."

Other details vary wildly. Crocker said the meeting lasted nearly an hour. Marion Davies recalled Hearst and Crocker claiming it spanned a mere five minutes. Considering translations, that barely allowed time for an "auf wiedersehen" or two.

To Marion, Hearst also claimed to be "not impressed" with Hitler. "I didn't understand a word Hitler was saying," she quoted him as telling her, "and I didn't understand his interpreter either."

But to Joe Willicombe, W. R. wrote:

> Hitler certainly is an extraordinary man. We estimate him too lightly in America. He has enormous energy, intense enthusiasm, a marvelous faculty for dramatic oratory, and great organizing ability.

Of course, all these qualities can be misdirected.

Nick Schenk's Loew's Inc. controlled Metro-Goldwyn-Mayer, longtime distributor of Hearst's (and Marion's) Cosmopolitan Productions studio's releases. Before meeting Hitler, Hearst contacted his old friend, MGM's Hollywood production chief Louis B. Mayer, to secure his assent. Mayer (like Schenk, a Jew) said to go ahead. Hearst later composed a memorandum (in the third person) of how events had transpired:

> After consulting his friend Louis B. Mayer as to the advisability of any discussion . . . Mr. Mayer had advised Hearst to have the interview and had said: "You may be able to accomplish some good. . . ." After the usual exchange of formal civilities, Hitler speedily came to the point. . . . He asked: "Why am I so misrepresented, so misunderstood, in America? Why are the people of America so antagonistic to my regime?"

Hearst answered that his countrymen were simply "averse to dictatorship." Hitler countered: "But I am entirely a product of democracy. I, as a private citizen, appealed to the people of Germany. I was elected to my office by a majority vote . . . I presented my proposals, my policies to the people. . . . They endorsed those policies by more than a two-thirds majority."

Crocker remembered Hearst replying, "That might be a democracy, but it is also a dictatorship in view of what those policies are."

Hearst now raised his real point. "There is," he advanced with some caution, "a very large and influential and respected element in the United States who are very resentful of the treatment of their fellows in Germany." Hitler knew exactly who Hearst meant: the Jews. Hitler, an ardent fan of sensational Western novels, counterattacked: "But what about the American Indians?" Hearst tried explaining that situation, though not particularly well, and quickly shifted back to questioning Nazi anti-Semitism. "[T]hese vigorous measures of the government were due to temporary circumstances," Hitler lied, "and that all discrimination is disappearing and will soon entirely disappear. That is the policy of my government, and you will soon see ample evidence of it."

To Davies, W. R. added that when Hitler had told him (in her words) "that the Jews should not have taken over the industries that were supposed to be for Germans," Hearst retorted, "I should think industries would belong to every nationality."

What Hitler made of it all, we know not—probably just another day at the office. Hanfstaengl departed, chortling to himself: "I only had to convince [Hearst] that we were interested in justice and he softens right up and went in to see Hitler. Hitler put on one of his acts—it is amazing how easy it is to impress these Americans."

Hearst believed he had accomplished some good for Germany's embattled Jews—and remained solicitous of their welfare. In December 1934, he wired his chief London correspondent to "go to Berlin and deliver personally the following message to Dr. Hanfstaengl; and while there you might incidentally get a little talk with Hitler. QUOTE 'Now that all citizens including Jews given political rights in Saar, why not grant this everywhere and give them representation in proportion to population? That is only one percent and surely the mouse need not terrify the elephant. Such action would strengthen Germany immensely in the United States and I think everywhere. But if you do this, do it strikingly by manifesto in [a] way to compel publication and attention everywhere . . . I think this would be wise, but please pardon me if I am unwarrantably interfering.'"

The Chief accomplished nothing, beyond naively accelerating his own popularity's nosedive—"a chain reaction," said his biographer John Winkler, "of tempestuous, percussive events . . . which all but accomplished his ruin."

Not ruined by *his* feelers to Hitler, however, was FDR.

Not ruined at all, because nary a soul knew of them—save for Hitler himself and his henchmen.

At least, that is, until August 2021, when certain German diplomatic files finally went on the auction block.

Eight pages of original documents revealed Franklin's secret personal outreach to Hitler on behalf of his former less-than-stellar first Federal Housing Administrator (and major 1932 campaign contributor), James

A. "Jimmy" Moffet (by 1936 vice president of Standard Oil of California), and a pair of Moffet's oil industry associates, Kenneth R. Kingsbury, the chairman of California Standard Oil (that company was indicted in 1934 for NRA oil code violations), and Texaco chairman Capt. Torkild Reiber. Reiber's eventual pro-Nazi reputation ("absolutely pro-German . . . a sincere admirer of the Führer") would force his resignation from the oil giant in 1940.

In August 1936, all three oil moguls craved to meet with Hitler personally, presumably to secure favorable business arrangements within the Reich—and FDR (who had met with Moffet earlier that month at Hyde Park) bent over backward to arrange their desired confab. As Germany's ambassador Hans Luther (once a chancellor of the Weimar Republic) advised the Chancellery on August 21: "Roosevelt has made known to the [Washington] embassy, via [Steve] Early . . . his request that we should make an effort to arrange for three very close friends of his to be received by the Führer. . . . In view of Roosevelt's personal interest . . . I recommend very strongly that his request should be granted." Hitler proved uninterested, fixated as he was on the upcoming annual party congress in Nuremburg.

FDR kept at it. Five days later, Early personally visited the embassy, and Luther wired Berlin, pleading that Moffet et al. "be received in audience as soon as possible after their arrival. The head of the President's office . . . asked it to be known once again what great importance Roosevelt attaches to Moffet being introduced to the Fuhrer."

Official German Foreign Ministry correspondence now reported that Hitler had personally advised Foreign Minister Konstantin von Neurath "that audiences are not welcome to him in the period prior to the Reichs Party Rally. But the letter [sic] from the U.S. President is an exceptional one, and reveals a particular interest in the matter." Foreign Ministry functionaries even pondered the possibility of the Reich footing the bill for the trio's transport from Berlin to Nuremberg. Nonetheless, Moffet's hoped-for rendezvous with the Führer slipped through the cracks, though not from FDR's lack of effort.

Meanwhile, Hearst threw his efforts into alienating big chunks of pro–New Deal readers, thanks, of course, in part to his own dealings with

Germany and Hitler. False rumors circulated that $400,000 in German money sugarcoated his coverage of the Nazi regime. His personal life remained as opulent as ever (thanks in part to shifting personal expenses to his corporations), but his corporate balance sheets were now a mess, trending more red than black.

Red.

W. R. saw Red. As he had prepared to decamp to Europe in March 1934, his papers unleashed a much-ballyhooed series alerting readers to the menace of domestic Bolshevism. "'Soviet Power in America,'" blared the headlines, "Slogan of Communist Drive Called to International Meet This Year." Another article warned "Communist Plan for May Drive to Seize All Property in United States Revealed." In early May 1935, Hearst commanded Ed Coblentz to produce an editorial "saying that the thing to do with communists is to deport them. . . . They are chronic troublemakers. They are a destructive element purely, and we should get rid of them as we would of any vermin . . . it is time to call in the cockroach man."

Crushing the Reds, Hearst theorized, would ultimately also defang the threat of domestic fascism. From Europe, he wrote Joseph Willicombe:

> Fascism seems to be spreading over here. We have got to keep crazy isms out of our country.
>
> If we can keep out Communism we can keep out Fascism. Fascism here [Germany] and elsewhere has sprung up to prevent the control of countries by Communism.
>
> Both are despotisms and deprive people of the liberties which democracy assures.

To W. R., Communism's virus bred most ominously in the colleges. Hearst reporters went undercover, sniffing out campus radical opinion. In November 1934, his *Syracuse Journal* unveiled the first of these exposés ("DRIVE ALL RADICAL PROFESSORS AND STUDENTS FROM THE UNIVERSITIES"), exposing supposed Reds at Syracuse University. Additional targets included New York University, Harvard, Yale, Dartmouth, Princeton, Amherst, Northwestern University, and the University of Wisconsin. The University of Chicago presented a particular target. By

July 1935, FDR was consoling its embattled president, Robert Maynard Hutchins, writing: "Private and Confidential"—"Dear Bob: You must have had a vile time with that inquisition. I sometimes think that Hearst has done more harm to the cause of Democracy and civilization in America than any three other contemporaries put together."

Hearst by now functioned as the liberals' and Leftists' favorite bête noire, not just the poster boy of capital "R" Reaction but the mastermind and pied piper of outright fascism. In 1936, a brace of highly critical Hearst biographies emerged. In his best-selling *Imperial Hearst*, author Ferdinand Lundberg ("As yet the world did not know that Hearst . . . had become converted to fascism") demanded "a Congressional inquiry into the Hearst enterprises from top to bottom lest they smash American democracy. . . . The American press can never be made free until it is made responsible to the people."

Twenty high-powered academics captained by Charles A. Beard (past president of the American Historical Association), the Riverside Church's Harry Emerson Fosdick, and philosopher John Dewey urged a probe into Hearst's "un-American activities." At New York's Central Opera House, a crowd of 2,500 (Heywood Broun among them) assembled under the auspices of "The Provisional Committee for Nonpartisan Labor Defense" to label him "Labor Enemy No. 1."

In July 1936, teachers gathered at Columbia University for summer sessions. A thousand of them, incensed by, among other things, Hearst's support for state-required teacher loyalty oaths, demanded that Senator Robert La Follette Jr. investigate Hearst's "vicious Fascist policies" and "un-American activities." Lacking much of a sense of irony, they charged that "his subversive influence threatens complete nullification of those clauses of the Constitution which guarantee freedom of speech, press and assembly."

In an April 1935 article titled "Heil Hearst," the Communist-dominated *New Masses* warned, "Hearst, even with today's keen competition from the Huey Longs and Father Coughlins, remains the outstanding demagogue of America." As the Communists lived in W. R.'s brain, so he noisily resided in their collective skulls, plotting every move against The Working Class, collaborating with each silk-hatted, moneybag-toting villain on Wall Street.

In August 1935, Washington columnist George Allen, home from five weeks crisscrossing the country, wrote his friend Eleanor Roosevelt that the only entity "effectively combating the Administration" was Hearst. Eleanor passed Allen's note on to Franklin, penciling in her own warning: "F.D.R. I'm sure this is true. E.R." It probably would have amused Mr. Hearst to know that Mr. Allen had, since January 1933, been supplying the KGB's New York office with information for $100 per month.

In February 1935, a 15,000-person Communist-front "Friends of the Soviet Union" rally at Madison Square Garden solicited funds to "bombard" Hearst facilities with literature. Boycotting Hearst papers became the thing to do—and it was effective. Traditionally, the bulk of Hearst readership lay with working-class and newer Americans—readers now resenting his constant sniping at Washington and/or Moscow.

In March 1935, Ed Coblentz finally warned W. R.: "The boycott, which is becoming more intense and widespread every day, is hurting our circulation. . . . Never a day passes that the Radicals do not hold a meeting; not [only] in Union Square, but in school houses, meeting halls, etc., and ask for a boycott of our papers. They are working among the young, the Jews and the parent teachers' organizations."

Hearst—either arrogantly bullheaded or strangely principled (or both)—plowed full steam ahead in capsizing his precious newspapers' circulation and advertising revenues. In April 1935, he directed Coblenz to "settle down to a consistent policy of opposition to this Administration. . . . If [FDR] is leading the country to disaster, we cannot oppose his policies and support him. . . . There is no knowing what may occur four years later. We could easily have a permanent dictatorship on this basis. We have practically a dictatorship now."

Perhaps he foresaw Franklin's upcoming tax proposals—hiking inheritance taxes and elevating the highest marginal income tax rate to 75 percent. Already battered by financial headwinds, these were the last things he needed. "It is of vital importance to me," he directed in November 1935, "that nothing shall be charged to me that is not necessary—so that I shall not have to pay any more income taxes than are necessary." Soon, he ordered, "I have got to keep my actual net income under a million dollars. *If it goes over a million dollars, they will practically confiscate the income.* I want $30,000 a week instead of fifty or whatever it is, deposited in my account. Out of that account, which is approximately a million and a half a year, I will be able to charge off, I should say about one-half—such as construction at ranch and similar expenditures that can legitimately be borne by the corporations, and leave me an income on which I will have to pay taxes of from $500,000 to $700,000. That is all the income I can afford to have, and it is all I am going to have."

"President's taxation program is essentially Communism," W. R. fumed to Coblenz and to his attorney Bainbridge Colby. "It is, to be sure, a bastard product of Communism and demagogic democracy, a mongrel creation which might accurately be called demo-communism, evolved by a composite personality which might be labeled Stalin Delano Roosevelt. . . . It divides a harmonious and homogeneous nation into classes, and stimulates class distinction, class discrimination, class division, class resentment, and class antagonism."

Whether FDR relished such divisions, we know not. He certainly enjoyed sticking it to Mr. Hearst. Harold Ickes noted that Franklin "thought [the tax bill] was the best thing he had done as President. . . . He looked up at me with a smile and said, 'That is for Hearst.'"

Hearst's vast organization sheltered many a New Deal sympathizer. In August 1935, more than one of them forwarded to administration functionaries a message addressed to one Hearst editor: "The Chief instructs that the phrase Soak the Successful be used in all references to the administration's tax program instead of the phrase Soak the Thrifty hitherto used, also he wants the words 'Raw Deal' used instead of 'New Deal.'"

FDR angrily commanded his press secretary, Steve Early, to publicly blast Hearst news policies. Early stood ready to say, "The President believes that it is only fair to the American people to apprise them of certain information which has come to him [about certain editors and] what is known as the deliberate coloring of so-called news stories, in accordance with orders issued to those responsible for the writing of news." FDR also ordered Early to reproduce the offending Hearst organization's instructions and to emphasize that they pertained "not to editorial expression but to news columns." Cooler heads prevailed, and Early remained silent.

August 1935 saw an unexpected salient open upon the FDR–Hearst battlefield—a by-product of unwelcome wrinkles in US–Soviet relations. When Roosevelt had recognized the "USSR." in November 1933, People's Commissar of Foreign Affairs Maxim Litvinov solemnly abjured any Soviet interference in US domestic affairs—a vow the Kremlin possessed not the slightest intention of keeping. Washington, of course, might have suspected that but, in the interests of statecraft, kept its suspicions to itself. In the summer of 1935, however, the ostentatious presence of such prominent American Communists as Earl Browder, William Z. Foster, and William Weinstone before the Comintern—to report to their actual bosses and to receive orders to accelerate their activities—threatened to upset everyone's applecart, particularly when Browder very publicly and proudly testified:

> The party has increased its membership by more than three times and numbers more than 30,000 members. . . . In 1930 native American-born citizens constituted less than 10 percent of the party; now they constitute more than 40 percent. In 1930 there were less than 100 Negroes in the ranks of our party; now there are over 2,500. . . . The party took upon itself the responsibility of directing the creation of mass organization of the unemployed. . . . We adopted the revolutionary traditions of 1776 . . . and came forward as [its] successors.

US ambassador William Bullitt, once quite sympathetic to Moscow, was by now shorn of his illusions. He pondered a break in relations but then reconsidered, advising Roosevelt to directly address the American people regarding Moscow's American puppets. FDR pointedly refused, instructing Bullitt to deliver the following note to Moscow:

> The . . . United States . . . anticipates the most serious consequences if the . . . Union of Soviet Socialist Republics is unwilling, or unable . . . to prevent further acts in disregard of the solemn pledge [to avoid interference in American internal affairs]. I may add that it is a source of regret that . . . development of friendly

relations between the Russian and American people will inevitably be precluded by the continuance on the territory of the Union of Soviet Socialist Republics, in violation of the promise of the [USSR], of activities involving interference in the internal affairs of the American people.

It was indeed a stern message, but an exceedingly vague one. The American people had no great idea of what had happened. Or where it had happened. In America? At Moscow? The Kremlin—aside from a powerful display of unctuous huffiness—ignored Bullitt.

And that was the end of it.

Or was it?

On Monday evening, August 26, 1935, James W. Fawcett, an editorial writer on Hearst's *Washington Evening Star*, shared a secret with his friend Harold Ickes. Fawcett possessed very personal reasons to assist Ickes and his boss. He was, like FDR, an avid philatelist. And in July 1934, Franklin had selected Mrs. Fawcett's etchings of Yosemite Park to adorn the Post Office's "National Park Year" First Day Cover offerings.

FDR, after all, was a *very* good politician.

Fawcett warned Ickes that the Hearst organization possessed copies of stenographic reports of Moscow's recent Comintern sessions and planned to expose the Reds' about-face on Roosevelt—something far more embarrassing to the White House than the existence of 2,500 Negro Communists. Ickes relayed said news to Steve Early. That morning's newspapers, however, reported a suspiciously related bombshell: Ambassador Bullitt's sharply worded warning to Moscow.

"This movement to sever diplomatic relations is a very sudden one," Ickes privately pondered. "At least there was no intimation of [it] at the last cabinet meeting or at any preceding one. My suspicion is that this is a shrewd counter-attack to destroy the effect of the anticipated Hearst blast against the president."

And perhaps it was that too.

•••

Communists about-faced to support "Wall Street tool" Franklin Roosevelt. Hearst, Raskob, and Coughlin stampeded in the opposite direction. Stamp-collecting Hearst editorialists leaked to the New Deal. It couldn't be any more confusing, unless . . .

. . . William Randolph Hearst endorsed Alfred Emanuel Smith . . . the same Al Smith who in 1919 had flayed W. R. as having not "a drop of good, clean, pure red blood in his whole body . . . a man as low and as mean as I can picture him . . . a pestilence that walks in the dark."

Yet, on Friday, in an August 29, 1935, front-page editorial (where else?), W. R. proposed a "Constitutional Democratic Party" designed to crush Franklin Delano Roosevelt and all his works:

> It is not for me to decide . . . who should be nominated on the genuine Jeffersonian Democratic ticket; but I think Alfred E. Smith would make a powerful candidate.
>
> He is the accredited leader of the genuine Democratic party.
>
> He was their latest presidential candidate.
>
> His principles are the storied principles of the party. . . .
>
> It is not for me, as an American believing devotedly in American principles of religious liberty, to know or care whether Mr. Smith is a Catholic, a Protestant, or a Jew.
>
> He is a good citizen.
>
> Nor do I care whether he pronounces the word "radio" in a manner to suit the professors of the Brain Trust.
>
> He pronounces the word "America" properly and patriotically.

But so did Republicans—and W. R. had a little to say about them as well.

· 11 ·

"The Old Deal"

The old gray elephant wasn't what it used to be.

New Dealers enacted program after program. What roadblocks ensued, as with 1935's World Court setback, were, more often than not, fashioned by Democrats—Coughlin, Long, and Hearst (and even Will Rogers), rather than by the minuscule cohort of Republicans still huddled together on Capitol Hill. Many Senate survivors were, in fact, highly independent progressives, essentially "Republicans In Name Only": Nebraska's George Norris, North Dakota's Gerald Nye and Lynn Frazier, California's Hiram Johnson, Michigan's James Gould Couzens, Kansas's Arthur Capper, New Mexico's Bronson Cutting, South Dakota's Peter Norbeck, and Idaho's Bill Borah—even Minority Leader Charles McNary of Oregon. Harry Hopkins funneled WPA appointments through Hiram Johnson rather than the state's Democratic senator, William Gibbs McAdoo. Ickes similarly favored Norris in Nebraska.

But hope springs eternal. And, while Roosevelt's list of accomplishments ran long, his list of setbacks was hardly negligible. The NRA and AAA were hardly world-beaters. Franklin was really better off without them. Spending and deficits rose higher than ever. Unemployment, while declining, hardly approached Coolidge-era levels. Most intriguingly, the gaggle of radicals to Roosevelt's left—Long, Coughlin, Townsend—might swipe enough votes from the New Deal coalition to transform the election into "No Deal 1936." And who exactly knew what mischief the much-derided big-circulation Hearst papers and big-bankroll Liberty Leaguers might yet accomplish?

Stranger things have happened, after all.

But who might Republicans run? With a paltry 128 members in both houses of Congress and a corporal's guard of governors, pickings were slim to avenge the much-maligned Herbert Clark Hoover.

Of course, as many noticed, no one hankered to avenge Herbert Clark Hoover more passionately (or, at least, more grimly) than Herbert Clark Hoover.

Mr. Hoover was the man who wouldn't go away, the true kiss of death to Republicans for decades and decades to come. In 1978's *Animal House*, Hoover's namesake "Robert Hoover" entreated Faber College's Dean Wormer for just "one more chance." In 1936, Herbert Hoover demanded just one more chance to get it right—or, more precisely, according to his jaundiced view, *for the American people* to get it right.

The Great Engineer, it must be admitted, had spruced up his act. No longer was he quite as starchy as his infamously starched white collars, no longer so weighed down by crushing responsibility and dismal failure. The critic's role, it turned out, was indeed far greater fun than that of the criticized. Moreover—as the nation tilted leftward—Hoover lurched personally rightward, "displaying in exile," as one historian discerned, "a commitment to laissez-faire doctrine he never articulated while in office."

"Hoover of 1932 was reserved," a reporter noted in June 1936, "his campaign speeches weighty discussions of economics and his administration. They did not sparkle and they did not reveal the president as a brilliant campaigner. Now . . . he has been hammering away at the New Deal with the same type of skill and brilliant wit and sarcasm that was typical of the attacks of which he was the target four years ago. His addresses sparkle, they sway audiences into roars of enthusiasm and approbation. They are inspiring and militant."

Vice President Garner *sort* of agreed. "The Republicans," the Hon. Cactus Jack privately argued, "used to do the politically smart thing most of the time. If they get back the knack I would imagine they will give Herbert Hoover a [second] try. He couldn't win, but he would carry more states than anyone else they can put up. . . . [I]n a year when they have little chance, Hoover would be their best nominee, because even though he would lose, he might carry a number of other Republican candidates to victory."

Numbered among Hoover's die-hard loyalists was MGM's Louis B. Mayer. Mayer owed Hoover big-time. It was Hoover's Department of Justice that blocked rival Fox Studio's bid to acquire MGM from Nick Schenk at Loew's (MGM's parent corporation), thus salvaging Mayer's position (and huge salary) as MGM's president. Repaying the favor, in 1932, Mayer had organized a last-minute series of pro-Hoover rallies, featuring such stars as Lionel and Ethel Barrymore, Wallace Beery, Buster Keaton, Al Jolson, Jimmy Durante, and even ten-year-old Jackie Cooper. In 1934, Mayer—just off a term as California state GOP chairman—solicited William Randolph Hearst's support for a Hoover comeback. Hearst possessed little use for The Great Engineer, his antipathy perhaps linked to Hoover's once rejecting an invitation to San Simeon—and Hearst surmising Marion Davies's presence fueling Hoover's rejection—but more likely, as noted earlier, fueled by the Hoover administration's prying into Miss Davies's tax foibles.

And so Hearst responded:

> Dear Louis:
>
> I am sorry but I cannot conscientiously support that man. He is selfish and stupid. He injects himself into the present situation for his own advantage. He will harm his own party, handicap the whole conservative movement, and strengthen the hands of the radicals. He has said nothing which has not been said better before and he accomplishes nothing but to make millions of people feel that the present incumbent [Roosevelt] would be immeasurably better than this discredited failure. . . . If you don't suppress this hoodoo, your party will lose its chance, too, of electing a Congress as well as a President. His name is an anathema to the American public.
>
> —W. R.

Franklin concurred with Hearst, accordingly favoring clay-pigeon Hoover as his 1936 opponent. "The real cause for mounting Republican panic is one Herbert Clark Hoover," deduced *Collier's* Washington staff writer George Creel in October 1935. "He is the cloud that threatens to blot out their sun; the skeleton that bids fair to make a mess of their feast. As one Republican leader confessed in a recent confidential interview, 'We know now just what the Democrats suffered with William J. Bryan. Lord, if Hoover would only get out and leave us alone.'"

All but the most sentimental (and dense) Republicans concurred. Agreeing on who to actually nominate was not easy. At first, it was impossible.

The party's first front-runner, Idaho's William E. Borah, was exceptionally impossible.

While Hoover was now too conservative for his times, Borah was definitely too liberal for his party—at least for its still-powerful, more-conservative Eastern wing. Many pundits believed the now seventy-one-year-old maverick ran less for the nomination and more to liberalize his party's platform.

Or just to annoy people.

Once briefly a teenaged touring Shakespearean actor, Borah possessed a flair for the dramatic, honing it early on in a series of high-profile Idaho court cases, once even as the defendant, accused of land fraud. Easily beating the rap, he leapt from the defendant's box to a seat in the United States Senate.

He quickly established himself as one of Washington's more interesting fellows, eventually hailed as "The Lion of Idaho." The *Literary Digest* described his home as "a mekka for the Capital's intelligentsia," praising the abode's hostess, diminutive, blue-eyed Mary McConnell "Little Borah" Borah "as an adept player in the game of politics over the teacups." Borah's biographer (who actually met Mary) differed. She described her as "the flightiest numbbrain that ever was."

Mrs. Borah was, however, the numbbrain daughter of a former Idaho governor.

Her story was an interesting one. Prior to being "The Lion of Idaho," the young Mr. Borah was accorded the title "The Stallion of Boise." Such virility was, in fact, how he got to Idaho in the first place—thanks to a highly unplanned pregnancy back in Kansas. Settled in Boise, he frequented most (if not all) of the city's twenty-eight brothels. Some said the Borah nuptials were hastened by yet another unplanned blessed event—though not so blessed as to avoid termination by abortion.

Such habits followed Borah to Washington. In 1916, Theodore Roosevelt briefly considered palming off Borah on his fast-expiring Bull Moose Party as their presidential nominee. Columbia University president Nicholas Murray Butler (a prominent Republican) responded, "The trouble with Borah (which I would not like even you to mention to anyone) is his personal habits in Washington. You can infer the rest. He has troubles in Washington of a very personal nature; personal habits that are objectionable."

TR protested that Butler was "speaking of a man I don't even know myself." If TR knew Borah not, his very precocious daughter "Princess Alice" did—or at least would. Despite Alice's marriage to future House Speaker Nick Longworth (himself "one of the great womanizers in history on Capitol Hill"), in February 1925, the fortyish Alice delivered Senator Borah's illegitimate daughter. Though first tempted to name the infant the rather-too-cute "Deborah," Alice eventually christened her Paulina.

Another Borah dalliance involved Eleanor "Cissy" Patterson, a member of the extended Chicago family that controlled both the conservative *Chicago Tribune* and the liberal *New York Daily News.* For good measure, she was also Nick Longworth's onetime lover. In 1930, Cissy assumed management of Hearst's *Washington Herald.* A short while later, her cousin Illinois US senator Joseph Medill McCormick's widow, Ruth Hanna McCormick, sought to succeed him in Washington. But Ruth McCormick violated campaign spending limits, and Borah vowed to oppose seating her. Cissy, no longer dallying with Nick but actively feuding with Alice, published the following editorial, with a meaning hardly lost on Washington's cognoscenti:

> Some weeks ago I wrote that Alice Longworth has no real gifts to bring Ruth Hanna McCormick's campaign. Ruth Hanna McCormick is Alice Longworth's close friend. I was in error. I spoke hastily. Senator Borah, another *close* friend of Alice Longworth, has said that if Ruth McCormick is elected he will vote to unseat her. . . . Mrs.

Longworth may now present her real gifts. She may use her political influence, of which the country has for so long heard so much. She may soften this decision of the frugal gentleman from Idaho.

Senator Borah is also a close friend of Mrs. Ruth McCormick.

They are all close friends.

But it is for Alice to come now bearing her offerings.

Will she? Can she?

Ahem.

In his earlier Senate days, Borah supported the standard progressive measures: female suffrage (though wobbling mightily on it at times); the direct election of US senators (some critics alleged from spite—after not being sent to Washington fast enough by Idaho legislators); and a fierce and enduring antipathy to monopoly. Though voting for war on Germany in 1917, his polestar remained isolationism. When Wilson submitted his League of Nations to the Senate, Borah (with Alice Longworth in the trenches beside him) successfully captained the "irreconcilable" faction in opposition. An avid supporter of recognizing the Soviet Union, he had, in December 1922, proclaimed, "Life is as safe under the Soviet government tonight as it is in Boston. . . . Property is as safe as in any other country." Conversely, as late as June 1936, he declared, "Mussolini is a remarkable man, a great statesman and leader who will undoubtedly go down in history."

Borah opposed the NRA, the AAA, and the World Court. He supported eleven of seventeen major portions of FDR's New Deal agenda, including the TVA, the Wagner Labor Relations Act, and Social Security. His appeal transcended progressivism, extending into radical and populist camps—even gaining grudging support from pro-Communist radical Vito Marcantonio. In 1934–35, Borah and Huey Long voted together 74 percent of the time. In August 1935, the Kingfish indicated he would sit out 1936 if Borah made the race.

Borah's support for his party's presidential candidates was spotty at best. He backed Hughes in 1916 and Hoover in 1928 (Borah, like so many Western progressives, was "dry"), but most often held himself aloof from GOP nominees. As a "Silver Republican," he opposed McKinley in 1896.

He sat out 1924's Coolidge–Davis–La Follette contest and had no compunction about shunning Hoover in 1932. A strong supporter of TR's bid to oust Taft in 1912, he nonetheless abstained from that year's third-party Bull Moose effort, affirming an awkward neutrality.

Always on the verge of running himself, he somehow never got around to it. When, in 1924, Coolidge offered him a place on the ticket, he snapped, "Which place, Mr. President?"

He always seemed to be opposing something. "Borah is first and foremost a prima donna," declared Nicholas Roosevelt; "he has all of the independence of spirit of a leading lady—and most of her inconsistencies and unreasonableness." Or, as Coolidge twanged, upon seeing Borah galloping through Washington's Rock Creek Park, "Must bother the Senator to be going in the same direction as the horse."

"Borah was not a great senator," concluded historian John Milton Cooper; "[he] contributed an often inspiring, always entertaining spectacle to American life, but he offered little else of real importance. What is worse, he deliberately strove to keep his contribution limited to that spectacle. . . . [H]e deliberately tried to reject every facet of the politician's function other than that of orator. . . . He refused to attend caucuses and paid almost no attention to committee work, even [as] chairman of the Foreign Relations Committee."

He was, in short, a windbag.

Borah's belated 1936 candidacy was yet another illustration of his vaunted contrariness. He was now seventy-one years old, well past contemporary standards for presidential hopefuls. Even William Henry Harrison was just sixty-eight on assuming office. Woodrow Wilson, at just fifty-six, was the oldest president since James Buchanan (sixty-five) in 1856. Moreover, Borah had just undergone a serious prostate operation—and made out his will. For years he had suffered from decreased energy.

Nonetheless, as one of the nation's shinier objects, his candidacy possessed a certain quotient of oomph. He was a name brand, and pundits estimated he'd arrive at June's convention holding 208 of the 501 delegates needed to nominate.

Orthodox Republicans distrusted him for all the above reasons. Worse, they suspected he was plotting hand-in-glove with Franklin

Roosevelt to disrupt both their parties' nominating process and the general election as they spied "The Lion of Idaho" visiting with FDR in the White House far too often for a senator of the opposite party. Borah's "loyal opposition" to the New Deal struck many Republicans as more "loyal" than "opposite."

On Tuesday, February 4, 1936, Borah announced his candidacy. Three days later, FDR invited him once more to lunch at 1600 Pennsylvania Avenue. Columnist Frank Kent voiced the suspicions of many regarding Borah's effort:

> His most enthusiastic supporters are the New Deal political managers, his best "publicity" from New Deal writers. No secret is made that nothing would delight Mr. Roosevelt and Mr. Farley more than success for Mr. Borah in various primary contests and . . . a big convention vote.
>
> FROM THE DAY Mr. Roosevelt had him to lunch at the White House he has been running with the New Deal blessing. They know, of course, there is no chance whatever of Mr. Borah's nomination. So does Mr. Borah. . . . What they hope and expect is that Mr. Borah will have enough convention strength to have a big nuisance value, and that, after he is turned down, true to the creed of the professional Liberal who can't get his way, he will howl to Heaven about the domination of the "mercenaries" and "reactionaries" of Wall Street.

Conservatives like Frank Kent weren't the only ones distrusting Borah. No other Northern senator generated so much hostility from the Black community. Following 1906's Brownsville Incident, TR had ignored legal niceties in cashiering 167 African-American infantrymen—and freshman senator Borah had rushed to his defense. He consistently opposed federal lynching laws and vowed to veto any as president. He mourned the Fifteenth Amendment, declaring it a "grave mistake" to assume that American Blacks were ready for suffrage so soon after "a thousand years of savagery, barbarism, of three hundred years of slavery."

"I will say very frankly," he intoned in 1914, ". . . it was a mistake to bestow upon the colored people at that particular time the right to vote."

Colored people, certainly, wouldn't vote for *him*.

• • •

Borah wasn't the only former TR acolyte in the field. There were several—including even Hoover, for that matter.

And neither was William Randolph Hearst the only newsman aiming to topple TR's cousin Franklin.

In 1898, a poor but promising young redheaded Michigander named Frank Knox answered Hearst's summons to "Remember the Maine." Abandoning his studies at tiny Alma College, he enlisted in the United States Army, eventually serving with Teddy Roosevelt's Rough Riders at San Juan Hill. His service, though honorable, was hardly Hearst front-page material: burial duty, a bout of dysentery, and a wardrobe so disgusting that on his return stateside a fellow soldier tossed Knox's pants ("They was almost walking by themselves") overboard. He disembarked pantless and wrapped in a blanket.

The war proved so short, Alma College allowed Knox to graduate anyway (by making up his courses—*not pantless*). Thereupon, he secured a $10-a-week reporting position with the *Grand Rapids Herald.* Within a year, he was its $15-a-week city editor. In 1902, he became his own boss, transforming a moribund Upper Peninsula weekly into a four-page daily, the *Sault Ste. Marie Journal.* A year later, he acquired the rival *News-Record*, combining both papers into the far more prosperous six-page *Sault Ste. Marie Evening News.* He succeeded in cleaning up wide-open Sault Ste. Marie, though not without first having his newspaper's windows shot out by hoodlums and being personally slugged by one unrepentant saloonkeeper.

He was already highly political. Returning from Cuba and armed with his war stories, he served as a warm-up act at rallies for local Republican US representative William Alden Smith (a minority shareholder in the *Herald*). In 1910, he successfully managed the gubernatorial campaign of another Sault Ste. Marie newsman, Chase S. Osborn (purveyor of 1934's Roosevelt/"Rosenvelt" theory). Catchy slogans can work wonders. Theirs was "Osborn, Harmony, and a New Deal."

Knox emerged as chairman of the Republican State Central Committee. Two years later, William Howard Taft invited him to chair his Michigan reelection campaign. Instead, Knox answered TR's request to round up GOP governors supporting his challenge to Taft. When Teddy bolted the GOP, Knox bolted with him.

In 1917, Knox founded New Hampshire's *Manchester Leader*. In 1917–18, he fought in France with the 153rd Artillery Regiment, mustering out as a lieutenant colonel, later making full colonel in the Reserves. Forevermore, he was "Col. Frank Knox."

Teddy expired in 1919, but Knox remained a Bull Moose Republican, serving, in 1920, as convention floor manager for yet another Rough Rider, TR's old friend and Spanish-American War comrade Gen. Leonard Wood. Wood failed to get the nomination. So did Knox when he sought New Hampshire's governorship in 1924.

He was, however, sufficiently expert to attract William Randolph Hearst, who recruited him to salvage his money-hemorrhaging *Boston American*. Knox, reluctant to depart New Hampshire, set his price at a presumably prohibitive $52,000 per year. Hearst, never a piker, responded: Why not? Knox so transformed the *American* that W. R. promoted him to general manager of his entire chain at $150,000 per year.

By 1931, some mysterious disagreement intervened. Nobody ever said exactly what. Knox strolled away, possessing rolls of Hearst cash but no great plans. Soon an opportunity arose to run the highly regarded—but massively debt-ridden ($12 million)—*Chicago Daily News*. Knox swept in, again working his tight-fisted magic. While Knox's *Daily News* was never as flashy as a Hearst paper, it met his goal to be "a good newspaper, suitable for its community, circulated in the proper field."

Not everything about Knox was above reproach. He was humorless (as the above goal might indicate). He cut too much slack for what remained of ex-mayor "Big Bill" Thompson's corrupt Chicago Republican machine. And there was . . . the *News*'s energetic women's editor, Leola Allard.

Knox fetched Miss Allard, a former Hearst staffer, with him to Chicago. She was, as *Daily News* reporter Mary Welsh (ultimately the *fourth* Mrs. Ernest Hemingway) griped, "one of the world's greatest bitches." Not inconsequentially, Leola was also the Colonel's girlfriend.

"Her presence," as the *Chicago Tribune*'s Walter Trohan recalled, "irked many a *News* reporter, especially when Knox gave her a car and a handsome salary, when salaries of other reporters had been cut."

Soon enough, Trohan cajoled a telephone operator into duping Knox that an incoming call had originated from Palo Alto, California, Herbert Hoover's current residence. He excitedly assumed the ex-president was calling.

"Hello," the Colonel answered.

"Is Leola there?" responded Trohan.

"Hello! Who is it?"

"Never mind who it is. Is Leola there?"

"Who wants her? Hello! Hello! Who is it?"

"This is your conscience, Frank," Trohan dramatically intoned—and hung up.

Essentially progressive (even aside from Miss Allard), Knox supported the very earliest of New Deal measures but quickly mutated into an energetic—and frenzied—Roosevelt critic.

Charitably explaining Knox's abrupt *volte-face, The Nation*'s Raymond Gram Swing posited that he was "fundamentally trusting in nature . . . often . . . a shade too ready to believe in the person he meets. Then, with disillusionment, he over-reacts. Behind his attacks on President Roosevelt, I imagine, is some episode in which he utterly believed in him and was fooled."

Thus, for example, in Los Angeles, in July 1935, Knox scored FDR:

> Upon what food does this, our Caesar, feed? What madness has seized him?
>
> Does he not see how dangerously close this comes to conspiracy to break down our institutions of government? . . .
>
> To Mr. Roosevelt's obviously sneering query—"Well, what do you suggest as a substitute?"—we may properly retort: "Why not try as a substitute, the program on which you were elected?"

Those who saw a Hearst under every bed—and there were many—spied Hearst still slithering beneath Knox's. But this was not the case.

When, for example, Hearst denounced radicalism at the University of Chicago, Knox's *Daily News* protested that such "hysteria" might cripple "academic freedom" and "the perennial quest for truth."

In February 1936, one Midwestern paper trumpeted Col. Knox's manly virtues thusly:

> Knox plays as he works and it is in his out-of-door life that he has shown a versatility even greater than that of Theodore Roosevelt. Knox has not only been a hunter and a fisherman, but has paddled his own canoe through most of the rapids of the upper Great Lakes. He has driven his own pack train over the plains and mountains of half-a-dozen Western States, ridden horse back over the mountains of New England and has followed a "chuck-wagon" and helped the Apaches in their fall roundup. He has visited every Indian reservation in the country. Knox can sail a boat, run a launch or automobile. He was an early devotee of the ski, the skate and the toboggan and is an expert swimmer. Nowadays he packs a heavy bag of golf clubs and has used them on links in all parts of the country.

But wait, as they say, there was even more to commend Colonel Knox:

> As a member of the board of Indian Commissioners he made his vacations riding expeditions to the out-of-the-way Indian reservations with Mrs. Knox. They studied the Indian then took steps in Washington to remedy their living conditions, an interest they still continue.
>
> While engaged in this work, Knox cleared the Montana range of thirty thousand useless wild horses which were canned and sent to Japan. In their place he had the Army remount service send blooded stallions to be bred with the rugged cowboy and Indian ponies of the Northwest. The result has been better mounts for the Army and better horses for the Indians.

This was all very admirable (unless you were one of those thirty thousand Japan-bound equines), but not enough to obscure the fact that newspaperman extraordinaire Col. Frank Knox—now seeking the highest public office in the land—had never even been elected dogcatcher.

Luckily, another Republican newsman was in the running: Michigan's cigar-puffing Arthur Hendrick Vandenberg. Like his friend William E. Borah, he was a member of the World's Greatest Deliberate Body. Like Franklin Roosevelt—more so, in fact, than Franklin Roosevelt—he was a Dutchman.

And like Frank Knox (and Hoover, for that matter), Sen. Arthur Hendrick Vandenberg ascended, in Horatio Alger fashion, from childhood hard times. Both Knox's and Vandenberg's fathers had been ruined by Grover Cleveland's Panic of 1893, forcing their sons to take work early. "I had no youth," recalled Vandenberg; "I went to work when I was nine, and I never got a chance to enjoy myself." Remarkably, however, as *Grand Rapids Herald* editor E. D. Conger hired Frank Knox as a $10-a-week cub reporter, he also engaged Arthur Hendrick Vandenberg as his state correspondent. Knox left. Vandenberg stayed. By March 1906, Conger was dead, and William Alden Smith tapped Vandenberg, just twenty-two, to succeed Conger as editor-in-chief and general manager. By 1919, Vandenberg had assumed presidency of the Herald Publishing Company. Ownership of three other Michigan papers followed.

Arthur Vandenberg was a true-blue Republican. His grandfather had voted to nominate Abraham Lincoln in 1860. His father's deathbed plea was, "My boy, I hope you'll always be a good Republican." Young Arthur, like Frank Knox, was an avid Square Dealer, an acolyte of the magnificent Teddy—and fired in October 1900 from his job as a Sears Biscuit Factory billing clerk for skipping out to march in a TR-for-vice-president parade down Grand Rapids's Main Street.

When, in 1910, Frank Knox assumed chairmanship of the state GOP, it was Vandenberg who nominated "that red-headed, red-blooded fighting man from the Soo." Two years later, Vandenberg remained aboard William Howard Taft's capsized ship. By 1916, he was state GOP convention chairman. Exempt from Great War service, he organized war-bond tours, including one with John Philip Sousa's band. On tour, he contracted the Spanish Flu.

He battled Wilson's League of Nations and championed Alexander Hamilton's memory, penning a trio of books in his honor. He loved to talk (in high school, classmates begged, "When will Vandenberg stop talking?") and orated across Michigan and the Midwest.

In 1928, he caught the break of a lifetime, being named to a US Senate seat when Democrat incumbent Woodbridge Ferris died. Capitol Hill possessed no shortage of unpleasant characters, but Vandenberg excelled on two fronts: his vanity, and his maddening fence-straddling.

A fellow senator lambasted him as "the only Senator who can strut sitting down." Journalist Fred Rodell opined that Vandenberg "looked and acted more like a strutting, orating Claghornesque caricature than any Northerner in history." The *Chicago Tribune*'s Walter Trohan sized him up as "one of the vainest men to serve in a body where the egos are often king size," and later informed a researcher, "I knew Vandenberg quite well. I was paid in part to know him. I confess I was not fond of him. . . . Politicians as a class are vain but he was vain beyond most of the tribe. His chief conversation was on his last speech or the one he had in preparation." Walter Lippmann dismissed him as "a pretty third-rate fellow."

Vandenberg excelled not merely in outsized pompous egotism but in world-class political obfuscation and fence-straddling—perhaps a natural legacy from decades of small-city editorial writing. Critics derided him as a "Yes and No Man."

"He has stood squarely on both sides of every issue, . . ." calculated Fred Rodell. "The Old Guard dies but never surrenders. Vandenberg surrenders but never dies." Anticipating a 1936 FDR–Vandenberg matchup, Senate Majority Leader Joe Robinson tartly proposed a Republican slogan: "Vacuity, Vacillation and Vandenberg."

Yet, despite his abundance of mind-numbing double-talk (he would, for example, advocate "Social-mindedness, not socialism"), he was not entirely without virtue. Unlike Bill Borah, he got things done. Early on, he moved Congress off the dime in reforming the House reapportionment process and obtained authorization for the long-stalled Ambassador Bridge connecting Detroit with Windsor, Ontario. Against all odds, he successfully challenged FDR's plans for an expensive (and potentially environmentally disastrous) cross-Florida canal. Most significantly, it was he—and not FDR or any of his brainy Brain Trusters—who promoted the remarkably simple, yet remarkably effective, concept of the Federal Deposit Insurance Corporation (FDIC). If anything restored public confidence in the banking system—and kept it restored—it was the FDIC. FDR hated the idea ("It won't work. . . . The weak banks will pull down the strong"), literally banged his fist on his desk, and vowed to veto it. Vandenberg dragged him into it, and, before long, FDR was vaingloriously boasting that the FDIC was "a gigantic task which the pessimists said could not possibly be done."

More importantly, Vandenberg was one of seven Senate Republicans triumphing in 1934's party bloodbath. Unlike Borah and many other Republican solons, Vandenberg had actually opposed the New Deal legislative juggernaut, voting for just three of its seventeen major measures: the gold reserve act, the stock exchange control bill, and Social Security. Yet, though his record might be conservative for 1936, he realized that such conservatism was no longer the most marketable of commodities. "If we make the New Deal the issue this election," he exclaimed to an interviewer in January 1936, "we can win. If we make the Old Deal the issue we'll lose!"

As might be imagined, a politician with Vandenberg's potpourri of calculation, obfuscation, and barely disguised false modesty might only warily divulge his own ambitions. To that same interviewer, he protested, "You don't think you're talking to a presidential candidate, do you? If you do, you are mistaken. There are plenty of candidates without me. But why any of them should want to shoulder that crucifixion . . . , I don't know."

And yet he *was* thinking of it and knew others were thinking of *him*—including (but only if things didn't work out for himself) Herbert Hoover. "They say Hoover is backing me," Vandenberg cannily confided to Cactus Jack Garner. "That's enough to whip anybody."

And so, with few other Republican hopefuls rating a first look, let alone a second, bloviating show horse Arthur Vandenberg entered 1936 as a dark horse

But one, certainly, in the race.

Kansas governor Alfred M. Landon was never a show horse—and, soon, neither a dark horse either.

Pennsylvania-born and Ohio-raised, Landon relocated to Independence, Kansas, in 1904, becoming, as author Irving Stone declared, "the apotheosis of Kansas; he changed his name to Alf, began to talk through his nose with a midwest twang, [and] later took to wearing his clothes with the farmer's disregard of elegance."

"I thought," recalled Alf's second wife, Theo Cobb Landon, "he was an insurance salesman when he first telephoned."

Graduating from the University of Kansas (where he earned the nickname "The Fox"), he settled into banking. Four years later, he shifted into independent oil production. It was the right move. By the late 1920s, he had achieved millionaire status—with a million dollars going a long way in both 1929 and Independence, Kansas.

He entered politics one step at a time, always inching forward. Raised Republican, he, too, caught the TR bug. Like Hoover and Frank Knox, Landon, along with his father, bolted the GOP to support 1912's Progressive crusade. Landon Sr. donated $1,000 to the Bull Moose cause.

In 1922, Alf emerged as personal secretary to Kansas governor Henry Allen, an opponent of the resurgent Ku Klux Klan. As Allen departed office in 1924, the state's nearly one hundred thousand Klansmen helped anoint both the Republican and Democratic gubernatorial candidates, disgusting *Emporia Gazette* editor William Allen White (like Harding, Knox, Vandenberg, Arthur Capper, *and* Henry Allen, part of the seemingly endless line of GOP newsmen-politicians; and, like Landon, a 1912 bolter), who reluctantly mounted a $25-per-week third-party run for the governorship to "spit in the face of the Klan." Landon not only bolted with White, he bolted Coolidge's national ticket to support 1924's Robert La Follette Sr.–Burton K. Wheeler Progressive slate.

Yet, by 1928, Landon was chairman of the state GOP and delivered to Herbert Hoover 72.02 percent of the Sunflower State vote—his highest state percentage anywhere. In 1932—a true *annus horribilis* for Republicans—Landon ran for governor as a champion of economy, and won.

His victory was as much fluke as fate. Incumbent Democratic governor Harry Woodring faced not only Landon, but the sinisterly goateed and bespectacled Dr. John R. Brinkley, a first-class strange one. Brinkley peddled a "goat gland" treatment via his own powerful radio station, Wichita's KFKB. Scores of hitherto healthy patients died (and even more took sick), while Brinkley grew rich. In 1930, campaigning in his private plane, Brinkley had captured 29.5 percent of the gubernatorial vote as a write-in. Had all his write-ins been counted, he would have won. An early 1932 straw poll showed him crushing both Woodring and Landon. Somehow, Landon pulled it out in a rare three-way nail-biter: Landon, 34.82 percent; Woodring, 34.12 percent; Brinkley, 30.58 percent.

Winning as a Republican in 1932 was difficult enough; winning two years later was damn near impossible. Yet Landon coasted to victory. First, in the GOP primary versus the ubiquitous Brinkley (79.90–20.10 percent), and that November with a fairly comfortable 53.61 percent.

Even by Kansas standards, Landon was hardly Mr. Excitement—Borah, Knox, and Vandenberg easily outpaced him as compelling figures. So unknown was he that, at first, Vandenberg kept referencing him as "Langdon." But he possessed a certain quiet friendliness, which, say, Herbert Hoover never enjoyed. He managed the state's affairs competently and economically.

Both Hoover and Roosevelt sent spending and deficits through the roof. Businessman Landon managed to balance economically devastated Kansas's budgets. From 1932 to 1935, per-capita state government spending fell from $15.68 to $13.41, earning Landon the admiring nickname "The Kansas Coolidge." Critics, however, charged that Landon's fiscal miracles derived not so much from him but rather from state laws mandating balanced budgets, massive infusions of federal aid (as benefited Georgia's Gene Talmadge), and a merciless shifting of costs to localities. They pointed out that his Democratic predecessor had also balanced his budgets.

Landon detested comparisons to Coolidge, hating them because he remained very much a progressive Republican, nowhere near as conservative as the laconic Coolidge. The Coolidges, Landon later pointed out, were "all regulars—my family were always insurgents."

In 1934, Eleanor Roosevelt's close friend Lorena Hickok visited Kansas. She found it to be "an interesting state. Even the Republican candidate for governor . . . is a sort of New Dealer. I read . . . one of his campaign speeches the other night, and I'll swear I'd have thought it was the Democrat talking! The Democratic candidate . . . is having a tough time of it, because the Republican has grabbed all his campaign material!"

Landon's January 1935 inaugural address sounded less like Silent Cal, and more like the Kingfish or "The Radio Priest." "Our problems have been intensified," Landon expounded, "by the great industrial plutocracy we have built since our last great depression of 1893. New adjustments must be made as a result of the development of machine production in the last quarter century."

Publishers seemed just crazy about him. The *Kansas City Star*'s Roy Roberts was an early presidential booster. Back in 1926, William Allen White wrote of Landon: "He is sane and sweet and very wise, incidentally I love him like a son."

William Randolph Hearst also took notice. In July 1935, Hearst magazine executive Richard Berlin assigned two of his more luminous writers—Hollywood's Adela Rogers St. John (aka both "The World's Greatest Girl Reporter" *and* "The Mother Confessor of Hollywood") and Broadway's Damon Runyon—to profile Mr. & Mrs. Landon for *Good Housekeeping* and *Cosmopolitan*, respectively.

Adela reported on how the frugal Mr. Landon had saved Kansas state taxpayers $33,000,000, but focused on Landon's thirty-six-year-old wife, Theo Cobb Landon. Rogers confessed that she had been expecting to meet a "large motherly sort of woman, weather-beaten and practical," but instead found Theo youthful and attractive and, for good measure, quite the talented harpist. Mrs. Landon, marveled Adela, possesses "amazing coloring . . . the blackest eyes and the whitest skin."

Damon Runyon commenced his own essay ("Horse and Buggy Governor") with reflections on the rough-hewn, aw-shucks aspects of Landon's wardrobe ("a pair of seer-sucker pants, somewhat crumpled. His black-and-white shoes were the worse for wear"). Irving Stone dismissed Runyon's effort as "another of his little fantasies on the subject of Why We Need an Unkempt President in the White House."

Broadway denizen Runyon queried Topeka denizen Landon regarding his stand on Prohibition. Kansas, after all, remained a "Dry" state.

Landon (guarding his Kansas base) quickly responded he was for it. Nonetheless, added Runyon, "it is said he has taken a drink. You can get all the beer you want in Kansas. It is sold openly, though hard licker is banned. That is, it's against the law in Kansas. So of course you can get hard licker there too, if you persist."

Hearst was smitten, and while his own electoral efforts consistently miscarried, his king-making efforts often succeeded. He had sponsored "Red Mike" Hylan as mayor of New York and Dr. Royal Copeland, a former Michigan Republican, as New York's Democratic US Senator. More significantly, he anointed both FDR and Garner in 1932. Governors, it seemed, were excellent presidential horses to bet on. Had not Cleveland, McKinley, TR, Wilson, Coolidge—and FDR—all galloped from state house to White House?

Yes, who might say Hearst's magic would not triumph once more in 1936?

By September 1935, Hearst was fully on board. A month later, supporters established a Landon headquarters at Kansas City's Hotel Muehlebach. That same month, Eastern Republican leaders read the riot act to their supposed natural candidate, Herbert Hoover. At a private Manhattan dinner, Hoover's former Treasury Secretary Ogden Mills spoke for those present to not only enlighten The Chief that he must not be the nominee—but that business would not support him if he were.

Also that October, Landon excitedly warned, "If we are going to stop the New Deal, it's 1936 or never. . . . This country is not far from fascism." The following month, when he addressed the Ohio State Chamber of Commerce, the *Cleveland Plain Dealer* gushed, "We are convinced that as Lincoln left a profound impression in the East in 1860, Landon left a similar impression in 1935."

In December 1935, three private railway cars, including Cissy Patterson's "chintz boudoir" car, chugged into Topeka. Aboard were Patterson, Arthur Brisbane, Paul Block of the Block newspaper chain, Marion Davies—and Hearst himself. Patterson and Block (whose idea the trip had been) pronounced themselves mightily impressed by The Kansas Coolidge. He "was simply grand," assessed Patterson. "He's just the solid, common type of man we need in the White House. And I think his wife is lovely." Said Block: "If the Republicans and those opposed to the New Deal united on a man like Governor Landon . . . a doer and not a promiser—the New Deal can be defeated."

"I think he is marvelous," Hearst gurgled. "To say I am favorably impressed puts it very mildly."

Yet Hearst and Landon hardly sang in perfect harmony. Landon supported many a New Deal program. He merely objected to their inefficiencies. "From the very first," he admitted, "I advocated the granting of unusual powers to the President because of the national emergency. . . . I have cooperated with the New Deal to the best of my ability."

Privately, he went further: "I do not think there is anything new or revolutionary about the distribution of wealth theory. Every wise statesman in every period of history has been concerned with the equitable distribution of property in his country."

In his 1935 inauguration, Landon orated: "America bids fair to join in the procession of nations of the world in their march toward a new social and economic philosophy. Some say this will lead to socialism, some communism, others fascism. For myself I am convinced that the ultimate goal will be a modified form of individual rights and ownership of property out of which will come a wider spread of prosperity and opportunity."

Internationally, he favored two Hearst bêtes noire: the League of Nations, and the World Court.

And, while W. R. lustily harpooned radicals and university professors, Landon had, in the spring of 1934, invited Norman Thomas to Topeka to speak. When Oklahomans protested a visiting "dangerous" radical professor from the University of Kansas, Landon tartly answered, "Under the academic freedom which we practice here in Kansas we do not attempt to control the thinking of . . . the faculties of our schools."

Hearst's definition of "marvelous" was very flexible.

In late 1935, the Left-leaning *The Nation* dispatched editor Raymond Gram Swing to ascertain just how great an ogre this "Kansas Coolidge" was. It turned out, he wasn't bad at all—at least, by liberal lights. Swing wrote:

> [Landon] is not much, if at all, less progressive in philosophy than Franklin D. Roosevelt. . . . Why Hearst and the East[ern conservative Republicans] have selected him baffles me. I am told that Hearst sent half a dozen men to Kansas to study his record before he came out for him. I can only wonder whether Hearst is more of a liberal than he shows himself in his newspapers or I am a worse reporter than I care to believe.

Roy Garvin, a staff member for the Black *Kansas City Call,* recalled that when Landon assumed control of the state GOP in 1928, Garvin's fellow African Americans, accustomed to second-class accommodations at party headquarters, pondered in what distant and shabby environs their assigned offices might lie. "Right here with the rest of us," Landon answered matter-of-factly.

"This first experience with him," Garvin noted, "convinced me that he was not only fair, but courageous and sincere."

African Americans, after all, needed all the friends they could get in 1936.

· 12 ·

"Anno Domini Father Divine"

Three groups had remained faithful to Herbert Hoover back in 1932.

The wealthy—a greatly shrunken and chastened demographic—held fast.

So did rural northeasterners in a band stretching from northern New England through northeastern Ohio.

And African Americans.

Blacks had reasons to shun the smiling FDR. First was sheer inertia. They had voted for the party of Lincoln for as long as they could vote. The Democratic Party remained solidly anchored to its segregationist Southern base. Blacks possessed no great reason to believe Franklin Roosevelt would be much (if any better) than Woodrow Wilson, the Southern-born segregationist he served as assistant secretary of the Navy from 1913 through 1920.

In 1932's primaries, northeastern Catholics remained loyal to Al Smith. FDR drew much of his support from influential Southerners. Huey Long might not have been the most racist Southerner in the world, but he was Southern enough so that his flamboyant support for FDR only aggravated African-American suspicions. So did the location of FDR's beloved second (or, rather, his third—or was it his fourth?) home, at Warm Springs, in violently Jim Crow Georgia. That FDR's running mate, "Cactus Jack" Garner, hailed from Uvalde, Texas, was hardly a selling point.

There were, however, rumblings of a major shift, as Blacks wearied of Republican apathy. A bitter Robert L. Vann, editor of the African-American *Pittsburgh Courier*, famously beseeched his compatriots: "My friends, go turn Lincoln's picture to the wall. That debt has been paid in full."

They didn't. But soon would.

Americans were flat on their backs in 1932. Blacks suffered most. Their unemployment soared to 50 percent. The New Deal provided jobs and relief for all, including African Americans. Three hundred thousand Blacks learned to read and write under FDR's literacy programs. One hundred and thirty-three of 367 New Deal housing projects were exclusively for Blacks. Another forty were integrated. "By the end of the thirties," wrote Doris Kearns Goodwin, "the WPA was providing basic earnings for one million Black families; three hundred thousand Black youths were involved in NYA [National Youth Administration] programs, and another quarter-million were serving in the CCC."

Franklin and Farley and Harry Hopkins and Ickes provided cold, hard cash. Eleanor provided the warmth.

There would be high-profile moments, as in May 1936 when she visited the ostensibly integrated District of Columbia Training School for Delinquent Girls. Her Scripps-Howard syndicated column, "My Day," usually involved noncontroversial pleasantries ("I think spring and autumn are my favorite seasons. There's beauty, of course, in every season."), but not following that trip. "Never have I seen an institution called a 'school' which had so little claim to that name," she exploded. "Buildings are unfit for habitation—badly heated, rat infested, with inadequate sanitary facilities, without an educational program or a teacher, children walled in like prisoners."

But many of her gestures were of simple courtesy. "She received Negro sharecroppers in the White House," recalled her friend and ally Joseph P. Lash, "and visited them in their tarpaper shacks in the cotton fields, and with kindly questions persuaded them to talk about themselves and their needs. . . . This was what the Negro wanted—that he be seen and recognized as an individual and accepted in the fullness of a humanity that he shared with the whites—and this was what the First Lady understood."

Three years prior to Black contralto Marian Anderson's appearance at the Lincoln Memorial, the Roosevelts invited her to entertain at the White House's Monroe Room. It was not their first invitation to African-American performers. Nor were Franklin and Eleanor the only such hosts: coloratura soprano Marie Selika Williams performed for President and Mrs. Hays in 1878; soprano Sisserietta Jones had performed for Benjamin Harrison, Cleveland, McKinley, and Theodore Roosevelt. Thus, while Miss Anderson's White House performance was hardly groundbreaking, Eleanor's attitude remained noteworthy. Anderson's longtime Finnish accompanist, pianist Kosti Vehanen, recalled: "After [Marian] sang there was a very touching scene. Mrs. Roosevelt, our charming hostess, took Marian's Mother by the hand, and led her over and introduced her to the President. I shall never forget seeing those two ladies enter the room. Mrs. Roosevelt's manner was sure and free, as becomes a woman of the world, happy to welcome [Marian's] mother. . . . In all of Mrs. Anderson's being, there was evident the feeling that this was one of the greatest moments in her life. Her face reflected her gratitude and the pride she felt."

A seemingly never-ending stream of such events and meetings transpired. Today they would seem commonplace. In 1936, they remained striking. "Blacks in the thirties," noted ER's biographer Blanche Weisen Cook, "found them impressive because there had been nothing like them in anyone's memory."

Yet Eleanor's racial attitudes would hardly pass later muster. Never anyone's idea of a Southern belle, she hardly shared her husband's fondness for Warm Springs. In fact, she had no use for it. But she—like her uncle Theodore Roosevelt—had antebellum Georgia ancestors and absorbed many a lesson at the knee of her great-aunt Anna Bulloch Gracie. "I quite understand the Southern point of view," Eleanor once explained, "because my grandmother was a Southerner from Georgia and her sister had a great deal to do with bringing us up when we were small children; therefore, I am familiar with the old plantation life."

Her everyday vocabulary reflected that upbringing. Rather than refer to the "Civil War," she employed the preferred Southern usage of the "War Between the States" and casually riddled her conversation with such terms as "pickaninny" and "darkies," having learned from Great-Aunt

Anna that such a word as "darky" counted "as a term of affection and I have always considered it in that light."

Miscegenation made her nervous. In 1928, she mollified a dubious potential Al Smith supporter: "I want to assure you that Gov. Smith does not believe in intermarriage between white and colored people. He has a full understanding of conditions as they are in the South and would never try to do violence to the feelings of Southern people . . . the Democratic Party has always better understood and sympathized with Southern feelings and prejudices than has the Republican."

A decade later, she reiterated: "Eating with someone does not mean you believe in intermarriage."

Arriving in Washington during Woodrow Wilson's administration, Eleanor always preferred "colored" help, finding them more tractable ("pleasanter to deal with and there is never any question about it not being their work to do this or that"). Returning to Washington in March 1933, she essentially instituted an all-Black staff ("a complete darky household"), thereby avoiding the prickly issue of segregating white and Black help. In February 1933, she wrote White House Head Usher Ike Hoover regarding the Herbert Hoover–FDR transition:

> I will also have my maid [Elizabeth "Lizzie" McDuffie] and my husband's valet [Irwin "Mac" McDuffie], both colored. They sleep in the house but I think could go to friends for a night or two or until the other changes in servants are made. They will, however, come to the White House and bring all of our bags, etc., on the afternoon of Inauguration Day. Will you let me know which will be the best door for them to enter by.

The inference was guarded but clear. The McDuffies would, of course, use the "colored" entrance.

Such incidents were, however, small potatoes, mere nitpicks, in the grand scheme of her attitudes and actions. "I believe," she would later say, "it never hurts to be kind."

She wore her heart on her sleeve. Franklin's heart lay somewhere else. "He was a New York patrician," griped the NAACP's Roy Wilkins, "distant, aloof, with no natural feel for the disabilities of black people. He had no compelling inner commitment to their cause . . . as a patron saint for Negroes he had plenty of red [Georgia] clay on his feet."

Eleanor employed the term "darky"; her husband told "nigger" jokes and wrote home to her from Jamaica that "a drink of coconut water, procured by a naked nigger boy from the top of the tallest tree, did much to make us forget the dust."

Franklin had his agenda in Washington, and if Blacks resided in it, they hardly dwelt in its better neighborhoods. Southern Blacks could not vote, so their desires took a back seat to Southern whites. Northern Blacks could. Their votes counted for much in swing states like New York, Illinois, and Ohio. They couldn't be ignored. They had to be wooed, though FDR never courted them with any enthusiasm or affection. In part, he knew full well that the white South—and powerful Senate Democrats—were peering sternly over his shoulder. In part, it seems, he just wasn't interested.

"In four White House terms," assessed one historian, "he neither advocated a single piece of civil rights legislation nor scarcely spoke a single word against Jim Crow. Nor did he even seem to think about or discuss privately the issue of race."

Aside from Eleanor, few members of Franklin's inner circle seemed prepared to push him along. Harold Ickes, a former Chicago NAACP leader, was one, but that was about it. Even liberals like Labor Secretary Frances Perkins and Agriculture's Henry Wallace seemed positively terrified of the issue. Perkins "dreaded" any discussion of Black labor relations in the South. Wallace asked, "Don't you think the New Deal is undertaking to do too much for the Negro?" Two key members of Roosevelt's palace guard—his short-tempered Virginia-born press secretary Steve Early (a grandson of Confederate General Jubal A. Early) and the much more likable but rail-thin and tubercular Kentucky-born appointments secretary Marvin McIntyre—proved predictably Southern in their attitudes. Equally unsympathetic to the Black agenda—either from prejudice or calculation—were New Yorkers Jim Farley and Louis McHenry Howe. Howe recommended favoring "our southern Brethren" over "our anxious colored brethren." FDR and Early ("no admirer" of E. R., and, like Marvin McIntyre no "New

Dealer at heart") barred Black reporters from presidential news conferences until February 1944. In September 1935, Eleanor attempted to allow Blacks into hers. Steve Early responded: "I have taken care of the Negro requests for the President's press conferences and if Mrs. Roosevelt opens hers it just makes the President more vulnerable. I think it is far the best thing to ignore the letter." Eleanor backed down.

She never quite won—but never quit trying—about lynching.

The lynching of Blacks had steadily drifted downward from its historic peak of 161 in 1892, to just 9 in 1929 but rebounded to 24 in 1933. Anti-lynching legislation had been stuck in Congress forever, blocked by Southern senators and questions of constitutionality. St. Louis Republican congressman Leonidas C. Dyer's version (ironically questioned by the NAACP on constitutional grounds) neared passage from 1922 through 1924, but failed thanks to the usual Southern filibusters. Not until 1933 would the NAACP launch another serious anti-lynching campaign, this one ultimately centered on a measure crafted by two Senate Democrats: Colorado's Edward Costigan and Al Smith's old Tammany pal Robert F. Wagner.

Eleanor worked with the NAACP's Walter F. White to enlist Franklin's support for the bill; for, absent a presidential boost, it had zero chance of passage. Predictably, FDR begged off. As far as the blue-eyed, exceedingly light-skinned White could tell, Marvin McIntyre was not even forwarding his correspondence to the president. Regarding a personal meeting, McIntyre wired White: "Cannot arrange appointment requested at this time. President extremely busy on matters requiring immediate attention."

White contacted Eleanor. She answered:

> The President talked to me rather at length about the lynching bill. As I do not think you will either like or agree with everything that he thinks, I would like an opportunity of telling you about it, and I would also like you to talk to the President if you feel you want to.

She arranged for White to visit the White House. He found Franklin absent, delayed in returning from cruising the Potomac aboard the presidential yacht *Sequoia*. FDR arrived to find his wife and mother chatting amiably with White on the South Portico. He turned on the charm, in part because he could not help being charming, but more importantly to short-circuit White from raising the topic at hand. When your life is a series of fifteen-minute meetings with people wanting something that you don't want to give them, cheerfully running out the clock ranks among the most cherished of skills.

A skill Franklin certainly had.

White finally forced FDR to explain his objections to Costigan–Wagner. "But, [Senate Majority Leader] Joe Robinson," Roosevelt argued, "tells me the bill is unconstitutional."

White persisted. Franklin protested—half-jocularly; not surprisingly, half-annoyed—"Somebody's been priming you. Was it my wife?"

White ignored Franklin's jibe, firmly suggesting their agenda remain fixed on Costigan–Wagner. FDR plied Eleanor with the same question. He got the same answer: stick to the bill. Exhausting his options, Franklin pled to his mother: "Well, at least I know you'll be on my side."

She wasn't.

FDR fell back to arguing practical politics. "I did not choose the tools with which I must work," he insisted. "Had I been permitted to choose them I would have selected quite different ones. But I've got to get legislation passed by Congress to save America. The Southerners by reason of the seniority . . . are chairmen or occupy strategic places on most of the . . . committees. If I come out for the anti-lynching bill now, they will block every bill I ask Congress to pass to keep America from collapsing. I just can't take that risk."

Franklin then retreated just a tad, informing White: "You go ahead. You do everything you can do. Whatever you can get done is okay with me, but I just can't do it."

White departed, and Eleanor asked, "Well, what about me? Do you mind if I [publicly] say what I think?"

"No, certainly not," FDR responded, taking the husbandly path of least resistance. "You can say anything you want. I can always say 'Well, that's my wife. I can't do anything about her.'"

Technically, FDR *had* spoken out against lynching. At Washington's Constitution Hall in December 1933, he not only decried lynching as "a vile form of collective murder," he added, "We do not excuse those in high places or in low who condone lynch law."

This was FDR's first rebuke of lynching. It concerned, however, not Blacks in the Democratic Deep South but two white kidnapper-murderers lynched in San Jose, California, and the comments of the state's Republican governor, James Rolph ("They [the mob] did a good job. I don't think anyone will be arrested . . . but if they are I'll pardon them.") in excusing this summary "justice." Thousands watched the lynching. A Los Angeles radio station broadcast it live.

FDR spoke. The violence continued. In October 1934, in Florida's Panhandle, a twenty-three-year-old Black farmhand named Claude Neal was accused of murdering and possibly raping a nineteen-year-old white woman. For his safety, authorities removed Neal to a jail in nearby Alabama. A white mob tracked him down, hauled him back to Florida, committed the all-too-usual barbarities, and lynched him at the farmstead where his alleged offense occurred.

The Atlanta-based Committee on Interracial Cooperation wrote FDR, describing the lynching as being "advertised hours in advance, bringing together thousands of men, women, and children eager to witness the spectacle. Lynching itself reported marked by unspeakable torture and mutilation. Local officers apparently indifferent throughout."

"Across the country," writes historian Isabel Wilkerson, "thousands of [other] outraged Americans wrote [to] Roosevelt demanding a federal investigation." Their pleas fell on deaf ears. As Wilkerson further noted: "The NAACP compiled a sixteen-page report and more files on the Neal case than any other lynching in American history. But Neal had the additional misfortune of having been lynched just before the 1934 national midterm elections . . . seen as a referendum on the New Deal itself. Roosevelt chose not to risk alienating the South with a Democratic majority in Congress at stake. He did not intervene in the case. No one was ever charged in Neal's death or spent a day in jail for it." That Neal's lynching coincided with a federal conference on crime—that pointedly avoided discussing lynching—only fueled Black outrage and frustration.

Claude Neal's death was only one of fifteen lynchings (all of Blacks) in 1934. Its interstate aspect, however, rendered it reasonably unique. Why couldn't Washington prosecute Neal's kidnappers under the recently enacted "Lindbergh Baby" anti-kidnapping act? Why couldn't Congress enact some stripped-down version of Costigan–Wagner to cover crossing state lines to commit lynchings or murders, paralleling the aforementioned Lindbergh kidnapping statute, 1910's Mann Act (barring the crossing of state lines with "any woman or girl for the purpose of prostitution or debauchery, or for any other immoral purpose") 1912's ban on transporting prize-fight films across state lines, or even 1919's federal anti-auto-theft law (coincidentally authored by Rep. Leonidas Dyer)? Nonetheless, nothing was done even in that modest regard.

The following month—November 1934—Walter White invited Eleanor to attend an anti-lynching rally at Carnegie Hall. FDR (he of "Well, that's my wife. I can't do anything about her.") vetoed the idea, relaying a message through Missy LeHand, "President says this is dynamite."

In February and March 1935, White and his NAACP helped stage an appropriately graphic exhibit at a Manhattan art gallery just blocks from the Roosevelts' East 62nd Street townhouse, entitled "An Art Commentary on Lynching." Franklin and Eleanor now reversed roles, and Eleanor wrote to White:

> The more I think about going to the exhibition, the more troubled I am, so this morning I went in to talk to my husband about it and asked him what they really planned to do about the [lynching] bill because I was afraid that some bright newspaper reporter might write a story which would offend some of the southern members and thereby make it even more difficult to do anything about the bill.
>
> My husband said it was quite all right for me to go, but if some reporter took the occasion to describe some horrible picture, it would cause more southern opposition. They plan to bring the bill out quietly as soon as possible although two southern Senators have said they would filibuster for two weeks. He thinks, however, they can get it through.

In the end, Eleanor did attend. She didn't care for the art.

Senator Borah also traveled to New York—to Brooklyn's Academy of Music. It was, by now, January 1936, and the former Stallion of Boise kicked off his presidential campaign in the Borough of Churches. The Northeast was not Borah country. Republicans remained too conservative. And there was, of course, his position on lynching, where he differed not only with the NAACP but with his own campaign manager (and FDR's own congressman), Rep. Hamilton Fish, who during the Great War had commanded Black troopers in France. Back in 1903, in Nampa, Idaho, Borah had risked his own life to successfully halt the lynching of an African-American bootblack and fellow Spanish-American War veteran, James Quarles, accused of shooting a white deputy sheriff in the chest. But that was long ago and far away, and Walter White described events:

> Icy winds from the East River cut like a jagged knife through the clothing of fifty pickets carrying signs attacking Borah for his stand on . . . Costigan–Wagner. . . . Borah's face blanched . . . and his shoulders seemed to shrink as with lowered head against the cold blast of weather and disapproval he entered the building. Instead of the vigor and boldness which had characterized his speeches in the Senate, he faltered and fumbled his words to such an extent that the audience and newspapermen looked at one another in amazement. Borah's campaign ended the night it opened. Opposition of the solid Negro Republican vote in the Ohio primary shortly afterward wrecked his presidential aspirations and his campaign died a-borning.

Other folks had better luck with African Americans in New York. These other folks were called Communists.

The Harlem Renaissance, like the Jazz Age, was over. Josephine Baker had left the building for Paris. But unrest seethed. Much of it revolved around employment. Blacks shopped in Harlem's many stores but often couldn't work there. "Don't Buy Where You Can't Work" became a popular slogan, as boycotts and resentment spread, sometimes led by flamboyant figures like Abdul Hamid, Harlem's anti-Semitic "Black Hitler." The *New York Times* described the powerfully built Hamid as decked out in "a white turban, a long dark green cloak decorated with gold braid and drawn in at the waist with an army belt, and black riding boots. He has a long black mustache and a Van Dyke beard." Focusing less on fashion, a former *New York Amsterdam News* reporter saw him as "a crude, racketeering giant . . . posing as a savior of black labor." In October 1936, police arrested Hamid for knifing Communist labor organizer Hammie Snipes at Lenox Avenue near 125th Street. He received twenty days.

In November 1934, a New York State Supreme Court judge ruled in local storeowners' favor:

> HARLEM STORE ACTS
>
> TO ENFORCE COURT'S BAN ON NEGRO PICKETS
>
> The A. S. Beck Shoe Corporation yesterday moved to halt picketing of its store at 264 West 125th Street by Negroes bent on coercing the management into replacing half of its white clerks by Negroes, following a . . . rul[ing] that the picketing was illegal, declaring the weapon's use must be restricted to labor conflicts and could not be called into play in racial disputes. He declared that, while the action was "born of an understandable desire" to increase Black employment, if the practice were permitted, white pickets might seek the discharge of colored help elsewhere, with resultant danger of race riots. The decision was viewed with satisfaction yesterday by Harlem merchants. . . .
>
> Isidore Schlesinger, Beck's attorney, announced he would shortly serve a copy of the court's order upon representatives of the Negroes, followers . . . of Abdul Hamid, Harlem's "Black Hitler."
>
> The attorney said he had refrained from raising the Jewish issue in court but added there could be no question that the Jewish issue entered into the fight.

The jurist ruling against picketing was Judge Samuel I. Rosenman—FDR's most trusted speechwriter.

Race riots followed in March 1935. Workers at West 125th Street's W. H. Kress Five and Ten Store nabbed a sixteen-year-old Black Puerto Rican, Lino Rivera, shoplifting, and things spun wildly out of control. Rivera bit an employee's hand, causing an ambulance to be summoned. Outside, a woman began shouting that Rivera had been murdered, which the ambulance's arrival only seemed to confirm. By complete coincidence, a hearse ominously halted nearby, and the seeds of riot were sown.

Instantly, pamphlets like this materialized:

> CHILD BRUTALLY BEATEN!
>
> WOMAN ATTACKED BY BOSS AND COPS
>
> CHILD NEAR DEATH
>
> One hour ago a 12-year-old Negro boy was brutally beaten by the management of Kress' Five and Ten Cent Store.
>
> The boy is near death, mercilessly beaten because they thought he had stolen a five-cent knife. A Negro woman, who sprang to defense of the boy had her arm broken by the thug and was then arrested.

It was all nonsense, even to the price of the knife. But three people died. At least a hundred more were injured. Rioters ransacked white businesses to the tune of an estimated $2 million in damages.

Some thought the Communists were behind it all. A few did belong to the group distributing the above leaflet (and the Young Communist League produced one with similar falsehoods), but by and large they actually proved a calming influence on events. It was, after all, part of their kinder, gentler Stalinism, the era of The United Front, though no portion of that front was ever stranger than with . . .

. . . Father Divine.

Actually, imagining the bald-headed 5'2" Father Divine allied with anyone was practically impossible, for Divine boldly proclaimed himself God Almighty walking the earth. For the Communists who believed in the latter (the earth) but not the former (God), that might have presented an insurmountable roadblock, save for the wonderful opportunity Divine presented to reach his numerous Harlem votaries (aka voters), not to mention his claimed two million worldwide acolytes. If that last number seemed nearly as dubious as his claims to divinity, well, there still remained sufficient members of Divine's flock to render the Communists' effort worthwhile.

From almost its very inception, the CPUSA had courted African Americans. As the nation's most oppressed group, Blacks seemed ripe for recruitment. In 1921, Lenin himself ordered the American party to accelerate the project. In 1928, the party—as usual, on orders from Moscow—proclaimed support for an autonomous African-American "Black Belt," stretching from Virginia to Texas. Few Americans thought much of the idea, and it was abandoned by 1934. CPUSA recruitment of Blacks was not.

Key to its drive were energetic efforts defending accused or harassed African Americans, including a minor *cause célèbre* stemming from labor organizer (and CPUSA member) Angelo Herndon's conviction in Atlanta in 1932 on charges of "subversion." Herndon's case—while big in party circles and eventually finding vindication in the Supreme Court—paled in comparison to the uproar created by the "Scottsboro Boys" case—nine Black teenagers convicted of raping two white women near Scottsboro, Alabama, in 1931.

Communist support, however, proved to be a double-edged sword for the accused. At one point, Scottsboro pickets angrily surrounded the White House, frightening those inside. "It was the first time we had seen mob hysteria . . ." recalled Louis Howe's assistant, the Kentucky-born former journalist Lela Stiles; "we expected them to charge the doors at any moment." Howe invited them in, and, while Stiles found them "grim" and "menacing," they dispersed peacefully. But Howe, wary not merely of normal New Deal political considerations (i.e., offending Southerners), but of the movement's obvious Communist influence, cautioned FDR against any action.

February 1936's session of the Communist-front National Negro Congress attracted 8,000 persons—817 formal delegates representing 585 organizations from 28 states. Dignitaries included James W. Ford (the CPUSA's 1932 and 1936 VP choice) but also poet Langston Hughes, Howard University's Ralph Bunche, the twenty-five-year-old Adam Clayton Powell Jr., and the Brotherhood of Sleeping Car Porters' A. Philip Randolph—even Bill Borah's campaign manager, Rep. Hamilton Fish Jr. Retired Howard University dean Kelly Miller worried that "the spirit of radicalism predominated. . . . [T]he reds, the Socialists and Communists were . . . in ascendancy, either in number or indominitable purpose, or in both." Randolph emerged as the new organization's president, but its executive secretary, the pro-Communist James P. Davis (a former Republican, the president of the National Federation of Colored Farmers, and a head field officer for the AAA), ran the show.

Walter White was too savvy to play footsie with the Communists. After all, if Eleanor Roosevelt would take your calls, why waste your nickel phoning James W. Ford?

From the Communists' viewpoint, reaching out to a raging anti-Semite and weirdo like "Black Hitler" Abdul Hamid remained verboten. As did any sympathy for Harlem's much-too-flamboyant, much-too-capitalist Marcus "The Black Moses" Garvey. Father Divine presented a different case altogether—to say the least. No one was quite sure where he came from. His admirers claimed from heaven. Less impressionable observers alternately theorized North Carolina, Georgia, or Maryland—and that his real name was "George Baker." By hook or crook, he had fallen into itinerant preaching, mostly in the South. First assuming the name "Major Jealous Divine" and then graduating to "Father Divine," his gospel was the very model of straitlaced evangelization: against alcohol and tobacco; even urging celibacy. Nearly as odd as his assertion of divinity were his finances. He never asked for money, never took up a collection, and yet had tons of cash—great rolls of greenbacks—often spent on free meals and lodgings for his followers. "I give everything," he boasted, "because I am omnipotent. I give you plenty of good food, clothes, shelter, work. And you are fat and merry."

A Long Island district attorney dispatched an undercover agent to discern what in hell went on with this strange operation. Nothing at all, she reported back. "As to the source of his income," one magazine noted, "Father answered all questions by biblical quotations having to do with ravens."

Many of his devotees were white. "Basic in the Divine program is the brotherhood of man," commented the *New Republic*. "The movement recognizes neither race nor creed. The word 'Negro,' and other words designating racial classifications, are tabu. No record of the color of adherents is kept."

It appears, however, that a significant number were *wealthy* whites. One was his white secretary, now known as "John Lamb," but, in reality, a former Brookline, Massachusetts, car dealer originally named J. Maynard Mathews, who early on bestowed upon Divine a new Cadillac. Divine's followers often assumed new names—not names like "John Lamb" or even "Major Jealous Divine"—but strange new concoctions like "Happy Boy Joe," "Sunny Sonny," "Quiet Love," "Wonderful Wisdom," "Gladness Darling," "Purity Love," "Heavenly Bouquet," "Sweet Inspiration," and "Orol Freedom."

The Journal of Educational Sociology dismissed many of those followers as "emotionally maladjusted." In Newark, three of them refused help while caught in a burning apartment, taking Divine's counsel—"We may take the words of Father Divine, eat and drink and live forever"—far too literally for their own good.

Political hopefuls courted Father's favor. At West 155th Street's Rockland Palace, in November 1933, a candidate dubbed "Shorty George" by Divine's followers embarrassingly groveled for his endorsement: "I say, I say. Father Divine, no matter what you want, I will support you. I am going to clean up this city and I came here tonight to ask Father Divine's help and counsel."

Said kowtowing failed. Father Divine remained neutral. Fiorello Henry La Guardia departed empty-handed.

Somehow, however, the Communists and Divine hit it off. Perhaps it was akin to two forlorn people at a dance, finding themselves alone, and pairing up after everyone else had partnered off. Whatever it was, in August 1934 four thousand Divine partisans attended a mass CPUSA-sponsored rally against war and fascism in Madison Square Park. Their banners read "God is peace; Father Divine is God." "Father Divine Is the Lord" and "Father Divine represents True Democracy. Justice, Freedom, Equality, Love." The *Daily Worker* confessed that "some of our comrades were startled and confused" but hastened to assure everyone that Lenin would have pronounced everything dialectically hunky-dory. "[W]e must," it editorialized, "under no circumstances allow ourselves to be side-tracked into a treatment of the religious question in the abstract."

For his part, Divine preached cooperation "with any party or group that stands for equality, brotherhood, and peace. The other parties have been in power and have failed to bring about that brotherhood in which Russia excels the rest of the world."

Some suspected the Reds had supplied some green to the Blacks—though, in Divine's case, that seemed unlikely. "I never got any money from Moscow," he protested. "It's the other way around, in fact. I don't altogether agree with them, but I've helped them, some."

March 1935's Harlem riots accelerated Divine's emphasis on the political—and toward the CPUSA. On May Day 1935, two thousand of his followers marched alongside Communists to Union Square, where he urged cooperation to "abolish racial discrimination, eradicate prejudice, and establish the fundamentals which stand for the good of humanity. . . . Unify yourselves with righteousness and justice." His acolytes roared back, "Amen, Father!"

That same month, his newspaper, *The Spoken Word*, proclaimed: "[I]ntelligent members of the Communist Party . . . are rapidly coming to the realization that violence or force cannot contain the answer to their problems. They are . . . becoming convinced that a united front and a peaceful orderly process of the electorate is the best means of obtaining their ends. The Communists are the only outstanding organization or party with enough courage to stand flatly for social equality or equal opportunity, regardless of race, creed, or color. . . . With the unrest gripping the world . . . every true American and Christian should unite himself with these principles of peace and equality, even if it brings upon him the label of 'Communist.'"

As 1936 ("A. D. F. D."—"Anno Domini Father Divine") opened, Divine presided over a three-day "International Righteous Government Convention" at West 69th Street's grimy St. Nicholas Arena, better remembered as the site of well over ten thousand boxing matches—and where, for good measure, at a CPUSA testimonial dinner, Pete Seeger later publicly debuted "If I Had a Hammer."

Divine's stronghold remained Harlem. But his five thousand delegates arrived from all over, with New Jersey, California, and Washington State noteworthy in their presence. By now, Divine grandly claimed that "twenty-two million have recognized [me] as their Saviour come to Earth again in Bodily Form."

The CPUSA's James Ford and Robert Minor addressed attendees. So did a representative of the Townsend Plan. FDR and Pope Pius XI received invitations to attend. They didn't.

John Lamb read the new movement's platform—for hours. "All [of its] sections, . . ." reported the *New York Amsterdam News*, "no matter how contradictory, were greeted enthusiastically with hand-clapping, led . . . by the little cult leader himself." Many planks dealt with race and discrimination, ranging from legislation "to abolish lynching" to "making it a crime for any employer to discharge an employee, even though insubordinate, when even circumstantial evidence can be introduced to show that it was on account of race, creed or color" to "making it a crime for any Newspaper, Magazine, or other Publication to use segregated or slang words referring to race, creed or color of any individual or group, or write abusively concerning any."

Its mish-mosh platform included:

> Abolition of all tariff schedules.
>
> Legislation limiting profit on manufactured articles.
>
> Government operation of the financial institutions of the country.
>
> Destruction of all counterfeit money, at the expense of whoever first finds out it is counterfeit. There must be no attempt to pass it on.
>
> True followers of Father Divine must immediately and henceforth stop buying on the installment plan.
>
> Enactment of laws against all newspapers and publications which employ words designating the difference in creeds, races and conditions of peoples.
>
> Enactment of a law prohibiting vaccinations and prohibiting all kinds of compulsory medical examinations.
>
> Immediate return of all stolen goods, either by individuals or by nations.
>
> Immediate enactment of the law fixing the maximum fee which can be charged by a labor union for membership; and a

law prohibiting labor unions from calling strikes unless they pay, during the strike, to all their members, the full wage for which they are striking.

The abolition of capital punishment.

All candidates, including the president must be nominated directly by the people. Immediate abandonment of a patronage system.

The enactment of laws requiring the government to take over all plants, factories and tools whose owners refuse to use or to operate them at their full capacity.

Many a wacky idea lay not-so-dormant. Divine, for example, opposed Social Security, not on any narrow bookkeeping, or even constitutional, grounds but upon more cosmic ones. "As far as taking out insurances," he orated, "we will not tolerate it and I would tell the President so," for to possess insurance was "to mistrust God and visualize disappointments, failures, accidents, and disasters."

And this: "The physicians and doctors must guarantee a cure, and a complete cure and the lives of the individuals. If not, they will be held responsible, and sued for the death of the person or persons. Remember this is RIGHTEOUSNESS and JUSTICE and TRUTH and we must have it. . . . When the physician takes charge of you physically, he must guarantee your health and complete happiness."

Not surprisingly, anyone posing as God (and managing to convince others of his claim) thought big—very big. "There will be one language, English," Divine blithered, "one speech and one flag, American, when the government which I have exemplified and brought to fruition shall have been established in all of the people. For I say, all of the nations of the earth politically must be brought into subjection of the government universally for the people, by the people, and through the people, shall perish from the earth without me."

Thus, the CPUSA and their newfound friend might not agree on *everything*. But in the Brave New World of United Fronts, such small points were hardly deal-breakers. What remained off-limits, however, was any significant friction on labor policy, on unions. Father Divine hated unions, fuming (occasionally ungrammatically):

> Why should the Unions try to control the people and put them in slavery? They must deal JUSTLY, and it may undoubtedly be a battle on hand. In the places where they work in different Factories, talking about the Unions coming in and snatching men and women up from their work, when they are working getting an honest living! It is Wonderful! I will call a STRIKE on the Unions if they will not deal justly. That is what I will do! I will call a strike on the Unions! They have oppressed the widow and the orphan, and the hireling in his wages, long enough. It is indeed Wonderful! Going under the name of Unions, and will not guarantee work for the people!
>
> Every Union that tries to bind the people and put them back in slavery, and prohibit them from working when they are trying to get an honest living—if they do not pay their dues how DARE they put their hands on an individual! Now tell them I Said KEEP THEIR HANDS OFF! This Country does not belong to the Unions, it belongs to GOD. It is indeed Wonderful! The very IDEA, talking about going into men's shops where they have paid for, and paid taxes in this City, and putting men and women out of the jobs. I will PUT A STOP TO IT! Now tell them I SAID it, and I MEAN IT!"

Communists, shall we say, disagreed, though expressing their reservations *very, very* gently: "We believe that Father Divine's trade union stand is a confused reflection of the discrimination which Negroes have suffered in many unions." The party's continuing soft-shoe with the messianic Divine, however, merely provided grist for the mill for rival Marxists. The Lovestoneite "Communist Opposition" splinter group taunted their old CPUSA comrades in their journal, *Workers Age*:

> That Divine is a Negro, that his demagogy demands the use of radical phrases and pretence of friendship for Communists, does not dilute his poison or change it into milk! Let us speak plainly: to play with a dangerous faker simply because he has mass support and because his color denotes membership of an oppressed race, is suicide for Communists. The anti-labor demagogues amongst the Negro masses must be exposed and fought!

> Marx defined the trade unions as the "elementary" training school of the working-class, where workers take the first firm steps forward on the road to liberation. Divine would crush these basic organizations of the mass of workers! Regardless of what or how he prattles about anything else, his bitter animosity to the trade union shows up his true colors. What makes him "Progressive," comrades of the CP?
>
> The Communist Party will reap a whirlwind of destruction for playing with Divine. The Divine movement is nourished by the enemies of Communism; its primary purpose is to annihilate Communist influence in Harlem. It is not accidental that the Divine movement arose and became powerful precisely when the Communists were beginning to make marked headway in Harlem.

Father Divine grew ever more political. He clearly eyed moving into more partisan spheres. But if his goals (and rhetoric) seemed murky, his political maneuvering proved totally opaque. His goal, said Divine, was not a new party, yet he boasted of "preparing thousands in New York City to pass the literacy test in the next presidential election."

Would they vote Communist? Or a business-backed junta? The *New York Amsterdam News* reported that one of the movement's top men, Paul Christian, stated that Divine would "back a president . . . through whom his spirit will work, and about whom he will place twelve good business men to direct the politics of the country."

Or FDR? "If President Roosevelt acts with righteousness, Justice and Truth," announced convention acting chairman Arthur Madison, "he will have the support of all the followers of Father Divine."

Or Father Divine himself? For, as Paul Christian also orated, "Hoover could not straighten out this country. President Roosevelt has failed to straighten out this country. But God Almighty Father Divine will straighten it out!"

Catholics, Communists, Democrats, Townsendites—Father reached out to them all. In 1932, like most Blacks, he had supported Herbert Hoover. It remained "essential," he then had exhorted, "for every man to accept, therefore, Mr. Hoover who promised to support and protect equal rights."

In 1936, however, he exhibited far less interest in a party, who, unlike the Communists or the Democrats, remained officially unsure of their choice of a candidate. The Party of Lincoln, the Grand Old Party, the much-battered Republicans, still had some deciding to do.

· 13 ·

"Dumb-bells, freaks, rubes and hicks"

It doesn't take very long, however, to sort things out when you don't have that much to sort.

Republicans had damned little to sort.

Competing in a compact, comparatively unknown field, Bill Borah assumed an early lead in an August 1935 survey of 3,200 party leaders:

	TOTAL VOTES	FIRST-PLACE VOTES
William E. Borah	368	247
Frank Knox	260	160
Frank Lowden (former governor of Illinois)	176	97
Arthur Vandenberg	126	88
Herbert Hoover	75	52

Former Illinois governor Frank Lowden's big moment had occurred way back in 1920, when he unsuccessfully competed for that year's GOP nod. Four years later, Republican delegates offered him the vice-presidential slot. He declined it. That contemporary Republicans favored a nearly seventy-five-year-old non-candidate like Lowden over Vandenberg and Hoover should have provided both with pause.

Real polling (in the form of Dr. George Gallup's Institute of American Politics) commenced in December 1935, revealing a two-man contest. Frank Lowden mercifully vanished. Alf Landon now assumed a substantial lead. Herbert Hoover bumped slightly up. Dr. Gallup reported:

Alf Landon	33%
William E. Borah	26%
Herbert Hoover	12%
Theodore Roosevelt Jr.	12%
Frank Knox	8%
Ogden Mills	5%
Arthur Vandenberg	3%
Iowa Sen. Lester J. "L. J." Dickinson	1%

Later that January, another private straw poll measured what might best be termed likely GOP voters. Prorating its percentages into raw votes, the totals were now:

Landon	8,400,000
Knox	3,900,000
Hoover	3,700,000
Borah	2,600,000
Vandenberg	1,400,000

Landon led everywhere except for the Northeast and the Pacific, peaking, not surprisingly, in the Midwest. Hoover's modest rise most likely stemmed from his increased visibility. Vandenberg led in Michigan but nowhere else.

On February 23, Gallup eliminated both TR Jr. and Ogden Mills and reported that Landon was for real:

Landon	43%
Borah	28%
Hoover	17%
Knox	7%
Vandenberg	4%
Dickinson	1%

Landon's effort accelerated. California governor Frank Merriam pledged support. Closer to home, Kansas's John D. M. Hamilton resigned from the Republican National Committee, announced he'd tour for Landon, bought some stationery, and opened a national headquarters in Washington. Hamilton's endorsement was indeed significant. Kansas's Republican Party was an ideological jumble: Landon, William Allen White, and former governor Henry Allen represented progressives. Former governor Clyde Reed lay beyond their Left. Hamilton, former vice president Charles Curtis, and Klan-backed former governor Ben Paulen staked out the Right. Hamilton's cross-ideological support for fellow Kansan Landon spelled trouble for both Knox and Hoover.

But nearly half of all Republicans remained undecided. Borah retained his supporters, but otherwise the ground was shifting steadily toward Landon. Author and psychologist Dr. Daniel Starch ran something called "Polling America"—which he billed as a "Nationally recognized Fact Finding Service." As 1936 opened, he found:

	JANUARY 4, 1936	MARCH 18, 1936
Landon	14.8%	25.1%
Borah	14.0%	14.5%
Hoover	15.3%	6.0%
Knox	8.2%	4.0%
Others	4.2%	4.3%
Undecided	45.9%	46.1%

The primaries commenced. Frank Knox had the field to himself in New Hampshire. Borah captured ultra-progressive Wisconsin, snaring twenty-one of its twenty-four delegates, the rest held by an Old Guard "uncommitted" slate.

In November, a win is a win. In presidential primaries, the wrong sort of victory spells defeat. In his new "home state" of Illinois, Frank Knox enjoyed considerable advantages. He was a "Favorite Son." Virtually every paper in the state backed him. So did 99 of 102 GOP county organizations, including the still-powerful Cook County group. He had money, and for weeks he crisscrossed the state, orating to whoever might hear him. Borah helicoptered in for a week and, with neither money nor manpower, made it a horse race. Knox took Cook County by 110,000 votes but bombed elsewhere, losing the rest of the state by 40,000 votes. Borah captured ten of fifteen downstate congressional districts and held Knox to 54 percent of the total vote. Bending the truth only a little, the maverick Idahoan bragged, "Frank Knox carried Chicago, but I carried Illinois."

Borah might crow in Illinois. But on the very same day, the identical principle of defeat-in-victory ambushed him in Nebraska. He captured an impressive 74 percent of the vote. But Alf Landon not only secured 25 percent via write-ins—he garnered twelve of fourteen uninstructed delegates.

By now, Dr. Gallup's polls revealed a commanding and sustained Landon advantage:

	APRIL 5, 1936	MAY 3, 1936
Landon	56%	56%
Borah	20%	19%
Hoover	14%	14%
Knox	5%	4%
Vandenberg	4%	5%
Dickinson	1%	1%
	100%	100%

The race turned ugly. Borah's forces began painting Landon as the "Old Guard" candidate. As Landon biographer Donald McCoy enumerated, they flung "flimsy accusations that Landon was linked with

Standard Oil, the American Liberty League, the Republican old guard, the Chamber of Commerce; . . . that he was a 'bolter' and an Anti-Saloon Leaguer [Kansas being dry], and a millionaire who favored big business and Wall Street." Less fancifully, they painted him as the Hearst candidate.

A string of small primaries followed. Landon avoided officially entering any—partly by design, partly by necessity—for, as William Allen White cautioned him in February 1936, "You have no money. You cannot get much honest money."

"I have no trouble with my enemies," Warren Harding once grumbled; "I can take care of my enemies in a fight. But my friends, my G-d Damn friends, they're the ones who keep me walking the floor at nights!" Alf Landon's most problematic friend was his most powerful friend—William Randolph Hearst. In early April 1936, William Allen White editorialized: "Professionally, Hearst is a form of poison. Politically, he has degenerated into a form of suicide. Whoever ties up with him begins to smell of lilies and attract the undertaker."

In California, Landon's—and Hearst's—allies entered Landon in their May 5 primary, outraging organization Republicans committed to an uncommitted slate (I know, that doesn't sound right). The blunder became readily apparent, but it was too late, and Landon captured just 43 percent of the vote versus favorite-son candidate—Alameda County's district attorney and Louis B. Mayer's successor as state GOP chairman—forty-five-year-old Earl Warren.

The last big contest transpired on May 12 in Ohio. Actually, there were two Buckeye State contests, the first being a meaningless "beauty contest" vote where Borah faced former comptroller of the currency Stephen A. Day. No one paid much attention to that. The real action, as always, lay for delegates, where Borah faced favorite son Robert A. Taft. Taft, out of office since losing his state senate seat in 1932, walloped Borah 3–2 in the popular vote and crushed him in securing delegates. Ohio Republicans, crowed Taft, chose "a candidate and . . . a platform uncompromisingly opposed to President Roosevelt and the New Deal."

Lost in the shuffle was this: Alice Roosevelt Longworth won election as a delegate—a Taft delegate.

Also, in Ohio, a candidate named "M. Herbert Hoover" trailed badly in the GOP primary for congressman-at-large. Nationwide, Herbert Clark Hoover seemed trapped in runner-up status. Perhaps comforted by the fact that Bill Borah also lay dead in the water, Hoover pondered his exit.

He did not exit gracefully.

On Saturday, May 16, 1936, at a summer resort at Blue Ridge Summit, Maryland, Hoover informed associates that he could support any Republican candidate save Borah—his actual preferences being Vandenberg, Knox, Iowa's L. J. Dickinson (running, it was said, only to salvage his embattled Senate seat), and, dead last, Alf Landon. Two days later, in Chicago, he withdrew in exceedingly Hooveresque fashion. As if conducting a news conference (which he wasn't), he composed a question-and-answer session grumpily detailing his exodus. From Hoover's Chicago hotel suite, his secretary, Paul Saxon, distributed typed copies to reporters. Its key provision read:

> I am not a candidate. I have stated many times that I have no interest but to get these critical issues before the country. I have rigidly prevented my friends from setting up any organization and from presenting my name in any primary or to any state convention, and not a single delegate from California or any other state is pledged to me. That should end such discussion.
>
> And get one thing straight. I am not opposing any of the candidates. My concern is with principles.

Hoover himself made no comment and boarded the 6:15 p.m. for Palo Alto.

Jim Farley entrained for Grand Rapids.

Farley served as the great utility man of the administration. He could play every position: chairman of the New York Democratic Committee, Democratic National Chairman, FDR campaign manager, cabinet member, and masterful dispenser of whatever patronage escaped Harold Ickes's or Harry Hopkins's eager grasp.

He journeyed to Grand Rapids in the last four of those capacities. Officially, he traveled as postmaster general, to anoint fifty-eight-year-old housewife Florence Abbott as postmistress of Ann Arbor, Michigan. That Mrs. Abbott was the widow of former Democratic National Committeeman Horatio J. Abbott was, of course, purely coincidental.

Distributing jobs to deserving Democratic widows and orphans was very nice. But what really propelled Farley westward (after all, as postmaster general, he could have easily *mailed* the appointment to Mrs. Abbott) was Michigan's Democratic state convention. Frank Murphy had been lured back from Manila to run for governor and anchor this key state for FDR. Hopes even flashed of enticing New Deal–leaning GOP US senator James Gould Couzens into the party. "You have never voted with the Republicans, . . ." Murphy now advised Couzens. "You can't win as a Republican. You can win as a Democrat"

Jim Farley was also there to bash Republican front-runner Alf Landon.

"This gentleman [Landon]," harangued Farley, "may be all his boosters present him as being, but he is nearly 50 years old, and it would be something new if he possessed all the magnificent qualities of administration, all the knowledge of public questions, all the noble attributes with which his champions endow him, without his fame getting beyond the borders of his own state."

So far, so good, but Farley continued:

> I am not, of course, in possession of exact knowledge of why the Republican Party chooses to put him on a pedestal, but if I were permitted to guess I would be inclined to believe it was because he was elected governor of a typical prairie state that has usually been Republican, and that the du Pont Liberty League crowd is less afraid of him than it is of the more widely known and more experienced statesmen . . . mentioned in connection with the Republican nomination.

. . . a typical prairie state . . .

Jim Farley was a good politician, but he was a good *New York* politician, and he should have realized that while one might denigrate opponents, one should tread warily in maligning entire states, let alone entire prairies.

"Perhaps," retorted the angry Kansas freshman congressman Frank Carlson, "Mr. Farley thinks that because the people out in the middle Midwest live in the prairie states, as did Lincoln, who was never heard of very much before his elevation to the presidency, they are all dumb-bells, freaks, rubes and hicks."

Angering Frank Carlson was one thing. Angering FDR was another. Jim Farley's boss—invariably as perceptive as any politician might be—was not amused:

> Memorandum for J. A. F. [James A. Farley]
> I thought we had decided that any reference to Landon or any other Republican candidate was inadvisable.
>
> Now that the water is over the dam, I told [Democratic National Committee publicity director Charles] Michelson that possibly a somewhat facetious reference to Frank Knox . . . by you might soften the effect of the Landon reference.
>
> Another good rule which should be passed down the line to all who are concerned with speech material is that no section of the country should be spoken of as typical but only with some laudatory adjectives. If the sentence had read "one of those splendid prairie states," no one could have picked us up on it, but the word "typical" coming from any New Yorker is meat from the opposition.
>
> F. D. R.

With Landon's nomination growing into a sure thing, Republicans anticipated giving FDR a run for his money—with a candidate unhindered by responsibility for the Great Depression. There had been "Hoover Blankets" and "Hoovervilles," but nary a "Landon Blanket" or "Landonville." Just sensible balanced Kansas budgets and huge cheerful Kansas sunflowers—the symbol of his campaign—festooned with his name.

Even ardent New Deal sympathizers now questioned Franklin's invulnerability. Journalist Ernest K. Lindley wrote:

> It has become almost a commonplace to blame [Louis] Howe's illness for Mr. Roosevelt's blunders during the past year or so.

> Now that Howe has gone to the shadows, many observers are wondering—some of them with ill-concealed hope—if Mr. Roosevelt will not begin to crack. For the legend held that Howe, a wise, shrewd, cautious and outspoken man, was the one force which held an "impulsive," "erratic" President in check.

In *The American Mercury*, H. L. Mencken chortled: "There was a time when the Republicans were scouring the country for a behemoth to pit against [Roosevelt]. Now they begin to grasp the fact that, if they can beat him at all, which seems most likely, they can best him with a Chinaman, or even a Republican. The only issue is Roosevelt. Is he a hero, as his parasites allege, or a quack[?] . . . Every vote will be cast either for him or against him. His opponent will be only the residuary legatee, the innocent bystander."

The Supreme Court was not bystanding—nor chortling. It continued stirring things up. On May 18, it invalidated the Bituminous Coal Conservation Act (the so-called Guffey Act), a measure about which FDR had famously and artlessly conceded having "doubts about [its] constitutionality" before his submitting it to Congress. On June 1, the Court struck again, overturning a New York State law regulating minimum wages for women and children. In a 5–4 decision, *Morehead v. New York ex rel Tipaldo*, Justice Pierce Butler wrote:

> The right to make contracts about one's affairs is a part of the liberty protected by the due process clause. Within this liberty are provisions of contracts between employer and employee fixing the wages. . . . In making contracts of employment, generally speaking, the parties have equal right to obtain from each other the best terms they can by private bargaining.

Previous High Court decisions had limited *federal* power to regulate hours and wages and business at large. *Tipaldo* struck at *state* power and was even too much for many Republicans. Editorial opinion ran almost unanimously negative. Only 10 of 344 newspapers approved. Herbert Hoover snapped, "Something should be done to give the states back the powers they thought they already had." A "frankly shocked" Rep.

Hamilton Fish damned it as "a new Dred Scott decision condemning millions . . . to economic slavery."

To his diary, Harold Ickes fumed, "If this decision does not outrage the moral sense of the country, then nothing will. . . . [I]f this decision is constitutional, we need either an entirely new or a radically amended Constitution. If it isn't constitutional, then we need a different Supreme Court."

Tipaldo accelerated New Deal complaints of an out-of-control High Court. It short-circuited any GOP defense of the Court. As Attorney General Homer Cummings consoled his chief, "While in a certain sense [these decisions] are a setback for America, they are a godsend to the administration. . . . We are no longer on the defensive."

Meanwhile, an invariably futile "Stop-[Fill-in-the-Blank]" movement arrived right on time. In June 1936, that "Blank" (in more ways than one) was Alfred Mossman Landon.

Convention delegates pulled in to Cleveland. Hollywood's Cecil B. DeMille (a "wet" defector to FDR in 1932) arrived as an Earl Warren delegate—his first foray to Cleveland since playing Hamlet in 1903: "I'm no politician," C. B. beamed, "but it's a wonderful experience."

William Allen White proposed amending the platform to neutralize *Tipaldo*, advocating a constitutional amendment allowing state regulation of hours and wages. "That need is the issue of the hour, . . ." urged White. "The Republican Party must not let the Democrats fire the first shot in the new battle for human freedom." Borah, being Borah, opposed him. So did Frank Knox. Until he didn't—which took a full day.

Ohioans seemed unusually busy. Robert A. Taft dropped out as a candidate. The state's delegates—as wary of "Herbert C. Hoover" as its voters had been of "M. Herbert Hoover"—dumped Hoover's old postmaster general (and patronage dispenser), the rather prissy Walter F. Brown, as their national committeeman. Concurrently, they nixed Alice Roosevelt Longworth's appointment to the resolutions committee, "for no reason that seemed significant in the larger convention sense," opined the *New York Times*'s Arthur Krock.

The print commentariat arrived in force, sharpening their wits and their daggers. Westbrook Pegler took aim at Governor Alf's homespun-oil-millionaire ways, down to his choice of a campaign song. Teddy

Roosevelt had marched to "Onward Christian Soldiers." Al Smith owned "The Sidewalks of New York." FDR won delegates and votes with "Happy Days Are Here Again." Landon, having neither come from Alabama, nor heading for Louisiana, or even possessing a banjo, selected the old chestnut "Oh, Susannah" (albeit with new lyrics) as his battle hymn. The tune played an estimated eight hundred times at the convention, driving Pegler to distraction:

> Alfred M. Landon's campaign song might be appropriate if you were running for the glee club, but for a man who wants to be president of the United States "Oh, Susanna," seems an unfortunate selection. This is a song reminiscent of the covered wagon, which antedates even the horse-and-buggy days that Mr. Roosevelt had in mind the time he flung his glove in the air and pulled a petulant snoot at the umpire because the Supreme Court ruled against him on a close one at the plate. It is a mandolin or guitar song, moreover, and is associated with ice tea and ginger snaps on the old front stoop. Surely someone in the Landon party should realize that this is an age of saxophones and swingy stuff and whiskey sours at the Lido Carbondale Supper Club or the Dallas Deauville Dine and Dance.
>
> Mr. Landon ought to get hot.

Henry Louis Mencken conversely professed Alfred Mossman Landon's hotness deficit as not merely inconsequential, but, perhaps, even, somehow highly utilitarian. "Assuming that the country is ready for a change," assessed the invariably erroneous Sage of Baltimore, "what it really wants is a president with no ideas at all. After more than three years of lunatic ideas, it is eager for a rest. I have always said that only a man of the type of Harding or Coolidge could beat Roosevelt, and I suppose it will be some fifth rate man like Landon. The Republicans need someone who never said anything that can be remembered, or did anything that can be recalled, and in consequence never offended anyone. This Landon has succeeded in ducking all the major issues, and such ducking requires skill."

Over NBC radio at 11:00 p.m. (ET) on Sunday, June 7, Harold Ickes unleashed a tirade against not so much Landon as against his most enthusiastic supporter, William Randolph Hearst, alleging not only that Hearst was the Kansan's "discoverer and principal backer" but also that W. R. would "do the final editing" of the proposed GOP platform.

Hearst in turn blasted Ickes's indictment as "rather absurd" and "particularly vapid," which, even by Washington standards, Ickes's supposedly humorous barbs often were. Landon, Hearst confidently projected, "will be elected. Mr. Ickes obviously believes this also. Otherwise he would not be working with the reactionaries in the Republican Party . . . to prevent Gov. Landon's nomination."

W. R. soon proclaimed:

> FORWARD WITH LANDON
>
> What the American people will have to decide this fall has never been more concisely and luminously expressed than by Alfred M. Landon in an address at the University of Kansas when he said:
>
> "WE WILL HAVE TO DECIDE WHETHER THIS RETREAT OF CIVILIZATION SHALL SPREAD TO OUR OWN COUNTRY OR WHETHER THIS RETREAT SHOULD BE TURNED BACK FROM OUR SHORES BEFORE IT IS TOO LATE."
>
> The retreat of European civilization began when Russia became Communistic instead of democratic in 1917.
>
> That was the first great thrust at DEMOCRATIC INDIVIDUALISM, which had been steadily evolving toward Jeffersonian principles since 1776—since Runnymede, in fact.
>
> Then followed the murder of democracy in Germany, Italy, Austria and Hungary and the MARCH BACK TO THE TOTALITARIAN NIGHT OF THE MIDDLE AGES.
>
> With the inauguration of President Roosevelt "the Retreat of civilization" reached America.
>
> The European invasion of America began with the NRA.

> REGIMENTATION and BUREAUCRACY—the twin tyrants—rear their heads for the first time in this country—sponsored by a party which was apostate to its great origins.
>
> Now comes Alfred M. Landon, who WILL turn back this tide away from Europe of MARXIAN COLLECTIVISM AND FASCIST BUREAUCRACY which is known as the New Deal—but which, in reality, is a deal as OLD as human slavery.
>
> FORWARD with Landon to a rebirth of AMERICAN CIVILIZATION!

Conversely, *The Nation*'s Heywood Broun declared that "the voters of America are being asked to preserve democracy by turning the rulership of this country over to William Randolph Hearst."

"Cleveland," the *New Masses*'s Marguerite Young revealed to her no-doubt terrified readership, "was a composite picture of the burgeoning forces of American fascism. You winced at the visible portents. Should fascism triumph, what barbarity, what death of culture. Here were vulgarity, banality, innate cruelty and violence."

Actually, Cleveland's environs were merely awash with unusual concentrations of Masons, Rotarians, county clerks, Methodists, former postmasters—and, not to be outdone, various relatives of either Theodore Roosevelt or William Howard Taft. Though it must be admitted that most, at one weak moment or another, might indeed have subscribed to a Hearst paper—at least its Sunday edition.

Before proceedings convened, a few GOP women attempted drafting Alice Roosevelt Longworth for president in an attempt "to consolidate the women's vote against the New Deal." Delegates weren't interested—and neither was she. "I am perfectly sure," she demurred, "that in one brief speech I could guarantee to antagonize militarists and pacifists, business and labor, wets and drys, sound-money men and inflationists, rugged individualists and economic planners. In fact I might easily be Exhibit A of the worst-defeated candidate who ever ran for office."

Backroom horse-trading commenced, much of it involving the hitherto lifeless Arthur Vandenberg. "Two conflicting psychologies took possession of Cleveland," Vandenberg mused. "The paradox is that most delegates believe both of them. One: Landon will be nominated on the first ballot. Two: if he isn't by the third ballot, I will be."

Borah, aloof from any stop-Landon cabal, trained his fire on the platform, demanding it ring even more isolationist than originally drafted. He opposed William Allen White's *Tipaldo* constitutional amendment. He opposed any attempt to revive the gold standard.

Landon, too, fretted over the platform committee, where the party's embattled Old Guard clung uneasily to power. Its sway would soon jeopardize the party's gossamer unity.

For those hoping against hope for a ninth-inning upset of Landon, two convention addresses gave—and quickly took away—hope. Oregon US senator Frederick Steiwer, a big man with a big, booming voice, delivered the keynote address. The *Washington Star* observed that he "looks like a candidate," and if Steiwer did not quite look *presidential*, he at least looked *vice* presidential. The Oregonian was good enough to bring the crowd to its feet but not himself to the ticket. As national politics shifted portside, the mildly progressive Steiwer blundered by steering too starboard a course. A deeply disappointed (and perhaps even shocked) Walter Lippmann viewed the Oregonian's talk as "profoundly reactionary. . . . [N]o Democrat who had any interest in principles could give active support to . . . the spirit and the ideas of Senator Steiwer's speech."

Less politely, Heywood Broun groused that "some had the audacity to refer to Senator Steiwer as an orator even after he had delivered his keynote speech."

Politics makes strange bedfellows. Rumormongers concoct stranger ones still. Whispers flew of a Hoover–Borah "Stop-Landon" tête-à-tête. Hoover, meanwhile, had actually suggested to Knox and Vandenberg that they surrender their few delegates to him—absolutely enraging Knox. Rumors also circulated of a Landon–Borah detente. All the while, Borah, Knox, and Vandenberg denied interest in any "Stop Landon" alliance.

Borah was not well. He had bestirred himself to a semblance of his old vigor for this campaign. But it was just that: a semblance, not a reality. One day around noon, William Allen White dropped into Borah's hotel suite. Decades previously, they had been classmates at the University of

Kansas. He now found Borah abed, attired in a striped gown, "sheltered by nurses in a darkened room." They chatted "amiably," concentrating on the few items of conversation they might agree upon. Borah bestirred himself to escort White out, two old warriors, their best days and most glorious battles almost entirely behind them. "Well, goodbye; I am glad you came," said Borah, his arm around White. He held White's hand. White, for once hard-pressed for words, responded, "Funny, isn't it?"

"It certainly is," the aged Lion of Idaho meekly responded.

Soon taking the podium was the Republican Party's very own version of "The Man Who Came to Dinner": Herbert Hoover. When Hoover last visited Cleveland in October 1932, he had blundered into the midst of a contentious strike, and workers' catcalls rang in his ears. Four years later, between six and eight thousand persons boisterously greeted his Union Terminal arrival. "Herbert Hoover," they shouted, "Hoover. Hoover, we want four more years of Hoover."

Later, at Cleveland's Public Auditorium, another throng hailed him with equal élan. "Wild lightning flashed over Lake Erie and rain poured down on the skylights of the Great Hall," reported Hearst's *New York Evening Journal*; "fifteen thousand persons alternated rapt attention and thunderous cheers as the graying man from California made perhaps the finest speech of his life.

"No orator, Mr. Hoover, and still baffled and beset with the difficulties of trying to read prepared copy before a microphone, so that to one-half of the hall his face was almost completely obliterated by his manuscript, the 'Savior of Belgium' nevertheless turned the hall into a screaming bedlam, and departed to the echo of long cheers that must have been sweet music and soft solace to a man for whom the cheers have not been too prolonged or thunderous through the past six years."

Convention organizers had installed a "demonstramoter," a ten-foot-high "applause barometer" to measure noise levels. Frederick Steiwer and House Minority Leader Bertram Snell ("as hard-shelled a reactionary who ever lived") both scored a middling 60. Hoover's mere arrival shot it up to 80. His speech hit the maximum 100.

"When [Hoover] finished speaking," his adviser David Hinshaw recalled, "the assembled delegates broke into round after round of applause and cheers which gained strength, as they swept along. State standards fell into line and the marching began. I was standing on the convention floor at the time and watching the swift growth of a stampede."

A Southern delegate (presumably African-American) inquired, "What's it mean, Mr. Dave?" Hinshaw answered, "I think these people are trying to tell Mr. Hoover that they are ashamed of the way they doubted him and deserted him and that now they know him to be their party's and the nation's finest and greatest man and are trying to convince him that their hearts are with him."

The delegate responded, "I think it means that they're going to nominate him!"

They weren't. Delegate noise means little. Hoover—efficiency expert to the end—wasted little time basking in his half-hour ovation, ducking out to his hotel room for a quick rest before catching yet another train, this time for New York.

Hoovermania aside, gloom pervaded the hall. New York's *Herald Tribune* spoke of a "soberness, bordering on the somber"—a glumness reaching down into even a lack of physical color, of flags and even a decent amount of bunting. "I started as a boy of eleven when my father took me to . . . Cincinnati in 1876," groused former US Senate Majority Leader James Watson. "This is the darndest [convention] I ever saw and the dullest."

Soon, everyone recognized that the triumph of the most lackluster candidate of recent memory—Alf Landon—was inevitable. Had Leni Riefenstahl filmed this rally, she would have titled her production *Triumph of the Dull.* It was an easy triumph, so easy that only he was placed in nomination. John D. M. Hamilton (his chin heavily bandaged from too hasty a shave) heralded his candidate as: "a man who met his payrolls . . . a modern American—unpretentious, unassuming, willing to serve—but not eager to dictate. Here is a homely record, if you will, and here are homely virtues and common sense aims. Here is no gilt and here no theatrical dramatics, no overwhelming egotism, no self-righteousness, no pretense of supremacy. Here is a man who is the product of our own country and our own time, who has made his way as we have had to make ours."

Blah.

Blah.

Blah.

Seconding speeches were limited to five minutes. Massachusetts's patrician former lieutenant governor Gaspar Griswold Bacon led off. In 1934, Bacon, son of a onetime TR Secretary of State, ran a losing race for governor against Boston mayor James M. Curley. Hoping to capitalize on Bacon's upper-crust image, Curley dispatched a Bacon look-alike to motor about Beantown in a huge limousine, barking at humble workmen (i.e., voters) to "stop leaning on your shovels." Well, that's the story, anyway.

Eleanor and Alice's cousin Corinne Robinson Alsop followed. So did African-American Perry W. Howard, Mississippi's "Black-and-Tan" national committeeman. With spread-eagle oratory, the light-skinned, mixed-race Perry proclaimed:

> Those who have preceded me represent the Nordic segment of the Grand Old Party. I speak for the segment, though darker, but to whom what is done here means more than to any others of the heterogeneous elements that make up this great political whole.
>
> I am able to speak for them because of what [Sen. Charles] Sumner did, [Preacher Elijah] Lovejoy did, John Brown did, and what the greatest of Americans did—Abraham Lincoln. (Applause) Lovejoy died for us. Sumner was assaulted into insensibility by a Southerner for us. John Brown sleeps as a martyr with a felon's rope around his neck. And Lincoln was a martyr to our cause. These men—these men—were all Republicans. . . .
>
> When God wanted to save the world He went to the lonely stalls of the manger and gave His only Son. When a leader was needed to safely lead the Israelites out of the wilderness, He went into the bushes and brought forth Moses. . . . [T]he great God who spoke on Mt. Sinai, has seen fit to call forth a leader, and the prairies of Kansas, the Kansas of John Brown, have furnished the atmosphere and the environment with which to choose a liberator from these conditions.

> I have studied his record in Kansas and to Governor Landon Negroes are American citizens—nothing more, nothing less. And with Landon in the White House we shall still be American citizens—representing a race that never fired on Old Glory or the flag of our country, and the race that never failed America in peace or war. . . .
>
> Ladies and gentlemen, this picture here tonight is not the work of man but the work of Divine Providence. For when has any man since the time of George Washington received the unanimous call of a people as this great Moses? And I want to assure you that with Landon in the White House, the American people in distress, the American Negroes in the breadlines, know that politics will not be played in their hunger and misery. For this man, who can balance budgets, will be able to balance justice and righteousness for all people.
>
> The twelve million in our group, in this hour, with aching heads and bleeding hearts, oppressed, and proscribed against, believe that in the wisdom of the Almighty, Landon "has come into the kingdom for such a time as this."

Only nineteen die-hard Borah Wisconsin delegates dared dissent as Landon's anointing triggered a near-hysteria. Cowbells rang. Parading delegates hoisted state banners high.

What passed for real excitement, however, had centered on the platform. The platform committee punted on William Allen White's proposed labor-and-hours amendment, contending that regulation could "be done within the Constitution as it now stands." This made no sense because, just eleven days previously, the Supreme Court had ruled it couldn't. John Hamilton issued a dramatic announcement: Landon had telegraphed from Topeka, pledging that if the Supreme Court struck down any new wages-and-hours law, he would "if nominated and elected" favor such an amendment. Furthermore, he provided additional "interpretations" of the platform's gold plank (after threats from Hoover to not otherwise support the ticket) and civil service plank. Only Alton Parker in 1904 and Al Smith in 1928 had previously dared question their party's platform—and then only after their nomination was assured. Landon had dared speak out before a single ballot had been cast or even before Hamilton placed his name in nomination. His unexpected boldness raised his stock nationwide.

Except . . . there *was* no Landon telegram. In reality, he had merely phoned in with a rough outline of his views. Hamilton, however, grasped that an actual document—a ringing declaration—was in order. Alongside the *Kansas City Star*'s Roy Roberts, he hurriedly scribbled its text and rushed out to the lobby's Western Union office—to send it to himself. Before completing his mission, however, he heard an announcement booming over auditorium loudspeakers: he—Hamilton—would now read Landon's "telegram" to the hall. He rushed back in, not reading from even his fake telegram but rather from the text he and Roberts had dashed off just minutes previously.

For his part, Borah fared fairly well on the platform front, scoring key points on foreign affairs, versus monopolies, and in helping stymie White's amendment. But, still sulking as usual, he departed Cleveland without once visiting the convention hall—this despite Hamilton's invitation to address the gathering. "Borah established a new high for disgruntlement," judged columnist John Lardner, "shattering the world's record which Al Smith set up in 1932 and bettered in his Liberty League speech of 1936. To do the Idahoan justice he had plenty of reason to be annoyed. His pledged delegates went around town saying that this here Landon was a pretty good guy, all in all. . . . Then, on top of everything else, somebody asked him if he wanted to be Vice-President.

"William kept his temper by a strong effort and replied, 'no, thanks,' but you could see how that last crack stung him. If Al Smith could take a walk, Borah is entitled to at least a small stroll."

Whether Borah might stroll all the way to Hyde Park remained unknown.

With Landon anointed, speculation accelerated on the second slot. Nearly everyone save Hoover drew at least some mention: Knox; Vandenberg; Frederick Steiwer; L. J. Dickinson; the Liberty League's James Wadsworth; Theodore Roosevelt Jr.; New Hampshire's conservative thirty-eight-year-old governor Styles Bridges; favorite sons former senator Walter Edge of New Jersey and Maryland's current governor Harry Nice, along with FDR's disgruntled first budget director Lewis Douglas and his former AAA director George N. Peek.

Liberty Leaguers hoped for a "coalition" ticket with Joseph Ely as the VP. That plan went nowhere. What Republican chieftains coveted was a disaffected Democrat third-party effort to siphon votes from FDR—by now, however, a total pipe dream.

Maryland GOP chairman J. Cookman Boyd droned on interminably, placing Gov. Harry Nice's name in nomination—and annoying the hell out of the crowd. Along the way, Boyd cited the candidate Nice had defeated for the governorship, the late Albert Ritchie. This, reported the *Dayton Herald*, merely "confused the delegates, . . . many of them thinking that a dead man was being put in nomination and a dead Democrat at that."

Perry Howard seconded the nomination of New York City's Col. Arthur W. Little ("the Anglo-Saxon Moses of the colored race"), a white officer with the Great War's famed "Harlem Hellfighters" regiment. Little very much wanted the nomination, even opening a campaign headquarters.

First to falter was Styles Bridges. *Cleveland Plain Dealer* sports columnist James Doyle pointed out the pitfalls of generating "Landon–Bridges falling down" jibes, and that was that. Arthur Vandenberg had long expressed his own disinterest. He amazed many by actually meaning it, grumpily resisting a midnight knock on the door from John D. M. Hamilton to bend his will. Democratic senator Bennett Champ Clark soon congratulated him on not choosing to ride in "the back seat of a hearse."

Harry Nice, Walter Edge, and even the obscure Colonel Little withdrew. Delegates unanimously nominated Knox, who was, shall we say, dumbstruck—and on the road. Assuming Vandenberg really would accept, he'd already skipped town before receiving news of his own nomination.

The newly fashioned Landon–Knox ticket was history's first fully bespectacled ticket. Knox's Rooseveltian pince-nez presented no great problem. His previous lack of campaign experience and public service did. He entered the political big leagues largely bereft of even minor league experience—and understudying a candidate with only modest "prairie state" credentials and expertise himself.

Critics already flayed Landon as a Hearst creation and puppet. And while Knox was not really one either, he had, in fact, served at the very apex of Hearst publishing. The GOP ticket possessed a huge target on its collective back—a huge bull's eye labeled, as the Lord of San Simeon himself might have styled it, **"HEARST!"**

The Landon–Knox slate was also this: a quarter-century-delayed victory for that old Rough Rider Theodore Roosevelt. In 1912, TR had challenged his former friend and ally William Howard Taft for the presidency. He failed, ran third-party, and managed to elect Woodrow Wilson in the process. Now, 1936's GOP ticket boasted not one but two Bull Moose bolters. Riding alongside was TR's great journalistic friend, William Allen White. And finishing right behind Bull Mooser Landon was Bill Borah—yet another TR-era progressive. Gaspar Bacon, Perry Howard (Teddy's seconder at 1912's GOP convention)—and, of course, Corinne Alsop—were all TR people to their core. Harold Ickes, Henry Wallace, Donald R. Richberg, and even Felix Frankfurter (four more TR bolters) might never admit it, but the Old Guard wing of the Grand Old Party was dead (or at least hibernating).

Yet all was not kosher in Bull Moose alumni land. Though reporters and columnists knew of it, and none would report of it, virtually all were cognizant of vice presidential nominee Knox's affections for Leola Allard. Washington's newspapers now, however, blazed with copious photos of Landon and Knox—with their families. Spying a photo of Col. and Mrs. Knox together, writer Myrtle Williams, herself the wife of a local newsman, exclaimed, "Politics sure does make strange bedfellows!"

Few institutions, however, make stranger bedfellows than Democratic national conventions.

· 14 ·

"It's myself"

Franklin Roosevelt could point with pride to a recovery that had clearly begun. Six million more Americans were working. National income was up by 50 percent. Deflation had vanished. Business was profitable again. The Dow Jones Industrial Index had risen by a full 80 percent. Rural electrification was increasing. A system of old-age pensions, though not yet in place, soon would be. Banks (except for those being robbed in the Midwest) remained open. A lot more Americans now warbled "Happy Days Are Here Again" than "Brother, Can You Spare a Dime?"

But really just how happy were people? The rise of the Kingfish and Father Coughlin, of Dr. Townsend and Upton Sinclair—and, yes, even to a lesser extent, of the Communists—indicated that millions of people were not happy at all. Frightened and angry and disappointed, they sought answers—and were not at all sure that Franklin Roosevelt had them. Or even that as he went on the radio and spoke to "My Friends," he really was anyone's friend.

To Republicans, a great question remained. Once banks had stabilized, how much of the subsequent recovery would have happened without Roosevelt—and without hundreds of millions of dollars of debt and deficits? Without so many pigs slaughtered and fields plowed under in the midst of want. Or without so many millions still unemployed. Had the New Deal actually impeded recovery—and threatened to impede it even more with an increasingly anti–big business rhetoric?

It was the classic question: Was the glass half-empty, or half-full?

Franklin Roosevelt had to convince roughly half the people that the glass was half-full.

He held many advantages. He oozed charm and reassurance. Despite his administration's many speed bumps, he could point to a record of amazing innovation. "[T]ake a method and try it," FDR promised in 1932: "If it fails, admit it frankly and try another." He hadn't always (if ever) admitted failure, but he possessed no shortage of new methods—and many of them delivered tangible benefits: dams, bridges, power lines, playgrounds, swimming pools, airports, golf courses, shiny new post offices chock-full of historic murals—and jobs, jobs, jobs. People liked that. After all, it wasn't their money (although Republicans kept pointing out that it was). His myriad of alphabet agencies employed millions of people and spent billions of dollars. As 1936 commenced, Franklin possessed at least half the vote, though not nearly as solidly as he liked. If Republicans surged and third parties rumbled, he might fall into an Electoral College trap and follow Herbert Hoover into a Depression-cursed, one-term oblivion.

On at least one front—the internal Democratic Party front—the news was uniformly positive. Huey Long had gone to his reward—taking his Share-Our-Wealth Club mailing lists with him. The Liberty League proved less of a threat than a gift. In March, Talmadge forces lost 5–1 (661–120) to FDR loyalists in a special Seminole County, Georgia, primary. A month later, a Mark Sullivan column highlighting anti-FDR Democrats bluntly proclaimed: "Roosevelt Opposition Dies."

It was, however, not officially defunct. Former Assistant Secretary of War Henry Breckinridge slogged away in a trio of state contests, with generally pathetic results: 4.68 percent in Ohio, 6.02 percent in Pennsylvania, and a comparatively whopping 15.11 percent in Maryland. Upton Sinclair (11.8 percent) and pro-Townsend representative John McGroarty (6.41 percent) polled some votes in always-interesting California.

Gene Talmadge chickened out of June's Florida primary. Instead, FDR faced a one-legged New Hampshire dentist named Joseph Coutremarsh. Coutremarsh, who still lived with his mother (a bit like Franklin, actually), favored $60-a-month national pensions, a $30-a-week minimum wage, printing $30 billion in new currency, plus a national lottery. Roosevelt got 89.67 percent of the vote, actually a good bit lower than his usual totals.

With a unified Democratic Party behind him, in mid-March, Dr. George Gallup reported fairly easy pickings for FDR against a generic Republican challenge:

TWO-PARTY VOTE		
	ROOSEVELT	GENERIC REPUBLICAN
All Voters	54.1%	43.4%
Women	56%	44%
Farmers	57%	43%
Young Persons	61%	30%
Reliefers	78%	22%

Not specifically polled were increasingly uneasy businessmen. In January's State of the Nation address, FDR vowed that "based on existing laws . . . no new taxes, over and above the present taxes, are either advisable or necessary." In early March, however, following invalidation of the AAA and passage of the veterans' bonus, he proposed a whopping $620 million levy on undistributed business profits. His forthcoming Revenue Act of 1936 hiked business taxes by $800 million.

As pro–New Deal *Collier's* Washington staff writer George Creel admitted: "Essentially an aristocrat, both by birth and environment, Franklin Roosevelt had the British squire's attitude to 'people in trade,' and as the great industrialists and financiers persisted in their antagonism to the New Deal, dislike deepened into prejudice and distrust. . . . [S]uccess in business or the professions became suspect. Only on park benches and ancestral estates was true nobility to be found."

In April, *Washington Times-Herald* editor Cissy Patterson visited the White House and queried Franklin as to how he might reassure business. "All right," FDR snapped, "you go ahead. Write out exactly what you think I could say that would banish fear. I'll dare you."

FDR picked the wrong woman to dare. She published an open letter to him, commencing:

> Mr. President— . . . You said once, with eternal truth, that the only thing to fear is fear itself. Fear is depressing industry. With due respect, you should concede the obvious. This fear is fear of you. It is fear of shifting policies; of a hostile attitude toward legitimate business; of insistence on discredited tax methods and other laws which prevent the earning and retaining of fair and honest profits.

She implored him to cease his "attacks on groups and individuals who happen to disagree with or criticize you." You should set a high example by clearing your mind of private hates . . . the chief thing is to eliminate fear and thus restore confidence. You alone can do that. But you must do it thoroughly, forsaking hate and vanity, and resuming that patience with which you so nobly and courageously conquered an illness that would have broken the spirit of most of us. You have been a great leader and a great man. You can be again."

He knew better than to respond—and knew he had a far more important document to compose: his acceptance speech.

FDR rarely wrote his own material. He was a raconteur, a motivator, in some sense an entertainer. Certainly a salesman. But not a writer. Like a successful Hollywood studio, he relied on—employed—a team of writers. Movies, it is remarked, are not written but rewritten. So were FDR's addresses, often with different sections pasted together from disparate drafts crafted by subalterns often at odds with each other.

It all worked because Roosevelt worked at it. He oversaw his homilies with a jeweler's eye, rehearsing them over and over, so his words flowed out clear and strong, armed with the right intonation, the proper emphasis, the best mixture of friendliness and wit, mockery and sarcasm and outright rage. In early 1936 he engaged the Radio and Film Methods Corporation to provide him with his addresses' recordings—not from vanity, but mindful of critiquing and ever-improving his already formidable style.

"The speeches as finally delivered were his—and his alone—," recalled his speechwriter Sam Rosenman, "no matter who the collaborators were. . . . No matter how frequently the speech assistants were changed through the years, the speeches were always Roosevelt's. They expressed the personality, the convictions, the spirit, the mood of Roosevelt. No matter who worked with him in the preparation, the finished product was always the same—it was Roosevelt himself."

Rosenman had once assisted Al Smith. He invented Franklin's famous encomium to Smith as "The Happy Warrior." Franklin hated the phrase but read it anyway and read it well, and two stars were born: Smith *and* FDR. Franklin also inherited speechwriter Raymond Moley from Smith, though Moley was never as much a Smith man as was Rosenman. As Ickes and Hopkins feuded, so did Rosenman and Moley. Rosenman found the pipe-puffing Moley "devious" and "morose"; Moley dismissed Rosenman as "smug" and "obsequious."

In 1932, Moley had composed FDR's famed "Forgotten Man" speech. Later, Moley, Rosenman—and Louis Howe (particularly jealous of Rosenman)—all worked on that year's acceptance speech promising a New Deal. By spring 1936, all three had vanished—at least temporarily—from the scene. Howe vanished eternally, of course. Moley traveled to Washington with FDR, but, after a disastrous experience at 1933's London Monetary Conference, departed to edit the newborn *Today* magazine and took an increasingly critical view of the administration. Rosenman, recipient of a coveted state Supreme Court judgeship, remained behind in New York. There, as we recall, he delivered his surprisingly anti-picketing ruling against Harlem protesters.

As the New Deal progressed, Rosenman largely faded away. Moley—despite increasing reservations—continued toiling with Howe, Rex Tugwell, Hugh Johnson, and others to craft presidential addresses.

Over Memorial Day 1936, however, Franklin invited Judge and Mrs. Rosenman to accompany him aboard the USS *Potomac* to cruise upon Chesapeake Bay. Rosenman assumed the visit a social one.

He feared for Roosevelt's reelection chances. "This is only May," Franklin assured him. "Lots of things can happen before November. Tides turn in politics; the sentiment of the voters changes very quickly. Wait until October comes around when we really get a chance to tell the people the facts—which they're not getting now from their newspapers."

Also aboard, as was often the case, was Missy LeHand. But so were relative newcomers Dr. and Mrs. Stanley High. High picked Rosenman's brain on how earlier Roosevelt campaigns had run. FDR's hidden agenda was to shove Rosenman and High together to see how they might soon function together. Rosenman found High pleasant enough and ultimately easy to work with, though still possessing no idea that they ever might.

Dr. High was another of the era's many influential religious figures, much like Father Coughlin, the Rev. Gerald L. K. Smith, Father Divine, Milo Reno, and the former Rev. Norman Thomas. Though never actually ordained, he had earned a degree in theology, served on a Methodist mission board, and also as editor of *The Christian Herald*. His fifteen-minute show, "Religion in the News," aired on NBC. Like many an FDR appointee, he was also a fallen-away Republican—as late as 1932, a prohibitionist supporting Hoover—no doubt earning references to "High and Dry." But, as Coughlin lurched away from FDR, High vaulted toward him. In February 1936, FDR set High to work, honchoing a major new effort—"The Good Neighbor League"—designed to snare more liberal churchgoers, good government types, and minorities (primarily Blacks) into his burgeoning New Deal coalition. The traditional Democratic troika of big-city bosses, Southerners, and prairie populists had pushed FDR over the top in 1932 and could easily do so again in 1936, but Franklin sought something far bigger and far more progressive than that.

Rexford Tugwell put it this way: FDR "saw no alternative, in the long run to creating a new force. A new progressivism . . . one capable of succeeding where that of Bryan, of Wilson, of La Follette the elder, of Uncle Ted had failed. He would be [its] founder. . . . The campaign of 1936 was not so much an election as an appeal for ratification of a progressivism quite as much Republican as Democratic."

Louis Howe had first approached Henry Wallace—another old Republican—to command this Good Neighbor League. But Wallace had other plans, re-registering as a Democrat in March 1936—perhaps, as some (including Rex Tugwell) deduced, as a prelude to his own presidential candidacy four years hence. In any case, Wallace thought little of the idea. "It was just a coverup for political purposes," he would recall, "to get folks who weren't Democrats. That method . . . never appealed to me. I thought it was a fraud and a fake."

Republicans concurred. Arthur Vandenberg, for example, damned High's Good Neighbor League as merely "a smokescreen for the Democratic National Committee [seeking] a piety which notoriously cannot attach to anything run by James A. Farley."

Farley.

Vandenberg got it only half right. FDR wasn't merely creating a smoke screen; he was once again fashioning a mechanism at war with itself, yet another rivalry for his affection, yet another explosive in the minefield of New Deal interoffice politics. How might Stanley High's new good-government effort mesh with Jim Farley's tried-and-true to-the-victor-belongs-the-spoils methodology? Did FDR even want them to mesh? Even now, with the party and the administration riding high, Big Jim Farley's star had commenced its inevitable descent. He relied too heavily on the old bosses and the old state organizations and thought too little of reaching out to these new coalition members. He was too visible, too voluble—even when not putting his foot in his mouth as with his unfortunate "typical prairie state" dig at Landon.

Sliding much further and faster downhill than Farley was Ray Moley. Accompanying Franklin to Washington in March 1933, he received a pledge that "no one in the Administration would have a more intimate relationship with the president. No one, except himself, would have more to do with making policy." He would be "Roosevelt's de facto minister of the moment."

Moley's influence was profound. Moley counseled Franklin to junk the gold standard . . . and gold was junked; to retain J. Edgar Hoover at the FBI . . . and Hoover was retained; to hire Joe Kennedy to salvage the SEC . . . and Joe was hired. The joke went around that visitors regularly beseeched FDR: "Franklin, can you do me just one favor, can you get me an appointment with Moley?"

Topical humor fades quickly. So did Moley. Two versions exist for what happened next. One (narrated by Moley) was that with 1936's convention approaching, FDR summoned him to assist on his acceptance speech. The other (Rosenman's) was that Moley, quite oblivious as to how drastically the old FDR–Moley partnership had cratered, volunteered to lend a hand, but his services were no longer desired. "Roosevelt's great failing," explained Rosenman, "was his inability to fire people close to him. He was loath to tell Moley he was about to use other people for help on speeches. . . . Moley's political and economic views were no longer close enough to his own. He thought that Moley had swung too far and too definitely to the right. It would have been a painful and embarrassing process . . . to work together on ideas and words when they were no longer together on purposes and objectives. But Roosevelt hated to make the break cleanly and definitely as he should have."

Roosevelt's rupture with Moley was fast coming—if not arrived already. On Thursday, May 28, the very day before Rosenman's introduction to Stanley High, Moley also conferred with Roosevelt, although "conferring" might not be the session's best description. "Brawling" works a lot better.

Moley was among the very few people *really* unafraid to speak his mind to Franklin. There might have been only four others: Louis Howe, Eleanor, Missy, and Sara. This evening's discussion was brutally frank. FDR wanted to vent about some recent Moley speeches plus a recent *Today* article, "Peeved at the Press." The article (not written by Moley) contended that "the lucubrations of critical columnists—unpalatable as they are to the New Dealers—are part of the freedom of the press. . . . A dispassionate observer would go still further and say that . . . opposition . . . is a most wholesome influence."

Perhaps it was the word "lucubrations" that set FDR off. More likely, it was "wholesome" as applied to the largely anti-FDR press. Newspaper criticism was getting to Franklin, whether from Hearst or Cissy Patterson or anyone else. As we've seen, only the following day, FDR would complain to Sam Rosenman of voters not getting the facts "*from their newspapers*." An early May conversation with Moley also centered on press duplicity.

FDR had simply swallowed all the press criticism he could. Moley stood his ground. Roosevelt got personal—jibing that the only reason anyone paid any attention to Moley was because of Moley's former attachment to *him*. FDR slammed Moley once more below the belt: "Oh, well, considering the circulation of *Today*, it was of no importance . . . what [Moley] said in it."

"I am not interested in talking about the tax proposal," he continued. "You can have any opinion you want on that. That's a detail." Here, he became particularly vexed: "You seem to be interested in personalities and details. I am not interested in personalities. It's not what you say or think about an individual in the administration or about a specific issue. There's one issue in this campaign. It's myself, and people must be either for me or against me."

This was not the Franklin Roosevelt Raymond Moley had come so much to admire in 1932.

A month later, Missy LeHand phoned Sam Rosenman. The Boss desired Sam to stay over during the approaching convention period. Rosenman protested that he'd be of little help. He'd been out of the loop for too long. Missy countered that FDR enjoyed working with him; Sam was one fellow who didn't make him nervous. Rosenman possessed an unstated reason for begging off: not only was White House food awful, its guest beds were worse. Nonetheless, he yielded and was assigned a second-floor bedroom directly across from the president's study.

He arrived on the Sunday preceding the convention. High bounced in, and they commenced work on the acceptance speech. A dizzying array of meetings followed—first with Senators Alben Barkley and Joe Robinson, then with FDR and members of the platform committee, including Robert Wagner and William Bullitt, by now relieved of his ambassadorial duties in Moscow and temporarily assigned to FDR's speechwriting team. Wagner's efforts seemed not good at all. From afar, Felix Frankfurter derided them as "wishy-washy, uninspiring mush . . . no inspiration, no generalized philosophy, no call to arms."

Thus, Rosenman also found himself stuck with the extra assignment of helping craft the platform. Nothing went well. Midnight passed, and Bill Bullitt punted. "We'll never get anywhere this way," he advised. "My suggestion is that we have someone sit down and spend the rest of the night getting up a draft to the platform which we can look at tomorrow. My nomination for this job is Sam Rosenman."

FDR had his own suggestion: "I have one thought . . . I would like to have as short a platform as possible this year, and . . . I would like to have it based on the sentence of the Declaration of Independence, 'We hold these truths to be self-evident.' Here are all the drafts which have been submitted by Wagner and some others. Try to put all the ideas together into one short one."

Rosenman and High labored through the night, blearily delivering a workable draft that Monday morning, though people like Harry Hopkins and former NRA administrator Don Richberg soon scurried in, bearing further planks and suggestions.

The day was chock-full of unpleasant surprises. FDR revealed that he had also requested Moley (of all people) and "Tommy the Cork" Corcoran to draft his address. Such an approach may have surprised High. It wasn't news to Rosenman, by now fully aware of Franklin's habit of surreptitiously assigning competing persons or groups of persons to the same task.

On Sunday, June 7, Corcoran had traveled to New York, bearing a message for Moley: FDR wanted him to assist Tommy with his acceptance speech. Moley declined, painfully cognizant that he and Franklin no longer inhabited the same ideological page. Corcoran was astonished. How could Moley surrender the chance to influence the president of the United States, to implant (however surreptitiously) his own ideas into a major presidential address? "You write the music," Corcoran argued. "He only sings it."

Moley blew up. "Tom," he lectured Corcoran, "I got you entree to the White House to serve Roosevelt's ideas, not yours. I've never, in my association with Roosevelt, insinuated anything into his speeches. He and I have argued endlessly over what the substance of a speech should be. But once he reached a decision, I've never slipped anything over on him. I can only plead with you to do the same. Remember, when you get to work on speeches, that you're a clerk, not a statesman."

Corcoran backtracked but finally cajoled Moley into at least reviewing his work before dispatching it to Roosevelt.

A fortnight later, Roosevelt summoned Moley to Washington. On June 24, Moley reviewed Corcoran's draft. It was awful—12,000 uninspiring words. It wouldn't do.

Two days later, Moley and Corcoran trekked to the White House. To Moley's relief, FDR was at his best, no longer petulant and defensive, but flashing all his considerable charm. "I want the speech to be only fifteen minutes long," he instructed Moley. "And it must rise to a very serious note."

Such calm would not last.

Moley and Corcoran retired to the Mayflower Hotel to toil upon a new draft, returning a few hours later to dine with FDR, Missy, Rosenman, and High.

Moley never admitted how ugly it had gotten. Rosenman and Corcoran did. It began with High needling Moley about Moley's new associates, and FDR joining in. "For the first and only time in my life," recalled Rosenman:

> I saw the President forget himself as a gentleman. He began twitting Moley about his new conservatism and about the influence of his "new, rich friends" upon his recent writings, which had been very critical of the Administration. Moley responded with what I thought was justifiable heat. The President grew angry, and the exchanges between them became very bitter.
>
> We all felt embarrassed; Missy did her best to change the subject but failed. The words became acrimonious. . . . While I knew how deeply Roosevelt had been stung by the unfriendly attacks on his policies by . . . Moley, I thought that his temper and language were particularly unjustified, not only because there were other people present, but because they were all his invited guests. It was an ordeal for all of us.

Perhaps Rosenman misremembered or misinterpreted what he saw. But he was no stranger to reading the Roosevelt tea leaves. Perchance Moley was too embarrassed to admit his humiliation. Or, perhaps, still recalling his greater savaging at Roosevelt's hands earlier in the month, he shrugged it all off. As Moley and Corcoran departed, Moley recollected Charles I's signing the death warrant for his major adviser the Earl of Stafford. Kings, Moley advised Corcoran, "exact complete loyalty from you but they never can afford to give you complete loyalty, personal loyalty in return—all promises of kings are presumptive and . . . and you have seen it tonight, Tommy, all of us are presumptive liquidable."

Larger battles, of course, remained regarding what shape this 1936 acceptance might assume. And what sort of convention—or, rather, coronation—might soon transpire in Philadelphia.

Liberty League types hoped against hope. Al Smith, Joseph B. Ely, Bainbridge Colby, former Missouri senator James A. Reed, and Tammany warhorse Daniel F. Cohalan all signed on to a fanciful letter demanding that the convention repudiate FDR. By now, the lot of them sounded like a broken, scratchy record playing a foxtrot in the swing era. John W. Davis, Lewis Douglas, and Bernard Baruch all refused to have anything to do with their challenge. New York's conservative senator Royal Copeland, never a Liberty Leaguer but similarly disgusted by FDR, did, however, refuse to attend the convention. "They have plenty of New Dealers," he snorted. "They don't need me."

Democrats—the party of sheer fractiousness, of 44 ballots in 1912 and 103 in 1924—arrived in the City of Brotherly Love for once meekly willing to do as they were told. Republicans in Cleveland had been placidly homogenized and moribund. Democrats in Philadelphia were the Stepford Wives of Modern Democracy, ready, willing, and able to be ready, willing, and able to cast their votes for Franklin Delano Roosevelt and the New Deal for which he stood—even following a stupefying fifty-eight seconding speeches lasting eight hours.

And why not? Fifty percent of all that year's delegates held federal jobs.

Delegates proved so pliant they *didn't even vote*. The convention recorded no roll calls. Every decision was by acclamation. Every decision unanimous.

Controversy, however, literally arose from a prayer. From 1868 onward, Republican conventions had hosted Black delegates. Southern "Black and Tan" votes had, in fact, proved crucial in securing the party's 1896, 1908, 1912, and 1928 nominations. Perry Howard's seconding speech at Cleveland was shocking merely for his fulsomeness, not for his race. Black delegates, however, had been historically verboten at all national Democratic gatherings. In 1936, however, everything (well, maybe not everything, but a lot) changed. Democrats seated twelve Negro delegates and twenty-two alternates.

Their convention's second day witnessed a local Black Baptist minister, the thirty-six-year-old Marshall L. Shepherd, providing the invocation. Republicans had broken the same ground just weeks previously by featuring Bishop James W. Brown of Harlem's New Mother African Methodist Episcopal Church, the city's largest Black congregation—but with no ill effect or even much notice. Even Blacks barely noticed.

That was not the case for the Democrats. At Philadelphia, a South Carolina reporter rushed up to his state's virulently racist senator Ellison D. "Cotton Ed" Smith, warning him that "a nigger is fixing to open the session with a prayer." Convention lighting, however, was so poor that the sixty-nine-year-old Smith remained unsure if Shepherd really was Black or if the reporter was just pulling his leg. He wasn't. "By God," the crusty Smith ("the last of the spittoon senators") blurted out, "he's as black as melted midnight! Get outa my way. This mongrel meeting ain't no place for a white man!"

"I am not opposed to any Negro praying for me, but I don't want any blue-gummed, slew-footed Senegambian praying for me politically! There isn't a man in America that has more regard for the Negro—*in his place*—than I have."

Smith stalked out. As did Charleston mayor Burnet Maybank, plus three other Palmetto State delegates. Remaining in place was their delegation's chairman, United States Attorney Claude Napoleon Sapp. "I don't care who prays for me," said Sapp. "I'm willing for anyone to pray for me who wants to." Also remaining was another Palmetto State delegate, a progressive young state senator—thirty-five-year-old J. Strom Thurmond. Virginia's conservative, anti–New Deal senator Carter Glass stayed put as well. "God knows," said the seventy-eight-year-old Glass, "I stand in need of prayer. I wish every Negro in the country would pray for me."

The following day, Smith fumed that "political equality means social equality and social equality means intermarriage and that means mongrelization of the American race. . . . [R]ealizing the unspeakable danger inherent in this thing, I cannot and will not be a party to the recognition of the Fourteenth and Fifteenth Amendments.

"Nor will I support any political organization that looks upon the Negro and caters to him as a political and social equal.

"We don't need it. I'm through so far as I'm concerned."

Cotton Ed vowed never to return—but did on the convention's fourth day—only to see Chicago Black congressman Arthur W. Mitchell on the podium. "This is another dose," Smith sputtered. "I have had enough. This time I'm leaving the convention to stay gone." This time he really did stay gone.

"I fear," retorted Mitchell, "the Senator is ignorant and steeped in prejudice. He belongs, probably, to the Ku Klux Klan, at least in mentality . . . and the sooner we get rid of his type the better. He is a disgrace to his state and to our party."

Party chieftains still, however, walked a fine line on courting Northern Negro votes. In Cleveland, Republicans maneuvered, showcasing Perry Howard but seating lily-white delegations from the South. Conversely, their platform, though not specifically mentioning lynching, had at least alluded to it and rendered some homage to African-American rights and issues:

> We favor equal opportunity for our colored citizens. We pledge our protection of their economic status and personal safety. We will do our best to further their employment in the gainfully occupied life of America, particularly in private industry, agriculture, emergency agencies and the civil service.
>
> We condemn the present New Deal policies which would regiment and ultimately eliminate the colored citizen from the country's productive life and make him solely a ward of the Federal Government.

Democrats uttered not a word.

Nonetheless, white Southern Democrats suffered a massive beating—as the party junked its 104-year-old rule requiring a two-thirds vote to select nominees. Missouri's senator Bennett Champ Clark spearheaded the move. Clark had a personal score to settle. In 1916, the rule had sidelined his father, House Speaker "Champ" Clark's nomination, ultimately delivering the nomination to Woodrow Wilson. Wilson would not keep us out of the war, but the rule kept the Clark family out of the White House.

Repeal proponents argued that the two-thirds rule had done little to supply stronger candidates. Deadlocks produced 1904's Alton B. Parker, 1920's James M. Cox, and 1924's John W. Davis—and November disaster. Repeal of the rule—rammed through on a very suspicious voice vote—forever ended the South's veto over nominees.

Some delegates grumbled that it might trigger something else: a Roosevelt third term. Jim Farley dismissed such murmurs as "asinine" and "ridiculous."

The Central Press Association's Charles P. Stewart noted:

> What the president [has] undertaken . . . many [Southerners] charge, is to gain absolute convention control in 1940, . . . making it perfectly possible for him to re-nominate himself or to designate his successor, anyway. . . .
>
> There are Anti-New Deal Northerners who whisper the same suspicions.
>
> I don't honestly suppose that there's definitely a deep-laid plot at this stage of the game to make Franklin D. Roosevelt America's first three-term president.
>
> Still when the time comes! If there's a demand for him and the thing's manageable? Who knows?
>
> It looks asinine to Chairman Farley now. But in 1940? The suggestion's been made anyhow, or Farley wouldn't have had to notice it.

Some stewed about a third term. Others fretted about securing a second. Pockets of doom pervaded the hall. "A few weeks ago," fretted Heywood Broun, "I said that Franklin D. Roosevelt could not possibly lose. Now, in my opinion, he is in grave danger of defeat. Indeed, I doubt he can win on points. . . . The political map of America has changed overnight. Now Mr. Roosevelt must make up his mind to get in there and slug."

Hugh Johnson, by now yet another Scripps-Howard columnist, nervously concurred: "If present trends continue the election is lost to the New Deal. The build-up propaganda of a new and liberalized Republican party is getting across in the farm states. The Smith–Ely grudge-blast will undoubtedly serve to stiffen the resentment of many old-line Democrats . . . torn between divided loyalties."

As with all conventions, there were diversions. Alice Roosevelt Longworth attended in her capacity as a national columnist. Dr. Townsend popped in just "to see the sideshow." Huey Long's oily former henchman Seymour Weiss supinely delivered Louisiana to FDR. "It was rather ludicrous," noted a disgusted Thomas Stokes, "to see Seymour Weiss . . . struggling . . . under a big banner 'I am for Roosevelt.' One of the [federal] income tax indictments which had been dropped was against Seymour Weiss."

The convention held its own beauty contest. The winner, twenty-year-old Miss Marion Fore of Floresville, Texas, arrived as "Texas Centennial Sweetheart." She departed literally transported upon an oaken throne "complete with statuary, fountains, a pale moon, and a mounted police guard." Sixty-two-year-old Reconstruction Finance Corporation chairman Jesse Jones joined his fellow Texans in hoisting her upon their shoulders.

Miss Fore wore a crown. Less-regal Florida delegates wore yellow jockey caps. Rhode Islanders sported red helmets. West Virginians clad themselves in "hillbilly overalls." Fifty women fainted and were hospitalized. A delegate from Scranton was among another twenty persons hospitalized (two hundred were injured) when their temporary stand collapsed on Broad Street during a specially staged mummer's Mardi Gras parade. Philadelphia police said they had never seen such an unruly crowd.

Collapsing stands were hardly the wildest occurrence in Philadelphia streets. On Thursday of the convention, feathers floated downward from the fourteenth floor of the city's Adelphia Hotel. On Broad Street, near the entrance of the Bellevue-Stratford, two taxicabs rolled by—both filled with more feathers. A man jumped out—wearing war paint, a feather headdress, blue swim trunks, and not much else. Grasping a bag of feathers, he flung its contents onto the busy street, snarling traffic.

Police gave chase, eventually capturing fiftyish Frank "Woody" Hockaday, recently escaped from the New Jersey State Hospital at Trenton. His goal: to spread feathers for peace.

Hockaday's case was particularly sad. Once a highly successful auto-parts and tire dealer, he had essentially invented the modern road sign (somebody had to) and popularized the slogan "Kansas Grows the Best Wheat in the Entire World." In October 1924—to promote said wheat—he distributed 24,000 sacks of it on the Atlantic City boardwalk. That's a lot of wheat on one boardwalk.

His feathers, however, were Philadelphia feathers, obtained for $300 from local feather dealer Benjamin Herdock.

"He didn't say what he wanted 'em for," said Herdock, which, under the circumstances, was probably the best answer.

In police custody, en route to Philadelphia General Hospital, curious officers asked Hockaday, "Do you have Indian blood in you?"

"Oh, no," he responded, "but I'm a fifth cousin of Abraham Lincoln."

• • •

As if to further incite Al Smith's ire (if that were possible), among those seconding John Nance Garner's nomination was former Alabama senator (but now an official of the FDR's Federal Housing Administration) Tom Heflin, whose hatred of Smith, the Catholic Church, and the pope infuriated him enough to endorse Herbert Hoover in 1928. "Since going on the New Deal payroll," reflected H. L. Mencken, "[Heflin] has mellowed and is now on fairly friendly terms with the Vatican."

Heflin had a past—but at least he still had a future. A donkey brought up from Garner's Uvalde, Texas, ranch got rambunctious on the convention floor and ended up with no future whatsoever. He was, reported the observant Mencken, "dispatched by a Bowie knife, and its carcass dragged out."

Joseph B. Ely's pro–New Deal successor as Massachusetts governor, James M. Curley, attended, announcing he'd accept the vice presidential nomination. Had "Cactus Jack" Garner swerved dead drunk into the convention with a swastika armband on one arm and a prostitute upon the other, there would still have existed zero chance of substituting Curley for Garner. Some likened his Bay State reign to Huey Long's Louisiana administration, though assessing it as far less competent. A critic noted that "eighteen thousand state employees dare not speak out against the governor. . . . With quick coups and an iron hand, he has usurped the power of all public officials and centered it in himself."

The *Boston Globe*'s Louis M. Lyons damned Curley's invariably Irish, invariably awful appointees, noting that, "Under him the Boston city machine has occupied the State House. The intolerance of the Irish politician in Boston for any sharing of political power or political liberties can be compared only to that of the early church magistrates of New England. Curley's regime is frankly racial beyond anything known elsewhere in America." Curley's underlings, Lyons added, were "the smallest and cheapest political [ward] heelers that ever shined their trousers in the seats of public office in Massachusetts."

At Philadelphia, Curley now dispatched an armed and uniformed personal honor guard to parade around the hall. "For the first time," *The Nation*'s Oswald Garrison Villard wrote, "I am sure, rifles and bayonets, even though only three or four, were seen on the floor of a political convention. The soldiers without guns, as well as those with them, were as perfect a potential fascist cell as ever delighted the heart of a Hitler or a Mussolini. Their uniforms were stunning and immaculate, their set-up and bearing worthy of the Kaiser's bodyguard."

But if such tactics faltered, Curley possessed a backup plan, attested to by his minions flaunting a banner proclaiming (or perhaps just warning), "Look Out for Curley in 1940."

High atop the galleries, some young men unfurled three Al Smith banners, chanting "We want Smith." They really didn't want Smith at all. They wanted Landon, being young Philadelphia Republicans. The hall erupted into booing. Pennsylvania Deputy Attorney General Joe Marinelli grabbed one of the offending banners, receiving a left hook to the jaw for his efforts, sending him tumbling downward through three rows of seats. The crowd angrily yelled "Lynch them!" as police hustled the Landonites off to jail. As Villard noted, they were openly "beaten up . . . with obvious brutality."

Despite such events, Villard still assessed the year's Democratic offering as "the dreariest, dullest, stupidest, loudest, most inane, most vulgar, most blatant, most idiotic, most depressing, most childish, most needless, most incredible, and generally most disgusting of political gatherings, bar none. If I had a few more adjectives I should apply them too."

Yet Villard still praised the party's platform as being "as clever and adroit a political document as we have had for a long time . . . a brilliant piece of political writing, avoiding every pitfall and giving the enemy nothing startling to pounce upon and twist." Gone were 1932's too-specific guarantees to slash spending and deficits. Inserted were FDR's suggested self-evident truths—and all with relative economy: 2,310 words in total to the GOP's 3,030. Yet pitfalls remained. Written near the high tide of American isolationism, the document promised:

> We shall continue to observe a true neutrality in the disputes of others; to be prepared, resolutely to resist aggression against ourselves; to work for peace and to take the profits out of war; to guard against being drawn, by political commitments, international banking or private trading, into any war which may develop anywhere.

Such was, of course, not to be. Neither was this solemn vow:

> We are determined to reduce the expenses of government. . . . Our retrenchment, tax and recovery programs . . . reflect our firm determination to achieve a balanced budget and the reduction of the national debt at the earliest possible moment.

Roosevelt remained in Washington while delegates endorsed his second nomination. In 1932, he flew to Chicago to impart his acceptance and inspire his legions. In 1936—alongside Eleanor, Missy, Marvin McIntyre, Steve Early, and a handful of other key staffers—he boarded a special Baltimore & Ohio train at Washington's Union Station. Destination: Philadelphia's Twenty-Fourth Street Station and then a brief motorcade through cleared streets heading toward the University of Pennsylvania's one-hundred-thousand-seat football stadium, Franklin Field.

At a dollar a head, Democrats also gathered in twenty-seven cities nationwide—in ballparks and in auditoriums—to bask in their president's remarks over the radio. Only 6,500 assembled inside 15,000-seat Madison Square Garden, however. Two to three thousand persons gathered in Topeka just outside Governor Landon's offices.

In Philadelphia, it rained—and then it didn't—and then it did. The band optimistically tootled "It Ain't Gonna Rain No More, No More." Diminutive thirty-eight-year-old soprano Lily Pons sang "Lo Hear Gentle the Lark" and "The Star Spangled Banner." A sopping wet H. L. Mencken thought the French-born Pons "trilled and gurgled beautifully." Majority Leader Joe Robinson pointed with confused pride to "this convention recently held in Chicago"—visibly flummoxing Philadelphia's Republican (but highly flexible) mayor Samuel D. Wilson.

That morning, as was his habit, Vice President Garner rose early. "I got up at six o'clock . . . and walked around the streets," he chatted to Eleanor as they traveled to the stadium. "That's about saddling-up time in Texas, but it's early here. The only people up were policemen, cab drivers and night workers. I talked to them and most of them are going to vote the Democratic ticket, and none of them have done that before. We will carry Pennsylvania." Eleanor disagreed and bet Garner a dollar on it.

On the podium, Garner pledged his "fealty" to FDR, with "the stars of heaven" as his witness. Introducing his boss, he somehow kept butchering his middle name, first as "Delaney," then as "Deluno."

The band blared "Hail to the Chief." FDR, bathed in the glare of overhead spotlights, entered, just behind ambassadors Josephus Daniels (his old Navy Department boss) and his Moscow man/speechwriter Bill Bullitt. At the mere flickering glimpse of Roosevelt, the joint exploded. The Democrats' own ten-foot-tall "demonstrometer" flashed wildly. Its white lights recorded a solid "100." It was, recalled Secret Service Agent Michael F. Reilly, "the greatest ovation I ever heard, and in ten years with FDR I heard an awful lot of ovations."

Reilly, James Roosevelt, and Franklin's loyal bodyguard, the beefy former New York City police officer Gus Gennerich, escorted Franklin as he hobbled toward the podium. Following his ascension to the presidency, the efforts to disguise his paralysis had taken on truly remarkable lengths. "As President, when he traveled, everything was planned for his convenience as carefully as humanly possible," historian Hugh Gregory Gallagher has noted. "The Secret Service would map the route . . . but making use of a checklist of details, ensuring complete accessibility for the President's wheelchair—measuring the width of doors, the angle of ramps, the height of toilets.

"The President moved quite literally in a ramped world. Wherever he went, the Secret Service went first. They built ramps for his use at every point. These were not merely simple ramps for the President's chair; upon occasion the Secret Service would actually raise the entire level of a street to the level of the building entrance by means of temporary but extensive wooden trestles and scaffolding."

Tonight's march to the podium thus looked like a comparative piece of cake—until everything went horribly wrong. Shuffling forward, FDR spied an elderly white-bearded man along his path: eighty-four-year-old Edwin Markham, author of 1898's wildly popular poem "The Man with a Hoe." That poem, published originally by Hearst's *San Francisco Examiner* (back in W. R.'s radical days), was a Roosevelt favorite, telling of a man bearing "on his back the burden of the world," suffering the "censure of the world's blind greed" and of its "masters, lords and rulers."

Good stuff indeed in 1898—and in 1936 as well.

As poet and president drew nearer, FDR flashed a smile of recognition. Perhaps Franklin recognized the aged Markham. Perhaps it was the false smile of false recognition that politicians so skillfully and falsely deliver. Markham beamed and extended his hand. And then . . .

Someone standing behind Markham shoved him forward onto James Roosevelt. James stumbled onto his father—bad enough—but then disaster really struck. The extra weight of James's body snapped a pin out of one of Franklin's leg braces, and he tumbled downward. Such mishaps could easily shatter a leg bone.

Secret Service man Reilly dropped downward, maneuvering his shoulder under FDR's right armpit, struggling to keep Roosevelt from hitting the ground. Yet not all was under control. Furiously flailing about, FDR had whacked his speech out of James's hand. "There I was hanging in the air," he later explained to the *Chicago Tribune*'s Walter Trohan, "like a goose about to be plucked, but I kept on waving and smiling, and smiling and waving. I called to Jimmy out of the corner of my mouth to fix the pin."

"Dad," his son protested, "I'm trying to pick up the speech."

"To hell with the speech," FDR muttered, "fix the G-d-damned brace. If it can't be fixed, there won't be any speech."

FDR did his best, at which he was always very good, to keep up appearances—waving and smiling, but underneath it all thoroughly infuriated ("the damndest, maddest white man . . . you ever saw . . . the most frightful five minutes of my life"). Jim Farley, Attorney General Homer Cummings, and other party bigwigs hurriedly gathered around, not so much to boost FDR up, but to shield his embarrassment from the immense crowd—and any press cameras. Franklin later recounted:

> By this time, I was mad clean through. First, I was mad because Jack Garner had mangled my name. . . . Then I was mad because Ed Halsey, the Senate secretary, got in front of me when I was waving to the crowd, and I must confide to you that Ed has the broadest beam in a body renowned for its posterior spread.
>
> I was mad at the mayor of Philadelphia, who kept leaning over to confide how many police they had on duty in the park, at the station and along the route. I have to tell you that the mayor has one of the worst cases of halitosis ever blown in my face. I was mad at the lights which were so bright I couldn't see a soul in the blackness beyond.
>
> I was mad at the speech which had scattered on the floor. Finally, and above all, I was mad at the damned brace, which had picked that particular moment of all moments to break down.
>
> I could feel Jimmy fumbling and then I heard the pin snap back into place [Gus Gennerich's work]. My balance was restored and the weight was lifted from poor Gus. Jimmy shuffled the pages into their proper order, but with some difficulty because he was flustered.

It could have been worse. Much worse. Reilly uttered "a fervent prayer that none of the Detail would shoot or hit the strange-looking old man with the flying white beard who stood in the middle of the melee. I think the number of poetry readers on the Detail is rather limited, so none of us recognized Markham. Three or four of us at the boss's side had seen him recognize Markham so we knew he was all right. But the men scattered nearby and in the crowd might not have seen FDR's smile of recognition. If our training worked, Markham was safe. If it didn't, and some trigger-happy agent cut loose, Markham and a lot of other nice people would be hurt."

No poets were harmed in presenting FDR's acceptance speech. Beyond that, FDR remained gracious enough to ensure that the aged Markham still got his handshake.

"None of the thousands out front knew what had happened," said Reilly, "and very few got a clear view backstage." Certainly, no one in the rest of America knew what drama had transpired. No radio announcers mentioned it. No journalists, not even the *Tribune*'s Walter Trohan (no friend of the New Deal) dared reveal it.

It took more than the possibility of pratfalling flat on his face before a hundred thousand people to fluster FDR. Forcing his renowned smile, he kept waving to the crowd. Still incensed—his hands still shaking—he commenced his address.

Pushing that address's text across the finish line were not only Rosenman, High, Moley, and Corcoran, but also Corcoran's twenty-four-year-old aide, Sam Beer (yet another Frankfurter alumnus), as well as the brilliant University of Pennsylvania law professor and assistant attorney general John Dickenson, a McAdoo protégé. Moley authored such conciliatory passages as:

> Faith—in the soundness of democracy in the midst of dictatorships. Hope—renewed because we know so well the progress we have made. Charity—in the true meaning of that grand old word. . . . In the place of the palace of privilege we seek to build a temple out of faith and hope and charity. . . . Governments can err. Presidents do make mistakes [definitely Moley's words], but the immortal Dante tells us that divine justice weighs the sins of the cold-blooded and the sins of the warm-hearted on different scales. Better the

> occasional faults of a Government that lives in a spirit of charity than the consistent omissions of a Government frozen in the ice of its own indifference.

Rosenman and High crafted tougher talk—a class-warfare message that Moley dreaded and hoped to avoid. In Philadelphia, Cradle of Independence, Roosevelt harkened back to Revolutionary days to bolster his war versus "[t]hese economic royalists [who] complain that we seek to overthrow the institutions of America. What they really complain of is that we seek to take away their power. Our allegiance to American institutions requires the overthrow of this kind of power. In vain they seek to hide behind the Flag and the Constitution. In their blindness they forget what the Flag and the Constitution stand for. Now, as always, they stand for democracy, not tyranny; for freedom, not subjection; and against a dictatorship by mob rule and the over-privileged alike." Roosevelt simply loved the phrase "economic royalists," recalled Sam Beer, and "rolled it off in great style."

Tommy Corcoran, among the least experienced of Franklin's scribes, provided one of FDR's most enduring and inspiring phrases. Recalling that Walter Lippmann had, back in March 1933, spoken of his generation's "appointment with destiny," he suggested cribbing the phrase. Someone objected that Republicans might lampoon FDR as orating about an "appointment with *the dentist*." A brainstorm struck Corcoran, and he countered: What about "*rendezvous* with destiny"?

Another objection: "rendezvous with destiny" sounded like World War I poet Alan Seeger's "I have a rendezvous with death." But Ray Moley stuck up for the phrase—and it stuck.

"There is a mysterious cycle in human events," Franklin proclaimed. "To some generations much is given. Of other generations much is expected. This generation of Americans has a rendezvous with destiny."

But, first, Franklin Roosevelt had a rendezvous with Alf Landon—and, come to think of it, Bill Lemke.

· 15 ·

"20,000 morons"

The vast majority of Democrats stood behind Franklin Roosevelt. And, in any one-on-one matchup versus Republicans, he enjoyed the very real, the very strong, likelihood of capturing a majority of all voters.

But strange things happen. Plagues. Earthquakes. Elections lost that should have been won. It happened to Bill Taft in 1912, and Woodrow Wilson waltzed through the back door of the White House. It happened to Samuel J. Tilden and once to Grover Cleveland. Both won the popular vote but neither the electoral vote nor the presidency itself. Their races were straight-up two-man races. With a third man in the race in 1936, and with Democrats fretting about losing key states like New York and Michigan, well, the impossible might just happen. FDR had his reasons for showcasing the deadly-dull Herbert Lehman in Philadelphia, desiring Lehman to run again in New York. If he didn't—Democrats might lose not just the state house but the White House. In Michigan, Franklin and Jim Farley basically shanghaied Frank Murphy back from Manila to run him for the governorship—and, again, to hold the state for the national ticket. Coughlin warned his old pal Murphy not to run: he'd never win on a Roosevelt-led ticket.

In mid-May, Gallup posed this question: "If there were only two political parties in this country—Conservative and Liberal—which would you join?" Fifty-three percent answered "Conservative." On Sunday, July 12,

1936, Gallup reported Landon sneaking ahead in the Electoral College 272–259. FDR's support was falling in thirty-eight states. Gallup pointed to three factors: Republicans had chosen their most popular candidate rather than some dark horse tapped by backroom bosses. Secondly, Al Smith's pre-convention telegram had actually shifted at least a few votes. Thirdly, and perhaps most importantly, New Deal spending had lost its charm. Economy was the new watchword, and the cheese-paring "Kansas Coolidge" seemed just like the sort of fellow to deliver it. Internal Democratic polling conducted by Emil Hurja, the party's crack analyst, verified Gallup's bad news: FDR was once again slipping. Hurja privately warned Harold Ickes that "the situation is very serious . . . the president [is] receiving slightly more than fifty per cent, but with Landon leading on electoral votes." He assessed FDR's chances in New York and Illinois as slim at best. In Ohio, Indiana, and Minnesota, Roosevelt possessed only an "outside" shot.

Two weeks later, Gallup pondered Roosevelt's maneuvering between competing poles of public sentiment. First, FDR had to please the Left's varied forces: old-line Socialists and Communists, traditional prairie and agricultural populists, and ever-more-popular (and noisy) mass movements represented by Coughlin, Townsend, and the late lamented Kingfish. These groups insisted on big business being punished—or at least reined in. They demanded pensions and wealth distribution and all kinds of things the New Deal had delivered—and more. Millions of others, however, wanted things to settle down—business as usual. Their most visible spokesmen might be Hearst or John Jakob Raskob, but they were not all rich or even all hoping to be rich. They merely trusted the old ways and distrusted the new—and feared what might eventually follow even the new.

FDR didn't need to win all these folk over—just enough of them to keep the New Deal wheels spinning. Gallup pointed out that it was precisely when Huey Long seemed most dangerous that Roosevelt proposed his own "soak-the-rich" bill. That gambit, however, contained risks, and FDR's popularity fell from 53 percent in March 1935 to a precarious 50.5 percent that summer. With Huey safely deceased, Roosevelt shifted rightward—announcing his so-called "breathing spell."

But now, in the summer of 1936, FDR's Left Front reopened, in the form of a grand coalition of malcontents with all manner of reasons to loathe and resent him: Charles Coughlin, Dr. Townsend, and Gerald L. K. Smith.

Al Smith, John Jakob Raskob, and the Liberty League knew the limits of dissent. They'd issue their pamphlets, hold their galas, and telegraph their protests. They'd been around the block more than once and understood the futility of third-party challenges. Coughlin, Townsend, and the Rev. Smith—drunk on the cheers of their admirers, intoxicated by the sound of their own voices, and completely inexperienced in electoral politics—did not.

Dr. Townsend's interest in presidential politics was of the meandering sort. He'd been for Borah and then against Borah, and then maybe, sort-of for Borah. He solemnly promised "I don't want to be President" and probably meant it. A man who still wears spats has, after all, probably ruled out higher office.

But Franklin Roosevelt seriously angered him. He had stolen much of the Townsend Plan's thunder by enacting Social Security. FDR had refused to even meet with him (Dr. Townsend, it seemed, was not as humble as he might appear). Adding injury to insult were the Bell Committee hearings, for which Townsend blamed FDR. Though he had absented himself from the Republican Convention, he soon issued guarded praise for the GOP's new standard-bearer: "I will say this much for Landon. He has done nothing in Kansas to indicate he was inclined to imprison those who differ with him concerning matters of government."

Which was more than he'd venture regarding Franklin D. Roosevelt.

Nonetheless, Townsend might have lain low, save for goading from his new Svengali, the Rev. Smith. In New York, back on June 2, Smith and Townsend had proclaimed that they would soon unite with Coughlin at Townsend's upcoming second annual OARP convention to back "Anybody but Roosevelt."

If party politics do not teach men to play well with others, they at least instruct them to *pretend* to play well with others. Franklin Roosevelt was living proof of that. Messianic mass-movement leaders rarely learn that skill—a shortcoming usually making their movements much less mass far too soon. Thus it was with Townsend and Smith and Coughlin.

Townsend and Coughlin had first met in November 1935, as Townsend traveled to Royal Oak. Coughlin was often prickly, but now it was the mild-mannered Townsend who popped off, carping to the *New York Times* that Coughlin was "stealing our stuff, anyway, organizing in congressional districts. When I saw Coughlin I told him the trouble with his program was that he had sixteen points, which were fourteen too many. And he told me that I had fourteen too few. But the great value of our plan is its simplicity, and I don't want to depart from that."

Nonetheless, when Townsend stormed out of his Bell Committee inquisition in May 1935, he took pains to send Coughlin his version of events. Coughlin printed their entirety in *Social Justice*.

By June 1936, Republicans had a candidate and a platform. Coughlin didn't like either. Its platform, he fussed, was "a step in the direction of the grave of democracy"; its pro-gold standard plank was akin to "slavery." But who would he support? Here the double-talk began—and it never really ended. The National Union, he averred, wouldn't *put up* a candidate *but* might *support* one. Coughlin admitted that said candidate just *might* be in discussions with Townsend and Smith *but* denied any coordination between Coughlinites and Townsendites. The Radio Priest denied even knowing Smith and averred that he "positively would not" attend Townsend's upcoming OARP convention.

Nonetheless, that very day witnessed Smith announcing that he and Townsend *would* combine with Coughlin and with followers of North Dakota congressman William Lemke in a twenty-million-person alliance combatting "Farleyism, dictatorship, and Communism."

Coughlin had affirmed that his NUSJ would not propose a candidate. It was obvious, however, that he alone would speak for it—and for everyone else in this quixotic axis—regarding its prospective nominee. Said candidate, certainly, would not be the dull septuagenarian Townsend. And, more certainly, not Smith, already tarnished by a reputation far more acrid than even Coughlin's or Townsend's. It would not be The Radio Priest. A personal candidacy would jeopardize both portions of his hard-won identity: "Radio" *and* "Priest." Moreover, his eligibility was suspect. Many considered his Canadian birth a bar to the office.

No such objections disqualified William Lemke. His populist credentials were impeccable. He was no priest and not even Catholic (though his mother was). He was, however, the least interesting, let alone charismatic, figure of this populist quartet. And compared to history's more prominent third-party hopefuls—TR, the elder La Follette, Eugene Debs, even Norman Thomas—well, Lemke rated as a two-term congressman from North Dakota.

Only 5'6", the balding, lantern-jawed, teetotaling Lemke sported a freckled, smallpox-scarred, often badly shaven face, further disfigured by a glass eye. His Germanic-tinged speaking voice was poor, his clothes disheveled. Gerald L. K. Smith, hardly a city slicker himself, dismissed his eventual comrade as "a complete composite of a hayseed; he wore a cap. He was not eloquent and all he could talk about was money and agriculture."

Lemke was actually a little more complex than that, but not by much. He had attended Georgetown and Yale and, until Mexico's revolution, held nearly a half million acres there. When Woodrow Wilson helped oust strongman Victoriano Huerta from power, Lemke lost it all, blamed Wilson, and, in 1915, penned a pro-Huerta book called *Crimes Against Mexico,* contending, among other things, that "the mistake that Huerta made was that he did not have Madero publicly executed immediately after he was arrested." He resumed his North Dakota law practice, aligned himself with the state's powerful agrarian movement, the Nonpartisan League, and assumed chairmanship of the state GOP. In 1920, he won the attorney generalship, but when he was accused of helping deposit state funds in an insolvent bank, a recall ejected him from office. He remained out of office until running for Congress in 1932. "He knew the farmer and he knew the law," as one historian noted, and that was enough to get him elected.

In mid-campaign, he traveled to Albany. The Republican Lemke and the Democrat Roosevelt conferred. FDR seemingly agreed with Lemke's thinking on agriculture ("Yes, yes, I am for all that"), and Lemke stumped for Franklin in seven Midwestern states. The North Dakotan believed he'd be Roosevelt's man on the farm; he wasn't even a needle in the haystack. He urged FDR to promote exporting farm surpluses abroad; FDR soon embraced Henry Wallace's contrary strategy of decimating farm production. FDR's eventual failure to support drastic inflationary policies or the Frazier–Lemke Farm Bankruptcy Act alienated both Lemke and Coughlin. For his part, FDR hated Lemke's Bankruptcy Act, privately damning it to Steve Early as "wild legislation" capable of wrecking the economy.

In May 1936, Coughlin forecast to Lemke a grand alignment of "progressive" anti–New Deal forces. In early June, he designated Lemke as this new party's North Dakota chairman, promising to soon divulge to him their standard-bearer's identity. Eight days later—much to Lemke's surprise—Coughlin revealed his choice: William Frederick Lemke. It was thus said that Lemke was nominated in a phone booth—with Coughlin at the other end of the line. Lemke, his head nonetheless turned by the "honor," graciously accepted. Presidential nominations, after all, do not grow on trees in North Dakota.

On Friday, June 18, Lemke proclaimed his candidacy, also revealing his running mate: former Boston district attorney Thomas "Hamburger Tom" O'Brien, a Catholic, a Democrat, a strong trade-union man, and—balancing Lemke's Yale bona fides—a Harvard man. That Lemke—not Coughlin—had selected O'Brien was yet another of the party's multiple charades.

At 10:45 p.m. (ET) that evening, Coughlin addressed a nationwide CBS radio audience. The big story was supposed to be Lemke and the new Union Party. But not until Coughlin concluded his 3,057-word address did he finally, begrudgingly, devote a mere 419 words to his newly minted Lemke–O'Brien ticket.

Lemke, for all his faults, was not entirely fooled by his new associates. In July 1935, he confided to a close friend:

> The fact that I may speak at Coughlin's or Long's meetings does not mean that I accept all of their ideas or ideals, but you surely know me well enough to know that I am not afraid to speak with the devil, if necessary, and I have been on platforms with some speakers for whose views I have not had the slightest respect, and which I did not hesitate to assail at the first opportunity.

Attending a 3,500-person OARP rally in Syracuse the day following Lemke's announcement, Townsend remained a tad blasé regarding their mutual adventure. "It's all right with me if [my upcoming convention] back[s] Lemke," he declared. "Whatever the convention says, we'll do. . . . It's up to them. Right now, however, I know of no talk whereby I would join a third party movement with Lemke. There may be later. That remains to be seen."

Smith had accompanied Townsend to Syracuse, as usual, displaying more pep. Essentially contradicting Townsend, he revealed that they'd soon confer with Lemke and fantasized victory with a "candidate who will permit . . . Charles E. Coughlin to define his money plank—Dr. Townsend to define his old age security plank—Gerald Smith to define his plank on labor, education and homesteads—the farmers union to define their plank on agriculture—this man will be the next President of the United States."

Insane optimism also gripped Lemke. Meeting with Coughlin on Thursday, June 25 at Royal Oak, he hallucinated he'd "carry Ohio, all of New England, Michigan, most of the Middle West, the extreme West, Pennsylvania and Illinois. Indiana will be nip and tuck. I see the Union party on top. I'm not concerned who will be next."

Well, who could resist a sure thing like that? Certainly not a visionary like Dr. Townsend. FDR, after all, was a nonstarter in his sights. Landon wasn't much better. "I saw Landon about a year ago," the doctor now explained, "and he thought we were on the lunatic fringe." The doctor proclaimed he'd rather "vote Socialist" than for either Roosevelt or Landon—"And Lord knows, I'm no Socialist or Communist."

Coughlin's, Townsend's, Smith's, and Lemke's legions would strike on all fronts—Smith's in the South; Townsend's on the West Coast; Lemke's in the Upper Midwest; and Coughlin's farther East—to trim Roosevelt's sails and votes. Maybe they really wouldn't elect Lemke, but they still might swing enough votes here and there to either elect Landon directly or, better yet, to send the process hurtling into the House of Representatives. It was the same game with different goalposts that Earl Browder's Communists played. Throw rocks at one opponent; pebbles at the other; and hope for the best. To the CPUSA, that meant reelecting Roosevelt;

to the new Coughlin-controlled "Union Party," it meant knocking the crutches out from under him.

The new party lacked many things—among them an actual convention. Thus, Townsend's July 15–19 Cleveland convention would have to substitute, to provide a whiz-bang mass-movement major-league kickoff for an essentially minor-league enterprise. Nonetheless, the stench of ruin still choked the air. Most ominously, OARP refused to formally endorse Lemke. Yes, Townsend and Smith individually would. Their organization per se would not. Even Townsend's purely personal endorsement remained strangely impersonal. Just days before the convention opened, he informed reporters that he "could name a dozen men in the United States who would make a better third party candidate [than Lemke] . . . but I don't think the delegates have decided by any means that they want a third party."

Precious few of Lemke's fellow politicians jumped on board: Ohio Coughlinite representative Martin Sweeney, North Dakota's senator Lynn Frazier and representative Usher Burdick, and Oklahoma's inflationist senator Elmer Thomas, an old Coughlin ally. Lemke's fellow Midwestern progressives kept their distance: Roosevelt remained their man. Lemke's largely North Dakota–centric campaign staff hardly befitted a national effort. Money proved pathetically short. By mid-July, less than $20,000 had arrived. Ballot requirements posed insurmountable hurdles. In Oklahoma and West Virginia, deadlines had already passed. Kansas's fell just twelve hours following Lemke's announcement. And, while Unionists anticipated a big splash upon launch, the national press either laughed or yawned. Many commentators were downright hostile, though not nearly as vehement as *Bridgeport Life*. "We believe the White House is and should be a typical American family home," it sniffed, "but not of the type inhabited by 'poor white trash.' We are afraid Mr. Lemke will not do."

The party's de facto debut—at Townsend's July OARP convention—was, nonetheless, loud and well populated. Eleven thousand "delegates" from thirty-eight states attended, shelling out a dollar a head to bask in the speeches and the excitement. They were largely old folks, not well off, a threadbare aggregation. They attended on their own dime, traveling in buses and rusted jalopies, lodging in cheap boardinghouses and run-down hotels, packing their own lunches, and, above all, still somehow trusting their leader and friend to deliver unto them their very own $200-a-month pension.

They came for pensions and to pay Townsend homage. They did not come to anoint William Lemke for anything. Gomer Smith, a partially Cherokee Oklahoma Townsendite and one of the movement's major (and more reputable) figures, denounced any third-party schemes, begging attendees to hold faithful to FDR. He ripped Coughlin and Gerald L. K. Smith for manipulating the Townsend movement to suit their own ends. FDR, testified Gomer Smith, was a "church-going, Bible-reading, God-fearing, golden-hearted man who has saved the country from Communism." Washington State congressman Martin Smith (yet another Smith in the same paragraph!) concurred, warning delegates, "My friends, we are not going to 'lose with Lemke,' we are going to 'triumph with Townsend.'" Fifteen state delegations voted *not* to endorse Lemke, causing the convention's permanent chairman to rage, "There will be no more free speech at these meetings."

Delegates cheered Roosevelt. They cheered attacks on Roosevelt. They cheered damn near everything. "There is a shout at the end of nearly every sentence of every speaker," noted the *Washington Post.* "It appears to make no difference what he has said. . . . The fine points make no difference to them. They don't want reason, but they love oratory."

They drew the line, however, when Norman Thomas showed up to boldly denounce the Townsend Plan as "a quack remedy which could not possibly work."

"I don't think," Thomas contended, "you cannot keep capitalism, and make the capitalist system pay you twice as much for not working at sixty as you got on the average before you were sixty."

Townsend implored his outraged followers not to boo. He failed.

Thomas was allowed in only as a pretext to authorize Lemke's appearance. Invitations went out to all the presidential candidates (though not Earl Browder). Thomas, always needing free publicity, accepted. Roosevelt and Landon, not nearly so desperate, didn't.

Dr. Townsend, of course, spoke. He was not scintillating. Clinton Wunder was, displaying what the *Washington Post* described as "pulpit manners on a par with the wildest of evangelists." Gerald Smith was no slouch either, thundering, "We must make our choice in the presence of these atheists. It is Tammany or Independence Hall! It is the Russian primer or the Holy Bible! It is the Red Flag or the Stars and Stripes! It is Lenin or Lincoln! Stalin or Jefferson! Stalin or Jefferson!"

Inventing yet another new conspiracy, he fulminated:

> The Democratic party won the election—the New Deal party took over the government—I am informed that there are not less than 1,000 planted delegates to this convention in the pay of the James A. Farley machine, to attempt to confuse the minds of the people gathered here for sincere purposes—I'm further informed that the same sabotage that cut the wires that led to the microphones in [the] recent [Republican] convention just before the keynote speech, is planning to do the same thing here—I am convinced that Huey Long was killed, murdered by the machine—Dr. Francis E. Townsend has assured me that he will stand with myself and others in the continued relentless attack on the Roosevelt-Farley machine.

The entire noisy shebang mightily impressed H. L. Mencken. "This Townsend show is really colossal," he wrote to a friend. "Imagine 20,000 morons penned up in one hall." Most wonderful of all was Gerald L. K. Smith. "His speech," marveled The Sage of Baltimore, "was a magnificent amalgam of each and every American species of rabble-rousing, with embellishments borrowed from the Algonquin Indians and the Cossacks of the Don. It ran the keyboard from the softest sobs and gurgles to the most ear-splitting whoops and howls, and when it was over the thousands of delegates simply lay back in the pews and yelled. Never in my life, in truth, have I heard a more effective speech . . . he waded in with the hearty, joyous confidence of a cop braining a Communist. . . . All the time-tried tricks of the best boob-bumpers were trotted out, and every one of them worked."

Mencken was thrilled. Father Coughlin was not, following Smith's act the next morning, an extremely unpalatable assignment—for anyone. Coughlin excelled as a radio speaker—but, as a stump speaker, clearly trailed Smith or Smith's mentor the Kingfish. He commenced his scheduled forty-minute address slowly, then broke loose. His delivery quickened. His rhetoric grew feverish. He seemed outright desperate to outperform Smith. Smith dramatically had shouted and sweated and gulped water straight out of a pitcher. Coughlin stripped off his coat and even his Roman collar. He lacerated the "money changers" manipulating our currency and financial systems. Frenetically, almost hysterically, he flung caution overboard, lacerating his old "friend" Franklin Roosevelt:

> As far as the National Union is concerned, no candidate who is endorsed for Congress can campaign, go electioneering for, or support the great betrayer and liar, Franklin D. Roosevelt. . . .
>
> I ask the Democrats from the South . . . to expel those Communists who have seized the party reins of the Democrats and who are flogging their party with destructional patronage.
>
> I ask you to purge the man who claims to be a Democrat from the Democratic Party—I mean Franklin Double-Crossing Roosevelt.

For the convention's final day, the show moved to Cleveland's cavernous eighty-thousand-seat Municipal Stadium (aka "The Mistake on the Lake")—for Bill Lemke's address to the throng. Such scheduling counted as yet another waterfront blunder. Most attendees had headed home before Lemke even got there. Only five thousand souls bothered showing up, and nobody past the largely empty bleachers paid much attention to what he had to say.

Again, Gerald Smith stole the show, vowing that, "If I have to take a candidate put up by William Randolph Hearst to have a Republican Party, then I say to hell with the Republican Party.

"If I have to drink milk warmed in Tammany from a bottle with a nipple put on by James A. Farley, in order to be a Democrat, then I say to hell with the Democratic Party.

"If Lemke forgets about the Townsend Plan, then I know a country doctor and a Louisiana preacher who will chop his dad-gummed head off."

Folks remained abuzz over Coughlin's recent performance—but not in a good way. Not good at all. His impromptu striptease (Gomer Smith: "I want my religion from a preacher with his shirt on") was the least of his problems. Publicly insulting the president of the United States as a "liar" and a "Double-Crosser" had set tongues wagging. Coughlin had crossed a dangerous new Rubicon. Would his Church finally discipline him? His bishop, Michael Gallagher (coincidentally on a trip to Rome), initially remained supportive, but reports swirled of increased Vatican pressure on Gallagher. On Thursday, July 23, Coughlin caved—sort of. Apologizing for the word "liar," he protested it referred not to FDR's broken assurances to him (though he implied FDR really had misled him), but to Roosevelt's discarded 1932 campaign promises—again still implying that FDR had lied. Pointedly, he concluded, "I deem it best for the welfare of our common country that you [FDR] be supplanted in office."

Rumors initially floated that Coughlin, Smith, and Townsend would barnstorm as a team. No one seemed to care what Lemke did. If the Union Party foursome was akin to Hollywood's Marx Brothers, Lemke was clearly Zeppo. Rep. Usher Burdick, having signed on to manage Lemke's campaign, quickly abandoned ship to salvage his own North Dakota House seat. Commencing his presidential campaign, Lemke promised an actual party convention. It never happened. Luckily for him, he could piggyback onto yet another mass meeting—again in Cleveland, this one sponsored by Coughlin's National Union for Social Justice.

In the month intervening between Townsend's and Coughlin's extravaganzas, however, this grand alliance had frayed like a cheap suit. OARP organizers Clinton Wunder and Jack Kiefer wanted no part of any Lemke adventure, so Townsend expelled them once more from his embattled organization's board. The rather-too-flexible Wunder now quickly landed a speaking birth with FDR's Good Neighbor League. Townsend himself remained hesitant, nonetheless. Coughlin's fragile ego barred sharing his spotlight with any interlopers. He resented the more hypnotic Smith and feared how he might steal his audience. He barely stirred to tout Lemke's candidacy. In their joint events, he seized top billing; Lemke was a footnote.

The movement's leadership denied any rifts. But each went their own way. Coughlin vowed to throw Communists out of the White House. Townsend swung by Topeka and, speaking to two thousand persons in the city auditorium, proclaimed, "I would vote for a native-born Chinaman or a Jap from Hawaii rather than vote for Roosevelt or Landon. William Lemke gets my vote."

In Newark, Smith spun a wild tale of New Deal henchmen offering him "everything from Maine to the Philippines to stop what I am doing." He claimed that in just the previous ten days alone, three attempts had been made on his life—in Atlanta, in North Carolina, and in Alabama.

Coughlin's NUSJ confab convened on Thursday, August 13, with undisguised sniping dividing his and the Townsend camps. Convention Grand Marshal Walter D. Davis urged the NUSJ to stay out of politics and wanted Townsend and Smith barred from its convention podium, claiming he feared a new version of Gomer Smith's earlier protests. "If one out of 12 apostles were a Judas Iscariot," warned Davis, "it was an even bet that one out of 1,200 delegates in the national convention will be a Gomer Smith!"

OARP executive secretary Gilmour Young, however, retorted that if Townsend and Smith couldn't speak, neither could Coughlin speak at any subsequent Townsendite gatherings. Coughlin caved.

Townsend's millions of adherents clearly adored him, but their ardor counted for nothing compared to Coughlinites' for their hero. Townsend promised them a check every month (and hadn't yet delivered). Coughlin visited their living rooms every Sunday night, soothed them, educated them, inspired them. He was their teacher and their friend. At Cleveland, in less than twenty-three hours, a single vendor sold 11,500 pastel-colored portraits of The Radio Priest for a quarter apiece. A resolution solemnly paid tribute to Coughlin's mother for having borne him.

An even more servile resolution followed:

> In the conduct of the [NUSJ], we endorse, without any exception whatsoever, all the acts of our president and great leader, Father Charles E. Coughlin. . . . Finally, lest specification detract from the fullness of our sanction, we publish our unreserved and unqualified

> endorsements of all public acts, radio addresses and statements of our leader, pledging our resources and our activities in his support and in support of our principles, even as he has thrown into the battle every ounce of his endurance.

Coughlin promised delegates that they—not he—would decide on Lemke's candidacy—he'd be no dictator. On Saturday, August 15, opposition from within the New York and Michigan delegations collapsed, and the convention endorsed Lemke 8,152 to 1. The lone dissenter was John J. O'Donnell, an alternate from Pittsburgh who, decrying the gathering's "mob psychology," claimed it "humbly and ignorantly serve[d] the purposes of the Liberty League and William Randolph Hearst." Police escorted O'Donnell out of the hall, as outraged Coughlinites screamed "Judas!" and "How much did Farley pay you?" One delegate threatened, "I don't want to see that monkey get out of here in one piece."

"The police kept Mr. O'Donnell in a locked room," noted *The Nation*'s Gerold Frank, "then took him for a motor ride and suggested he spend the rest of the day at the Great Lakes Convention, which is also a big show, but less dangerous."

Coughlin now arrived in Cleveland—pleasantly startling reporters with his bonhomie. Queried regarding O'Donnell's lone dissenting vote, Coughlin viewed the glass as 8,152/8,153 full rather than 1/8,153 empty. He had feared tougher sledding: a mere 80-to-1 victory.

He boasted—and far too rashly: "If I can't deliver my radio audience—and that's 9 million voters—if I can't deliver them for Lemke and O'Brien in November, I'm through. . . . I'll be a washout and I'll quit broadcasting."

Rarely are political conventions—even real ones—about voting. They're about orating. As a speaker, Townsend remained leaden. Smith remained gold, so Coughlin schemed on downgrading Smith's performance, scheduling him at suppertime, calculating that delegates would be tired, hungry, and wanting to rest and dine rather than endure another speech—even a rip-snorter. It didn't work: Smith retained his magic, infuriating Coughlin. As one historian noted, Coughlin petulantly "squirmed in his seat, talked to his friends, grinned slyly at those around him, and elaborately pretended to go to sleep—anything to detract attention from the spellbinding Smith."

On Sunday, August 16, Coughlinites moved two blocks north to Municipal Stadium for the really big three-and-a-half-ring circus. Unlike July's OARP fiasco, a much bigger crowd attended—somewhere between 25,000 and 40,000 persons—but the huge new ballpark still remained better than half-empty. But even a 40,000-person crowd was nothing near the 100,000 throng the organizers had boldly predicted earlier that month.

Cleveland's Catholic auxiliary bishop James McFadden provided the invocation. VP choice "Hamburger Tom" O'Brien followed, as did Lemke, who predicted he'd win fifteen million votes and at least fifteen states. "Roosevelt," he charged, "is a bewildered Kerensky not knowing where he is going. Landon represents the dying shadows of a past civilization and doesn't know it."

A broiling sun beat down as Coughlin commenced his own forty-minute address. He said little about Lemke, but much about Roosevelt, avoiding the word "liar" but not the concept:

> I believed that inaugural address. I believed those peerless lips which enunciated golden words in that campaign of 1932. "Why, here was a new voice. Here was the reincarnation of Christ's voice which spoke on Tuesday of Holy Week and was stilled on Friday of Holy Week which had said: 'Drive the money changers out of the temple.'"
>
> This peerless president of ours issued an edict for the nationalization of gold. By 1934, at Christmas time, forgetting the Babe that was born in Bethlehem, this peerless President passed over the coins that he had confiscated from the men and women of the country to the private owners of the Federal Reserve Bank, your masters and his cordial advisers.
>
> Then I knew he was using you and me on the chess board of life.

He seemingly branded FDR a Communist: "Roosevelt and Tugwell and the rest of the Communists are destroying us." Somehow, no one seemed to notice.

He spoke of the Jews. At first, sympathetically. But, as with Roosevelt and the "money changers," he suddenly lashed out, bizarrely challenging:

> We are a Christian organization in that we believe in the principle of "love thy neighbor as thyself." With that principle I challenge every Jew in this nation to tell me that he does or does not believe in it. I am not asking the Jews of the United States to accept Christianity and all of its beliefs, but since their system of "a tooth for a tooth and an eye for an eye" has failed, that they accept Christ's principles of brotherhood.

The day's main program had commenced at 4:00 p.m. sharp, to be wrapped up by 5:15 due to the limits of a major radio hookup. With eight minutes to go, however, the sweat-drenched Coughlin abruptly halted. "I must apologize to you. I have been ill all night and I shall not be able to proceed any further."

Coughlin claimed that, ten minutes previously, he had gone black: "I couldn't see anything although I knew I was in bright sunshine." Suffering from the intense heat, from overwork, and from intestinal problems of the previous evening, and unshielded by any canopy, he turned his back on the microphone and collapsed into the arms of a nearby policeman.

His audience thought he had merely concluded, not knowing how expensive eight minutes of air time was—or of his condition. Soon they stood stunned, in silent prayer.

Coughlin staggered to a waiting car to recuperate in his hotel room before a full week of rest. The crowd slowly trudged out. A convention was over. A campaign would commence.

Lemke and O'Brien campaigned—both with a twist. Lemke remained on the North Dakota ballot, running to retain his old House seat. O'Brien also performed double duty, competing as a write-in Democratic primary candidate against Boston mayor James M. Curley for an open US Senate seat. Curley would claim that Coughlin had once offered his support, but their alliance unraveled, at least partially thanks to Curley's refusal to repudiate Franklin Roosevelt. O'Brien lost the primary (garnering only 10.01 percent of the vote) but stayed in the race. Curley later declared that he offered "Hamburger Tom" $10,000 to quit—but that Republicans offered him $25,000 to stay in.

Coughlin continued to attract huge crowds. On September 8, he drew somewhere between eighty thousand and one hundred thousand admirers to Chicago's Riverview amusement park, speaking from a specially built podium designed by a twenty-eight-year-old NUSJ staffer—the future internationally renowned architect Philip Johnson.

In December 1934, the upper-crust, high-culture Johnson (Harvard '27) had abandoned his post as chairman of the newly formed Museum of Modern Arts's Department of Architecture to head south in a twelve-cylinder Packard convertible and attach himself to Huey Long, taking with him a pal, the museum's executive director, Alan Blackburn (Harvard '29). "I'm leaving to be Huey Long's Minister of Fine Arts," Johnson joked (only perhaps) to friends as the pair departed.

Actually, his sights were set at a far greater altitude. Previously, he and Blackburn had fancied forming their own party, "The National Party," with a symbol of its own—not a swastika or a Blue Eagle but, of all things, a flying wedge. Like the Nazis and Fascists and Communists, they sported their own wardrobe. In their case, shirts of gray, though they denied any connection to any of the other shirt outfits. "We are a separate shirt," protested young Mr. Blackburn.

"We're adventurers with an intellectual overlay," Johnson flippantly explained to the *Herald Tribune*'s Joseph Alsop (Corinne Alsop's son; Eleanor's first cousin once removed), "so we're almost articulate but not quite articulate."

As Johnson's secretary later informed the FBI, he somehow believed that "the fate of the country" fell upon him—and not upon the bumptious Long. Johnson—not the Kingfish—would be "the 'Hitler' in the United States. . . . By joining with Huey Long he could eventually depose Huey Long from control of the country and gain control of it for himself."

Easier said than done, since neither Long nor Long's secretary Earl Christenberry had much use for Johnson and Blackburn's services or for the speechwriting and researching talents Johnson claimed he brought with him. Huey's speechifying already seemed quite adequate, thank you, and Christenberry bluntly informed his uninvited Yankee visitors,

"How many votes have you got? You come back with a million votes, or a hundred thousand votes, and you can see Huey any time. But you ain't got nothin'."

And so Christenberry shuffled Johnson and Blackburn (aka "The Gold Dust Twins") off to menial Share-Our-Wealth field work in Johnson's native Ohio.

Long's September 1935 demise upended that gig. Soon, Johnson and Blackburn had shifted to plugging the Townsend Plan and then Father Coughlin's NUSJ and, soon after that, the new Union Party. Not surprisingly, Johnson found Lemke to be "a crashing boor" but nonetheless soldiered on to assist Coughlin as a correspondent and in design work. "A special stand" is how the *Chicago Tribune* described Johnson's Riverview Park brainstorm, "bordering on the modern . . . at one end of the field . . . a glaring white background 50 feet wide and 20 feet high for the solitary figure of the priest."

That Johnson's Riverview Park inspiration looked uncomfortably Nazi understates the matter wildly—he modeled it after one he'd seen Hitler employ at a Hitler Youth rally (Putzi Hanfstaengl helped secure his ticket) in October 1932. Johnson savored not merely Hitler and all "the excitement" but "all those blond boys in black leather."

Coughlin marched on. On September 10, before 10,000 at Detroit's Olympia Stadium, Lemke, midway through his own speech, instantly surrendered the microphone to the late-arriving Coughlin, again confirming Coughlin's top-dog status. The following day, Coughlin headlined a mile-long parade in Brooklyn. At Ebbets Field, he and Thomas O'Brien addressed a paid crowd of 22,000, speaking from atop a twelve-foot-high dais, which, it was said, "strikingly resembled a gallows."

But speeches were not votes, and votes were not coming the Unionists' way. A few days later, New York State held congressional and state legislative primaries. All fifteen Townsendite and Union challengers suffered defeat. In one Democratic state senate race, they fell by a 25–1 margin.

Four thousand persons in Des Moines paid 50 cents each to hear Coughlin excoriate Earl Browder's sub-rosa support for FDR and how "Roosevelt grins and likes it." Later, at a local radio-station studio, he delivered a rambling impromptu, unguarded interview, blustering, "We are at the crossroads. One road leads towards fascism, the other towards communism. I take the road towards fascism."

Coughlin was unraveling. A week later, he hit Cincinnati. "When any upstart dictator . . . succeeds in making of this nation a one-party form of government, and the ballot becomes useless," he exploded, "I shall have the courage to stand up and advocate the use of bullets." Slamming FDR's farm policies as "unchristian and radical," he proclaimed, "The Bible commands 'increase and multiply,' but Roosevelt says 'destroy and devastate,' and therefore I call him anti-God and radical." Cincinnati, Cleveland, and Omaha's bishops all condemned him.

At Boston, on Monday, October 12, *Boston Globe* reporter John J. Barry questioned his labeling of David Dubinsky and Felix Frankfurter as Communists. Barry then traveled with Coughlin to Providence, where Coughlin cornered him in a hotel corridor, berated him for "lacking common decency," accused him of "sticking your nose into a private meeting," and allegedly assaulted him before being restrained by Tom O'Brien.

Returning to Boston, Coughlin remained on the warpath, threatening to "get" Barry and "tear him to pieces." Soon, however, he calmed down, claiming Barry was drunk and that he had merely "harmlessly held [Barry] against the wall. . . . Lifting his glasses I advised him that he should have his face slapped for impudence."

Six days later, Coughlin addressed eight thousand at Michigan's State Fair Grounds, mere miles south of his home parish. GOP governor Frank D. Fitzgerald introduced him; Coughlin returned the favor by endorsing Fitzgerald against his erstwhile friend Frank Murphy.

"Communism," Coughlin thundered, "takes its principle that the earth is the state's and the people's thereof."

Whatever that meant.

A man attired in white trousers, a bright red shirt, and a white cap trimmed with feathers loitered at the rear of The Radio Priest's platform. Coughlin continued: "Christianity takes as its principle that the earth belongs to God."

Which was a lot clearer.

That was as far as he got. The man sprang forward, sprinkling Coughlin with feathers. Seizing Coughlin's microphone, he boomed, "You can't mix religion and politics."

Frank "Woody" Hockaday had struck again. Now calling himself "Chief Pow-Wow," he'd been more than busy since the Democrats' National Convention, scattering forty pounds of feathers and shouting "Feathers instead of Bullets!" at Acting Secretary of War Harry Woodring, at various American Legion gatherings, and on Wall Street. In between featherings, he escaped from St. Elizabeth's Hospital in Washington; Long Island's's Chestnut Lodge Sanitarium; and a third institution in Hutchinson, Kansas. At various times he announced plans to bring his "mission" to the Supreme Court or to war-torn Madrid. On October 8, traveling light (just twenty pounds of feathers), he invaded Alf Landon's office. A pair of bodyguards seized him and ushered him out.

Twice.

The feathers he tossed at Coughlin, Hockaday explained, were "brown feathers from Boston," where he had lain in wait to ambush The Radio Priest.

Resourceful as Hockaday was, he underestimated Coughlin's reaction. The priest swung wild and hard. Hockaday ducked a right to his chin before a solid punch to his shoulder landed and the priest pinned him to the floor. As police led Hockaday through the hostile crowd, angry Coughlinites shouted, "Lynch him!" "Hold him!" "Kill him!" "Don't let him get away!" Bloodying him, they shoved feathers down his throat. "[O]ne elderly gray-haired woman, . . ." noted a press report, "was among the loudest."

Coughlin shouted, "Don't touch that man. Don't touch that man! We'll bring him up here and let him talk. I love to talk with communists and NewDealocrats."

From his jail cell, Hockaday announced plans to discuss peace with Hitler and Mussolini. No mealy-mouthed appeaser, he mused, "If they have the wrong ideas on the subject, I'll pull out my feathers again."

Coughlin weathered such embarrassments. He was, after all, "The Radio Priest," and even though Pius XI's personal representative Eugenio

Cardinal Pacelli soon arrived stateside to rein him in, Coughlin still enjoyed his bishop's support and a weekly audience in the millions.

Gerald L. K. Smith remained as formidable a speaker as ever. When he appeared before the National Press Club that August, columnist Mark Sullivan marveled that he was "as good as Bryan. . . . He is much better at his art than the Rev. Billy Sunday." Smith remained as unapologetic as ever:

> If you say "the flag" you are a rabble-rouser. The very first reference to the Stars and Stripes makes you a rabble-rouser. And never refer to the Bible; never refer to the Constitution. That makes you a demagogue and a rabble-rouser. . . .
>
> I am a symbol. I am a symbol of a state of mind. When politicians and practitioners on the gullibility of the population overplay their hand, certain nerve centers in the national population begin to scream—and I am one of the yellers.
>
> I have lived for many years with the masses. I know the people of America. . . . I understand a certain section of the great forgotten group of middle-class people and poverty-stricken people in the United States of America, and because of my understanding of these people I am interested in this campaign. . . . We know how poor people live and we know what our people want. . . . I say to America, "Hear my cry, for it is the cry of 75,000,000 poor people of America."

Infighting, however, within Townsend's inner circle remained fierce, and Smith's high-profile presence irked many veteran Townsendites, particularly those hostile to the increasingly shaky Lemke–Union Party gambit.

But for all his oratorical skills, Smith never hauled in the big crowds. Townsend and Coughlin drew far more. By October, he was desperately maneuvering to regain the spotlight. In mid-month, his spokesman, Harry J. Costello, announced that Smith was now raising funds from four hundred "financial leaders" for "a $1,500,000 nationalist front against Communism."

"He has changed his idea of his own role before the public," Costello, a former Georgetown star quarterback, a reluctant participant in American intervention in Russia, and more recently LSU's director of sports communications, explained, "declaring he took to the Union party only for a forum. He now sets himself up as a nationalist and as spokesman for a new force against Communism."

Which, while interesting—and, perhaps, even true—was not particularly horrible.

Within days, however, Smith demolished what little store of respectability he retained.

Booking himself into Manhattan's six-thousand-seat Hippodrome Theatre, he found that few New Yorkers bothered to catch his act. To rows of empty seats, he raged that "when the Reds dynamite the tunnels and bridges of New York and cut off all lines of communication; when the [William] Bullitt Reds and the [David] Dubinsky Reds and all the rest of that crew join forces to seize America, us cotton choppin', corn huskin', baby havin' God-fearin', Bible readin' [people] are goin' to have our own united front—we'll save America."

All pretty standard Smith stuff. He was pretty good at saving America. But when he proclaimed he was creating an independent movement of ten million followers "to seize the government of the United States," Townsend hit the roof.

> "If the press reports concerning the Fascist actions of Gerald L. K. Smith are true," the doctor exploded, "then I hereby disavow . . . Mr. Smith. . . . I am against fascism: it is un-American and smacks of the New Deal and President Roosevelt. . . . I repeat, Gerald Smith shall henceforth have no connection with our organization. This is definite and final. . . .
>
> "The Townsend organization is American in its foundation and ideals, and I do not propose to allow any person with dictatorial tendencies, whether they be under the guise of the New Deal or nationalization, to stampede the Townsend movement in whole or in part into even partial endorsement. . . .

> "[N]ationalism and centralization are both definite trends toward Fascism. As a matter of principle his connection with our National Recovery Administration must be automatically severed."

More and more people cut their losses, moving on to better, less fanciful worlds. Lemke largely retreated to North Dakota, determined to salvage his House seat and salary. Townsend advised his followers in the fourteen states where Lemke had failed to secure ballot access, to cast their votes for Landon. "Roosevelt," he ordered, "must be defeated."

The election was heating up.

Though, Alf Landon clearly wasn't.

· 16 ·

"Innocuous as a watermelon . . . boiled in a bathtub"

Alf Landon was hardly the type of fellow to seize power.

Contrary to descriptions of him as the puppet/ally/hireling of a vast Liberty League/Hearst/fascisti conspiracy, he was pretty much what he looked like, a bespectacled, middle-aged Republican from a typical prairie state.

He would need a lot of luck to best Franklin Roosevelt. But much luck had already clung to him. He won the governorship thanks to a quack "goat gland" doctor's third-party bid. He captured the presidential nomination with precious little heavy lifting. His opponents had not so much as fallen *by* the wayside but started *in* the wayside and then wandered off into the woods to die. The nation's most powerful publisher devoted thousands upon thousands of column inches to his cause. Though Hearst's support was not without drawbacks, there was much to be said for such free publicity, the operative principle being "Don't look a gift Hearst in the mouth."

But what of the future? Good things might again miraculously transpire. Franklin Roosevelt's popularity had a way of sliding up and down. It seemed to be slipping once more, and might slip still further between summer and fall. Though Lemke's candidacy turned out to be largely a bust, it had certainly held potential in the early summer. A few votes stolen away here and there—either by Lemke or Norman Thomas—might yet filch a state or two or more from the Democratic column. Al Smith might finally convince enough of his old friends and admirers of what a scoundrel this Roosevelt fellow was. Last, but not least, there were still millions of unemployed men and women, destitute farmers, and ruined businessmen whose wounds Dr. New Deal had not yet salved.

But all these were external factors. What would *Landon* do?

Having chosen not to contest the primaries or attend the convention, he went on vacation.

In early June, Landon rented the 1,200-acre McGraw Ranch, at the foot of the Rockies, six miles north of Estes Park, Colorado. Settling into a large rustic cabin, two miles from the main gate, were the candidate and his thirty-seven-year-old wife; her sixty-one-year-old mother; Landon's three children: nineteen-year-old Peggy Ann (his daughter by his first wife who had died in 1918), nineteen-year-old Nancy Jo, and three-year-old Jon Cobb ("Jack"); their nurse; Mrs. Landon's secretary; plus their two dogs, Jerry, a blue terrier, and Spooky, a Scottie pup.

A thousand Coloradans greeted their arrival—all on horseback. His campaign beckoning, Landon went fishing. "I'm doing a good job of loafing right now," he confessed. "I came out to get a real rest. I need it, too."

At Estes Park's Stanley Hotel, he faced forty reporters—peppering him with questions concerning his farm policy. He wasn't good. "[H]e got tongue-tied," noted one Eastern reporter, "stammered and racked his brain for words that . . . did not come. He was in a quandary."

They asked him about his approaching acceptance speech. He languidly responded, "I was just nominated a week ago today, you know. There hasn't been time enough yet to settle that question."

Landon actually did spend a fair amount of time on this vacation working on his acceptance speech and on other official and political business, but valuable time remained forfeited. A disturbing message of a dangerously lackadaisical campaign—and candidate—was being sent. Frank Knox and John D. M. Hamilton hit their respective campaign trails on June 26; Landon kept his powder dry for another month, until his formal acceptance in Topeka on July 23. In between, Landon—still Governor Landon—summoned a special session of the Kansas legislature.

He recruited his own version of the "Brain Trust." Roosevelt's worked. His didn't—for multiple reasons. It was very late in the game, almost the ninth inning. Franklin's team of expert advisers—Moley, Tugwell, Rosenman, et al.—had all been on board well before his 1932 nomination and, despite their inevitable squabbles, remained on the same page until their electoral mission was accomplished.

"None of these Landon 'brain trusters' [however]," scoffed *The Nation*'s Paul Ward, "has as yet any precise knowledge as to what his duties are to be. Several of them had never seen the Governor before they reached Topeka and are as much in the dark as to his talents and inclinations as is the rest of the country."

And, while FDR's own "Brain Trust" was marvelously compact and efficient, Landon's was simply too unwieldy to get out of its own way, let alone block Franklin Roosevelt's. Logistics also posed a problem. Topeka, Kansas, while literally the center of the country, is nonetheless hardly the center of anything else.

Yet perhaps such problems were mere quibbles. On July 6, Landon wrote to Ogden Mills that "the tide is running very strong in our direction," and Landon's opinion was hardly indefensible. July 12's Gallup Poll reported a 272–259 Landon electoral vote lead. Two weeks later, the *Farm Journal* straw ballot, having correctly called every election since 1912, reported Landon besting FDR by a 5-to-4 margin. As noted earlier, Emil Hurja's internal Democratic polling confirmed such ill winds—and had been doing so since as far back as February. On July 26, Farley privately predicted significant losses in the House. DNC publicity director Charlie Michelson foresaw the party losing "nearly, if not quite, one hundred seats."

The *Boston Herald* reported that a Boston newsreel audience displayed two to three times more enthusiasm for images of Landon silently fishing in Colorado than for FDR rendezvousing with destiny in Philadelphia.

More than a fair amount of people remained nervous of the New Deal. An August Gallup poll asked: "Do you believe the acts and policies of the Roosevelt administration may lead to dictatorship?" Forty-five percent answered yes. Fifty-eight percent of New Englanders agreed—including 73 percent of those living in towns under 2,500 in population. Even 47 percent of Franklin's fellow New Yorkers concurred. The majority (52 percent) of those living in small towns nationwide answered yes.

In late September, the *Herald Tribune* reported on pollster Rogers C. Dunn's prediction of a Landon landslide. Only twelve states remained in the Roosevelt camp. Only three wobbled on the fence. Everyplace else, seered Mr. Dunn, was Landon territory, representing a hefty 377 votes and victory. Dunn drew his figures and predictions upon an entire new system—devised by himself; his wife, Betty; and a friend from toney Southampton—based not on straw ballots or any Gallup-style "scientific" method but solely upon newspaper circulation and what each paper's editorial policy was. "The wonder," sputtered an obviously dumbstruck and outraged *Montgomery Advertiser*, "is not that a fool would put any faith in such a farce of his own invention but that a supposedly reputable newspaper of the metropolitan area would give credence to his fantasy by printing it as news."

In mid-October, the *Literary Digest* finally gathered data from all forty-eight states. The verdict: Landon led in thirty-two states, boasting a 370–161 electoral vote lead, and a 55.4–40.1 percent popular vote edge—though that last percentage had by now declined for six straight weeks.

By late July, reports had reached Washington of Landon pondering major cabinet appointments. In view of the increasing controversy over Jim Farley's dual role as Democratic national chairman and postmaster general, John D. M. Hamilton decided he would not take the postmaster generalship, preferring either attorney general or to function as a healthier, more hygienic GOP edition of Louis Howe. Ogden Mills would reclaim his old Treasury post. Kansas representative Clifford Hope, a former chair of the House Agriculture Committee, would take Agriculture. Herbert Hoover could have his choice: either the State Department or his old bailiwick Commerce.

Hoover now hankered to support Landon. His old ally Louis B. Mayer didn't. On July 3, Mayer lunched with FDR's Comptroller of the Currency James F. T. O'Connor and MGM producer John Considine Jr., an ardent Democrat and the brother of the rising young Hearst columnist Bob Considine. O'Connor and Considine angled to discover Mayer's plans for the election. Mayer reassured them: if he did not actually support Roosevelt, he wouldn't actively oppose him either. Mayer also confided that the film industry's previous plans to support Landon were now dead.

A greater—or at least a more continuing—difficulty was John Hamilton. Hamilton had his talents. He was a very skilled organizer and (when not predicting Landon had it in the bag) an articulate spokesman. But he was far to the right of the moderate-to-liberal Landon, and, certainly, much further to the right than any image the party now dared project.

The Landon–Hamilton relationship was a mystifying one. Not only were they ideologically opposites, but Landon had served as Clyde Reed's campaign manager in 1928, sinking Hamilton's hopes in the state's GOP gubernatorial primary.

Still, Hamilton retained Landon's great trust. "[T]hough he is five years Hamilton's senior," noted Paul Ward, "Landon looks up to Hamilton with the admiration of a young boy for his elder brother. He openly refers to Hamilton as 'our leader' and eagerly takes a back seat whenever Hamilton puts in an appearance. Nor does he wince when Hamilton says boldly, 'I'm running this show.'"

Colorado ranch houses and the special legislative session behind him, Landon opened his campaign—in 104-degree (in the shade) heat—before the Kansas State House on Thursday, July 23. A hundred thousand (some said 200,000) Republicans cheered him, having arrived via at least 20,000 automobiles and 400 special trains. It was, as not even Harold Ickes could deny, the largest crowd Topeka had ever seen. Cecil B. DeMille helped organize the shindig in true DeMille style, with klieg lights, a hundred bands, and 200 cowboys, 500 Indians from 50 tribes, 3 elephants (one genuine; two papier-mâché), 4,000 musicians, 15 drum-and-bugle corps, various massed choirs and decorated floats, stagecoaches and prairie schooners, fireworks, an ornate gold-leaf trimmed podium, and a 40-by-60-foot, 900-pound (including 496 pounds of paint) banner of the not-quite-smiling Landon draped over a nearby office building.

Counted among marchers in the hour-and-forty-five-minute parade was a contingent advertising themselves as "five hundred economic royalists and princes of privilege from Clay County, Kansas." The president of the Shawnee County farm bureau did not march—he rode a cow.

"The crowd," noted William Allen White, "which was attentive and in a receptive mood, was liberal with its cheers and gave a big hand to John D. M. Hamilton, . . . who has a big grin and also a big mouth which often makes him look as if he were grinning when he isn't." It may be inferred that Mr. White did not care much for John D. M. Hamilton.

H. L. Mencken, dispirited because it was "simply too hot for alcohol," struggled mightily to extend something akin to praise or enthusiasm for Landon's own remarks. "There was," he wrote, "little slurring of syllables. . . . The effect was not that of a trumpet or a violin cello, but rather that of a muted xylophone. . . . There was applause at the end, but not much."

Nonetheless, Landon's forty-minute talk drew seventy-one rounds of either cheers or applause as he articulated the campaign's themes of constitutional government, efficiency, and patronage reform, while avoiding any concrete criticism of the New Deal. But the day also exposed the strange sluggishness dogging Landon's effort. The Associated Press noted that the candidate had taken "several hours of rest during the day." Theo Cobb Landon spent much of her own day in seclusion while announcing she would not personally join her husband's campaign. Aside from a natural shyness, her decision may have stemmed from other factors. The first was political: to provide a demure contrast with the very public Mrs. Roosevelt. The second may have stemmed from a fear for her family's safety. In September 1933, authorities had uncovered a plot to kidnap Mrs. Landon's step-daughter Peggy.

The family then announced plans for . . . *two* additional Colorado vacations. Only one transpired, and it was marred by yet another kidnapping threat against Landon's children. Also delaying matters was a bout of pleurisy striking Landon himself.

By August, the bloom was vanishing from the Landon Sunflower. Democratic forces displayed greater optimism. Two factors contributed to their cheer. In Spain, civil war now raged between Communist-backed Loyalists and Mussolini-supported Nationalists, fueling fears of a wider European conflict. FDR's incumbency provided greater foreign-policy credibility than anything the Topeka-based Landon might ever boast.

Secondly, Landon's acceptance address, broadcast nationally, impressed neither in content nor delivery. "[Landon's] voice on the air was monotonous," noted historian Irving Stone, "without any semblance of the warmth and humor and human quality of the man. Chairmen tried to anticipate Landon's poor speaking by telling audiences that he was no radio crooner, which drew laughter and a cheer but did not fully prepare the listener for the jerky, halting, almost dismal manner of his public speaking. The fine magnetism that drew people to Alf Landon vanished when he approached a microphone or loud-speaker; he became nervous; then formal, then cold, reading his speeches with his head buried in the manuscript. He took lessons from voice coaches; he improved somewhat as the campaign waxed hotter, but he developed no sense of vocal showmanship, could not think fast or wittily or graciously on his feet. Had his texts been revolutionary he might have fired his audience in spite of the poor delivery; as it was he received but scant applause even from Republican gatherings."

Such deficiencies earned merciless ridicule. "Do you know," Alice Roosevelt Longworth confided to Mrs. Ogden Reid, "J. P. Morgan won't allow the name Franklin Roosevelt to be mentioned in his presence because it raises his blood pressure. I'm for Landon, but I do wish he'd stop lowering my blood pressure." Columnist Dorothy Thompson jibed to Democratic fundraiser George Allen that if Landon delivered one more speech, Roosevelt would carry Canada.

In late August, Westbrook Pegler unleashed a column of absolutely withering mockery:

> Considerable mystery surrounds the disappearance of Alfred Landon of Topeka, Kansas, who has been missing from his regular haunts for some time. The Missing Person Bureau has sent out an alarm bulletin bearing Mr. Landon's photograph and other particulars, and anyone having information of his whereabouts is asked to communicate direct with the Republican National Committee. The bulletin adds that he might be found in the vicinity of a trout stream or throwing snowballs in Estes National Park, Colorado. The bulletin describes Mr. Landon as follows:
>
> *Height, average.*
> *Weight, average.*

Appearance, average.
Complexion, average.
Habits, average.
Distinguishing characteristics, scars, birthmarks, etc., average.

Mr. Landon suddenly dropped from view a few days after a party of friends called on him in Topeka and notified him that he had been nominated for president by the Republicans, in a ceremony known as Landon Astonishment Day.

He seemed rather startled, if not shocked, by the news, and intimate friends express the belief that he has been brooding over this development. However, his personal affairs are said to be in average shape at the time of his disappearance, and those who know Mr. Landon, insist that not even his worst enemy would have wished to do him harm.

In fact, his enemies have expressed only the kindliest sentiments toward him. One—the Rev. Charles Coughlin—went out of his way to describe him as an honorable man and Mr. James Farley is known to be worried over his disappearance.

"What a soft life this would be," Mr. Farley said, "if all our opponents were Landons. I could not have chosen any more desirable Republican nominee if the Republicans as well as the Democrats had left it to me."

Mr. Landon's disappearance might be traced to this very lack of enmity in his opponents. He was heard to say, only a few days before his absence was noted, that nobody gave him credit for his dangerous potentialities.

• • •

Mr. Landon recently has been engaged in promoting the professional career of John D. M. Hamilton, a Kansas attorney, and is given credit for a remarkably fine job. Within three months, Mr. Landon has raised Mr. Hamilton from comparative obscurity to national prominence.

Pressed for the exact hour of Mr. Landon's disappearance, Mr. Hamilton said he was unable to establish the time within four or five days.

...

"He was around the place in Topeka as usual," Mr. Hamilton said, "nobody seems to notice that he was gone for quite some time. Then one day somebody said, "Where is Alf?" and nobody remembered seeing him for some time.

"I remember, now, however," Mr. Hamilton said, that he seemed depressed over the way his opponents were treating him." One day he went around singing: 'Nobody hates me; everybody loves me; I guess I will go out in Estes Park and throw some snowballs.' I said, 'Oh, cheer up; you probably have some faults,' and passed the matter up.

"I certainly hope we find him soon. I don't know what I am going to do without him."

Colonel Frank Knox, of Chicago, was mystified when reporters asked him if he had seen Mr. Landon lately.

"Never heard of him," said Colonel Knox, "What does he do? He sounds like the forgotten man."

The official description of Mr. Landon has led to unfortunate confusion for men are being turned up all over the country who resemble the person described in the bulletin. These have included, to date, 11,382 vice presidents of trust companies and real estate firms and 2,836 presidents and secretaries of chambers of commerce.

The police are baffled.

Colorado was relatively cool. Much of the country was damned hot. The country had survived the Dust Bowl of the early '30s, but horrid drought and heat returned ferociously in the summer of 1936. By mid-July, record temperatures were recorded at Bismarck, North Dakota (114°), Keokuk, Iowa (108°), Rapid City, South Dakota (106°), Concordia,

Kansas (106°), Miles City, Montana (108°), Moorhead, Minnesota (114°), Omaha, Nebraska (110°), Phoenix, Arizona (114°), and Wishek, North Dakota (120°).

"Hot winds, tearing up the top-soil, leave thousands of acres of unfertile fields," reported the *Literary Digest.* "Then the dust is deposited in drifts on fields perhaps hundreds of miles away, doing double damage by killing growing crops. Highways are blocked, motoring and aviation are made dangerous, humans and cattle are seriously afflicted. The dust permeates everywhere. People put ointment in their nostrils, wear wet cloths over their mouths, sleep with their windows shut. But the dust creeps in, irritating throat and eyes and lungs, spoiling food, covering furniture and floors till housekeeping becomes a nightmare."

The year 1936 witnessed Kansas's hottest summer ever. Topeka endured thirty-one days of temperatures reaching between 90° and 100°—plus fifty-nine days *over* 100°.

The damage was hardly confined to the West and Midwest. The *Literary Digest* reported that "the wave of heat swept on, scorching much of the East. Day after day of relentless heat took suffering to congested metropolitan areas where the unfortunate sweltered on fire escapes and blistering pavements and stoops. Some . . . sought relief at watering places—and died. Two hundred dead from drought, heat, drowning, was the Eastern toll as the week began—sixty-eight in New York City and thirty-nine more in other parts of New York State; twenty-eight in New Jersey, thirty-one in Pennsylvania, five in Delaware and thirty in New England. The killing heat of the direct sun was so intense it weakened huge steel beams of Manhattan bridges, warped raised sections so they could not be lowered."

The crisis triggered the first face-to-face meeting of presidential nominees in campaign history. In Des Moines, on September 3, Roosevelt conferred with five Midwestern governors—from Missouri, Nebraska, Iowa, Oklahoma, and, most significantly, Kansas. FDR and Landon conversed privately and cordially for forty minutes. FDR relied on his extraordinary political memory (he amazed Landon by recalling their one previous conversation) and upon his finely honed gift for small talk. "Governor," FDR chatted, "if you get my job at the White House you had better get a small boat to take weekend fishing trips up on the Potomac. Large ones hold too many people, and it is a pretty hard job without these trips."

"Thanks, Mr. President," Landon responded. "I will remember that."

"Landon is a swell guy," thought Rexford Tugwell. "He's a very fine, charming gentleman," Landon informed reporters regarding Roosevelt. "Harmony," mused Sen. Arthur Capper, "dripped so steadily from every rafter that I expected one of the candidates to withdraw."

Well funded and well supported, Landon, of course, was not about to withdraw. In mid-September, newly appointed GOP "Speaking Bureau" chief Fred S. Purnell announced he would soon unleash eight hundred speakers nationwide on behalf of the ticket. In late September, Washington columnist Robert S. Allen reported from Chicago: "The GOP campaign staff here is one of the largest and most diverse in history. There are 776 persons on the payroll. This does not include the large staffs in the New York and Washington offices. The Chicago set-up is so big that it startled Governor Landon when he learned of its size. On his birthday recently, a large scroll of greetings was got up and each member of the Chicago office signed it.

"Presented to Landon in Topeka, he scrutinized it open-eyed. 'Do all these people work in the Chicago headquarters?' he asked. 'Yes, Governor.' 'Gosh, what do they do?' he pleaded."

Chicago was also home to Col. Robert "Bertie" McCormick's staunchly conservative *Chicago Tribune*—a rival to Frank Knox's *Daily News*. Some said that McCormick (privately advised by FDR in 1932 that he hoped to reduce federal expenditures by 20 percent) had coveted 1936's GOP VP slot but was too restrained to seek it out. In any case, his *Tribune* remained tough competition to Knox's *Daily News.* (Once, Knox ordered his underlings to differ with the *Tribune* on "everything," triggering McCormick's quip "He'll be at a disadvantage next week when we start our campaign against syphilis.")

Hearst endured as the man everyone loved to hate, drawing the lion's share of blame for concocting Landon. But McCormick was also an early and influential Landon backer, endorsing him back on January 26, 1936. For most of the campaign, his *Tribune* ran daily headlines pleading "Only [fill in the appropriate number of] days left to save your country! What are you doing to save it?" Briefly, *Tribune* telephone operators even greeted callers with that same desperate message. McCormick—not Hearst, nor any Liberty Leaguer—delivered the campaign's largest donation—$100,000—to the Landon campaign, extending particular generosity to a largely female group known simply as the "Volunteers," who rang doorbells, licked stamps, and worked like hell for the Landon ticket, albeit to increasingly less effect. *Chicago Times* columnist Gail Borden (not a woman, by the way) taunted their efforts (and haute bourgeois mid-Atlantic accents) thusly:

There was a young man from Topeka
Whose campaign grew weakah and weakah
Till the Volunteers came
And made every old dame
A bell-ringa, singah, or speakah.

Bill Borah rang no bells. In patented Borah mode, he provided neither the Republican nominee nor his platform a second thought. Facing both a Townsendite primary challenge plus popular three-term Democratic governor C. Ben Ross in the general election, he had his work cut out for him. He retreated to Idaho (his first visit since 1935) and stayed there.

Al Smith, Joseph Ely, James Reed, and company all endorsed the Landon effort. As had Oklahoma's populist former governor, "Alfalfa Bill" Murray, like Smith a 1932 dark horse, and former Maryland senator William Cabell Bruce, cousin to the late governor Albert Cabell Ritchie and himself a Pulitzer Prize–winning biographer. John W. Davis nonetheless remained not "greatly impressed by Brother Landon." Only reluctantly did he take to the radio on October 21 to blister the New Deal, though not mentioning Landon once.

H. L. Mencken, scourge of all things rural, Rotarian, Republican, and respectable, came on board, though by now he proved exceedingly skeptical of GOP chances. Landon, assessed Mencken, "probably knows a great deal less than the Hon. Mr. Roosevelt, but much more of what he knows is true."

An even more surprising boost than Mencken's emanated from Walter Lippmann, no iconoclast nor reactionary, but rather a former FDR friend, now increasingly weary and fearful of Roosevelt's penchant for creating "unreal and unnecessary divisions . . . when solidarity and union are of the utmost importance." Lippmann, however, remained wary of Landon's stated positions on the tariff, John Hamilton's too-prominent role in the campaign, and the efficacy of Al Smith and the Liberty League. Nonetheless, he privately assisted FDR's former budget director Lewis Douglas in drafting an anti–New Deal statement of principles. Privately, he praised John W. Davis's October 21 speech as "Nobly Done."

"We believe," he publicly declared, "that [Hoover's] New Era and the New Deal are two streams from the same source. The one fostered private monopolies in the name of national prosperity. The other has fostered state-controlled monopolies in the name of the national welfare. We believe that both are an aberration from the basic principles upon which this nation has grown great and has remained free."

Lippmann's decision probably shocked even Lippmann himself, who later privately admitted that the Kansan was "a dull and uninspired fellow, an ignorant man . . . of no account." His endorsement, he ultimately admitted, amounted to nothing more than "a protest vote."

Occasionally, celebrity endorsements materialized. Hall of Fame shortstop Honus Wagner visited with both Landon and Knox in Topeka. Alf bummed a three-for-a-dime "Pittsburgh stogie" from him. Other baseball legends signed on as well: former fireballing Washington Senators pitcher Walter "The Big Train" Johnson and voluble current St. Louis Cardinals star Jerome Herman "Dizzy" Dean. "I'm going to wear [a] sunflower to the ball-park," Dean pledged, "and let folks know where I stand."

Very late in the campaign, Henry Ford signed on. "Landon is like Coolidge," he declared. "I am for Landon. I haven't voted for twenty years, but I am going to vote this time." Regarding Landon's running mate, Ford chuckled, "Knox won't keep his mouth shut." Mr. Ford thought that was a good thing. Evidently an administration could tolerate only so much reticence.

Less welcome was an endorsement ("Bund Command #2") from New York, from the newly formed German-American Bund's Fritz Kuhn—a former Ford employee. Fresh from a visit to Germany (and essentially a brush-off from Hitler), the Munich-born Kuhn directed his fifty thousand

Bundists to cast their votes for the GOP as the nation's best bulwark against Communism and "to create a friendly understanding between our adopted country and Germany, our native land." Landon had not been Kuhn's first choice. That honor fell to William Lemke (well, actually, to Adolf Hitler), but with Lemke missing from numerous state ballots, Kuhn shifted his poisonous embrace to the GOP. Josephus Daniels's *Raleigh News and Observer* (obviously pro-FDR) surprisingly reassured readers to forsake any fears that Landon had "sold out to the Fascists."

"[I]f Governor Landon were elected," contended the *News and Observer*, "we should have no Hitler, Nazi fools to the contrary notwithstanding. . . . If Roosevelt is elected we shall have no Stalin, Communist fools to the contrary notwithstanding."

The GOP may not have been playing footsie with Fritz Kuhn. It did with Father Coughlin. That autumn, Coughlin approached Landon adviser and radio spokesman William Hard, seeking assistance in recruiting "Washington correspondents" for a projected new magazine. Hard forwarded the news ("Are you free to take on a little more journalistic work? It would be quite left-wing") to a friend of his, journalist Gardner Jackson. Harold Ickes got ahold of the news (probably from Jackson), using it to publicly savage Landon's campaign.

Escaping Democrats' notice, however, was John D. M. Hamilton's clandestine meeting at Manhattan's Waldorf Towers with Coughlin—accompanied, as Hamilton recalled years later, by two obvious bodyguards that to Hamilton resembled "hoodlums."

Coughlin was clearly alarmed. Not by anything requiring bodyguards—but by the mild-mannered Landon: "the poorest radio speaker he ever heard . . . the only man I know of in public life who uses his voice so that he makes a climax in the middle of every sentence that he utters."

Coughlin beseeched Hamilton to simply yank his candidate off the air. Hamilton refused. People, after all, would demand to know why. Coughlin snorted "let him break a leg." Hamilton assumed Coughlin meant that figuratively. Much to Hamilton's amazement, he meant it quite literally. "Landon rides a lot," Coughlin explained, "and all you got to do is issue a statement . . . that he had been thrown by a horse, broken a leg and cannot make any further campaign speeches."

Hamilton still wasn't buying such an unprecedented, desperate—and weird—strategy. Reporters, he argued, wouldn't either. At which point, Coughlin alleged that his fainting spell at Cleveland was an outright fake—devised to dodge an unwanted Gerald L. K. Smith–scheduled event in Louisiana.

Climbing aboard the increasingly off-key Landon bandwagon was *The Clansman* author Thomas Dixon, an erstwhile star of Gene Talmadge's ill-received Macon conference. Still professing to be "an old-fashioned, dyed-in-the wool Democrat," he graced June's GOP convention as a delegate from his home state of North Carolina. In October, he rendezvoused with Frank Knox, as Knox pointlessly campaigned in the heavily Democratic Tar Heel State. Dixon, himself, was about to commence his own statewide series of pro-Landon (or rather anti–New Deal) orations. "For 50 years, I fought to destroy the Republican Party," Dixon admitted to a Raleigh reporter. "I'm glad I didn't now because that is the only instrument that can be used to destroy the New Deal. I think this New Deal is all wrong. I am full of fire and pizen."

Recalling his old Johns Hopkins classmate and friend Woodrow Wilson, Dixon informed one audience that Wilson would "suffer his right arm to be cut off before he would touch a New Deal ticket. I've looked in vain for a Democratic candidate for the presidency . . . I bring you a challenge tonight to find me a Democratic Party. . . .

"Communism is no idle threat. Not by one word has [Roosevelt] condemned the Socialists or the Communists since he became President. . . . He has carried out 27 planks of the Socialist platform. . . . One plank of the Democratic Party he has carried out, that providing for the more abundant flow of liquor."

"This is Bull Run," he warned another gathering. "Gettysburg is to follow. If Roosevelt is elected it will be by the South, and if he returns to office the South will be crucified as it has never been before. . . . A great blow was struck . . . when the two-thirds rule was junked. That was Farley's plan to pave the way for a Roosevelt third term and a dictatorship. When that comes another civil war will follow."

On Saturday, August 22, Landon returned from his second Colorado vacation. Finally invading the East, he addressed a crowd of somewhere between 75,000 and 110,000 at his West Middlesex, Pennsylvania, birthplace. He spoke of still ordering maple syrup each winter from local producers. He proclaimed, "Wherever I have gone in this country, I have found Americans."

From his New Hampshire summer home, Frank Knox praised the talk as "direct and vigorous," not to mention "wholesome." Visiting with the *Washington Herald*'s Cissy Patterson at her Long Island estate, Harold Ickes also listened in. "Literally," wrote the dumbfounded Ickes, "he did not say a thing. . . . It was . . . schoolboyish." Patterson had to agree. The following day, George Gallup announced that FDR had overtaken Landon in the Electoral College, 274–257.

The following day, Monday, August 24, Landon addressed ten thousand at Chautauqua, New York, distancing himself from a pet Hearst project: loyalty oaths. "In Kansas," he proclaimed, "we insist that no teacher should be required to take any oath not required of all citizens." Such independence might have garnered some Democratic respect, save for his usual dismal delivery. "The first five minutes you could see the advantage of the coaching," acknowledged FDR pollster Emil Hurja, "but it wore off after that." Texas congressman Sam Rayburn wouldn't even concede five minutes to the Kansan. "[T]he worst I have [ever] heard," Rayburn concluded.

A few days later, Jim Farley convened a Democratic Party conference at Manhattan's Hotel Biltmore. A party operative reported recent audience reaction at Madison Avenue's Trans-Lux newsreel theatre: Landon "made such a miserable appearance . . . there were more people laughing than anything else."

To Republican newspaper publisher Frank Gannett (a former Borah man), the candidate confessed that he often never even saw his speeches before delivering them. It showed. "Over the radio," Gannett's biographer later cracked, "Landon sounded like a fighting rabbit."

What Landon initially lacked in fire (eventually he did display more oomph—delivering as many as twenty-eight whistle-stop talks in a single day), Knox provided, whacking the New Deal with frenzied glee. "I see," he orated in Ottumwa, Iowa, "where Mr. Farley has been talking . . . about the way the administration carried out the 1932 platform. They carried it out, all right. They carried it out and put it in the ash pile and set it afire."

Frenzied glee was one thing. Outright stupidity was something else. Knox proved profoundly embarrassing, at Allentown, Pennsylvania, by bizarrely alleging that, under the New Deal, "no life insurance policy is secure; no savings account is safe"—an accusation proven immediately, completely, and irrefutably untrue. A panicked Landon phoned Knox, imploring greater caution. "Boys," the annoyed Knox carped to reporters over drinks, "I've got another McKinley on my hands."

In Washington, reporters joshingly queried FDR: Were Democrats, by chance, paying Landon and Knox to deliver such counterproductive orations? "Strictly off the record," Franklin joshed back, "it is a question of how much longer we can afford to pay them. They have been so successful that they are raising their prices."

The mercurial, bushy-browed United Mine Workers president John L. Lewis (ostensibly a Republican), jibed that his party had nominated a candidate "just as empty, as inane, and innocuous as a watermelon . . . boiled in a bathtub."

The emptiness ran deep. Landon, perceived historian Arthur Schlesinger Jr., "simply did not see the New Deal, as Hoover did, as a conspiracy to subvert American institutions. He . . . had offered to enlist with Roosevelt in 1933, . . . supported the administration's agricultural and conservation programs, endorsed the principle of social security, had never criticized the securities or banking or holding company or labor legislation, and seemed to hold against the New Deal chiefly its administrative inefficiency and its fiscal deficits."

Landon's basic pitch—that a firmer, more competent hand was needed to settle things down in Washington, to progress further, spend less, and recover more—was not entirely indefensible, but it neither inspired nor convinced the millions of voters he needed for victory.

In mid-October, John L. Lewis shifted gears, no longer seeing Landon as merely innocuous, to fume: "The interests supporting the Republican Party seek a centralized control in the hands of a few. They would control money, natural and material resources, and the people. They would establish an economic and financial dictatorship: they would denude and exploit the many to enrich the few. Their plans are equivalent to setting up a Fascist state. They would place in the seat of power a quavering, quaggy dummy."

It must have been a dummy, however, who concocted one particular GOP stunt in late September. In New York, the "Landon First Voters League" engaged three fashion models, each posing as a "Victim of Future Taxes." Two wore attire with certain portions missing—supposedly indicating a percentage lost to taxes. The third model, Miss Bonnie Clare, attired more modestly in academic gown and mortar board, displayed a placard reading:

YOU PAY $10.00
for Lounging Pajamas,
of which
$1.98 goes for TAXES
TAXES TAKE
$5.00 of every $25.00
Evening Gown.

"At the end of the show," noted Irving Stone, "a cute young thing, ostensibly naked, tripped out in a barrel with a placard which read, IF THE NEW DEAL WINS, while another Beauty sauntered about in evening gown and white fur cape with a placard reading, IF THE NEW DEAL LOSES. . . . From thirty to forty million Americans had lost their homes, their jobs, their security, were facing endless suffering and desperation, and the Republican managers were concerned only in terms of the fluff of expensive evening gowns for young women."

An outraged female reader fired off a letter to the *Brooklyn Eagle*: "So the Landon Voters League had to use professional models to pull off their 'Victim of Future Taxes Barrel Show.' Couldn't they find in their ranks enough young women who have the courage of their convictions?

"That's not so strange when you consider the convictions that they are supposed to have. 'You pay $10 for lounging pajamas, of which $1.98 goes for taxes,' one placard read. Hmmp! Who pays $10 for a pair of lounging pajamas?"

• • •

Alf Landon could not stand Herbert Hoover.

Hoover's inept handling of the Depression alienated the Kansan. Hoover's equally futile bid for the 1936 nomination and his anti-Landon machinations in that year's California primary only fueled his angst. Hoover's personality repulsed voters, reminding them why they'd elected Roosevelt in the first place, possessing all the easy warmth of *It's a Wonderful Life*'s crankily parsimonious Mr. Potter.

Thus Landon exhibited little, if any, inclination to employ The Great Engineer in his own great adventure. Hamilton and Hearst general counsel Francis Neylan, however, argued that Hoover would be the best person to rebut Democratic blasts aimed at the former administration—as if the GOP's current campaign somehow needed to re-litigate those issues. It was not, however, until September 2 that Landon and Hoover even spoke together over the phone.

Landon's nervous staff then denied that they had, infuriating Hoover. "If this denial is persisted in," Hoover erupted, ". . . I will . . . have published the complete stenographic notes of my conversation . . . with Governor Landon."

Hoover momentarily triumphed. Not only would he participate in the campaign, but on Thursday, October 1, he would arrive in Topeka to confer with the candidate. It was not a session Landon looked forward to. Dining on fried chicken and smoking big cigars, they tuned in to FDR's talk from Pittsburgh's jam-packed Forbes Field. "Hoover and Landon listened with sour looks on their faces," noted Landon's de facto official biographer Donald McCoy, "Hoover because of Roosevelt, and Landon perhaps because of Hoover." Landon hustled Hoover out of the executive mansion to his train for Chicago. "We had better rush if we're going to catch the train."

The Great Engineer needn't have rushed. At Chicago, as his adviser and biographer David Hinshaw noted, he "found the headquarters cool toward him [and] delayed making arrangements for any Hoover speeches. According to them they found it extremely difficult to work out a satisfactory schedule. They also indicated that local party officials were loathe [*sic*] to arrange meetings for him. After a few such rebuffs Mr. Hoover arranged for his own speeches and broadcasting and operated throughout the campaign entirely as an independent unit."

Arthur Vandenberg took up what remained of Landon's cudgel. Nineteen thirty-six's campaign, though anti-climactic in many ways, witnessed several firsts. There had been that first face-to-face meeting of rival nominees—back in Des Moines on September 3. Earlier, there was the first public exchange of correspondence between candidates, as Norman Thomas entreated Landon to clarify his position on labor issues, specifically support for unionization "free from interference from any source." Saturday, October 17 witnessed the first presidential debate—commencing with an asterisk—and concluding with an exclamation point.

The time: 7:30 p.m. Central Time.

The scene: Chicago's Medinah Athletic Club.

The players: Arthur Vandenberg and an "orthophonic" phonograph record of Franklin Roosevelt.

The idea: Broadcasting nationwide over the CBS and Mutual networks, Vandenberg would debate the Roosevelt record in more ways than one, countering recorded snippets from FDR's 1932 campaign promises with a barrage of facts, figures, and cutting asides, such as this exchange:

> *Roosevelt's Recorded Voice:* Through this program of action, we address ourselves to putting our own national house in order and making income balance outgo.
>
> *Vandenberg:* But, Mr. Roosevelt, this is 1936 and we are still spending two dollars for every dollar the Treasury takes in. We have had plenty of programs for more income, but none for less outgo. Where is the promised "balance?" Even our relief costs go up as our relief necessities go down. Former Comptroller General [John R.] McCarl bluntly condemns many of your "programs of action" as I quote: "Loosely and extravagantly set up and tax-consuming in the extreme." Red ink flows across your ledgers in a sinister stream.

Mutual had no problem with Vandenberg's stunt. CBS pulled the plug in mid-broadcast, yanking him off the air in twenty-three of eighty-five stations, including such major markets as New York, Philadelphia, Boston, Buffalo, Cleveland, and Detroit.

"This is just another example," fulminated Republican National Committee public relations director Hill Blackett, "of the intimidation of the radio stations by this Administration. There is no ruling by the Federal Radio Commission to prevent a broadcast of this kind. Moreover, this sort of thing has been done by stations before. It was the President's voice, of course, and in a way you can't blame the radio people. All our stations now operate on a six months' license and they know that they may have their licenses taken away from them."

As gimmicky as Vandenberg's stunt was, it was hardly unique among anti-FDR efforts. As 1936 commenced, the Sentinels of the Republic had produced an anti-FDR animated cartoon titled "The Amateur Fire Brigade—A Fable of the New Deal," screening publicly in such places as Chicago and Philadelphia and privately for Al Smith and former Missouri senator James A. Reed at Palm Beach. Ohio authorities censored portions of it for disrespecting the president. Chicago censors tried banning it entirely.

The Sentinels tried approaching the Liberty League to help fund distribution. The League wasn't interested. Instead, it explored its own weekly fifteen-minute anti–New Deal radio series featuring a character who, while lollygagging in a country store, kept sniping about various administration programs. Costing $100,000 to produce—money the League (its moneybags reputation to the contrary) did not have—it never got off the ground. The GOP, however, did launch its own half-hour radio effort, "Liberty at the Crossroads," featuring a more varied cast of grumblers, including a young couple obtaining a marriage license and worrying about their tax-burdened future. While CBS and NBC refused to run it, Mutual did. "If you did not hear it, you missed a lot—," observed one presumably Democratic critic, "a lot of dreary dialogue, insipid intonations, and mournful attempts at wisecracks."

Heywood Broun had a little fun composing alternative dialogue:

CLERK: Who was that statesman I saw you walking down the street with?

JOHN: That was no statesman, you dope. That was a Republican Presidential candidate.

State of Maine voters still cast ballots for non-presidential elections each September. In 1936, that included GOP US senator Wallace White's seat, the governorship (being vacated by Democrat Louis Brann, busy challenging White), and the state's three House seats (two of which rested in Democratic hands). The GOP (aided by Liberty League supporters) poured money and manpower into those races, including visits from Knox and then Landon. In Portland, on September's Election Eve, Landon addressed 25,000. Bathed in klieg lights, atop a twenty-foot-high platform, he proclaimed, "Americans everywhere are waiting for the majorities you will pile up. . . . You will start a victory parade that will span the Nation."

Victory was indeed theirs. Republicans narrowly reelected White, easily recaptured the governorship, and swept all three House seats. Democrat Louis Brann groused, "If they had given me the money spent by the Republican State Committee, I could have elected a Chinaman governor of Maine." Landon crowed: "As Maine goes, so goes the nation"—and Republicans prayed very, very hard for his dream to come true.

Landon, however, followed Maine's triumph with a trio of disastrous speeches. To twenty thousand at Des Moines's State Fairgrounds, on September 22, he addressed farm policy, simultaneously out-promising the New Deal on spending while vowing to slash expenditures and deficits. "[A]s I listened . . . over the radio," discerned Harold Ickes, "I got the impression that he was for anything that any farmer anywhere might conceivably want."

To an overflow Minneapolis crowd two nights later, Landon jettisoned his previous pro-free-trade positions—getting his basic facts wrong to boot.

Two weeks earlier, the normally Democratic *Baltimore Sun* revealed that it could not support Roosevelt. It now ditched Landon. Both candidates, it complained, "are tarred heavily with the same stick . . . of authoritarian government." Also recoiling in dismay were such potential Democratic allies as Dean Acheson and James Warburg and two former

GOP cabinet members, Secretary of State Frank Kellogg and Secretary of War and Secretary of State Henry L. Stimson. So was Woodrow Wilson's former Secretary of War Newton D. Baker, grumbling to William Allen White that Landon's new tariff views reminded him of McKinley at his worst.

Initially, Landon had no plans to campaign in the staunchly pro–New Deal Far West. But, in a last-gasp play for Townsendite votes—and despite California polling numbers remaining solidly Democratic—he suddenly re-jiggered his schedule to include the Golden State. Even by his standards, the results proved dismal. He hoped to speak at Los Angeles's 6,700-seat Shrine Auditorium—but that was already rented out to the Communist-front Hollywood Anti-Nazi League. They weren't about to step aside. He received similar brush-offs at Olympic Stadium and the Pan-Pacific Auditorium before finally settling for the 101,574-seat Hollywood Coliseum. As Los Angeles Police Commissioner (and *The Jazz Singer* screenwriter!) Alfred A. Cohn wired Jim Farley:

> LANDON BITTER DISAPPOINTMENT [TO] REPUBLICANS ESPECIALLY TOWNSENDITES BECAUSE HIS REFUSAL TO MENTION PLAN. NET RESULT WILL GREATLY INCREASE ROOSEVELT MAJORITY BECAUSE OF FAILURE TO IMPRESS PERSONALLY AND PERHAPS WORST POLITICAL SPEECH ANYONE EVER MADE. COLISEUM LESS THAN HALF FILLED DESPITE AUTO CARAVANS FROM ALL OVER STATE. LANDON BOOED IN EVERY BLACK DOWNTOWN SECTION UPON ARRIVAL.

Cohn wasn't exaggerating. It wasn't just Blacks who booed Landon. Catcalls greeted him throughout his mile-long journey from the train. Arriving at his hotel, he seemed "crushed." Later, at the Coliseum, "the boos began again, creating a deep, ominous undertone in every burst of cheers." Twice, police waded into the crowd to break up altercations. As Landon and California State GOP Chairman Earl Warren departed, an empty liquor bottle crashed against a stadium wall, showering their vehicle's running board with shards of glass. "I just couldn't resist the impulse," sixteen-year-old John Dobbins confessed to police.

Landon's worst move was yet to come. In Milwaukee, on Saturday, September 26, he trained his bespectacled sights on Social Security. Republicans hadn't invented Social Security. But they hadn't really opposed it either. The great majority of the party's surviving senators and congressmen voted for it. Alfred du Pont (cousin of the Liberty League du Ponts) had long supported the idea. Compared to two competing non-contributory schemes—the Townsend Plan and the more comprehensive and Communist-endorsed Lundeen–Frazier "Workers Unemployment Insurance Bill" (approved by the House Labor Committee in March 1935; to be administered not by the government but rather by "workers' and farmers' organizations," something sounding suspiciously like soviets)—FDR's original Social Security Act (SSA) was relatively modest. It was, however, hardly perfect. It was, for one thing, yet another break with 1932's Democratic platform, which supported old-age pensions on a state rather than a federal level. But that was small potatoes compared to the issue of funding. From the start, FDR instructed subordinates to construct a plan based on "contributions" rather than on general tax revenues. Social Security's employee and employer contributions had the effect of taking money out of the economy and raising prices during a Depression. Beyond that, as Rexford Tugwell (and a great many other people) also complained, this contributory scheme "was very little different than a sales tax." In an era of soak-the-rich and "Share-our-Wealth" agitation, Social Security marched off in a radically (well, actually, in a non-radical) opposite trajectory, constituting a classically regressive tax. Economist Abraham Epstein would later damn it as "a system of compulsory payments by the poor for the impoverished" that exempted "the well-to-do from their share of the social burden." Even pro–New Deal historian William Leuchtenburg would eventually skewer the legislation as, "In many respects . . . astonishingly inept."

Yet, in other aspects, it remained politically brilliant. As FDR later confided to a critic: "I guess you're right on the economics, but those taxes were never a problem of economics. They are politics all the way through.

We put those payroll contributions there so as to give the contributors a legal, moral and political right to collect their pensions and their unemployment benefits. With those taxes in there, no damn politician can ever scrap my social security program."

Had Landon been elected and had more time to work on it, he might have fashioned a better plan, though what would have survived congressional input remains an entirely different story. But starting from a draft composed by *The Nation*'s Raymond Gram Swing, he eventually delivered a speech that, while attempting to ride two horses, angered just about everyone. Conservatives thought little of his overall endorsement of the plan and less of his idea to junk the payroll tax in favor of a more liberal broadly based tax. Liberals were offended by his slashing attacks on the program's shortcomings and inefficiencies. Few took seriously his dystopian, Big Brother predictions for enforcement: "the Republican party will have nothing to do with any plan that involves prying into the personal records of 26 million people . . . a government agent must keep track of [them] . . . federal snooping follows."

"[W]ith doomed ingenuity," assessed Arthur Schlesinger Jr., Landon "contrived to alienate at once both [the SSA's] friends and its enemies."

Social Security's old-age pensions were originally not scheduled to commence until 1942. More significantly politically, while its enabling legislation had passed back in early August 1935, no payroll taxes were to be collected before the 1936 election. And only about half of all workers were covered—including just 10 percent of the Black workforce. The 25 percent of Blacks remaining unemployed obviously paid no payroll tax. Employed Blacks remained largely in agricultural or domestic work. The former category was exempted outright; the latter largely through a provision exempting entities with eight or fewer employees. Yet those employed, but not covered, faced the burden of increased prices generated from the program's payroll levies. "Such taxes, Negroes contended," as scholar Raymond Wolters noted, "were essentially indirect sales taxes that employers would pass on to consumers in the form of higher prices, causing greatest discomfort among the low-waged domestics and agricultural wage hands who would be 'doubly exploited' because they did not receive any benefits from the new program but still had to pay higher prices for the necessities of life."

Neither Franklin nor Eleanor Roosevelt paid much attention to African-American concerns regarding Social Security.

They paid much more attention to African-American votes.

ABOVE: On the campaign trail: Secretary of Agriculture Henry Wallace (extreme left) along with Franklin and Eleanor Roose (COURTESY OF THE LIBRARY OF CONGRESS) BELOW LEFT: Brain Truster Rexford Guy Tugwell. "The young brain trusters," Al Smith, "caught the Socialists in swimming and ran away with their clothes." (COURTESY OF THE LIBRARY OF CONGR BELOW RIGHT: The Works Program Administration's Harry Hopkins slamming Alf Landon to reporters in November Landon, says Hopkins, "balanced his budget in Kansas by taking money out of the hides of the needy . . . [Landon's adm tration] "had never put up a thin dime for relief." (COURTESY OF THE LIBRARY OF CONGRESS)

LEFT: Ex-President Herbert C. Hoover. He wants his old job back in 1936. He won't get it. (COURTESY OF THE LIBRARY ONGRESS) ABOVE RIGHT: Mr. & Mrs. William Randolph Hearst in 1923. Hearst, assessed Al Smith in 1919, was "a man as nd as mean as I can picture him . . . a pestilence that walks in the dark." (COURTESY OF THE LIBRARY OF CONGRESS) w: Anti-New Deal Georgia Governor Eugene Talmadge (right) with Atlanta Constitution publisher Clark Howell. adge, sneers Harold Ickes, looks "more like a rat than any other human being that I know . . . with all of the mean, nous and treacherous characteristics of that rodent."

Wheeler-dealer Joseph P. Kennedy. Kennedy provides a bridge between FDR and such eventually-alienated supporters as publisher William Randolph Hearst and Father Charles E. Coughlin. (COURTESY OF THE LIBRARY OF CONGRESS)

New York City Mayor Fiorello P. LaGuardia, a skilled advocate in obtaining New Deal funding, leaving the White House. (COURTESY OF THE LIBRARY OF CONGRESS)

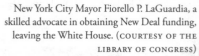

Franklin Roosevelt inspecting his prized sta collection. (COURTESY OF THE LIBRARY OF CONGRESS)

Franklin Roosevelt's White House secretarial staff. Missy LeHand, appropriately, resides front and center. (COURTESY OF THE LIBRARY OF CONGRESS)

FDR's January 1934 Birthday rty privately poked fun at his "imperial presidency" image. is McHenry Howe and Press cretary Stephen Early crouch e extreme right. FDR's valet rwin McDuffie stands at the r top. FDR's daughter Anna FDR's right. Missy LeHand he first person kneeling from the left. (COURTESY OF THE NATIONAL ARCHIVES AND RECORDS ADMINISTRATION - 47-96:1756)

Vice President and Mrs. John Nance Garner host Franklin and Eleanor Roosevelt at a gala February 1936 Hotel Washington dinner. George Burns and Gracie Allen entertained. Newspapers cropped out the military aide supporting FDR. (COURTESY OF THE LIBRARY OF CONGRESS)

BELOW LEFT: Socialist Party presidential nominee Norman Thomas chats with Eleanor Roosevelt, who would have voted for Thomas in 1932 "if I had not been married to Franklin." (COURTESY OF THE LIBRARY OF CONGRESS) BELOW RIGHT: Communist Party presidential standard-bearer Earl Browder, in jail for twenty-five hours at Terre Haut, Indiana in Septembe 1936. "Communism," Browder argues during the campaign, "is Twentieth Century Americanism." (COLLECTION OF THE AUTHOR) BOTTOM: "There's one issue in this campaign," FDR lectures his erstwhile supporter Ray Moley, "It's myself, and people must be either for me or against me." (COURTESY OF THE LIBRARY OF CONGRESS)

Interior Secretary Harold Ickes and Brain Truster and FDR speechwriter "Tommy the Cork" Corcoran. (COURTESY OF THE LIBRARY OF CONGRESS)

Interior Secretary Harold Ickes Interior Department's Division nvestigation chief Louis Russell lavis, his personal spy regarding irs of the heart. (COURTESY OF THE LIBRARY OF CONGRESS)

Works Program Administration (WPA) Harry Hopkins and Interior Secretary Harold Ickes. They were not always so agreeable. (COURTESY OF THE LIBRARY OF CONGRESS)

Maverick Idaho Senator (and 1936 GOP president hopeful) William E. Bora and Brain Truster Raymo Moley (COURTESY OF TH LIBRARY OF CONGRESS)

Mrs. Mary Borah and Alice Roosevelt Longworth, mother of Mrs. Borah's husband's illegitimate daughter Paulina. (COURTESY OF THE LIBRARY OF CONGRESS)

GOP dark horse presiden hopeful, Michigan Senat Arthur Vandenberg (wid known as "the only Senat who can strut sitting dow and WPA chief Harry Hopkins. (COURTESY OF THE LIBRARY OF CONGR

Left-wing Scripps-Howard newspaper columnist (and former Algonquin Round Table wit) Heywood Broun. "We've got to sink our differences—," Broun informs the *Daily Worker*, "Socialists, liberals, Communists and other progressives—faced with a very real threat of fascism, and I don't believe there can be any really important Farmer-Labor Party without Communists included." (COURTESY OF THE LIBRARY OF CONGRESS)

The Baltimore Sun's H. L. Mencken—a Landon supporter—testifying before Congress. His 1936 topsy: "If we have prayed instead of boozing, Alf ht be in the White House today, and [we] might be training for ambassadorships. As it is, we'll be ucky if we escape Alcatraz." (COURTESY OF THE LIBRARY OF CONGRESS)

The progressive Republican publisher of the *Emporia Gazette*, William Allen White. Despite souring on Landon as the campaign praises, he still finds FDR's arguments "slick as goose grease and false as hell." (COURTESY OF THE LIBRARY OF CONGRESS)

· 17 ·

"Keep on running"

Votes are won, and votes are lost.

Republicans had forfeited millions of votes overall since steamrolling Al Smith in 1928. They risked losing more votes—particularly Black votes—in 1936.

The party recognized the problem. They tried fixing it. It was too late.

For three-quarters of a century, Blacks had remained loyal to the GOP—loyal, even in 1932. Blacks in cities like Philadelphia, Pittsburgh, and Chicago stubbornly voted for Hoover. The year 1934, however, witnessed a small but significant break in the Republican dike when the nation's only Black congressman, Chicago's Oscar De Priest, fell to a Black Democratic challenger, Arthur Mitchell, a defector from the city's fast-expiring GOP machine. That same year, Philadelphia's middle- and upper-class Blacks commenced their own exodus. "I can beat the Democrats," complained one local Black Republican ward leader, "but that d— Roosevelt has taken Lincoln's place."

The sheen was fast falling off Republicans. But Blacks remained painfully aware of Southern influence on the GOP's rivals. "The Democratic Party," exclaimed one Black Republican, "is controlled by devils from below the Mason–Dixon line." Even the most ardently New Deal African Americans could hardly deny that.

For all the largesse showered upon Blacks—an estimated 40 percent were on relief or were employed by the PWA—discrimination, particularly regarding skilled or managerial government positions, remained endemic. NRA wage codes displaced Black workers with whites. Many Blacks jeered that NRA stood for "Negro Removal Act," "Negro Rarely Allowed," "Negroes Ruined Again," "Negro Rights Abused," "Negroes Robbed Again," "Negro Rights Assassinated," "Negro Run-Around," and "No Roosevelt Again." And that hardly exhausts the list of bitter jibes. Within the NRA's bureaucracy, hardly any Blacks held "a rank equal to that of clerk."

AAA acreage reductions similarly impacted poor sharecroppers of both races, but particularly Blacks. Beyond that, federal allotments were rarely paid directly to sharecroppers but rather to landowners, fostering widespread abuse and corruption. In segregated CCC camps, FDR requested the program's Tennessee-born director, Robert Fechner, "to put in colored foremen, not of course on technical work, but on ordinary manual labor."

The Urban League's T. Arnold Hill pointed out that the Negro "remains the most forgotten man in a program planned to deal new cards to the millions of workers neglected and exploited in the shuffle between capital and labor. . . . [T]he will of those who have kept Negroes in economic disfranchisement has been permitted to prevail, and the government has looked on in silence and at times with approval. Consequently, the Negro worker has good reason to feel that his government has betrayed him under the New Deal."

Among the administration's highest-level African-American appointees was Robert L. Vann, he who had famously urged Blacks to turn Lincoln's portrait to the wall. Yet even Vann found himself shunted aside. "I'm not doing anything down here," he complained. "It looks like they put me down here in Washington to shut me up."

Despite all such problems, frustrations, and disappointments, Blacks didn't just edge toward once-hated Democratic banners, they scurried there. The discrimination they suffered under New Deal administrations was nothing new. They'd seen it before—and worse. What they (or anyone else, for that matter) had never seen were so many checks from Washington. The bottom line, as Raymond Wolters chronicled, was this:

> The share of FERA [Federal Emergency Relief Administration] and WPA benefits going to Negroes exceeded their proportion of the general population. The FERA's first relief census reported that more than two million Negroes were on relief in 1933, a percentage of the Black population (17.8) that was nearly double the percentage of whites on relief (9.5). By 1935, the number of Negroes on relief had risen to 3,500,000, almost 30 percent of the Black population, and an additional 200,000 Blacks were working on WPA projects. Altogether, then, almost 40 percent of the nation's Black people were either on relief or were receiving support from the WPA.

The *Baltimore Afro-American* put it bluntly: "Relief and WPA are not ideal, but they are better than the Hoover bread lines and they'll have to do until the real thing comes along."

One African-American minister waxed more poetically: "Let Jesus lead you and Roosevelt feed you!"

Black votes (what few there were) counted for little in the South. The Northeast and Midwest proved decidedly different. In early October 1936, an article in the Black press calculated that African-American votes held the balance of power in six key states, accounting for 139 electoral votes:

	REGISTERED BLACKS	ELECTORAL VOTES
Pennsylvania	277,000	38
Illinois	218,000	29
Indiana	7,000	15
Ohio	200,000	24
Michigan	134,000	15
Missouri	150,000	18

"While the Democrats might win even if losing these states," one Black analyst calculated, "it is almost inconceivable that the Republicans . . . could be victorious if these half-dozen commonwealths are placed in the opponent's column."

"If the Republicans," said a "prominent white G. O. P. official," "had the colored votes in the six pivotal states as we used to have them, there wouldn't be any question about all . . . being insured for Governor Landon."

"Neither side," the Los Angeles–based Black weekly newspaper *California Eagle* reported in October, "has claimed any of the six controversial states except by a small margin."

Beyond those six key states, four other states recorded large Black registrations:

	REGISTERED BLACKS	ELECTORAL VOTES
New York	287,000	47
New Jersey	141,000	16
Maryland	165,000	8
West Virginia	67,000	8

To avert further Black defections, Republicans outspent Democrats by a two-to-one margin. Their special "Colored Divisions" contained subdivisions for women, legal, and labor issues. Thousands of Blacks—arriving on thirty specially chartered trains—attended Landon's Topeka notification. Traditionally Republican Black Baptist and Methodist clergy provided endorsements. National GOP committeeman Perry W. Howard stumped for Landon, pointedly reminding voters of how "crackers" controlled New Deal programs in the South so as "to make cotton-pickers of us" and how FDR's Warm Springs Institute had "refuse[d] black boys treatment . . . THIS PLACE IS CONTROLLED BY PRESIDENT ROOSEVELT." He boldly predicted Landon winning 75 percent of the Black vote.

For screening in Black movie theatres, Republicans commissioned a series of three-minute "newsreels," highlighting famous Blacks endorsing Landon. One featured the Negro Elks' Grand Exulted Ruler J. Finley Wilson. Two musical editions showcased the pioneering Blues recording artist Mamie Smith and the very popular quartet "The Beale Street Boys" (harmonizing, of course, to "Oh, Susanna").

But how effective were such efforts? "Republicans," theorized the NAACP's *Crisis* magazine, "listen to a lot of people on this Negro problem, but *The Crisis* suspects they still pay most attention to the old-line southern Negro Republicans [like Perry Howard]. These Dixie delegates cannot speak for the three million Negroes in the North who have the vote.

"Anyone ought to know by now that unless a Roman Catholic, a Jew or a Negro is nominated for President, the South is going to stay Democratic. Therefore the Negroes who are going to do the Republican party any good are the Negroes in the North."

Not helping matters was Landon himself. On his first Colorado vacation, a *Baltimore Afro-American* reporter had queried him about lynching and the federal requirements for photographs to accompany civil service applications (a not-particularly subtle way of weeding out Black applicants). He refused to answer. The "absolutely stunned" Landon's "face turned red," reported the paper. "It was just like a bolt of lightning out of [a] clear blue sky."

His noises about respecting states' rights, particularly in distributing relief measures, panicked Blacks. "If Governor Landon were older and more experienced in government," jibed the *Afro-American*, "he'd know that there are fourteen states that can't be trusted to administer relief, old-age pensions or unemployment insurance for colored people. . . . HE PROPOSES TO SELL US DOWN THE RIVER."

Help arrived for Landon . . . right off the boat from far-off Berlin. . . .

In August 1936, Hitler's Nazis hosted the Olympic Games, capturing the bulk of medals and inventing the system of scoring national medal hauls and the Olympic Torch ceremony, but also struggling to convince a rightly suspicious world that they were not such bad Aryans after all. Concurrently, their theories of racial superiority ran into a Black American buzzsaw named Jesse Owens. The twenty-two-year-old Ohioan not only helped capture a record-setting four gold medals, he made it look easy.

Owens, grandson of a slave and the child of sharecroppers, was now an international sensation, wildly popular even among the largely Master Race audience at Berlin's hundred-thousand-seat Olympic Stadium. Landon and Roosevelt forces jostled to secure his endorsement. Even before Owens departed Berlin, Democratic operatives led by Robert L. Vann (now back with the *Pittsburgh Courier*) attempted enticing him into the Democratic camp. And why not? Just a year previously, Owens had—under Democratic auspices—served as a page in the Ohio legislature.

Fifty thousand persons greeted his return to New York Harbor aboard the Cunard liner *The Queen Mary.* So did additional entreaties—and controversies. Song-and-dance man Bill "Bojangles" Robinson (representing Mayor La Guardia) and former heavyweight champion Jack Dempsey attempted to recruit him for FDR. Robinson also angled to represent Owens on the vaudeville stage and for a possible role in an upcoming Shirley Temple flick. Reports floated of Al Jolson offering Owens $20,000 for a gig—and of another blackface comedian, Eddie Cantor, bidding $40,000 for ten weeks' work alongside him on the radio and in person. Rumors circulated of a two-film deal with Hollywood's Fox studios. And for a series of shorts with Paramount.

Two competing Ohio delegations jockeyed for favor. Cleveland Alderman Herman H. "The Little Napoleon of Ward 12" Finkle commanded Republicans. State party chairman Francis W. "Big Frank" Poulson led Buckeye Democrats. On the government cutter sailing out to meet *The Queen Mary,* however, the tousle-haired, cigar-puffing Poulson proved bumptiously aggressive, annoying (among others) "Bojangles" Robinson. "Listen here," Robinson threatened Poulson, "you may be a big shot in Ohio, but you don't amount to much around here. I'll punch you in the eye."

Back in Manhattan, meanwhile, Eighth Avenue's New Yorker Hotel had refused lodgings to Owens's parents and to his twenty-year-old wife, Ruth. As did the Biltmore, the Lincoln, and the McAlpin. Alderman Finkle finally pled the Owenses' case with the Hotel Pennsylvania. They got rooms, but only by agreeing to use its service entrance.

Eddie Cantor's offer turned out to be fake—a cheap headline-grabbing stunt by his press agent. Similar offers also proved chimerical since, as Owens soon confessed, "I haven't any talent. I can't dance. I can't sing." Nothing panned out. Not even for a featured role in 20th Century Fox's upcoming feature *Charlie Chan at the Olympics.*

In early September, Owens finally signed on the dotted line—for a Landon speaking tour. One press report stated he got $15,000; others hiked it to $30,000. In reality, it was $10,000, personally supplied by the conservative, anti-NRA millionaire Joseph Pew of the Sun Oil Company.

Said Owens, in pitching Landon: "The country was made largely by the sweat of the Negros. I do not want to knock the present Administration; President Roosevelt has done something, but not enough to benefit the people of the colored race. But I believe the election of Governor Landon would be good for America and for the . . . colored race. Governor Landon does not promise much but what promises he makes, I think he will keep."

Soon, however, Owens's white business manager, Marty Forkins (also Bill Robinson's longtime manager), was pressuring Owens to abandon Landon, and Jesse was reportedly zigzagging away from the endorsement. The press quoted him as saying, "Almost every Negro I have talked to has told me I was foolish and has told me I ought to retract . . . I will not stump for Landon or anybody else."

He soon retracted his retraction. "These reports," he quickly declared, "are not only untrue, but serve to indicate the lengths New Deal press agents will go to to discredit those forces [of Republican principles and real Americanism]."

Traveling to Chicago, he conferred with Frank Knox; at Topeka, with Landon for two hours, though, mostly talking sports. With Kansas City's African-American *Kansas City Plaindealer*, he discussed his Olympic experience:

> My trip to Germany was one of the most enjoyable experiences of my life. I was never treated more royally. Segregation was forgotten, until I hit the shores of the United States. . . . Hitler is O. K. as far as I know. He did not show any signs of unwelcome to me. He waved his hand at me from his box seat, after I finished a major event. I can't see why the newspapers always play the wrong thing up. I did not go to Germany to visit Hitler, my mission was to run. I think that Hitler treated me better than the President of the United States. Mr. Roosevelt did not even send me a message of congratulations for winning honors for the United States. Hitler did wave his hand at me.

". . . Hitler treated me better than the President of the United States."

Perhaps not quite true—but not quite false, either.

Cleveland Baptist minister Ernest Hall had married Jesse and Ruth Owens. More pertinently to Roosevelt, he had once pastored FDR's valet Irvin McDuffie. In August, Hall personally requested FDR that US Olympic medalists "be officially received by yourself upon their return home without regard to race or color." FDR, again fearing Southern reaction, refused. The Democratic Party's Good Neighbor League's Bishop R. R. Wright telegraphed Franklin, asking him to dispatch greetings to Jesse to be presented by the League. Again—nothing happened.

Campaigning for Landon, Owens drew crowds of Blacks, Republicans, and just-plain autograph seekers in such cities as Boston, Providence, New Haven, Newark, Philadelphia, Harrisburg, Pittsburgh, Buffalo, Niagara Falls, Columbus, Cleveland, Detroit, and Omaha. In both Chicago and Baltimore, he attracted crowds of ten thousand. In Baltimore, enthusiastic autograph seekers tore the door off his wife's parade vehicle.

Prior to his appearance at Cincinnati's Music Hall, (presumably) Democratic operatives drove a truck around Black neighborhoods, with a banner falsely proclaiming "Jesse Owens Has Left Town. Meeting Called Off." At the session itself, members of the Glee Club of the Sixteenth Ward Republican Women's Club—"24 Negro women smartly clad in white, with gold and blue capes and berets"—belted out not only spirituals but also such parodies as "Wail, Wail, the New Deal is Here" and "The Daring New Dealers They Do As They Please."

Not all, however, was harmonious. In Indianapolis, four of the nine cars in Owens's caravan were spotted sporting FDR stickers. The *Washington Tribune*'s Frederick S. Weaver (a great-grandson of Frederick Douglass) jeered that Owens "admits he knows nothing about politics. His statement proves it. He should therefore keep his mouth shut. Because a person has swift feet does not mean he qualifies as an adviser of an entire race on problems political and social. So keep on running, Jesse."

A parade honoring Owens in Harlem turned into a bust. Many held his family's previous acceptance of essentially segregated hotel quarters against him. Aggravating matters was Jack Dempsey's presence. Dempsey (a pro–New Deal Democrat) was infamous in Harlem for never accepting a Black challenge to his heavyweight crown. Onlookers (and they were sparse) ripped down American flags along 125th Street, jeering "Jesse Owens. Jim Crowed. Jesse Owens. Jim Crowed."

Toward campaign's end, Owens again returned to Manhattan, as an honored guest at a Brown Bombers football game at far-northern Manhattan's Dyckman Oval, again facing a decidedly "cool reception." Hecklers shouted, "Jesse is trying to keep Roosevelt beef steaks out of Harlem."

"Poorest race I ever ran," Owens himself admitted years later. "But they paid me a lot. No, I won't say how much—but a *lot*!"

The CPUSA's James Ford blasted any Black daring to support Landon. In a late September NBC Red Network nationwide broadcast, Ford declared, "A colored voter who supports the Republicans is helping to put a lynch rope around the neck of his people."

Black Republicans saw it differently. For his part, Landon accused the administration of employing "relief rolls as modern reservations on which the great colored race is to be confined forever as a ward of the Federal Government, excluded from the productive life of the country."

Just prior to Election Day, Republicans ran full-page ads in such outlets as the African-American weekly newspaper *The New York Age* and the Urban League's *Opportunity* magazine, exhorting readers:

> THE CONTINUATION OF THE NEW DEAL MEANS THE GHETTO, THE RESERVATION, JIM CROW, SERFDOM AND EXTINCTION FOR THE NEGRO. . . .
>
> COLORED VOTERS SHOULD SHOW THEIR RESENTMENT AGAINST PRESIDENT FRANKLIN D. ROOSEVELT'S SILENCE ON THE ANTI–LYNCHING BILL BY VOTING AGAINST HIM.

Democrats faced the reverse of GOP problems: to reassure people formerly long repulsed by their party that the causes for their revulsion were no longer operative—or were outweighed by newer, weightier factors.

They pointed with pride to Roosevelt's supposed "Black Cabinet," a group of roughly four dozen African-American New Deal appointees, most prominently Mary McLeod Bethune, the National Youth

Administration's Director of the Division of Negro Affairs and a close friend of Eleanor Roosevelt.

As 1936 opened, Eleanor wrote to the fading Louis Howe urging a wide variety of initiatives for the upcoming campaign, including targeting African-American voters: "The *negroes* of this country are in a more definitely friendly attitude toward the Administration than I have ever known them to be to a Democratic Administration and we should add to our organization . . . a unit that will supervise and keep in touch with them." Her proposal went nowhere.

Numerous hurdles had to be overcome: Howe's death, the reluctance (if not antipathy) of such Roosevelt advisers as Steve Early, and, truth be told, Black factionalism. African-American leaders might suddenly like Franklin Roosevelt. They did not necessarily like one another. Farley papered over such difficulties, much as FDR divided up spheres of influence between his advisers, eventually staffing two separate "Colored Democratic Divisions"—in the East under Robert L. Vann, with the assistance of Boston attorney Julian Rainey (another former Republican, and a Mayor Curley patronage appointee); and in the West, out of Chicago, under first-term congressman Arthur W. Mitchell. An uneasy peace reigned until Rainey—in his cups in a Harlem saloon—vented his drunken anger at Mitchell, climaxing in his solemn wish for the congressman's November defeat. Mitchell heard about it and was not pleased. Neither was he delighted to hear that Kansas's Democratic chairman had named a white man to head the state's Colored Democratic division.

Neither Vann nor Rainey nor Mitchell was the Democrats' equivalent of Jesse Owens. Heavyweight boxer Joe Louis might have been. Like Owens, Louis's career intersected with international implications. Owens triumphed in Berlin. In June 1936, however, Joe "The Brown Bomber" Louis fell to Germany's Max "The Black Uhlan of the Rhine" Schmeling in a twelfth-round Yankee Stadium knockout. Louis, nonetheless, remained an endorsement worth having. Republicans failed landing him. Democrats succeeded, but found the twenty-two-year-old less than articulate. At a rally sponsored by Jersey City boss Frank "I Am The Law" Hague, Louis stammered, in a voice so low and halting that few heard him, "Although I have trained in New Jersey it is the first time I have been in Newark . . . uh, Patterson, uh, Jersey City. I wish I could speak as hard as I can punch. But I'm glad to be here in the interests of Mayor Hague." Queried earlier at the Newark airport regarding how often he might campaign for the president, Louis blankly answered, "I dunno."

Joe Louis would not do.

Elizabeth "Lizzie" McDuffie, the college-educated wife of FDR's valet Irvin "Mac" McDuffie, would.

The Georgia-born Lizzie—the linchpin of Eleanor's army of Black maids and housekeepers—was a bit of a live wire. "Lizzie treated FDR like one of her family," recalled White House maid and seamstress Lillian Rogers Parks, "kidding him and teasing him by kissing the bald spot of his head."

From her earliest days, friends appraised Lizzie as a natural for the stage—and she, in fact, majored in theatre at Atlanta's Morris Brown College. At the White House, she often entertained the Roosevelts with a pair of puppets named "Suicide" and "Jezebel." As producer David O. Selznick prepped *Gone with the Wind*'s blockbuster film version, a movie executive visiting the White House caught McDuffie's "histrionic talent" and "robust and healthy" 140-pound physique. He joyfully wired Selznick, "I have found Mammy!"

Eleanor footed Lizzie's travel expenses for five screen tests for the role of Scarlet O'Hara's sassy servant "Mammy." Newspapers reported she got the part. Friends planned a testimonial in her honor. The stories were no truer than those of Eddie Cantor hiring Jesse Owens.

Lizzie had, however, landed the featured role of 1936 campaign spokesperson.

With FDR's expressed permission, she toured Black communities in such cities as Chicago, Springfield, St. Louis, East St. Louis, Cleveland, Columbus, Cincinnati, Indianapolis, and Gary, Indiana. An estimated fifty thousand persons heard her speak.

Part of her pitch remained very serious, defending FDR's enduring alliance with the white South: "Like in President Lincoln's time, all those who were in his party did not believe in absolute equality for the colored race. There have been many during the past three years who have been slow to see the light and to depart from the old traditional lines of thought. President Roosevelt, as you know, has not been afraid to act when necessary. Executive orders wiping out discrimination and unfair practices have been sent out on more than one occasion by him."

She boasted: "Hundreds of our brightest young men have been put in places of high Authority, in every major department of our government. Distinguished leaders of our own race like Mrs. Mary McLeod Bethune . . . have been called to Washington. She has seen to it that more than 30,000 of our own boys and girls benefited from the federal government student-aid program under the NYA."

Which sounded good—and certainly the number of jobs handed out was true—but as historian Jill Watts has assessed, "The reality was that there weren't 'hundreds' of new black appointees and that the 'brightest young men' who made up the black cabinet constantly encountered obstructions 'in every major department of the government.' They had no 'authority,' and the White House had little interest in their advice."

Robert Vann or Congressman Mitchell or Mrs. Bethune herself could easily have provided the talking points Lizzie McDuffie cited. Her audiences craved something more, the "scoop" on life deep within the White House (where the childless McDuffies lived on the East Wing's second floor) and about the Roosevelts themselves—"President and Mrs. Roosevelt as I Know Them," as Lizzie titled her talk.

At St. Louis, for example, "gowned in black lace over a pink slip, her bobbed hair straightened and combed straight back, long pearl earrings dangling," she addressed a 750-person audience in the gymnasium of the YWCA's local African-American branch.

"From her husband, Mrs. McDuffie . . . had it that the President reads from the Bible each night," the *Baltimore Afro-American* reported. "By her own knowledge, only light wines and beer are served at the White House, and members of the family are temperate in their use."

She reported FDR reassuring her, "For years your people have been drawers of water and hewers of wood. But now they are going to get the rights that are theirs."

Audiences laughed when she revealed that Mrs. Roosevelt did not like sunflowers and had advised her: "Lizzie, I believe the Negro race has many things to contribute to our nation. Certain things, such as song and rhythm, come to them naturally, whereas we have to work for those accomplishments."

Lizzie McDuffie had her appeal, but the Roosevelt campaign was not about to place all their African-American hopes in her limited basket. Among Louis Howe's final legacies to Franklin was his work in setting up a high-toned (but highly political) "Good Neighbor League," targeting such groups as Republicans, progressives, women, peace activists, social workers, businessmen—and African Americans. The League's "Colored Committee" membership would be limited to the African-American middle class: clergy, editors, businessmen, and so on. Its efforts would include such publications as *Why I, A Colored Citizen, Will Vote for the Reelection of President Roosevelt; Has the Roosevelt New Deal Helped the Colored Citizen?; The Second Emancipation Proclamation;* and *What the Negroes of Kansas Think of Governor Landon.* It ultimately issued a quarter-million copies of such pamphlets.

Stanley High assumed command of the League in February 1936. Not, however, until August 1 did he write to Rev. Adam Clayton Powell Sr., pastor of Harlem's immense (ten-thousand-parishioner) Ebenezer Baptist Church, requesting him to chair the League's "Colored Committee." The light-skinned, blue-eyed Powell, formerly an intensely proud Republican (and a former statewide GOP elector), had more recently also allowed his church to host events protesting the Scottsboro Boys' incarceration.

Once again, Democrats divided up African-American leadership, though this time along denominational lines, tapping African Methodist Episcopal Bishop R. R. Wright as co-chair.

Powell quickly jumped ship. A press report noted that he "announced from the pulpit he had been misled by the purpose of the league. As he had understood it was a body of white and colored ministers interested in . . . the Good Neighbor policy. When he learned he was tied up with a jim crow movement within the organization, he withdrew."

More likely, it was a pure power struggle. A huge number of other African-American New Yorkers, including many clergy, followed Powell Sr. ("I do not believe in ministers around political offices") out the door. Some claimed that the League had touted them as members, but that they had either never even been contacted by it or had refused to join. Others complained of being falsely listed as attending a League event.

On September 21, 1936, the eve of the seventy-fourth anniversary of Lincoln's Emancipation Proclamation ("Emancipation Eve"), the Good Neighbor League's Colored Committee presented a spectacular nationwide series of events—twenty-five meetings in all, with an anticipated audience of one hundred thousand in Pennsylvania, Delaware, Maryland, Michigan, Ohio, Illinois, New York, West Virginia, Kentucky, and the District of Columbia—commemorating not Lincoln but Roosevelt.

Madison Square Garden hosted the evening's pièce de résistance—the largest African-American political rally to date. Somewhere between 15,000 and 18,000 persons attended the admission-free event, though it was hardly billed as a Democratic rally:

FREE! TO EVERYONE!
Come join in this monster tribute!
74th Anniversary Celebration
of Negro Progress
A Dramatic Spectacle Extolling
THE NEGRO AND HIS ACHIEVEMENTS

There were the usual political speeches. But if you think thousands trooped down from Harlem to receive the reading of a decidedly tepid message from the conspicuously absent but still nearby (at Hyde Park) FDR, think again. Nor, may it be assumed, were they all that interested in hearing Stanley High, Sen. Robert F. Wagner (of Wagner–Costigan Anti-Lynching Bill fame—a last-second drop-in), or white Westchester congresswoman Caroline O'Day (the wealthy, blue-eyed Episcopalian daughter of a Confederate general). Or even the wide array of ministers plugging FDR. They could hear their own ministers on Sundays.

Rather, the evening presented four hours of pure spectacle, in essence one of the great Black vaudeville bills of all time.

Leading off was the flamboyant radio preacher Elder Lightfoot Solomon Michaux, the pastor with the "Million Dollar Smile," who transported 300 of his flock via special train from Washington. Beseeching his huge audience to fight "not with carnal but spiritual weapons," Elder Michaux led his famed white-gowned and -capped 156-voice "Happy I Am Choir" in song. More spectacularly, he brought with him a 20'x24' oil painting titled "The Three Emancipators."

"Christ," reported the *Baltimore Afro-American*, "was termed the emancipator from sin; Lincoln emancipator from bondage and Roosevelt, the emancipator from social injustices."

Stanley High recalled seeing the twenty-foot-high image of FDR, "his hands outstretched in benediction over a kneeling group of Negroes and with the spirit of Abraham Lincoln hovering . . . in the shadows."

But Michaux's massive artwork was a mere warm-up act. Harlem's forty-piece Monarch Elks Band played (among other things) FDR's theme song, "Happy Days Are Here Again." Juanita Hall's (often WPA-funded) sextet, "The Negro Melody Singers," sang spirituals. Actor Rex Ingram, "De Lawd" in the recent Warner Brothers hit all-Black film *The Green Pastures,* took a bow. W. C. Handy reminisced about composing "The St. Louis Blues" and how he hadn't thought it would ever amount to much. Bringing the house down was Cab Calloway and his Cotton Club Orchestra, belting out "Copper Colored Gal o' Mine," "Frisco Flo," and (naturally) "Minnie the Moocher." The immense throng joined in for "Minnie."

"20,000 Harlemites Hi de Ho for Roosevelt," headlined the *Baltimore Afro-American.*

One Black newspaper, however, derided the evening as a "minstrel mass meeting." Two hundred Black Republican ministers slammed it as one of a series of "religious jazz shows."

It was not until late October that FDR himself delivered his first address to a Black audience, dedicating a new PWA-funded chemistry building at Washington's Howard University. In his brief comments, FDR contended that, "As far as it was humanly possible, the Government has followed the . . . policy that among American citizens there should be no forgotten men and no forgotten races. It is a wise and truly American policy. We shall continue faithfully to observe it." A straw poll of Howard students favored FDR to Landon 289–91. The integrated Browder–Davis ticket trailed with sixty-two votes. Prohibitionist D. Leigh Colvin bested Norman Thomas six votes to four.

Yes, things were looking good for the Democrats. The normal Democrat machines could be counted on to do their part to woo Black voters, though often roughly—and at arm's length. They might indeed want Black hands to pull down their party's voting machine levers. They might not actually want to shake them.

Such, it appeared, was Empire State Democrats' attitude in mid-September when Jim Farley convened a private campaign conference at the Biltmore. "The Republicans," gushed Farley just ten days before the Good Neighbor League's gala, "have said so much about the administration's favoritism toward the colored people that it has seeped through to them. We will get all of Harlem. . . . This generation of negroes is grateful for what Roosevelt has done for them."

His underlings concurred. Nassau County chairman John S. Thorp was optimistic—but not *that* optimistic. He anticipated winning 40 percent of the African-American vote: "It is not so much the work we have done for them. They are just for Roosevelt."

"What they get from the relief, the WPA, is just about what they are capable of earning in good times," Thorp added. "The colored fellow has been living at the top of the world."

"I think," Farley reckoned, "we ourselves will be amazed at the percentage of the colored vote for Roosevelt." Professing amazement at how well Democrats were doing, he nonetheless left little to chance—even buying ads in the *New York Amsterdam News* to secure its key endorsement and creating a sixteen-minute campaign film, "We Work Again," specifically highlighting the Black experience in the Works Progress Administration.

Farley tracked things statewide—including normally Republican upstate. At the Biltmore, he queried Albany County boss Edward J. O'Connell: "Are there many coons in your town, Ed?"

For the increasingly confident Jim Farley, such votes may have been a luxury; but other parties were scrambling for every vote they could get.

· 18 ·

"The very essence of un-Americanism"

Father Divine was not running for anything. After all, if you're God—or at least just pretending to be God—why accept a demotion?

But still dabbling in left-wing politics, he hoped to be a player, if not in world events (Pius XI never did get back to him), at least north of 110th Street.

August 1936 witnessed two hundred of his disciples join in a Communist-led League Against War and Fascism parade. That September, thousands of his devotees converged on Madison Square Park, where Divine introduced Coughlinite vice presidential hopeful "Hamburger Tom" O'Brien, who, in turn, likened Divine to the great Lincoln. Despite such flattery, Divine issued no Lemke–O'Brien endorsement—a full acceptance of his Peace Mission platform being necessary for that occurrence.

Voter registration was expanding throughout the city, and Divine's International Peace Mission Movement acolytes were not to be left behind, though their custom of adopting, shall we say, unconventional names created unprecedented hurdles at the city's board of elections. Males bearing such names as "Providence Star," "Sunny Sonny," and "Happy Boy Joe," and females named "Quiet Love," "Wonderful Wisdom," "O Beautiful Revelation," "Gladness Darling," "Ruth and Naomi," and "Purity Love" were rejected as prospective voters. When three hundred of Divine's adherents jammed their local polling place, refused to leave, and kept chanting "Peace,

Father," they were accordingly arrested, hustled off to 229 West 123rd Street's 28th Precinct House, and posthaste to night court.

At which point, Divine's female followers objected to riding in the same paddy wagon as their male counterparts. "Father Divine," they primly explained, "has redeemed us from men." Police proved flexible—flexible enough to order male detainees to walk to night court.

At night court, "Happy Boy Joe" (née Harold Martin) vouched for Father Divine, averring that Father had reformed him of many a vice, even including playing the numbers.

"Well," marveled Magistrate Michael A. Ford, "if he cured you of the policy playing, he's done something that the Police Department and the mayor have not been able to do."

Ford—noted for his often-interesting rulings—dropped all charges. A subsequent state Supreme Court decision allowed Peace Movement members to register in the name of their choice. The *Baltimore Afro-American* rejoiced:

> **PRZEMIELEWKSI**
>
> Quiet Love, Mary Light, Abundant Life, Peaceful Love, Beacon Light, Pleasant Day and other spiritual names of divine followers, rejected by a New York election board, were ordered registered by the court last week.
>
> And why not?
>
> What is there in the state constitution or the laws of New York, which prevents a person from adopting an unheard-of name as his or her own?
>
> After all, didn't clerks of election register all Zschieches, Zizwareks, Zinsetos, Przemielewksis [sic], and Goeterdammerungs who appeared before them without hesitation? If we had to choose between these tongue twisters and the simple names of the Divine followers, we choose, let us say, Pleasant Day.

But who might the "Pleasant Days" of the world vote for? So queried at police court, they replied: "Father has not yet told us how to vote. We are guided by the Father." The following day, however, his devotees filed petitions for six candidates on a new "All Peoples Party" ticket, including East Harlem's radical Republican congressman Vito Marcantonio, two Harlem Assembly candidates (one being the embattled Communist Party activist Angelo Herndon), and three Court of Special Sessions hopefuls. Their petitions included such signatories as "Jonah Whale," "Love, Love, Love," "Holy Hannah," and "Flowery Bed of Peace."

No politician, however, sported less of a Father Divine–like name than Norman Thomas.

As Thomas launched his third straight presidential campaign, his crusade seemed more doomed than ever. True, he retained such notable endorsements as the railway workers' union's A. Philip Randolph, the United Auto Workers' Walter Reuther, and theologian Reinhold Niebuhr. But they amounted to slim pickings contrasted to a George Norris or an Al Smith—or even celebrities like Jesse Owens or Cab Calloway. They barely surpassed Honus Wagner. Thomas had polled a reasonably impressive 884,885 votes four years previously, but intervening events hardly improved his chances, as he simultaneously spurned Earl Browder's United Front blandishments while still alienating his party's anti-Communist Old Guard. "I can no longer be identified with a party which is making alliances with Communists," complained longtime Socialist David Dubinsky, president of the International Ladies Garment Union. Thomas's 1928 and 1932 running mate, former Federation of Labor president James H. Maurer, also decried his party's "trend toward Communism" and similarly bolted. Old Guard Socialist Louis Waldman summed it up: "Norman Thomas won a nomination and lost a party."

Old Guard defections, however, only paled compared to a much-larger problem named Franklin D. Roosevelt. New Dealers might never admit it, but Al Smith's charge that "the young Brain Trusters caught the Socialists in swimming and they ran away with their clothes" contained more than a kernel of truth. And just as Woodrow Wilson's "New Freedom" hobbled the Gene Debs Socialist Party of old, FDR's New Deal rendered Norman Thomas's nostrums increasingly less relevant.

Disaffected Socialists migrated to the Democratic Party—or something very much like it. New York's Old Guard elements invented their own party, the "American Labor Party," specifically designed to safeguard

Empire State electoral votes for Franklin Roosevelt—but also to feather their own political nests. The game was this, as David Dubinsky recalled: "The C.I.O. was worried that it would be shut out of any leadership role in the campaign, because Jim Farley . . . wanted to give all the spotlight to Dan Tobin of the A.F.L.'s Teamsters Union, who was going to be appointed chairman of the Democratic Party's labor committee." Dubinsky's allies in the C.I.O. strategized to counterattack the relatively more conservative Tobin. Their new American Labor Party helped do the trick.

Jim Farley even named six American Labor Party honchos (including Dubinsky; the millinery union's Max Zaritsky; the Amalgamated Clothing Workers' Sidney Hillman; and New York State Federation of Labor president George Meany) to a combined forty-seven-member combined Democratic-ALP slate of FDR Empire State electors alongside Farley himself.

The ALP boosted FDR. Norman Thomas did not. Unlike the CPUSA, which trained its fire on Landon, Thomas largely ignored the Kansan. "He typifies reaction," Thomas reassured a national radio audience in late July. "He gives no evidence as yet of knowing what it is all about . . . but it is absurdly and dangerously misleading to call this modest conservative, rather bewildered Kansan, a Fascist."

His strategy made some sense. There were precious few votes for a Socialist to steal from a Republican, but far more to filch from FDR. In Providence, he once more excoriated Franklin for "running as a radical in the west, as a safe and sane friend of good business in the east," and for, when governor, ignoring Robert Moses's plan to avert major bank failures.

Moreover, he scored New Deal fumblings:

> Last year there was a 36 percent increase in the profits of the great corporations. The increase in employment was exactly 2½ percent.
>
> This could not happen under a Socialist government. There are twelve million men and women out of work. A sixth of our population is on relief. There has been no increase at all in the . . . wage of the average worker.
>
> This is not socialism. No, indeed! I would hate to think of a socialism which sanctioned a steadily increasing burden of

> debt. . . . In my wildest flights of imagination I cannot imagine a Socialist government closing its eyes to the exploited peons of the cotton fields or to the slaves of Florida's flogging belt; nor of a Socialist government's paying for the destruction of food when little children are hungry.

Thomas's campaign took him south, to a luncheon in Nashville where restaurant management refused to serve Blacks alongside whites—"We are still in the South and can't mix the two races socially"—but allowed Thomas to "bring colored people along to entertain, but not to eat."

He went north—to Schenectady, New York's Union College, scolding his audience that "even in the age of innocence, college men never fell harder than they do today for political guff" and warning them that "this generation of college students is probably headed for war."

In a midnight radio address from New York, he skewered all the major (and minor) parties: Democrats, Republicans, Coughlinites, Communists. "Bitterly as these parties quarrel," he jibed, "all of them alike are trying to cure tuberculosis with cough drops. Their brands are different, some better, some worse, but none can do the job."

In September, he telegraphed a debate challenge—not to FDR, nor Landon, but to Lemke, who, he explained, "is getting away with more murder. I feel kind of sorry for poor Alf. He isn't going across with any kind of a bang even with the people who hate Roosevelt." If Lemke, who Thomas feared might very well carry Minnesota, the Dakotas, and Oregon, couldn't oblige, Thomas said he'd be happy to debate a "proxy": Father Coughlin.

Lemke wired back: no, thanks, "Your telegram which you made public apparently for publicity purposes received. . . . My time is otherwise occupied especially since you and your comrade Browder are both giving aid and comfort to Jim Farley's candidate for the presidency."

Earl Browder.

For the representative of a party that drew a paltry 0.26 percent of the vote four years previously, Earl Browder seemed everywhere. This was, indeed, his moment. Perhaps he was not quite respectable, but doors were flinging open to him all over the place. Three thousand heard him at Denver. Fifteen hundred greeted his mere arrival in Los Angeles. A combined 12,000 heard him at two Philadelphia meetings. In July, he spoke alongside Norman Thomas, Harold Ickes, and former GOP Senator Hiram Bingham at the University of Virginia's Institute of Public Affairs roundtable. The National Press Club hosted him in late August. He logged 26,000 miles, barnstorming through twenty-six states.

At campaign's end, he boasted, "No other Communist candidate has seen such hospitality as that accorded me this year"—and was being modest. "Not since Eugene Debs's day," assessed his biographer James G. Ryan, "had an American leftist received such frequent favorable publicity."

In early September, painter Rockwell Kent unveiled the "Committee of Professional Groups for Browder and Ford." Membership included composer Aaron Copland, novelist Waldo Frank, poet Langston Hughes, humorist S. J. Perelman, authors Max Weber and Michael Gold, *New Masses* editor Granville Hicks, and the officially heretical Episcopal bishop William M. "Bad Bishop" Brown.

Later that month, Browder and James Ford took to the airwaves: Browder, with a series of eight paid broadcasts over NBC; Ford, speaking on "The Negro People and the Elections," over the more modest NBC Red Network, a circuit nonetheless with ten stations in the South. The *New York Herald Tribune* provided yet another nationwide Browder hookup, hosting him as part of its Annual Forum at Manhattan's Waldorf Astoria. When Pittsburgh's Hearst-owned station WCAE refused to honor its contract to broadcast three Browder speeches, the Federal Communications Commission ordered him back on.

Yet, to every revolution a little rain must fall.

Browder—and Ford—were in fact *not* welcomed everywhere.

On Saturday, September 12, Browder invaded the Deep South. It went as well as might be expected. Four plainclothes detectives met him at Atlanta's train station with orders to arrest him ("We don't like that stuff in Atlanta") if he made any "communist utterances." He wired Franklin Roosevelt demanding federal protection. Attorney General Homer Cummings responded, denying that any federal issues were at stake.

Browder canceled his engagement and caught the next train to Tampa, only to find his venue, the United Secret Orders Hall, padlocked in a comedy of errors. Also using the hall were local Odd Fellows, and Odd Fellow member Salvador Llosa, unaware of Browder's meeting being hastily rescheduled there, had innocently locked up the place to secure his group's equipment. Browder's organizers finally hunted down the Cuban-born Llosa at a local movie theatre. An hour and forty-five minutes after the meeting was scheduled to commence, he removed the padlocks, apologizing profusely. Frustrated organizers, nonetheless, advised three hundred prospective audience members to just go home.

Not missing a chance to grandstand, Browder and three local Communists sued the city for $100,000. Topping it off, they also sued the *Tampa Tribune*, the Concord Baptist Church, Lodge No. 12 of the Knights of Pythias, and the local Optimists Club. The three organizations had passed resolutions opposing his talk. The *Tribune* had published them. They somehow neglected to sue the Odd Fellows or any of the other organizations running the hall.

On Sunday afternoon, October 25, Browder returned to Tampa. Now, lock-shy, he was slated to speak in a padlock-free downtown vacant lot. A dozen men wearing American Legion caps rushed in to assault crowd members. Browder pled: "I am not here to attack any individual and I hope no one else is here except to listen to an orderly discussion of political questions. There is one issue in this campaign. It is the defense of democracy." The mob overturned Browder's makeshift speaker's platform, and he fled into a nearby car. A dozen persons—some pistol-whipped—sustained injuries. Four, including a woman, were hospitalized. Authorities arrested three men (a Tampa constable, his deputy, and a former deputy sheriff) for assault and battery, aggravated assault with a deadly weapon, and something called "affray" ("an instance of fighting in a public place that disturbs the peace"). The national commander of the American Legion condemned the violence as "the very essence of un-Americanism."

Browder fared better at Birmingham, where city fathers allowed him access to the city's 3,000-seat Ben-Hur Hall. That was the good news. The bad news: only 350 listeners (230 white, 120 Black) bothered attending. Later he met with the nine jailed Scottsboro Boys, providing them with $2.00 each for candy and cigarettes.

Worse news greeted Browder at Terre Haute—home to the legendary Eugene Debs, but more recently the scene of a July 1935 general strike requiring Indiana Democratic governor Paul V. McNutt to mobilize National Guardsmen to restore order.

On Wednesday morning, September 30, Mayor Samuel O. Beecher and Police Chief James C. Yates (both Republicans) first barred Browder from speaking at either State Teachers' College Auditorium or over local radio stations WBOW and WGFB. Which was just the beginning. As Browder, novelist Waldo Frank, and four comrades detrained, Chief Yates arrested the lot of them. "We do not want radicals stopping here," Yates explained. "We've had our share of labor troubles from such agitators."

"Now these Communists know we mean business," proclaimed Mayor Beecher, arguing, "Both . . . Mr. Roosevelt and Mr. Landon recognize Communism as a menace. . . . Therefore, Communistic speakers are not welcome in Terre Haute."

Authorities detained Browder *et al.* for "investigation" of vagrancy. Jailed for twenty-five hours, they sued for false arrest. The American Civil Liberties Union protested. From New York, Jack Dempsey condemned the arrests as "a lousy stunt . . . shabby treatment . . . not at all fair and sporting."

Since Mayor Beecher had approvingly cited FDR for his actions, CPUSA Campaign Chairman William Z. Foster telegraphed the White House and demanded clarification, generously allowing the president to "wire reply collect." FDR didn't respond. Nor did Landon. Attorney General Cummings again ducked federal jurisdiction: "Browder is in conflict with the local authorities. There is no Federal question involved. Anyway, that's not our matter."

Norman Thomas also telegrammed FDR, condemning the episode as "an act of high-handed tyranny which advertises Communism and disgraces America." Soon, he arrived in town to harvest his own publicity, joking that "Landon was as much of a vagrant as Browder," as both men were out "looking for jobs." Half-fearfully (and probably half-hopefully), he "half expected" his own arrest.

Browder himself returned on Tuesday, October 20, the tenth anniversary of Eugene Debs's passing, armed with a copy of the Constitution and—as evidence he really wasn't a vagrant—a certified check for $1,000. That night, he was again scheduled to broadcast from WBOW. A mob pelted him with eggs and rotten tomatoes. A news photographer climbed to the roof of a car to get some shots. Protestors kicked the camera from his hands, smashing it to bits. Browder scurried back into his cab, fled to his hotel room, and petitioned Franklin Roosevelt and Governor McNutt for recourse. Nothing came.

Communists, small-town radio stations, and mobs simply did not play well together. On Friday evening, October 23, in Southern California's Imperial Valley, a two-hundred-man mob invaded the studios of El Centro radio station KXO to block a broadcast by the CPUSA's 20th District congressional candidate, a thirty-two-year-old San Diego oil field laborer named Esco L. Richardson. With Police Chief J. Sterling Oswalt conveniently absent in Los Angeles and every law-enforcement officer in town equally conveniently unreachable at a local high school football game, absolute mayhem erupted. "He [Richardson] was interrupted," noted a press report, "when someone pulled a plug from a controlling meter outside the station. An engineer plugged it in again, and Richardson resumed.

"Meanwhile, the mob was gathered in the street outside. An unidentified member of it produced a pistol and shot out the light meter. Five more bullets were fired into the meter itself, disabling the station.

"Engineers rushed out to repair the damage, and the mob surged in, jammed through a narrow corridor and broke the glass door to the studio to get at Richardson. He went down under a pile of men and was dragged out into the street, his eyes blackened, bleeding from the nose. . . .

"Richardson was pushed in the direction of the railroad station. When he slowed, he was pushed again. The mob followed a few paces behind throwing rotten eggs and vegetables."

Browder's running mate, James W. Ford, endured no actual violence, yet often met hostility along the campaign trail. As he informed the *Daily Worker*:

> I want to give you just a few examples. Certainly the every-day experiences of the Negro people are much more dismal. . . . At the YMCA hotel in Scranton, Pa. . . . I was refused admission.

> At Columbus, Ohio, I almost had a fist fight at one of those White Tower restaurants. They refused to serve me a glass of milk, and when the state statute was thrown in their face they wanted to charge 21 cents for a five-cent glass.
>
> At Uniontown, Pa. the Ku Klux Klan has been revived to bring the Mason and Dixon Line into Pennsylvania. . . . Leaflets were spread to frighten the Negro people, stating that this town will "ooze with nigger blood."
>
> . . . at Springfield, the home or shrine of Abraham Lincoln I was refused a room at the Abraham Lincoln Hotel. At a local movie house, . . . carrying the name "Lincoln" I was refused admission. . . . I stopped to get my shoes shined and was told that they could not take patronage from colored people.

Earl Browder had a greater difficulty than the occasional idiotic mayor or mob (who, after all, were the CPUSA's best publicity agents). It was his campaign slogan. No, not "Communism is Twentieth Century Americanism." No, that was fine—at least until the twenty-first century rolled around. It was the party's widely derided cri de coeur: "Defeat Landon at all cost—Vote for Earl Browder."

In late August, *Daily Worker* managing editor James Casey (formerly of the *Times*) had had enough. He resigned his post and his party membership, and abandoned his Bronx congressional race, decrying the party's "hypocritical" attitude on the election, and charging that it had worked to "swing the support of its membership and affiliated mass organizations to President Roosevelt." Essentially retorting "you can't quit, we fire you," the party expelled the hard-liner Casey for "deserting to the camp of the enemies of the working class."

William Randolph Hearst saw it differently.

As far back as August 1935, as we might recall, Hearst had been digging into the Comintern's newfound regard for Franklin Roosevelt and its eagerness to support his reelection. Hearst's investigation had, of course, been torpedoed by the State Department's sudden ostentatious warning to Moscow to avoid any "interference in the internal affairs of the American people."

The story lay dormant until August 1936, when *Chicago Tribune* correspondent Donald Day (brother of Catholic activist Dorothy Day and a royal anti-Semite) filed a story from Riga, Latvia, titled "Moscow Orders Red in U.S. to Back Roosevelt, Sees Landon as Bitter Foe of Class Warfare."

"We are going to work for the election of Roosevelt," Day quoted the Comintern as directing its American subordinates, "because we wish to strengthen our influence among America's many radical groups.

"We all have a common aim. It is to defeat Landon."

Day got it wrong, but not *too* wrong. He wasn't quoting orders from the Comintern—at least, not directly—but mistakenly quoting a translation of a May 29, 1936, radio speech by Earl Browder. The pro-FDR *Chicago Times* jumped into the fray, refuting the story, even offering a $5,000 reward for anyone able to prove its accuracy. Nobody collected.

By Saturday, September 19, 1936, however, the Hearst chain essentially repeated Day's charges, getting the May 1936 Browder speech part right, and supplementing its narrative with the details of a much more recent Browder pronouncement, delivered in Detroit that September 5. "We have working agreements," Browder publicly proclaimed, "with all 'progressives' definitely committed to Roosevelt. . . . We are 100 percent opposed to Landon. . . . Some of our closest associates favor Roosevelt and my Communist candidacy will not prevent our working together. We have common objectives . . . and are constantly working with units favorable to Roosevelt."

For good measure, Hearst added a report of an August 1935 Georgi Dimitroff speech ("His [FDR's] defeat might enable forces now opposing our forces to give us a body blow"). Browder, bellowed Hearst, "is the "TITULAR nominee" of the Communists but "the REAL CANDIDATE—the UNOFFICIAL candidate of the Comintern—is FRANKLIN D. ROOSEVELT."

Roosevelt could ignore the *Tribune*. He dared not ignore such front-page tirades from the mighty Hearst. On Saturday, September 19, 1936, he ordered Steve Early to issue this statement:

> My attention has been called to a planned attempt, led by a certain notorious newspaper owner, to make it appear that the President

passively accepts the support of alien organizations hostile to the American form of government.

Such articles are conceived in malice and born of political spite. They are deliberately framed to give a false impression—in other words to "frame" the American people.

The President does not want and does not welcome the vote or support of any individual or group taking orders from alien sources.

This simple fact is, of course, obvious. . . .

The American people will not permit their attention to be diverted from real issues to fake issues which no patriotic, honorable, decent citizen would purposely inject into American affairs.

From far-off Amsterdam, Hearst shot back via cablegram on Sunday, September 20, 1936: "THE President has issued a statement. . . . He has not had the frankness to say to whom he refers, . . . nor . . . the sincerity to state his complaint accurately. . . . I have not stated at any time whether the President willingly or unwillingly received the support of the Karl Marx Socialists, the Frankfurter radicals, Communists and Anarchists, the Tugwell Bolsheviks and the Richberg Revolutionists who constitute the bulk of his following. I have simply said and shown that he DOES receive the support of these enemies of the American system of government, and that he has done his best to DESERVE the support of all such disturbing and destructive elements."

James Casey, Hearst, and the *Chicago Tribune* and the GOP weren't the only ones noticing the CPUSA's strange affinity for Franklin Roosevelt. So was Norman Thomas. From New York, he accused the Comintern of ordering its American vassals to supply FDR with their "indirect support."

"If correctly quoted," Earl Browder howled, Thomas's charge "sounds as if it were borrowed from the Hearst editorial pages."

"Technically," notes historian Harvey Klehr, "Browder was absolutely correct. The Comintern had not ordered the Americans to give 'indirect support' to Roosevelt. It had wanted direct support."

Hearst dug in his heels deeper: "Mr. Roosevelt declares that he is not a Communist, but the Communists say he is one. The Communists ought to know. Every cow knows its own calf. . . . The Communists may be misguided in many ways, but they are at least sincere. . . . Must we become Europeanized, Communized, Socialized, Bolshevized absolutely and on all occasions? Must we give up our own institutions, our own welfare, our own customary progress and prosperity? The good Lord forbid. Let us rather give up Roosevelt. . . . Let us have a 'New Deal' in Americanism, in the fine American policy of looking out first for the American people, and in minding our own American Business."

Accompanying Hearstian prose was Hearstian poetry, specifically an offering by veteran *New York American* sportswriter George E. Phair:

A Red New Deal with a Soviet Seal
Endorsed by a Moscow hand
The strange result of an alien cult
In a liberty-loving land.
The truth is out, and there is no doubt
Of the trend of the New Deal heads
Their plans are made and their courses laid
With the blessings of the Reds.
All free men shrink as they pause to think
Of the threatening Moscow tide
But the evidence there stands red and bare
And it cannot be denied.

But, though Mr. Phair might have you believe otherwise, not all free men were shrinking, and Franklin Roosevelt stood ready, willing, and able to capture their votes.

· 19 ·

"I welcome their hatred"

Franklin Roosevelt departed Philadelphia's Franklin Field with the cheers of a hundred thousand loyal Democrats vibrating in his heart.

But also a nagging doubt.

His home base wobbled. New York's forty-seven electoral votes seemed too shaky for comfort. Hoover swept rural upstate New York in 1932. Republicans recaptured the state Assembly in 1935. More astoundingly, a Republican won Gotham's aldermanic presidency in 1933. Al Smith loyalists threatened a walk to Landon. The Socialist vote, though declining precipitously in 1933's mayoral election, remained a wild card. In 1932's special mayoral contest, veteran Socialist Morris Hillquit polled an impressive 249,887 votes—12.4 percent of the total. If Norman Thomas polled just half that statewide, he might sabotage FDR in a close contest. Mid-July saw John D. M. Hamilton boldly forecast a Landon Empire State sweep by 350,000 to 500,000 votes.

FDR needed help—from Herbert Lehman. As early as May 1934, the popular New York governor informed FDR of his intentions to retire in 1936, thus placing the entire state ticket (Franklin included) at greater risk. FDR talked him back on the reservation—but only temporarily. In early 1936, Lehman was at it again, and, in the words of Lehman biographer Alan Nevins, Franklin was "greatly disturbed."

"He simply cannot be permitted to withdraw," FDR desperately wrote Henry Morgenthau.

In late May 1936, Lehman made his intended departure public. FDR swung into action, showcasing him at the national convention with, as Nevins also noted, a "spectacular half-hour demonstration; . . . the delegates cheering and parading in a tribute that was mainly prearranged by Farley and others to influence the governor to run again. . . . Lehman knew that it had been contrived, he found it heart-warming nevertheless."

Pouring it on, FDR invited Lehman onto his private train to Hyde Park, where he schmoozed him for a full three hours, following up with essentially a political mash note (which "comes more deeply from my heart than I can adequately express on paper"). He praised "all the things you have done in these four years," concluding "the more I look at it from every angle the more I'm convinced of the very great importance of your running—important to the social security of the whole nation in all that implies."

On July 1, Lehman capitulated. "American political history," editorialized the *Buffalo Courier-Express,* "has witnessed no stranger spectacle than . . . a President . . . and his advisers, plucking frantically at the coat tails of a governor of the President's own state and imploring him to run for office just once more, . . . to save the national ticket."

Far less displeased, of course, was Jim Farley. "Victory definitely assured," he wired associates.

Whether overconfident from his Lehman coup, or simply desiring to pace himself and his campaign on terms and terrain of his own choosing, FDR—like Landon—rolled out of the box very slowly.

On Saturday, July 11, he arrived in New York to celebrate an awkward triumph—the dedication of the city's massive Triborough Bridge—the East's largest PWA project, a complex of four bridges connecting the Bronx, Queens, and Manhattan.

Overseeing the Triborough Bridge Authority (TBA) was the ubiquitous Robert Moses. Back when Al Smith was governor, and Moses was Smith's trusted aide, Moses had blocked Louis Howe from obtaining a $5,000-per-year state sinecure, designed so Louis might continue promoting his master's political work on the public dime. Howe and FDR never forgot that, and, for that matter, Moses never forgot how much he loathed both of them. So much so that Moses (in his capacity as head of New York City's Parks Commission) attempted to block naming a new Lower East Side park after FDR's mother, though what the aristocratic Sara had to do with the Lower East Side was anybody's guess.

Lower East Side parks were one thing; control of a $45 million bridge and all the contracts and jobs (and glory) accompanying it was quite another. But underlying everything was FDR's abiding hatred of Moses—a fact somehow escaping Mayor Fiorello La Guardia. "[O]f all the people in the City, . . ." "The Little Flower" bewailed himself to a friend, "I had to pick the one man who Roosevelt won't stand for and he won't give me any more money unless I get rid of him."

Following Moses's November 1934 gubernatorial loss to Herbert Lehman, FDR hectored PWA boss Harold Ickes into canning Moses from the TBA. Ickes played hardball. As Moses's biographer Robert Caro noted, "Honest Harold" now threatened La Guardia that unless he jettisoned Moses, he would not (in Caro's words) "approve a single new PWA project of any type in New York City—not hospital, school, or subway" or, for good measure, neither would he requisition funds "for projects already underway in the city—[displacing] the tens of thousands of men now employed on them." In late December, Ickes (with FDR's direct collaboration) followed up with "Administrative Order 129," a thinly veiled subterfuge aimed at finally prying Robert Moses from his TBA perch.

Virtually anyone else would have quit. The wily Moses fought back, manufacturing a near-unanimous firestorm of press criticism skewering FDR's administration for playing politics at the expense of a then-nearly-universally admired public servant. Ickes, forced to publicly cover up his boss's complicity ("I was asked whether the President [had ever spoken to me about Moses]. I had to lie"), considered it to have been a "great mistake" to have made "a martyr" out of Moses. When an embattled FDR queried an old friend, "Isn't the President of the United States entitled to one personal grudge?" the blunt answer came back: "No." In late February 1935, when Al Smith jumped in to publicly defend his old pal Moses, FDR knew the jig was up and surrendered. The Triborough Bridge Authority rolled forward under Bob Moses's direction.

In July 1936, the Triborough finally opened—a wonderful ceremony for any president, and, particularly, for one hustling toward another term. But Robert Moses remained in command, dammit! And FDR, though scheduled to be in nearby Hyde Park that day, petulantly refused to attend. Ickes pled, and FDR's political instincts finally surmounted his "one personal grudge." He'd attend—but only on one condition. Robert Moses could introduce everyone else. But not Franklin Roosevelt. That honor fell to Mayor La Guardia.

FDR, requiring a rest after sharing a podium (let alone four bridges) with Bob Moses, took one. He loved the open water. Whether it was extended houseboating with Missy LeHand in the 1920s; a New England cruise aboard the rented 37-foot yawl *Myth II* immediately following his July 1932 nomination; on his Hudson Valley neighbor Vincent Astor's immense 264-foot-long yacht *Nourmahal* following that year's triumph; as an excuse in October 1935 to reconcile the feuding Ickes and Harry Hopkins; for two weeks aboard the brand-new presidential yacht USS *Potomac* in March–April 1936, scouring the Caribbean for barracuda; or aboard that same vessel in late May to cautiously introduce Sam Rosenman and Stanley High.

On Monday morning, July 13, Franklin departed Hyde Park for Maine. The next morning, along with three of his four sons, James, John, and Franklin (Elliott remained in Texas, awaiting the birth of seven-pound Elliott Jr.), he'd board the two-masted, fifty-six-foot schooner *Sewanna.* Among the *Sewanna*'s two-man non-Roosevelt crew was an unlikely adjunct, cook and handyman Joseph Emmerz, an Imperial German Navy veteran of the World War's Battle of Jutland. Along for part of the voyage was Eleanor's brother Hall Roosevelt.

Trailing the *Sewanna* was the *Potomac*; another schooner, the 114-foot *Liberty* (for use by the press); the destroyer USS *Hopkins*, from which Secret Service agents would deploy in smaller boats; and the USS *Owl*, which provided air support and served as mail tender. All in all, the deeply tanned, quite scruffy, and unshaven FDR absented himself for two weeks, sailing off the Maine and Nova Scotia coasts. Like his crutches and wheelchair, his short-lived mustache, muttonchops, and growth of beard remained off-limits to photographers.

"I'll be in old clothes and cool by morning—the oldest clothes I've got," he had chortled as he departed Hyde Park, adding a day later, "I'm just going to loaf."

Not exactly.

"I can look forward now," he had said a few days earlier, "to two or three weeks of freedom from official cares except, possibly for the reading and acting on some forty or fifty dispatches a day, the signing of a bag full of mail once every four or five days unless, of course, I get caught in a fog down the coast of Maine, and I am rather praying for fog."

From the *Sewanna*'s Marconi radio, Roosevelt listened to rival Alf Landon's Topeka acceptance speech. We have no record of his reaction. Vacationing at FDR's twenty-three-room, eighteen-bedroom Campobello "cottage" (despite its size, remarkably, neither electrified nor possessing a telephone), Eleanor was not impressed. "We listened to Landon's speech over her [Sara Roosevelt's] radio, . . ." she wrote her daughter Anna, "not well delivered & in spots it faded out but it was effective if you didn't say 'how.' I'm sorry for them if they get in & after all the promises have to do just about what has been done."

Better accomplished was FDR's sailing. A master of small boating since his youth, he refused to pull rank (or age or infirmity) and took his two daily watches at 9:00 p.m. and 3:00 a.m. This current voyage, assessed James Roosevelt, was his father's "prize cruise."

From aboard the *Liberty*, the *New York Times*'s Charles Hurd concluded something else: "Ten days on board the *Sewanna* have not only given the president a heavy coat of tan but a renewed vigor that has put him thoroughly in shape for the rigors of his campaign for re-election."

Roosevelt's colleagues in Washington must have found that preposterous, as FDR's leisurely pace simply alarmed them. Hugh Johnson remained pessimistic, worrying that, "If the present adverse trends continue, the reelection of President Roosevelt is extremely doubtful."

Harold Ickes confided to his diary: "[T]he President smiles and sails and fishes and the rest of us worry and fume. . . . [T]he whole situation is incomprehensible to me. It was loudly proclaimed that Louie Howe had supplied most of the political strategy that resulted in the nomination and election of President Roosevelt and I am beginning to believe that this must have been true." Steve Early further alarmed Ickes's fears by confiding that their boss's campaign functioned (if that was the word) bereft of concrete funding or even a real budget. To Eleanor, Early complained of "apparent confusion all over the place and a lack of competent staffs."

In August, Lynn, Massachusetts, congressman William P. Connery Jr. warned Jim Farley, "From where I sit at present time it looks like 60–40 in favor of Landon."

The ticket itself, however, remained upbeat. John Nance Garner firmly believed Landon's nomination "set the stage for a party debacle." Roosevelt calculated that Republicans had gotten out of the box too early and repeated their charges too often. After a while the public would simply stop listening. He would hold his fire—and not wear out his considerable welcome. In March 1935, he explained his strategy to journalist (and Woodrow Wilson biographer) Ray Stannard Baker: "The public psychology and, for that matter, individual psychology, cannot, because of human weakness, be attuned for long periods of time to a constant repetition of the highest note on the scale. . . . People tire of seeing the same name day after day in the important headlines of the papers, and the same voice night after night over the radio." Roosevelt held true to that. For seventeen months between April 1935 and September 1936, he went without delivering a single one of his famed Fireside Chats. The latter talk—addressing the year's massive drought—was, in fact, only his eighth such talk.

And so, on August 2, Franklin confidently inscribed his Electoral College prediction for November: "FDR, 340, AML, 191."

He waited until Thursday, August 13 to seriously hit the road once more, again playing the non-political chief-of-state role to tour flood-ravaged portions of New York, Pennsylvania, and Ohio. En route, he paused to speak at western New York's venerable Chautauqua Institute. Here, at perhaps the apogee of American isolationist and anti-war sentiment, the formerly Wilsonian FDR tacked once more to prevailing political winds. Thanks to Bill Bullitt's speechwriting skills, he now proclaimed:

> We shun political commitments which might entangle us in foreign wars; we avoid connection with the political activities of the League of Nations. . . .

> We are not isolationists except in so far as we seek to isolate ourselves completely from war. Yet we must remember that so long as war exists on earth there will be some danger that even the Nation which most ardently desires peace may be drawn into war.
>
> I have seen war. I have seen war on land and sea. I have seen blood running from the wounded. I have seen men coughing out their gassed lungs. I have seen the dead in the mud. I have seen cities destroyed. I have seen two hundred limping exhausted men come out of line—the survivors of a regiment of one thousand that went forward forty-eight hours before. I have seen children starving. I have seen the agony of mothers and wives. I hate war.

His timing and strategy were excellent, getting ahead of the curve, staking an advance claim to whatever anti-war stance Landon might eventually expound, and cementing the loyalties (or at least the silence) of such staunch Republican and progressive isolationists as Borah, Robert LaFollette Jr., Gerald Nye, Hiram Johnson, and George Norris. Just days afterward, George Gallup queried respondents: "To declare war, should Congress be required to obtain the approval of the people by means of a national vote?" Seventy-one percent said yes.

Following this brief tour, FDR again hunkered down at the White House. In early September, he pondered the unthinkable: What if he lost to Alf Landon? What if a triumphant Landon then invited Democrats and New Dealers into his cabinet? *What if he requested FDR's own assistance and participation?* Harold Ickes advised Franklin against accepting anything like that. FDR should steer clear of tying himself to Landon, retaining his options to lead any opposition. Roosevelt agreed, theorizing that if Landon won, the country would collapse within "two or three months." Ickes exhibited more confidence in the American experiment: it would hold together for a good six.

Roosevelt finally commenced his campaign's official debut on Tuesday evening, September 29. The scene: his state's annual Democratic convention at Syracuse.

Two evenings previously, Raymond Moley—celebrating his fiftieth birthday—visited Hyde Park, his first call on Franklin since their pre-Philadelphia contretemps. Since then, Moley had aggravated FDR even further thanks to a column in his *Today* magazine, referencing FDR's recent precipitous 55.8 to 51.8 percent drop in the latest Gallup poll. Moreover, Moley had dared critique Franklin's convention speech, thusly: "It seemed to thoughtful people that the warlike note struck in Philadelphia, which could only be interpreted as the assurance of a continuation of Leftist reform, was unsound politically because the country was temporarily tired of reform."

At Hyde Park, FDR perfunctorily attempted to lure his erstwhile ally back into the fold, but really wasn't all that interested in rapprochement. Neither, really, was Moley. Behind the scenes, a different sort of game played out: hide-and-seek. Sam Rosenman, Stanley High, and Tommy Corcoran were present, too, toiling all day to craft Franklin's upcoming Syracuse address. FDR kept them well secreted from Moley—a full two miles away, in fact, at Eleanor's hideaway Val-Kill Cottage. He didn't invite Ray to rejoin his team this day—or ever.

Harold Ickes also arrived. Together, he and Franklin would travel five hours by rail to Syracuse. Also en route were train car after train car of Tammany, Brooklyn, and Bronx delegates. At Syracuse, buffeted by bad weather, FDR donned hat and overcoat to ride through crowded streets to dedicate a building at Syracuse University's $825,000 Academy of Medicine. It was, of course, a PWA project.

At Syracuse's armory, before a packed, uproarious crowd, FDR's two-thousand-word, half-hour speech displayed him at top form. "No trick of inflection or shading of emphasis was overlooked," observed the *St. Louis Post-Dispatch,* including "a syrupy voice, edged with sarcasm." The *Philadelphia Inquirer* also noted the "full force of . . . withering sarcasm."

To two thousand delegates (plus a paid, two-network radio audience) Franklin wove through a variety of themes. His first: a counterattack to the mounting charges of pro-Communist influence within his administration—and of covert CPUSA support for his ticket. Steve Early's rebuttal of Hearst's charges (allegations soon echoed by John D. M. Hamilton) had proven less than effective. Jim Farley warned FDR that no GOP charge had proven so damaging as these latest Hearst salvos.

"Here and now," Franklin thundered, "once and for all, let us bury that red herring and destroy that false issue. . . . I have not sought, I do not seek, I repudiate the support of any advocate of Communism or of any other alien 'ism' which would by fair means or foul change our American democracy. That is my position. It has always been my position. It always will be my position."

Secondly—and more importantly—Franklin issued a reminder of economic conditions four years previously, accusations of Republican failure, and a very thinly veiled anti–Liberty League parable:

> In the Summer of 1933, a nice old gentleman wearing a silk hat fell off the end of a pier. He was unable to swim. A friend ran down the pier, dived overboard and pulled him out; but the silk hat floated off with the tide. After the old gentleman had been revived he was effusive in his thanks. He praised his friend for saving his life. Today, three years later, the old gentleman is berating his friend because the silk hat was lost.

That, as the *Philadelphia Inquirer* noted, "brought the house down." Which set the stage for skewering Landon:

> You cannot be an old Guard Republican in the East, and a New Deal Republican in the West. You cannot promise to repeal taxes before one audience and promise to spend more of the taxpayers' money before another audience. You cannot promise tax relief for those who can afford to pay, and, at the same time, promise more of the taxpayers' money for those who are in need. You simply cannot make good on both promises at the same time.

Such words were, to say the least, a fair criticism of Landon's confused message, but they also remained suspiciously near to plagiarizing Norman Thomas's repeated criticisms of FDR himself: that he campaigned "as a radical in the west, as a safe and sane friend of good business in the east."

But more than that, FDR was running as a liberal *and* a conservative *in the same speech*—this speech. His actions, he argued, would "provide insurance against radicalism of the sort which the United States has most to fear":

> The true conservative is the man who has a real concern for injustices and takes thought against the day of reckoning. The true conservative seeks to protect the system of private property and free enterprise by correcting such injustices and inequalities as arise from it. The most serious threat to our institutions comes from those who refuse to face the need for change. Liberalism becomes the protection for the far-sighted conservative.
>
> Never has a nation made greater strides in the safeguarding of democracy than we have made during the last three years. Wise and prudent men—intelligent conservatives—have long known that in a changing world worthy institutions can be conserved only by adjusting them to the changing time. In the words of the great essayist: "The voice of great events is proclaiming to us—reform if you would preserve."
>
> I am that kind of a conservative because I am that kind of a liberal.

Sharing the stage with FDR was his usual entourage: Jim Farley; a "severely" black-clad Eleanor (as was so often the case, delayed by duties at New York's Todhunter School); Herbert Lehman (embarrassingly placed in nomination by Supreme Court Justice Thomas Dowd as "Herbert Hoover"); Senator Wagner; Secretary of Labor Perkins; and the confident flotsam and jetsam of the state Democratic ticket. But also a surprising new name: aviatrix Amelia Earhart.

Amelia had first met Eleanor at Springwood in late November 1932. She and her husband, publisher George P. Putnam, lunched with Sara and Eleanor and Lord and Lady Astor in anticipation of Amelia's "Flying for Fun" talk at nearby Poughkeepsie. By August 1935, Earhart was an adviser with the National Youth Administration.

Before arriving in Syracuse, she busied herself stumping for the Democrats. At upstate Mechanicville, appearing as part of a "Women's Caravan," the 5'8" aviatrix ordered a desk hauled out on to the street so she might stand atop it to be better still seen and heard. At nearby Ballston Spa, she handed out Roosevelt campaign buttons and explained the differences between the Republican and Democratic parties as similar to that of a small, wooden airplane and a larger modern metal craft. "The one was all right at one time, but the larger, more efficient plane is better today. And that is why I urge you to vote for Franklin D. Roosevelt, as pilot of the nation." At Syracuse, she delivered a radio address over NBC before seconding the nomination of her Rye, New York, friend and neighbor, Representative Caroline O'Day.

Yet Miss Earhart might not have been present at all. On September 15, she furiously telegraphed Eleanor—threatening to bolt the campaign. For while Amelia was still George Putnam's second wife (the first being heiress to the Crayola Crayon fortune), she was also the lover of fellow aviator Gene Vidal, son-in-law of Oklahoma senator Thomas Gore, father of author Gore Vidal, and, currently, the director of the federal Bureau of Air Commerce. Said bureau was being reorganized, and Vidal was about to be sacked, infuriating Earhart. Eleanor hurried Amelia's telegram to Franklin, who, being Franklin, found the contretemps highly amusing. Within two days, however, Vidal had his job back (at least temporarily), and Amelia returned to the campaign hustings.

Franklin faced a less salacious but a hardly less vexing problem, speaking at Pittsburgh's Forbes Field the following night. To a crowd of thirty thousand at that very same venue, back in October 1932, he had delivered another major talk, this one largely drafted by the unfortunate Hugh Johnson. It had easily been the most conservative address of that campaign, perhaps of Franklin's entire career, not only approvingly citing Al Smith but, remarkably, even Calvin Coolidge. A carload of facts and figures had skewered Hoover's fiscal policies. Salvos flew against spending, taxes ("paid in the sweat of every man who labors because they are a burden on production and can be paid only by production"), debt, and waste. FDR savaged "the idea that we ought to center control of everything in Washington as rapidly as possible" and vowed to "reduce the cost of (the) current Federal Government operations by 25%. . . . I regard reduction in Federal spending as one of the most important issues of this campaign . . . the most direct and effective contribution that government can make to business."

To say the least, FDR now regretted such enthusiasms. Summoning Sam Rosenman, he requested: "I'm going to make my first major campaign speech . . . in exactly the same spot I made that 1932 Pittsburgh speech; and in that speech I want to explain my 1932 statement. See whether you can prepare a draft giving a good and convincing explanation of it."

Rosenman reviewed 1932's text. He pondered alternatives. Returning to FDR, he answered: yes, he knew exactly how it might be done, what excuse might work.

"Fine," responded a comforted (and, actually, surprised) FDR. "What sort?"

"Mr. President, the only thing you can say about the 1932 speech is to categorically deny that you ever made it."

That would have made for too short—and too newsworthy—a speech, so Rosenman crafted a far different address—not denying Roosevelt's previous words, but placing them, shall we say, into context.

Five thousand cheering souls greeted FDR at Pittsburgh's Baltimore and Ohio freight station. Thousands more stood four or five deep along the three-mile route to Forbes Field. A few blocks distant from the park hung a huge portrait of Roosevelt—reading "The Man Who Saved America" in electric lights. Inside Forbes Field itself, a fifty-piece WPA band was among the score of bands entertaining the wildly cheering fifty thousand enthusiasts present.

Before Roosevelt's arrival, state senator Warren R. Roberts, an ardent New Dealer running for state auditor general, sternly fired up the crowd, slowly ticking off the names of hated millionaires—Andrew Mellon, Joe Grundy, J. Howard Pew, the du Ponts—dramatically pausing after each name to allow the multitude to bellow its hatred for each. "You could almost hear the swish of the guillotine blade as it fell," observed columnist Thomas Stokes. Democratic governor Howard Earle III followed Roberts. Though no poor man himself (personages with Roman numerals trailing their surname rarely are), Earle knew a good thing when he saw one and essentially regurgitated Roberts's tirade. "[T]he crowd vented its scorn on its enemies," noted Stokes, "like the whine of the hurricane before it strikes. He stood, smiling and confident, enjoying the tempest he had produced. Again, you could almost hear the swish of the guillotine blade as it fell. The mob was whipped into a frenzy ready for the Deliverer. He entered in an open car. It might have been the chariot of a Roman Emperor. They drowned him with paeans of joy."

But FDR wasn't in a Roman Coliseum. He was in an American ballpark, and he—and Sam Rosenman—were politically smart enough to know that. Relying heavily on baseball "box score" imagery, he argued:

> If the national income continues to decline, then the Government cannot run without going into the red. The only way to keep the government out of the red is to keep the people out of the red. We had to balance the budget of the American people before we could balance the budget of the national government. That makes common sense, doesn't it? . . . To balance our budget in 1933 or 1934 or 1935 would have been a crime against the American people. . . .
>
> [W]e didn't just spend money—we spent it for something. America got something for what we spent—conservation of human resources through Civilian Conservation Corps camps and work relief; conservation of natural resources of water, soil and forest; billions for security and a better life. While many who criticize today were selling America short, we were investing in the future of America.

It was indeed a busy night. Six blocks away, a florid-faced Frank Knox harangued eight thousand supporters, frantically pummeling FDR and all his works ("If I find any better words than 'appalling' and 'staggering' and 'breath-catching,' I'll use them"). Eleanor remained in New York, speaking to the NYA. Landon and Hoover grumpily conferred in Topeka. At Carnegie Hall, hecklers twice interrupted Al Smith ("You're no better than Jimmy Walker!"). Fervently lambasting FDR, Al failed to formally endorse (or even mention) Landon until his very last sentence.

That morning's *New York Times* delivered a body blow to Landon, guardedly endorsing Roosevelt, hoping he would "make his second

Administration more conservative than his first, in the sense that conservatism means consolidating ground already gained and perfecting measures hastily enacted. We believe this because the tide of public opinion is now running with steadily increasing strength against hasty experimentation and because the President himself has moved definitely in this direction." FDR's policies, the *Times* argued, provided "insurance against radicalism of the sort which the United States has most to fear."

Franklin kept on dedicating things. On Friday, October 2, he traveled to Frank Hague's Jersey City to christen a $5 million medical building. Hague (for Smith in 1932 and fervently hoping FDR might forget that unpleasant fact) declared a school holiday, and some 250,000 people (including 72,000 schoolchildren) turned out for Roosevelt, requiring 800 cops and 300 firemen to keep order. Hague claimed that as many as 700,000 watched, but that seemed a stretch.

From Jersey City, FDR headed straightaway for a luncheon at Democratic National Committee headquarters at 42nd Street's Biltmore Hotel. From there, he motorcaded northward, into East Harlem and a stop at yet another ballpark, the New York Giants' Polo Grounds, for Game Two of their World Series versus the Yankees. Harold Ickes recalled that they went "through the Bronx and there were large and enthusiastic crowds all along the line. It was especially interesting to see the turnout of Negroes. Senator Wagner remarked . . . that in former times Negroes would not turn out to see any Democratic candidate. There were thousands of them and they displayed great enthusiasm."

FDR threw out the ceremonial first pitch. In Topeka, the best Alf Landon could do was listen on the radio. In the seventh inning, Franklin departed, this time to dedicate the $58 million, PWA-funded Queens–Midtown Tunnel. Again, the response on the streets was overwhelming. Boarding his train that night for Hyde Park, FDR observed to Ickes that he had been booed only twice all day, in the morning near Fifth Avenue before reaching the Biltmore, and later passing the Yale Club. A Harvard man and a Democrat could take incidents like that in stride.

Franklin nestled into Hyde Park for three days of rest. On Sunday morning, both Roosevelts motored to services at tiny St. James Episcopal Church, where FDR served as senior warden. Perusing the *Herald*

Tribune, Eleanor spied a column by their mutual distant cousin Nicholas Roosevelt. The headline read:

His "Mollycoddle Philosophy"
Is Called Typical of Roosevelt.
Contrast Drawn Between Earlier Roosevelt, Who
Preached "The Strenuous Life," And President,
Who Popularizes Dependency and Easy Life

Eleanor always remained ambivalent regarding Franklin's ambitions and triumphs—and, most of all, toward himself. But not about her own goals. As her son Elliott once wrote, "Mother, in a widely quoted interview, told [her friend, reporter Lorena Hickok] 'I never wanted to be a president's wife, and I don't want to now.' But she did want power and influence, provided it was in her own right and her own name."

Not long after cousin Nick's "mollycoddle" slur, Eleanor also confided to Hickok, now off touring the nation as a "confidential investigator" for Harry Hopkins's Federal Emergency Relief Administration, "I realize more & more that F.D.R. is a great man & he is nice to me but as a person, I'm a stranger & I don't want to be anything else." Regarding Franklin's triumph at Franklin Field, she added, "I felt entirely detached." From Campobello, back in July, she had already declared her apathy, writing Hick, "I have a feeling that the tide is setting pretty hard against F.D.R. just now but there is time to turn it. I feel as usual, completely objective & oh! Lord, so *indifferent*!"

Detached.

Indifferent.

"All your personal inclinations would be to rejoice in defeat," an infuriated and disgusted Hick had fired back from South Dakota in July. "And so far in evaluating the president and his administration go—you 'can't see the woods for the trees.' I think I may have a little better perspective now. I've been out of the mess [of Washington], more or less for a couple of months. With all [his] faults—and the faults of some of the people around him—I still think [FDR] is a very great man. His defeat—and I'm awfully afraid he may be defeated—will be a terrible calamity for millions of people in this country. The poor and the lowly. Forgive me if I have offended you."

But Eleanor could also be highly engaged, as when she sat in to plot campaign strategy with FDR, Farley, Stanley High, Democratic National Committee publicity director Charlie Michelson, and DNC treasurer (and, not inconsequently, her uncle by marriage) W. Forbes Morgan. In mid-July, with the campaign floundering, it was she (at FDR's direction) who essentially ordered everyone—Farley, High, Michelson, Steve Early, and the DNC Women's Division's very talented head, Molly Dewson—to shape up, pointedly labeling her missive "a matter of record," and demanding "answers in black and white." Shortly thereafter, she wrote daughter Anna deriding DNC publicity efforts as a "disgrace. . . . Steve has answered my memo with explanations and excuses and I await the others."

And so Nicholas Roosevelt's "Mollycoddle" jibe caused Eleanor to hit the roof. In her next "My Day" newspaper column, she exploded: "No one who really knew both men [TR and FDR] could have made that contrast. . . . No man who has brought himself back from what might have been an entire life of invalidism to strength, and activity, physical and mental and spiritual can ever be accused of preaching or exemplifying a mollycoddle philosophy.

"My acquaintances who exemplify the philosophy of the mollycoddle are not amongst those to whom my husband is trying to bring greater security and ease of life. Most of my mollycoddles have had too much ease, too much dependency, too much luxury of every kind."

As midnight struck on Thursday, October 8, Franklin and Eleanor commenced their Western campaign swing. Their presidential train—the largest ever, nine cars plus two dining cars—transported a hundred persons, including forty reporters. The gang was pretty much all aboard: Sam and Dorothy Rosenman, James Roosevelt, Missy LeHand and her fellow presidential secretary Grace Tully, military adviser Edwin "Pa" Watson, Marvin McIntyre, Henry Wallace, FDR's physician Dr. Ross McIntyre, and three Western senators, Montana's Burton K. Wheeler, Nevada's Key Pittman, and Wyoming's Joseph C. O'Mahoney.

A question remained: What to do with Eleanor? She herself had long avoided boilerplate campaign oratory. Traditionally, First Ladies were, well . . . more . . . ladylike. Edith Roosevelt was no slouch. Grace Coolidge and Lou Hoover were college graduates. Edith Wilson actually ran the country for a while for her incapacitated husband, Woodrow. But none gave campaign speeches. Plus, Eleanor was damn controversial, particularly in the South. Many within FDR's campaign advised a policy not only of her discreet silence but even downplaying her very presence.

The GOP deluded itself in viewing her as a liability to Franklin. Americans, they calculated, really did not favor such behavior as Mrs. R's. They proudly pitched Theo Landon as her very antithesis. The largely silent Theo accompanied her husband's "Sunflower Express" campaign train only rarely and under extreme pressure.

Eleanor thus boarded Franklin's train anticipating a full ration of anonymity. This was, after all, Franklin's show. And alongside Franklin on his rear platform, there was only so much room—and never any shortage of local politicians lusting to fill it (a detail to which Franklin paid immense attention). But, as Scripps-Howard columnist Ruth Finney recorded, the "crowds wanted Mrs. Roosevelt. If she failed to appear on the platform they shouted for her until she did appear, and they cheered her just as heartily as her husband, sometimes more heartily. She smiled and waved but made no speeches. She never does when her husband is about."

In St. Paul, Franklin spoke of foreign trade. From Iowa, he rode into Nebraska with the latter state's seventy-five-year-old senator, George Norris, a former progressive Republican now scrambling to survive as an independent. Before slamming Alf Landon's "inconsistent, campaign-devised, half-baked" agriculture promises, FDR spoke of never making state endorsements outside of New York, but "I have made—and so long as he lives I always will make—one magnificently justified exception. George Norris's candidacy transcends State and party lines."

In Denver, his topic was water projects. On October 12–13—at Jim Farley's urging, he invaded enemy territory—campaigning at Dodge City, Wichita, Emporia, and Kansas City, Kansas.

In William Allen White's Emporia bailiwick, Franklin playfully wished that "Bill White . . . were here because he is a very old friend of mine. No,

I'll qualify that; he's a good friend of mine three and a half years out of every four." White was indeed present, and the huge crowd boisterously pointed out his presence.

"Hello, Bill," FDR bellowed. "Now that I see you, I won't talk about that other six months. Come on up, I want to see you a minute."

"Please make way for Mr. White—the man with the gray hat," the event's public address announcer boomed.

White pushed forward, as Roosevelt joked, "Shoot not this old gray head. Make way for Mr. White."

"Two great Americans are now shaking hands," exclaimed the voice on the loudspeakers.

Small pleasantries followed. Musing that he might have been "predestined to be a traveling salesman," Franklin rattled on, "I hope I can come back here again in one of those three-and-a-half-year periods when Bill White is with me."

When this is over, White shot back, come back for a three-inch Kansas steak.

"You come down and visit us," said Roosevelt with a grin.

The next day, however, White roasted not steaks but Roosevelt. Observing that "our old American smiler declared that Kansas would not have pulled through the last few years of drouth [sic] and depression if it had not been for 'federal aid in many fields of endeavor,'" White scorned FDR's argument as:

> slick as goose grease and false as hell. . . . Who in the world thinks it is wrong to give federal assistance? We Republicans are just as much for . . . it as the slick old thimble-rigger who passed so felicitously through Kansas yesterday. . . . Where the Republican plan differs from the Democratic practice is in our promise that this federal aid shall be administered by the states, counties, and cities . . . following local knowledge and wisdom. [Otherwise, you] build up a great political machine centered in Washington and pay for it with waste and extravagance. . . . It's sensible if you are a Democrat but mad as a hoot owl if you are a taxpayer.

Roosevelt—the "old American smiler"—was, after all, a friendly fellow, an accommodating fellow. Soon after Emporia, Tommy Corcoran joined the troupe. One evening, aboard their train, Franklin asked Corcoran (still only thirty-five): "Tommy? Did you learn anything about politics today?"

Corcoran confessed that he was puzzled by just one thing: that every local politician who departed FDR's beaming presence exited "with the idea that if you are elected, he would become an assistant secretary of Agriculture."

Franklin laughed, mumbling something about it not being a "precise promise," but admitted, "Yes; I had hoped that would happen."

This only disturbed Corcoran further: "How do you make a decision after you're elected, to . . . keep what they thought was a promise and you knew perfectly well was not a promise?"

FDR chortled once more, answering, "That's the difference between being a campaigner and the President and furthermore, it's one of the problems of the Presidency."

"Well," Corcoran bore on, "how do you resolve it?"

Franklin's practical politics solution: "You give the job to the fellow who will make the most trouble if he doesn't get it."

On Wednesday evening, October 14, Roosevelt hit Chicago. George Gallup's polls revealed comfortable leads for FDR in nine of ten major cities, but only a slim 52 to 48 percent lead in Chicago's Cook County, not necessarily enough to overcome the Republican vote elsewhere in Illinois, where he trailed 52 to 48 percent. "Roosevelt," posited Gallup, "must change nearly 75,000 votes in his Chicago speech . . . to carry the State."

From Grant Park, 100,000 loyal Democrats (largely on the city payroll) escorted FDR to Chicago Stadium, site of 1932's Democratic Convention, including 2,900 persons just from the 21st Ward's Democratic machine. Ignoring rules barring military participation in politics, a local National Guard unit provided its mounted band. In a city of ethnics, even "Canadians for Roosevelt" processed. Spectators booed press cars for Hearst's *Herald-Examiner* and Bertie McCormick's even more vociferously anti–New Deal *Tribune*. "Down with the *Tribune*!" they screamed. "To hell with the *Tribune*!"

Thirty thousand persons jammed Chicago Stadium. Fifteen thousand more listened outside via loudspeakers and sound trucks. Fifty thousand balloons headed skyward. Fireworks filled the sky above Michigan Avenue.

Right above Roosevelt, a pair of huge national maps proclaimed "Bank suspensions before Roosevelt—8,935," and "Bank suspensions during Roosevelt—66." A banner added, "Not a national bank failure from Oct., 1935 to Oct., 1936, a record for fifty-five years."

Introduced by Mayor Ed Kelly, Roosevelt ripped into business elements now opposing his reelection:

> Some of these people really forget how sick they were. But I know how sick they were. I have their fever charts. I know how the knees of all of our rugged individualists were trembling four years ago and how their hearts fluttered.
>
> They came to Washington in great numbers. Washington did not look like a dangerous bureaucracy to them then. Oh, no, it looked like an emergency hospital. All of the distinguished patients wanted two things—a quick hypodermic to end the pain and a course of treatment to cure the disease. We gave them both.
>
> And now most of the patients seem to be doing very nicely. Some of them are even well enough to throw their crutches at the doctor.

Back at Harvard, Felix Frankfurter wired his protégé Tommy Corcoran to forward these words to Franklin: "HEARD YOUR CHICAGO SPEECH WITH HIGH REPUBLICAN AUTHORITY WHO AT END OF IT SAID, MORE IN ANGER THAN IN CONTENTMENT, 'THIS IS THE DAMNEDEST BEST SPEECH HE HAS MADE. IT LEAVES US VERY LITTLE.' THEY HAVE BEEN A SUCCESSION OF VIBRANT, HEARTENING, TAKE-THE-OFFENSIVE SPEECHES."

Felix Frankfurter, it must be admitted, *always* liked Franklin's speeches (and moreover always ensured to *tell* him so), but other folks did too. The campaign—molasses-like in commencing—was roaring to a finish.

Where Roosevelt left off, his aides and allies filled in the gaps.

In St. Paul, Burton Wheeler eviscerated not only Landon's fluctuating positions, but his utter lack of them: "After careful study, I conclude that Governor Landon is in favor of good health, sunshine, a temperate climate and a long happy life. I do not wish to misquote him. I believe he is in favor of sunshine, but only when accompanied by adequate precipitation, a temperate climate, but one sufficiently bracing, a long and happy life, but not too long nor too happy."

Harold Ickes maintained his running war on Landon, rapping him as the "changeling candidate" who prior to his anointing as GOP standard-bearer had traveled "farther on the road toward State Socialism than any other responsible public official in the United States." The great majority of Ickes's fellow cabinet members, however, were either too dull—or too unpopular—to take the stump. Henry Wallace might only be safely dispatched to the Midwest. Jim Farley kept plugging away, but "Farleyism" remained a somewhat tainted concept—so tainted that at one point, FDR plotted to temporarily ditch "Big Jim" as postmaster general, replacing him with renegade GOP Michigan senator James Gould Couzens. Only Couzens's refusal sank the plan.

Harry Hopkins wasn't actually in the cabinet. In power and influence, however, he outranked most of its members. While not a career politician like Farley, he was hardly immune from playing the political game. At Roosevelt's request, he diligently required his WPA field offices to file regular reports on local political conditions.

"I thought at first I could be completely non-political," he later recalled. "Then they told me I had to be part non-political and part-political. I found that was impossible, at least for me. I finally realized that there was nothing for it but to be all-political."

"Loyalty to the WPA and to the New Deal became indistinguishable for Hopkins," admitted an admiring biographer. "He was willing to hire Republicans, or indeed anyone with the proper professional credentials. But they had to support the New Deal. Word that a Pennsylvania official had spoken against it sparked a warning from his boss: 'I am not going to have people on our payroll who are openly working against us here in Washington.'"

Hopkins remained a favorite target of Republican editorialists and the party's dwindling cadre of officeholders. The *Chicago Tribune* spoke for many when it opined, "Mr. Hopkins is a bull-headed man whose high place in the New Deal was won by his ability to waste more money in quicker time on more absurd undertakings than any other mischievous wit in Washington."

And it was not just Republicans who found Hopkins profligate. "The trouble with Harry," assessed the pro–New Deal *Collier's* writer George Creel, "as with so many others that Franklin Roosevelt gathered around him, and even with the President himself, was that he had never spent his own money. A social worker throughout his adult life, he had obtained his funds from municipal treasuries or foundations, so that dollars were never associated in his mind with work and thrift. Just figures in a budget."

Jim Farley, wary of Hopkins's "injudicious wisecracks," apprised him that "about 75 percent of the complaints we [at national Democratic headquarters] were receiving were about WPA" and suggested he keep silent until campaign's end. Outraged, Hopkins appealed to Roosevelt—and remained on the political trail.

Few examples of Hopkins's oratory remain, though this impassioned example, delivered in Los Angeles during 1936's campaign, bears repeating:

> I am getting sick and tired of these people on the W. P. A. and local relief rolls being called chiselers and cheats. It doesn't do any good to call these people names, because they are just like the rest of us. They don't drink any more than the rest of us, they don't lie any more, they're no lazier than the rest of us—they're pretty much a cross-section of the American people. . . .
>
> I want to finish by saying two things. I have never liked poverty. I've never believed that with our capitalistic system people have to be poor. I think it is an outrage that we should permit hundreds and hundreds of thousands of people to be ill-clad, to live in miserable homes, not to have enough to eat; not to be able to send their children to school for the only reason that they are poor. I don't believe ever again in America are we going to permit the things to happen that have happened in the past to people. We are never going back again, in my opinion, to the days of putting the old people in the

almshouses, when a decent dignified pension at home will keep them there. We are coming to the day when we are going to have decent houses for the poor. When there is genuine and real security for everyone. I have gone all over the moral hurdles that people are poor because they are bad. I don't believe it. A system of government on that basis is fallacious. I think further than that, that this economic system of ours is an ideal instrument to increase its national income of ours, not back to 80 billion where it was, but up to 100 billion or 120 billion. The capitalist system lends itself to providing a national income that will give real security for all.

Now I want to say this, I have been at this thing for three-and-a-half years. I have never been a public official before. I was brought up in that school of thought that believes that no one went on the public payroll except for political purposes or because he was incompetent or unless he had a job that he didn't work at. One of the most insidious things is the propaganda that something is wrong about one that works for the people. I have learned something in these three-and-a-half years. I have taken a look at a lot of these public servants. I have seen these technical fellows working for three or four thousand a year—not working seven hours a day but working fifteen hours a day. I've seen these fellows in the Army Engineer Corps. The motivation can't be money—they don't get very much. I have seen them work just as hard as any engineers in America and just as qualified and just as competent, and I have come to resent an attitude on the part of some people in America that you should never be part of this business of public service. I am proud of having worked for the government. It has been a great experience for me. I have signed my name to about six billion dollars in the last three and a half years. None of it has stuck to the fingers of our administrators. You might think that some of it has been wasted. If it has been wasted it was in the interest of the unemployed. You might say we have made mistakes. I haven't a thing to apologize for about our so-called mistakes. If we have made mistakes we have made them in the interest of the people that were broke.

There was altruism, and there was politics. In September, Jim Farley addressed the state's Democratic county chairs. "This is very confidential—extremely confidential," he warned. "There won't be anything I will say that should be treated more confidentially. The day before the election, the foremen on the WPA projects—you know them—you know the fellows you can talk to—they should be able to move around on the WPA projects . . . the day before the election they should [speak] to the Republicans [and tell them]. If it wasn't for Roosevelt and his desire to help everybody this money wouldn't have been appropriated for this kind of relief. Landon is talking extravagance. You ought to be interested enough in yourself and your future to know that the President . . . has indicated his desire to keep on . . . helping people. You ought to tell people to think of themselves and not the Republican Party."

An upstate Democratic county chairman concurred, suggesting that his fellow Democrats work through local WPA paymasters: "I think that the last night before, or the last check he pays them before election, he should go around and say 'Now, gentlemen, I don't know that you shall see me again, because if Roosevelt is defeated, you know my job is gone. We won't any of us have any jobs left if Roosevelt is not elected.'" Farley advised caution, because "if you do it too far before election and it gets in the papers, it will just be too bad."

"But my Lord," as Lorena Hickok once exclaimed to Harry Hopkins regarding the WPA following her tour of its Pennsylvania operations, "it's political!"

Joseph P. Kennedy, having departed the Securities and Exchange Commission in September 1935, went back (as usual) to making money hand over fist—consulting first with RCA and then (less happily) at Paramount. He hankered to reenter the political fray. "[I]f I can be of any service . . . please let me know," he importuned Missy LeHand. His own idea (aside from becoming Secretary of the Treasury) was to "author" a book defending the administration.

FDR gave the OK. The *Times*'s Arthur Krock provided the title and the actual writing. In early August, *I'm for Roosevelt* ($1.00 per copy) debuted under Joe's byline. *Saturday Review* judged it to be "an enthusiastic and amazingly sweeping endorsement of Mr. Roosevelt's policies . . . he expresses no disapproval even of the NRA . . . a savage attack on . . . Mr. Hearst and Old Dealers." The highly pro-FDR *New York Daily News* dubbed it "a masterpiece."

The most treasured review, however, came from Franklin himself, autographing a copy for its purported author: "Dear Joe: . . . The book is grand. I am delighted with it."

The best line in the book had nothing to do with FDR or his policies. It was this: "I have no political ambitions for myself or my children."

It is certainly the most quoted since.

Kennedy was, however, just getting started. Roosevelt recommended that he host a series of "Businessmen for Roosevelt" dinners to cajole his fellow businessmen into aligning with FDR. Joe hated the idea—but, being the good soldier—went along. In September he "authored" articles for both the *New York Times Magazine* and the *Review of Reviews*. That October, he delivered three radio addresses. Krock drafted each one; the White House vetted each script.

The "Progressive National Committee Supporting Franklin D. Roosevelt for President" sponsored Kennedy's third talk. Being the foremost (or, at least, wealthiest) Catholic remaining in the Roosevelt camp, it fell to Joe to jab his erstwhile companion Father Coughlin—and he did—excoriating "the efforts made for low, political purposes to confuse a Christian program of social justice for a Godless program of communism."

Whispers nonetheless floated that Joe's glittering enthusiasm was not quite all gold. Some alleged income-tax problems. The administration, after all, was very good at pursuing such matters, as it had done with the Long machine, John J. Raskob, Andrew Mellon, the Stock Exchange's Richard Whitney, Robert McCormick, Philadelphia publisher Moses Annenberg, and *Liberty*'s Fulton Oursler. Jim Farley, in fact, eventually passed such rumors of Joe's difficulties on to the *Chicago Tribune*'s Walter Trohan. They even involved the Vatican and massive money laundering.

Income taxes aside, not everyone was all that wild about Joe. True, he had his utility, assisting in swinging Hearst's support to FDR at 1932's convention (a fact he never let FDR forget), providing that year's campaign with a $50,000 "loan," and raising even more money from the business community. As SEC chairman, he was, indeed, among FDR's better appointments. But he was not loved. Neither Louis Howe nor Eleanor Roosevelt could stand him. It was said that Eleanor was particularly aggrieved by the name-dropping Joe's crassness in putting FDR on the phone to his mistress, actress Gloria Swanson. Eleanor, after all, had ample cause for such sensitivities.

While Kennedy toiled, FDR groused. To Harold Ickes, on October 7, he derided both Kennedy and Raymond Moley as "prima donnas," complaining (in Ickes's words) of how "he had to send for Joe every few days and hold his hand."

Yet Roosevelt often drew back from that hand. Autographing *I'm for Roosevelt* was not his cup of ink at all. He signed at Joe's written request—and only after said entreaty lay upon his desk for a month and until Missy LeHand finally demanded, "You must do this!"

Joe Kennedy, none the wiser, framed his prized trophy to hang on his Hyannisport wall.

Publishing was the name of the game. In August, former AAA chief official George N. Peek issued *Why Quit Our Own?* A month later, the anti-radical crusader Elizabeth Dilling self-published *The Roosevelt Red Record and Its Background*, a 456-page exposé of all things New Deal. "Do REDS Run Roosevelt?" asked the ads for Peek's 50-cent-per copy effort. "Is the New Deal Communistic?" echoed the ads for Mrs. Dilling's.

Henry Wallace composed *Whose Constitution?: An Inquiry into the General Welfare*—a surprisingly open 327-page defense of court packing. Jim Farley thought it a risky move and vetoed its issuance. In May 1936, Wallace went over Farley's head, receiving a rather spirited presidential OK. "I have not had a chance to read it very carefully," wrote FDR, "but what I have read I like enormously. May you sell 100,000 copies!" *Whose Constitution?* listed for $1.75 per copy. Vendors at the Democratic National Convention let it go for a buck a throw. The Constitution itself fetched only 50 cents.

In late October, Harry Hopkins published a slim, largely ghostwritten effort, *Spending to Save: The Complete Story of Relief*. It passionately argued that "the one most truthful allegation is never made except by the families who depend upon us. We have never given adequate relief."

In July 1935, Macmillan had published Harold Ickes's *Back to Work: The Story of PWA*, a 276-page encomium to his agency, drawing the ire of the Hearst press for non-literary reasons. The *San Francisco Examiner* headlined:

'HONEST HAROLD'S' SIDELINE:
TAXPAYERS PAY FOR ICKES' BOOK

HE WILL TAKE PROFITS

**Written and Advertised
By Men on WPA Payroll**

Ickes made excuses. To his diary he attempted a lame justification. Hearst's exposé, he explained, "was to be expected [as] I have been criticizing him and linking him up with Landon. Several questions were asked . . . at my press conference . . . and I told them that I availed myself of the same service that was furnished to any citizen by this department. I pointed out the fact that Mr. Hearst's correspondents have the free use of Government stationery, Government telephones, Government office space, Government typewriters as well as Government stenographers if they want them. I pointed out also that, on demand, my staff was prepared to furnish anything from a rough draft to a finished product. In other words, I was taking only the services that were freely rendered to anyone else who wanted to avail himself of those services."

Some people provided words—others provided manpower and cash.

Progressive, radical, and labor forces coalesced behind Roosevelt. Many had once hoped that Minnesota's Farmer-Labor Party governor Floyd Olson would lead a national third-party Farmer-Labor Party, but Olson was biding his time and running for the US Senate. He had won reelection in 1934 with FDR's support. He would have won a Senate seat in 1936 with his continued support. In December 1935, however, Olson's stomach started acting up. He thought it was ulcers; but it was stomach cancer.

Warning, just days before he expired, against the election of a "Fascist Republican," he endorsed FDR. "The defeat of Landon," he counseled, "is of the utmost importance to the great masses."

Democrats and Farmer-Laborites mourned Olson. So, too, did his Communist allies. In Hibbing, Minnesota, as the *Daily Worker* reported, "thousands of workers and farmers listened to . . . Robert Minor, [New York] Communist leader, and then raised their right hands and with bared heads pledged that Olson's place should not fall to the hands of reaction. . . . Minor analyzed the policies of 'another Governor, quite different from Olson—Governor Landon.'"

In Michigan, pro–New Deal Republican US senator James Gould Couzens, now primaried for his seat by former governor William M. Brucker, suddenly endorsed FDR. The move sank his primary chances—already slim after his having spent the entire campaign aboard a rented yacht on Lake Michigan. But the ailing Couzens didn't really care. His endorsement was nice—as was that of South Dakota's Republican senator Peter Norbeck—but the endorsement Franklin really coveted was Bill Borah's. It was not to be.

"I should have asked a hundred to one odds from you when last May I bet you one dollar that Borah would come out for me," FDR later wrote Jim Farley. "I made the dollar bet on even terms on the doctrine of chances—that Borah, for the last twenty-five years or more, had threatened regularly . . . to bolt his party nominee—only to backslide to said nominee during the few months before the national election. I was wrong. He ran true to form."

FDR's explanation wasn't exactly true. In fact, it wasn't true at all. But Jim Farley probably knew better than to argue the point.

In August, Old Guard Socialist leader Louis Waldman endorsed FDR. Labor leaders like the Amalgamated Clothing Workers' Sidney Hillman, the United Mine Workers' John L. Lewis, and the Pressman's Union's Major George L. Berry organized "Labor's Nonpartisan League" to support Franklin's reelection. Union money—probably $2 million in all—largely fueled Roosevelt's campaign.

Early in the campaign, the bushy-browed Lewis had materialized at the White House, bearing a check for $250,000—plus a photographer to snap his photo bestowing it upon his candidate. Roosevelt was aghast. Such an image and such a large check—a literal embarrassment of riches—would only play into the hands of Franklin's many enemies. "No, John," FDR responded, "I don't want your check, much as I appreciate the thought. Just keep it, and I'll call on you if and when any small need arises." The need kept arising, in smaller, but by no means negligible, amounts. By campaign's end, FDR had tapped Lewis for a phenomenal $469,870.

A hundred and fifty thousand persons cheered FDR in downtown Detroit. The seriously ill senator Couzens left his sickbed to appear alongside FDR, while Franklin plugged his "old friend" Frank Murphy.

Huge crowds greeted Franklin in Albany, rendering egress through its centuries-old streets nearly impossible. A few days later, he commenced two days through southern New England. At Worcester, he confronted a nagging issue. Landon and John D. Hamilton hammered away at Social Security. So did Hearst and the *Chicago Tribune*. "The evidence speaks for itself," averred the Republican National Committee, claiming that the administration had already let contracts for "dog tags" for each covered worker to wear around his or her neck.

Worse, workers discovered messages in their pay envelopes, warning of the program's future pitfalls:

> Effective January, 1937, we are compelled by a Roosevelt "New Deal" law to make a 1 per cent deduction from your wages and turn it over to the government. Finally, this may go as high as 4 per cent. You might get this money back . . . but only if Congress decides to make the appropriation for this purpose. There is NO guarantee. Decide before November 3—election day—whether or not you wish to take these chances.

Farley and his publicity chief, Charlie Michelson, theorized that Republicans had struck too far in advance of Election Day, allowing Democrats ample time to counterattack. They were right. Democrats struck back—hard.

FDR counterpunched at Worcester: "I want to say a word also to the wage earners who are finding propaganda about the security tax in their pay envelopes. I want to remind them that the new social security law was designed for them, for the greater safety of their homes and their families. The fund necessary to provide that security is not collected solely from workers. The employer, too, pays an equal share. And both shares—yours and the employer's—are being held for the sole benefit of the worker himself."

The pro-FDR *New York Daily News* pounced from an opposite angle: "The Republicans are squawking because workers were compelled to contribute for their pensions they themselves are to collect under the Social Security Act.

"What is wrong with that? Do the Republicans want the **employer** to pay for the old age pension of the worker? We can hardly believe that. Or do the Republicans want the money pulled out of the thin air as old Doc Townsend proposes? We can hardly believe they are that dumb."

FDR's old 1920 running mate, James M. Cox, rebutted: "Why didn't the boss put any political propaganda in your pay envelopes four years ago? Because there wasn't any pay envelopes."

Republicans countered with reminders of the administration's own strong-arm tactics. "WPA workers are being intimidated and coerced," Landon reminded five thousand supporters at Charleston, West Virginia. "In many cases approval of party leaders is necessary to get relief work, and workers on relief are told they must vote for the Administration in power or lose their jobs."

Republicans also reminded voters of a raft of previously broken New Deal vows to bondholders, veterans, and pensioners. A GOP ad proclaimed:

THE DEPENDABILITY OF YOUR GOVERNMENT IS MEASURED BY THE INTEGRITY OF THOSE WHO ADMINISTER AND EXECUTE THE LAW.

The government issued bonds on which the interest and principal were to be paid in gold. What did Roosevelt's New Deal administration do with this agreement? It went "out the window."

Ask any Spanish-American War veteran how good the word of the present administration is. Thousands of Spanish-American War veterans were living on pensions the government gave them

> in 1920. They had no other income. President Roosevelt took these pensions away a few weeks after he took office and thousands of these veterans either committed suicide or went to the poorhouse.
>
> Ask the disabled World War veterans who were in government hospitals when Mr. Roosevelt took office. Thousands of these helpless men were thrown into the streets.
>
> What about the platform of 1932 upon which Mr. Roosevelt was almost unanimously elected? Was not that repudiated, too? Yet he said he was 100 per cent for it and that he considered it a covenant with the people.

Franklin and Eleanor continued slogging through southern New England. Immense crowds greeted them wherever they went—"the most amazing tidal wave of humanity," as Franklin put it—200,000 in Providence, 150,000 at both New Bedford and the Boston Common, 100,000 at Fall River. Never anticipating anything approaching such numbers, organizers made little preparation for them. "There was a real danger that people might be run down or that some of our party would be cut off, . . ." Eleanor remembered. "To this day I look back on those trips, triumphant in that they augured well for the election, as nightmares of anxiety not for myself or Franklin, but for the people in our party and in the crowds. No matter what your fears, however, you must smile and bow; and if you stop to receive flowers, or some remembrance of the place you must appear to be enjoying yourself and carefree."

It looked like everyone (save for four hundred or so Harvard undergraduates catcalling from their dorms) supported FDR. But someone was missing. At Providence's rail station café, Eleanor seemed uneasy. She knew very well who that was—Louis McHenry Howe. She mourned to Tommy Corcoran, "I could see his little figure walking through that familiar station with the coat hanging from the sagging shoulders and the clothes looking much too big for him."

As FDR counterpunched on one issue—Social Security—he wisely ignored a smaller, but potentially far more personally embarrassing, controversy. November 1933 had seen him recognizing the Soviet Union—in part to create US jobs by facilitating exports to Stalin. The

Kremlin, however, largely lacked the resources to buy our products. So the following February, yet another New Deal program sprang to life, the Export-Import Bank, designed (by executive order) to provide credit specifically to poverty-stricken Latin America—and the Soviets. Among the capitalist goods Moscow coveted were bombers, and it negotiated a complicated deal to purchase fifty ostensibly commercial Lockheed aircraft to eventually be converted to warplanes. Soon emerging as a middleman in that deal (with hopes of a $500,000 commission) was none other than Franklin's thirty-three-year-old son Elliott, mysteriously conducting negotiations in code—"Mosley" for Moscow; "Rochelle" for his father; and "New Rochelle" for himself. Dutch aircraft manufacturer Anthony H. G. Fokker (also in on the deal) later claimed that when Elliott had personally phoned FDR to confer on the matter, Franklin vetoed a planned Moscow trip by his gallivanting son—while okaying the deal itself. Ultimately, however, the Kremlin (clearly knowing the value of a ruble) nixed the scheme, fearing they were now being stung on costs. Though the isolationist Nye Committee sat on the story for two years, it finally broke in early October 1936, when *Aero Digest* magazine published details—including questions regarding a $5,000 payment not reported on Elliott's income-tax form. "Since no sales were made," Senator Nye then piously intoned, "it is obvious that the President's son did nothing illegal, and so far as [my] committee is concerned the incident is closed."

And so it was.

In St. Louis, on Halloween, a crowd of 18,000 greeted Alf Landon. But *Time* magazine described him as "halting frequently with eyes searching anxiously for his place in the manuscript." He was, they assessed, "not a much better orator" than when he started.

Yet Landon's words (if not his delivery) finally managed to compete with the folksy, easy-to-understand phrasing of his masterful opponent, countering FDR's claim to have repaired the economic train wreck inherited from Republicans and addressing those workingmen and -women whom the New Deal had not yet pulled "out of the ditch":

> I should like to [comment] on this parable of the derailed train. The president assumes that his administration deserves all the credit.

> Surely, the courage, industry and sacrifices of our people had something to do with getting the train out of the ditch.
>
> Further, the president fails to state that after the train got into the shop, it stayed there for nearly two years. It stayed there nearly two years because the repair work was entrusted to "thumble-fingers" who were long on theory but short on practical experience. And it wasn't this administration which finally got the train out of the shop. It was the Supreme Court, when it decided the NRA was unconstitutional.
>
> Then there is the repair bill, which is not taken into account. This bill is a large part of the 25 billion dollars spent by this administration of which 13 billion dollars has not been paid.
>
> Finally, the train was in the shop so long that it is far behind its schedule. It is so far behind that 11 million unemployed men and women are still standing along the tracks, waiting to be carried to their destination—the destination of full time work and full time pay.

At Albany, Al Smith addressed a 3,500-person crowd jammed into 3,000-seat Harmanus Bleecker Hall. Once more, decrying the New Deal's hijacking of his old Democratic Party, he cited Roosevelt's pattern of alliances with Floyd Olson's Farmer-Laborites, Nebraska's George Norris, and New York's newborn American Labor Party. He warned that his old pal Franklin was "neither a Communist nor a Socialist—any more than I am—but there has been something taking place to this country, there to some certain kind of a foreign 'ism' crawling over this country. What it is I don't know. What its first name will be when it is christened I haven't the slightest idea. But I know that it is here and the sin about it is that he don't seem to know about it. If he does then he is satisfied with it."

Smith and Landon broadcast nationwide. Frank Knox, winding up his 24,000-mile, 250-speech campaign, broadcast from the Chicago Stockyards. John Hamilton addressed a 20,000-person Boston Garden "Jumbo Jubilee." He hammered away at Social Security, brandishing an alleged sample of a government-issued Social Security Administration worker "dog tag." Father Coughlin spoke from Manhattan's WOR studios over the Mutual network.

The previous evening, yet another tumultuous throng greeted FDR as he energized three thousand Brooklyn Democrats at their borough's Academy of Music. Police had never seen such a crowd at the joint. Inside, Jack Dempsey capped a series of appearances for the Democrats and vaulted onstage to shake the president's hand. Disgraced New York City mayor Jimmy Walker introduced Governor Lehman and blasted his old Tammany chum Al Smith. The Democracy Glee Club and the Friendly Sons of St. Patrick double quartet entertained. From the Metropolitan Opera came a bevy of performers, including soprano Alma Gluck (mother of future TV star Efrem Zimbalist Jr.). Contralto Hilda Kosta sang "negro spirituals." Hilda Kosta was white. But then again, the Romanian-born Gluck's recording of "Carry Me Back to Ol' Virginny" had sold two million copies. Crossover stars were crossover stars back then.

All, however, did not go smoothly. As FDR's car not-so-gingerly navigated a ramp approaching the hall, it demolished a two-by-four, painfully hurling wooden shards into the knee of nearby police officer Carl Scholle.

Scheduled to broadcast at nine, Franklin arrived after ten, with Herbert Lehman still at the mike, and waited for Lehman's conclusion before finally commencing his own talk. He returned to his 49 East 65th Street townhouse for the evening. The next morning, Eleanor shopped on crowded Fifth Avenue. Though E. R. strode at her normal fast pace, a woman managed to thrust something into her hand—an Alf Landon palm card festooned with the Kansan's campaign button. "It struck me as so funny," Eleanor chortled in her daily column, "that I looked up with a smile and as I walked along, looked back over my shoulder and laughed at them. They still looked absolutely solemn and I don't know now whether they knew to whom they were trying to hand a Landon button."

At noon at the Biltmore, she reconnoitered with Franklin for an intimate little lunch with 1,500 campaign workers. Both whizzed north for another luncheon with 1,440 more women at the Bronx's Concourse Plaza Hotel, as FDR lamented that "this is probably my last campaign as a candidate." He rode uptown and down. He traveled twice through enthusiastic crowds on Harlem's Seventh Avenue before returning to his townhouse to rest and polish his speech.

Eleanor kept going: to the Commodore Hotel to five hundred more Democratic women—and a third lunch. Four more events followed—with five hundred semi-enthusiastic Tammanyite women at the Commodore, a thousand pro-Roosevelt women lawyers at the Essex House, another thousand Southern women at the Waldorf Astoria, and who knows how many more women and children at the Hotel Roosevelt. She billed all her talks as non-political, though each featured as much partisan rhetoric as possible.

All that after a morning shopping on Fifth Avenue.

The day witnessed a rather puzzling—but quite true—report: rumors of an impending engagement between twenty-one-year-old Franklin Delano Roosevelt Jr. and twenty-year-old Miss Ethel du Pont, of *those* du Ponts (Ethel's father, Eugene Irénée du Pont being a cousin to frères Lamont, Pierre, and Irénée). Franklin and Ethel's relationship already had had its moments. In April 1934, young Franklin smashed the camera of a photographer attempting to snap them at a Philadelphia wrestling match.

That evening, a frenzied throng of twenty thousand packed Madison Square Garden. Attending, of course, was Senator Robert Wagner. Naturally wanting to attend was his twenty-eight-year-old secretary and speechwriter, Leon Keyserling. a Tugwell protégé. Wagner said no. "You don't go, . . ." he ordered Keyserling. "You stay and work on the next [event]. There's some delicatessen in the icebox."

"Delicatessen" aside, Keyserling thought that was baloney, and, when the boss was gone, he hightailed it for the Garden. There he approached a policeman, pleading, "I'm Senator Wagner's secretary. I've got an important telegram for him."

"Go on in," said the cop—though he soon smelled a rat and took the precaution of escorting Keyserling straight to Wagner. To Wagner he explained, "Here's a man who says he's your secretary and he's got a telegram for you." Growled Wagner: "I never saw that man before in my life."

Onstage, an excited Herbert Lehman introduced FDR as "the bearer of our destiny," generating a twelve-minute ovation from the equally energized multitude.

FDR had ordered speechwriters Rosenman, High, Corcoran, and Ben Cohen to blast Republicans with both barrels. They—and he—did, unveiling an impassioned defense of his tenure and a more impassioned—and often heated—counterattack, reiterating his ire at GOP efforts to denigrate his Social Security program.

At Philadelphia, he had desired a speech constructed around a single phrase: "We hold these truths." Tonight's theme was a single word: "Peace."

"What was our hope in 1932?" Franklin now asked. "Above all other things the American people wanted peace. They wanted peace of mind instead of gnawing fear." He played upon that theme, both at home and abroad, all the while maintaining an increasingly warlike stance toward his political adversaries. He had traveled not very far at all since January's State of the Union, when he warned of a "resplendent economic autocracy" bent on achieving "power for themselves, enslavement for the public." Some tunes and notes had changed. Franklin's hymnal remained the same.

As the *New York Herald Tribune* concluded in January, Roosevelt, while preaching peace abroad, incited "hatred at home . . . a smiling president has been replaced by a bitter one who will omit no appeal to prejudice or selfishness or passion in his effort to stave off defeat."

"[D]esperate men," he now dubbed his opponents, "with their backs to the wall . . . aliens to the spirit of American democracy. Let them emigrate and try their lot under some foreign flag in which they have more confidence."

Climaxing, Franklin grew downright angry:

> We have not come this far without a struggle and I assure you we cannot go further without a struggle.
>
> For twelve years this Nation was afflicted with hear-nothing, see-nothing, do-nothing Government. The Nation looked to Government but the Government looked away. Nine mocking years with the golden calf and three long years of the scourge! Nine crazy years at the ticker and three long years in the breadlines! Nine mad years of mirage and three long years of despair! Powerful influences strive today to restore that kind of government with its doctrine that that Government is best which is most indifferent.

> For nearly four years you have had an Administration which instead of twirling its thumbs has rolled up its sleeves. We will keep our sleeves rolled up.
>
> We had to struggle with the old enemies of peace—business and financial monopoly, speculation, reckless banking, class antagonism, sectionalism, war profiteering.
>
> They had begun to consider the Government of the United States as a mere appendage to their own affairs. We know now that Government by organized money is just as dangerous as Government by organized mob.
>
> Never before in all our history have these forces been so united against one candidate as they stand today. They are unanimous in their hate for me—and I welcome their hatred.

Fury consumed FDR. The crowd exploded as he poured it on: "I should like to have it said of my first Administration that in it the forces of selfishness and of lust for power met their match. I should like to have it said of my second Administration that in it these forces met their master."

Had Franklin finally gone too far? Some thought so. Not all were Republicans.

"Many people found his performance distressing," reflected Frances Perkins's biographer George Martin, "in particular members of the old Progressive party, some of whom had been campaigning for social justice before Roosevelt had entered the New York legislature. By and large they supported [his] programs. . . . But they disliked his public relations posturing, his cult of himself as a hero, his constant and divisive appeals to interest groups and his language of class warfare. It was the age of dictators, and to take the public's general feelings of insecurity, distill them into a hatred and focus them on a small minority was a totalitarian technique."

Even back at Philadelphia, Franklin's "economic royalist" rhetoric had positively stunned Perkins herself. "This is going to be used against him," she whispered to DNC Women's Division's head Molly Dewson. She gingerly conveyed those fears to Franklin himself, adding that they were not just her worries but those of her friends—many of whom were artists or widows surviving on trust funds.

FDR literally laughed her off. "Of course they do not know what I had in mind," he responded, "but perhaps it was a lucky choice of words. Anyhow, I don't think people ought to be *too* rich."

Perkins didn't quite know what that meant. She wasn't sure he knew either.

Columnist Thomas Stokes, a liberal Roosevelt fan, caught FDR's Madison Square Garden words over the radio—and could not bring himself to believe he had heard them correctly. The next morning, he carefully checked the newspapers. "Yes, there it was," thought Stokes. "It was true. He had said it, all right"—Franklin Roosevelt would be his opponents' "master." Stokes didn't like that at all—"Nor was it altogether what [FDR] said. There was a vengefulness in his voice when he said it."

"Thoughtful citizens," Ray Moley later wrote, "were stunned by the violence, the bombast, the naked demagoguery of these sentences. No one who has merely read them can half know the meaning conveyed by the cadences of the voice that uttered them." Even the usually combative New Dealer Donald Richberg confessed himself "frankly horrified" by FDR's battle cry.

At Madison Square Garden in October, Tommy Corcoran departed alongside Democrat pollster Emil Hurja. "Tommy," a worried Hurja warily inquired, "is that your line—next term they'll find their master?"

"No," Corcoran answered, denying responsibility, "that's Stanley High's . . . the so-called punch-line man."

"Well," Hurja confessed, "I have a hunch that punch is going to hurt the President more than it is going to help him."

"I accept the president's judgment as the best we have," he added; "but as for myself, I wish he hadn't felt he had to say that."

Sometimes pollsters have it right.

And sometimes they don't.

· 20 ·

"Send for a priest"

Political polling had been around longer than radio or talking pictures or pop-up toasters or any number of newfangled things. Back in 1916, customers at the eight-thousand-store Rexall Drug chain slipped their ballots into in-store boxes overseen by specially hired clerks. Rexall not only forecast Woodrow Wilson's eyelash victory; it pinpointed his razor-thin New Hampshire and California margins.

Rexall's, of course, wasn't the only big straw poll. Not at all. The weekly *Literary Digest* mailed out millions of ballots each election—including ten million in 1936, with 2,376,523 persons actually responding. It had predicted Harding, Coolidge, and Hoover's Roaring Twenties victories—plus The Great Engineer's 1932 fall to earth. In 1924, the *Digest* projected 56.50 percent for Coolidge. He received 54.03 percent. It called forty-seven of forty-eight states accurately, misfiring only on Kentucky. In 1932, it forecast a 474–57 FDR electoral vote victory. He conquered Hoover 472–59.

And so it was that in that year, Josephus Daniels's *Raleigh News and Observer* reflected: "[I]t might be a good idea hereafter quadrennially to quit holding elections and accept the *Digest*'s polls as final. It would save millions in money and in time."

"Self-selecting" in its methodology, the *Literary Digest*'s sampling—though often accurate—was not considered "scientific." And, while it might correctly forecast outcomes, it might not accurately forecast their scope. A 1934 *Digest* poll had predicted California Republican Frank

Merriam's victory over Upton Sinclair, but wildly overshot its margin. The *Digest* forecast 62.31 percent for Merriam. He received 48.87 percent.

The early 1930s witnessed scientific polling's rapid ascent. Emil Hurja, a former Alaskan gold miner and Texas newsman, had volunteered to poll for Al Smith in 1928 but had been rejected by John Jakob Raskob. Jim Farley took him on, however, with remarkably good results in both 1932 and 1934. He remained onboard in 1936, assisting Farley not only in matters of public opinion but in doling out patronage.

"You do the same test to public opinion that you do to ore," Hurja explained in 1936. "In mining you take several samples from the face of the ore, pulverize them, and find out what the average pay per ton will be. In politics, you take sections of voters, check new trends against past performances, establish the percentage of shifts among different voting strata, supplement this information with reports from competent observers in the field, and you can accurately predict an election result."

In 1935, Columbia University journalism professor Dr. George Gallup unveiled his own "scientific" poll, sampling only fifty thousand respondents. The *Digest* enjoyed a solid track record. Dr. Gallup remained the new untested kid on the block, but he soon wielded a fairly large megaphone, syndicated in roughly seventy newspapers, including such major outlets as the *New York Herald Tribune*, the *Boston Globe*, the *Philadelphia Inquirer,* the *Atlanta Constitution,* the *Minneapolis Tribune,* the *Oakland Tribune,* the *Cincinnati Enquirer,* and the *Richmond Times-Dispatch*. In *Today* magazine, Raymond Moley vouched for Gallup methodologies as "scrupulously honest [and] better indications of public opinion than the *Literary Digest* poll, for reasons too technical and numerous to set forth."

Throughout 1936, the *Digest* reported on New Deal weakness, commencing with its January poll showing 61.89 percent ominously answering "no" to the query "Do you NOW approve the acts and policies of the Roosevelt New Deal to date?"—a complete reversal of 1934 polling on essentially the same question.

In early September 1936, the *Digest* reported its first FDR–Landon matchup. Landon led in Maine, New Jersey, New York, and Pennsylvania, although "none of these ballots came from any of the great metropolitan areas where President Roosevelt's strength is . . . greatest.

So, . . . if Landon's adherents feel elated, Roosevelt supporters need not feel depressed."

By early October, the *Digest* had tallied 713,451 Landon responses to just 485,302 for Roosevelt—a whopping 56.9 percent for the Kansan. On October 17, 1936, the *Digest* finally reported samplings from all forty-eight states. Landon held a solid 55.4 to 40.1 percent popular vote lead, giving him thirty-two states and an equally commanding 370–161 electoral vote edge. The *Digest*'s final tally gave Landon a 1,293,669–977,897 edge over Roosevelt and the identical 32 state, 370 electoral vote lead. Dr. Gallup remained dubious, pointing out (through one of his own surveys) that only 15 percent of Roosevelt supporters bothered returning their *Literary Digest* ballots, compared to 33 percent of Landon's.

Yet the *Digest* hardly stood alone. The *Cleveland News* aggregated totals from a variety of straw polls and calculated a 310–217 Landon electoral vote triumph. A compilation of collegiate polls indicated a popular preference for FDR but a 233–206 Landon electoral victory. Landon swept Yale's student body 1,814–704. The *Farm Journal*'s straw vote projected Hoover in 1928 and Roosevelt in 1932. Its 1936 132,000-response survey called it for Landon 277–160. In September, "voting research expert" Rogers C. Dunn forecast a minimum of thirty-three states for Landon. That same month, Dr. Daniel Starch ("Director of America's Leading Research Organization") conceded a 46.1 to 43.1 percent popular vote lead to FDR, but with so great a portion of it emanating from the lopsided Solid South, Starch awarded the electoral vote to Landon. "PRESENT STANDING INDICATES VICTORY FOR GOP" headlined his results.

On Sunday, July 12, Gallup had reported a narrow 51.8 to 48.2 percent edge for Roosevelt—who had dropped four points since June polling, declined in thirty-eight states, and now trailed Landon 272–259 in the Electoral College. Publicly, DNC publicity director Charlie Michelson cast cold water on the results. Behind the scenes, Emil Hurja's private Democratic polling confirmed Gallup's findings.

At Wellesley College five days earlier, Gallup warned that Father Coughlin's new Union Party might "be the deciding factor in the election—in favor of Landon."

"It will be the closest election . . . since Wilson defeated Hughes in 1916 and one of the closest elections in the political history of the country.

"The middle class, older people of the country are swinging away from Roosevelt, and more in New England are turning away from him than in any other part of the country. If Roosevelt loses the election it will be because he alienated too many of the conservatives. . . .

"Roosevelt will not receive the huge majority he did in 1932. It is inconceivable that he will get as many votes as he did then, and it is inconceivable that Landon will win by a landslide.

"If the *Literary Digest* conducted this poll today it would show Landon winning the election."

On August 9, Gallup reported a 276–255 Electoral College Landon edge, though Landon had slipped slightly in the popular vote (Roosevelt 52.4 percent–Landon 47.6 percent). Within two weeks, however, everything shifted, and FDR now led Landon 274–257. Below that seemingly slight shift, however, lay serious danger for the GOP. Landon commanded a piddling 56 electoral votes solidly, compared to 257 votes in Gallup's shaky "leaning" category. Democrats, conversely, possessed a mere 54 "leaning" votes, but an imposing 220 "solid" votes. Gallup's final survey revealed FDR commanding a 53.8 to 42.8 percent popular vote advantage. Only three states—Maine, Vermont, and New Hampshire—rated "sure for Landon–Knox." Another fourteen remained "Too Close for Accurate Prediction": South Dakota, Massachusetts, Kansas, Connecticut, Rhode Island, Illinois, Iowa, Michigan, New Jersey, Pennsylvania, West Virginia, Wyoming, Indiana, and Ohio.

On October 14, *News-Week* reported the results of a survey of "political news writers." Nineteen foresaw an easy Roosevelt 374–157 victory. Eight writers, including Republicans David Lawrence and Mark Sullivan, declined comment.

Back in Kansas, William Allen White was also privately hedging his bets. In early October, he had publicly predicted Landon would not only carry Kansas by fifty thousand votes, he would best Roosevelt in the combined Kansas–New York vote totals. In mid-October, he affixed his name, alongside other former Teddy Roosevelt Progressives, in an open letter to Harold Ickes endorsing their fellow Bull Mooser Alf Landon.

Later that month, at a New York TR birthday commemoration, White even directed a slight dig at Theodore's cousin Franklin. "Americans of future years," he orated, "will be able to distinguish which Roosevelt was the valiant, gorgeous, splendid personality, the cloud by day and the pillar of flame by night. I want our Roosevelt to stand out as a unique distinct Roosevelt. I'm jealous of that name—I want it to mean all that is honest, brave, chivalrous, and true."

Yet, behind the scenes, White faltered. A publisher queried him regarding the *Literary Digest*'s rosy forecasts, and he scoffed, "You have a quaint sense of humor. If Landon is elected, I'll write you a book about him, bind it in platinum, illustrate it with apples of gold and pictures of silver, and won't charge you a cent."

But the bloom was off the rose, the rodent about to depart the capsizing vessel. Having once more jumped the GOP ship to endorse Nebraska's George Norris, White now distanced himself from the man he had once professed to love "like a son."

"I have seen Alf Landon but three times since last June," White suddenly and publicly protested. "I am not one of his advisers. I am not on his board of strategy and have never been on his train."

Worse was to come. Just four days following his imputations that Hyde Park's Roosevelt was not quite "the valiant, gorgeous, splendid personality" his Oyster Bay cousin was, White secretly contacted FDR confidant Felix Frankfurter:

> I am sending you today a little batch of cold potatoes in the shape of a little book. It is what I wrote about the campaign and its inception. My idea of the campaign as it should have been and was not. I am sending it to you, hoping you will look it over after the election and understand how I should like to have seen this campaign go if I had been on Landon's board of strategy.
>
> As I think I told you, I have not been in Landon's entourage. He has invited me to go on every trip and I have refused each time. I

have written none of his speeches. The only paragraph I contributed was his denunciation of the teachers' oath.

I was not on his board of strategy. I would have conducted a different kind of a campaign. And the reason why I have not visited him in Topeka since his nomination is that I did not want to go in and fight for my ideas with a bunch of conservatives and take the responsibility for what looked like an inevitable defeat. That on the one hand. On the other hand, I did not want to stay and be a part of a compromise which would get nowhere, stultify me, and at the same time leave me with no liberty of action which would not be misconstrued as involving Landon.

For instance, I have supported George Norris . . . heartily. I supported Jim Couzens in Michigan before the primaries. . . . If I had been next to the throne, my support would have involved Landon. So I have kept away. But I do respect him. He is forthright, courageous, honest. He is new at the game of economics. If he had won, perhaps I should have been happy to help him if he had let me. I don't know whether he would or not. This is all confidential between two American citizens who, if they had been nearer each other during the years, would have been dear friends, I think.

Always most cordially yours,
W. A. WHITE

William Allen White had leaped feetfirst into the next three-and-a-half years of his life.

Other Republicans remained more optimistic—or at least claimed they were. In New York, John D. M. Hamilton predicted Landon would outperform his *Literary Digest* numbers. At another point, he boasted, "We are going to break the Solid South; it might happen that we will carry all 48 States. . . . Get that on record."

It was all nonsense, and Hamilton didn't believe a word of it. A month previously, he had met with columnist David Lawrence and Chicago advertising executive Albert Lasker, an architect of Warren Harding's historic 1920 landslide. Landon, Hamilton confided, wasn't about to carry anything beyond Maine, Vermont, the Dakotas, Nebraska, and Kansas.

Landon harbored his own doubts. He kept them similarly secret, a secret he came dangerously—nearly fatally—close to revealing.

On October 26, internal GOP polling, conducted by the Nielsen organization, called it 50 to 33 percent for Roosevelt. Two days later, just before his Madison Square Garden swan song, Landon swung through New Jersey. Following a listlessly received talk at Newark's Mosque Theatre, he lunched with former US senators Joseph Frelinghuysen and Walter Edge. A third man accompanied them. Landon assumed he was an associate of Edge.

Landon asked: What are my chances in the state?

"No chance," assessed Edge, before countering, "What's the chance in the country?"

"No chance." Landon shrugged.

Only at this rather belated point did Landon bother to learn that his mystery companion was actually a reporter for a Newark newspaper. If said reporter printed Landon's gaffe, several thousand naïve Republicans would have catapulted themselves off of Al Smith's Empire State Building.

"I'll call his publisher," Edge exclaimed. "I know him. He's a Republican. I'll stop it."

"Sit down," Landon snapped. "I'll handle this." By now, even the reporter in question was scared. "Your reporter is perfectly entitled to that story," Landon stepped in to inform his editor. "And if you print it, I won't deny one word of it. But you might as well call off the election. I'm not going to call your publisher or anyone else. Your reporter is standing here, and it's up to you."

The story died. False optimism survived.

Yes, it did. Forty-four-year-old Rockland County attorney Miss Natalie F. Couch, eastern manager of the women's division of the Republican National Committee (and Caroline O'Day's opponent for Congresswoman-at-large) foresaw Landon capturing 70 percent of the women's vote. The Republican National Committee projected a gain of at least 53 House seats—possibly as many as 123.

From his home in Detroit, Henry Ford warned that if FDR won, workingmen "will be put still further under the control of international financiers. . . . Anyone who thinks that the real inside finances are opposed to the New Deal doesn't know what is going on.

"Every American—especially every American workingman—should understand clearly that industry is one thing finance is another thing."

"International financiers" might really have meant "international financiers" to Ford. More likely, it meant Jews.

Another Detroit automaker, Packard's former president (and Liberty League advisory board member) Henry B. Joy ("There is decidedly too much Jewish power in our government by presidential appointment and approval"), now desperately mailed out anti-Semitic pamphlets raging against "the formidable sect [Jews] in control of the White House."

The whiff of anti-Semitism also permeated a GOP ad running in at least two Pittsburgh papers. "**Dubinsky, Zaritsky and Hillman are for Roosevelt**," it headlined, concluding with "There can be no clearer hand-writing on the wall. Dubinsky, Zaritsky, and Hillman (and all their kind) stand with Roosevelt. Where do you stand?"

. . . "*and all their kind.*"

Indeed.

Dubinsky, in particular, worried that his presence on New York's electoral slate might bring more harm than good. He nervously dispatched Mayor La Guardia to carry a message to Roosevelt: if FDR desired it, he would step aside. "Tell that little-son-of-a-bitch," Roosevelt bluntly informed La Guardia, "to mind his own business. This is my business. I'll take care of it. Let him stay where he is." Dubinsky stayed.

As Election Day neared, candidates edged closer to home. For a brief moment, hope rekindled within Alf Landon's heart, and he paused to reflect upon upcoming cabinet appointments. Such fantasies soon passed. He returned to Topeka, where, on the Sunday before Election Day, the Landons attended Methodist services before scurrying back to Independence.

Immediately following FDR's "they have met their master" jeremiad, the Roosevelts headed north to Hyde Park, arriving home at 12:20 a.m. but still managing to worship the following morn at a packed two-hour St. James Episcopal Church service. The *Herald Tribune* reported that Franklin looked "well and fresh."

That evening, William Randolph Hearst steamed toward American shores aboard the Cunard White Star liner *Queen Mary.* Nine dachshunds and Marion Davies accompanied him. From shipboard, he broadcast a message over the NBC network, deriding FDR as "by nature a spender and waster, a political playboy."

That same Sunday, at Cambridge, Felix Frankfurter—sycophant par excellence—had kinder words for FDR and, as usual, shared them with him:

> And now, Dear Frank, you have fought your fight and ours—and the Nation will crown it with victory. But the enduring victory is always within. As you pause, before you go on with the terrific tasks that lie ahead, surely you must feel, as you are entitled to feel, securely serene.
>
> When, a good many years ago, I read all of Lincoln's speeches and writings, what struck me most, apart from his felicity, was the temper of what he said, that in the midst of war he said nothing which fifty years later he would want to change. I've heard or read all that you publicly spoke during this campaign, and I do not recall a single word that the understanding historian of the future would want unsaid.
>
> I have no doubt that in your second Administration you will prove yourself the master of the dark and ignorant forces of our country. Nor have they! But what is no less true, and what is indispensable to the realization of your objectives, you have proved anew in this campaign that in a democracy the essence of true politics is popular education. And so, you will enter your second term not only with the confidence of our people but with that informed intelligence, for you have informed it, which is indispensable for bringing nearer the dream of brotherhood to which America was dedicated.
>
> May your strength and contagious
> spirit remain unabated.
> Devotedly yours, F.F.

Felix Frankfurter bet on FDR. So did most of the smart money, though Alice Roosevelt Longworth (not a particularly wealthy woman) wagered a hefty $100 on Landon with her unlikely friend, the critic and CBS radio personality Alexander Woollcott, who, soon enough, not only twitted her miserable judgment on his weekly broadcast—but demanded she tender prompt and full payment at contest's end. "It may comfort Mrs. Longworth," jeered the invariably waspish Mr. Woollcott, "to know that the entire sum will be devoted to feeding and clothing a poor, broken-down old newspaperman—named Alexander Woollcott."

Monday, November 1 opened with odds on FDR at 2–1, climbing to 2½–1, then to 4–1, before closing 3–1. In 1932, Hoover commenced the year at 2–1. By November 1932, it was FDR 7–1. Rumors flew that Republicans—hoping to avoid similar dispiriting odds—raised a pool of $200,000 to shore up Landon's embattled odds. *Daily News* columnist Ed Sullivan reported that *Herald Tribune* publisher John Hay "Jock" Whitney personally ponied up $30,000.

That same Monday, less well-heeled Landon Republicans—four men, four women, and a child—gathered within sixty-three-year-old Mrs. Clara F. "Sister Cora" Bogue's modest third-floor apartment, located at 1361 Main Street, Hartford, Connecticut. They represented the larger membership of something called the "Hartford Praying Band." From 10 p.m. through dawn, they, as their septuagenarian leader and founder, the walrus-mustached Brother George W. Smith, explained, planned on loudly praying (and periodically singing "America") to "put this miserable New Deal Heresy to a perpetual end."

"I'm sure the good Lord will not let us down," said Smith. "If He should decide against us, the Lord's will be done—but we will go right on praying."

Mrs. Smith's displeased landlord, Chauncey N. Leroy, wasn't crazy about this. Nor was his attitude improved when local jokers rounded up some equally local drunks with bogus promises of free booze at Mrs. Bogue's. "Nearly 40 persons," noted a press report, "not members of the band and many of them drunk, crowded into Sister Cora's apartment . . . at 10 o'clock. One carried a bagful of rotten eggs. Others plastered New Deal posters on the door of the house." Eventually the eggs went airborne, one landing upon a "fellow inebriant." Brother Smith attempted persuasion. By midnight, he found that calling the cops worked far better. He also suspected that Landlord LeRoy was a Democrat.

In New Orleans, another Smith—one of our more frequently encountered Smiths, Gerald—was also interacting with police, jailed for two hours for "disturbing the peace, reviling the police and using obscene language" following an inflammatory radio address alleging a corrupt oil deal between state and federal authorities. "When this oil deal is finally uncovered," Smith roared, "it will make the Teapot Dome scandal look like a copper kettle."

In the *Herald Tribune*, columnist George Sokolsky, a former radical turned anti-Communist, tepidly endorsed Landon—well, no, not really. He really dis-endorsed FDR. He wrote:

> I fear Roosevelt. To me his famed smile is not sweetness and light; it is the cynicism of a man who is putting something over for the fun of it. I don't like fun in the White House. . . . I like the White House to be a serious place for serious-minded people. The president's sense of humor leaves me cold, because he is amused by things that are too sacred to laugh about.
>
> I am afraid of him because he is afraid of nothing. He does not fear extravagance; he does not fear bankruptcy; he does not fear the effects of as much inflation as we already have; he does not fear the effects of undermining the Constitution and the Supreme Court. He is fearless.
>
> I prefer a president who is not so fearless. . . .
>
> I am really voting against Roosevelt, against Farley and Tugwell, against the New Deal. I am also voting against cheap tricks on the radio, against the misuse of the income tax investigation, against wisecracks that [playwrights] George Kaufman and Morrie Ryskind can do better, against government by threat, intimidation and mass pressure.
>
> I'm voting against these things—therefore, I vote for Landon. There will be millions like me tomorrow.

Millions more actually planned on voting for FDR. Not only Gallup was projecting a second Roosevelt term, so were two other new polling kids on the block: the Crossley and Roper surveys. Crossley, backed by the Hearst organization, gave FDR 53.8 percent of the popular vote and 406 electoral votes. Elmer Roper's *Fortune* magazine survey calculated 61.7 percent for

Roosevelt. Emil Hurja now forecast Roosevelt with 376 electoral votes to 155. FDR scribbled down his own estimate: a 360–171 triumph.

Hugh Johnson had by now reversed his pessimism and predicted just four states for Landon. Columnists Drew Pearson and Robert S. Allen gave "The Kansas Coolidge" three. Thomas Stokes forecast between eight and eleven states for Landon. Jim Farley, no great believer in either scientific or unscientific polling ("Polls go wrong and that's all there is to it"), wrote FDR regarding their chances in New York:

> We should carry New York City by at least one and a quarter million . . . and [if] we come down [from upstate] with less than 200,000 loss, this will give us a million majority in the State. This may seem to you like a crazy figure, but I think we are going to get a tremendous vote in the cities, and I think this is true of the villages because . . . every village and every community has been helped in some way by your Administration, and that should be reflected by the increased vote for you. In every community in the State there have been Public Works Programs and WPA projects. In every county and surely in every community hundreds of thousands have been benefited directly or indirectly . . . I feel that you will run at least 100,000 ahead of Lehman.

The same tide surged through the Midwest. In late October, *Davenport Democrat and Leader* editor Hugh Harrison wrote Farley regarding the groundswell of Iowans registering to vote. "Men and women stood for hours in lines which extended far out into the street, . . ." noted Harrison. "Most of them were wearied and tired, but they clung tenaciously to their position in the lines. And why? There can be but one answer. They were swayed by the humanitarianism of President Roosevelt and want to vote for him."

Some Election Eve FDR supporters got a tad bumptious at Times Square. A screaming mob of four hundred Democrats clogged the area around West 42nd Street at Seventh Avenue. They hailed passenger cars and taxis. They pasted Roosevelt stickers on vehicles. They jumped on fenders and running boards and demanded to know who drivers and passengers were voting for. Things got particularly ugly if they spied a

Landon button. At 43rd Street, they stormed a pro-Landon sound truck, smashing its windows. Seven women in the truck fled. At 45th Street, the mob disrupted a Young Republican rally.

Earlier that Monday, a report arrived from London. The famed Swiss psychologist Dr. Carl Jung had recently distantly observed Roosevelt at Harvard's recent tercentenary celebrations. He now published an article in the *London Sunday Observer*, titled "Psychology of Dictatorship; Stalin and Mr. Roosevelt."

"I have just come from America," diagnosed the mustachioed, pipe-puffing Jung, "where I saw Roosevelt. Make no mistake, he is a force—a man of superior and impenetrable mind, but perfectly ruthless, a highly versatile mind which you cannot foresee. He has the most amazing power complex, the Mussolini substance, the stuff of a dictator absolutely."

Jung couldn't vote. America could.

A foot of snow blanketed South Dakota. Minnesota got eight inches. Indiana and a few other states had rain, but otherwise the day was clear. Formerly sweltering Kansas saw record lows overnight; in some areas as cold as eighteen degrees. The East remained quite warm, unseasonably so. The Far West clear and cold. Overall, a good day for turnout—and turnout there would be.

Arthur E. Gehrke voted. Ordinarily, the voting habits of a fifty-three-year-old Watertown, Wisconsin, tavern owner hardly counted for much. But this was no ordinary fifty-three-year-old Watertown, Wisconsin, tavern owner. This was "Turkey" Gehrke, the 215-pound "human hibernator," internationally known (or, so it was claimed) for a quarter-century of not emerging from his bed from October through April. The cold, it seemed, vexed him mightily. Gehrke had, however, aroused himself just the previous February—to select the casket for his wife Grace's funeral. She had died unexpectedly of a heart attack while reading in a chair. "Turkey" had been, of course, asleep at the time.

"I may like to sleep," he now explained, "but when election comes around I like to get up early and cast my ballot." Queried as to who he voted for, Gehrke chuckled "The winner."

Some old-timers voted. Some didn't. In Orting, Washington, ninety-four-year-old Civil War veteran Daniel Horace Delano stayed abed but sent his eighty-eight-year-old wife to vote for his fourth cousin Franklin Delano Roosevelt. Delano vowed to "continue to vote for Cousin Frank as long as he behaves himself." Cousin Dan, a lifelong Republican until 1932, had originally planned on driving five blocks to the polls, but didn't feel quite up to it. "This cold weather," he alibied, much as any politician might, "brings out my rheumatism every time."

Theodore Roosevelt's seventy-five-year-old widow, Edith Kermit Roosevelt, was made of sterner stuff. Sporting a brace on her fractured right hip, she traveled with her chauffeur and her Black servant Clara Lee to an Oyster Cove, Long Island stable to cast her anti–New Deal ballot—a mere few hundred yards from her husband's grave.

In Cincinnati, 115-year-old former slave "Uncle Mark" Thrash cast his vote for FDR. It was hardly the white-bearded Thrash's "last hurrah," however, living as he did until just days shy of his 123rd birthday in December 1943.

On Sunday, in Chicago, Francis Townsend counseled his supporters to vote for Landon in states where Lemke lacked ballot position, arguing that "democratic government is at stake." On Tuesday, he voted by absentee ballot. Back in California, an erstwhile OARP official, Los Angeles's George Highley, challenged it.

In midafternoon, Father Coughlin, accompanied by his handpicked US Senate candidate, Louis B. Ward, voted at Royal Oak's Woodland School. Earlier in the year, Coughlin had inserted Ward into the year's Democratic primary, and Ward had nearly upset organization candidate, Rep. Prentiss Brown, so narrowly that he had received a recount. Now he was running third party on an outfit called, rather too prosaically and generically, "The Third Party." State officials, it seemed, had barred using the Union Party name. In Royal Oak, voters already in line preceding Coughlin's arrival, nonetheless, allowed him to vote first. He cast his votes for Ward, plus the Republican candidates for secretary of state, attorney general, lieutenant governor, and—even rejecting his old friend and altar boy Frank Murphy—for governor.

Unorganized, remote, largely uninhabited Armstrong County in central South Dakota was a rare Democratic stronghold in the state. In 1932, FDR had bested Hoover there 17–0, which by Armstrong County standards was actually pretty normal, having similarly cast zero Republican votes in both

1928 and 1930. Populated (if that is the word) largely by "cowboys and Indians," nary a soul—Democrat nor Republican—bothered voting in 1936.

But then again, thanks to long-standing tradition, neither did any of the nine members of the Supreme Court. Franklin Roosevelt probably gave thanks for that.

At a polling place in Kentucky's eastern mountains, Policeman W. V. Hood attempted to arrest forty-four-year-old Republican precinct worker M. M. Coleman for carrying a concealed weapon. Coleman protested that it wasn't concealed at all and drew. Hood shot him twice through the stomach, was later arrested and released on $15,000 bail. Coleman died four days later. All in all, doings were quieter in Kentucky than four years earlier, when six persons died in Election Day violence.

A *lot* of the voting transpired in New York.

After a half-hour wait, Jim Farley and his wife, Elizabeth Finnegan Farley, voted at 9:00 a.m. at East 85th Street's Public School 6, very near to their 1040 Fifth Avenue home. Farley then motored north to his old Rockland County haunts before returning to the city and to the Biltmore and Democratic headquarters to receive returns from the nation's roughly 3,100 Democratic county chairmen. Before departing, he reminded reporters of his February election prediction: FDR would not only increase his 1932 vote—he'd carry Kansas.

At 9:25 a.m., Norman Thomas, his diminutive wife, Frances, and family members waited five minutes to vote at a store at 197 Third Avenue, telling reporters he'd be spending the day quietly at home. He ended up touring sixty Socialist party headquarters and storefronts.

Governor and Mrs. Herbert Lehman voted at Henry Roth's upholstery shop at 767 Madison Avenue, not far from their 820 Park Avenue apartment. They waited forty-five minutes.

At 9:30 a.m. on the Upper West Side's Morningside Avenue, Columbia University president (and the state GOP's favorite-son candidate back at the convention) Nicholas Murray Butler found sixty people ahead of him and left. He got his hair cut, came back—and left again, to golf. The third try was the charm. At 3:25, he finally cast his presumably Republican ballot.

Al Smith voted at a vacant store at 678 Madison Avenue near his 820 Fifth Avenue home. In 1920's election, Al's old Lower East Side assembly district had been the only one statewide supporting the Cox–Roosevelt ticket. In 1932, his new home lay within the only Manhattan assembly district remaining loyal to Hoover. This morning, Al wore his trademark brown derby. His wife, Catherine Dunn Smith, brightened her Persian lamb coat with a large Landon sunflower. Some in the waiting crowd cheered him. Others razzed. The precinct's Republican watcher scrambled to escort Smith to the head of the line, angering The Happy Warrior's critics. He took two minutes to vote; Catherine, a while longer.

In Brooklyn, every vote in the large Schechter family went for Roosevelt. The four immigrant Schechter brothers—Joseph, Martin, Alex, and Aaron—had toppled FDR's NRA, but today eldest brother Joe confessed himself an enthusiastic New Dealer. "I wonder if it would be possible," he asked visiting reporters, "to congratulate President Roosevelt through the newspapers and tell him that sixteen votes in our family were cast in his favor."

Another fellow with no hard feelings against FDR was our pre-war ambassador to Imperial Berlin, James W. Gerard. Back in 1914, before Franklin had mastered the art of vote-getting, the Tammany-backed Gerard demolished him in that year's Democratic US senatorial primary. Twenty-two-years later, Gerard wagered $20,000 to win $10,000 on FDR's reelection—only to discover Section 152, Article 7 of New York State Election Law: "No person who shall . . . make . . . any bet or wager depending upon the result of an election, shall vote at such an election." Gerard, accordingly, paid off two gamblers $1,700 apiece to annul those bets and legally ballot for FDR.

Some people could vote for free—and didn't.

Election officials had finally allowed Father Divine's followers to register under their own unconventional yet harmonious "Peace Movement" names; but by Election Day, their leader had reconsidered this whole election concept as, "Not one of the major parties, officially and nationally, or conventionally, has come to me and accepted my righteous government platform."

"We must stay our hands until I give the command," Divine explained. "No doubt it will be 1940."

Accordingly, a hundred of Divine's most trusted followers patrolled Harlem polling places, dissuading his acolytes from wasting their ballots. His right-hand man, John Lamb, claimed fifty thousand voters were thus dissuaded, a dubious estimate at best.

At 12:25, at a West 38th Street barbershop, forty-eight-year-old Rabbi Nathan Wolf of that street's Times Square Temple voted—and a lot of people thought *that* was a waste. It wasn't personal. Through a quirk in drawing the city's election districts, Rabbi Wolf constituted the entire electoral strength of Manhattan's 10th District's 40th Precinct. This went on year after year, with four women from the board of elections, two clerks, and two policemen all stationed to oversee the Austrian-born Wolf's exercising his franchise (hardly a secret ballot). Total annual cost: $500. Not until 1939 did a second voter reside in the district.

"Last year," Rabbi Wolf mused in 1936, "I thought that maybe if the city offered me a house, I might move. But now, not even for a house would I move."

Fresh from addressing 17,000 comrades at Chicago Stadium the night previously, Earl Browder voted at 8:00 a.m., at a garage just down the street from his 7 Highland Avenue, Yonkers home. His party's campaign, Browder judged, was "the most successful and satisfactory the Communist Party ever entered into. On the whole we have been very well received by the country."

In Fargo, North Dakota, reality finally dawned on Bill Lemke. Father Coughlin had left him high and dry, providing virtually nothing for his campaign. His Union Party raised but $92,033 in total, including a $7,000 personal loan from Lemke himself. Even the oppressed workers and peasants of the CPUSA raised more—$266,000.

Lemke's congressional seat lay in jeopardy. His attacks on Franklin Roosevelt made him a New Deal target, and local Democrats pounded him for simultaneously seeking two offices. Lemke ingeniously denied that obvious fact. "Some of my so-called friends, . . ." he countered, "even suggest that I am running for two offices. . . . I am not running for President. The Union Party electors are running for presidential electors. . . . I am running as a nonpartisan candidate for Congress on the Republican ticket. . . . I want to be there to help elect myself president."

Of course.

Two thousand people and a nineteen-gun salute greeted Alf and Theo Landon; his daughter, Peggy; and his seventy-eight-year-old father, John Landon, when their special train chugged back into Independence at 8:00 a.m., Election Day. Ensconced aboard the Sunflower Special, father and son breakfasted earlier—on kidney and bacon on toast. At Independence, the Landons maneuvered through crowded streets (or at least as crowded as streets get in a town of 15,000) to vote at 8:49 in a local automobile showroom packed with another 500 well-wishers. Alf, Theo, and John marked their ballots simultaneously in the precinct's three voting booths. They deposited them into what looked suspiciously like a tall tin garbage can.

Vice President Garner hadn't bothered delivering a campaign speech until October 17. And didn't want to. "I know my weakness," he alibied, ". . . and I know if I get to 'swashbuckling' around speechmaking I am likely to do something . . . which would destroy whatever I accomplished." But that was just the half of it. In fact, he was no longer quite so thrilled by the New Deal, nor with FDR's treatment of his old pals in the Congress. And didn't really want to lie (too much) that he was.

Finally presented with the text of a campaign speech prepared by Hugh Johnson, he flushed purple with rage, flinging it aside in disgust. Only a quick edit by Charlie Michelson brought him on board—and that relied heavily on praise for Garner's deceased House Republican colleague Alice Longworth's husband, Nick. "That," recalled Michelson, "was all we could get him to do, however. He went back to Uvalde, to his fishing and hunting and his banks." To entreaties that Garner do more, Michelson also recollected, "We got back only salty comments to the effect that in his country when you had a steer roped and branded there is no sense in lassoing him some more."

An inveterate early riser, Garner somehow concluded that the polls in Uvalde, Texas, opened at 7:00 a.m. After hiking the first of the three blocks from their North Park Street home to their schoolhouse polling place, he and his wife, Ettie, learned otherwise: the polls were scheduled to open at eight. The Garners trudged home, then back again. Tempting fate, he finally voted as Voter Number Thirteen—an unlucky number that some believed had helped sink Charles Evans Hughes in 1916. As

Ettie (Number Fourteen) marked her ballot, Cactus Jack hectored her to "hurry up." The Veep had his reasons. People voted from the *outside* of the schoolhouse, with ballots handed through a window. And it was *cold.* Overcoat-weather cold.

"I need a little more time," Mrs. Cactus Jack protested.

"Oh," Garner ordered her, "just put an 'x' after each Democrat."

"I'll do my own voting," she retorted, and meant it. When the couple had first met in 1893, they had, after all, been primarying each other for Uvalde County judge.

On Monday, Franklin, as was his habit, toured the lower Hudson Valley, almost as if still seeking a state senate seat rather than a second-floor White House bedroom. He toured Poughkeepsie and Beacon and Rhinebeck and then motored across the river to Newburgh and Kingston. At Poughkeepsie, 12,000 heard him. At Beacon, he crowed, "I am glad to see from signs here not only that more people are working, but that the factories are running two shifts. I just want to say 'How-di-doo.'"

"Three times," Eleanor's Republican cousin the *Herald Tribune*'s Joseph Alsop reported, "he told the grinning grown-ups and cheering schoolchildren of traditionally Republican Ulster and Dutchess counties that he would talk no politics, and then reminded them that jobs are more plentiful and money is easier to come by now than it was four years ago. Once, at Newburgh, he varied the formula by adding to it a reminder that the junior high school was a present from the federal government."

At eleven the following morning, all manner of Roosevelts converged upon Hyde Park's little green-and-white wood-frame church-like town hall. A hundred locals and a gaggle of fifty or so reporters and photographers awaited them. Franklin and his mother arrived together in an open touring car. Eleanor, a white silk scarf tied around her hair, drove her own tan roadster, providing a lift to son Franklin Jr., daughter Anna, and Anna's second husband, John Boettinger, a former *Chicago American* and *Chicago Tribune* reporter, now with Hollywood's Hays office. FDR (number 312 of 768 voters in his district) voted first.

All was not smooth sailing.

Sara somehow assumed she could storm into the booth next without benefit of providing her name or signing the registrar's book. "Darling, you have to stop here," Eleanor warned her. Eleanor, Anna, Franklin Jr., and Boettinger balloted behind Sara, followed by Eleanor's friend and Val-Kill partner Miss Nancy Cook, Eleanor's secretary Mrs. Malvina "Tommy" Schneider, and, finally, Missy LeHand. Normally much savvier, Missy had departed Washington for Hyde Park, nearly in tears, dreading not only a Roosevelt defeat—but losing her Pennsylvania Avenue lodgings. And this was FDR Jr.'s first trip to the ballot box, and, having left his required prep school graduation certificate behind at the White House, he underwent a mandatory literacy test at the local high school.

On Election Eve, Franklin had followed his own little custom by touring the area. On Election Day, he followed another. Decades previously, Sara had engaged two house painters for Springwood. Franklin made small talk with one of them, an English-born fellow named Tom Leonard. Leonard thought this wealthy young man to be a decent enough chap, most particularly on discovering that he was also a Democrat. Leonard, Hyde Park's Democratic town chairman, encouraged FDR to attend the committee's meetings. The rest, as they say, was history, but more so since each year following Roosevelt's paralysis, it was Leonard and no one else who ever assisted FDR into Hyde Park's polling booth.

The afternoon proceeded. Eleanor retreated to answer her mail. "Reached by phone, . . ." noted the *Times*'s thirty-eight-year-old Kathleen McLaughlin, a veteran Eleanor watcher, "Mrs. Roosevelt assured reporters that they would be welcomed after the first returns have been received, indicating that a buffet supper would be awaiting callers about 10:30 P. M. Minor bets were being made among the usual press retinue that the First Lady would have scrambled eggs on the menu."

By late evening—win or lose—the storm would break loose at Hyde Park. Phone calls. Telegrams. An avalanche of results from Jim Farley. More reporters and more photographers.

Here and there, Landon marked gains from Hoover's 1932 showing; but overall, voters somehow resisted GOP blandishments. Even at 3:40 p.m. Eastern time, in scattered returns from sixteen states, FDR enjoyed a 41,016–29,078 lead—including a 17,230–16,143 advantage in Kansas.

The CPUSA kept up its game. The *Daily Worker* headlined:

American People: Defeat Landon!
Build Farmer-Labor Party! Vote Communist!

In the tiny far-southern Indiana town of Georgetown, local Republicans found their headquarters trashed. Vandals had ripped portraits of Landon and Knox from the wall, replacing them with those of FDR and Garner. "Barnyard debris," euphemistically noted one report, "littered the floor." On Election Eve, intruders had invaded the small schoolhouse in Ripon, Wisconsin, that had served as birthplace of the Republican Party, tearing apart its front steps, smashing its windows, and hurling lime onto its walls.

Things were quieter in New Ashford, Massachusetts.

Each midnight, as the clock ticked into Election Day, and votes might finally be cast and counted, various remote, minuscule communities developed the idea of everyone voting at midnight, counting the ballots, and grabbing fifteen minutes of national fame. Back then, pride of place in such voting fell to New Ashford, nestled just north of Pittsfield in the Bay State's Berkshires.

In 1928, New Ashford voted 28–3 for Hoover over Smith; in 1932, 24–8 for Hoover. On the Saturday night before Election Day, 1936, its citizens conducted a "dress rehearsal" for their quadrennial first-Tuesday-following-the-first-Monday-in-November midnight frolic. With twenty voting booths (a bit of overkill) cluttering up their 150-year-old one-room schoolhouse, they feasted on turkey and conducted a dry run of the voting. Landon bested FDR 32–12. Some wiseacre (probably the village atheist) "voted" for John Aiken, a Chelsea, Massachusetts, furniture finisher and standard-bearer for the largely moribund Socialist Labor Party.

New Ashford had a pretty good racket going. It would not last. Even tinier (four families) Millsfield, New Hampshire, had other plans, and, not even enjoying a polling place before 1936, the element of surprise was all theirs. At midnight Election Eve, residents gathered over sandwiches, sweet cider, and doughnuts in the Nadig family's kerosene-illuminated farmhouse before trooping through fog and drizzle to vote at a nearby tarpaper-roofed shack. Eighty-six-year-old Quincy Nadig, old enough to recall Lincoln's assassination, voted first. Landon bested FDR 5–2. Five residents said to hell with such foolishness and, though polls remained open all the way to 12:35 a.m., stayed home.

New Ashford took such news not well at all.

The larger news—the big story—arrived largely via radio. At 5:15 p.m., New York City's WOR ominously hosted a show called "Election Day Complaints from Police Headquarters." Hearst's *San Francisco Examiner* broadcast results on KYA, also transmitting them to over a score of theatres and "amusement places."

Coverage from Washington's NBC affiliate, WMAL, emanated from a makeshift studio at the *Washington Star*. The *Star* itself posted returns on a neon sign festooned upon a Goodyear blimp gliding over the city. Sixteen *Star* reporters answered two thousand calls per hour.

Nearby, an army searchlight at the base of the Washington Monument flashed returns to "New Deal bureaucrats" (as the *Chicago Tribune* termed DC residents). A beam pointing north over the White House signaled Roosevelt's triumph; east over the Capitol, Landon's. If the beam merely pulsated in one direction or the other, that candidate was ahead but had not yet sealed the deal.

The *Boston Globe* flashed returns on a giant screen across from its headquarters. *Chicago Tribune* switchboard operators fielded 15,000 calls—a record.

Times Square's Palace Theatre blasted out songs and results from loudspeakers mounted on its marquee. The zipper—the great moving message board circling the *New York Times*'s headquarters—kept viewers up to date minute by minute. Farther uptown, management at the Hotel St. Regis periodically broadcast returns into its swank Iridium Room, filled mostly with Landon supporters—save incongruously for Harry Hopkins. Finally, with victory at hand, Hopkins arose to toast his boss. Everyone ignored him.

Alf Landon departed Independence, Kansas, boarding the Sunflower Special for Topeka's Executive Mansion just after 1:00 p.m. The press busied itself, filing what stories it could and establishing a headquarters in a garage behind the mansion. The candidate napped after dinner, not emerging until 9:00 p.m. He spied a huge floral arrangement, festooned with sunflowers. "Theo," he beckoned his wife, "better have our picture taken while we've got a chance."

Mrs. Landon had prepared a red-, white-, and blue-frosted "Landon Victory Cake." It lay on a sideboard, uncut, as increasingly forbidding returns trickled and then flooded in. "However it comes out," Theo informed reporters rather haltingly, "I'm proud of him." Her eyes misted over. Alf seemed cheerier, even laughing, as he chatted with friends. "I know he has put up a brave fight," she continued. "I went into this thing with him prepared to accept the outcome—whatever it may be."

Suddenly she remembered her cake—the "victory" cake. "Maybe—just maybe—," she mourned, "we have waited too long to cut it."

In Chicago, John D. M. Hamilton maintained an insanely brave front. At eleven, he consoled fellow Republicans that they could "go to bed assured that in the morning there would be a totally different outlook," comparing 1936 to 1916's Woodrow Wilson–Charles Evans Hughes nail-biting tussle where "Hughes appeared to be a certain winner, but morning found Wilson had won the office."

"The rural vote," asserted Hamilton of this year's contest, "has in a large measure not yet been reported."

Even supposedly dumb peroxide blonde chorus girls knew better. A few days earlier, someone (probably a press agent) sampled opinion from the chorus line of Florenz Ziegfeld's *Follies*. The tally: FDR, 36; Landon, 12; Lemke, 1 (due to his support of old-age pensions). Three didn't know who was running (dumb peroxide blonde stereotypes do have their root causes). By intermission on Election Night, however, all had climbed aboard the New Deal bandwagon. Featured singer Jane Pickens (a brunette) remained the entire cast's sole holdout, earning a mighty razzing from headliners Fanny Brice and comedian Bobby Clark. In, no doubt, another publicity stunt, top-hatted William Gaxton supposedly lost a bet and ended up rolling Brice—attired in her trademark "Baby Snooks" costume—in a giant baby carriage down Broadway.

No stunt, at all, was the money won on Roosevelt in real bets. Wall Street "betting commissioners" estimated $20,000,000 was wagered on the contest, perhaps the largest sum in thirty years. MGM President Nick Schenck (a $15,000 contributor to FDR's effort) won $90,000. Former *New York World* editor Herbert Bayard Swope won $97,000. Professional bookmaker and NFL New York Giants owner Tim Mara scooped up $100,000. Former Brooklyn vaudeville theatre owner Frank Keeney won $110,000. Bookmaker Frank Erickson, formerly an associate of the late gambling kingpin Arnold Rothstein, took home nearly $500,000. Where they found so many suckers remains a mystery.

Around midnight, Election Night, the scope of the evening's disaster had become apparent to even the five hundred or so faithful but naïve souls staffing and volunteering at the Republican National Committee's 41 East 42nd Street national headquarters. "Demand a recount," someone shouted. Forty-five-year-old real estate man Rodney Dean vainly barked out returns from a small Kansas town Landon had won—until a flood of truly awful returns swamped his optimism. "Remember," he now cried, "the Constitution of the United States provides a way to get rid of [Roosevelt]—by impeachment."

Miss Kathleen R. Livingston of 241 East 49th Street possessed a clearer head than the lot of them. "I think we're buried, don't you?" she asked. "Better send for a priest."

In Times Square a million people gathered.

They'd been assembling for hours, there to celebrate the Democrats' victory. Some store windows—including a liquor store's—were boarded up for fear of the night's immense crowd. New York's polls—normally shuttered at six—remained open three additional hours in anticipation of greater turnout. The Times Square crowd was unusually good-natured—thanks in part to the army of four hundred police on scene, including a hundred mounted officers. But most observers also credited state liquor laws barring the serving of beer, wine, or alcohol until the polls closed at 9:00 p.m.

A hundred thousand revelers remained until 1:15 a.m., when a light rain finally chased even the hardiest of New Dealers away. Hours earlier, police had arrested seventeen-year-old Joseph Fallon, in town from Los Angeles and packing a .25-caliber pistol along with some blank cartridges.

When he was booked in night court for disorderly conduct, Magistrate Louis B. Brodsky edified him: "You're not in the Far West now. Guns at election time are past history in New York."

Fallon seemed astonished by this news.

"Who were you rooting for?" Brodsky continued.

"Roosevelt," Fallon responded quietly.

"I can understand that," Brodsky deliberated. "Sentence suspended."

• • •

You didn't have to be in Times Square to celebrate.

Richmond residents tore a banner from the local Jeffersonian Democrats' headquarters, tied it to the back of a car, and dragged it down Broad Street. On Chicago's Michigan Avenue, celebrants hurled eggs at the *Tribune* building. They set fire to a truckload of its bulldog edition.

Much like the Schechter brothers, Jersey City tailor Jacob Maged—once jailed for violating NRA pants-pressing codes—displayed no hard feelings. "My heartiest congratulations," he wired Roosevelt. "Yours was a deserved victory. This comes from the much-publicized Jacob Maged, NRA tailor at Jersey City. I trust that a new NRA will once again become a law for the protection of the little man."

Asked how a new NRA code would work, Maged answered:

> How should I know? Roosevelt will figure out the way. He's a smart president. Landon's a dope. He said on the radio if you're poor that's your hard luck. Is that a way for a man to talk? I never heard such foolish radio speeches in my life as Landon's. All he did was knock Roosevelt. I knew he would never be anything for the common people.

Tammany Hall finally seemed reconciled to FDR—or at least pretended to be. On the Lower East Side, Charles Schneider's Wigwam Democratic Club delivered Manhattan's Eighth Assembly District to Roosevelt by an 8–1 margin. To the oompahs of the Boys' Band of East

7th Street's St. Stanislaus Church, they marched 1,800 strong in a torchlight parade down to Union Square and Tammany Hall itself.

Among the livelier members of the seemingly endless stream of Democratic has-beens endorsing Landon was former Oklahoma governor "Alfalfa Bill" Murray, once so popular in his state that folks named a county after him ("Murray County," not "Alfalfa County").

That was then.

Now, its residents petitioned to rename it "Roosevelt County."

In Dutchess County, the inner circle gathered. Among the eighty or so guests awaiting returns with Franklin were his friend Vincent Astor, Henry Morgenthau, his former law partner Basil "Doc" O'Connor, his next-door neighbors Mr. and Mrs. Gerald Morgan (Gerald was a Groton man), Dexter Cooper (an engineer who also enjoyed a Campobello summer home), Franklin's seventy-three-year-old uncle Frederic A. Delano, the British governor of Bermuda, and author Fannie Hurst, as well as his trusted confidante Daisy Suckley. Present, too, were speechwriters Rosenman, High, and Corcoran. But not, of course, Ray Moley. Corcoran's main duty this enchanted evening was entertainment: parading about the house, parodying "Oh, Susanna" on his accordion. His efforts, however, were nowhere near as mirth-provoking as John D. M. Hamilton's 11:00 p.m. prediction of a Landon comeback.

The great house buzzed with activity. Eleanor in her white chiffon gown, bedecked with an immense red rose in her belt. Teletype machines clattering here. Telephones ringing there. Reporters everywhere. Sandwiches, doughnuts, and apple cider for the press in FDR's wood-paneled library. At nine thirty, the president's family took tea; at ten, they dined on salad, and . . . scrambled eggs.

Eleanor reverted to her usual distant attitude toward her husband's fortunes. "I was expected to show interest in the returns," she muttered in her memoirs—phrasing too revealing for its own good. Franklin closeted himself alone with pencil and paper and voting charts. The great clue that this would not just be a victory but a *great* victory arrived with returns from New Haven. Franklin won the city by 15,000 votes. The numbers puzzled him. They couldn't be accurate. They "must be wrong," he puzzled; "they couldn't be that large."

They *were* that large, and FDR exclaimed "Wow!" Rosenman, High, and Corcoran might have written something better. But "Wow!" summed it up quite nicely, thank you.

Numbers like New Haven's rolled in all night—from virtually everywhere.

The mood shifted from nervous expectancy to utter jubilation.

"Who are the fourteen persons who voted against you in Warm Springs?" Jim Farley chortled. "You ought to raise hell with them."

The great buzz centered on Farley's unshakable predictions that Roosevelt would sweep all in his path save Maine and Vermont. He had reiterated it even on Election Eve. And he was right.

"I knew," Franklin teased Eleanor, "I should have gone to Maine and Vermont, but Jim wouldn't let me."

Despite a light drizzle, a huge enthusiastic torchlight-bearing crowd gathered on Sara's lawn. A small band accompanied them, blaring "Happy Days Are Here Again." At 11:00 p.m., Franklin and Eleanor, Sara, sons John and Franklin Jr., and daughter Anna emerged to greet them. News photographers' flashbulbs popped. Franklin, supported on FDR Jr.'s arm, crowed that it "looks as if we are going to have one of the largest sweeps ever heard of in the history of the United States.

"I can't say anything official, but it appeared that the sweep was covering every section—the South, the Coast, the Mountain States, and New England."

Flashbulbs kept popping. Photographers demanded more poses. FDR grew impatient. "Hurry it up," he growled. "I've got to get back and get the returns from California."

"Four more happy years with Roosevelt," someone shouted.

"I'm awfully glad Hyde Park got here ahead of Poughkeepsie," Franklin continued. "Poughkeepsie is on the way. I believe we will carry Poughkeepsie." He did. He carried Poughkeepsie—and his own precinct in Hyde Park. But not the town.

Franklin mused that "this has been my sixth election experience. There was 1910, 1912, 1928, 1930, and now 1936."

"And there'll be 1940, too," someone shouted. The *Chicago Tribune*'s Willard Edwards noticed that Franklin "beamed."

Eighty-two-year-old Sara Roosevelt stepped forward, bareheaded in the rain. The shout went out: "Three cheers for Mrs. James Roosevelt, Sr.

"And three more for Mrs. Franklin Roosevelt."

Smoke from the throng's blazing torches choked FDR, who stifled a cough. "I'm swallowing a lot of red fire," he explained.

But before ducking inside, he added, "I hope in the next four years, with the worst part of the emergency over, I'll be able to spend a little more time in Hyde Park."

Actually, that had been the Republican plan. It obviously hadn't worked.

Late in the evening, the phone rang. It was for Anna Roosevelt's husband, John Boettinger, for ten years a reporter with Hearst's *Chicago American*. It had been re-routed from the White House.

"Hello, John, this is Marion Davies. I just wanted to tell you that I love you. We know that a steamroller has flattened us out, but there are no hard feelings at this end. I just wanted you to know that."

Then Hearst interrupted. "Hello, is that you, Boettinger? Well, I just wanted to repeat what Marion said, that we have been run over by a steamroller, but that there are no hard feelings at this end."

Indeed not. By month's end, Hearst had engaged Boettinger to run his *Seattle Post-Intelligencer* at $30,000 (plus a bonus) annually and Anna as its $10,000-per-year women's editor.

A wag wrote:

CARES OF A PRESIDENT
WITH A BIG FAMILY.

One son has gone Du Pontish,
My daughter's man's with Hearst;
The ties I once thought fine
Are very quickly burst. . . .
Last night I had a nightmare
—It was the shock of shocks:
My wife had had an offer
To write for Colonel Knox!

GOP dreams to capture House seats fared no better than their hopes for Messrs. Landon and Knox. They forfeited fifteen seats, reducing them to an infinitesimal eighty-eight seats—their worst total since 1890. Surviving were North Dakota's "Liberty Bill" Lemke and his erstwhile campaign manager Usher Burdick. In New York, Hamilton Fish managed to annoy FDR by coasting to reelection as his Hyde Park congressman. Harlem's Vito Marcantonio narrowly, but only temporarily, lost his seat. Statewide, Caroline O'Day trounced the unduly optimistic Natalie Couch. With the exception of one North Chicago district and a few surrounding Boston, Republican House representation in the larger cities essentially vanished.

Republicans fared equally horridly in the Senate, though Bill Borah (fighting a bad chest cold) waltzed to victory with 63.4 percent of the vote. In mid-campaign, he had received two $5,000 checks, quietly brought to him by John D. M. Hamilton—and written by progressive bêtes noir Joseph Pew Jr. and Lammot du Pont. Later, Borah startled Hamilton by publicly belittling Pew and du Pont, leading Hamilton to assume that Borah had rejected their contributions.

He assumed wrong.

Other GOP incumbents faced tougher sledding. Arthur Capper and Minority Leader Charles McNary (who, like Borah, refused to endorse Landon) barely survived. Presidential dark horse Lester J. "Dick" Dickinson of Iowa lost with 47.1 percent of the vote. Thanks to FDR's boost and a well-timed exit from the Republican Party, Nebraska's George Norris survived with a mere 43.8 percent. The most interesting Senate result was the year's solitary Republican pickup. Thirty-four-year-old Henry Cabot Lodge Jr. upended Boston mayor James M. Curley 48.5 to 41.0 percent.

Republicans, as always, faced the toughest slog in South Carolina, where the party's rival "Black and Tan" and "Lilywhite" factions fielded separate candidates versus pro–New Deal incumbent senator Jimmy Byrnes, harvesting infinitesimal totals of 0.8 and 0.6 percent of the vote, respectively.

All in all, Senate Republicans forfeited a net five seats, dropping to just sixteen, the smallest quotient by either major party since the Democrats' twelve in post–Civil War 1868—and the GOP's poorest showing since electing its first senator in 1854. Even the doomed Whigs garnered twenty seats in their swan song of 1852.

"Our ignominious defeat," assessed H. L. Mencken to a friend, "is unquestionably due to our neglect of God's word. If we had prayed instead of boozing, Alf might be in the White House today, and you and I might be training for ambassadorships. As it is, we'll be lucky if we escape Alcatraz."

Third-party senatorial candidates enjoyed only a singular success: in Minnesota, where Rep. Ernest Lundeen won on the Farmer-Labor ticket.

Coughlin's hopeless Union Party Senate hopefuls failed to even crack double digits. Their party's best showing came in Massachusetts, where Coughlinite vice presidential candidate Thomas C. O'Brien competed via write-in versus Mayor Curley and Henry Cabot Lodge. His 7.4 percent of the vote capsized Curley's chances. Curley's secretary, Frank L. Kane, angrily wired Coughlin: "As Christ had his Judas and Caesar his Brutus, Washington his Arnold, so has Governor Curley his Father Coughlin."

In Coughlin's Michigan stronghold, his close ally Louis B. Ward garnered only 4.43 percent. In Illinois, the party's most famous senatorial hopeful, corrupt former Chicago mayor "Big Bill" Thompson, lassoed just 3.31 percent. Improbably, however, Coughlinites fashioned a direct and significant impact on New York State governance. Voters swept five Republican incumbent assemblymen out of office, jeopardizing their party's slim, newly won majority. But in ultra-Democratic Albany County, Republican County Coroner John C. McBain ousted Democratic Assemblyman S. Earl McDermott. GOP control survived by just a single vote—with his absolutely stunning upset achieved only through his Union Party endorsement.

Of thirty-four governorships in play, Republicans captured just four. Third-party candidates (Progressives in Wisconsin and Farmer-Laborites in Minnesota, and the Non-Partisan League in North Dakota) took three. Reinforcing the utter futility of Republican efforts, the three third-party states outnumbered the GOP's four states in population 6,183,804 to 2,315,176.

The GOP's net loss of two governorships ratcheted them down to just seven. Recapturing Maine in September and South Dakota in November, they had nonetheless lost Michigan, Delaware, and Kansas to the Democrats and North Dakota to the Non-Partisan League's "Wild Bill" Langer. Particularly painful was Kansas, where Alf Landon's former secretary Will G. West met narrow defeat to an absolute Democrat nonentity, Walter A. Huxman, who had run merely after being promised a lucrative New Deal job following his anticipated walloping.

FDR's strategy of recruiting Herbert Lehman and Frank Murphy to run in New York and Michigan, respectively, had little impact on his own showing in either state. He ran ahead of Lehman 58.65 to 53.45 percent. He outpaced Murphy 56.33 to 51.02 percent.

Democrats now boasted an overwhelming 74 Senate seats, 334 House seats, and 38 governorships. A rising Roosevelt tide indeed lifted all (or virtually all) Democratic boats, including many an outright bozo. "Democrats," privately fretted Harold Ickes, "gained Governors and Senators and Congressmen where already they had too many Congressmen and Senators, and with respect to some states, too many Governors. The President pulled through to victory men whose defeat would have been better for the country."

The minor parties' boats largely sunk.

In a year and an election where if you weren't being called a Communist you risked being dubbed a fascist, only one bona fide fascist was on the ballot—Silver Shirt leader William Dudley Pelley, and only in Washington State. His 1,598 "Christian Party" votes placed him not merely behind Lemke, Thomas, and Browder but also substantially trailing a pair of Prohibitionist Party lawyers, D. Leigh Colvin and Claude A. Watson (37,646 votes). Back in May, their party had nominated Great War hero Sgt. Alvin York as Colvin's running mate. York nonetheless kept his powder dry, leaving Prohibitionists to tap the far less valiant Mr. Watson. Also besting Pelley (with 12,799 votes) were the Socialist Labor standard-bearers, the aforementioned hardwood finisher John W. Aiken and his running mate, Emil Teichert. Mr. Teichert seemed momentarily unemployed.

Anti-Semite Louis McFadden never made it onto any ballot. His "Independent Republican National Christian-Gentile Committee" vanished as soon as it appeared. A bid to recapture his old House seat faltered in the primary stage. In any case, he never made it to Election Day even to vote, keeling over in his Manhattan hotel room and dying that October.

Bill Lemke failed to approach anything near Father Coughlin's reckless 9 million-vote goal, garnering just 892,378 votes or a minuscule 1.95 percent. He might have done better had he appeared on more than thirty state ballots—being barred, as he was, in such major battlegrounds as New York and Townsendite California. In his native North Dakota, he scored a disappointing 13.41 percent and failed to carry a single county. Only in Minnesota, Massachusetts, and Rhode Island did he score more than 6 percent; only in Oregon, Wisconsin, Ohio, and Michigan more than 4.

Having failed to secure ballot access in twelve states (most prominently Ohio), Norman Thomas collected just 187,720 votes, the worst Socialist Party showing since 1900—free-falling from his own 881,951-vote total just four years previously. He hadn't really wanted to run this year—or even wanted his party to run anyone—and he had been right.

In 1928, Bella Bernstein Waldman, wife of his SP gubernatorial running mate, Louis Waldman, observed, "Roosevelt is the most formidable opponent that the Socialist Party will ever have." Nineteen thirty-six proved her right as well.

A bigger loser than Norman Thomas's Socialists was the du Ponts' Liberty League. It was never nearly as flush as its many detractors supposed it to be, and never quite sure of what it was supposed to be, nor how it was supposed to slay the great dragon Roosevelt. By mid-1936 campaign, it had floundered on its last legs. The du Ponts still spent money on their great crusade, but now funneled it directly into the Landon campaign or into radio broadcasts of the so-called Jeffersonian Democrats—Al Smith, Joseph Ely, James A. Reed, Bainbridge Colby, Breckinridge Long, "Alfalfa Bill" Murray, and former Texas congressman Joseph W. Bailey Jr. By September 30, it had formally (though privately) suspended operations. It survived the election, but just barely. In December, Jouett Shouse found his salary slashed from $30,000 to $12,000. All branch offices shut up shop.

Also down—but sort of up—were the fortunes of the CPUSA. Its Browder–Ford tally of 80,159 votes was down from 1932's Foster–Ford

102,785 total. It was, moreover, a relatively expensive exercise for the Reds—$2.02 per vote compared to Norman Thomas's shoestring 11 cents.

Yet the Communists had not really been trying to win votes—at least, not for Earl Browder. Browder didn't run to win votes. He ran to win publicity and converts, and he succeeded—though, thanks to his party's damnable acquiescence in 1939's Hitler–Stalin pact, its relative popularity proved fleeting.

A shining Red Star, however, hung over the City College of New York. There, a late poll of students found Browder not only outpolling Norman Thomas 1,039–49—but also swamping the decidedly un–New York Alf Landon 1,039–196.

Nineteen thirty-six's great third-party winner is least remembered: New York's American Labor Party provided Franklin Roosevelt with 274,924 votes and Herbert Lehman with 262,192. Bankrolled with a massive $142,000 in contributions from David Dubinsky's International Ladies Garment Union, it essentially dispatched the Socialist Party into perennial obscurity. The following year, 21.6 percent of Gotham voters supported Fiorello La Guardia's reelection on the ALP line. But in its success lay the seeds of its own destruction. In 1936, CPUSA New York gubernatorial candidate Robert Minor had run so poorly (35,609 votes) that Communists lost their status as an official Empire State political party, forfeiting their right to automatic ballot access—or the ability to officially register anyone as a Communist voter. Communists poured into the ALP, eventually capturing it.

The star of the evening was Franklin Roosevelt, for, as Rexford Tugwell perceived, "In 1932 it could be said that the voters had been against Hoover. This time they were for Franklin."

FDR spoke much truth when he lectured Ray Moley, "There's one issue in this campaign. It's myself, and people must be either for me or against me."

And, thus, Democrats largely kept their powder dry, not allowing themselves to be sucked into fighting on battlefields of their enemies' choosing. They would *not* respond to attacks on FDR's allies. That would only magnify voters' concerns about his often-controversial underlings. Republicans, theorized Farley's publicity chief Charlie Michelson, "took as their targets

Chairman Farley and Rex Tugwell; they invoked the communism issue on the basis of a New York Democratic elector [David Dubinsky].

"Farley was not a conscienceless villain; Tugwell was not a Socialist gone mad, and Dubinsky was not a Communist; but if the Republicans could get us arguing on such points they had a much better chance. . . . So Farley took it on the chin and we made no replies to the collateral assaults."

The big picture was this: 27,747,636 votes for FDR; 16,679,543 for Landon; 60.8 percent of the vote for FDR; a pathetic 36.5 percent for Landon; and, most famously, 523 electoral votes for FDR; an even more pitiable 8 for Landon.

Officially, Republicans outraised Democrats $7,761,039 to $5,206,159, though some (including John Hamilton) calculated GOP spending to be somewhere in the range of $12,000,000. Both parties ran deficits—officially $445,250 for the Democrats; $915,314 for Republicans. Old money and big money remained a factor for both camps. Bankers and brokers contributed $578,910 to GOP coffers; manufacturers added another $1,162,934. Democrats still attracted $220,000 in old money, from such individuals as the polo-playing Cornelius Vanderbilt Whitney, W. Averell Harriman, and the Biddles of mainline Philadelphia. But Democrats leaned far more heavily on union funding: $770,218 from organized labor, with the aforementioned $469,870 from John L. Lewis's United Mine Workers.

Democrats spent their money on radio ($540,000—some said $840,000) and on an estimated one hundred million pieces of printed material. And did surprisingly well with the nation's newspapers. Republicans, revealed Charlie Michelson, had "the support of a majority of the big newspapers, and so the stories along that line got wide publicity. But this advantage was more apparent than real. There were 7,000 small dailies and weeklies that took our clip sheets and printed our cartoons, and most of them used what went out to them—articles . . . modestly headed 'editorial suggestion.'"

FDR loved playing the underdog—and bashing the press—later famously whining that 85 percent of the papers were opposed to him. He exaggerated, as *Editor and Publisher* found when it surveyed 1936's scene: 36.1 percent for Roosevelt; 57.10 for Landon; and 5.80 percent uncommitted. In fact, Landon enjoyed the smallest percent of editorial support of any of FDR's four hapless opponents. A survey, which FDR personally ordered via the Democratic National Committee, had yielded similar results, even though it excluded data from the almost uniformly Democratic South.

Most of all, Roosevelt retained his job thanks to other people again having jobs. November 1936's unemployment rate of 13.9 percent, while hardly wonderful, was the lowest since 1931. Beyond that were the hundreds of thousands of jobs and checks handed out from Washington via the WPA, the PWA, FERA, the CCC, the AAA, etc. etc. etc.—a fact that FDR, for all his patrician advantages, understood very well. "You tell [PWA assistant administrator] Corrington Gill," Franklin ordered Henry Morgenthau as the election approached, "that I don't give a g-d damn where he gets the money from but not one person is to be laid off on the first of October!" Intent on capturing Kansas's electoral votes (and embarrassing Landon), the administration pumped WPA money into the state, its spending skyrocketing from $15,820,351 in fiscal year 1935–36 to $27,888,660 the following year. Between June 27 and that November, the number of Kansas WPA relief recipients soared from 46,966 to 69,163. FDR carried 73 of 105 Kansas counties; he captured Landon's home county by seven votes.

Overall—despite a trumpeted "recovery"—federal relief rolls had steadily increased, from 3,566,842 in 1933 to 4,324,953 in 1934 to 4,681,828 in 1935. Combined federal, state, and local relief efforts affected twenty-one million persons in 1934—and twenty-four million in early 1936.

"You cannot beat Santa Claus," summarized Hamilton Fish, "with a Communist bogey man or by stupid attacks on social security legislation which most Republican members of Congress, including myself, favored." And he was right on both levels.

Behind Roosevelt's big numbers lay a series of spectacular smaller numbers and achievements: he carried Pennsylvania, the first Democrat doing so since James Buchanan in 1856, bringing with him both houses of the state legislature—another first since Civil War days. Democratic registration in Pennsylvania skyrocketed from 21 percent in 1934 to 42 percent in 1936. In Pittsburgh, for the first time ever, Democrats now outnumbered Republicans—a statistic made all the more remarkable by an even more startling figure: in 1929, enrolled Democrats comprised just 3 percent of city voters.

FDR won 78 percent of the Catholic vote, with an estimated 103 of 106 US bishops behind him. He captured 90 percent of the Jewish vote. In 1936, the nation finally became officially Democratic, GOP enrollment having skidded from 59 percent in 1932 to 52 percent in 1934 to now just 42 percent.

Roosevelt won 68 percent in the Far West. He held Landon to under 30 percent of the vote in Washington, Oregon, Nevada, Arizona, Montana, and North Dakota and just over 30 percent in California, Minnesota, Wisconsin, and Tennessee. Fueling FDR's immense regional popularity were the piles of New Deal money pumped into the West. A 1939 study revealed that figure as 60 percent more per capita than in Southern states.

Even while failing to carry Maine and Vermont, he took 54 percent of New England's vote. Landon, once comfortably ahead in the region, tumbled to just 43 percent.

Michigan witnessed remarkable Democratic advances. Flint voted 28 percent Smith in 1928. By 1936, it was 72 percent Roosevelt. Statewide, the party's vote surged from 152,000 in 1924 to 1,017,000 for FDR in 1936. Moreover, as Detroit's Polish-American newspaper, *Dziennek Polski*, predicted, "Hundreds of thousands of votes of citizens of Polish extraction will be cast for Roosevelt in Michigan. They, in a great majority, were staunch Republicans who turned Democrats because the Republicans rated them as lower-class citizenry."

In 1928, Al Smith achieved significant inroads in the nation's big cities. Roosevelt built upon them—and built to the sky. His margin of victory in the nation's twelve largest cities exploded from 1.8 million votes in 1932 to 3.5 million four years later. Of the nation's 106 largest cities, Landon carried only Pasadena and Syracuse, Syracuse being the only city Republicans managed to flip from 1932. Hoover carried 15 of those 106 cities in 1932.

The cities were changing—they *had* changed. And people should have seen it coming a long time previously. As public opinion analyst Samuel Lubbell noted:

> In . . . 1910 Congress received the longest report ever submitted by a government investigating body up to that time. From early 1907 a special commission [studied] almost every imaginable aspect of immigration . . . [it] showed that a majority of the children in the schools of thirty-seven of our leading cities had foreign-born fathers.
>
> In cities like Chelsea, Fall River, New Bedford, Duluth, New York and Chicago more than *two out of every three* children were the sons and daughters of immigrants . . . those figures forecast a major political upheaval some time between 1930 and 1940.

They certainly did in 1936.

This translated into a much greater voting pool. Thus, while Landon performed horribly (a fact even John Hamilton might now concede), he outpolled Hoover's 1932 showing by a respectable 923,547 votes (rising from 15,760,684 to 16,684,231). Simultaneously, however, people of all stripes (immigrant, rural, on relief, etc.) stormed out of the woodwork to cast their ballots for FDR, who ratcheted up his own totals by a whopping 4,927,832 votes (from 22,829,501 to 27,757,333). The trend was particularly pronounced in Pennsylvania, where Hoover hung on to defeat FDR 1,453,540 to 1,295,948 in 1932. Landon improved on Hoover's totals, recording 1,690,300 votes. Roosevelt walloped him with 2,353,788.

Beyond geography and national origin, FDR achieved remarkable results with certain economic strata, taking over 60 percent of the Northern Protestant lower-income vote. The lower the income level, the greater his vote: 42 percent of upper-income voters; 60 percent middle-income; a whopping 76 percent of lower-income voters.

Beyond even that, save for Al Smith's 1928 debacle, the Republican vote had been flatter than Alf Landon's Kansas; Democratic totals skyrocketed, particularly in urban areas:

	REPUBLICAN	DEMOCRATIC
1920 (Harding–Cox)	16,152,200	9,147,353
1924 (Coolidge–Davis)	15,725,016	8,386,503
1928 (Hoover–Smith)	21,391,381	15,016,443

1932 (Hoover–FDR)	15,761,845	22,821,857
1936 (Landon–FDR)	16,679,853	27,757,333

A big earthquake shook the Black electorate, with FDR receiving an estimated 71 percent of its vote. Republican appeal evaporated throughout the North:

REPUBLICAN SHARE OF PRESIDENTIAL VOTE IN HEAVILY AFRICAN-AMERICAN PRECINCTS, 1928–1936

	1928	1932	1936
Chicago	72%	75%	51%
Cleveland	72%	82%	38%
Knoxville	56%	70%	44%
New York	66%	46%	17%
Philadelphia	82%	71%	30%

Democrats were building a base of support for a post–FDR/New Deal world, electing twenty Black state legislators in nine Northern states. Their success came with a rush—but not cheaply, as Democrats expended a hefty $500,000 on appropriating the Northern Black vote. They fared not badly in the South as well. "Every Negro I registered so far has said he would vote for President Roosevelt," admitted one Columbia, South Carolina, voting registrar. "They say Roosevelt saved them from starvation, gave them aid when they were in distress."

As Blacks North and South entered, white Southerners departed—or at least their once powerful influence on their ancestral party receded. Not long previously, Southern-born Woodrow Wilson's cabinet had been chock-full of Southerners. Following 1920's Cox–Roosevelt debacle, 107 of 131 surviving Democratic congressman were Southerners. Certainly, FDR relied on Southern support for his 1932 nomination and remained ever fearful of alienating Dixie's powerful congressional forces. But even in 1936, things were changing, with FDR carrying less of the Southern popular vote than four years previously. In 1936, only 235 of FDR's 523 electoral votes came from the South, and, with Democrats sweeping all before them in the Northeast, Midwest, and West—only 35 percent of all House Democrats now emanated from Dixie.

Perhaps the year's least-noticed poll belonged to Elmer Roper's modest *Fortune* magazine poll, which, every three months from January on, surveyed a mere 1,600 people. In January, Roper tabulated Roosevelt 59 percent; Landon 37 percent, and 4 percent undecided. At campaign's end it was pretty much all the same at 61.7 for FDR. All the analysis, the speeches, the money expended had barely moved the needle.

And yet while Roosevelt indeed won big, the depth of his support was not quite as fervent as history remembers it—at least according to Roper, a former jeweler and clock salesman. In October 1936, he also tabulated these surprisingly lukewarm figures regarding the public's perception of FDR:

Roosevelt's re-election essential for the good of the country	35%
He may have made mistakes but no one else can do as much good	26%
He did many things that needed doing, but most of his usefulness is now over	14%
About the worst thing that could happen to this country is another Roosevelt administration	23%

Among Franklin's most fervent supporters (the 35 percent in the above table's first row), Roper—four years later a Roosevelt pollster—also reported that "people in general did not expect him to lead the nation very much farther to the left, nor did they want him to. Most of his supporters thought his policies would continue about as they had been [59 percent] or, if they did change, would become more conservative [17 percent]."

• • •

Franklin scored fairly well in his final 360–171 electoral vote prediction, though not nearly as prescient as Jim Farley, George Gallup, or even Drew Pearson. As many as two hundred thousand persons lined the streets to greet his return to Washington. At an informal press conference, a reporter queried FDR as to why he so missed the mark: "What frightened you?"

"Oh," Roosevelt quipped, "just my well-known conservative tendencies."

FDR laughed. Mr. Wilfred J. Funk, the recently installed editor-in-chief of the *Literary Digest*, cried. "I'm simply astounded, . . ." he confessed. "It's beyond comprehension to explain away the *Digest* poll. I couldn't possibly do that now. That would take time—and a lot of pencils and paper and figuring."

"Don't get me wrong," the fifty-three-year-old Funk added, almost as an afterthought; "my personal belief was that Roosevelt would win. I thought it would be close."

It was dinnertime, Wednesday, November 4, 1936, and Election Day 1936 had passed into history. On New York's West 52nd Street, two young men passed through the doors of Jack White's fashionable "Club 18." They hoped to drown their sorrows. They hoped not to be recognized. Being William Randolph Hearst's sons—twenty-eight-year-old William Jr. and twenty-seven-year-old John Randolph "Jack" Hearst—they had good reason.

"Club 18" boasted a master of ceremonies on the way up, Brooklyn-born John Herbert Gleason, a wisecracking twenty-year-old Broadway personality in the manner of Gotham's late speakeasy hostess "Texas" Guinan. One evening, spying Olympic figure-skating star Sonja Henie's entrance, the young Mr. Gleason grabbed an ice cube, presented it to Henie, and demanded, "Okay, now do something."

Tonight, he recognized the Hearst boys. Without missing a beat, John Herbert Gleason—better known to history as Jackie Gleason—called out, "Ah, here come Maine and Vermont!"

Somewhere, Louis McHenry Howe couldn't stop laughing.

ACKNOWLEDGMENTS

Getting a country out of a Great Depression is no easy task, and neither is writing a history of said endeavor—particularly in a pandemic, when setting a physical foot in a physical library was a virtual thing of the past.

But thanks to the Internet, such things can be done, and particular thanks are extended to the New York Public Library, the New York State Library, the now-departed online research service Questia, and, particularly, to the increasingly magnificent effort known as archive.org. When things opened up a little at the conclusion of this process, we received assistance from the Schenectady County Public Library, the Schaffer Library of Union College, and from Kristine Krueger of the Academy of Motion Picture Arts and Sciences' Margaret Herrick Library.

Major-league huzzahs are certainly extended to Tom Tryniski, operator of the website fultonhistory.com. With nary a cent of public funding, Mr. Tryniski had posted over fifty million searchable pages of historic newspapers online—largely, but not exclusively, from New York State. If I handed out medals for selfless public service, I would hand one out to him and make it solid gold.

Appreciation also goes out to my friends San Francisco radio host John Rothmann; author Kathryn Smith; Cliff Laube, Public Programs Manager at the Franklin D. Roosevelt Presidential Library and Museum; Adam Dias, Cataloger at Alexander Historical Auctions LLC; and to the *Washington Examiner*'s David Mark.

Many thanks to my agent, Philip Turner of Philip Turner Book Productions, and, not entirely coincidentally, editor-in-chief of Carroll & Graf Publishers when my earlier *Rothstein* and *1920: The Year of the Six Presidents* first saw the light of day and an editor at Sterling Publishing when it acquired my *1960* and *1948*.

Thanks as well to another veteran of my publishing odyssey, Keith Wallman, executive editor and editor-in-chief at Diversion Books, who has been on board in various capacities for even more of my titles, not only at Diversion and Carroll & Graf, but also at Lyons Press. And to Phil Gaskill, *1920*'s copy editor at Carroll & Graf and *Roosevelt Sweeps Nation*'s line editor at Diversion and to Shannon Donnelly and Alex Sprague of Diversion's publicity and marketing department.

Thanks also to Steve Leard, who designed the book's magnificent cover, to publishing coordinator Evan Phail and to *Roosevelt Sweeps Nation*'s design team at Neuwirth & Associates: Noah Perkins, Beth Metrick, and Jeff Farr.

And, of course, to my wife, Patty.

BIBLIOGRAPHY

BOOKS

Abt, John J., and Michael Myerson. *Advocate and Activist: Memoirs of an American Communist Lawyer.* Urbana: University of Illinois Press, 1993.

Allen, George E. *Presidents Who Have Known Me.* New York: Simon and Schuster, 1950.

Allison, Robert. *James Michael Curley.* Beverly (MA): Commonwealth Editions, 2011.

Alter, Jonathan. *The Defining Moment: FDR's Hundred Days and the Triumph of Hope.* New York: Simon & Schuster, 2006.

Amenta, Edwin. *When Movements Matter: The Townsend Plan and the Rise of Social Security.* Princeton (NJ): Princeton University Press, 2006.

Anderson, William. *The Wild Man from Sugar Creek: The Political Career of Eugene Talmadge.* Baton Rouge: Louisiana State University Press, 1975.

Asbell, Bernard. *Mother and Daughter: The Letters of Eleanor and Anna Roosevelt.* New York: Penguin Adult, 1982.

Baker, William J. *Jesse Owens: An American Life.* New York: Macmillan College Division, 1986.

Barnard, Harry. *Independent Man: The Life of James Gould Couzens.* New York: Charles Scribner's Sons, 1958.

Barzman, Sol. *Madmen and Geniuses: The Vice-Presidents of the United States.* Chicago: Follette, 1974.

Beard, Patricia. *Newsmaker: Roy W. Howard, The Mastermind Behind the Scripps-Howard News Empire from the Gilded Age to the Atomic Age.* Guilford (CT): Lyons Press, 2016.

Beasley, Norman. *Frank Knox, American: A Short Biography.* Garden City (NY): Doubleday, Doran and Company, 1936.

Beatty, Jack. *The Rascal King: The Life and Times of James Michael Curley 1874–1958.* Reading (MA): Addison-Wesley, 1992.

Beauchamp, Cari. *Joseph P. Kennedy Presents: His Hollywood Years.* New York: Alfred A. Knopf, 2009.

Beekman, Scott. *William Dudley Pelley: A Life in Right-Wing Extremism and the Occult.* Syracuse (NY): Syracuse University Press, 2005.

Beienburg, Sean. *Prohibition, the Constitution, and States' Rights.* Chicago: University of Chicago Press, 2019.

Bell, C. Jasper. *The Story of a Missourian.* Kansas City: Self-Published, 1971.

Bennett, David H. *Demagogues in the Depression: American Radicals and the Union Party, 1932–1936.* New Brunswick: Rutgers University Press, 1969.

Beschloss, Michael. *Kennedy and Roosevelt: The Uneasy Alliance.* New York: W. W. Norton & Co., 1981.

Best, Gary Dean. *Pride, Prejudice, and Politics: Roosevelt Versus Recovery, 1933–1938.* New York: Praeger, 1991.

Black, Conrad. *Franklin Delano Roosevelt: Champion of Freedom.* New York: Public Affairs, 2003.

Blackorby, Edward C. *Prairie Rebel: The Public Life of William Lemke.* Lincoln: University of Nebraska Press, 1963.

Blair, Joan, and Clay Blair. *The Search for JFK.* New York: Berkley, 1976.

Blum, John Morton (ed.). *Public Philosopher: Selected Letters of Walter Lippmann.* New York: Ticknor & Fields, 1985.

——— (ed.). *From the Morgenthau Diaries.* Boston: Houghton Mifflin, 1959.

Bowers, Claude G. *My Life: The Memoirs of Claude Bowers.* New York: Simon and Schuster, 1962.

Braeman, John, Robert H. Bremner, and David Brody (eds.). *The New Deal.* Columbus: Ohio State University Press, 1975. (Published in two volumes: I. The National Level; II. The State and Local Levels.)

Briggs, John A. *High Tension: FDR's Battle to Power America.* New York: Diversion Books, 2020.

Brinkley, Alan. *Voices of Protest: Huey Long, Father Coughlin, & The Great Depression.* New York: Alfred A. Knopf, 1982.

Brough, James. *Princess Alice: A Biography of Alice Roosevelt Longworth.* Boston: Little, Brown & Co., 1975.

Browder, Earl. *Communism in the United States.* New York: International Publishers, 1935.

———. *Democracy or Fascism: Earl Browder's Report to the Ninth Convention of the Communist Party.* New York: Workers Library Press, 1936.

———. *What Is Communism?* New York: Workers Library Press, 1936.

Browder, Robert Paul, and Thomas G. Smith. *Independent: A Biography of Lewis W. Douglas.* New York: Alfred A. Knopf, 1986.

Brown, Robert J. *Manipulating the Ether: The Power of Broadcast Radio in Thirties America.* Jefferson (NC): McFarland & Co., 1998.

Brownell, Will, and Richard N. Billings. *So Close to Greatness: A Biography of William C. Bullitt.* New York: Macmillan, 1987.

Bulger, William M. (edited by Robert J. Allison). *James Michael Curley: A Short Biography with Personal Reminisces.* Carlyle (MA): Commonwealth Publications, 2009.

Burk, Robert Fredrick. *The Corporate State and the Broker State: The Du Ponts and American National Politics, 1925–1940.* Cambridge (MA): Harvard University Press, 1990.

Burke, Robert E. (ed.). *The Diary Letters of Hiram Johnson, 1934–1938.* New York: Garland, 1983.

Burns, James MacGregor. *Roosevelt: The Lion and the Fox.* New York: Harcourt, Brace and Company, 1956.

Burrough, Bryan. *The Big Rich: The Rise and Fall of the Greatest Texas Oil Fortunes.* New York: Penguin, 2010.

Butler, Susan. *East to the Dawn: The Life of Amelia Earhart.* New York: Da Capo Press, 1999.

Carlisle, Rodney P. *Hearst and the New Deal: The Progressive as Reactionary.* New York: Garland, 1979.

Carlson, John Roy. *Under Cover: My Four Years in the Nazi Underworld of America.* New York: E. P. Dutton & Co., 1943.

Casey, James. *The Crisis in the Communist Party.* New York: Three Arrows Press, 1937.

Chalmers, David M. *Hooded Americanism: A History of the Ku Klux Klan.* Chicago: Quadrangle Paperbacks, 1965.

Charles, Searle F. *Minister of Relief: Harry Hopkins and the Depression.* Syracuse (NY): Syracuse University Press, 1963.

Coblentz, Edmond D. (ed.). *William Randolph Hearst: A Portrait in His Own Words.* New York: Simon and Schuster, 1952.

Cohodas, Nadine. *Strom Thurmond & the Politics of Southern Change.* Macon (GA): Mercer University Press, 1995.

Colby, Gerard. *Du Pont Dynasty.* Secaucus (NJ): Lyle Stuart, 1984.

Collier, Peter (with David Horowitz). *The Roosevelts: An American Saga.* New York: Simon & Schuster, 1994.

Conradi, Peter. *Hitler's Piano Player: The Rise and Fall of Ernst Hanfstaengl, Confidant of Hitler, Ally of FDR.* New York: Carroll & Graf, 2004.

Considine, Bob. *It's All News to Me: A Reporter's Deposition.* New York: Meredith Press, 1967.

Cook, Blanche Wiesen. *Eleanor Roosevelt, Volume II: The Defining Years, 1933–38.* New York: Viking, 1999.

Cook, Raymond A. *Thomas Dixon.* New York: Twayne Publishers, 1974.

———. *Father Coughlin's Radio Sermons: October, 1930–April, 1931.* Baltimore: Knox & O'Leary, 1931.

Cordery, Stacy A. *Alice: Alice Roosevelt Longworth from White House Princess to Washington Power Broker.* New York: Viking Penguin, 2007.

Cortner, Richard C. *The Kingfish and the Constitution: Huey Long, the First Amendment, and the Emergence of Modern Press Freedom in America.* Westport (CT): Greenwood Press, 1996.

Costigliola, Frank. *Roosevelt's Lost Alliances: How Personal Politics Helped Start the Cold War.* Princeton (NJ): Princeton University Press, 2012.

Coughlin, Rev. Charles E. *The New Deal in Money.* Royal Oak (MI): The Radio League of the Little Flower, 1933.

Cramer, C. H. *Newton D. Baker: A Biography.* Cleveland: World Publishing Co., 1961.

Creel, George. *Rebel at Large: Recollections of Fifty Crowded Years.* New York: G. P. Putnam's Son's, 1947.

Crocker, Harry. *That's Hollywood.* (Unpublished Manuscript—held by the Margaret Herrick Library of The Academy of Motion Picture Arts and Sciences, Beverly Hills, CA).

Crowther, Bosley, *Hollywood Rajah: The Life and Time of Louis B. Mayer.* New York: Holt, Rinehart & Winston, 1960.

Culver, John, and John Hyde. *American Dreamer: The Life and Times of Henry A. Wallace.* New York: W. W. Norton & Co., 2000.

Curley, James Michael. *I'd Do It Again: A Record of All My Uproarious Years.* Englewood Cliffs (NJ): Prentice Hall, Inc., 1957.

Dallek, Robert. *FDR: Franklin D. Roosevelt and American Foreign Policy: 1932–1945.* New York: Oxford University Press, 1979.

Daniels, Roger. *Franklin D. Roosevelt: Road to the New Deal, 1882–1939.* Urbana: University of Illinois Press, 2015.

Davies, Marion (edited by Pamela Pfau and Kenneth S. Marx). *The Times We Had: Life with William Randolph Hearst.* Indianapolis: Bobbs-Merrill, 1975.

Davin, Eric Leif. *Crucible of Freedom: Workers' Democracy in the Industrial Heartland, 1914–1960.* Lanham (MD): Lexington Books, 2010.

Davis, Kenneth S. *FDR: The New Deal Years 1933–1937: A History.* New York: Random House, 1979.

DeMille, Cecil B. (edited by Donald Hayne). *The Autobiography of Cecil B. DeMille.* Englewood Cliffs (NJ): Prentice Hall, 1959.

Douglas, Paul H. *Social Security in the United States: An Analysis and Appraisal of the Federal Social Security Act.* New York: Whittlesey House, McGraw-Hill, 1939.

Draper, Theodore. *The Roots of American Communism.* New York: Viking Press, 1957.

Dubinsky, David, with A. H. Raskin. *David Dubinsky: A Life with Labor.* New York: Simon and Schuster, 1977.

Dunning, John. *On the Air: The Encyclopedia of Old-Time Radio.* New York: Oxford University Press, 1998.

Eaton, Herbert. *Presidential Timber: A History of Nominating Conventions, 1868–1960.* New York: The Free Press of Glencoe, 1964.

Eccles, Marriner S. (edited by Sidney Hyman). *Beckoning Frontiers: Public and Personal Recollections.* New York: Alfred A. Knopf, 1951.

Ekirch, Arthur A., Jr. *Ideologies and Utopias: The Impact of the New Deal on American Thought.* Chicago: Quadrangle Books, 1969.

Ellis, Edward Robb. *A Diary of the Century: Tales from America's Greatest Diarist.* New York: Union Square Press, 2008.

Faber, Doris. *The Life of Lorena Hickok: ER's Friend.* New York: William Morrow, 1980.

Farber, David. *Everybody Ought to Be Rich: The Life and Times of John J. Raskob, Capitalist.* New York: Oxford University Press, 2013.

Farley, James A. *Behind the Ballots: The Personal History of a Politician.* New York: Harcourt Brace and Company, 1938.

———. *Jim Farley's Story: The Roosevelt Years.* New York: Whittlesey House, 1948.

Farr, Finis. *FDR.* New Rochelle (NY): Arlington House, 1972.

Felsenthal, Carol. *Alice Roosevelt Longworth.* New York: G. P. Putnam's Sons, 1988. (Re-issued by St. Martin's Press as *Princess Alice: The Life of Alice Roosevelt Longworth.*)

Ferrara, Peter, and Michael Tanner. *A New Deal for Social Security.* Washington (DC): Cato Institute, 1998.

Ferrell, Robert H. *The Dying President: Franklin D. Roosevelt, 1944–1945.* Columbia: University of Missouri Press, 1998.

Filler, Louis. *The Unknown Edwin Markham: His Mystery and Its Significance.* Yellow Springs (OH): Antioch Press, 1966.

Finan, Christopher M. *Alfred E. Smith: The Happy Warrior.* New York: Hill and Wang, 2002.

Fine, Sidney. *Frank Murphy: The New Deal Years.* Chicago: University of Chicago Press, 1979.

Flynn, Elizabeth Gurley. *Earl Browder: The Man from Kansas.* New York: Workers Library Publishers, 1941.

Foster, William Z. *Toward Soviet America.* New York: Coward-McCann, 1932.

Freedman, Max (ed.). *Roosevelt & Frankfurter: Their Correspondence, 1928–1945.* Boston: Atlantic Little, Brown, 1967.

Freidel, Frank. *Franklin D. Roosevelt: A Rendezvous with Destiny.* Boston: Little, Brown, 1990.

Fried, Albert. *FDR and His Enemies.* New York: Palgrave, 1999.

Fried, Amy. *Pathways to Polling: Crisis, Cooperation and the Making of Public Opinion Professionals.* New York: Routledge, 2012.

Gallagher, Hugh Gregory. *FDR's Splendid Deception: The Moving Story of Roosevelt's Massive Disability—And the Intense Efforts to Conceal It from the Public.* Arlington (VA): Vandermere Press, 1994.

Gallup, Dr. Frank H. *The Gallup Poll: Public Opinion, 1935–1948* (Volume 1). New York: Random House, 1972.

Garraty, John A. *Right-Hand Man: The Life of George W. Perkins.* New York: Harper & Brothers, 1960.

Gies, Joseph. *The Colonel of Chicago.* New York: E. P. Dutton, 1979.

Gitlow, Benjamin. *I Confess: The Truth About American Communism.* New York: E. P. Dutton and Company, 1940.

———. *The Whole of Their Lives: Communism in America, a Personal History and Intimate Portrayal of Its Leaders.* New York: Charles Scribner's Sons, 1948.

Guiles, Fred Lawrence. *Marion Davies: A Biography.* New York: McGraw-Hill, 1972.

Hadju, David. *Love for Sale: Pop Music in America.* New York: Farrar, Straus and Giroux, 2016.

Hair, William Ivy. *The Kingfish and His Realm: The Life and Times of Huey P. Long.* Baton Rouge: Louisiana State University Press, 1991.

Hallgren, Mauritz A. *The Gay Reformer: Profits Before Plenty Under Franklin D. Roosevelt.* New York: Alfred A. Knopf, 1935.

Hamilton, Virginia Van der Veer. *Hugo Black: The Alabama Years.* Baton Rouge: Louisiana State University Press, 1972.

Hansen, Chris. *Enfant Terrible: The Times and Schemes of General Elliot Roosevelt.* Tucson: Able Baker Press, 2013.

Harbaugh, William H. *Lawyer's Lawyer: The Life of John W. Davis.* New York: Oxford University Press, 1973.

Harris, Sara (with the assistance of Harriet Crittendon). *Father Divine.* New York: Collier, 1971.

Harwood, Michael. *In the Shadow of Presidents: The American Vice-Presidency and Succession System.* Philadelphia: J. P. Lippincott, 1966.

Hart, George L. *Official Report of the Proceedings of the Twenty-First Republican National Convention Held in Cleveland, Ohio, June 9, 10, 11, and 12, 1936 Resulting in the Nomination of Alfred M. Landon, of Kansas, for President and the Nomination of Frank Knox, of Illinois, for Vice President.* New York: Tenny Press, 1936.

Hawley, Ellis W. *The New Deal and the Problem of Monopoly: A Study in Economic Ambivalence.* Princeton (NJ): Princeton University Press, 1966.

Higham, Charles. *Merchant of Dreams: Louis B. Mayer, M.G.M. and the Secret Hollywood.* New York: Donald I. Fine, 1993.

Hiltzik, Michael. *The New Deal: A Modern History.* New York: Free Press, 2011.

Hinshaw, David. *A Man from Kansas: The Story of William Allen White.* New York: G. P. Putnam's Sons, 1945.

———. *Herbert Hoover: American Quaker.* New York: Farrar, Straus & Co., 1950.

——— (ed.). *Landon: What He Stands For—The Republican Presidential Candidate Interpreted by Henry J. Allen, John Hamilton, Malcolm W. Bingay, Roy Roberts, Arthur Capper, Wm. Allen White.* New York: Mail & Express Publishing Co., 1936.

Hoge, Alice Albright. *Cissy Patterson: The Life of Eleanor Medill Patterson, Publisher and Editor of the Washington Times-Herald.* New York: Random House, 1966.

Holli, Melvin G. *The Wizard of Washington: Emil Hurja, Franklin Roosevelt, and the Birth of Public Opinion Polling.* New York: Palgrave Macmillan, 2002.

Holtzman, Abraham. *The Townsend Movement: A Political Study.* New York: Octagon Books, 1975.

Hoover, Herbert (edited by George H. Nash). *The Crusade Years, 1933–1955: Herbert Hoover's Lost Memoir of the New Deal Era and Its Aftermath.* Stanford (CA): Hoover Institution Press, 2013.

———. *The Memoirs of Herbert Hoover: The Great Depression 1929–1941.* New York: Macmillan, 1952.

Hopkins, Harry L. *Spending to Save: The Complete Story of Relief.* New York: Norton, 1936.

Horan, James D. *The Desperate Years: A Pictorial History of the Thirties.* New York: Bonanza Books, 1962.

Hutchins, Grace. *The Truth About The Liberty League.* New York: International Publishers, 1936.

Ickes, Harold L. *The Secret Diary of Harold L. Ickes, 3 vols.* New York; Simon & Schuster, 1954.

Ingalls, Robert P. *Herbert H. Lehman and New York's Little New Deal.* New York: New York University Press, 1975.

Irey, Elmer L. (as told to William J. Slocum). *The Tax Dodgers: The Inside Story of the T-Men's War with America's Political and Underworld Hoodlums.* New York: Greenberg Publisher, 1948.

Jackson, Kenneth T. (ed.). *The Encyclopedia of New York City.* New Haven (CT): Yale University Press, 1995.

Jeansonne, Glen. *Gerald L. K. Smith: Minister of Hate.* New Haven (CT): Yale University Press, 1988.

Jeffers, H. Paul. *The Napoleon of New York.* New York: John Wiley & Sons, 2002.

Johnpoll, Bernard K. *Pacifist's Progress: Norman Thomas and the Decline of American Socialism.* Chicago: Quadrangle Books, 1970.

Johnson, Claudius O. *Borah of Idaho.* New York: Longmans, Green and Co., 1940.

Johnson, Walter (ed.). *Selected Letters of William Allen White, 1899–1943.* New York: Henry Holt and Company, 1947.

Josephson, Matthew, and Hannah Josephson. *Al Smith: Hero of the Cities (A Political Portrait Drawing on the Papers of Frances Perkins).* Boston: Houghton Mifflin, 1969.

Kahn, Albert E. *High Treason: The Plot Against the People.* New York: Lear Publishers, 1950.

Kane, Harnett T. *Louisiana Hayride: The American Rehearsal for Dictatorship, 1928–1940.* New York: William Morrow, 1949.

Keiler, Allan. *Marian Anderson: A Singer's Journey.* Urbana: University of Illinois Press, 2002.

Kennedy, David M. *Freedom from Fear: The American People in Depression and War 1929–1945*. New York: Oxford University Press, 1999.

Kennedy, Joseph P. *I'm For Roosevelt.* New York: Reynal & Hitchcock, 1936.

Kennedy, Stetson. *Southern Exposure.* Garden City (NY): Doubleday & Company, 1946.

Kessler, Ronald. *The Sins of the Father: Joseph P. Kennedy and the Dynasty He Founded.* New York: Warner, 1996.

Kessner, Thomas. *Fiorello H. La Guardia and the Making of Modern New York.* New York: McGraw-Hill, 1989.

Klehr, Harvey. *The Heyday of American Communism: The Depression Decade,* New York: Basic Books, 1984.

Knopf, Terry Ann. *Rumors, Race, and Riots.* New Brunswick (NJ): Transaction Books, 1975.

Koskoff, David E. *Joseph P. Kennedy: A Life and Times.* Englewood Cliffs (NJ): Prentice Hall, 1974.

Kramer, Dale. *Heywood Broun: A Biographical Portrait.* New York: A. A. Wyn, 1949.

Kurth, Peter. *American Cassandra: The Life of Dorothy Thompson.* Boston: Little, Brown & Co., 1990.

Kurzman, Paul A. *Harry Hopkins and the New Deal.* Fair Lawn (NJ): R. E. Burdick, Inc., 1974.

Lamster, Mark. *The Man in the Glass House: Philip Johnson, Architect of the Modern Century.* New York: Little, Brown and Company, 2018.

Lash, Joseph P. *Dealers and Dreamers: A New Look at the New Deal.* Garden City (NY): Doubleday, 1988.

———. *Eleanor and Franklin: The Story of Their Relationship, Based on Eleanor Roosevelt's Private Papers.* New York: W. W. Norton & Co., 1971.

———. *Love, Eleanor: Eleanor Roosevelt and Her Friends.* Garden City (NY): Doubleday, 1982.

Latham, Earl. *The Communist Controversy in Washington: From the New Deal to McCarthy.* New York: Atheneum, 1969.

Leighton, Isabel (ed.). *The Aspirin Age: 1919–1941.* New York: Simon and Schuster, 1949.

Lemke, William. *Crimes Against Mexico.* Minneapolis: Great West Printing Company, 1915.

Leuchtenburg, William E. *Franklin D. Roosevelt and The New Deal.* New York: Harper & Row, 1963.

———. *The FDR Years: On Roosevelt and His Legacy.* New York: Columbia University Press, 1995.

———. *The White House Looks South: Franklin D. Roosevelt, Harry S. Truman, Lyndon B. Johnson.* Baton Rouge: Louisiana State University Press, 2005.

Levin, Linda Lotridge. *The Making of FDR: The Story of Stephen T. Early, America's First Modern Press Secretary.* Amherst (NY): Prometheus Books, 2008.

Lewy, Gunther. *The Cause That Failed: Communism in American Political Life.* New York: Oxford University Press, 1990.

Lichtman, Allan J. *White Protestant Nation: The Rise of the American Conservative Movement.* New York: Grove Press, 2008.

Long, Huey Pierce. *My First Days in the White House.* Harrisburg (PA): Telegraph Press, 1935.

Long, Huey P. *Share Our Wealth: Every Man a King.* Washington (DC): H. P. Long, 1935.

Lord, Russell. *The Wallaces of Iowa.* Boston: Houghton Mifflin, 1947.

Louchheim, Katie (ed.). *The Making of the New Deal: The Insiders Speak.* Cambridge (MA): Harvard University Press, 1983.

Louis, Joe (with Edna and Art Rust). *Joe Louis: My Life.* New York: Harcourt Brace Jovanovich, 1978.

Lowitt, Richard, and Maureen Beasley (eds.). *One Third of a Nation: Lorena Hickok Reports on the Great Depression.* Urbana: University of Illinois Press, 1981.

Lubbell, Samuel. *The Future of American Politics.* New York: Harper and Brothers, 1952.

Lundberg, Ferdinand. *Imperial Hearst: A Social Biography.* New York: Modern Library, 1936.

Lyons, Eugene. *The Red Decade: The Stalinist Penetration of America.* Indianapolis: Bobbs-Merrill, 1941.

Mahl, Thomas E. *Desperate Deception: British Covert Operations in the United States, 1939–44.* Dulles (VA): Potomac Books, 2000.

Manchester, William. *H. L. Mencken: Disturber of the Peace.* New York: Collier, 1962.

Mangione, Jerre. *The Dream and the Deal: The Federal Writers' Project, 1935–1943.* Syracuse (NY): Syracuse University Press, 1995.

Marcus, Sheldon. *Father Coughlin: The Tumultuous Life of the Priest of the Little Flower.* Boston: Little, Brown and Company, 1973.

Martin, George. *Madame Secretary: Frances Perkins.* Boston: Houghton Mifflin, 1976.

McCoy, Donald R. *Landon of Kansas.* Lincoln: University of Nebraska Press, 1966.

McJimsey, George. *Harry Hopkins: Ally of the Poor and Defender of Democracy.* Cambridge (MA): Harvard University Press, 1987.

McKean, David. *Tommy the Cork: Washington's Ultimate Insider from Roosevelt to Reagan.* Hanover (NH): Steerforth, 2003.

McKee, John Hiram. *Coolidge Wit and Wisdom: 125 Short Stories About "Cal."* New York: Frederick A. Stokes Company, 1933.

McLynn, Frank. *Carl Gustav Jung.* New York: St. Martin's Press, 1997.

McRae, Donald. *Heroes Without a Country: America's Betrayal of Joe Louis and Jesse Owens.* New York: Ecco, 2003.

Meijer, Hendrik. *Vandenberg: The Man in the Middle of the American Century.* Chicago: University of Chicago Press, 2017.

Michaels, Tony (ed.). *Jewish Radicals: A Documentary History.* New York: New York University Press, 2012.

Michelson, Charles. *The Ghost Talks.* New York, G. P. Putnam's Sons, 1944.

Miles, Jonathan. *The Dangerous Otto Katz: The Many Lives of a Soviet Spy.* New York: Bloomsbury, 2010.

Miller, Adrian. *The President's Kitchen Cabinet Book: The Story of the African Americans Who Have Fed Our First Families, from the Washingtons to the Obamas.* Chapel Hill: University of North Carolina Press, 2017.

Milne, Richard. *That Man Townsend.* Long Beach (CA): Prosperity Publishing Company, 1935.

Moley, Raymond. *27 Masters of Politics: In a Personal Perspective.* New York: Funk & Wagnalls Company, 1949.

———. *After Seven Years.* New York: Harper & Bros., 1939.

——— (with the assistance of Elliot A. Rosen). *The First New Deal.* New York: Harcourt, Brace & World, Inc., 1966.

Monagan, John S. *A Pleasant Institution: Key—C Major.* Lanham (MD): University Press of America, 2001.

Morgan, Ted. *FDR: A Biography.* New York: Simon and Schuster, 1985.

———. *Reds: McCarthyism in Twentieth Century America.* New York: Random House, 2003.

Morison, Elting E. (ed.). *The Letters of Theodore Roosevelt.* Cambridge (MA): Harvard University Press, 1954.

Morris, George. *The Black Legion Rides.* New York: Workers Library Publishers, Inc., 1936.

Morris, Sylvia Jukes. *Edith Kermit Roosevelt: Portrait of a First Lady.* New York: Coward, McCann & Geoghegan, 1980.

Mugglebee, Ruth. *Father Coughlin of the Shrine of the Little Flower: An Account of the Life, Work and Message of Reverend Charles E. Coughlin.* Garden City (NY): Garden City Publishing Co., 1933.

Naison, Mark. *Communists in Harlem During the Depression.* Urbana: University of Illinois Press, 1983.

Nasaw, David. *The Chief: The Life of William Randolph Hearst.* Boston: Houghton Mifflin, 2000.

———. *The Patriarch: The Remarkable Life and Turbulent Times of Joseph P. Kennedy.* New York: Penguin Press, 2012.

Navasky, Victor S. *Naming Names.* New York: Viking Press, 1980.

Nevins, Alan. *Herbert H. Lehman and His Era.* New York: Charles Scribner's Sons, 1963.

Newman, Roger K. *Hugo Black: A Biography.* New York: Fordham University Press, 1997.

Nordin, Dennis S. *The New Deal's Black Congressman: A Life of Arthur Wergs Mitchell.* Columbia: University of Missouri Press, 1997.

O'Connor, Richard. *Heywood Broun: A Biography.* New York: G. P. Putnam's Sons, 1975.

———. *The First Hurrah: A Biography of Alfred E. Smith.* New York: G. P. Putnam's Sons, 1970.

Ohl, John K. *Hugh S. Johnson and the New Deal.* Dekalb (IL): Northern Illinois University Press, 1985.

Opotowsky, Stan. *The Longs of Louisiana.* New York: E. P. Dutton, 1960.

O'Reilly, Kenneth. *Nixon's Piano: Presidents and Racial Politics from Washington to Clinton.* New York: The Free Press, 1995.

Ottanelli, Fraser M. *The Communist Party of the United States: From the Depression to World War II.* New Brunswick (NJ): Rutgers University Press, 1991.

Ottley, Roi. *"New World A-Coming": Inside Black America.* Boston: Houghton Mifflin, 1943.

Oursler, Fulton (Fulton Oursler Jr., ed.). *Behold This Dreamer! An Autobiography by Fulton Oursler.* Boston: Little, Brown and Company, 1964.

Parks, Lillian Rogers (with Frances Spatz Leighton). *The Roosevelts: A Family in Turmoil.* Englewood Cliffs (NJ): Prentice Hall, 1981.

Parmet, Robert D. *The Master of Seventh Avenue: David Dubinsky and the American Labor Movement.* New York: New York University Press, 2005.

Patenaude, Bertrand M. *The Big Show in Bololand: The American Relief Expedition to Soviet Russia in the Famine of 1921.* Stanford (CA): Stanford University Press, 2002.

Patterson, James T. *Congressional Conservatism and the New Deal: The Growth of the Conservative Coalition in Congress, 1933–1939.* Lexington: University of Kentucky Press, 1969.

Pauwels, Jacques R. *The Myth of the Good War: America in the Second World War.* Toronto: J. Lorimer, 2009.

Perkins, Frances. *The Roosevelt I Knew.* New York: Viking, 1946.

Persico, Joseph E. *Franklin and Lucy: President Roosevelt, Mrs. Rutherfurd, and the Other Remarkable Women in His Life.* New York: Random House, 2008.

Peyser, Marc, and Timothy Dwyer. *Hissing Cousins: The Lifelong Rivalry of Eleanor Roosevelt and Alice Roosevelt Longworth.* New York: Anchor Books, 2016.

Pizzitola, Louis. *Hearst Over Hollywood: Power, Passion, and Propaganda in the Movies.* New York: Columbia University Press, 2002.

Procter, Ben. *William Randolph Hearst: The Later Years, 1911–1951.* New York: Oxford University Press, 2007.

Proskauer, Joseph M. *A Segment of My Times.* New York: Farrar, Straus and Company, 1950.

Pumphrey, R. Mack. *False Messiah: The Ministry of Father Divine and the Influences of New Thought Theology on The Ministry of Father Divine.* n.p.: Xulon Press, 2007.

Quirk, Lawrence J. *The Kennedys in Hollywood.* New York: Cooper Square Press, 2004.

Radosh, Ronald, and Allis Radosh. *Red Star Over Hollywood: The Film Colony's Long Romance with the Left.* San Francisco: Encounter Books, 2005.

Reilly, Michael F., with William J. Slocum. *Reilly of the White House.* New York: Simon and Schuster, 1947.

Rigueur, Leah Wright. *The Loneliness of the Black Republican: Pragmatic Politics and the Pursuit of Power.* Princeton (NJ): Princeton University Press, 2016.

Ripley, William Z. *Main Street and Wall Street.* Boston: Little, Brown and Company, 1927.

Rodgers, Marion. *Mencken.* New York: Oxford University Press, 2005.

Rollins, Alfred B. *Roosevelt and Howe.* New York: Alfred A. Knopf, 1962.

Roosevelt, Eleanor. *The Autobiography of Eleanor Roosevelt.* New York: Harper & Brothers, 1961.

———. *This I Remember.* New York: Harper & Brothers, 1949.

Roosevelt, Elliott (ed.). *F.D.R.: His Personal Letters, 1928–1945.* New York: Duell, Sloan and Pearce, 1947.

Roosevelt, Elliott, and James Brough. *An Untold Story: The Roosevelts of Hyde Park.* New York: G. P. Putnam's Sons, 1973.

———. *Mother R.: Eleanor Roosevelt's Untold Story.* New York: G. P. Putnam's Sons, 1977.

———. *Rendezvous with Destiny: The Roosevelts in the White House.* New York: G. P. Putnam's Sons, 1975.

Roper, Elmer. *You and Your Leaders: Their Actions and Your Reactions, 1936–1956.* New York: William Morrow and Company, 1957.

Rosenman, Samuel I. *The Public Papers and Addresses of Franklin D. Roosevelt, Volume 5.* New York: Random House, 1938.

———. *Working with Roosevelt.* New York: Harper & Row, 1952.

Rosenman, Samuel I., and Dorothy Rosenman. *Presidential Style: Some Giants and a Pygmy in the White House.* New York: Harper & Row, 1976.

Ross, Jack. *The Socialist Party of America: A Complete History.* Lincoln (NE): Potomac Books, 2015.

Ross, Steven J. *Hollywood Left and Right: How Movie Stars Shaped American Politics.* New York: Oxford University Press, 2011.

Rothbard, Murray. *America's Great Depression.* Princeton (NJ): Van Nostrand, 1963.

Ryan, James G. *Earl Browder: The Failure of American Communism.* Tuscaloosa: University of Alabama Press, 1997.

Ryskind, Allan H. *Hollywood Traitors: Blacklisted Screenwriters—Agents of Stalin, Allies of Hitler.* Washington: Regnery, 2015.

Saposs, David Joseph. *Communism in American Politics.* Washington: Public Affairs Press, 1960.

Savage, Sean J. *Roosevelt: The Party Leader, 1932–1945.* Lexington: The University Press of Kentucky, 2015.

Schlesinger, Arthur M. *The Politics of Upheaval: 1935–1936, The Age of Roosevelt, Volume III.* Boston: Houghton Mifflin, 1960.

Schlesinger, Robert. *White House Ghosts: Presidents and Their Speechwriters.* New York: Simon & Schuster, 2008.

Schroeder, Alan. *Celebrity-in-Chief: How Show Business Took Over the White House.* New York: Basic Books, 2004.

Schruben, Francis W. *Kansas in Turmoil: 1930–1936.* Columbia: University of Missouri Press, 1969.

Schulze, Franz. *Philip Johnson: Life and Work.* Chicago: University of Chicago Press, 1996.

Seldes, George. *One Thousand Americans.* New York: Boni & Gaer, 1947.

Sheppard, Si. *The Buying of the Presidency? Franklin Roosevelt, the New Deal, and the Election of 1936.* Santa Barbara (CA): Praeger, 2014.

Sherrill, Robert. *Gothic Politics in the Deep South: Stars of the New Confederacy.* New York: Ballantine Books, 1968.

Sherwood, Robert E. *Roosevelt and Hopkins, an Intimate History.* New York: Harper, 1948.

Shilling, Donovan A. *They Put Rochester on the Map: Personalities of Rochester's Past.* Rochester (NY): Pancoast Publishing, 2012.

Shlaes, Amity. *The Forgotten Man: A New History of the Great Depression.* New York: HarperCollins, 2007.

Sinclair, Andrew. *The Available Man: The Life Behind the Masks of Warren Harding.* New York: Macmillan, 1965.

Sitkoff, Harvard. *A New Deal for Blacks: The Emergence of Civil Rights as a National Issue.* New York: Oxford University Press, 1978.

Slide, Anthony. *American Racist: The Life and Films of Thomas Dixon.* Lexington: University Press of Kentucky, 2004.

Smith, Amanda. *Newspaper Titan: The Infamous Life and Monumental Times of Cissy Patterson.* New York: Alfred A. Knopf, 2011.

Smith, Gerald L. K. *Huey P. Long: A Summary of Greatness, Political Genius, American Martyr.* Dandridge (TN): Dewey H. Tucker, 2015.

Smith, Jean Edward. *FDR.* New York: Random House, 2007.

Smith, Kathryn. *The Gatekeeper: Missy LeHand, FDR, and the Untold Story of the Partnership That Defined a Presidency.* New York: Touchstone, 2016.

Smith, Richard Norton. *The Colonel: The Life and Legend of Robert R. McCormick 1880–1955.* Boston: Houghton Mifflin, 1997.

Smith, Rixey, and Norman Beasley. *Carter Glass: A Biography.* New York: Longman, Green and Co., 1939.

Smith, Webster. *The Kingfish: A Biography of Huey P. Long.* New York: G. P. Putnam's Sons, 1933.

Social Security Board. *Security in Your Old Age.* Washington: Government Printing Office, 1936.

Solomon, Burt. *FDR v. the Constitution: The Court-Packing Fight and the Triumph of Democracy.* New York: Bloomsbury USA, 2009.

Solomon, Mark I. *The Cry Was Unity: Communists and African Americans, 1917–36.* Jackson (MS): University Press of Mississippi, 1998.

Spivak, John L. *The Shrine of the Silver Dollar.* New York: Modern Age Books, 1940.

Steed, Hal. *Georgia: Unfinished State.* New York: Alfred A. Knopf, 1942.

Steel, Ronald. *Walter Lippmann and the American Century.* Boston: Little, Brown & Co., 1980.

Steinberg, Alfred. *Sam Rayburn: A Biography.* New York: Hawthorn Books, Inc., 1975.

———. *The Bosses.* New York: Macmillan, 1972.

Stiles, Lila. *The Man Behind Roosevelt: The Story of Louis McHenry Howe.* Cleveland: World Publishing Company, 1954.

Stokes, Thomas L. *Chip Off My Shoulder.* Princeton (NJ): Princeton University Press, 1940.

Streitmatter, Rodger (ed.). *Empty Without You: The Intimate Letters of Eleanor Roosevelt and Lorena Hickok.* New York: The Free Press, 1998.

Stuckey, Mary E. *Voting Deliberatively: FDR and the 1936 Presidential Campaign.* University Park: Pennsylvania State University Press, 2015.

Sutton, Matthew Avery. *Aimee Semple McPherson and the Resurrection of Christian America.* Cambridge (MA): Harvard University Press, 2007.

Swanberg, W. A. *Citizen Hearst: A Biography of William Randolph Hearst.* New York: Simon and Schuster, 1961.

———. *Norman Thomas: The Last Idealist.* New York: Scribner's, 1976.

Swing, Raymond (Gram). *"Good Evening!": A Professional Memoir.* New York: Harcourt, Brace & World, 1964.

Taylor, Nick. *American-Made: The Enduring Legacy of the WPA: When FDR Put the Nation to Work.* New York: Bantam Books, 2008.

Teichmann, Howard. *Alice: The Life and Times of Alice Roosevelt Longworth.* Englewood Cliffs (NJ): Prentice Hall, 1979.

Terkel, Studs. *Hard Times: An Oral History of the Great Depression.* New York: Pantheon Books, 1986.

Thayer, George. *The Farther Shores of American Politics.* New York: Simon and Schuster, 1967.

Thomas, Norman. *After the New Deal—What?* New York: Macmillan, 1936.

Thomas, Richard W. *Life for Us Is What We Make It: Building Black Community in Detroit, 1915–1945.* Bloomington: Indiana University Press, 1992.

Timmons, Bascom N. *Garner of Texas: A Personal History.* New York: Harper, 1948.

Tompkins, C. David. *Senator Arthur H. Vandenberg: The Evolution of a Modern Republican, 1884–1945.* East Lansing: Michigan State University Press, 1970.

Trende, Sean. *The Lost Majority: Why the Future of Government Is Up for Grabs—and Who Will Take It.* New York: Palgrave Macmillan, 2012.

Trohan, Walter. *Political Animals: Memoirs of a Sentimental Cynic.* Garden City (NY): Doubleday & Co., 1975.

Tugwell, Rexford Guy. *A Chronicle of Jeopardy.* Chicago: University of Chicago, 1955.

———. *In Search of Roosevelt.* Cambridge: Harvard University Press, 1972.

———. *Roosevelt's Revolution.* New York: Macmillan, 1977.

———. *The Art of Politics: As Practised by Three Great Americans: Franklin Delano Roosevelt, Luis Muñoz Marín, and Fiorello H. La Guardia.* Garden City (NY): Doubleday & Company, 1958.

———. *The Brains Trust.* New York: Viking, 1968.

———. *The Democratic Roosevelt.* Garden City (NY): Doubleday & Co., 1957.

Tull, Charles J. *Father Coughlin and the New Deal.* Syracuse (NY): Syracuse University Press, 1965.

Tully, Grace. *F. D. R.: My Boss.* New York: Charles Scribner's Sons, 1949.

"Unofficial Observer" (pseud. of John Franklin Carter). *American Messiahs.* New York: Simon & Schuster, 1935.

———. *The New Dealers.* New York: The Literary Guild, 1934.

US Department of Commerce. *Statistical Abstract of the United States 1937.* Washington: Government Printing Office, 1938.

Vinyard, JoEllen M. *Right in Michigan's Grassroots: From the KKK to the Michigan Militia.* Ann Arbor: University of Michigan Regional, 2011.

Waldman, Louis. *Labor Lawyer.* New York: E. P. Dutton, 1944.

Wall, Joseph Frazier. *Alfred I. du Pont: The Man and His Family.* New York: Oxford University Press, 1990.

Ward, Geoffrey C. *Closest Companion: The Unknown Story of the Intimate Friendship Between Franklin Roosevelt and Margaret Suckley.* Boston: Houghton Mifflin, 1995.

Ward, Louis B. *Father Charles E. Coughlin: An Authorized Biography.* Detroit: Tower Publications, 1933.

Warren, Donald. *Radio Priest: Charles Coughlin, The Father of Hate Radio.* New York: Free Press, 1996.

Watkins, T. H. *Righteous Pilgrim: The Life and Times of Harold L. Ickes, 1874–1952.* New York: Henry Holt & Co., 1990.

Watts, Jill. *God, Harlem U.S.A.: The Father Divine Story.* Berkeley: University of California Press, 1992.

———. *The Black Cabinet: The Untold Story of African Americans and Politics During the Age of Roosevelt.* New York: Grove Press, 2020.

Weed, Clyde P. *The Nemesis of Reform: The Republican Party During the New Deal.* New York: Columbia University Press, 1994.

Weinstein, Allen, and Alexander Vassiliev. *The Haunted Wood: Soviet Espionage in America—The Stalin Era.* New York: Random House, 1999.

Weiss, Nancy Joan. *Farewell to the Party of Lincoln: Black Politics in the Age of FDR.* Princeton (NJ): Princeton University Press, 1983.

Weyl, Nathaniel. *The Jew in American Politics.* New Rochelle (NY): Arlington House, 1968.

Wheeler, Burton K. (with Paul F. Healy). *Yankee From the West: The Candid, Turbulent Life Story of the Yankee-Born U. S. Senator from Montana.* Garden City (NY): Doubleday & Company, 1962.

White, Graham J. *FDR and the Press.* Chicago: University of Chicago Press, 1979.

White, Richard. *Kingfish: The Reign of Huey P. Long.* New York: Random House, 2006.

White, Walter F. *A Man Called White: The Autobiography of Walter White.* New York: Viking Press, 1948.

White, William Allen. *The Autobiography of William Allen White.* New York: Macmillan, 1946.

Wilkerson, Isabel. *The Warmth of Other Suns: The Epic Story of America's Great Migration.* New York: Vintage Books, 2011.

Wilkins, Roy. *Standing Fast: The Autobiography of Roy Wilkins.* New York: Viking Press, 1982.

Williamson, Samuel T. *Imprint of a Publisher: The Story of Frank Gannett and His Independent Newspapers.* New York: R. M. McBride, 1948.

Winfield, Betty Houchin. *FDR and the News Media.* Urbana: University of Illinois Press, 1990.

Winkler, John K. *William Randolph Hearst: A New Appraisal.* New York: Hastings House, 1955.

Winters, Kathleen C. *Amelia Earhart: The Turbulent Life of an American Icon.* New York: Palgrave Macmillan, 2010.

Wolfskill, George. *The Revolt of The Conservatives: A History of the American Liberty League 1934–1940.* Boston: Houghton Mifflin Company, 1962.

Wolfskill, George, and John A. Hudson. *All But the People: Franklin D. Roosevelt and His Critics, 1933–1939.* New York: Macmillan, 1969.

Wolters, Raymond. *Negroes and the Great Depression: The Problem of Economic Recovery.* Westport (CT): Greenwood, 1970.

Woodbury, Marda Liggett. *Stopping the Presses: The Murder of Walter W. Liggett.* Minneapolis: University of Minnesota Press, 1998.

Wunder, Clinton. *Crowds of Souls.* New York: Fleming H. Revell Company, 1926.

Zucker, Norman L. *George W. Norris: Gentle Knight of American Democracy.* Urbana: University of Illinois Press, 1966.

DOCTORAL DISSERTATIONS

Barnes, Roma Penelope. *"Blessings Flowing Free": The Father Divine Peace Mission Movement in Harlem, New York City, 1932–1941.* York (UK): University of York, Department of History, January 1979.

Daniel, Edward O. *Sam Rayburn: Trials of a Party Man.* Denton: North Texas State, 1979.

Kopp, Eliot A. *Fritz Kuhn: The American Fuehrer and the Rise and Fall of the German-American Bund.* Boca Raton: Florida Atlantic University, 2010.

Marshall, Paul Michael. *The Union Party and the 1936 Presidential Election.* Brighton (UK): The University of Sussex, 2013.

Powell, David Owen. *The Union Party of 1936.* Columbus: Ohio State University, 1962.

PAMPHLETS

American Liberty League. *The Facts of the Case: Speech of Alfred E. Smith—American Liberty League Dinner, Washington, D.C., January 25, 1936.* Washington: American Liberty League, 1936.

American Liberty League. *The Redistribution of Power: Speech of John W. Davis—Member of the National Executive Committee of the American Liberty League*

Before the New York State Bar Association, New York City, January 24, 1936. Washington: American Liberty League, 1936.

CONGRESSIONAL DOCUMENTS

Hearings Before the Committee on Finance, United States Senate (NRA Hearings)s. *Seventy-Fourth Congress, First Session, Pursuant to S. Res. 79 A Resolution for an Investigation of Certain Charges Concerning the Administration of Industrial Codes by the National Recovery Administration Volume 1 Pages 1 to 1182, March 7 to April 4, 1935.* Washington: US Government Printing Office, 1935.

House Committee on the Judiciary. *Hearings Before Subcommittee No. 1 of the Committee on the Judiciary House of Representatives 83rd Congress 2nd Session.* Washington: US Government Printing Office, 1954.

House Committee on Un-American Activities (Testimony of Lucille Désirée Ball Arnaz), Committee on Un-American Activities, House of Representatives, 83d Cong., 1st sess., *Investigation of Communist Activities in the Los Angeles Area – Part 7*, Washington: United States Government Printing Office, 1953.

House Special Committee on Communist Activities in the United States (Fish Committee). *Investigation of Communist Propaganda. Hearings Before a Special Committee to Investigate Communist Activities in the United States of the House of Representatives, Seventy-First Congress, Second Session, Pursuant to H. Res. 220, Providing for an Investigation of Communist Propaganda in the United States.* Washington: US Government Printing Office, 1930–31.

Investigation of Lobbying Activities: Hearings Before a Special Committee to Investigate Lobbying Activities (Black Committee), United States Senate, Seventy-Fourth Congress, First[-Second] Session, Pursuant to S. Res. 165, a Resolution Providing for an Investigation of Lobbying Activities in Connection with the So-called "Holding Company Bill" (S. 2796).

Select Committee to Investigate Old-Age Pension Plans and Organizations (Bell Committee). *Hearings Before the Select Committee to Investigate Old-Age Pension Plans and Organizations Seventy-Fourth Congress, Second Session, Pursuant to H. Res. 443, Volume 1.* Washington: US Government Printing Office, 1937.

Select Committee to Investigate Old-Age Pension Plans and Organizations (Bell Committee). *Hearings Before the Select Committee to Investigate Old-Age Pension Plans and Organizations Seventy-Fourth Congress, Second Session,*

Pursuant to H. Res. 443, Volume 2. Washington: US Government Printing Office, 1937.

Select Committee to Investigate Old-Age Pension Plans and Organizations (Bell Committee). *Report of the Select Committee to Investigate Old-Age Pension Plans and Organizations Seventy-Fourth Congress, Second Session, Pursuant to H. Res. 443, Volume 1*. Washington: US Government Printing Office, 1937.

Special Committee to Investigate Lobbying Activities (Black Committee Digest Part 1). *Digest of Data from the Files of a Special Committee to Investigate Lobbying Activities, United States Senate, Seventy-Fourth Congress, Second Session Pursuant to S. Res. 165 and S. Res 184 Resolutions Resolution Providing for an Investigation of Lobbying Activities and Propaganda during the Seventy-Fourth and Succeeding Congresses, Part 1: List of Contributions*. Washington: US Government Printing Office, 1936.

Special Committee to Investigate Lobbying Activities (Black Committee Digest Part 2). *Digest of Data from the Files of a Special Committee to Investigate Lobbying Activities, United States Senate, Seventy-Fourth Congress, Second Session Pursuant to S. Res. 165 and S. Res 184 Resolutions Resolution Providing for an Investigation of Lobbying Activities and Propaganda During the Seventy-Fourth and Succeeding Congresses, Part 1: List of Contributions*. Washington: US Government Printing Office, 1936.

NEWSPAPERS

Akron (OH) Beacon Journal
Albany (NY) Evening News
Albany (NY) Knickerbocker-Press
Albany (NY) Times-Union
Alexandria (LA) Town Talk
American Israelite (Cincinnati)
Amsterdam (NY) Evening Recorder
The Arizona Republic (Phoenix, AZ)
Atlanta Constitution
Auburn (NY) Citizen-Advertiser
Ballston Spa (NY) Daily Journal
Baltimore Afro-American
Baltimore Evening Sun
Baltimore Sun
Bangor (ME) Daily News
Battle Creek (MI) Enquirer
Beacon (NY) News
Berkshire Evening Eagle (Pittsfield, MA)
Binghamton (NY) Press
Boston Globe
Boston Pilot
Brattleboro (VT) Reformer
Bridgewater (NJ) Courier-News
Brooklyn Times Union
Buffalo Courier-Express
Buffalo Evening-News
California Eagle (Los Angeles)
Cattaraugus (NY) Republican

Chicago Tribune
Cincinnati Enquirer
Cleveland Gazette
Coshocton (OH) Tribune
Cumberland (MD) Evening Times
Dayton (OH) Daily News
Dayton (OH) Herald
Decatur (AL) Daily
Decatur (IL) Daily Review
Des Moines Register
Des Moines Tribune
Detroit Free Press
Detroit Jewish Chronicle
Detroit Times
Dothan (AL) Eagle
Elmira (NY) Star-Gazette
El Paso (TX) Herald-Post
Elyria (OH) Chronicle-Telegram
Emporia (KS) Gazette
Eugene (OR) Register-Guard
Fort Myers (FL) News-Press
The Forum (Dayton, OH)
Geneva (NY) Daily Times
Glens Falls (NY) Post-Standard
Gloversville (NY) Morning Herald
Great Falls (MT) Tribune
Greenville (SC) News
Hackensack (NJ) Record
Hagerstown (MD) Morning Herald
Hammond (IN) Times
Hanover (PA) Evening Sun
Harrisburg (PA) Sunday Courier
Helena Daily (MT) Independent
Hutchinson (KS) News
Jefferson City (MO) Capital News
Jewish Advocate (Boston)
Jewish Daily Bulletin
Jewish Telegraphic Agency
Kansas City (KS) Plaindealer
Kansas City (MO) Times
Kingston (NY) Daily Freeman
Knoxville (TN) News-Sentinel
Lancaster (OH) Eagle-News
Lancaster (PA) New Era
Lawrence (KS) Daily Journal-World
Lockport (NY) Union-Sun and Journal
Los Angeles Evening Citizen News (Hollywood, CA)
Los Angeles Record
Los Angeles Times
Louisville Courier-Journal
Manhattan (KS) Mercury
Manhattan (KS) Morning Chronicle
Massillon (OH) Evening Independent
The Michigan Daily (The University of Michigan)
Milford (UT) News
Millbrook (NY) Round Table
Moberly (MO) Monitor-Index
Montgomery (AL) Advertiser
Muncie (IN) Evening Press
Nashville Tennessean
Nebraska State Journal
Negro Star (Wichita, KS)
New Militant
New York Age
New York Amsterdam News
New York Daily News
New York Daily Worker

New York Evening Post
New York Herald Tribune
New York Sun
New York Times
New York Tribune
Niagara Falls (NY) Gazette
Norfolk (VA) Journal and Guide
North Shore (NY) Daily Journal
North Tonawanda (NY) Evening News
Oakland (CA) Tribune
Oklahoma News (Oklahoma City, OK)
Oshkosh (WI) Northwestern
Palm Beach (FL) Post
Park City Daily News (Bowling Green, KY)
Pasadena (CA) Post
Patterson (NJ) Morning Call
Philadelphia Inquirer
Philadelphia Public Ledger
Pittsburgh Courier
Pittsburgh Post-Gazette
Pittsburgh Press
Pittsburgh Sun-Telegraph
Plainfield (NJ) News-Courier
Poughkeepsie (NY) Eagle-News
Poughkeepsie (NY) Star-Enterprise
Racine (WI) Journal-Times
Raleigh (NC) News and Observer
Randolph (NY) Register
Reading (PA) Times
Richmond (VA) Times-Dispatch
Rochester (NY) Democrat and Chronicle
Rochester (NY) Times-Union
Rome (NY) Daily Sentinel
Sacramento Bee
Salamanca (NY) Republican
San Bernardino (CA) Sun
Sandusky (OH) Register
Saratoga Springs (NY) Saratogian
Schenectady (NY) Gazette
Scott County (Scottsburg, IN) Journal
Scranton (PA) Times
Shreveport (LA) Times
Socialist Call (NYC)
St. Joseph (MO) Gazette
St. Louis Post-Dispatch
St. Louis Star and Times
Spokane (WA) Spokesman-Review
Stevens Point (WI) Daily Journal
Summer Texan (University of Texas, Austin, TX)
Tampa Bay Times (St. Petersburg, FL)
Thomasville (GA) Times-Enterprise
Uniontown (PA) Standard
Utah Labor News (Salt Lake City)
Utica (NY) Observer-Dispatch
Valparaiso (IN) Vidette-Messenger of Porter County
Victoria (BC) Daily Times
The Wall Street Journal
Washington (DC) Evening Star
Washington (DC) Examiner
Washington (DC) Post
Washington (DC) Times-Herald
Washington (DC) Tribune
The Weekly People (New York, NY)
Wilmington (DE) Evening Journal
Wilmington (DE) Morning News
Wilmington (DE) News Journal
Windsor (ON) Star

Wisconsin Jewish Chronicle (Milwaukee)
Workers Age
Wyandotte Echo (Kansas City, KS)
Yonkers (NY) Herald-Statesman

PERIODICALS

American Heritage
The American Historical Review
American Jewish History
The American Magazine
The American Mercury
The American Political Science Review
Arthuriana
Broadcasting
California History
Collier's Weekly
Comparative Studies in Society and History
Congressional Record
Comparative Studies in Society and History
The Communist
The Crisis
Explorations in Economic History
The Forum
The Georgia Historical Quarterly
Historic Journal of Massachusetts
Indiana Magazine of History
The Journal of Blacks in Higher Education
The Journal of Negro History
The Journal of Policy History
The Journal of Southern History
Labor Defender
The Literary Digest
Michigan Historical Review
The Modern Monthly
The Nation
The National Corporation Reporter
The New International
The New Masses
The New Outlook
New Theatre
New York History
The New Yorker
News-Week
Oklahoma Law Review
The Pacific Northwest Quarterly
Pennsylvania Magazine of History and Biography
Phylon
Political Science Quarterly
Public Opinion Quarterly
Records of the American Catholic Historical Society of Philadelphia
Reviews in American History
The Saturday Evening Post
Social Justice
Social Science History
The "Spoken Word"
The Student (Wake Forest University)
Time
The Western Political Quarterly

⁋ SOURCES ⁋

CAST OF CHARACTERS

vii. "is by nature . . . scratching himself." *American Mercury*, May 1936, p. 5. **vii.** "The Bookkeeper" Morgan (*Reds*), p. 168. **vii.** "mastermind of the Townsend plan." Bell Committee, p. 18. **viii.** "impossible and preposterous." *Washington Star*, 26 January 1936, p. 6. **viii.** "an able brilliant . . . another Harvard man [FDR]." McKean, p. 68. **viii.** "an intellectual crook . . . could see him." McKean, p. 72. **viii.** "He just used me." Marcus, p. 70. **ix.** "the end of western civilization." *The Forum*, October 1939, p. 188 **ix.** "I can no . . . alliances with Communists." Parmet, p. 130. **ix.** "Steve the Earl." Parks & Leighton, p. 61. **ix.** "every state except Maine and Vermont." *Binghamton Press*, 4 November 1936, p. 10. **x.** "ooze with nigger blood." *NY Daily Worker*, 1 September 1936, p. 2. **x.** "no claim to infallibility" *Buffalo Evening News*, 30 October 1936, p. 37. **x.** "Rally round it." Tull, p. 144; Marcus, p. 127. **x.** "what ages, what economic groups." *Philadelphia Inquirer*, 9 August 1936, p. 7. **x.** "dead mouse in a mince pie." "Unofficial Observer" (*New Dealers*), p. 271. Words of John Franklin Carter. **x.** "would be in no way surprising." *Binghamton Press*, 4 November 1936, p. 10. **xi.** "smell of lilies and attract the undertaker." *Emporia Gazette*, 9 April 1936, p. 4. **xi.** "That's why I . . . with this stuff." Marcus, p. 135. **xi.** "a pitiable spectacle . . . none—except himself." Beard, pp. 155, 314. **xi.** "The trouble with . . . his own money." Creel, p. 296. **xi.** "Felix the Cat." Parks & Leighton, p. 86. **xi.** "I think it . . . my husband sustained." Roosevelt (*Remember*), p. 144. **xi.** "If present trends . . . the New Deal." *Charlotte News*, 25 June 1936, p. 8. **xii.** "professional public nuisance in Chicago." *American Mercury*, October 1936, p. 264. **xi.** "for myself or for my children." Kennedy (*Roosevelt*), p. 3. **xi.** "never liked me . . . found me useful." Blair & Blair, pp. 16–17. **xi.** "Jewish bacillus-carriers." *NY Times*, 1 April 1936, p. 22; Kopp, p. 41. **xiii.** "He comes to . . . fifty million dollars." Kessner, pp. 336–37. **xiii.** "I have found Americans." Schlesinger (*Upheaval*), p. 607. **xiii.** "all he could . . . money and agriculture." Marcus, p. 114. **xiii.** "The interests supporting . . . a Fascist state." *NY Daily Worker*, 19 October 1936, p. 5. **xiii.** "a damned sight . . . is a radical." Woodbury, p. 67. **xiii.** "unreal and unnecessary . . . the utmost importance." *NY Herald Tribune*, 8 September 1936, p. 21. **xiv.** "We got the . . . have the graft." *The Atlantic*, November 1935, p. 526. **xiv.** "one-third mush and two-thirds Eleanor." "Unofficial Observer" (*New Dealers*), p. 215. **xiv.** "bootlegger and alleged 'dope peddler.'" Bell Committee, p. 48. **xiv.** "chief right hand men." *Schenectady Gazette*, 18 July 1936, p. 4. **xiv.** "Lizzie, I believe . . . for those accomplishments." *St. Louis Post-Dispatch*, 17 October 1936, p. 3. **xiv.** "There was a . . . even a Republican." *American*

Mercury, March 1936, p. 265. **xv.** "Charlie the Mike**"** Michelson, p. 192. **xiv.** "nearly, if not . . . one hundred seats." Weed, p. 106. **xiv.** "A truly gifted . . . a political hack." Draper, p. 126. **xiv.** "out-Huey Longing Huey Long." Terkel, p. 253. **xiv.** "I don't trust . . . don't like him." Caro, p .426. **xiv.** "I am a . . . for white supremacy." Schlesinger (*Upheaval*), p. 522. **xiv.** "Hamburger Tom" Steinberg (*Bosses*), p. 182. **xiv.** "will be wiped out forever." *Social Justice*, 29 June 1936, p. 5. **xiv.** "from the capitol to the White House." Tull, p. 109. **xv.** "I am . . . am a radical." Wolfskill & Hudson, p. 136. **xv.** "will save us from a dictatorship here." *California Eagle*, 2 October 1936, p. 1 **xv.** . "Fear is depressing . . . fear of you." *Washington Times-Herald*, 6 April 1936, p. 1. **xv.** "Mr. Landon ought to get hot." *Oklahoma News*, 5 June 1936, p. 8. **xvi.** "very definite organization . . . to get rich." *American Historical Review*, October 1950, p. 19; Farber, p. 295. **xvii.** "So long as . . . was with them." Patterson, p. 65. **xvii.** "I realize more . . . be anything else." Lash (*Love*), p. 242. **xvii.** "Jay the Rose.**"** Parks & Leighton, pp. 62, 86. **xvii.** "people must be . . .or against me." Schlesinger (*Upheaval*), p. 578. **xvii.** "even more . . . than her son." Trohan, p. 102. **xvii.** "Lots of things . . . changes very quickly." Rosenman (*Working*), p. 99. **xvii.** "do not believe . . . or revolutionary changes." *Hagerstown Morning Herald*, 19 February 1936, p. 1. **xviii.** "certainly isn't anti-New Deal . . ." *LA Times*, 23 August 1934, p. 1. **xviii.** "There can be . . . of Communistic Russia." *NY Times*, 26 January 1936, p. 36. **xviii.** "greatest rabble-rouser since Peter the Hermit." Schlesinger (*Upheaval*), p. 627. **xviii.** "I am a . . . of the yellers." *NY Herald Tribune*, 16 August 1936, p. A-2. **xviii.** "church-going, Bible-reading . . . country from Communism." *Victoria Daily Times*, 29 June 1936, p. 4. **xviii.** "prim spinster" Ward (*Companion*), p. *ix*. **xviii.** "The President is . . . can I say." Ward (*Companion*), p. *x*. **xix.** "more like a . . . of that rodent." Ickes (*Diary*), p. 675; Schlesinger (*Upheaval*), p. 521. **xix.** "Mr. Roosevelt did . . . on a stretcher." *NY Times*, 3 February 1936, p. 6. **xix.** "Just think. They. . . liberated all mankind." *NY Post*, 16 July 1936, p. 4. **xix.** "The Sweetheart of the Regimenters." *American Mercury*, September 1936, p. 77. **xix.** "It has already . . . is literally meant." *The American Economic Review*, March 1932, Vol 22, p. 89. **xix.** "the only Senator . . . strut sitting down." Meijer, p. 57. **xix.** "more like a . . . Northerner in history." *American Mercury*, January 1947, p. 6. **xix.** "My friends, go . . . paid in full." *Pittsburgh Courier*, 13 February 1952, p. 5. **xix.** "crazy but he gets his way" Stiles, p. 251. **xix.** "Weiss, Dr. Weiss . . . shoot me for?" Williams, p. 866. **xx.** "[A] converted pocketbook . . . a good beginning." Wunder, p. 115; Bell Committee Hearings, Vol. 1, p. 850.

I "FRANKLIN IS ON HIS OWN NOW"

1. "I don't care". *NY Post*, 8 November 1928, p. unknown; Lash (*Eleanor*), p. 320. **1.** "[W]hen Eleanor was . . . a certain kind." Costigliola, p. 680. **1.** "an armed truce . . . enter his embrace." Lash (*Love*), pp. 71–72. **1.** "Do you think . . . chances of re-election?" Faber, pp. 189, 358. **2.** "So would I . . . married to Franklin." Lash (*Eleanor*), pp. 347–48, 736. **2.** Description of Howe's suite. Oursler, pp. 405–06. Fulton Oursler counted a dozen portraits of Eleanor; only one of Franklin. **3.** Wheelchair. Roosevelt & Brough (*Hyde Park*), p. 300. **2.** "I had never . . . last day alive." Oursler, pp. 404–05. **2.** "Why in Hell . . . me a cigarette?" Rollins, p. 443. **2.** Telephone. Roosevelt & Brough (*Hyde Park*), p. 300. **3.** Howe in bed. Stiles, p. 291; Ickes (*Diary*), p. 552. **4.** Polio. Smith (*Gatekeeper*), p. 174. **4.** "The way we . . . cared too much." Parks & Leighton, p. 238. **4.** "not one to . . . form of shyness." Stiles, p. 289. **4.** "despite his very . . . a long period." Goodwin, p. 245. Perhaps even more interesting than what Ickes writes is what he does not write, who he does not mention as anyone FDR might, even fleetingly, care about: Eleanor. **4.** "Roosevelt had absolutely . . . it didn't exist." Goodwin, pp. 245, 668. **4.** "I have been . . . hero to me." *Saturday Evening Post*, 12 October 1940, p. 422. **5.** Eleanor at bedside. Lash (*Eleanor*), p. 434. **5.** "when F.D.R. was . . . *anyone else has!*" Faber, pp. 281, 367. On November 15, 1940. **5.** "I think it . . . my husband sustained." Roosevelt (*Remember*), p. 144. **6.** "The young brain . . . with their clothes." *Washington Star*, 26 January 1936, p. 6. **7.** "No one has . . . the Federal Government." *NY Times*, 11 August 1935, p. E1. **7.** "the consolidation of . . . transition to Fascism." *New International*, March 1935, pp. 40–43. **7.** "great and earnest . . . across the seas." *NY Daily News*, 24 October 1935, p. 6. **7.** January 1936 poll. *Literary Digest*, 18 January 1936, pp. 10–11. **8.** Battleground states. *Richmond Times-Dispatch*, 19 January 1936, p. 33. **8.** "Roosevelt's strength has been waning rapidly." *New Republic*, 29 January 1936, p. 325. **8.** Keller description. Monagan, p. 87. **8.** "Plant Protection Administration." *Saturday Evening Post*, 12 October 1940, p. 134. **8.** "Of course, you'll . . . his own now." *Saturday Evening Post*, 12 October 1940, p. 42; Stiles, p. 298.

2 "TRY SOMETHING"

10. Michigan. https://www.ssa.gov/history/reports/ces/cesbookc3.html. **10.** "Members find it . . . cannot be accepted." *NY Times*, 5 March 1933, p. E6. **10.** Eleanor. Morgan (*FDR.*), p. 373. **10.** "We are at . . . we can do." Joslin, p. 366. **10.** "No secret of . . . ever escaped her" "Unofficial Observer" (*New Dealers*), p. 232. John Franklin Carter's words. **10.** "That's his political . . . madder than hell." Persico (*Lucy*), p. 223. **11.** "voracious . . . in his . . . a flypaper mind." Burns, p. 155. **11.** "His character was. . . . quarrelsome, recalcitrant men." Sherwood, p. 11. **11.** "You see, I'm . . . it at first!'" Creel, p. 332. **12.** "Never let your . . . way he works." Blum (*Morgenthau*), p. 127. **12.** "a consummate actor and an unmitigated liar." Browder & Smith, p. 129. **12.** "that FDR's first . . . bit of it." Trohan, p. 60. **12.** "Long had made . . . myself any longer." Ickes (*Diary*), p. 606. **13.** Spending cuts. Hallgren, p. 305; Morgan (*FDR*), p. 378; Brands, pp. 320–22. **13.** "The federal government . . . courage and determination." Taylor, pp. 160–61. **13.** "Before long the . . . and perfectly plausible." Brands, p. 320. The payment of benefits and the collection of taxes often seemed politically timed. Bonus checks—averaging $583 to 3,518,191 for eligible war veterans—did not go out until mid-June 1936, during the GOP Convention (Sheppard, pp. 15, 59). Conversely, Social Security payroll taxes, enacted back in August 1935, were not collected until following the 1936 election. **13.** "Take a method . . . means, try something." *NY Times*, 23 May 1932, pp. 1, 6. **14.** Production increases. *Explorations in Economic History*, July 2016, p. 54; https://www.sciencedirect.com/science/article/abs/pii/S0014498316300122. **14.** Hourly employment. *Explorations in Economic History*, July 2016, p. 54; https://www.sciencedirect.com/science/article/abs/pii/S0014498316300122. **14.** "People don't realize . . . trouble after that." Terkel, pp. 250–51. It was an old idea, actually. William Jennings Bryan advocated deposit insurance in his 1908 campaign. (*Chicago Tribune*, 27 October 1908, p. 4) **16.** "by all means . . . again broken down." *NY Times*, 23 May 1932, pp. 1, 6. **16.** "[T]he Oglethorpe speech . . . of collectivism." Tugwell (*Democratic*), p. 219. **16.** "a great cooperative . . . and disastrous overproduction." Rosenman (*1933*), p. 202. **16.** "To plan or . . . be the question." *Wall Street Journal*, 5 May 1933, p. 1. **16.** "large measure of . . . anti-trust law prosecutions." *Wall Street Journal*, 5 May 1933, p. 1. **16.** "the murderous doctrine . . . take the hindmost." Schlesinger (*Coming*), p. 88. **16.** Maged. *NY Times*, 22 April 1934, p. 36; *NY Times*, 1 April 1939, p. 19. **17.** "Unless labor is . . . escape from it." Swing, p. 173. **17.** *The Corporate State*. Perkins, p. 206; Ohl, p. 122. **17.** "If I were . . . the United States." Lowitt & Beasley, p. 218. **17.** "I am much . . . of restoring Italy." Schivelbusch, pp. 44–46. **17.** in the event . . . a foreign foe." *Pittsburgh Press*, 4 March 1933, p. 3. **17.** "As new commander-in-chief . . . now confronts us." Alter, p. 4. **18.** "This was dictator . . . explicit power grab." Alter, p. 5. **18.** Drinking. Ohl, pp. 29–30, 74, 106, 122, 151–52, 167–68, 170, 234–35. **18.** Robinson. Ohl, pp. 152–57, 170–71. **18.** "This is the end . . . do their work." Schlesinger (*Upheaval*), p. 280. **18.** "We have been . . . of interstate commerce" *Minneapolis Star*, 14 March 1938, p. 10. **18.** "You know the . . . will be over." Perkins, pp. 252–53. **18.** Farm prices. Sheppard, p. 13. **19.** "Henry, through July . . . Is that clear?" Culver & Hyde, p. 163. **19.** "The Greatest Butcher in Christendom." Barzman, p. 234. **19.** "By some means . . . sort of chance." Lowitt & Beasley, p. 212. **19.** AAA Gallup poll. *Philadelphia Inquirer*, 5 January 1936, p. 9. **20.** "He is at . . . let them down." *Political Quarterly*, July-September 1950, p. 262. **19.** "the best actor . . . voice in radio." Best, p. 2. **20.** "Roosevelt is the . . . destroy that fate." Best, p. 6. **20.** "[T]he braintrust is . . . in public affairs." Best, p. 6. **21.** "Roosevelt laughs and . . . is no ash." *Pittsburgh Press*, 26 October 1936, p. 23. **21.** "I felt that . . . and how able." Best, pp. 3, 226. **21.** "I have gathered . . . make America over!" Schlesinger (*Crisis*), p. 194. **21.** Hopkins. Morgan (*FDR*), p. 384. **21.** "one of the . . . untidy—impossible socially." Ward (*Companion*), p. 23. **21.** "forever putting chips . . . to knock off." Trohan, p. 145. Trohan's view. **21.** "insinuated" *Saturday Evening Post*, 26 October 1935, p. 85. **21.** "happy hot dogs." *Saturday Evening Post*, 26 October 1935, p. 7. **21.** "obscure but key . . . [New Deal] department." *Saturday Evening Post*, 26 October 1935, p. 85. **21.** "[H]e had been . . . had totalitarian leanings." Tugwell (*Democratic*), p. 414. **22.** Teetotaler. Michelson, pp. 132, 135. **22.** "You kiss the . . . as we choose." Wolfskill & Hudson, p. 25. A noteworthy Eleanor kiss was of Black NYA official Mary McLeod Bethune (Weiss [*Lincoln*], p. 122). "Eleanor kissed very few people, seldom even her children. She rarely even kissed her husband," noted White House maid Lillian Rogers Parks (Parks & Leighton, p. 220). **22.** "The Rosenvelts in . . . they were both." *Detroit Jewish Chronicle*, 15 March 1935, p. 1. Not all the racial rumors were aimed at Roosevelt. The *Chicago Tribune*–backed gubernatorial candidate "Curley" Brooks (so nicknamed because of his "kinky" hair") found himself pilloried for possessing "Negro blood" (*Time*, 27 April 1936, pp. 12–13). **23.** "He comes to . . . fifty million dollars." Kessner, pp. 336–37; Taylor, p. 187. **23.** *Macbeth*. Taylor, pp. 255, 261–63. **23.** 700,000. Jackson, pp. 1274–75. **23.** One-seventh. Caro, p. 453; Taylor, p. 187. **23.** "You can't imagine . . . with post offices." *Saturday Evening Post*, 26 September 1936, p. 5. **24.** "dumb people criticize . . . need any apologies!" Sherwood, p. 60. **24.** "Who's going to . . . pay for it." Taylor, p. 183. **24.** "We Poke Along" Smith (*Gatekeeper*), p. 162. **24.** "thousands of inconsequential . . . of the country." Smith (*Gatekeeper*), p. 162. As liberal as Ickes might be on the big issues (and he was *very* liberal), he remained stubbornly conservative in expending public funds. "One of my favorite stories," chortled Arthur Goldschmidt, who ultimately worked for both Hopkins and Ickes, "is that he took the doors off the booths in the men's room so people couldn't sit and read the newspaper too long" (Louchheim, p. 248). **24.** "a lawless individual . . . the President's re-election." Ickes (*Diary*), p. 434. **24.** Hopkins leaked. Trohan, p. 144. Henry Wallace was also ratting on Ickes. **25.** "a virtual OGPU . . . employing 1,000 detectives." *Tampa Bay Times*, 10 February 1940, p. 4. **25.** "Glavis became a . . . it was wired." *Pacific Northwest Quarterly*, April 1964, p. 74. **24–26.** Ickes affair. Watkins, pp. 355–57, 360–62; *Reviews in American History*, December 1991, p. 548. **26.** "the character we . . . on the outside." *New Yorker*, 5 June 1954, p. 126. **26.** Hopkins-Ickes feud resolved. Sherwood, pp. 78–79; Davis (*FDR*), pp. 582–88; Taylor, pp. 201–02. **26.** "I'm not criticizing . . . forestry is a joke" Oursler, pp. 396–98. **26.** C.C.C. popularity. *Philadelphia Inquirer*, 5 July 1936, p. 7. Seventy-seven percent of all those polled, however, also favored "military training" as part of the C.C.C. camp regimen. This, of course, was at a time when isolationist sentiment was reaching a peak. Go figure. **27.** Numbers employed. U.S. Department of Commerce, p. 333; Sheppard, p. 135. **27.** "[T]he elections would . . . as campaign fodder." Smith & Beasley, p. 370. **27.** Patronage. Sheppard, p. 131. **27.** Postmasters. Sheppard, p. 131. **27.** "F.R.B.C." "Unofficial Observer" (*New Dealers*), p. 145. **27.** "The vast maneuver . . . and transform it." Tugwell (*Democratic*), p. 415. **28.** "Mr. Roosevelt in . . . escape from it." *Literary Digest*, 7 April 1934, p. 10. **28.** "We'll have eight . . . a progressive one." Tugwell (*Democratic*), p. 412. **28.** Johnson/WPA. McJimsey, p. 92. **29.** "a Democrat of convenience." Tugwell (*Democratic*), p. 413. **29.** "saw no alternative . . . Republican as Democratic." Tugwell (*Democratic*), p. 410. **29.** "The transmission from . . . the American people" Rosenman (*1935*), p. 272. **30.** "it is disgusting . . . we will adjourn." Patterson, pp. 60–61. **30.** "For the moment . . . his political gains." Kennedy (*Fear*), p. 284. **30.** "jubilation. Over ten . . . that of 1929." Hawley, pp. 131–32. **30.** "any experienced reporter . . . recover its losses." Rosenman (*1935*), p. 353. Former Republican National Chairman Charles D. Hilles observed to James Wadsworth in June 1935: "In the old days we were opposed by a party whose slogan was 'a tariff for revenue only.' Now the fact is, whatever the slogan may be, that it is a party which favors a tax not only for revenue, but for revenge" (Patterson, p. 59). **31.** "very considerable legislative . . . breathing spell." Rosenman (*1935*), p. 357; Moley (*Seven*), p. 318. **31.** "The Communist road . . . the new world." *New Masses*, September 1932, p. 22. **31.** "The American People . . . take the label." Landa, p. 120. **31–32.** Townsend, 1932. *NY Herald Tribune*, 23 March 1936, p. 31. **32.** "the money changers in the temple." Warren, pp. 47, 52. FDR himself employed the term "money changers" not once but twice in his first inaugural address.

3 "ONE BULLET"

33. "He is the . . . appear before me." Deutsch, p. 25; Smith (*Long*), p. 10. **33.** The Comrade. *Louisiana History*, Winter 2012, p. 52. **34.** "Every man a . . . wears a crown." Steinberg (*Bosses*), p. 221. **34.** Socialists. *Journal of Southern History*, August 1954, pp. 316, 322; *Louisiana History*, Winter 2012, p. 53; Taylor, p. 149. **34.** Sedition Act. *Louisiana History*, Winter 2012, pp. 51–67; Williams, pp. 113–15. **35.** "We got the . . . have the graft." *The Atlantic*, November 1935, p. 526. **35.** 2%-5%. Irey, p. 117. **35.** "[I]mpeachment did something . . . made him vicious." Williams, p. 410. **35.** Nicknames. *Saturday Evening Post*, October 12 1935, p. 82.

35. "Constipational League." *Saturday Evening Post,* October 12 1935, p. 82. **35.** "have to grow . . . crop of legislators." *Saturday Evening Post,* October 12 1935, p. 82. **35.** "I want to . . . there myself someday." Williams, p. 107. **35.** "It almost gave . . . measuring it all." Williams, p. 107. **36.** "a nuisance without becoming a power." "Unofficial Observer" (*New Dealers*), p. 359. Quote from John Franklin Carter. **36.** "circus hitched to a tornado." Williams, p. 591. **36.** Lose to Hoover. Williams, p. 553. **37.** "I don't like . . . be for him." Wheeler, p. 285; Williams, p. 573; Brands, p. 399. To Burton K. Wheeler. **37.** "We never again underestimated him." Farley (*Ballots*), p. 171. **37.** "When I talk . . . 'Fine!' to everybody." Schlesinger (*Old Order*), p. 619. **37.** Voting record. Brinkley, p. 76. **37.** "Every fault of . . . last blind vote." *Congressional Record,* 7 June 1933, p. 5178. **37.** "Men it will . . . lead the mob." Schlesinger (*Upheaval*), p. 66. **37–38.** "What the hell . . . decision over him?" Farley (*Ballots*), pp. 240–42. H. W. Brands places this meeting in June 1933, but FDR's appointments calendar indicates it transpired on July 25. **38.** "What Huey was . . . out of Roosevelt." Williams, p. 537. **38.** "pay them my . . . go to hell." Williams, p. 639. **39.** "It is here . . . still weep here." Leighton, p. 349. Delivered in St. Martinsville, Louisiana. **39.** "The American people . . . want more money." *The Nation,* 25 September 1935, p. 344. **39–40.** "enough for a . . . educate their children." Long (*Share*), p. 14. **39–40.** "to maintain a family in comfort." Brinkley, p. 72. **39–40.** "Old Age Pensions . . . have never failed." Long (*Share*), p. 1. **39–40.** "God invited us . . . of it back." *Congressional Record,* 14 January 1935, p. 412. Harry Hopkins paralleled Long's thinking in August 1934, in stating: "We ought to get rid of the present relief scheme and get a permanent relief scheme in its place. It will cost a lot more for this permanent scheme, and we won't get it without doing away with a larger percentage of the luxuries now taking up or consuming so much of our national income. . . . I am sure that in the future the national income will be so divided that people can get a decent living. We cannot deliver an American civilization and let millions of people live as we have permitted them to live. . . . Some have far more than they need" (*Baltimore Sun,* 24 August 1934, p. 19). **40–41.** "'They' tell you . . . not till then." Smith (*Kingfish*), p. 271. **41.** Tax plan. Brinkley, p. 72. **41.** Economist estimate. Bennett, p. 121. **41.** "It must be . . . to give anything." Long (*Share*), p. 4. **41.** Membership/circulation. "Unofficial Observer" (*Messiahs*), p. 23. **41.** Mailing list. "Unofficial Observer" (*Messiahs*), p. 22. **41.** 25 million. Williams, p. 810. **42.** "Long had less . . . in the Senate." Wheeler, p. 282. **42.** "I'm not working . . . for themselves." *The Crisis,* February 1935, p. 41. **42.** "Don't say I'm . . . specially for niggers." *The Crisis,* February 1935, p. 52. **42.** "One of . . . voting? No sirree!" *The Crisis,* February 1935, p. 41. **42.** "Well, I don't . . . right to boast?" Wheeler, p. 284. **42.** "a grown-up bad boy." Swing, p. 179. **42.** "not boring." Davis (*FDR*), p. 494; Leuchtenburg (*New Deal*), p. 98. **42–43.** "Huey Long had . . . the great tragedies." Terkel, p. 253. **42–43.** "is so high-strung . . . whatever he says." "Unofficial Observer" (*Messiahs*), p. 6. **42–43.** "Every serious blunder . . . influence of liquor." Smith (*Long*), p. 39. **42–43.** Hutton's race. Hajdu, p. 64. **42–43.** "I'll eat this . . . too fat already." White (*Kingfish*), p. 185. **43.** "It is not . . . the assault themselves." Schlesinger (*Upheaval*), pp. 57–58. **44.** World War I. Leighton, p. 347; Williams, p. 115. **44.** "yellowest physical coward . . . ever let live." *Alexandria Daily Town Talk,* 12 February 1940, p. 11. **44.** "Well, I don't . . . to catch him." Wheeler, p. 282. **44.** "Long and his . . . on the loot." Irey, p. 91. **44.** "Why have you . . . on the Louisiana job." Irey, pp. 91–92. **44.** Indictments. "Unofficial Observer" (*Messiahs*), p. 25. **44.** "Don't put anybody . . . and every agency." Davis (*FDR*), p. 494. "Roosevelt also toyed with . . . making a deal with . . . Long," noted FDR biographer Frank Freidel. ". . . [O]n two occasions Long approached Attorney General Homer Cummings to find out how he could avoid being charged with corruption. The president never had to decide whether to make Long an offer" (Freidel [*Rendezvous*], p. 186). **44.** "The Vice-President said . . . the Vice-President." *Morgenthau Diary*, Book 4. p. 143 (22 March 1935). **44.** "Hell, if Jim Farley . . . in the Senate." *The Atlantic*, November 1935, p. 523. **45.** "need either to . . it to quietly!" Ward (*Companion*), p. 17. As in the case of Missy LeHand, controversy remains heated regarding the exact nature of FDR's close relationship with Daisy Suckley. A tantalizing hint to some is Daisy's August 1933 diary entry: "The President is a man—*mentally, physically* & *spiritually*. What more can I say" (Ward [*Companion*], p. *x*). **45.** "the bankers have . . . Supreme Court decision." Bowers, pp. 288–89. FDR exaggerated his predicament with the metropolitan press, particularly since plans were afoot (though never realized) for Bowers to return home to write for one or the other of Democrat J. David Stern's two most prominent dailies, the *Philadelphia Record* or the *New York Evening Post* (*Indiana Magazine of History*, March 1996, p. 34). **45.** "I was so . . . and hurting them." Freidel (*Rendezvous*), p. 185. **45.** "1940 will be my real year." Bennett, p. 127. **45.** Edsel Ford. Bell, p. 158. **46.** Borah, Talmadge, Sinclair. *The Atlantic*, November 1935, p. 523. **46.** "So the Democratic . . . but skin 'em!" *Saturday Evening Post*, 15 August 1932, p. 90. **47.** "It was easy . . . might spell disaster." Farley (*Ballots*), pp. 249–50. **47.** "Hoover is the . . . chance on anything." *The Atlantic*, November 1935, p. 523. **47.** Hoover, Borah. Long (*White House*), p. 6. **47.** Smith. Long (*White House*), p. 8. **47.** "What in the . . . qualified to fill." Long (*White House*), p. 18. **48.** National Guard, police. White (*Kingfish*), p. 208. **48.** "I am not . . . made poor slaves." Leighton, p. 343. **48.** "There is no . . . not just showmanship." "Unofficial Observer" (*Messiahs*), p. 7. **48.** Shotguns. Krock, pp. 174–75. **48.** "This is a . . . money they needed." *Pittsburgh Press*, 10 August 1935, p. 3. **48.** "I would draw . . . who killed Long." *Washington Star*, 10 August 1935, p. 2. **48.** "As far as . . . is drunk again." *Pittsburgh Press*, 10 August 1935, p. 3. **48.** "I attended the . . . make no objection." *Pittsburgh Press*, 10 August 1935, p. 3. At a public anti-Long meeting in June 1934, Mayor Hardy proclaimed, "If it is necessary for us to teach them fairness and justice at the end of a hempen rope, I, for one, am ready to swing that rope" (Williams, p. 717). **49.** "Mr. Long was . . . of flashlight batteries." *NY Herald Tribune*, 16 August 1935, p. 5. **49.** "twin bed mates of disaster." *Alexandria Weekly Town Talk*, 17 August 1935, p. 2. **49.** "The country can't . . . never find out." *NY Herald Tribune*, 16 August 1935, p. 5. **49.** "If either Hoover . . . in the bargain." *NY Herald Tribune*, 16 August 1935, p. 5. **49.** "Borah would carry forty-eight states." *NY Herald Tribune*, 16 August 1935, p. 5. **49.** Eight choices. *Alexandria Weekly Town Talk*, 17 August 1935, p. 2. **49.** Black blood, Kane, p. 134. Arthur Schlesinger writes that it was Judge Pavy himself about whom these rumors swirled, but this was not the case (Schlesinger [*Upheaval*], p. 339). In 1928, Huey played the race card in arguing to Al Smith that Southerners supported Prohibition "because there are some people we don't want to get [liquor]." A disgusted Smith walked away and advised "come and get this fellow" before I throw him "off the roof" (Beienburg, p. 391). **49.** "You remind me . . . old nigger woman." Cortner, p. 155. **50.** "I've been shot." *New Orleans Times-Picayune*, 9 September 1935, p. 1. **49.** "like a hit deer." Brinkley, p. 248. **49.** Short straw. De Soto Hotel. Williams, pp. 871–72. **49.** "He wanted it . . . the nigger business." Williams, p. 872. Others said Weiss Jr. was not at the DeSoto meetings (which were by no means all about assassination), but that his father—also a "Dr. Weiss"—attended (Hair, pp. 321–22). **50.** "God, don't let . . . much to do." Williams, p. 876.

4 "FIVE NEGROES ON MY PLACE . . ."

53. "his strong right hand." Farber, p. 225. **53.** "Smith felt there . . . statecraft by ear." Proskauer, pp. 65, 70. **54.** "This is no . . . rich against poor." *NY Times*, 14 April 1932, pp. 1, 6, 8; *Literary Digest*, 23 April, 1932, p. 11; *Time*, 27 June 1932, p. 14. **54.** RFC. Finan, pp. 295–96. **54.** Cummings. *NY Times*, 14 January 1924, p. 1. **54–55.** "Scurrying through *Who's* . . . and a woman." O'Brien (*Rogers*), p. 155. **55.** "I am for . . . as against experiment." *NY Times*, 25 November 1933, pp. 1, 8; *NY Times*, 26 November 1933, p. E4. **55.** "the end of western civilization." *The Forum*, October 1939, p. 188; Cook (*Eleanor, Vol. 2*), p. 92. **55.** Bafflement. *NY Times*, 14 April 1932, p. 8. **55.** Raskob an independent. Farber, p. 220. **55.** Raskob's $100,000. *Chicago Tribune*, 17 June 1930, p. 3. Henry Ford's son Edsel donated $25,000 (Smith [*Gatekeeper*], p. 75). **56.** $50,000. Caro, p. 293. Smith biographer Richard O'Connor places his salary at $65,000 (O'Connor [*Smith*], p. 240). **56.** "Five negroes on . . . as a painter." Wolfskill, pp. 23–24. **56.** "You haven't much . . . businessmen are crooks." *American Historical Review*, October 1950, p. 19. **56.** "some very definite . . . to get rich." *American Historical Review*, October 1950, p. 19; Farber, p. 295. **57.** Naming the Liberty League. Farber, p. 298; Harbaugh, p. 344. **57.** "double-crossed his . . . shameless, and effective." Alter, p. 101. **57.** Roach. Burk, p. 157. **57.** Hutton Wet. Finan, p. 277. **57.** Wadsworth a nominee. *LA Times*, 23 August 1934, p. 1. The Wadsworths evidently had a thing about the Roosevelts. Jim Wadsworth's father had been driven from office by Franklin's cousin Theodore. **57.** Root. Harbaugh, p. 346. **57.** Membership. *NY Times*, 23 August 1934, p. 4. **57.** "the blessing of . . . profession of aims." *NY Times*, 23 August 1934, p. 12. **58.** Current office holders. *NY Times*, 24 August 1934, p. 2. **58.** "I've been hoping . . . behind your back." *NY Times*, 24 August 1934, p. 2; *Chicago Tribune*, 27 August 1934, p. 5. Wolfskill, p. 33. **58.** "right-thinking people . . . ever find them." *Baltimore Evening Sun*, 24 August 1934, p. 15. **58.** "All the big . . . take it club.'" Freidel (*Rendezvous*), p. 140; Wolfskill, p. 35. **58.** "Love thy God . . . property is God." *Cincinnati Enquirer*, 25 August 1934, p. 1. **58.** "rough going." *NY Times*, 25 August 1934, p. 12. **58.** "It certainly isn't . . . would be helpful." *LA Times*, 23 August 1934, p. 1. **58.** "I am most . . . in due course." *NY Times*, 24 August 1934, p. 2. **59.** "I can subscribe . . . it is fine." Wolfskill, p. 27. **59.** "Mac, Jouett has . . . the Association." Wolfskill, p. 28. On August 15, 1934. Shouse unveiled the League on August 22. **60.** "This is the . . . the cause of Liberty." Hoover (*Memoirs*), p. 454. Hoover may not have known the following, but if he had he would have been even more incensed: Shouse had attempted to recruit Charles Michelson for the League—Michelson, who had so successfully orchestrated the Democratic National Committee's post-1929 campaign against Hoover (Michelson, pp. 141–42). **60.** Liberty League. Lost in the shuffle of tarring the Liberty League as fascist was the fact that the du Pont brothers were one-eighth Jewish (Seldes, p. 208). If economics were not deterrent enough, this fact provides a further reason why Liberty Leaguers avoided such anti-FDR, anti-Semitic radicals as Father Coughlin or Gerald L. K. Smith. **60.** 36,055.

Temple Law Review, Winter 2014, p. 296*fn*. **60.** 70,000/124,856. Colby, p. 356. **60.** Knudsen, Sloan. Burk, p. 180; Farber, p. 307. **60.** Hutton. Farber, p. 302. **61.** "a naive amateur . . . the political game." *Scribner's*, March 1932, p. 131. By *Baltimore Sun* columnist Frank Kent. In July 1928, FDR warned Smith against appointing Raskob as national chairman, as Raskob would "permanently drive away a host of people in the south and west and rural east" (Schlesinger [*Crisis*], p. 127). **61.** "the long-time, privileged . . . might even help." *NY Times*, 6 August 1935, p. 25. **61.** IRS. Burk, p. 168. **61.** GM stock. *NY Times*, 20 August 1935, p. 30. **61.** Stock transfers. Wolfskill pp. 144–45; Burk, pp. 66–67, 213, 271; Farber, p. 317. **61.** Staff. Wolfskill, p. 57; Colby, p. 342. **62.** League pamphlets. *Temple Law Review*, Winter 2014, p. 297. **62.** "you can't eat the Constitution." *NY Times*, 9 November 1934, p. 2.

5 "A GREAT PITY"

63. Farley offer to Ritchie. Eaton, p. 344. **63.** "somehow like a . . . a show window." Stokes, p. 319. **64.** "[F]reedom of persons . . . by Federal mandate." *New Outlook*, October 1933, p. 12. **64.** "began to believe . . . the New Deal." Finan, p. 304. **64.** Primaries. *Boston Globe*, 9 March 1931, p. 1; *NY Times*, 29 March 1931, p. 24; Finan, pp. 300–01. **65.** Hutton. Burk, p. 175. **65.** *The Citizen and His Government.* Slayton, p. 378. **65.** 1936. *NY Times*, 19 May 1935, p. BR1. **65.** Not speaking against FDR. Finan, pp. 310–11. **65.** Jackson Day Dinners. *Washington Star*, 8 January 1936, p. 1. **65.** "the retention of . . . will not retreat." *Washington Star*, 9 January 1936, pp. 1, A9. **65.** "the Democratic organization . . . so nearly exhausted." *NY Times*, 22 January 1936, p. 18. **66.** "If the boys . . . in next July." Stuckey, pp. 28, 127. Dispatched in January 1936. **66.** 1934 national poll. *Literary Digest*, 10 October 1934, p. 8. **66.** January 1936 poll. *Literary Digest*, 11 January 1936, pp. 9–10. **66.** 1924 Smith campaign. Roosevelt (*Yesterday*), p. 164; Perkins, p. 68. **66.** "If the rest . . . make to me?" *NY Post*, 8 November 1928, p. unknown; Lash (*Eleanor*), p. 320. **66.** "I felt Gov. . . . comparatively little." Cook (*Vol. 1*), p. 554. Elinor was Mrs. Henry Morgenthau Jr. **67.** "I see by . . . come and go." Slayton, p. 386. **67.** 1932 Invitation. Josephson & Josephson, p. 436; Bowers, p. 136. **67.** "It is a matter . . . stay with them." Slayton, p. 386. **67.** Kaplan. *Glens Falls Post-Standard*, 31 December 1935, p. 1. **67.** Ely would support. *NY Herald Tribune*, 31 December 1935, p. 5; *Glens Falls Post-Standard*, 31 December 1935, p. 1. **67.** "back him to the sky." *Baltimore Evening Sun*, 31 December 1935, p. 2. **67.** 32nd Floor. Josephson & Josephson, p. 241. **67–68.** "I notice by . . . the record straight." *NY Times*, 31 December 1935, p. 1. **68.** "The only statement . . . any other friend." *NY Herald Tribune*, 31 December 1935, p. 5. **68.** "There is no . . . October of '33." *NY Herald Tribune*, 31 December 1935, p. 5. **68–69.** "The newspapers seem . . . without an invitation." Slayton, p. 386. **69.** "Personal and Confidential . . . the new year." Slayton, pp. 386–87. **69.** "Probably that of . . . talks too much." *Baltimore Evening Sun*, 31 December 1935, p. 2. **69.** "Franklin, get in . . . lap it up!" Stiles, p. 293. **70.** Attire. Burns, p. 266. **69.** "a political rally . . . his studio audience." *The Nation*, 15 January 1936, p. 60. **69.** "cannot hope to . . . do for them." Moley (*New Deal*), p. 544; Davis (*FDR*), p. 606. **70.** "a thoughtful discussion . . . of the union." *The Nation*, 15 January 1936, p. 65. **70–71.** "growing ill-will, of . . . of general war" *Buffalo Courier-Express*, 4 January 1936, p. 8. **71.** "the general sentiment . . . of the Administration." Davis (*FDR*), p. 603. **71–72.** "[W] e have invited . . . for the public." *Buffalo Courier-Express*, 4 January 1936, p. 8. **73.** "strain of manner . . . stave off defeat." *NY Herald Tribune*, 4 January 1936, p. 14. **73.** "Much talk says . . . who cherishes traditions." *Rochester Democrat and Chronicle*, 8 January 1936, p. F1. **73.** Breckinridge. *Dayton News*, 13 January 1936, p. 1. **73.** Lindbergh. *Manhattan Morning Chronicle*, 21 March 1936, p. 4. **74.** "leeches and bloodsuckers . . . rascals and crooks." *NY Daily News*, 24 January 1936, p. 343. **74.** "the least responsible . . . arrogant and tyrannical." *NY Times*, 25 January 1936, p. 6. **74.** "it will become . . . occasional rubber stamp." *NY Times*, 25 January 1936, p. 6. **74.** Bar association dinner. *NY Times*, 25 January 1936, pp. 1, 6. **74.** "The more favors . . . they can operate?" *NY Times*, 25 January 1936, p. 6. **74.** "Unlike [the Democrats'] . . . us are crooks." *Washington Star*, 26 January 1936, p. 6. **75.** Menu. *Chicago Tribune*, 26 January 1936, p. 7. **75.** "The Democrats can . . . to be re-elected." *Washington Star*, 26 January 1936, p. 1. **75.** "colored, former judge . . . of the District." *Washington Star*, 26 January 1936, p. 6. **76.** "two-thirds mush and one-third Eleanor." "Unofficial Observer" (*New Dealers*), p. 215. **76.** "black silk with . . . her shapely shoulders." *Chicago Tribune*, 26 January 1936, p. 7. **76.** "evening jacket made . . . crepe graced her." *Chicago Tribune*, 26 January 1936, p. 7. **76.** du Ponts. *New Masses*, 4 February 1936, p. 6. **76.** "Few of the . . . four-in-hands." *Chicago Tribune*, 26 January 1936, p. 7. **77.** Drunk. *The Nation*, 5 February 1936, p. 153. **77.** "This is not . . . a lobster mallet." *Chicago Tribune*, 26 January 1936, p. 7. **77.** Ghosted by Moses. Caro, p. 574. **77.** Moses refused. Slayton, p. 381. **77–79.** Text of Smith speech: *Washington Star*, 26 January 1936, p. 6. **79.** "The Al Smith . . . of good faith." *The Nation*, 5 February 1936, p. 153. **79.** "A good technical . . . but otherwise lousy." *Washington Star*, 26 January 1936, p. 1. **79.** "traitor," "Judas" Slayton, p. 388. **79.** Effigy. Slayton, p. 388; Finan, p. 321. **79–80.** "I was struck . . . unintelligible to me." Ickes (*Diary*), p. 524. Ickes, still barely a nominal Republican, voted Bull Moose in 1912 and Democratic in 1920, 1924, 1928, and 1932 (Watkins, pp. 189, 213, 215, 268). **80.** Town Talk Forum. Ickes (*Dairy*), p. 526. **80.** "The brown derby . . . the high hat." *Sacramento Bee*, 29 January 1936, pp. 1, 5. **80.** "From all of . . . be a dud." *Contemporary Speeches*, Vol. 22, 1936, Issue 2, p. 340.

6 "COMMON, IGNORANT, AND HALF-TIGHT"

81. "Sure, I stole . . . it for you." *Current Biography 1941*, p. 850. **81–82.** "[T]here is one . . . 'Wool-Hat Boys' . . ." https://www.saturdayeveningpost.com/2016/08/wool-hat-dictator/. **82.** "You folks only . . . and Ol' Gene!" Sherrill, p. 39. Often cited as a quote from Talmadge himself, his son, Sen. Herman Talmadge, denied they were his father's words (https://docsouth.unc.edu/sohp/html_use/A-0331-1.html). **82.** Cost of tags. *Georgia Historical Quarterly*, Fall 1995, pp. 674–75. **82.** "I gotta Eugene . . . a three-dollar car." *Georgia Historical Quarterly*, Fall 1995, p. 676. **82.** Unit system. "Unofficial Observer" (*Messiahs*), p. 176. **82.** Relief figures "Unofficial Observer" (*Messiahs*), p. 179. **83.** "mad course of socialism," "Unofficial Observer," p. 179. **83.** 1934. Steinberg (*Bosses*), p. 289; Anderson (*Talmadge*), pp. 108–09. **83.** Strikers. "Unofficial Observer" (*Messiahs*), p. 175. **83.** "I reckon I'm . . . dictator in him?" https://www.saturdayeveningpost.com/2016/08/wool-hat-dictator/. **83.** "The greatest calamity . . . two-by-four plank." *Thomasville Times-Enterprise*, 18 April 1935, p. 1. **83.** "Listen, my countrymen . . . high on pensions." Steed, p. 107; Steinberg (*Bosses*), p. 262.

83. "hunting something to . . . processing tax on." *Indianapolis Star*, 30 November 1935, p. 10. **83.** Effigy. *Indianapolis Star*, 30 November, 1935, p. 10; Steinberg (*Bosses*), p. 291. **83.** SCUC claims. *Buffalo Courier-Express*, 16 September 1935, p. 3. Supporters supposedly included former US senator John W. Harreld, an Oklahoma Republican, and former New Mexico Democratic governor James F. Hinkle (*Philadelphia Inquirer*, 4 August 1935, p. 8). As one scholar noted, the SCUC was "a creature of nouveau riche Texas oilmen." such as H. R. Cullen, George Strake Sr., and Clint Murchison Sr. though even they did little more than grace its letterhead (Burrough, p. 131). **84.** Ritchie, Byrd, Glass, Baker. *Buffalo Courier-Express*, 16 September 1935, p. 3. **84.** Jones. *Philadelphia Inquirer*, 19 January 1936, p. 2. **84.** Long. Burrough, p. 132. **84.** Talmadge. *Buffalo Courier-Express*, 16 September 1935, p. 3. Briefly, Talmadge enjoyed a mysterious appeal. In November 1935, Pittsburgh mayor William Nissley McNair (elected in 1933 on a vociferously pro-New Deal platform), announced his support for Talmadge—"the man to rescue the Democratic Party from the Communistic tendencies of the administration" (*Boston Globe*, 6 November 1935, p. 17). **84.** "That Talmadge ain't . . . suit his ambition." Brinkley, p. 217. **84.** "g-ddamn bush league outfit." Anderson (*Talmadge*), p. 118. **84.** "doctrine of share-the-wealth . . . out Rooseveltting Roosevelt." *Tampa Tribune*, 23 April 1935, p. 10. **84–85.** "The blood which . . . to lose him." Smith (*Long*), p. 30. **85.** "Huey Long is . . . love him most." *The Nation*, 13 February 1936, p. 15. **85.** La Follette, Bryan. *Rome Daily Sentinel*, 15 August 1936, p. 4. **86.** "Governor, some of . . . them do it?" *Rome Daily Sentinel*, 15 August 1936, p. 4. **86.** Bodyguard. *Washington Post*, 4 February 1934, p. M22. **86.** "I am embracing . . . their greedy ambition." Smith (*Long*), p. 8. **86.** Klan. Holtzman, p. 171; Bennett, p. 115. **86.** Silver Shirts. Carlson, pp. 304, 317–18; Thayer, p. 49; Jeansonne, pp. 28–30; Bennett, p. 116. Smith's lectures included "Some Day 100 Million Americans Will Hide Behind the Silver Shirt for Protection" and "Why I Left the Conventional Pulpit to Join the Christian Militia of the Silver Shirts." **86.** "The Semitic propaganda . . . in the world." Jeansonne, pp. 30–31. **86.** Two million. Bennett, p. 114. **86.** "the only man . . . than I am." Jeansonne, p. 130. **86–87.** "A steam locomotive . . . from our ideal." *Saturday Evening Post*, October 12 1935, p. 27. **87.** "Wall Street and . . . go marching on." *New Republic*, 13 February 1935, p. 13. **87.** "He assured me . . . in generous liberalism." Swing, p. 176. **87.** "I think that . . . I cared to attend." Swing, p. 177. **87.** "If I had printed . . . news in Louisiana." Swing, p. 177. **88.** "He had changed . . . being a menace." Swing, p. 180. **88.** "If God was . . . the public till." Terkel, p. 321. **88.** "Second Louisiana Purchase." *Washington Post*, 24 March 1937, p. 6. The term was coined by Westbrook Pegler (Kane, p. 183). Part of the deal involved allowing Harry Hopkins's WPA to remain in business in the state (Stokes, p. 404). **88.** Grand jury protest. Stokes, pp. 405–06. **88.** "Peace, it was . . . and PWA goodwill." Kane, p. 201. **88–89.** "divine providence for . . . the United States." Kane, p. 185. **88–89.** $10,000. Bennett, p. 132; Jeansonne, p. 43. **89.** Christenberry. Kane, pp. 196–97. **89.** "get out of . . . be carried out." Bennett, p. 134. **89.** Plans announced. *Buffalo Courier-Express*, 5 January 1936, p. 5. **89.** "I've made 432 . . . before the convention." *NY Times*, 28 January 1936, p. 7. **90.** "about 150 professional soreheads." *Time*, 10 February 1936, p. 17. **90.** "a plumed knight . . . for Federal Gold." Burrough, pp. 132–33. **90.** "nominate a Democrat . . . platform of 1932." *NY Times*, 28 January 1936, p. 7. **90.** "every true Democrat . . . in the South." *Atlanta Constitution*, 30 January 1936, p. 3. **90.** "Franklin Lenin Roosevelt." *Pittsburgh Sun-Telegraph*, 30 January 1936, p. 6. And "James Stalin Farley."

90. "We're going to . . . his dead mouth." *Time*, 10 February 1936, p. 17. **90.** "a Rasputin in the White House." *Hammond Times*, 30 January 1936, p. 21. **91.** "Those who have . . . his own people." *Hammond Times*, 30 January 1936, p. 21. **91.** "Too many . . . that omitted work." *Collier's Weekly*, 1936, 2 May 1936, p. 33. Among the few respectable folks attending was Henry Breckinridge (Wolfskill, p. 179). **91.** Dixon's fortunes. Cook (*Dixon*), p. 125; Slide, p. 185. **91.** "a Magna Carta of human rights." Slide, p. 185. **91.** "it would make . . . bayonets at our breasts." *Pittsburgh Sun-Telegraph*, 30 January 1936, p. 6. **91.** "incredibly common, ignorant, and half-tight." *The Nation*, 11 February 1936, p. 318. **92.** "Andrew Jackson didn't . . . old United States." *NY Times*, 30 January 1936, p. 8. **92.** "Mrs. Roosevelt being . . . that with niggers?" *Collier's Weekly*, 1936, 2 May 1936, p. 34. The photo bore the caption: "A picture of Mrs. Roosevelt, going to some nigger meeting, with two escorts, niggers, on each arm" (Sitkoff, p. 106). **93.** "in Dixie . . . to be condemned." *Hammond Times*, 30 January 1936, p. 21. **93.** "heart is in the right place." *NY Times*, 2 February 1936, p. E4; *NY Times*, 12 July 1936, p. E7; Black Committee, Part 6, p. 1987. **93.** "an automobile owned . . . of the paper." *NY Times*, 12 July 1936, p. E7. **93.** "Despicable and Stupid." **93.** *The Crisis*, March 1936, p. 81. **93.** "could provide good . . . in larger quantities." Riggs, p. 47. **93.** "could also apply . . . from their actions." Riggs, p. 47. **93–94.** "serious defect of . . . of nefarious dealings." Ripley, p. 303. Ripley also gained fame as a prominent racial anthropologist, presaging the work of the more-remembered Madison Grant. **94.** "abolition of the . . . of holding companies." Schlesinger (*Upheaval*), p. 305; Riggs, p. 123. **94.** Rayburn, Wheeler opposed. Steinberg (*Rayburn*), p. 126; Daniel, p. 55. **94.** 1932 Convention. Davis (FDR), p. 92*fn*. **94.** Willkie. Shlaes, p. 237; Riggs, p. 125. **94.** "[R]egulation of public . . . in their welfare." Daniel, p. 50. **95.** House, Senate votes. Steinberg (*Rayburn*), p. 128; Riggs, p. 129. Twenty-eight Senate Democrats opposed the "death penalty." **95.** "a blood-sucking business, a vampire." Riggs, p. 130. **95.** Witness, 1:00 a.m. Hamilton, p. 247. The witness admitted to circulating rumors of FDR's mental incapacity. **95.** "There is no . . . right to lobby." *Oklahoma Law Review* 1975, p. 551. **95.** "general blanket order." *Journal of Policy History*, Vol. 30, Number 2, 2018, p. 173. **95.** "Most of the . . . by a decade." *Journal of Policy History*, Vol. 30, Number 2, 2018, p. 174. **95.** Lawrence, Wadsworth, Huddleston. *Journal of Policy History*, Vol. 30, Number 2, 2018, p. 174. Huddleston had dared deliver an impassioned anti–"death sentence" floor speech that triggered three minutes of applause from fellow Democrats. He failed to win re-nomination (Patterson, pp. 54–55). **95.** "vindictive spirit . . . consideration of legislation." *NY Times*, 6 March 1936, p. 20. **95.** "threat to liberty . . . of the press." *Brooklyn Eagle*, 19 April 1936, p. 1; Best, p. 123. **96.** "the philosophies of . . . defend civil rights." *NY Times*, 24 March 1936, p. 15. Particularly upsetting to Baldwin was Black's investigating Alice Paul and the National Women's Party (*Journal of Policy History*, 2 November 2018, p. 186). **96.** "went too far." Newman, p. 189. **96.** "subpoena goes way . . . to be protected." *NY Times*, 15 March 1936 p. E10. **96.** "I simply wanted . . . of the administration." Moley (*Seven*), pp. 338–39. **96.** "This nightmarish conversation . . . businessmen—re-elect him." Moley (*Seven*), p. 339. **96.** Wheeler-Rayburn passes. *Oklahoma Law Review* 1975, p. 567. **96.** "While a strait-jacket . . . which to work." Riggs, p. 133. **96–97.** Other organizations funded. Black Committee (*Digest, Part 1*), *passim*; *NY Times*, 21 June 1936, p. 2. In 1937, Minute Men and Women of Today President Benjamin W. Blanchard was arrested in Philadelphia for inciting to riot, conspiracy, and carrying concealed weapons (*Baltimore Sun*, 9 October 1937, p. 9). **97.** "The American Liberty . . . guilty by association." Wolfskill, p. 228. **97.** Prominent donors. Black Committee (*Digest, Part 1*), *passim*; *NY Times*, 21 June 1936, p. 2. Over an eighteen-month period. Numerous interesting names appear on this list, though they triggered little interest at the time. They included Bernard Baruch ($100, National Economy League), Walter Chrysler ($376.28, The Crusaders), John Foster Dulles ($100, Liberty League), Andrew Mellon ($1,000, Liberty League), John D. Rockefeller Jr. ($1,000, National Economy League), Philip K. Wrigley ($100, American Taxpayers League), and Arthur Hays Sulzberger ($100, National Economy League). No donations appear from Alfred E. Smith, John W. Davis, Joseph Ely, James Wadsworth, or Albert Ritchie. John Henry Kirby, who supposedly spent $100,000 to elect Al Smith in 1928 (*Pittsburgh Sun-Telegraph*, 30 January 1936, p. 6;), expended just $500 on SCUC and nothing at all on any other of these organizations. **97.** "an analysis . . . and utility companies." *NY Times*, 21 June 1936, p. 2. **97–98.** "Black's hatred of . . . of constitutional rights." Newman, p. 193. **97–98.** Few farmers. *New Republic*, 2 September 1936, p. 96. **97–98.** "Wall Street Farmers." Newman, p. 185. **98.** "The fight for . . . want a Hitler." *NY Times*, 18 April 1936, p. 4. The Sentinels did not appear to have much, if any, of a Liberty League connection, though, at one point, a merger was discussed. Its only du Pont donation came from Irénée du Pont in the amount of $100. The group functioned largely as an organ of the Pittsburgh Plate Glass Co.'s Raymond Pitcairn (Burk, pp. 174, 177, 206). Other prominent contributors prior to the incident included Alfred P. Sloan, Robert McCormick, and Nicholas Roosevelt. Interestingly enough, Runyon (later a prominent anti-fluoridation activist) had worked alongside Felix Frankfurter in Henry Stimson's US Attorney's Office for the Southern District in 1910 (*The National Corporation Reporter*, 2 June 1910, p. 551). **99.** Plan to run Black Democrats. *Boston Globe*, 29 May 1936, p. 18; Wolfskill, p. 233. **99.** Scar-faced. *Time*, 27 April 1936, p. 11. **99.** "I went with . . . which he prefers." *Austin American*, 13 November 1929, p. 2. The Caraway subcommittee on lobbying investigated Muse's "blackening" plan. Caraway invited Hugo Black to sit in as a special "guest assistant" to its proceedings (*Oklahoma Law Review* 1975, p. 551). **99.** "I am fighting . . . I was 19." *Amsterdam Evening Recorder*, 15 April 1936, p. 9. **99.** "you are putting . . . I can't answer." Black Committee, Part 6, p, 1966. **99.** "I think I . . . have implicit faith." Black Committee, Part 6, p. 1963. **99.** "I decline to . . . discuss these things." Black Committee, Part 6, pp. 1970, 1971. Wrote Texas historian Bryan Burrough: "By 1935, thanks to Muse, the Kirby Building . . . was home to a warren of shadowy, interconnected ultraconservative groups, all devoted to white supremacy, fighting labor unions and communism, and above all defeating Roosevelt's re-election. . . . The Kirby groups were little more than the Ku Klux Klan in pinstripes, a kind of corporate Klan: the Texas Tax Relief committee, the Texas Election Managers Association, the Sentinels of the Republic, and the Order of American Patriots" (Burrough, p. 129). **99–100.** "BLACK: Can you . . . of Confederate gray)." Black Committee, Part 6, p. 1973. Contemporary press accounts (e.g., *NY Herald Tribune*, 16 April 1936, p. 11) have Muse using the word "negro." That was not the case. **99–100.** Filibuster. Hamilton, pp. 237–38; Newman, p. 575. **99–100.** Southern Committee to Uphold the Constitution contributions. Black Committee (*Digest, Part 6*), p. 37. **99–100.** "didn't know anything about." *Black Committee*, Part 6, p. 1986; *Auburn Citizen-Advertiser*, 15 April 1936, p. 1. **99–100.** Sloan. *Black Committee*, Part 6, pp. 1987, 2013; Burk, p. 218. **100.** "God's gift to Franklin Roosevelt." Sheppard, p. 23. **101.** "In my opinion . . . of the people." *Buffalo Evening News*, 2 July 1936, p. 6. **101.** Cuts. Champagne, p. 69. **102.** "Unofficial Observer" (*New Dealers*), p. 271. Words of John Franklin Carter. **102.** "My Dear John: . . . Jno. N. Garner." *Buffalo Evening News*, 2 July 1936, p. 6.

7 "METHODIST PICNIC PEOPLE"

103. "one of the . . . speakers on earth." Bennett, p. 14. **103.** Log cabin. *NY Times*, 2 September 1960, p. 23. **103.** Oldest. Bennett, p. 149. **103–105.** "The Land Filled . . . the country hears." Milne, p. 2. **105.** Letter. Amenta, p. 35; Powell, p. 31. **105.** "the Townsend Plan . . . after receiving it." *The Forum*, May 1936, p. 282. **106.** "compel attention, and . . . a higher amount." Milne, p. 28. **103.** "by 1928, 11 . . . cost of assistance." http://www.socialwelfarehistory.com/programs/old-age-pensions-a-brief-history. **103.** 1934. Douglas, pp. 7, 10. **103.** Dill-Connolly. *Law and Contemporary Problems,* Vol. 3, No. 2, pp. 188–89; Douglas, pp. 9–11; Ferrara & Tanner, p. 19. Adding to Dill-Connolly's charms was the fact that the Supreme Court had no problems with the idea of federal matching funds for the states. **103.** "Old age pensions! . . . not go broke." Oursler, p. 417. **103.** "Age for leisure; youth for work." Holtzman, p. 84. That slogan sounded suspiciously like the words of author Bruce Barton ("Let the young do the work and the old men loaf."), who in *Vanity Fair*'s August 1931 issue satirically proposed a similar plan ("How To Fix Everything"). Townsend always denied any inspiration from Barton. **103.** "velocity of money." Bennett, p. 152. **106.** "people over 60 . . . more buying experience." Bennett, p. 165. **107.** Office opened. Bell, p. 107; Powell, p. 32. **103.** "Old-Age Revolving Pension, Ltd." Bell Committee Report, p. 4; Powell, p. 32. **103.** "Prosperity Publishing Co., Ltd." Bell Committee Report, p. 8. **103.** First Townsend Club. Bell Committee Report, p. 4; Bell, p. 107; Powell, p. 33. In Huntington Park, California. **103.** Staff, letters. Bennett, p. 154. **103.** McGroarty. Powell, p. 33. **103.** More fashionable. *Law and Contemporary Problems,* Vol. 3, No. 2, p. 189. **103.** "now is the . . . possibly be fulfilled." *NY Times*, 15 November 1934, pp. 1–2. **103.** 2,000 clubs, 300,000 members. Amenta, p. 58. **103.** $.25. Amenta, p. 53; Bennett, p. 154. **103.** 3,000 clubs. Douglas, p. 73. **103.** 7,000 clubs, 1.5–2 million members. Amenta, p. 116. **107.** 30 million. Bell, p. 117; Bennett, p. 174. **108.** "left few stones . . . in the Legion.'" Bennett, p. 171. **108.** $300,000. *The Modern Monthly*, June 1936, p. 11. **108.** $79,000. Bell Committee Report, p. 19; Bell, p. 137. **108.** "You and I . . . work it right." Bell Hearings, Vol. 1, pp. 596, 600. **108.** Night club. Bell Committee Report, p. 42; *Chicago Tribune*, 22 May 1936, p. 12. **108.** Gambling, dope. *NY Times*, 3 June 1936, p. 4; Bell Committee Hearings, Vol. 1, pp. 962, 963. **108.** Indictments. *NY Times*, 2 April, 1936, p. 11; Bell Committee Report, p. 43; Amenta, p. 141; Holtzman, p. 165. **108.** Einstein. *LA Times*, 7 February 1933, p. A5. **108.** Darrow, WGOD. Shilling, p. 53. **109.** "a converted pocketbook . . . the proportion increase." Wunder, p. 115. **109.** Fund raiser, Hollywood. *Rochester Democrat and Chronicle*, 20 April 1930, p. 18. **109.** "The Liberal Voice of Los Angeles" *LA Record*, 12 April 1933, p. 3. **109.** "a fortune from . . . purchased by Townsendites." *Modern Monthly*, June 1936, p. 11. **109.** *Soviet Russia Today*. Bell Committee Report, p. 14. **109–110.** "MARRIED AT 120. . . or hermetic philosophy—" Bell Committee Report, p. 13. **110.** "just folks . . . Methodist picnic people." Bennett, p. 168. **110.** "We [he and his wife] . . . old to vote!" Powell, p. 32. **110.** "utterly impractical. It . . . accomplished. It cannot." *Los Angeles Evening Citizen News*, 24 December 1934, p. 1. **110.** "Roosevelt has raised . . . house this session." *NY Times*, 17 January 1935, p. 5. **110.** Social Security. *NY Times*, 17 January 1935, p. 5. Not only could FDR have introduced Social Security much earlier, he had refused to support Robert Wagner's 1934 bill creating it. **111.** "would accomplish two . . . the present time." Holtzman, p. 222; Sheppard, p. 18. **111.** "from the very . . . income eroded character." Tugwell (*Democratic*), p. 280. **111.** Cost, revenues. *NY Times*, 2 September 1960, p. 23. **111.** "In the comparatively . . . 250 per cent." *The Forum*, May 1936, p. 286. **111.** "Even the man . . . crust of bread." Bell, p. 114. **111–112.** "its witnesses—Townsend . . . by a different name."*American Sociological Review*, April 1991, p. 56. **112.** 256–66.. *NY Times*, 19, 1935. p. 1. **112.** House Social Security vote. Two members voted present; 25 did not vote. A mere handful of House conservatives like New York's James Wadsworth voted "nay," but so had Townsend's man John S. McGroarty, the far-left (indeed, Communist-leaning) New Yorker Vito Marcantonio, and North Dakota's agrarian radicals Usher Burdick and William Lemke. **112.** "nondrinking, nonsmoking and Bible-reading" (Historian David Bennett's words). Bennett, p. 8. **112.** Chicago Convention. Bennett, p. 8; Powell, pp. 37–38. **112.** "beloved leaders." *Chicago Tribune*, 25 October 1935, p. 12. **112.** "We believe God is on our side." *LA Times*, 25 October 1935, p. 8. **112.** "sure thing." *Chicago Tribune*, 25 October 1935, p. 12. **112.** "end not only . . . save the country." *LA Times*, 25 October 1935, p. 8. **112.** "Onward Townsend Soldiers." *LA Times*, 25 October 1935, p. 8. **112.** "We're all . . . in many years." *Chicago Tribune*, 24 October 1935, p. 10. **112.** Verner M. Main. *NY Daily News*, 15 December 1935, p. 50. **112.** "As Main goes, so goes the nation." *News-Week*, 1936, 28 December 1935, p. 1. **113.** "Townsend plan converts . . . the Republican Party." *NY Times*, 29 December 1935, p. E11. **113.** "an insult that . . . people should resent." Holtzman, p. 170. **113.** "the most extraordinary . . . our entire history." Schlesinger (*Upheaval*), 40. **113.** Borah, inches away. *Sacramento Bee*, 29 January 1936, pp. 1, 9; Holtzman, p. 135; Amenta, pp. 111, 136. **113.** Sickbed. *Sacramento Bee*, 29 January 1936, p. 9; Amenta, p. 136. **113.** Endorses Borah, changes registration. *NY Herald Tribune*, 23 Mar 1936, p. 1. **113.** 1932. *NY Herald Tribune*, 23 Mar 1936, p. 31. **113.** "If twenty billion . . . on the way." *Collier's*, 20 June 1936, p. 46. **114–115.** "Considering the fact . . . grand big spree." *Washington Star*, 26 January 1936, p. 6. **115.** Wunder. Bell Committee Report, pp. 34–36; Bell Committee Hearings, Vol. 1, p. 859; *NY Times*, 2 April 1936, p. 11. **115.** California delegates. Holtzman, p. 142. **115.** "private political ambitions . . . like a fool." Bennett, p. 180. **115.** "Just think. They . . . liberated all mankind." *NY Post*, 16 July 1936, p. 4. **115–116.** "almost wholly political . . . the 1936 elections." Bennett, p. 179. **116.** Clements resigned. *NY Times*, 2 April 1936, p. 11. **116.** "You and I . . . work it right." Bell Hearings, Vol. 1, pp. 596, 600. **116.** Merriam. Bell Committee Hearings, Vol. 1, pp. 484–85. **116.** Klan. Bell Committee Hearings, Vol. 1, pp. 518, 535; Holtzman, p. 165. **116.** Dyer. Bell Committee Hearings, Vol. 1. pp. 664–65; Holtzman, p. 165. **116.** "old fossils." Bell Committee Hearings, Vol. 1, pp. 460, 471, 735. **116.** "We don't give . . . about poor people." *NY Times*, 22 May 1936, p. 1. Some accounts say "poor people," others "old people." **116.** "We of . . . sins of another?" Bell Committee Hearings, Vol. 1, p. 858. **117.** "DEAR HELENE You . . . virginal pal, 'Clint.'" Bell Committee Hearings, Vol. 1, p. 837; Bell Committee Report, pp. 33–34. **117.** "impress me as . . . minister of the Gospel." Bell Committee Hearings, Vol. 1, p. 899. **117.** "Dr. Wunder bore . . . money, money, money."

Bell Committee Hearings, Vol. 4, pp. 577–78. **117–118.** "Mrs. JACKSON: . . . the second edition." Bell Committee Hearings, Vol. 4, p. 577. **118–119.** Thelma Mills. *LA Times*, 18 March 1935, p. 17; *Rochester Democrat and Chronicle*, 18 April 1935, p. 18; *Cincinnati Enquirer*, 20 April 1935, p. 11; *LA Times*, 22 April 1935, p. 2; *Fort Worth Star-Telegram*, 1 May 1935, p. 15; *Birmingham News*, 16 May 1935, p. 2; *LA Times*, 29 May 1937, p. 3. **119.** Ignore subpoenas. Bell Committee Hearings, Vol. 1, p. 831; *LA Times*, 23 May 1936, p. 1. **119.** "After reading . . . before this committee." Bell Committee Hearings, Vol. 1, p. 867; *NY Times*, 2 June 1936, p. 7. **119.** "the humiliation of its leader." Bennett, p. 179. **119.** "You can't . . . would be harmless." Bennett, p. 180. **119.** "When forced to . . . an inexpensive toy." Bennett, p. 180. **119–120.** "Unable to uncover . . . most simple terms." Holtzman, p. 166. **120.** "Isn't that nice." *Baltimore Sun*, 22 May 1936, p. 1. **120.** "plagiarist" Bell Committee Hearings, Vol. 1, p. 764; *Chicago Tribune*, 22 May 1936, p. 12; *Baltimore Sun*, 22 May 1936, p. 2. **120.** "atheist." Bell Committee Hearings, Vol. 1, pp. 580, 752; *NY Daily News*, 22 May 1936, p. 56. Years later, Gerald L. K. Smith commented, "They called in a bunch of neurotic women to testify against him. . . . They had a Roman holiday with the old man" (Terkel, p. 325). **120.** "No written statements . . . kept us waiting?" *Chicago Tribune*, 22 May 1936, p. 1. **120.** "In view of . . . good-bye, gentlemen." Bell Committee Hearings, Vol. 2, p. 1064; Powell, pp. 43–44. **120.** Downey. *Baltimore Sun*, 22 May 1936, p. 1. **120.** "Shut that door!" *Chicago Tribune*, 22 May 1936, p. 1. **120.** "Stop him!" *NY Times*, 22 May 1936, p. 8; *Chicago Tribune*, 22 May 1936, p. 1. **121.** Police officer. *Washington Star*, 22 May 1936, p. 2. **120.** "A hurrying reporter . . . a big fist." *Chicago Tribune*, 22 May 1936, p. 1.

8 "A VOICE MADE FOR PROMISES"

122–123. "Doc, they're going . . . You've got him." Terkel, p. 325. **123.** "Isn't that right? . . . That's all right." *NY Daily News*, 22 May 1936, p. 56. **123.** Smith-Townsend-Coughlin alliance. *NY Daily News*, 22 May 1936, p. 56. **123.** 1923. Marcus, p. 21. **124.** Royal Oak parish. Fish Committee, p. 18; Powell, p. 5; Warren, pp. 14–15. **124.** 28 families. *American Heritage*, October 1972, p. 41; Warren, p. 15. **124.** Klan. Tull, p. 3; Marcus, pp. 22–23; Warren, pp. 18–19, 310–11. Coughlin biographer Donald Warren expressed serious doubts regarding the incident. For some reason, journalist John L. Spivak incorrectly amplified the episode into the Klan "burn[ing] Coughlin's church to the ground" (Spivak, p. 4). **124.** Ballplayers. Marcus, pp. 23–24; Warren, p. 16. **124.** WJR. Warren, p. 23; Powell, p. 5; Bennett, p. 32; Marcus, pp. 25–26. **124.** "avoid prejudicial subjects . . . and especially bigotry." Mugglebee, p. 169. His words in 1927. **124.** "a voice of . . . made for promises." Leighton, p. 234. **124.** "League of the Little Flower." Spivak, p. 83; Powell, p. 8; Bennett, p. 32; Warren, p. 16. Later renamed/reincorporated as the "*Radio* League of the Little Flower." **124.** Dues, deposits. Warren, p. 27. **124.** "It is either . . . brothel of Lenin!" *Atlantic Monthly*, December 1935, pp. 660–61. **124.** Attacking Bolshevism and socialism. Mugglebee, pp. 183–84; Marcus, p. 31. **124.** "Only the soft-brained . . . against the millionaire." Mugglebee, p. 184. **124.** Fish Committee. Fish Committee, pp. 18–25; Warren, pp. 32–34. **124.** Weishaupt, Illuminati. Fish Committee, p. 19. **124.** "instrumental in subsidizing . . . the Russian country." Fish Committee, pp. 20–24. **124–125.** "it does happen . . . Jews are communists." Fish Committee, p. 25.

125. CBS network. Dunning, p. 242; Powell, p. 8; Bennett, p. 33; Marcus, p. 36. **125.** 80,000 letters, 96 clerks. Warren, p. 34. **125.** Post Office. Warren, p. 34. **125.** "Modern capitalism as . . . detriment to civilization." Schlesinger (*Upheaval*), pp. 18–19. **125.** "Hoover tried to . . . people of Michigan." *NY Times*, 24 August 1933, p. 7. **125.** "Another Roosevelt shall . . . of our country!" Powell, p. 12. **125.** McFadden. *Detroit Jewish Chronicle*, 12 April 1934, p. 2; Ward (*Coughlin*), pp. 83–85; Tull, pp. 6–7; Fried, pp. 41–42. **125.** Versailles broadcast. Ward (*Coughlin*), pp. 84–85; Marcus, pp. 35–36; "Unofficial Observer" (*Messiahs*), p. 39; Fried, pp. 41–42. **125.** Hoover. Warren, p. 36. **125.** 350,000 letters. Warren, p. 34. Some said 1,250,000 (Tull, p. 7). **125.** Server. *American Heritage*, October 1972, p. 101; Beschloss, p. 116. **126.** "Father Coughlin is . . . 'yes' or 'no.'" Marcus, p. 45. **126.** "the banker's friend . . . of Wall Street." Bennett, p. 33. **126.** "driving the money . . . of the temple." Tull, p. 24. **126.** "The Catholic Church . . . is for all." *Boston Pilot*, 23 April, 1932, p. 2. **126.** Supports Bonus March. *Chicago Tribune*, 13 April 1932, p. 10. **126.** $5,000. *Chicago Tribune*, 11 June 1932, p. 11. **126.** First met. Marcus, p. 46; Warren, p. 41. **126.** "a member of the Klan." Tull, p. 16. **126.** Mother. *Literary Digest*, 28 March 1936, p. 8; *American Heritage*, October 1972, p. 40; Warren, pp. 19–20. **126.** "disliked and distrusted . . . or trusted him." Warren, p. 42. Joseph P. Lash noted how much he was "struck by her hostility to the Catholic Church, not as a matter of faith or religious doctrine, but because of its political activities." Lash (*Eleanor*), p. 242. Elliott Roosevelt recalled, "Mother did not take to Tom [Corcoran]. He was too pungent a personality to suit her. He was also one more Catholic in the President's entourage" (Roosevelt & Brough [*Rendezvous*], p. 100). Elliott further mused that Lucy Mercer's Catholicism hardly improved her attitude (Roosevelt & Brough [*Mother R.*], p. 162). Joseph Alsop recounted, "Eleanor still believed the anti-Catholic nonsense she had heard during her childhood" (McKean p. 76; Smith [*Gatekeeper*], p. 166). **127.** Testifying with Murphy. *San Antonio Light*, 27 June 1932, p. 5-A; Marcus, p. 46. **127.** "Carpenter from Nazareth . . . engineer from Palo Alto." *NY Times*, 30 June 1932, p. 17. **127.** Coughlin's assessment. *American Heritage*, October 1972, p. 100. **127.** "I do hope . . . about many things." Powell, p. 14. **127.** Demagogue. Tugwell (*Democratic*), p. 349. **127.** "We must tame . . . useful to us." Tugwell (*Democratic*), p. 350. **127.** "I have twenty-six . . . the common man." Marcus, p. 47; Brinkley, p. 108. **127.** "the banksters" Ward (*Coughlin*), p. 170; Warren, p. 54. **127.** Banking controversy. Tull, pp. 24–29; Bennett, p. 41. **128.** "angry as hell . . . in that mess." Marcus, p. 59. **128.** "should run for . . . he think he is?" Marcus, p. 64. **128.** Morgan. Coughlin (*New Deal*), pp. 84, 92. **128.** Morgenthau Sr. *Detroit Free Press*, 29 April 1934, p. 1. **128.** Hippodrome. *NY Times*, 28 November 1933, p. 17; Marcus, pp. 62–63; Warren, pp. 60–61. **128.** "Mr. Roosevelt is . . . the Dark Ages." *NY Times*, 19 January 1934, p. 7. **128.** "President Roosevelt is . . . Roosevelt or ruin." *NY Times*, 17 January 1934, p. 17. **128.** "I will never . . . is Christ's deal." *NY Times*, 9 April 1934, p. 27. **128.** "Sometimes, I am . . . being with him." Beschloss, p. 116. **128–129.** "Unless the Democrat . . . regulate its value." *NY Times*, 24 April 1934, p. 4. **129.** Morgenthau list. *NY Times*, 27 April 1934, p. 14. **129.** 500,000 ounces. *NY Times*, 29 April 1934, p. 10. **129.** "one week's expenses." *Detroit Free Press*, 29 April 1934, p. 1. **129.** "the gold advocates . . . the international bankers." *Detroit Free Press*, 29 April 1934, p. 1. **129.** Black anti-Semitism. Diner, p. 78. In 1938, Gallup polled various groups regarding support for Father Coughlin, including Jews (10%), Protestants (19%), Lutherans (29%), Catholics (42%), and African Americans (50%). (Weyl, pp. 135–36). **129.** "only one fit . . . against the Jews." *NY*

Times, 9 October 1934, p. 2. **129.** "the Independent Republican . . . Christian-Gentile Committee." *Jewish Daily Bulletin*, 23 January 1935, p. 1; *Modern View*, 31 January 1935, p. 16. **129.** "keep the Jew . . . the Republican Party!" *Jewish Daily Bulletin*, 23 January 1935, p. 1. McFadden's candidacy, however, quickly evaporated—as did his friendship with Coughlin. By April 1935, having tired of Coughlin's vacillations regarding the New Deal, McFadden denounced Coughlin as "not careful of the facts. . . . [He] has led himself out on many limbs" (*Elmira Star-Gazette*, 26 April 1935, p. 18). **129.** Description of True. *Saturday Evening Post*, 27 May 1939, p. 72. **130.** "'Karl Marx' Professor . . . and his legal kikes." Wolfskill & Hudson, p. 69. **130.** "even a Negro's skull wide open." *New Masses*, 18 August 1936, p. 8. **130.** "Kike-Killer." *New Masses*, 18 August 1936, p. 8; Wolfskill & Hudson, p. 69. **130.** "We're not going . . . 'em right here." *New Masses*, 18 August 1936, p. 8. **130.** Black Legion. *Jewish Telegraphic Agency*, 2 August 1936, p. 4; Morris (*Legion*), p. 20. **130.** Yom Kippur. *Comparative Studies in Society and History*, July 1983, p. 512. **130.** "to defranchise the . . . in the population." Thayer, p. 49*fn*. **130.** Edmondson. *NY Times*, 9 June 1936, pp. 1, 4; *NY Times*, 12 June 1936, p. 2; *New Masses*, 23 June 1936, p. 3; *American Jewish History*, September 1981, pp. 79–102. **130.** "hook-nosed and bloated . . . German anti-Semitic newspaper." Weyl, p. 120. **130.** *Fortune* poll. Weyl, pp. 236, 255–56. **130.** "naturally . . . in America today." *New Masses*, 18 August 1936, p. 9. **131.** "the Hebrew, Karl Marx" Warren, p. 32. **130.** "if there is . . . for our independence." *Jewish Daily Bulletin*, 2 November 1934, p. 2. **130.** "either dead or dying." *Jewish Daily Bulletin*, 14 November 1934, p. 1. **130.** "I know Mr. . . . and his honesty." *Jewish Daily Bulletin*, 14 November 1934, p. 1; *Detroit Jewish Chronicle*, 16 November 1934, pp. 1, 10. **131.** "will no doubt . . . the anti-Jewish axe." *Jewish Daily Bulletin*, 14 November 1934, p. 1. **132.** "Listen, I was . . . that silver business." Marcus, pp. 60, 70. **132.** NUSJ. Spivak, p. 32; Tull, p. 142; Marcus, p. 71; Bennett, p. 68. **132–133.** "1. I believe in . . . care for themselves." Tull, p. 63. Paraphrased in "Unofficial Observer" (*Messiahs*), pp. 44–45 and Warren, pp. 62–63. **132.** "limit the amount . . . shall be limited." Tull, p. 66. **132.** $10 billion plan. Tull, pp. 69–70. **133.** "old parties are all but dead." Powell, p. 21. **134.** "Rockefeller millions are . . . World Court alive." *Pittsburgh Press*, 17 January 1935, p. 1. **134.** "old-fashioned enough . . . love of minorities." *NY Times*, 21 January 1936, p. 16. **134.** "an internationalism which . . . Soviet Third International." Bennett, p. 76. **134.** Telegrams. Tull, p. 76; Warren, p. 64. Some claimed 20,000 telegrams (Bennett, p. 76). **134.** "You are right . . . or our objectives." Roosevelt & Brough (*Rendezvous*), p. 98. **134.** 150 per minute. *Elmira Star-Gazette*, 10 May 1935, p. 1. **134.** "Mr. Roosevelt now . . . is Father Coughlin." *Elmira Star-Gazette*, 10 May 1935, p. 1. **135.** "If Coughlin kept . . . in each country." *Morgenthau Diaries*, p. 255. The three cardinals: O'Connell of Boston, Hayes of New York, and Mundelein of Chicago. **135.** Des Moines event. *Chicago Tribune*, 24 July 1966, p. 22. **135.** Coughlin declined. *Des Moines Tribune*, 26 April 1935, p. 7; Brinkley, p. 210. **135.** "I like Coughlin . . . ideas are sound." *NY Times*, 28 April 1935, p. 24. **135.** "Coughlin is just . . . tired of him." *The Nation*, 25 September 1935, p. 344. **135.** "going through a . . . in every bone." Beschloss, pp. 113–14, 294. **135.** "first two years . . . business and finance." Tull, p. 82. **135.** "There comes burring . . . Irish-Canadian priest." Tull, p. 83; Powell, p. 25; Ohl, p. 260. **135–136.** "the chocolate soldier . . . Deal's greatest casualty." Mugglebee, p. 349. FDR himself later berated Johnson as "a liar, a coward, and a cad." To his face—*twice* (Roosevelt & Brough [*Rendezvous*], p. 96). **136.** Ickes talk. Powell, p. 25. **136.** "no objections." Powell, p. 40. **136.** "broken every promise . . . the present advisers." Warren, pp. 67, 317.

136. "Not one New . . . of the Democrats." Warren, pp. 67, 317. **136.** Cleveland. Powell, p. 26. **136.** Madison Square Garden. *NY Post*, 23 May 1935, pp. 1, 7; Marcus, pp. 95–96; Powell, p. 26; Warren, p. 65. **136.** "snowed under" *NY Times*, 23 May 1935, p. 19. **136.** 59–10. Tull, p. 100; Bennett, p. 76. **136–137.** "shining star among . . . of the Administration." *Social Justice*, 6 July 1936, p. 2; *Pittsburgh Post-Gazette*, 11 July 1936, p. 6; Beschloss, p. 127. **137.** "Joseph Kennedy agrees . . . in this analysis." Beschloss, p. 118. **137.** "Home, I'm busy . . . next night then." Beschloss, p. 118. **137.** "holding his own." *NY Post*, 10 September 1935, p. 3. **137.** "the most regrettable . . . in modern history." *Philadelphia Inquirer*, 11 September 1935, p. 5; Tull, p. 101. According to a press report, "Travelling on the same train from Detroit to Albany was Mrs. Franklin D. Roosevelt" (*NY Post*, 10 September 1935, p. 3). **137.** "My Washington . . . have finally succeeded." *NY Times*, 11 September 1935, p. 15. **137.** "The Boss was . . . a shock to him." Marcus, p. 99. What Roosevelt thought of Long's death beyond his forthcoming ultra-bland official statement remains a mystery. We do know, however, that he was soon denying learning of Long's death from Coughlin, claiming instead that Missy LeHand had already informed him (*NY Times*, 12 September 1935, p. 13). **137.** "go look at the pigs." Beschloss, p. 119; Nasaw (*Patriarch*), p. 235; Warren, p. 69. **138.** "Cards on the . . . I told him?" Marcus, p. 99. It is not impossible that such an improbable document did exist—but most likely only as a forgery. In 1927, the Hearst papers famously published a series of articles claiming that the Mexican government had issued the then-fabulous sum of $1.15 million in bribes to four unnamed senators (they turned out to be Borah, Norris, Heflin, and La Follette). Their supporting documents were forgeries, and once Hearst ascertained that, he promptly repudiated the tale (Swanberg [*Hearst*], pp. 394–403; Nasaw [*Hearst*], pp. 381–85; Procter, pp. 142–44; McKenna, pp. 231–32). **137.** Summer 1935 version. *American Heritage*, October 1972, p. 103. **137.** "Joseph B. Kennedy & Father Coughlan." http://www.fdrlibrary.marist.edu/daybyday/daylog/september-10th-1935/. **137.** "social visit." Tull, p. 101. **137.** "I was there . . . with his President." *NY Times*, 12 September 1935, p. 13. **137.** "Not that I know of." Beschloss, p. 120; Warren, p. 68. **137.** "I went down . . . he told me." Beschloss, pp. 119–20. **137.** "a friend in Great Barrington." Warren, p. 71; Nasaw (*Patriarch*), p. 235. **139–140.** "According to the . . . to the president." Ickes (*Diary*), pp. 536–37. **140.** Basil O'Connor. Trohan, p. 38. **140.** "The truth is not . . . Come on!" *NY Times*, 17 February 1936, pp. 1–2. **140.** "He accepts your . . . o'clock tomorrow morning." *NY Times*, 18 February 1936, p. 1. **140–141.** "Every decent Catholic . . . operator in the Capital." *NY Times*, 18 February 1936, p. 1. **141.** Johnston. *Syracuse Journal*, 18 February 1936, p. 2. **141.** McCoy. *Syracuse Journal*, 18 February 1936, p. 2. **141.** 235–142. Tull, p. 120. **141.** "The Last Straw." *Social Justice*, 29 May 1936, p. 1.

9 "SHIRT MANIA"

142. Utilities. Davis (*New York*), pp. 97–99. **142.** Tammany. Davis (*New York*), p. 102. **141.** Banking. *The Nation*, 11 February 1931, pp. 147–49; *Oakland Tribune*, 22 August 1932, p. 2; Freidel (*Triumph*), p. 190. **141.** "an evil genius . . . hence, ineffectual measures." Davis (*New York*), p. 108. **141.** "[T]he least defensible . . . his Socialist beliefs." "Unofficial Observer" (*Messiahs*), pp. 161–62. **141.** "He is today. . . his approach to life." "Unofficial

Observer" (*Messiahs*), p. 163. **141.** Coughlin attack. Warren, p. 28; Powell, p. 7. **143.** "headed for hell or something worse." *Oakland Tribune*, 22 August 1932, p. 2. **144.** "the ablest and . . . of American Fascism." *Oakland Tribune*, 10 September 1935, p. 3. **144.** "Norman, I'm a . . . than you are." Gregory, p. 128; Johnpoll, p. 151. **144.** "The President and . . . they were silent." Thomas (*New Deal*), p. 4; Gregory, p. 136. **144.** Manhattan vote. Klehr, p. 172. **144.** 125,826. Weyl, p. 112. **144.** 11,922. Ross (*Socialist*), p. 365. **144.** Surpassed by CPUSA. Ross (*Socialist*), p. 365. **144.** "bogus democracy of capitalist parliamentarism." Ottanelli, p. 91. **145.** "symptoms of a . . . almost uncontrollable frenzy." Waldman, pp. 194–95. **146.** Bernard. Klehr, p. 291. **146.** Lundeen. Klehr, p. 285. **146.** "a paid under . . . the Communist Party." Gitlow (*Whole*), pp. 260, 361. Officially, the CPUSA was known as the "Workers Party" when Gitlow ran in 1924 and 1928. **146.** "unscrupulous demagogue." Klehr, p. 257. **146.** "Build the FLP." Klehr, p. 259. **146.** "For two short . . . that controlled it." Klehr, p. 259. **146.** Chicago Conference. Ryan, p. 111. **146.** "the truth about . . . with the underworld." Woodbury, p. 60. **146.** Townley. *The Nation*, 17 October 1934, p. 436. **146.** "press censorship by shotgun." *Minneapolis Star*, 7 September 1934, p. 1. **146–147.** "the Farmer-Labor press . . . their unpaid labor." Woodbury, pp. 62–64. **147.** "in Minnesota, *hands* . . . Shipstead and Oleson [sic]." Burns, p. 202; Schlesinger (*Upheaval*), p. 103. The Democratic nominee versus Olson was an Al Smith Democrat, thus further motivating FDR (*The Nation*, 17 October 1934, p. 436). **147.** "a damned sight . . . is a radical." Woodbury, p. 67. **147.** "I don't think . . . Howard Guilford's case." Woodbury, p. 66. **147.** Edith testified. Woodbury, p. 216. Several years later, former veteran high-ranking Soviet agent D. H. Dubrowsky alleged the murder was the work of "Communist agents." Dubrowsky and the pro-Moscow Liggett had worked together for Soviet recognition in the 1920s (*Collier's*, 20 April 1940, p. 64). **147.** "You bet your . . . radical as hell!" Schlesinger (*Upheaval*), p. 99. **147.** "capitalism has failed . . . of the few." *The Nation*, 17 October 1934, p. 436. **147.** "You can't have . . . a third party." *Brooklyn Times Union*, 16 November 1936, p. 2. **148.** Old Guard SP. Ross (*Socialist*), p. 371. **148.** Tugwell. Morgan (*FDR*), p. 416. **148.** "radical enough." Schlesinger (*Upheaval*), p. 104. **148.** Farmer-Labor platform. "Unofficial Observer" (*Messiahs*), pp. 92–93. **148.** Schall's death. *Chicago Tribune*, 23 December 1935, pp. 1, 6; *LA Times*, 23 December 1935, pp. 1–2. **148.** Debs. *American Heritage*, December 1971, p. 100. **148.** Imprisonment. Draper, p. 309. **148.** "bookkeeper." Morgan (*Reds*), p. 168. **149.** "Browder, a very . . . a native American." Gitlow (*I Confess*), pp. 328–29, 330. In 1929, Communist organizer Jack Stachel (himself Jewish) observed (not approvingly) that in Los Angeles "practically 90 percent of the membership is Jewish" (Weyl, p. 118). Not until October 1936 was a majority of CPUSA members native-born. Not until September 1938 did that happen in New York (Lewy, p. 7). **149.** "In Browder, Stalin . . . on his own." Lyons, p. 64. **149.** "all the capitalist . . . [be] functioning alone." Foster, p. 275. **149.** "the main social . . . open fascist dictatorship." *NY Workers Age*, date unknown, p. 5; Klehr, p. 99. **149.** "step in the direction of fascism." Lewy, p. 22. **149.** "to preserve the . . . imperialist war abroad." Browder (*Communism in the United States*), p. 14. **149.** "carrying out more . . . against the masses." Wolfskill & Hudson, p. 123. **149.** "slave legislation." Klehr, p. 123. **149–150.** "from beginning to . . . of Wall Street." Wolfskill & Hudson, p. 124. **150.** "Mussolini-schooled boys of the Administration." *New Masses*, 11 December 1934, p. 4. **150.** "Social-Fascist Enemies of Jobless Get Answer." Klehr, p. 113. **150.** "Socialist ushers, about . . . a general battle." *NY Times*, 17 February 1934, p. 1.

150. "won't last long . . . be civil war." Latham, p. 45*fn*. **151.** "to deceive the . . . the chief enemy." Latham, p. 45. **151.** "broad people's anti-fascist . . . proletarian united front." Klehr, p. 170. **151.** "Comrades: you remember . . . of his cutthroats." Latham, p. 47. **151.** "If one is . . . socialism at all." Klehr, p. 171. **151.** "humiliating . . . not a revolutionary." Latham, p. 47. **152.** "applaud democracy and . . . birth of Lenin." Morgan (*Reds*), p. 168. **152.** Homosexuality, abortion. Ryan, p. 98. **152.** "Under Browder's leadership . . . on formal occasions." Ryan, p. 99. **152.** "to the fascist . . . bamboozle the masses." Latham, p. 47. **152.** "by continuing the . . . the American Revolution.'" Lyons, p. 173. **152.** Fifth generation. *American Heritage*, December 1971, p. 59. **153.** "Communism is Twentieth Century Americanism." *New Masses*, 14 July 1936, p. 18. **153.** "Innocents' Clubs" Morgan (*Reds*), p. 169. **153.** West Side Mothers for Peace. Morgan (*Reds*), p. 169. **153.** "In the country's . . . influence and power." Lewy, p. 56. **153.** League of American Writers. Lyons, pp. 146–48. Many intellectuals had already jumped on the Communist bandwagon. Endorsing the 1932 Foster–Ford CPUSA ticket were Sherwood Anderson, Waldo Frank, Theodore Dreiser, John Dos Passos, Malcolm Cowley, Erskine Caldwell, Lincoln Steffens, Granville Hicks, Mathew Josephson, Sidney Hook, Clifton Fadiman, Edmund Wilson, Upton Sinclair, and Frederick L. Schuman (Schlesinger [*Crisis*], pp. 436–37). **153.** Hollywood Anti-Nazi League. *LA Daily News*, 3 June 1936, p. 3; *LA Times*, 18 October 1936, p. 50; *California Eagle*, 31 December 1936, p. 1; Radosh & Radosh, pp. 43–44, 47–54; Ryskind, pp. 35–42; Miles, pp. 161–64. After spending part of his honeymoon in Leningrad and Moscow in 1936, Lubitsch permanently soured on the Soviets—and eventually on the Anti-Nazi League, which he saw as a Communist front (McCormick, p. 247). **154.** "In those days . . . be a Republican." HCUA (Los Angeles), p. 2571. **154.** "only game in town." Navasky, p. 244. **154.** American Student Union. Ryan, p. 91. **154.** "the Stalinists and . . . of conservative newspapers." *New Leader*, 10 December 1938, p. 8. **154.** "[I]t was in . . . at that time." *American Heritage*, December 1971, p. 61. **154.** "wanted [us] . . . Roosevelt in fact." *American Heritage*, December 1971, p. 61. **155.** "In California . . . even greater results." *The Communist*, July 1936, p. 584. **155.** 1930 Congress. Kramer, pp. 206–24; O'Connor (*Broun*), pp. 160–65. **155.** Expulsion. Kramer, p. 241; O'Connor (*Broun*), p. 179. **155.** "in getting out . . . to the left." *Pittsburgh Press*, 29 April 1933, p. 1; Klehr, p. 102. **155.** "We've got to . . . without Communists included." *NY Daily Worker*, 18 June 1936, p. 1. Charles Michelson described Broun as "an extreme liberal possibly with communistic ideals" (Michelson, p. 125). **155.** "I'm not a . . . and government is okay." *NY Daily Worker*, 19 June 1936, p. 2. **156.** 20,000. *NY Times*, 28 November 1935, p. 36. **156.** Singing. *NY Times*, 28 November 1935, p. 36. **156.** "the maximum possible . . . and good faith." *NY Times*, 28 November 1935, p. 36. **156.** "to make Socialists . . . and unsocialist folly." *NY Times*, 28 November 1935, p. 36. **156.** "Mr. Browder considered . . . good Communist doctrine." *NY Times*, 28 November 1935, p. 36. **156.** "Is Russia so . . . Ethiopians are killed." Swanberg (*Thomas*), p. 91. **156.** "a love feast. . . . the Communist party." *NY Times*, 28 November 1935, p. 36. **156.** "did not think . . . formal united front." *St. Louis Post-Dispatch*, 28 November 1935, p. 17. **157.** "Under French conditions . . . worth its cost." *New Republic*, 6 May 1936, p. 374. **157–158.** "SHADES OF LENIN! . . . happiness to all." (!)" *New Militant*, 8 February 1936, p. 4. **158.** Browder attends. *St. Louis Post-Dispatch*, 25 May 1936, p. 1. **158.** "America's foremost apostle . . . of the land." *St. Louis Post-Dispatch*, 25 May 1936, p. 2. **158.** "honeycombed with Communists." *St. Louis Post-Dispatch*, 25 May 1936, p. 2. **158.** Honorary

Presiding Committee. *NY Daily Worker*, 25 June 1936, p. 2. **158.** "The delegates from . . . looking forward to.'" *NY Daily Worker*, 25 June 1936, p. 2. **158.** Bloor. *NY Times*, 25 June 1936, p. 11. **159.** Ware. Klehr, pp. 140–43, 229; Latham, pp. 103–04, 106–11; Morgan (*Reds*), pp. 154–55. **159.** "Twenty-five thousand . . . revolutionary movement. . . ." *NY Herald Tribune*, 29 June 1936, p. 4. **159.** "Frederick Douglass of 1936." *NY Daily Worker*, 29 June 1936, p. 1. **159.** "Communist version of . . . grey flannel suit." Naison, p. 99. **159.** "The dictatorship of . . . It is tyranny." Draper, p. 125. **159.** "A truly gifted . . . was his business." Draper, p. 126. **159.** "a true son . . . to those traditions." *Allentown Morning Call*, 29 June 1936, p. 4. **160.** 2.25 hours. *NY Times*, 25 June 1936, p. 11. **160.** Radio. *NY Herald Tribune*, 29 June 1936, p. 4. **160.** "the Soviet Union . . . enough to boast." *NY Daily Worker*, 29 June 1936, p. 2. **160.** "At the head . . . William Randolph Hearst." *NY Daily Worker*, 29 June 1936, p. 1.

10 "HEIL HEARST"

162. Hearst holdings. *American Magazine*, March 1912, p. 545; Winfield, p. 21. **162.** $100 million. Beasley, p. 122. **163.** "William Also-Randolph Hearst." Carlyle, p. 4. **163.** "in league with . . . lack of milk." O'Connor (*Smith*), p. 110. **163.** "an agitator we . . . in American politics." *NY Evening Post*, 1 March 1904, p. 6. **163.** "a loyal American . . . and sincere Democrat." *NY Times*, 3 January 1932, p. 3. **163.** Curley. Curley, p. 237. **164.** $25,000. Nasaw (*Patriarch*), p. 183. **165.** "ROOSEVELT ASKS DICTATOR'S ROLE." Farr, p. 191. **165.** "Please tell the . . . stop the presses." Procter (*Later*), pp. 179–80. **165.** Hearst mollified. Nasaw (*Hearst*), p. 479. **165.** Broun. Nasaw (*Hearst*), p. 482; O'Connor (*Broun*), pp. 181–90. **165–166.** "a menace to . . . supposed to serve." *San Francisco Examiner*, 29 October 1933, p. 1. **166.** "No Recovery Allowed." *Albany Times-Union*, 31 October 1933, p. 2; Procter (*Later*), p. 181. From Germany, in 1934, he also blasted the NRA as "Nonsensical, Ridiculous, Asinine" (*NY Times*, 2 September 1934, p. 12). Communists termed it the "National Run Around" (Lundberg, p. 360). **166.** "The people elected . . . say unconstitutional, interruption." *Albany Times-Union*, 31 October 1933, pp. 1–2. **166.** "all wet . . . of hard men." *NY Times*, 3 December 1933, p. 32. **166.** May 1934 overnight. http://www.fdrlibrary.marist.edu/daybyday/daylog/may-24th-1934/. **166.** Misquoted. Coblentz, p. 111; Swanberg (*Hearst*), p. 442. **166.** Millicent. http://www.fdrlibrary.marist.edu/daybyday/daylog/may-31st-1934/. **166–167.** "much of the administration . . . is not good." *Syracuse American*, 23 July 1934, p. 2. **167.** "I am told. . . . The President agreed." Nasaw (*Hearst*), p. 500. Davies's tax problems, largely involving Manhattan real estate, dated back to the Hoover administration. In 1931, she settled with the government for $825,000. **167.** Elliott Roosevelt. Collier with Horowitz, pp. 373–75; Hansen (kindle edition). **167.** Keehn, Astor. Nasaw (*Hearst*), p. 501. **167.** Kennedy. Roosevelt (*Letters*), Vol. 1, p. 424; Swanberg (*Hearst*), p. 529. **167.** "a period of genuine recovery." *SF Examiner*, 10 October 1934, p. 1. **167.** "Government cannot continue . . . wholesale a manner." *SF Examiner*, 10 October 1934, p. 1. **167–168.** "told [FDR] that . . . the Hearst matter." Ickes (*Diary*), p. 354. **168.** "Huey Longism, Coughlinism . . . just too bad." Nasaw (*Hearst*), p. 513. **169.** "Tell Mr. Hearst to go to hell." Eaton, p. 288. **169.** the most sinister . . . and most dangerous." Morison, p. 1249. **169.** Hired Hitler. Nasaw (*Hearst*), p. 474. **169.** Dachshunds. Procter (*Later*), p. 184. **169.** "Everybody is for . . . evidences of disturbance." Nasaw (*Hearst*), p. 494. Hearst's biographer David Nasaw contended that Hearst's opinion was "not inaccurate." **170.** "The results represent . . . the world. "*NY Times*, 23 August 1934, p. 10. In Hearst's defense, while this might simply be a case of translation from English to German and back again, somehow this passage just doesn't quite read like Hearst. **170.** Misquoted. Swanberg (*Hearst*), p. 444; Conradi, p. 173. **170–171.** "When you are . . . week or so." Conradi, p. 173. **171.** "has not been . . . subject to criticism." *The Guardian*, 15 September 1934, p. 15. **171.** "Hitler is surrounded . . . off the catastrophe!" Crocker, p. XXI-10. **172.** Hearst opposed. Procter (*Later*), p. 185. **172.** "no matter what . . . talked to Hitler." Crocker, p. XXI-11. Before leaving for Europe, however, Hearst did express interest in meeting with Hitler (Pizzitola, p. 311). **172.** Mussolini. Guiles, p. 275. **172.** "I'd heard his . . . imagined. Possibly worse." Davies, pp. 205–06. **172.** "Have a heart . . . this mysterious person." Guiles, p. 276. **172.** Selwyn. Davies, p. 205; Guiles, p. 277. **172.** "Marion! I can't . . . can't get out." Guiles, p. 277. **172.** "didn't, and was . . . for two days." Davies, p. 205. **173.** "a stout, red-faced, gay fellow." Pizzitola, p. 313; Nasaw (*Hearst*), p. 487. **173.** "No communism—no . . . —no unemployment!" Pizzitola, p. 313. **173.** "Hanfstaengl has been . . . be Bismarck's study!" Crocker, p. XI-14. **173.** "asked Hitler whether . . . go with you." *Buffalo Evening News*, 17 September 1936, p. 12. **173.** "Visiting Hitler is . . . it for publication." *SF Examiner*, 17 September 1936, p. 2. **173.** An hour. Crocker, p. XI-17. **173.** Five minutes. Davies, p. 206; Guiles, p. 277. **173.** "not impressed." Davies, p. 207. **173.** "I didn't understand . . . his interpreter either." Davies, p. 206. **173–174.** "Hitler certainly is . . . can be misdirected." Procter (*Later*), p. 187. **174.** "after consulting . . . to my regime?" Crocker, p. XI-14. **174.** "But I am . . . a two-thirds majority." Crocker, p. XI-15. **174.** "That might be . . . those policies are." Crocker, p. XI-15. **174.** "averse to dictatorship . . . Germany?" . . . fellows in Germany." Crocker, p. XI-16. **174.** "But what about the American Indians?" Guiles, p. 277. **174–175.** "[T]hese vigorous measures . . . evidence of it." Crocker, p. XI-16. **175.** "that the Jews . . . to every nationality." Davis, p. 207. **175.** "I only had . . . impress these Americans." Conradi, pp. 173–74. **175.** "go to Berlin . . . am unwarrantably interfering." Nasaw (*Hearst*), p. 499. Absolutely no one is quite sure where Hearst got the notion that Hitler had granted the Saarland's Jews any rights at all. **175.** "a chain reaction . . . accomplished his ruin." Winkler, p. 270. Scripps-Howard publisher Roy Howard similarly met with Hitler in February 1936, escaping, however, with no public ill effects. His subsequent interview with Stalin earned him a Pulitzer Prize (Beard, pp. 180–96). **175–176.** Contributor. *NY Times*, 1 November 1932, p. 18; *NY Times*, 5 January 1933, p. 27. Robert Allen and Drew Pearson later noted that Moffet "probably did as much to retard housing as anyone with the possible exception of the building and loan associations" (*Pittsburgh Press*, 6 December 1937, p. 2). **176.** Indicted. *NY Times*, 31 March 1934, p. 7. **175.** "absolutely pro-German . . . of the Führer." Pauwels, p. 33. "All three were wealthy oilmen and were very likely considering business arrangements with Hitler—not unlike that made by Standard Oil of New Jersey, which had secret arrangements with the Nazis selling oil through a series of shell companies and third-party traders," commented the documents' auctioneer. (https://www.alexautographs.com/auction-lot/franklin-roosevelt-asks-that-his-friends-be-grant_30D469DBC1/; *Washington Examiner*, 17 August 2021, p. 43). **175.** Resignation. *Detroit Free Press*, 24 August 1940, p. 1. **176.** Quotes from German correspondence. https://www.alexautographs.com/auction-lot/franklin-roosevelt-asks-that-his-friends

-be-grant_30D469DBC1/; *Washington Examiner*, 17 August 2021, p. 43. **177.** $400,000. Nasaw (*Hearst*), pp. 510–11. The *New York Times* printed an account of this story, then quickly deep-sixed all copies of the paper for fear of a Hearst libel suit. **177.** "Soviet Power in . . . Meet This Year." Nasaw (*Hearst*), p. 486. **177.** "Communist Plan for . . . United States Revealed." Nasaw (*Hearst*), p. 486. **177.** "saying that the . . . the cockroach man." Nasaw (*Hearst*), pp. 486, 647. **177.** "Fascism seems to . . . which democracy assures." Coblentz, p. 106; Swanberg (*Hearst*), p. 446. **177.** "DRIVE ALL RADICAL . . . FROM THE UNIVERSITIES." Procter (*Later*), p. 195. **177.** College investigation begins. *Syracuse Journal*, 22 November 1934, pp. 1–2; Nasaw (*Hearst*), p. 504. Concurrently, Hearst also supported state-mandated teacher loyalty oaths. **178.** "('Private and Confidential . . . contemporaries put together." Nasaw (*Hearst*), pp. 514–15. **178.** "As yet the . . . converted to fascism." Lundberg, p. 347. **178.** "a Congressional inquiry . . . to the people." Lundberg, p. 380; *North American Review*, Autumn 1936, p. 184. **178.** "un-American activities." Procter (*Later*), p. 196. **178.** "Labor Enemy No. 1." *NY Post*, 4 February 1935, p. 5; *New Militant*, 9 February 1935, p. 1. **178.** Loyalty oaths. Lundberg, p. 352; Procter (*Later*), p. 195. **178.** "vicious Fascist policies . . . press and assembly." *NY Post*, 31 July 1936, p. 1. By 1935, the New York City Teachers Union (Local 5 of the American Federation of Teachers) had fallen under Communist control. **178.** "Heil Hearst . . . demagogue of America." *New Masses*, 9 April 1935, p. 9. **179.** "effectively combating the . . . this is true. E.R." Nasaw (*Hearst*), p. 515. **179.** KGB. Haynes, Klehr & Vassilev, pp. 159–60. **179.** Carnegie Hall rally. *NY Times*, 26 February 1935, p. 8. While the CPUSA railed against Hearst (and vice-versa) the *Daily Worker* enriched his coffers by subscribing to the photographic services of the Hearst empire (Casey, pp. 9–10). **179.** "the boycott, which . . . parent teachers' organizations." Nasaw (*Hearst*), pp. 507, 648. **179.** "settle down to . . . a dictatorship now." Nasaw (*Hearst*), pp. 511, 649. **179.** "It is . . . than are necessary." Nasaw (*Hearst*), pp. 514, 649. **179–180.** "I have got . . . going to have." Nasaw (*Hearst*), pp. 514, 649. Hearst was not the only one calculating how to sidestep FDR's tax plan. In the end, it delivered relatively little revenue—just $45 million from its upper bracket increases and $250 million overall. Within three years, only one individual, John D. Rockefeller Jr., fell into the $1 million bracket (Burk, p. 187). So, why did Roosevelt propose it? Probably from an imprecise combination of three factors. Pure politics—bashing the rich often works like a charm in any era, but particularly well in 1935–36; a cavalier ignorance of basic economic laws; and sheer pique following business criticisms of his New Deal. **180.** "President's taxation program . . . and class antagonism." Coblentz, p. 179. **180.** "thought [the tax] . . . is for Hearst." Ickes (*Diary*), p. 384. To his ally, publisher Roy Howard, however, FDR dismissed the tax bill as "lousy," proposed "solely because of [the] political campaign year" (Beard, p. 197). **180.** "The Chief instructs . . . of 'New Deal.'" Levin, p. 154. **180.** "The President believes . . . to news columns." Nasaw (*Hearst*), p. 515. Hearst biographer David Nasaw indicates this FDR blast was released to the press. This does not appear to be the case (Nasaw [*Hearst*], p. 515). **181.** "The party has . . . as [its] successors." Brownell & Billings, pp. 179–80. **181–182.** The . . . United States . . . of the American people." *Philadelphia Inquirer*, 1 September 1935, p. 2. **181–182.** Philatelist. *Fort Myers News-Press*, 2 December 1968, p. 2A. **181–182.** Etchings. *Plainfield News-Courier*, 20 July 1934, p. 7. **181–182.** Fawcett call. Ickes (*Diary*), p. 428. **182.** "This movement to . . . against the president." Ickes (*Diary*), pp. 428–29. Heywood Broun (presumably not in on what was astir) saw it differently: "The position taken by the State Department . . . seems to rest on the wholly erroneous point of view that nobody in America ever has a radical thought or utters a radical word unless he has received a picture postcard from Joseph Stalin. Severance of relations with Russia would not abate radical propaganda by one jot. My own impression is that, all Russian officials in this country have bent over backward in an effort to keep to the strict letter of the . . . agreement" (*NY Daily Worker*, 28 August 1935, p. 2). Leftist journalist Mauritz Hallgren saw FDR's move as a "surrender to the Hearst press . . . made in that spirit of joyous unconcern for its effects that had marked all Rooseveltian ballyhoo from the start. . . . That the President should have gone to such dangerous lengths in seeking to prove, for the sake of his own political future, that he was no friend of the Communists was characteristic of the man" (Hallgren, p. 314). **183.** "a drop of . . . in the dark." *NY Sun*, 30 October 1919, p. 3; *NY Tribune*, 30 October 1919, p. 6. **183.** "Constitutional Democratic Party." *SF Examiner*, 29 August 1935, p. 1. **183.** "It is not . . . properly and patriotically." *SF Examiner*, 29 August 1935, p. 2. This was not Hearst's first volte-face regarding Smith. Following their "Milk Trust" contretemps in 1920, Hearst endorsed him against future Liberty Leaguer Nathan Miller. W. R. supported William Gibbs McAdoo for president versus Smith in 1924 and Ogden Mills for governor against him in 1926 (Lundberg, p. 254).

11 "THE OLD DEAL"

184. Rogers. Warren, p. 64. **184.** Johnson/PWA. McJimsey, p. 92. **184.** Norris. Patterson, p. 48. **185.** "displaying in exile . . . while in office." Sheppard, p. 327. **185.** "Hoover of 1932 . . . inspiring and militant." *Rock Island Argus*, 10 June 1936, p. 3. **185–186.** "The Republicans used . . . candidates to victory." Timmons, p. 209. **186.** 1932. *LA Daily News*, 29 October 1932, p. 5; Ross (*Hollywood*), p. 69. In *The Champ*, Jackie Cooper's stepfather was played by Hale Hamilton, John D. M. Hamilton's older brother. **186.** Hoover/Davies. Pizzitola, p. 290. According to Mayer biographer Charles Higham, however, Hoover instead refused Mayer's request for Hearst to be received at the White House (Higham, p. 178). **186.** "Dear Louis: I . . . —W. R" Crowther pp. 196–97; Swanberg (*Hearst*), p. 443. **186.** FDR favors Hoover. Trohan, p. 83; Ickes (*Diary*), p. 467. **186–187.** "The real cause . . . leave us alone." *Collier's*, 12 October 1935, p. 8. **186.** "a mekka for the Capital's intelligentsia." *Literary Digest*, 1 February 1936, p. 9. **186.** "as an adept . . . over the teacups," *Literary Digest*, 1 February 1936, p. 9. **186.** "the flightiest numbbrain that ever was." Felsenthal, p. 148. **187.** Borah in Boise. Felsenthal, pp. 147–49; Cordery (*Alice*), pp. 303–04, 525. **186.** "The trouble with . . . that are objectionable." Garraty, p. 347. **186.** "speaking of a . . . even know myself." Garraty, p. 347. **186.** "one of the . . . on Capitol Hill." Felsenthal, p. 135. "Fishbait" Miller's words. **186.** Paulina. Cordery, pp. 303–25; Felsenthal, pp. 155–59; Peyser & Dwyer, pp. 153–58. Unverified rumors also eventually connected Alice romantically to *Baltimore Sun* columnist Frank Kent, Burton K. Wheeler, and John L. Lewis (Teichmann, pp. 160, 192; Felsenthal, pp. 191–93, 197; Cordery, pp. 413–16). **186.** Borah/Patterson. Cordery (*Alice*), pp. 303, 313. **186.** Nick/Patterson. Cordery (*Alice*), pp. 303–04, 314. **188–189.** "Some weeks ago . . . she? Can she?" Brough, pp. 282–83. Ruth Hanna McCormick was the daughter of famed McKinley adviser Marc Hanna. **189.** Suffrage. *Modern Monthly*, July 1936, p. 21. **189.** Direct election. *Crisis*, March 1936, p. 64. **189.** "Life is as . . . other country." *Hazleton Plain Speaker*, 4 December 1922, p. 5. **189.** "Mussolini is a . . . down in history." *Modern Monthly*, July 1936, p. 21. **189.** 11 of 17. *Richmond Times-Dispatch*, 26 January 1936, Sect. IV, p. 5. **189.** Marcantonio. *Daily Worker*, 27 March 1936, p. unknown. **189.** 74%. Brinkley, p. 174. **189.** Long would step aside. *Alexandria Weekly Town Talk*, 17 August 1935, p. 2. **190.** "Which place, Mr. President?" McKenna, p. 211. **190.** "Borah is first . . . inconsistencies and unreasonableness." *Randolph Register*, 5 June 1936, p. 7. **190.** "Must bother the . . . as the *horse*." McKee, p. 2. **190.** "Borah was . . . the Foreign Relations Committee." *Pacific Northwest Quarterly*, October 1965, pp. 145–46. **190.** Operation. McKenna, pp. 306–07. **190.** 208 votes. *Literary Digest*, 4 January 1936, p. 6. **191.** Lunch with FDR. *Louisville Courier-Journal*, 8 February 1936, pp. 1–2. **191.** "his most enthusiastic . . . of Wall Street." *Wall Street Journal*, 1 May 1936, p. 2. **191.** "grave mistake . . . years of slavery." *Modern Monthly*, July 1936, p. 21. **191.** "I will say . . . the right to vote." *Crisis*, March 1936, p. 64. **192.** Burial detail. Beasley, pp. 18, 19. **192.** "They was almost walking by themselves." Beasley, p. 26. **192.** *Grand Rapids Herald. Chicago Tribune*, 29 April 1944, p. 5; Beasley, pp. 29–36. **192.** Windows, saloonkeeper. *NY Times*, 29 April 1944, p. 8. **192.** "Osborne, Harmony, and a New Deal." *Detroit Free* Press, 31 October 1910, p. 44. **193.** State chairman. *Detroit Free Press*, 29 April 1944, p. 1. **193.** 1924 governorship. *NY Times*, 4 November 1923, p. E14. **193.** $52,000. Beasley, p. 126. **193.** $150,000. Beasley, p. 126; *NY Times*, 29 April 1944, p. 8. **193.** $12 million. Beasley, p. 132. **193.** "a good newspaper . . . the proper field." *NY Times*, 29 April 1944, p. 8. **193.** $52,000. Beasley, p. 126. **193.** "one of the world's . . . girlfriend." *The Student*, Winter 1978, p. 18. **194.** "her presence irked . . . had been cut." Trohan, p. 147. **194.** "Hello, Is Leola . . . your conscience, Frank." Trohan, p. 147; Smith (*Colonel*), p. 343. **194.** "fundamentally trusting in . . . and was fooled." *The Nation*, 19 February 1936, p. 219. **194.** "Upon what food . . . you were elected?" *Arizona Republic*, 26 July 1935, p. 17. **195.** "hysteria . . . quest for truth." *The Nation*, 19 February 1936, p. 220. **195.** "Knox plays as . . . for the Indians." *Scott County Journal*, 12 February 1936, p. 4. **196.** "I had no . . . to enjoy myself." Tompkins, p. 2. **196.** Editor-in-chief. *Battle Creek Enquirer*, 19 April 1951, p. 3. **196.** "My boy, I . . . a good Republican." *Battle Creek Enquirer*, 19 April 1951, p. 3. **196.** Fired. *Battle Creek Enquirer*, 19 April 1951, p. 3; Tompkins, p. 4. **196.** "red-headed, . . . from the Soo." Beasley, p. 57. **197.** "When will Vandenberg stop talking?" Meijer, p. 5. **197.** "the only Senator . . . strut sitting down." Tompkins, pp. 45–46. **197.** "looked and acted . . . Northerner in history." *American Mercury*, January 1947, p. 6. **197.** "one of the . . . often king size." Trohan, p. 142. **197.** "I knew Vandenberg . . . had in preparation." Mahl (ebook). **197.** "a pretty third-rate fellow." Blum (*Lippmann*), p. 346. **197.** "Yes and No Man." *American Mercury*, January 1947, p. 6. **197.** "He has stood . . . but never dies." *American Mercury*, January 1947, p. 6. **197.** "Vacuity, Vacillation and Vandenberg." *Philadelphia Inquirer*, 18 November 1934, p. A5. **197.** "Social-mindedness, not socialism." *NY Sun*, 23 November 1937, p. 14. **197.** Borah a friend. Tompkins, pp. 132–33. **197.** "It won't work . . . down the strong." Tompkins, p. 85; Meijer, p. 79. **197.** "a gigantic task . . . possibly be done." *St Louis Post-Dispatch*, 2 January 1934, p. 1. **197.** 3 of 17. *Richmond Times-Dispatch*, 26 January 1936, Sect. IV, p. 5. **197.** "If we make . . . issue we'll lose!" *Richmond Times-Dispatch*, 26 January 1936, Sect. IV, p. 5. **197.** "You don't think . . . I don't know." *Richmond Times-Dispatch*, 26 January 1936, Sect. IV, p. 3. **198.** "They say Hoover . . . to whip anybody." Meijer, p. 114. **199.** "the apotheosis of . . . disregard of elegance." Stone, p. 307. **199.** "I thought he . . . he first telephoned." *SF Examiner*, 21 June 1936, p. 17. **199.** $1,000. *Cosmopolitan*, November 1935, p. 176. **199.** 100,000 Klansmen. Chalmers, p. 144. **199.** $25. Chalmers, p. 147. **199.** "spit in the . . . of the Klan." Johnson, p. 245. White captured 22.71 percent of the vote. **199.** La Follette. Schlesinger (*Upheaval*), p. 533. **199.** Poll. *Literary Digest*, 24 September 1932, p. 8. **199.** "Langdon" Tompkins, p. 133; Meijer, p. 120. **199.** $15.68 to $13.41. Schlesinger (*Upheaval*), p. 531. **199.** "all regulars— . . . were always insurgents." Schlesinger (*Upheaval*), p. 532. **200–201.** "an interesting state . . . his campaign material!" Lowitt & Beasley, p. 341. **201.** "Our problems have . . . last quarter century." *The Nation*, 15 January 1936, p. 70. **201.** "He is sane . . . like a son." McCoy, p. 34. **201.** "The World's Greatest . . . Confessor of Hollywood." *Arizona Republic*, 14 April 1988, p. E3. **201.** St. John/Runyon. *Cosmopolitan*, November 1935, pp. 30–31, 172–74; *Good Housekeeping*, November 1935, pp. 24–25, 174–80. **201.** "large motherly sort . . . the whitest skin." *Good Housekeeping*, November 1935, p. 177. **201.** Stone on Runyon. Stone, p. 310. **201.** "it is said . . . if you persist." *Cosmopolitan*, November 1935, p. 174. **201.** Hearst on board. McCoy, p. 232. **201.** Headquarters. Schruben, p. 192; McCoy, p. 223. **201.** Mills/Hoover. McCoy, pp. 225–26. **201.** "If we are . . . far from fascism." McCoy, p. 223. **201.** Ohio State Chamber. Schruben, p. 193; McCoy, pp. 227–28. **201.** "We are convinced . . . impression in 1935." *Somerset Daily American*, 21 November 1935, p. 4. **201.** "chintz boudoir." Hoge, p. 173. **201.** Visit to Topeka. McCoy, p. 232; Nasaw (*Hearst*), p. 516. **201.** Block's idea. Carlisle, pp. 167–68. **201.** "He's just the . . . wife is lovely. **201.** *Buffalo Courier-Express*, 11 December 1935, p. 4. **202–203.** "If the Republicans . . . can be defeated." *Buffalo Courier-Express*, 11 December 1935, p. 4. **201.** "I think he . . . it very mildly." *Buffalo Courier-Express*, 11 December 1935, p. 4. **201.** "From the very . . . of my ability." Schlesinger (*Upheaval*), p. 533. **201.** "I do not . . . in his country." Swing, p. 182. **201.** "America bids fair . . . prosperity and opportunity." Swing, pp. 182–83. **201.** League/Court. Schlesinger (*Upheaval*), p. 538. **201.** Thomas. *The Nation*, 15 January 1936. p. 72; *Richmond Times-Dispatch*, 1 March 1936, p. 42; *San Bernardino County Sun*, 30 September 1936, p. 13; Swing, p. 182; Davis (*New Deal*), p. 625. **201.** "Under the academic . . . of our schools." *The Nation*, 15 January 1936, p. 72. **203–204.** "[Landon] is not . . . care to believe." *The Nation*, 15 January 1936, p. 72. **204.** "Right here with . . . courageous and sincere." *The Crisis*, May 1936, p. 139.

12 "ANNO DOMINI FATHER DIVINE"

206. "My friends, go . . . paid in full." *Pittsburgh Courier*, 13 February 1952, p. 5. **206.** Literacy, housing, schools. *Journal of Blacks in Higher Education*, Winter 2002/2003, p. 45; Braeman et al (*Vol. 1*), p. 186. **206.** "By the end . . . in the CCC." Goodwin (*Ordinary*), p. 163. **206.** "I think spring . . . in every season." *Pittsburgh Press*, 16 September 1940, p. 19. **206.** "Never have I . . . in like prisoners." *Pittsburgh Press*, 8 May 1936, p. 39. **206.** "She received Negro . . . First Lady understood." Lash (*Eleanor*), p. 522. **207.** Previous Roosevelt invitations. Keiler, p. 166. **207.** "After [Marian] sang . . . pride she felt." Keiler, pp. 166–67. **207.** "Blacks in the thirties . . . in anyone's memory." Goodwin (*Ordinary*), p. 163. **207.** Hated Warm Springs. *Allentown Morning Call*, 20 November 1977, p. D13. Warm Springs was originally named "Bullochville." It was FDR who renamed it. Local Bullochs, however, were not related to Eleanor and TR's Bulloch kin (www.bullochhouse.com/history). **207.** "I quite understand . . . the old plantation life." Lash (*Eleanor*), p. 522. **207.** "War Between the States" Lash (*Eleanor*), p. 522. **207.** "pickaninny." Lash (*Eleanor*), p. 522. **207.** Lash (*Eleanor*), p. 522. **208.** "as a term . . . in that light." Lash (*Eleanor*), p. 522. Corrected on the term "darky," she apologized, "I am sorry if it hurt you. What do you prefer?" **208.** "I want to . . . has the Republican." Lash (*Eleanor*), p. 519. In 1941, however, a Black quartet, "The Grand Central Red Caps," captured the New York City championship of The National Society for the Encouragement and Preservation of Barber Shop Quartet Singing in America, but was barred from the national competition. Al Smith and Robert Moses resigned their memberships. Moses was particularly irate (*NY Times*, 13 July 1941, p. 1). **208.** "Eating with someone . . . believe in intermarriage." Lash (*Eleanor*), p. 521. **208.** "pleasanter to deal . . . this or that." O'Reilly, p. 110. **208.** "a complete darky household." O'Reilly, p. 110. **208.** Eleanor Roosevelt to Ike Hoover, 9 February 1933. Original at the Roosevelt Houses, NYC. FDR's lack of concern for his black valet Irvin "Mac" McDuffie outraged Rexford Tugwell. In 1939, McDuffie suffered a nervous breakdown (Tugwell [*Brains*], p. 28). Walter Trohan recorded that "FDR let Mrs. R. bring an occasional Negro into the White House but almost never saw one himself. Roosevelt had his personal valet, Irwin McDuffie, thrown into the Navy brig for looking on gin when it was white [i.e., drinking heavily]. That smacked more of Simon Legree than the friend of the common man. Mrs. R. persuaded her husband to give McDuffie a number of chances, but finally had to agree to his replacement" (Trohan, pp. 101–02). **208.** "I believe it . . . to be kind." Lash (*Eleanor*), p. 521. **208–209.** "He was a . . . on his feet." Wilkins, p. 127. Wilkins's reference to "red clay," no doubt, refers to the famous red clay of segregationist Georgia, FDR's Southern home base. Harry Truman, while still considering FDR a great president, concurred regarding his aloofness. "He was the coldest man I ever met," HST assessed in 1970. "He didn't give a damn personally for me or you or anyone else in the world as far as I could see" (Ferrell, p. 168; Costigliola, p. 680). As did journalist George Creel: FDR "joked and joshed and gibed, but what a change occurred when anyone took a liberty with him! The atmosphere chilled instantly to the freezing point" (Creel, p. 335). **209.** "a drink of . . . forget the dust." O'Reilly, p. 110. **209.** "In four White . . . issue of race." O'Reilly, p. 111. **209.** "dreaded" Lash, p. 514; O'Reilly, p. 111. **209.** "don't you think . . . for the Negro?" Lash (*Eleanor*), p. 528. **209.** Jubal Early. "Unofficial Observer" (*New Dealers*), p. 223. **209.** Rail-thin, tubercular. Smith (*Gatekeeper*), p. 112. Tuberculosis also afflicted Missy's assistant Grace Tully and previously afflicted Raymond Moley. **209.** "our southern Brethren . . . anxious colored brethren." O'Reilly, p. 114. **209–210.** "no admirer . . . Dealer at heart." Trohan, pp. 67, 137. **210.** Reporters barred. Lash, p. 519; O'Reilly, p. 115. **209–210.** "I have taken . . . ignore the letter." Lash (*Eleanor*), pp. 519, 742. **209–210.** "Cannot arrange appointment . . . requiring immediate attention." Lash (*Eleanor*), p. 515. **210.** "The President talked . . . you want to." Lash (*Eleanor*), p. 515. **211.** "But, Joe Robinson . . . bill is unconstitutional." Lash (*Eleanor*), p. 516. **210.** "Somebody's been . . . it my wife?" Lash (*Eleanor*), p. 516. **210.** "Well, at least . . . on my side." White (*Kingfish*), p. 169. **210.** "I did not . . . take that risk." Braeman et al (*Vol. 1*), p. 201. Scholar Raymond Wolters makes an interesting point about NAACP involvement in the anti-lynching movement: "Regardless of what the president had done, there was no real chance of cloture being voted and the anti-lynching bill passed. Indeed, there is considerable evidence suggesting that the leaders of the NAACP themselves recognized there was no realistic possibility of securing the legislation; they launched the anti-lynching campaign to keep the name of their organization before the public, to raise funds, and, most importantly, to outmaneuver militant black critics who were demanding that the association deemphasize agitation, courtroom activities, and congressional lobbying and devote more of its attention to the economic problems that plagued the masses of Negroes" (Braeman et al [*Vol. 1*], p. 201). **210.** "You go ahead . . . can't do it." Braeman et al (*Vol. 1*), p. 201. **211.** "Well, what about . . . anything about her." Braeman et al (*Vol. 1*), p. 201. **211–212.** "a vile form . . . condone lynch law." *Washington Star*, 7 December 1933, p. 3. Author Kenneth O'Reilly writes: "Roosevelt finally condemn[ed] such crimes after a mob executed a white man in San Jose, California, as 'a vile form of collective murder.' Two days later in St Joseph, Missouri, when vigilantes tortured, burned, and hung a nineteen-year-old black man, the president returned to a policy of silence." This implies that the Missouri lynching occurred two days after Roosevelt spoke. It did not. It occurred two days after the San Jose lynching, and news coverage of FDR's remarks referenced not only the San Jose and Missouri lynchings but one also in Maryland. **212.** "They did a . . . I'll pardon them." *Oroville Mercury Register*, 27 November 1933, p. 1. **212.** Neal lynching. Lash (*Eleanor*), p. 516; Wilkins, pp. 132–33. **212.** "advertised hours in . . . apparently indifferent throughout." Lash (*Eleanor*), p. 516. **212.** "Across the country . . . jail for it." Wilkerson, p. 61. **212.** Crime Conference. Wilkins, pp. 132–36. **213.** Lindberg Act. Wilkins, p. 133. **213.** "any woman or . . . other immoral purpose." *Brooklyn Daily Eagle*, 25 October 1913, p. 6. **213.** Carnegie Hall invitation. Lash (*Eleanor*), pp. 516–17. **213.** "President says this is dynamite." Lash (*Eleanor*), pp. 517, 742. **213.** "The more I . . . get it through." Wilkins, p. 130. Eleanor might also have fretted about the impact of the exhibition's cosponsors, the Communist-front groups, the John Reed Club, the League of Struggle for Negro Rights, and the International Labor Defense. **213.** Attended. Wilkins, p. 130. **214.** Quarles. *Congressional Record*, 10 February 1936, p. 1712; McKenna, pp. 31–32; Johnson (*Borah*), pp. 77–78. **214.** "Icy winds from . . . campaign died a-borning." White (*Kingfish*), pp. 171–72. **215.** "a white turban . . . Van Dyke beard." *NY Times*, 9 October 1934, p. 2. **215.** "a crude, racketeering . . . of black labor." Ottley, p. 116; *Journal of Negro History*, Summer-Autumn 1984, p. 139. **215.** Snipes. *NY Daily Worker*, 19 October 1936, pp. 1, 4. **215.** "HARLEM STORE ACTS . . . into the fight." *Jewish Daily Bulletin*, 2 November 1934, p. 1. **216.** "CHILD BRUTALLY BEATEN! . . . was then arrested." Knopf, p. 46. **216.** Young Communist League. Solomon (*Unity*), p. 273. **216.** Calming influence. Knopf, p. 47. **217.** "It was the . . . menacing." Stiles, p. 256. **217.** Howe wary of Reds. O'Reilly, p. 114. **217.** National Negro Congress. Wolters, pp. 358–76; Solomon (*Unity*), pp. 304, 336; *American Quarterly*, Winter 1970, pp. 883–91. The convening of the National Negro Congress followed a similar conference at Howard University, of which Kelly Miller complained that "the sessions were communistic in nature and . . . the overthrow of the United States Government by force was openly advocated" (Wolters, p. 377). Chicago Democratic Congressman Arthur Mitchell, the sole Black in Congress, concurred that "a house cleaning is most urgently needed" (Solomon [*Unity*], p. 250). **217.** Fish. *Daily Worker*, 22 January 1936, p. 2. **217–218.** "the spirit of . . . or in both." Wolters, p. 363. **218.** Davis. Wolters, pp. 373–74; Solomon (*Unity*), p. 237. **218.** "I give everything . . . fat and merry." *The Nation*, 6 February

1936, p. 153. **218.** "As to the . . . do with ravens." *The Forum*, April 1936, p. 213. **218.** "Basic in the . . . adherents is kept." *New Republic*, 16 September 1936, p. 148. **219.** "John Lamb." *New Yorker*, 20 June 1936, p. 36; Pumphrey, p. 107. **219.** New names. *The "Spoken Word,"* 8 September 1936, p. 22; *NY Amsterdam News*, 10 October 1936, p. 1. **219.** "emotionally maladjusted." *Journal of Educational Sociology*, January 1937, p. 303. **219.** "We may take . . . and live forever." *Journal of Educational Sociology*, January 1937, p. 298. **219.** "Shorty George." Harris, p. 197. **219.** "I say, I . . . help and counsel." *The Forum*, April 1936, p. 212. The Rockland Palace's most famous interracial event, however, was the annual "Faggots Ball," featuring what the *New York Amsterdam News* described as "some of the most notoriously degenerate white men in the city. . . . The judges were imported from Greenwich Village especially for this occasion" (*NY Amsterdam News*, 20 February 1929, p. 2). **219.** "God is peace. . . . Freedom, Equality, Love." *NY Daily Worker*, 6 August 1934, p. 6. **219.** "we must under . . . in the abstract." *NY Daily Worker*, 6 August 1934, p. 6. **220.** "with any party . . . in which Russia." *New Republic*, 16 September 1936, p. 148. **220.** "I never got . . . helped them, some." *The Forum*, April 1936, p. 212. **220.** May Day 1935. *New Republic*, 16 September 1936, p. 148; Barnes, pp. 480–81. **220.** "abolish racial discrimination . . . Amen, Father." Barnes, p. 481. **220.** "[I]ntelligent members of . . . label of 'Communist.'" Naison, pp. 150–51. **220.** "A. D. F. D."—"Anno Domini Father Divine." *NY Amsterdam News*, 18 January 1936, p. 1. **220.** Divine followers' locations. *The "Spoken Word,"* 8 September 1936, p. 32. **220–221.** "twenty-two million have . . . in Bodily Form." *The "Spoken Word,"* 8 September 1936, p. 7. **221.** Ford. *NY Amsterdam News*, 18 January 1936, p. 16. St. Nicholas Arena also hosted Mother Bloor's August 1951 funeral (*NY Times*, 15 August 1951, p. 24). **221.** Townsend. *NY Amsterdam News*, 18 January 1936, p. 16. **221.** FDR, Pius XI. Harris, pp. 197–98; Barnes, p. 498. **221.** "All [of its] . . . cult leader himself." *New York Amsterdam News*, 18 January 1936, p. 1. **221.** "to abolish lynching." *The "Spoken Word,"* 8 September 1936, p. 10. **221.** "making it a . . . creed or color." *The "Spoken Word,"* 8 September 1936, p. 10. **221.** "making it a . . . abusively concerning any." *The "Spoken Word,"* 8 September 1936, p. 10. **221–222.** "Abolition of all . . . their full capacity." *NY Times*, 8 January 1936, p. 19. **222.** "As far as . . . accidents, and disasters." *The "Spoken Word,"* 8 September 1936, p. 8. **222.** "The physicians . . . and complete happiness." *The "Spoken Word,"* 8 September 1936, p. 9. **222.** "There will be . . . earth without me." Harris, p. 199. **223.** "Why should the . . . I MEAN IT!" *The "Spoken Word,"* 8 September 1936, p. 9. *Workers Age* asked: "Is Father Divine offering his racket as a strike-breaking agency to the employers? Is Father Divine working behind the scenes with the bosses in the New York garment center?" (*Workers Age*, date unknown 1936, p. 2). **223.** "We believe that . . . in many unions." *Daily Worker*, 6 July 1936, p. 7. **223–224.** "That Divine is . . . headway in Harlem." Watts (*Divine*), pp. 66–67; *Workers Age*, date unknown 1936, p. 2. **224.** "preparing thousands in . . . next presidential election." *New Republic*, 16 September 1936, p. 148. **224.** "back a president . . . of the country." *NY Amsterdam News*, 18 January 1936, p. 16. **224.** "If President Roosevelt . . . of Father Divine." *NY Times*, 8 January 1936, p. 19. **224.** "Hoover could not . . . straighten it out!" March of Time Newsreel (1936). https://search.alexanderstreet.com/preview/work/bibliographic_entity%7Cvideo_work%7C1792740. **224.** "essential for every . . . protect equal rights." Watts (*Divine*), p. 108.

13 "DUMB-BELLS, FREAKS, RUBES AND HICKS"

226. Straw Vote. *NY Times*, 12 August 1935, p. 2; McCoy, p. 220; Schruben, p. 196. **227.** December 1935 Gallup poll. *Philadelphia Inquirer*, 1 December 1935, p. 3; Gallup, p. 4. **227.** Straw votes pro-rated totals. *Philadelphia Inquirer*, 31 January 1936, p. 5. **228.** Merriam. McCoy, p. 244. **228.** Hamilton. *Nebraska State Journal*, 10 March 1936, p. 1; McCoy, pp. 237–38. **228.** Starch Poll. *Detroit Free Press*, 4 January 1936, p. 4; *Atlanta Constitution*, 18 March 1936, p. 36. **229.** 99 of 102. Sheppard, p. 36. **229.** "Frank Knox carried . . . I carried Illinois." *Time*, 27 April 1936, p. 15. https://www.cnn.com/ALLPOLITICS/1996/analysis/back.time/9604/26/index.shtml. **229.** Nebraska. McCoy, pp. 245–46. **229.** April & May 3 polls. *Philadelphia Inquirer*, 5 April 1936, p. 9; *Philadelphia Inquirer*, 3 May 1936, p. 9. **229–230.** "flimsy accusations that . . . and Wall Street." McCoy, p. 236. **230.** "You have no . . . much honest money." McCoy, p. 237. **230.** "I have no . . . floor at nights!" Sinclair, p. 283. **230.** "Professionally, Hearst is . . . attract the undertaker." *Emporia Gazette*, 9 April 1936, p. 4. While tying Hearst to Landon ranked as a favorite pastime in 1936, Walter Lippmann devoted an April 1936 column opposing the practice of damning candidates—whether Landon, Hoover, Borah, Knox, or Vandenberg—because of their respective supporters or even quasi-supporters (the same principle could, of course, be applied to Roosevelt and the Communists). "It would seem," Lippmann argued, "to be a good deal fairer to judge [a candidate] as he is. By what he is, by what he has done, by what he proposes to do, rather than by the hitchhikers on his bandwagon" (*NY Herald Tribune*, 4 April 1936, p. 17). **230.** "a candidate and . . . the New Deal." *Lancaster Eagle-Gazette*, 13 May 1936, p. 1. **230.** Longworth. *Dayton Daily News*, 13 May, 1936, p. 1; *Time*, 25 May 1936, p. 14. Alice actually leaned toward Knox based on his Rough Rider connection to her father, though she eventually did become very close to Robert Taft and his outspoken wife (Sheppard, p. 27). **231.** "M. Herbert Hoover." *Akron Beacon Journal*, 13 May 1936, p. 6. **231.** Dickinson. *Collier's*, 11 April 1936, p. 56. **231.** Hoover's preferences. *NY Times*, 20 May 1936, p. 15. **231.** "I am not a . . . is with principles." *St. Louis Post-Dispatch*, 19 May 1936, p. 1. **232.** Florence Abbott. *St. Joseph Herald-Press*, May 1936, p. 1. **232.** "You have never . . . as a Democrat." Barnard, p. 307. **232.** "I am not . . . the Republican nomination." *Detroit Free Press*, 21 May 1936, p. 1. **233.** "Perhaps, Mr. Farley . . . rubes and hicks." *Kansas City Times*, 22 May 1936, p. 7. **233.** "Memorandum for J. A. F. . . . the opposition. F. D. R." Farley (*Story*), p. 62. **233–234.** "It has become . . . President in check." *Today*, 9 May 1936, p. 8; Best, p. 127. **233.** "There was a . . . the innocent bystander." *American Mercury*, March 1936, p. 265. **233.** Guffey Act. Davis (*FDR*), p. 612. **233.** *Tipaldo. New York History*, Winter 2014, p. 49. **233.** "The right to . . . by private bargaining." 298 U.S. 587 (56 S.Ct. 918, 80 L.Ed. 1347). MOREHEAD, Warden, v. PEOPLE OF STATE OF NEW YORK ex rel. TIPALDO. **233.** 10 of 344. Shlaes, p. 276. **234–235.** "Something should be . . . they already had." Shlaes, p. 276. **235.** "a new Dred . . . to economic slavery." *Poughkeepsie Star-Enterprise*, 5 June 1936, p. 2. **235.** "If this decision . . . different Supreme Court." Ickes (*Diary*), p. 614. **235.** "while in a . . . on the defensive." Solomon (*Court-Packing*), p. 87. **235.** DeMille. DeMille, pp. 326, 353. **235.** "I'm no politician . . . a wonderful experience." *Akron Beacon Journal*, 8 June 1936, p. 17. **235.** Proposed amendment. McCoy, p. 253. **235.** "That need is . . . for human freedom." *Emporia Gazette*, 3 June 1936, p. 4. **235.** Borah opposed. McCoy, p. 253. **235.** Knox opposed. *Washington Star*, 9 June 1938, p. A-8. **235.** Knox for. *Washington Star*, 10 June 1938, p. A-9. **235.** Taft drops out. McCoy, p. 250. **235.** Prissy. Stokes, p. 423. **235.** "for no reason . . . larger convention sense." *NY Times*, 10 June 1936, p. 14. **236.** New Lyrics. *Baltimore Evening Sun*, 8 June 1936, p. 3; Lyrics included such lines as "Alf Landon's learned a thing or two, he knows the right solution/And in the White House he will stay within the Constitution." **236.** 800 times. Stone, p. 311. **236.** "Alfred M. Landon's . . . to get hot. *Oklahoma News*, 5 June 1936, p. 8. **236.** "Assuming that the . . . ducking requires skill." *St. Louis Post-Dispatch*, 8 June 1936, p. 1. **237.** "discoverer and principal . . . the final editing." *Pittsburgh Press*, 8 June 1936, pp. 1, 4. **237.** "rather absurd . . . Gov. Landon's nomination." *Pittsburgh Press*, 8 June 1936, p. 4. **237–238.** "Forward with Landon . . . of AMERICAN CIVILIZATION!" *SF Examiner*, 11 June 1936, p. 4. **238.** "The voters of . . . William Randolph Hearst." *The Nation*, 24 1936, p. 800. **238.** "Cleveland was a . . . and violence." *New Masses*, 23 June 1936, p. 9. **238.** "to consolidate the . . . the New Deal." *Dayton Daily News*, 2 June 1936, p. 2; Brough, p. 296. **238.** "I am perfectly . . . ran for office." Brough, p. 296. **238.** "Two conflicting psychologies . . . I will be." Tompkins, p. 134. **239.** Platform Committee. *Washington Star*, 10 June 1936, p. A-9. **239.** "looks like a candidate." *Washington Star*, 10 June 1936, p. A-9. **239.** "profoundly reactionary . . . Senator Steiwer's speech." *Chattanooga Times*, 11 June 1936, p. 6. **239.** "Some had the . . . his keynote speech" *The Nation*, 24 1936, p. 800. **239.** Hoover-Borah. *Washington Star*, 10 June 1938, p. 1. **239.** Knox rage. Tompkins, p. 135. **240.** "Well, goodbye; I . . . It certainly is." *Emporia Gazette*, 22 January 1940, p. 4. **240.** 1932 visit. *Akron Beacon Journal*, 11 June 1936, p. 8. **240.** "Herbert Hoover. Hoover . . . years of Hoover." *Washington Star*, 10 June 1938, p. 1. **240.** "Wild lightning flashed . . . the past six years." *Akron Beacon Journal*, 11 June 1936, pp. 1, 8. The author was sports columnist Bill Corum. **240.** "demonstramoter." *New Masses*, 23 June 1936, p. 10; Sheppard, p. 40. **240.** "as hard-shelled . . . who ever lived." Tugwell (*Politics*), p. 95. Rex Tugwell's words. **240.** "Applause barometer." *Akron Beacon Journal*, 11 June 1936, p. 12. **240–241.** "When [Hoover] finished . . . to nominate him!" Hinshaw (*Hoover*), p. 314. **241.** "soberness, bordering on the somber." *NY Herald Tribune*, 11 Jun 1936 p. 5. **241.** "I started as . . . and the dullest." *NY Herald Tribune*, 11 Jun 1936 p. 2A. **241.** Bandage. *Portsmouth Times*, 12 June 1936, p. 5. **241.** "a man who . . . to make ours." *Philadelphia Inquirer*, 12 June 1936, p. 11. **242.** "stop leaning on your shovels." Bulger, p. 67. **242–243.** "Those who have . . . time as this." Hinshaw (*Convention*), pp. 167–68. **243.** "be done within . . . it now stands." *Cincinnati Enquirer*, 12 June 1936, p. 8. **243.** Hoover. Hoover (*Crusade*), p. 105. **243.** "in conscience . . . interpretations." *Brooklyn Daily Eagle*, 12 June 1936, p. 5. **243.** Fake telegram. Stokes, pp. 430–31. **243.** Not visited. *Baltimore Sun*, 12 June 1936, p. 12. **243.** Hamilton. Schruben, p. 196; Stokes, p. 434. **243.** "Borah established a . . . a small stroll." *Baltimore Sun*, 12 June 1936, p. 12. **244.** VP possibilities. *Akron Beacon Journal*, 11 June 1936, p. 12; *NY Herald Tribune*, 11 June 1936, p. 2. **243.** Liberty League. Burk, p. 233. **243.** "confused the delegates . . . Democrat at that." *Dayton Herald*, 12 July 1936, p. 3. **243.** "the Anglo-Saxon . . . of the colored race." *Atlanta Constitution*, 9 June 1936, p. 12. **243.** "Landon-Bridges falling down." *Dayton Daily News*, 12 June 1936, p. 44. **243.** "the back seat of a hearse." Tompkins, p. 137; Meijer, pp. 121–22. **245.** Knox left town. *St. Louis Post-Dispatch*, 12 June 1936, p. 2. **246.** "Politics sure does make strange bedfellows!" Trohan, p. 148.

14 "IT'S MYSELF"

248. Georgia primary. *Valparaiso Vidette-Messenger of Porter County*, 5 March 1936, p. 2. **248.** "Roosevelt Opposition Dies." *Decatur Review*, 17 March 1936, p. 10. **248.** Maryland. *NY Times*, 10 May 1936, p. E3. **248.** Talmadge, Florida. *Tampa Times*, 1 May 1936, p. 28. **248.** Coutremarsh. *Tampa Times*, 1 June 1936, p. 1. **249.** March Gallup poll. *Philadelphia Inquirer*, 15 March 1936, p. 37. Also aiding FDR was the drop in support for third parties. **249.** "based on existing . . . advisable or necessary." FDR biographer Roger Daniels contends that FDR's "carefully hedged no-new-taxes statement in his message to Congress, issued before the expected bonus-veto override, suggests that he knew in January that he would have to ask for some new taxes" (Daniels, p. 256). **249.** $620 million. *St. Louis Post-Dispatch*, 3 March 1936, p. 2. **249.** $800 million. Daniels, p. 262. FDR biographer Conrad Black terms the bill as Roosevelt "at his imperious, crypto-Socialist worst, in manner reminiscent of Frances Perkins' recollections of his haughtiness twenty-five years before . . . a shabby but minor bit of Huey Long-style grandstanding" (Black [*Champion*], p. 379). Eighteen Senate Democrats voted against the bill; only Byrd (VA), Bilbo (MS), and Russell (GA) were Southern (Patterson, p. 78*fn*). **249.** "Essentially an aristocrat . . . to be found." Creel, pp. 296–97, 337. **249.** Patterson at White House. *Buffalo Courier-Express*, 6 April 1936, p. 1. **249–250** "All right, you . . . can be again." *Washington Times-Herald*, 6 April 1936, p. 1. **250.** Recordings. *Broadcasting*, 16 April 1936, p. 11; Brown, p. 16. **250–251.** "The speeches as . . . was Roosevelt himself." Rosenman (*Working*), p. 56. **251.** Moley and Rosenman. Schlesinger (*Ghosts*), p. 8. Numerous other rivalries pervaded the Roosevelt inner circle. Both Eleanor and Stephen Early disliked Tommy Corcoran. Henry Morgenthau considered Corcoran "an intellectual crook . . . I would not trust him as far as I could see him" (McKean, pp. 72, 73, 76). According to Elliott Roosevelt, Sara Roosevelt "despised [Louis Howe] as much as anyone in the world" (Roosevelt & Brough [*Rendezvous*], p. 21). **251.** "This is only . . . from their newspapers." Rosenman (*Working*), p. 99. FDR long possessed unbounded optimism regarding his chances. In late December 1935, he informed his Cabinet: "We will win easily next year, but we are going to make it a crusade" (Burns, p. 266). **252.** Rosenman-High. High did not wear as well with the rest of Franklin's team. "He was a forceful and picturesque writer," conceded Charlie Michelson, "but could not keep his feet on the ground. I still have in mind his prancing through Democratic headquarters at the Biltmore proclaiming that he was off to write a speech for the President—a rather shocking violation of the rules of the game, as a ghost writer is never supposed to admit that he is the author of a great man's utterances. . . . The [eventual defection] of Dr. High caused no great mourning among his one-time confreres" (Michelson, pp. 193–94). **252.** Clergy. Even the leader of the German-American Bund's predecessor organization, the Friends of the New Germany's Heinrich Spanknöbel, was an ordained Seventh Day Adventist minister. **252.** "Religion in the News" Moley (*Seven*), p. 334. **252.** "saw no alternative . . . Republican as Democratic." Tugwell (*Democratic*), p. 410. **252.** 1940. Culver & Hyde, p. 163. **252–253** "It was just . . . and a fake." Culver &Hyde, p. 163. **252–253.** "a smokescreen for . . . by James A. Farley." *NY Times*, 4 February 1961, p. 19. **252–253.** "no one in . . . of the moment." *NY Times*, 19 February 1975, p. 35. **252–253.** "Franklin, can you . . . appointment with Moley?" *NY Times*, 19 February 1975, p. 35. **254.** "Roosevelt's great failing . . . he should have."

Rosenman (*Working*), p. 104. **254.** "the lucubrations of . . . most wholesome influence." Moley (*Seven*), p. 342. **255.** "Oh, well, said . . . said in it." Moley (*Seven*), p. 342. **255.** "I am not . . . or against me." Moley (*Seven*), p. 342. **255.** "wishy-washy, uninspiring . . . call to arms." Freedman, p. 344; Lash (*Dealers*), p. 275. **255.** "We'll never get . . . is Sam Rosenman." Rosenman (*Working*), p. 101. **256.** "I have one . . . one short one." Rosenman (*Working*), p. 102. Henry Morgenthau found FDR "far more interested . . . the subject matter" (Best, p. 131). **256.** "I can't participate . . . not a statesman." Moley (*Seven*), p. 343. **256.** Promises to review. Moley (*Seven*), p. 343. **257.** High needling. McKean, p. 70. **257.** "I saw the . . . all of us." Rosenman (*Working*), p. 105. "Moley," recalled Corcoran, "being an Irishman fought back" (McKean, p. 70). **257–258.** "exact complete loyalty . . . are presumptive liquidable." Lash (*Dealers*), p. 274. **258.** Liberty League protest. *Buffalo Courier-Express*, 1 July 1936, p. 7; Wolfskill, pp. 182–83, 186; Burk, p. 234. **258.** "They have plenty . . . don't need me." *NY Times*, 16 June 1936, p. 1; Patterson, p. 47. **258.** Seconding speeches. *Chicago Tribune*, 28 June 1936, p. 29; Burk, p. 235. **258.** Federal jobs. Savage, p. 120. **258.** Crucial to GOP nominations. *Phylon*, 3rd. **258.** Quarter 1975, pp. 270, 272–73. **258–259.** Black delegates. *NY Daily News*, 26 June 1936, p. 35; *Phylon*, 3rd Quarter 1975, p. 274; Sheppard, p. 65. They came not just from the North, but also from Virginia and Kentucky. One African American served as an alternate in 1924; ten in 1932 (*Phylon*, 3rd). **259.** Quarter 1975, pp. 269, 274). **259.** Bishop Brown. *NY Times*, 12 June 1936, p. 12; Weiss (*Lincoln*), p. 185*fn*. **259.** "the last of the spittoon senators." *New Republic*, 14 September 1938, p. 157; Patterson, p. 43. **259.** "By God he's . . . a white man!" Cohadas, p. 47. **259.** "I am not . . . than I have." Sheppard, p. 66. **259.** "I don't care . . . who wants to." *Greenville News*, June 1936, p. 1. **259.** "God knows I . . . pray for me." Sheppard, p. 67. **259–260.** "Political equality means . . . as I'm concerned." *Greenville News*, June 1936, p. 6. **260.** "I have had . . . to stay gone." Cohadas, p. 47. **260.** "I fear the . . . to our party." Nordin, p. 158. **260.** "We favor equal . . . the Federal Government." *The Crisis*, July 1936, p. 209. **261.** Voice vote. Sheppard, p. 68. **261.** "asinine . . . ridiculous." *Chicago Tribune*, 24 June 1936, p. 4. **261.** "What the President . . . to notice it." *Brooklyn Times Union*, 27 June 1936, p. 6. In her column, Alice Roosevelt Longworth wrote, "The talk is quite general that Mr. Roosevelt now is laying the groundwork for a third term." FDR and Farley were right to duck any third-term talk. In May, Gallup found 64 percent opposed (Gallup, p. 25). Farley eventually admitted: "I discovered later that the reason President Roosevelt wanted the change was that he had a third term in mind" (*NY Times*, 10 August 1958, p. 28). **261.** "A few weeks . . . there and slug." *Charlotte News*, 25 June 1936, p. 8. **262.** "If present trends . . . between divided loyalties." *Charlotte News*, 25 June 1936, p. 8. **262.** "to see the sideshow." *St. Louis Star-Times*, 25 June 1936, p. 8. **262.** Weiss. *NY Daily News*, 26 June 1936, p. 35; Stokes, p. 405. **262.** "It was rather . . . against Seymour Weiss." Stokes, p. 405. **262.** Fore. *NY Daily News*, 26 June 1936, p. 34; *Philadelphia Inquirer*, 26 June 1936, p. 1: *Summer Student*, 28 June 1936, p. 1. **262.** Headgear. *Carlisle Sentinel*, 26 June 1936, p. 1. **262.** "hillbilly overalls." *Literary Digest*, 4 July 1936, p. 4. **262.** Injuries. *Carlisle Sentinel*, 26 June 1936, p. 1; *Chicago Tribune*, 28 June 1936, p. 29. **263.** "Kansas Grows the . . . the Entire World." *Hutchinson News*, 11 October 1924, p. 13. **263.** "He didn't say . . . of Abraham Lincoln." *Philadelphia Inquirer*, 2 July 1936, p. 4. **263.** "Since going on . . . with the Vatican." *Baltimore Sun*, 28 June 1936, p. 2. **263.** "dispatched by a . . . carcass dragged out." *Baltimore Sun*, 28 June 1936, p. 2. **263–264.** Curley angles for VP. *Buffalo Evening News*,

23 June 1936, p. 4. **264.** "Eighteen thousand state . . . it in himself." Braeman et al (*Vol. 2*), p. 22. **264.** "Under him the . . . office in Massachusetts." *The Nation*, 29 April 1936, p. 540. **264.** "For the first . . . bodyguard in 1914." *The Nation*, 4 July 1936, p. 11. **264.** "Look Out for Curley in 1940." *The Nation*, 4 July 1936, p. 11. **264.** "We want Smith." *Carlisle Sentinel*, 26 June 1936, p. 1; Burk, p. 235. **264.** "Lynch them!" Wolfskill, p. 185. **264.** "beaten up . . . with obvious brutality. *The Nation*, 4 July 1936, p. 10. **265.** "For the sake . . . apply them too." *The Nation*, 4 July 1936, p. 10. Henry Wallace also appraised it as "very dull" (Culver & Hyde, p. 165). **265.** "as clever and . . . upon and twist." *The Nation*, 4 July 1936, p. 11. **265.** "We shall continue . . . may develop." *Brooklyn Times Union*, 26 June 1936, p. 2. **265.** "We are determined . . . earliest possible moment." *Brooklyn Times Union*, 26 June 1936, p. 2. **266.** Radio gatherings. *Cincinnati Enquirer*, 28 June 1936, p. 21; Scruben, p. 202. **266.** Wet Mencken. Manchester, p. 325. **266.** "trilled and gurgled beautifully." *Baltimore Sun*, 28 June 1936, p. 2. **266.** "this convention recently held in Chicago." Sheppard, p. 75. **266.** "I got up . . . will carry Pennsylvania." Timmons, p. 209. **266.** "Delaney," "Deluno" Trohan, p. 83. **266.** "demonstrometer." *Literary Digest*, 4 July 1936, p. 5. **266.** "the greatest ovation . . . lot of ovations." Reilly, pp. 100–01. **267.** "As President, when . . . trestles and scaffolding." Gallagher, p. 97. **267.** "The Man with a Hoe." Sheppard, p. 73. Yet Markham, another old TR Progressive, possessed limited enthusiasm for FDR, disappointed that the New Deal didn't go far enough. Roosevelt, Markham thought, was merely an American Kerensky (Filler, pp. 129, 149, 194–95). In 1933, Hearst's *New York American* commissioned Markham to compose "a Prayer for the President" (*San Francisco Examiner*, 13 March 1940, p. 31). **267.** Markham. Reilly, pp. 99–100; Schlesinger (*Upheaval*), p. 583. **267.** Leg bone. Gallagher, p. 104. **268.** "the damndest, maddest . . . be any speech." Trohan, p. 82. **268.** "By this time . . . he was flustered." Trohan, p. 83. **268–269.** "a fervent prayer . . . would be hurt." Reilly, p. 99. **269.** "None of the . . . clear view backstage." Reilly, p. 100; Sheppard, p. 74. **269.** "Faith—in the . . . its own indifference." Rosenman (*1936*), p. 235. **270.** "[t]hese economic royalists . . . the over-privileged alike." Rosenman (*1936*), p. 234. **270.** "rolled it off it great style." Lash (*Dealers*), p. 275. Of his own efforts, Beer recalled: "I had helped produce a truthful, factual, specific, long, and very dull draft." *Harvard Magazine*, Volumes 86–87, p. 67. **270.** "appointment with destiny," etc. Lash (*Dealers*), p. 276. **270.** "There is a . . . rendezvous with destiny." Rosenman (*1936*), p. 235. Commentators quickly picked up Lippmann's earlier use of "appointment with destiny" (*Reading Times*, 15 July 1936, p. 6).

15 "20,000 MORONS"

271. Coughlin. Fine, p. 227. **271.** Conservative/Liberal. Gallup, p. 26. **271–272.** July 12 poll. *Philadelphia Inquirer*, 12 July 1936, p. 7. **272.** Three reasons. *Philadelphia Inquirer*, 12 July 1936, p. 7. **272.** Hurja. Davis (*FDR*), p. 638. **272.** "the situation is . . . on electoral votes." Ickes, p. 621. Ickes's words. **272.** Gallup analysis. *Philadelphia Inquirer*, 26 July 1936, p. 7. **273.** "I don't want to be President." *NY Post*, 16 July 1936, p. 4. **273.** "I will say . . . matters of government." *LA Times*, 14 June 1936, p. 8. **273.** "Anybody but Roosevelt." *NY Times*, 2 June 1936, p. 7. **274.** November 1935 meeting. Marcus, p. 103. **274.** "stealing our stuff . . . depart from that." *NY Times*, 29 December 1935, p. 15; *Modern Monthly*, June 1936,

p. 10. **274.** May 1936. *Social Justice*, 29 May 1936, p. 3. **274.** "a step in . . . slavery." *Buffalo Evening News*, 17 June 1936, p. 1. **274.** Coughlin doubletalk. *Buffalo Evening News*, 17 June 1936, p. 1. **274.** "Farleyism, dictatorship, and Communism." *Buffalo Evening News*, 17 June 1936, p. 1. **275.** Tee-totalling, unshaven, glass eye. Schlesinger (*Upheaval*), p. 560; Warren, p. 68. **275.** "a complete composite . . . money and agriculture." Marcus, p. 114. **275.** "The mistake that . . . he was arrested." Lemke, p. 145. **275.** "He knew the . . . knew the law." Bennett, p. 93. **275.** "Yes, yes, I am for all that." Bennett, p. 92. **276.** "wild legislation." Bennett, p. 97. **276.** Phone booth. Bennett, p. 18; Brinkley, p. 255. **276.** Text of Coughlin address. *Social Justice*, 22 June 1936, p. 15. **276.** "The fact that . . . first opportunity." Blackorby, pp. 220–21. **277.** "It's all right . . . to be seen." *Buffalo Evening News*, 21 June 1936, p. 5. **276.** "candidate who will . . . the United States." *Buffalo Evening News*, 21 June 1936, p. 5. **276.** "carry Ohio, all . . . will be next." *NY Times*, 26 June 1936, p. 11. **276.** "I saw Landon . . . the lunatic fringe." *Spokane Spokesman-Review*, 14 June 1936, p. 5; Bennett, p. 199. **276.** "vote Socialist . . . Socialist or Communist." *NY Times*, 15 July 1936, p. 12. **278.** "could name a . . . a third party." *Niagara Falls Gazette*, 17 July 1936, p. 19. **278.** $20,000. Bennett, p. 211. **278.** Ballot hurdles. Bennett, p. 212; Schruben, pp. 207–08. **278.** "We believe the . . . will not do." *Social Justice*, 13 July 1936, p. 3. **278.** Thirty-eight states. Amenta, p. 145. **279.** "church-going, Bible-reading . . . country from Communism." *Victoria Daily Times*, 29 June 1936, p. 4. **279.** "My friends, we . . . 'triumph with Townsend.'" *Rochester Times-Union*, 15 July 1936, p. 1. **279.** Delegations against. *Niagara Falls Gazette*, 17 July 1936, p. 19; Amenta, p. 146; Bennett, p. 10. **279.** "There will be . . . at these meetings." *Time*, 27 July 1936, p. 19; *Victoria Daily Times*, 29 June 1936, p. 4; Bennett, p. 10. **279.** "There is a . . . they love oratory." *Washington Post*, 17 July 1936, p. 7. **279.** "a quack remedy which could not possibly work." Bennett, p. 9. **279.** "I don't think . . . you were sixty." Johnpoll, p. 173. **279–280.** "pulpit manners on . . . wildest of evangelists." *Washington Post*, 17 July 1936, p. 7. **280.** "We must make . . . Stalin or Jefferson!" *Chicago Tribune*, 16 July 1936, p. 4. **280.** "The Democratic party . . . Roosevelt-Farley machine." *Cincinnati Enquirer*, 16 July 1936, p. 7. **280.** "This Townsend show . . . in one hall." Manchester, p. 326. **280.** "His speech was . . . of them worked." *Baltimore Sun*, 16 July 1936, p. 1. **281.** "As far as . . . Franklin Double-Crossing Roosevelt." *Boston Globe*, 17 July 1936, p. 8. **281.** "If I have . . . dad-gummed head off." *Cattaraugus Republican*, 22 July 1936, p. 4. **282.** "I want my . . . his shirt on." *Buffalo Evening News*, 17 July 19, p. 6. **282.** "I deem it . . . supplanted in office." *St. Louis Post-Dispatch*, 23 July 1936, p. 1. **282.** Wunder, Kiefer expelled. Amenta, p. 288. Townsend also accused Wunder and Kiefer of drunkenness and "obscene correspondence," and "personal misconduct and inefficiency." Kiefer sued Townsend for libel in the amount of $250,000 (*LA Daily News*, 24 September 1936, p. 3; *Oakland Tribune*, 24 September 1936, p. 7). **282.** Good Neighbor League. *LA Times*, 12 August 1936, p. 1; *NY Herald Tribune*, 12 August 1936, p. 9; *NY Daily News*, 28 September 1936, p. 35. **283.** Rift denial. *Buffalo Evening News*, 25 July 1936, p. 1; *NY Herald Tribune*, 26 July 1936, p. 5. **283.** "I would vote . . . gets my vote." *NY Times*, 4 August 1936, p. 1. **283.** "everything from Maine . . . I am doing." *NY Herald Tribune*, 26 July 1936, p. 5. **283.** "If one out . . . a Gomer Smith!" *Buffalo Evening News*, 13 August 1936, p. 8. **283.** Gilmour Young. *Buffalo Evening News*, 13 August 1936, p. 8. **283.** Coughlin relents. Marcus, p. 124. **283.** Portraits. *The Nation*, 22 August 1936, p. 204; Tull, p. 139. **283.** Mother honored. *The Nation*, 22 August 1936, p. 204. **283–284.** "In the conduct . . . of his endurance." Bennett, p. 17. **284.** New York, Michigan. *Utica Observer-Dispatch*, 15 August 1936, p. 1. **284.** 8,152–1. *NY Times*, 16 August 1936, p. 1. **284.** "mob psychology . . . William Randolph Hearst." *NY Times*, 16 August 1936, p. 1. **284.** "Judas! . . . but less dangerous." *The Nation*, 22 August 1936, p. 204. **284.** 80–1. *North Shore Daily Journal*, 16 July 1936, p. 7. **284.** "If I . . . I'll quit broadcasting." Tull, p. 141; Bennett, p. 16. **284–285.** "squirmed in his . . . the spellbinding Smith." Bennett, p. 19. **285.** 100,000. *NY Post*, 5 August 1936, p. 5. **285.** "Roosevelt is a . . . doesn't know it." *Schenectady Gazette*, 18, July 1936, p. 1. **285.** "I believed that . . . board of life." *Brooklyn Daily Eagle*, 17 August 1936, p. 3. **285.** "Roosevelt and Tugwell . . . are destroying us." *Kingston Daily Freeman*, 17 August 1936, p. 1. **286.** "We are a . . . principles of brotherhood." *Jewish Telegraphic Agency*, 19 August 1936, p. 5. **286.** "I must apologize . . . proceed any further." *Schenectady Gazette*, 18, July 1936, p. 1. **286.** "I couldn't see . . . in bright sunshine." *Brooklyn Daily Eagle*, 17 July 1936, p. 3. **286–287.** Curley. Curley, p. 298; Beatty, p. 396; Steinberg (*Bosses*), p. 182. **287.** "We are a separate shirt." *Rochester Democrat and Chronicle*, 23 December 1934, p. 5A. **287.** "We're adventurers with . . . not quite articulate." *NY Herald Tribune*, 18 December 1934, p. 17. **287.** "the fate of . . . it for himself." Lamster, p. 139. **288.** "How many votes . . . ain't got nothin'." Lamster, p. 143. **288.** "A special stand . . . of the priest." *Chicago Tribune*, 7 September 1936, p. 1; Schulze, p. 126. **288.** "the excitement . . . in black leather." Schulze, p. 90. **288.** Olympia Stadium. *Rochester Times-Union*, 10 September 1936, p. 12. **288.** "strikingly resembled a gallows." *Brooklyn Times-Union*, 12 September 1936, p. 3. **288.** NYS primary. *Buffalo Evening News*, 16 September 1936, p. 14. **288.** "Roosevelt grins and likes it." *Detroit Times*, 20 September 1936, p. 1. **289.** "We are . . . road toward fascism." *NY Daily Worker*, 24 September 1936, p. 2; Schlesinger (*Upheaval*), p. 629. **289.** "When any upstart . . . anti-God and radical." *Gloversville Morning Herald*, 26 September 1936, p. 1. **289.** Bishops. *Des Moines Register*, 27 September 1936, p. 4; *Patterson Morning Call*, 26 September 1936, p. 2. **289.** "lacking common decency . . . a private meeting." *San Bernardino Sun*, 14 October 1936, p. 2. **289.** O'Brien. *Historic Journal of Massachusetts*, Summer 2015, page unknown. **289.** "get . . . him to pieces." *Palm Beach Post*, 14 October 1936, p. 12. **289.** "harmlessly held [Barry] . . . slapped for impudence." *Louisville Courier-Journal*, 18 October 1936, p. 13. **289.** 8,000. *Detroit Free Press*, 18 October, p. 1. The *Daily Worker* reported only 4,500. The United Press reported 5,000 (*NY Daily Worker*, 19 October 1936, p. 1; *Knoxville News-Sentinel*, 18 October 1936, p. 8). **289.** Endorsed Murphy. *Detroit Free Press*, 18 October 1936, p. 7. **289.** "Communism takes . . . belongs to God." *Pittsburgh Press*, 18 October 1936, p. 1. **290.** "You can't mix religion and politics." *NY Daily Worker*, 19 October 1936, p. 1. **290.** "Feathers instead of Bullets!" *Detroit Free Press*, 18 October 1936, p. 2. **290.** Washington, Rockville Center, Hutchinson. *Battle Creek Enquirer*, 18 October 1936, pp. 1, 6. Hockaday wasn't the year's most unstable figure. June 1936 saw often-erratic Seattle Democratic congressman Marion Zioncheck being committed to a Washington, DC, psychopathic ward. August saw him jump to his death from a downtown Seattle office building. **290.** Supreme Court. *Battle Creek Enquirer*, 18 October 1936, p. 1. **290.** Madrid. *Battle Creek Enquirer*, 18 October 1936, p. 6. **290.** Landon. *Davenport Times*, 8 October 1936, p. 1. **290.** "brown feathers from Boston." *Detroit Free Press*, 18 October 1936, p. 1. **290.** Ducked. *Pittsburgh Press*, 18 October 1936, p. 1. **290.** Two swings. *Syracuse American*, 18 October 1936, p. 1. **290.** Shouts of the crowd. *Detroit Free Press*, 18 October 1936, p. 2; *Lansing State Journal*, 18

October 1936, p. 10. **290.** "[O]ne elderly woman . . . among the loudest." *Buffalo Courier-Express*, 18 October 1936, p. 1. **290.** "Don't touch that . . . communists and NewDealocrats." *Buffalo Courier-Express*, 18 October 1936, p. 1. **290.** "If they have . . . my feathers again." *Battle Creek Enquirer*, 18 October 1936, p. 1. **291.** "If you say . . . people of America." *NY Herald Tribune*, 16 August 1936, p. A-2. **291.** "a $1,500,000 nationalist . . . front against Communism." *Washington Post*, 18 October 1936, p. M6. **292.** "When the Reds . . . we'll save America." *NY Herald Tribune*, 21 October 1936, p. 9. **292.** 10,000,000. *NY Times*, 20 October 1936, p. 7. **292.** "to seize the . . . the United States." *NY Times*, 20 October 1936, p. 7. **292.** "If the press . . . and President Roosevelt." *NY Times*, 21 October 1936, p. 16. **292.** "I repeat, Gerald . . . definite and final." *NY Herald Tribune*, 21 October 1936, p. 9. **292.** "The Townsend organization . . . be automatically severed." *NY Herald Tribune*, 21 October 1936, p. 9. **293.** "Roosevelt must be defeated." *Cattaraugus Republican*, 28 October 1936, p. 7.

16 "INNOCUOUS AS A WATERMELON . . . BOILED IN A BATHTUB"

295. Family. *Chicago Tribune*, 19 June 1936, p. 4. **295.** "I'm doing a . . . need it, too." *LA Times*, 26 June 1936, p. 13. **295.** "[H]e got tongue-tied . . . in a quandary." *Baltimore Afro-American*, 11 July 1936, p. 1. **295.** "I was just . . . settle that question." *Chicago Tribune*, 19 June 1936, p. 4. **295.** June 26/July 23. McCoy, p. 267. **296.** "None of these . . . of the country." *The Nation*, 27 June 1936, p. 832. **296.** "The tide is . . . in our direction." McCoy, p. 268. **296.** Gallup Poll. *Philadelphia Inquirer*, 12 July 1936, p. 7. **296.** *Farm Journal. NY Sun*, 20 July 1936, p. 4. **296.** Hurja, February. Holli, pp. 70–71; Best, pp. 124, 133. **196.** Farley. Weed, p. 106. **296.** "nearly, if not . . . one hundred seats." Weed, p. 106. **296.** Newsreel audiences. *Amsterdam Evening Recorder*, 13 July 1936, p. 4. **296.** "Do you believe . . . lead to dictatorship?" *LA Times*, 2 August 1936, p. 14. **297.** Dunn poll. *NY Herald Tribune*, 28 September 1936, p. 4. **297.** "The wonder is . . . it as news." *Montgomery Advertiser*, 1 October 1936, p. 4. **297.** Mid-October *Digest* poll. *Literary Digest*, 17 October 1936, pp. 7–8. In August, a reporter queried Alice Longworth regarding the *Digest*'s encouraging partial returns favoring Landon. "If they're not right," she sniffed, "I shall be forced to cancel my subscription" (Teichmann, p. 174). **297.** Cabinet. *N. Tonawanda Evening News*, 27 July 1936, p. 4. **297.** Mayer. Higham, p. 249. The Considine brothers' father, John W. Considine Sr., was the partner in the West Coast Sullivan–Considine vaudeville circuit with the notorious Lower East Side Tammany kingpin "Big Tim" Sullivan. In late October, Democrats released a straw poll of movie executives showing Roosevelt with a 7–1 lead, with 319 of them formally endorsing him (*NY Times*, 31 October 1936, p. 5). **298.** 1928. *The Nation*, 27 June 1936, p. 831; McCoy, pp. 37–43. **298.** "[T]hough he is . . . running this show." *The Nation*, 27 June 1936, p. 831. **298.** 104 degrees. *Baltimore Sun*, 24 July 1936, p. 2; Sheppard, p. 85. **298.** 200,000. Sheppard, p. 85; Brown, p. 85. **298.** Cars, trains. *Baltimore Sun*, 24 July 1936, p. 2. **298.** "one of the . . . used in Kansas." *Emporia Gazette*, 25 July 1936, p. 4. **298.** DeMille extravaganza. *St. Joseph Gazette*, 18 July 1936, p. 2; *Lancaster New Era*, 23 July 1936, p. 14; *Pittsburgh Sun-Telegraph*, 23 July 1936, p. 3; *Emporia Gazette*, 25 July 1936, p. 4; McCoy, pp. 271–72: Sheppard, p. 85. **298.** "Five hundred economic . . . Clay County, Kansas." *Baltimore Sun*, 24 July 1936, p. 2. **298.** Cow. Schruben, p. 199. **298–299.** "The crowd which . . . when he isn't." *Emporia* Gazette, 25 July 1936, p. 2. **299.** "simply too hot . . . but not much." *Baltimore Sun,* 24 July 1936, p. 2. **299.** 40-minute. *Baltimore Sun,* 24 July 1936, p. 2. **299.** 71 rounds. McCoy, p. 273. **299.** "several hours of . . . during the day." *Lancaster New Era,* 23 July 1936, p. 14. **299.** Mrs. Landon. *Pittsburgh Sun-Telegraph,* 23 July 1936, p. 3. **299.** Kidnapping. McCoy, p. 158. **299.** More vacations. McCoy, pp. 276–77. **299.** Pleurisy. McCoy, p. 276. **299.** Spain; acceptance speech. *Albany Evening News,* 20 August 1936, p. 19. **299–300.** "[Landon's] voice . . . from Republican gatherings." Stone, p. 312. **300.** "Do you know . . . my blood pressure." Teichmann, pp. 169–70, 263. **300.** Thompson. Allen, p. 72. **300–302.** "Considerable mystery surrounds . . . police are baffled." *El Paso Herald-Post,* 20 August 1936, p. 6. **302–303.** Record temperatures. *Literary Digest,* 18 July 1936, p. 4. **303.** "Hot winds, tearing . . . becomes a nightmare." *Literary Digest,* 18 July 1936, p. 4. **303.** Topeka temperatures. McCoy, p. 277. **303.** "the wave of . . . not be lowered." *Literary Digest,* 18 July 1936, p. 4. **303–304.** "Governor, if you . . . will remember that." McCoy, p. 289. **304.** "Landon is a swell guy." Schlesinger (*Upheaval*), p. 610. **304.** "He's a very fine, charming gentleman." *Pittsburgh Press,* 4 September 1936, p. 11. **304.** "Harmony dripped so . . . candidates to withdraw." Schlesinger (*Upheaval*), p. 610. **304.** 800 speakers. *Bangor Daily News,* 18 September 1936, p. 20. **304.** "The GOP campaign . . . do?' he pleaded." *Rome Daily Sentinel,* 21 October 1936, p. 4. **304.** 1932. Smith (*Colonel*), p. 131. **304.** "everything, . . . campaign against syphilis." Gies, p. 135. **305.** Telephone operators. Winfield, p. 130. **305.** "There was a . . . singah, or speakah." Gies, p. 137; Smith (*McCormick*), p. 346. Another version of this went: "There was a young man from Topeka / Whose chances grew weaker and weaker, / So the Democrats thought / 'Til the figures were brought / And they saw it would be a close squeaka" (*Harrisburg Evening News,* 31 July 1936, p. 14). Pro–New Deal papers proved equally partisan. Both the *Chicago Times* and the *New York Daily News* distributed Roosevelt campaign buttons (Winfield, p. 130). Following the election, FDR gushingly wrote to *Daily News* publisher Joseph Patterson that his paper had won him more votes in the city than all the Democratic speeches and rallies put together (White [*Press*], p. 54). **305.** 1935 visit. McKenna, p. 337. **305.** Murray. *Madison Capital Times,* 28 October 1936, p. 24; Braeman et al (*Vol. 2*), p. 184; Schruben p. 207. **305.** Bruce. *Hanover Evening Sun,* 13 July 1936, p. 1; Schruben, p. 207. **305.** "greatly impressed by Brother Landon." Harbaugh, p. 354. Expressed privately in September 1936. **305.** Landon omitted. *NY Times,* 21 October 1936, p. 18. **305.** Mencken skeptical. Manchester, pp. 324–25; Rodgers, p. 431. **305.** "probably knows a . . . knows is true." *American Mercury,* October 1936, p. 134. **306.** "unreal and unnecessary . . . the utmost importance." *NY Herald Tribune,* 8 September 1936, p. 21. **306.** Tariff. Blum (*Lippmann*), pp. 352–53. **306.** Hamilton. Blum (*Lippmann*), p. 353. **306.** Anti-Liberty League. Blum (*Lippmann*), p. 348. **306.** "Nobly Done." Harbaugh, p. 355. **306.** "We believe that . . . has remained free." Blum (*Lippmann*), p. 350. **306.** "a dull and . . . a protest vote." Steel, p. 318. **306.** Wagner. *Buffalo Courier-Express,* 18 October 1936, p. 2. **306.** Johnson. *NY Times,* 26 August 1936, p. 12; Schruben, p. 206. **306.** "I'm going to . . . where I stand." *Marion Star,* 9 October 1936, p. 21. **306.** "Landon is like . . . his mouth shut." *Kansas City Star,* 30 October 1936, p. 6. Landon's appearance at Detroit's Navin Field proved so inept, Michigan's Republican governor Frank D. Fitzgerald literally fled the Sunflower Special to board FDR's campaign train (Sheppard, p. 172). **306–307.** Kuhn. *NY Daily News,* 15 October 1936, p. 10. **307.** "sold out to . . . the contrary notwithstanding."

Raleigh News and Observer, 16 October 1936, p. 4. **307.** Coughlin/Hard/Ickes. *Pittsburgh Press*, 10 October 1936, p. 3. Jackson was quite left-wing. In 1935, he was fired from the AAA for agitation on behalf of sharecroppers. **307–308.** Coughlin/Hamilton. Sheppard, pp. 125, 258. **308.** "an old-fashioned, dyed-in-the wool Democrat." *Raleigh News and Observer*, 13 October 1936, p. 2. **308.** "For 50 years . . . fire and pizen." *Raleigh News and Observer*, 13 October 1936, p. 2. **308.** "suffer his right . . . flow of liquor." *Raleigh News and Observer*, 13 October 1936, p. 2. **308.** "This is Bull . . . war will follow." *Charlotte News*, 23 October 1936, p. 27. **309.** 75,000–110,000. McCoy, p. 283. **309.** "Wherever I have . . . have found Americans." *NY Times*, 23 August 1936, p. 35. **309.** "direct and vigorous . . . wholesome." *Philadelphia Inquirer*, 23 August 1936, p. 13. **309.** "Literally, he did . . . it was . . . schoolboyish." Ickes (*Diary*), p. 665. **309.** Gallup poll. *Philadelphia Inquirer*, 23 August 1936, p. 7; Gallup, pp. 23–24. **309.** "In Kansas we . . . of all citizens." McCoy, p. 286. New York did have such a law—signed by Governor Lehman (Stokes, p. 439). **309.** "The first five . . . off after that." **309.** *New York History*, Winter 2014, p. 58; Sheppard, p. 104. **309.** "[T]he worst I have [ever] heard." *New York History*, Winter 2014, p. 58; Sheppard, p. 104. **309.** "made such a . . . than anything else." *New York History*, Winter 2014, p. 57. **309.** Not having read speeches. Williamson, p. 239. "[L]ike all ghost-written stuff," assessed Herbert Hoover, "sooner or later, the people smelled it and lost all interest" (Hoover [*Crusade*], p. 107). **309.** "Over the radio . . . a fighting rabbit." Williamson, p. 239. **309.** Twenty-eight talks. Stone, p. 312. **309.** "I see where . . . set it afire." *St. Louis Globe-Democrat*, 26 September 1936, p. 4. **310.** "no life insurance . . . account is safe." *Philadelphia Inquirer*, 6 September 1936, p. 20; Schlesinger (*Upheaval*), p. 618. **310.** "Boys, I've got . . . on my hands." McCoy, p. 304. **310.** "Strictly off the . . . raising their prices." Boller, p. 248. **310.** "just as empty . . . in a bathtub." *Time*, 9 November 1936, p. 14; Kennedy (*Fear*), p. 290. **310.** "simply did not . . . its fiscal deficits." Schlesinger (*Upheaval*), p. 603. **310–311.** "The interests supporting . . . quavering, quaggy dummy." *NY Daily Worker*, 19 October 1936, p. 5. **311.** "YOU PAY $10 . . . $25 Evening Gown." N*Y Sun*, 24 September 1936, p. 23; *LA Times*, 30 September 1936, p. 20. **311.** "At the end . . . for young women." Stone, p. 314. **311.** "So the Landon . . . of lounging pajamas?" *Brooklyn Daily Eagle*, 11 October 1936, p. 32. **312.** "If this denial . . . with Governor Landon." Hinshaw, p. 316; Schlesinger (*Upheaval*), p. 605. **312.** Hoover visit. *NY Times*, 2 October 1936, pp. 1, 7; Hoover (*Crusade*), pp. 106–07. **312.** Chicken, cigars. *Bluefield Daily Telegraph*, 2 October 1936, p. 1; *Pittsburgh Post-Gazette*, 3 October 1936, p. 4. **312.** "Hoover and Landon . . . because of Hoover." McCoy, p. 309. **312.** "We had better . . . catch the train." McCoy, p. 309. Landon's forces were just as wary regarding dealing with Hoover's Treasury Secretary Ogden Mills. "The men around Landon," recalled Hoover, "insisted that Mills be taken from the train at a station before Topeka and brought secretly into his headquarters so that the press would not know of this leprous association. Mills was more deeply offended by this act than by anything that had happened in his long and useful life" (Hoover [*Crusade*], p. 107). **312–313.** "found the headquarters . . . an independent unit." Hinshaw (*Hoover*), p. 316. **313.** Thomas/Landon. *Emporia Gazette*, 30 July 1936, p. 1; McCoy, pp. 274–75. **313.** "Roosevelt's Voice: Through . . . a sinister stream." *Chicago Tribune*, 18 October 1936, p. 5. McCarl served every president from 1921 through 1936. **313–314.** Stations pulled. *Philadelphia Inquirer*, 18 October 1936, p. 25. **314.** "This is just . . . away from them." *Philadelphia Inquirer*, 18 October 1936, p. 25. **314.** Cartoon. *Chicago Tribune*, 1 February 1936,

p. 6; *LA Times*, 1 February 1936, p. 1; *Chicago Tribune*, 15 February 1936, p. 8; *Baltimore Sun*, 18 April 1936, p. 2; *Akron Beacon Journal*, 9 May 1936, p. 15; Wolfskill, p. 232; Burk, pp. 203, 219; Lichtman, p. 73. **314.** Radio. *Moberly Monitor-Index*, 13 January 1936, p. 10; Burk, pp. 236–37. **314.** "If you did . . . attempts at wisecracks." *Utah Labor News*, 31 January 1936, p. 5. **314–315.** "CLERK: Who was . . . Republican Presidential candidate." *Pittsburgh Press*, 17 January 1936, p. 23. **315.** "Americans everywhere are . . . span the Nation." *Bangor Daily News*, 14 September 1936, p. 12A. **315.** "If they had . . . governor of Maine." *Bangor Daily News*, 18 September 1936, p. 20. **315.** "As Maine goes, so goes the nation." *Bangor Daily News*, 14 September 1936, p. 12A. **315.** "[A]s I listened . . . might conceivably want." Ickes (*Diary*), p. 683. **315.** "are tarred heavily . . . of authoritarian government." *St. Louis Star and Times*, 1 October 1936, p. 1. **315–316.** Acheson, Warburg, Baker, Kellogg. Sheppard, p. 110; Schlesinger (*Upheaval*), p. 612; Stokes, p. 446. Charles P. Taft, William Allen White, and Lewis Douglas also disapproved. **316.** Baker. Cramer, p. 269. **316.** Townsend California votes. Sheppard, p. 172. **316.** Refused venues. *Rochester Democrat and Chronicle*, 20 October 1936, p. 9. **316.** "LANDON BITTER DISAPPOINTMENT . . . SECTION UPON ARRIVAL." Sheppard, p. 268. **316.** "crushed . . . burst of cheers." *Time*, 2 November 1936, p. 8. **316–317.** Altercations. *Scranton Times*, 21 October 1936, p. 2. **317.** "I just couldn't resist the impulse." *Time*, 2 November 1936, p. 8. **317.** Alfred du Pont. Wall, p. 546. **317.** "workers' and farmers' organizations." Douglas, p. 75. The House defeated the bill 204–52 (Douglas, p. 109). **317.** "was very little . . . a sales tax." *Journal of American History*, September 1983, p. 363. **317.** "a system of . . . the social burden." *Journal of American History*, September 1983, p. 364. **317.** "In many respects . . . astonishingly inept." Leuchtenburg (*New Deal*), pp. 132–33. **317–318.** "I guess you're . . . social security program." *Journal of American History*, September 1983, p. 374. **318.** "the Republican party . . . federal snooping follows." *Minneapolis Star*, 28 September 1936, p. 7. **318.** "[W]ith doomed ingenuity. . . and its enemies." Schlesinger (*Upheaval*), p. 613. Ironically, this most "conservative" of Landon speeches was crafted largely by his most liberal adviser, Charles P. Taft. **318–319.** "Such taxes, Negroes . . . necessities of life." Braeman et al (*Vol. 1*), p. 195.

17 "KEEP ON RUNNING"

320. Philadelphia. Braeman et al (*Vol. 2*), p. 57. Philadelphia's Italians followed a similar pattern, their Democratic vote rising from 22.6 percent Democratic in 1932 to 52.2 percent in 1934. Again, middle- and upper-class voters deserted first. **320.** "I can beat . . . taken Lincoln's place." Braeman et al (*Vol. 2*), p. 60. **320.** FDR snub. Rigeur, p. 13. **321.** NRA Pejoratives. Weiss (*Lincoln*), p. 56; Solomon (*Unity*), p. 234; Braeman et al (*Vol. 1*), p. 185. Conversely, some dubbed the NRA the "Negro Relief Administration" (Sitkoff, p. 104). **321.** "a rank equal . . . that of clerk." Solomon (*Unity*), p. 235; Wolters, p. 162; Braeman et al (*Vol. 1*), p. 185. **321.** "to put in . . . ordinary manual labor." O'Reilly, p. 114. **321.** "Whether [the Negro's] . . . the New Deal." Wolters, p. 155; Braeman et al (*Vol. 1*), p. 185. **321.** "I'm not doing . . . shut me up." Watts (*Cabinet*), p. 184. **322.** "the share of . . . from the WPA." Braeman et al (*Vol. 1*), pp. 188–89. **322.** "Relief and WPA . . . thing comes along." *Baltimore Afro-American*, 24 October 1936, p. 4. **322.** "Let Jesus lead . . . Roosevelt feed you!" Rigeur,

p. 17. **323.** "If the Republicans . . . for Governor Landon." *Capitol Plain Dealer*, 4 October 1936, p. 2. **323.** "Neither side has . . . a small margin." *California Eagle*, 2 October 1936, p. 1. **323.** Twice as much. Braeman et al (*Vol. 1*), p. 209. **323.** "Colored Divisions." *Capitol Plain Dealer*, 4 October 1936, p. 2. **323.** Notification day. *Kansas City Plaindealer*, 24 June 1936, p. 1. **323.** "crackers . . . BY PRESIDENT ROOSEVELT." *Cleveland Gazette*, 31 October 1936, p. 2. **323.** 75%. *Philadelphia Inquirer*, 3 September 1936, p. 15. **323.** Newsreels. *Public Opinion Quarterly*, April 1937, p. 35; Braeman et al (*Vol. 1*), p. 209; Weiss (*Lincoln*), p. 187. **324.** "Republicans listen . . . Negroes in the North." *The Crisis*, July 1936, p. 209. **324.** "absolutely stunned . . . clear blue sky." *Baltimore Afro-American*, 11 July 1936, pp. 1–2. **324.** "If Governor Landon . . . DOWN THE RIVER." *Baltimore Afro-American*, 3 October 1936, p. 4. **325.** Vann. Baker, p. 132. **325.** Page. *California Eagle*, 18 September 1936, p. 1; Baker, p. 132. **325.** Robinson/Dempsey. *Chicago Defender*, 29 August 1936, p. 2; Weiss (*Lincoln*), p. 191; Rigeur, p. 19. **325.** Jolson. McRae, p. 165. **325.** Cantor offer. *Norfolk Journal and Guide*, 22 August 1936, p. 14; *Brooklyn Times Union*, 25 August 1936, p. 1; McRae, pp. 165, 173; Baker, p. 115. **325.** Fox. *Washington Post*, 22 October 1936, p. X21. **325.** Paramount. Baker, p. 118. **325.** "Listen here. You . . . in the eye." *Chicago Defender*, 29 August 1936, p. 2; Baker, p. 133. **325.** Owens's parents. *Chicago Defender*, 29 August 1936, p. 1; McRae, p. 169; Baker, p. 123. **325.** Cantor. *Chicago Defender*, 12 September 1936, p. 13; *Chicago Defender*, 19 September 1936, p. 1; McRae, p. 173; Baker, p. 129. **325.** "I haven't any . . . I can't sing." *Chicago Defender*, 19 September 1936, p. 2. **325.** Chan. McRae, p. 175. **325–326.** $15,000/$30,000. *Norfolk Journal and Guide*, 7 November 1936, p. 1; *Chicago Defender*, 14 November 1936, p. 1; Baker, p. 135. **326.** $10,000. Baker, p. 136. **326.** "The country was . . . he will keep." *NY Times*, 3 September 1936, p. 10. **326.** "Almost every Negro . . . or anybody else." *NY Amsterdam News*, 19 September 1936, p. 1. **326.** "These reports are . . . and real Americanism]." *Negro Star*, 2 October 1936, p. 1. **326.** Knox. Baker, p. 136. **326.** "My trip to . . . hand at me." *Kansas City Plaindealer*, 11 September 1936, p. 8. Robert L. Vann supported Owens's claims: "I saw Herr Adolf Hitler salute this lad. I looked on with a heart which beat proudly as the lad who was crowned king of the 100 meters event, got an ovation the like of which I have never heard before. I saw Jesse Owens greeted by the Grand Chancellor of this country" (*Pittsburgh Courier*, 8 October 1936, p. 1). **327.** "be officially received . . . race or color." Hall to FDR, 5 August 1936; https://rediscovering-black-history.blogs.archives.gov/2016/08/05/jesse-owens-american-hero-2/. **327.** Wright. https://rediscovering-black-history.blogs.archives.gov/2016/08/05/jesse-owens-american-hero-2/. **327.** Owens tour. *Wyandotte Echo*, 1936, 2 October, p. 1; *Buffalo Courier-Express*, 5 October 1936, p. 4; *Cleveland Gazette*, 10 October 1936, p. 1; *Cleveland Gazette*, 11 October 1936, p. 8; *Kansas City Plaindealer*, 16 October 1936, p. 1; Rigeur, p. 19. **327.** Chicago. Baker, p. 137. **327.** Torn door. *Baltimore Afro-American*, 10 October 1936, p. 18. **327.** "Jesse Owens Has . . . Meeting Called Off." *Cincinnati Inquirer*, 8 October 1936, p. 12. **327.** Glee Club. *Cincinnati Inquirer*, 8 October 1936, p. 12. **327.** Indianapolis. *NY Times*, 26 October 1936, p. 2. **327.** Douglass. *NY Times*, 5 April 1982, p. D9. **327.** "admits he knows . . . on running, Jesse." *Washington Tribune*, 13 October 1936, p. 1. **327–328.** Dempsey. Baker, p. 127. **328.** Onlookers. *Chicago Defender*, 12 September 1936, p. 12; McRae, p. 172; Baker, p. 127. **328.** Dyckman Oval. *Baltimore Afro-American*, 2 November 1936, p. 1. **328.** "Poorest race I . . . but a *lot*!" McRae, p. 285; Baker, p. 138. **328.** "A colored voter . . . of his people." *NY Amsterdam News*, 26 September 1936, p. 4. **328.** "relief rolls as . . . of the country." Braeman et al (*Vol. 1*), p. 210. **328.** "THE CONTINUATION OF . . . VOTING AGAINST HIM." *NY Age*, 31 October 1936, p. 3. **329.** "The Negroes of . . . touch with them." Watts (*Cabinet*), pp. 193–94. **329.** "Colored Democratic Divisions." Braeman et al (*Vol. 1*), p. 209. **329.** Rainey drunk. Nordin, p. 170. **329.** Kansas. Nordin, p. 162. **329.** GOP effort. *California Eagle*, 2 October 1936, p. 1. **329–330.** "Although I have . . . I dunno." *St. Louis Post-Dispatch*, 30 September 1936, p. 1. In 1940, Louis "campaigned all over" for Willkie, arguing that Roosevelt "promised a lot but he didn't always come through. He wouldn't even sign [sic] the antilynch bill" (Louis, p. 159). **330.** College-educated. Parks & Leighton, p. 20; Watts (*Cabinet*), p. 110. McDuffie's husband was also college-educated. **330.** "Lizzie treated FDR . . . of his head." Parks & Leighton, p. 20. **330.** Theatre major. Watts (*Cabinet*), p. 110. **330.** Puppets. Parks & Leighton, p. 25; Miller, p. 134. **330.** "histrionic talent." *NY Age*, 8 January 1938, p. 9. **330.** "robust and healthy." *Pittsburgh Courier*, 14 March 1936, p. 8. **330.** "I have found Mammy!" *Philadelphia Inquirer*, 3 January 1937, p. 7. **330.** Eleanor paid. *Batavia Daily News*, 3 January 1938, p. 2; *California Eagle*, 20 January 1937, p. 6-A. **330.** Got the part. *Philadelphia Inquirer*, 3 January 1937, p. 7; *NY Age*, 8 January 1938, p. 9; Parks & Leighton, p. 25. **330.** Not cast. *Washington Post*, 4 January 1936, p. X1; *Norfolk Journal and Guide*, 15 January 1937, p. 1; *California Eagle*, 20 January 1937, p. 6-A. Adding insult to injury, the ultimate "Mammy," Hattie McDaniel, publicly endorsed Wendell Willkie in 1940 (Schroeder, p. 121). **330.** Permission. *St. Louis Post-Dispatch*, 17 October 1936, p. 3. **330.** 50,000. *California Eagle*, 13 November 1936, page unknown. **330–331.** "Like in President . . . occasion by him." *NY Amsterdam News*, 17 October 1936, p. 1. **331.** "Hundreds of our . . . under the NYA." *NY Amsterdam News*, 17 October 1936, pp. 1–2. Like so many Blacks, Bethune supported Hoover in 1928 and 1932 (Watts [*Cabinet*], pp. 46, 48, 174). **331.** "The reality was . . . in their advice." Watts (*Cabinet*), p. 196. **331.** White House quarters. *Pittsburgh Courier*, 14 March 1936, p. 8; *NY Amsterdam News*, 14 March 1936, p. 2. **331.** "President and Mrs. . . . I Know Them." *St. Louis Post-Dispatch*, 16 October 1936, p. 1. **331.** "gowned in black . . . pearl earrings dangling." *St. Louis Post-Dispatch*, 17 October 1936, p. 3. **331.** "From her husband . . . in their use." *Baltimore Afro-American*, 31 October, 1936, p. 17. **331.** "For years your . . . that are theirs." *St. Louis Post-Dispatch*, 17 October 1936, p. 3. **331–332.** "Lizzie, I believe . . . for those accomplishments." *St. Louis Post-Dispatch*, 17 October 1936, p. 3. Conversely, Landon's four Black servants (particularly his chauffeur) allegedly complained of being underpaid; his cook was quoted saying "Roosevelt is the man for the job" (*Baltimore Afro-American*, 18 July 1936, p. 7). **332.** Membership limited. *Journal of Negro History*, Vol. 63, No. 4 (October 1978), p. 309. **332.** Pamphlets. *Journal of Negro History*, Vol. 63, No. 4 (October 1978), p. 309. **332.** "announced from the . . . organization, he withdrew." **332.** *The Forum* (Dayton), 2 October 1936, p. 6. **332.** "I do not . . . around political offices." *Norfolk Journal and Guide*, 26 September 1936, p. 10. **333.** Other resignations. *NY Age*, 19 September 1936, p. 2; *Norfolk Journal and Guide*, 26 September 1936, p. 5; *The Forum* (Dayton), 2 October 1936, p. 6; *Journal of Negro History*, October 1978, p. 310. **333.** 100,000. *NY Daily News*, 18 September 1936, p. 17. **333.** 25 cities. *Buffalo Courier-Express*, 22 September 1936, p. 5. **333.** "Free! To Everyone! . . . and His Achievements!" Weiss (*Lincoln*), p. 194. **334.** "Christ was termed . . . from social injustices." *Baltimore Afro-American*, 26 September 1936, p. 1. **334.** "his hands outstretched . . . in the shadows." Weiss (*Lincoln*), p. 195. **334.** Entertainment program. *NY Herald Tribune*, 22 September 1936, p. 12; *Washington*

Tribune, 25 September 1936, p. 14; *NY Age*, 26 September 1936, p. 1; *Baltimore Afro-American*, 26 September 1936, p. 1; *The Forum* (Dayton), 2 October 1936, p. 6; *Journal of Negro History*, Vol. 63, No. 4 (October 1978), p. 311; Weiss (*Lincoln*), p. 194. **334.** "20,000 Harlemites Hi de Ho for Roosevelt," *Baltimore Afro-American*, 26 September 1936, p. 1. **334.** "the minstrel mass meeting." *The Forum* (Dayton), 2 October 1936, p. 6. **334.** "religious jazz shows." *Journal of Negro History*, Vol. 63, No. 4 (October 1978), p. 311. **334–335.** "as far as it . . . to observe it." *Baltimore Afro-American*, 31 October 1936, p. 21. **335.** Howard poll. *Baltimore Afro-American*, 7 November 1936, p. 8; Daniels, p. 274. Colvin ran against FDR once previously, for vice president in 1920. **335.** Ads for endorsement. Weiss (*Lincoln*), p. 195. **335.** "We Work Again." Weiss (*Lincoln*), p. 199; Watts (*Cabinet*), pp. 201–02. **335.** "The Republicans have . . . your town, Ed?" *New York History*, Winter 2014, pp. 50–51.

18 "THE VERY ESSENCE OF UN-AMERICANISM"

336. Parade. *NY Amsterdam News*, 29 August 1936, p. 9. **336.** O'Brien. *Washington Post*, 14 September 1936, p. X6; *NY Amsterdam News*, 10 October 1936, p. 24. **337.** "Przemielewksi . . . say, Pleasant Day." *Baltimore Afro-American*, 24 October 1936, p. 4. **338.** "All People's Party" nominees. *NY Times*, 8 October 1936, p. 25. **338.** Endorsements. Ross (*Socialist*), p. 376. **338.** "I can no . . . alliances with Communists." Parmet, p. 130. **338.** "trend toward Communism." *NY Times*, 8 July 1936, p. 7. **338.** "Norman Thomas won . . . lost a party." *Washington Post*, 31 May 1936, p. B-4; *NY Times*, 7 June 1936, p. 107. **339.** "The C.I.O. was . . . Party's labor committee." Dubinsky, p. 262. **339.** Combined electors. *NY Times*, 19 August 1936, p. 12; Parmet, p. 138; Dubinsky, p. 268. **339.** "He typifies reaction . . . Kansan, a Fascist." *St. Louis Post-Dispatch*, 29 July 1936, Part 3, p. 1. On at least one occasion, Earl Browder conceded that Landon was not quite the essential threat to human existence that CPUSA propaganda portrayed. "Landon is no Mussolini or Hitler," Browder admitted at the University of Pennsylvania. "That's why he was chosen as the Republican candidate. He is the most colorless candidate seen in American politics in the memory of living man" (*St. Louis Post-Dispatch*, 17 October 1936, p. 2). **339.** "running as a . . . in the east." *Oakland Tribune*, 22 August 1932, p. 2. **339–340.** "Last year there . . . Florida's flogging belt." *NY Times*, 7 June 1936, p. 107. DuPont profits rose by 72 percent from 1935 to 1936; General Motors by 70 percent (Daniel, p. 270). In 1936, General Motors issued a record $200 million in stockholder dividends (Burk, p. 251). **340.** Nashville. *California Eagle*, 2 October 1936, p. 4. **340.** "even in the . . . headed for war." *Malone Evening Telegram*, 31 October 1936, p. 1. **340.** *NY Post*, 11 July 1936, Second Section, p. 1. **340.** "is getting away . . . who hate Roosevelt." *San Pedro News-Pilot*, 8 September 1936, p. 1. **340.** Thomas challenge. *Boston Globe*, 8 September 1936, p. 9. **340.** "Your telegram which . . . for the presidency." *Corsicana Daily Sun*, 9 September 1936, p. 7. **340–341.** Denver. *NY Daily Worker*, 9 August 1936, p. 2. **341.** Los Angeles. *NY Daily Worker*, 10 August 1936, p. 1. **341.** Philadelphia. *NY Daily Worker*, 19 October 1936, p. 4. **341.** University of Virginia. *Brooklyn Times Union*, 21 July 1936, p. 6. **341.** National Press Club. *NY Daily Worker*, 13 August 1936, p. 1; *Washington Post*, 16 October 1936, p. X8; Ryan, p. 113. **341.** 26,000 miles, 26 states. Ryan, p. 113. **341.** "No other Communist . . . me this year." *NY Post*, 2 November 1936, p. 2. **341.** "Not since Eugene . . . frequent favorable publicity." Ryan, p. 94. **341.** "Committee of Professional Groups." *NY Daily Worker*, 2 September 1936, p. 2. **341.** Eight NBC broadcasts. *NY Daily Worker*, 21 August 1936, p. 1. **341.** Ford on NBC. *NY Daily Worker*, 10 September 1936, p. 3. **341.** Southern stations. *NY Amsterdam News*, 26 September 1936, p. 4. **341.** *Herald Tribune* forum. *NY Daily Worker*, 24 September 1936, p. 1; Ryan, p. 113. **341.** WCAE. *NY Daily Worker*, 14 September 1932, p. 5; *Buffalo Evening News*, 21 September 1936, p. 8; Ryan, pp. 113–14. **341.** Atlanta. *Philadelphia Inquirer*, 14 September 1936, p. 39; *Tampa Tribune*, 14 September 1936, p. 2; Ryan, p. 114. **341.** September Tampa trip. *Tampa Tribune*, 14 September 1936, pp. 1–2; *Tampa Tribune*, 17 September 1936, p. 1; *Decatur Daily*, 17 September 1936, p. 1; Ryan, p. 114. **341–342.** October Tampa trip. *Washington Post*, 26 October 1936, p. X1; Ryan, pp. 114–15. **342.** Arrests. *Washington Post*, 27 October 1936, p. X3; *Labor Defender*, 1 December 1936, p. 17. **342.** "the very essence of un-Americanism." *Labor Defender*, 1 December 1936, p. 17. **342.** Birmingham. *NY Daily Worker*, 15 September 1936, p. 6; *California Eagle*, 18 September 1936, p. 1; *Dothan Eagle*, 24 September 1936, p. 4. **343.** "We do not . . . from such agitators." *NY Daily Worker*, 1 October 1936, p. 1. **343.** "Now these Communists . . . in Terre Haute." *Washington Post*, 2 October 1936, p. X8. **343.** Sues. *Washington Post*, 2 October 1936, p. X8. The case was finally thrown out of court in 1940 (Ryan, p. 119). **343.** ACLU. *Washington Post*, 1 October 1936, p. X2. **343.** "a lousy stunt . . . fair and sporting." *NY Daily Worker*, 1 October 1936, p. 2. **343.** "wire reply collect." *NY Daily Worker*, 1 October 1936, p. 2. To reporters, Landon refused comment (*NY Times*, 2 October 1936, pp. 1, 7). **343.** Landon. *NY Times*, 2 October 1936, p. 1, 7; *New Masses*, 13 October 1936, p. 9. **343.** "Browder is in . . . not our matter." *NY Daily Worker*, 1 October 1936, p. 1. **343.** "an act of . . . and disgraces America." *Hackensack Record*, 1 October 1936, p. 7; Ryan, pp. 117, 291. **343.** Thomas. Ryan, p. 117. **343–344.** Terre Haute, October. *Washington Post*, 21 October 1936, p. X1; *Rome Daily Sentinel*, 21 October 1936, p. 1; Ryan, pp. 118–19. **344.** "He was interrupted . . . eggs and vegetables." *Albany Evening News*, 24 October 1936, p. 7; *Utica Observer-Dispatch*, 24 October 1936, p. 1. **344–344.** "I want to . . . from colored people." *NY Daily Worker*, 1 September 1936, p. 2. Also, in Springfield in 1936, Chicago's representative Arthur Mitchell was refused service in a hotel's main dining room, with the explanation "they could not serve Colored people in the regular dining room, as Springfield is a small town and purely Southern in sentiment, as far as the mixing of the races is concerned" (Nordin, pp. 168–69). **344.** "hypocritical . . . to President Roosevelt." *NY Times*, 30 August 1936, p. 13; Klehr, p. 195. **344.** "hypocritical . . . the working class." *NY Times*, 30 August 1936, p. 13; Klehr, p. 195; *New International Year Book* (1937), p. 180. **344.** "interference in the . . . the American people." *Philadelphia Inquirer*, 1 September 1935, p. 2. **346.** "Moscow Orders Red . . . to defeat Landon." *Chicago Tribune*, 9 August 1936, p. 16. **346.** May 29 speech. Wolfskill & Hudson, p. 189; White (*Press*), p. 97. **346.** *Times* debunks. Wolfskill & Hudson, p. 189. **346.** $5,000 reward. Wolfskill & Hudson, p. 189; Winfield, p. 130. **346.** "We have working . . . favorable to Roosevelt." *Detroit Times*, 20 September 1936, p. 3. **346.** "His [FDR's] defeat . . . a body blow." *Detroit Times*, 20 September 1936, p. 3. **346.** Dimitroff speech. *Detroit Times*, 20 September 1936, pp. 1, 3. **346.** "is the "TITULAR . . . FRANKLIN D. ROOSEVELT." *San Francisco Examiner*, 20 September 1936, p. 1. **346–347.** "My attention has . . . into American Affairs." *San Francisco Examiner*, 20 September 1936, p. 1. **347.** "THE President has . . . and destructive elements." *Syracuse Journal*, 21 September 1936, p. 1. **347.** "indirect support." *NY Times*, 22 October

1926, p. 12. **347.** "If correctly quoted . . . Hearst editorial pages." Klehr, p. 135. **347.** "Technically, Browder was . . . wanted direct support." Klehr, p. 135. **347–348.** "Mr. Roosevelt declares . . . own American Business." *San Francisco Examiner*, 1 October 1936, pp. 1–2. **348.** "A Red New . . . cannot be denied." *Pittsburgh Sun-Telegraph*, 25 September 1936, p. 44.

19 "I WELCOME THEIR HATRED"

349. NYS Assembly. Weed, p. 92. **349.** Hamilton. *Cattaraugus Republican*, 22 July 1936, p. 4. **349.** "greatly disturbed." Nevins, p. 187. **350.** "He simply cannot be permitted to withdraw." Nevins, p. 187. **350.** Lehman retires. *Brooklyn Daily Eagle*, 30 June 1936, p. 1. **350.** "spectacular half-hour demonstration . . . heart-warming nevertheless." Nevins, p. 188. **350.** "comes more deeply . . . all that implies." Nevins, p. 188. In 1937, when Lehman opposed Franklin's court-packing scheme, a furious FDR, nonetheless, privately sneered to reporters, "What else would you expect from a Jew?" (Trohan, p. 99). Interestingly, son Elliott Roosevelt also noted "the anti-Semitism of [Eleanor's] earlier days" (Roosevelt & Brough [*Rendezvous*], p. 96). **350.** "American political history . . . the national ticket." *Binghamton Press*, 1 July 1936, p. 27; *New York History*, Winter 2014, p. 48. **350.** "Victory definitely assured." Sheppard, p. 67. **350.** Sinecure. O'Connor (*Smith*), p. 230; Caro, p. 287. **351.** "of all the . . . rid of him." Watkins, p. 374. **351.** "approve a single . . . employed on them." Caro, p. 428. **351.** Order 129. Ickes (*Diary*), pp. 307, 317; Caro, pp. 430–32. **351.** "I was asked . . . had to lie." Ickes (*Diary*), p. 268. **351.** "great mistake . . . a martyr." Ickes (*Diary*), p. 268; Caro, p. 434. **351.** "Isn't the President . . . No." Caro, p. 438. **352.** 1932 post-nomination. Cross, pp. 57–65, 94. **352.** March–April 1936. Cross, pp. 93–94. **352.** Emmerz. *NY Times*, 10 July 1936, p. 20; *Brooklyn Times Union*, 26 July 1936, p. 3. **353.** "I'll be in . . . clothes I've got." *NY Times*, 14 July 1936, p. 1; Cross, p. 95. **353.** "I'm just going to loaf." *NY Times*, 15 July 1936, p. 1; Cross, p. 95. **353.** "I can look . . . praying for fog." Rosenman (*Vol. 5*), pp. 259–60; Cross, p. 95. **353.** "We listened to . . . has been done." Asbell, p. 70. Sara had her own "cottage" just to the north. **353.** Watches. Cross, p. 97. **353.** "prize cruise." Cross, p. 101. **353.** "Ten days on . . . campaign for re-election." *NY Times*, 26 July 1936, p. N1. **353.** "If the present . . . is extremely doubtful." *Albany Times-Union*, 17 July 1936, p. 3. **353–354.** "[T]he President smiles . . . have been true." Ickes (*Diary*), p. 640. **354.** Early to Ickes. Levin, p. 149. **354.** "apparent confusion all . . . of competent staffs." Levin, p. 149. **354.** "From where I . . . favor of Landon." Schlesinger (*Upheaval*), p. 608. **354.** "set the stage . . . a party debacle." Timmons, p. 209. **354.** "the public psychology . . . over the radio." Burns (*Fox*), p. 214; Black, p. 354. **354.** Fireside Chats. Daniels, p. 277; Winfield, pp. 119–20. Depending on who was counting, FDR delivered, at most, thirty-two Fireside Chats—or as few as twenty-one. **354.** "FDR, 340, AML, 191." *NY Times*, 7 November 1936, p. 3; Schlesinger (*Upheaval*), p. 608. **354.** Bullitt. Brownell & Billings, p. 186. **354–355.** "We shun political . . . I hate war." *NY Post*, 15 August 1936, pp. 1, 4. **355.** Gallup. Gallup, p. 35. **355.** FDR–Ickes conversation. Ickes (*Diary*), p. 679. **355.** "It seemed to . . . tired of reform." *Rochester Democrat and Chronicle*, 17 July 1936, p. 3. **355.** Val-Kill. Lash (*Dealers*), p. 278. **355–356.** Moley. Schlesinger (*Ghosts*), p. 18. **356.** PWA project. *Buffalo Courier-Express*, 27 September 1936, p. 7; *St. Louis Post-Dispatch*, 30 September 1936, p. 2. **356.** "No trick of . . . edged with sarcasm." *St. Louis*

Post-Dispatch, 30 September 1936, p. 2. **356.** "full force of . . . withering sarcasm." *Philadelphia Inquirer*, 30 September 1936, p. 8. **356.** Farley warning. *Philadelphia Inquirer*, 30 September 1936, p. 8. **357.** "In the Summer . . . hat was lost." *NY Times*, 30 September 1936, p. 17. **357.** "brought the house down." *Philadelphia Inquirer*, 30 September 1936, p. 8. **357.** "as a radical . . . in the east." *Oakland Tribune*, 22 August 1932, p. 2. When FDR trotted out that line in Omaha, a local reporter blurted out, "No—it's the same old bull everywhere" (Stokes, p. 454). **357–358.** "provide insurance against . . . than his first." *NY Times*, 1 October 1936, p. 24. **358.** "the true conservative . . . of a liberal." *Boston Globe*, 30 September 1936, p. 14. **358.** "severely." *St. Louis Post-Dispatch*, 30 September 1936, p. 2. **358.** Todhunter. *Albany Evening News*, 28 September 1936, p. 4; *Albany Knickerbocker-Press*, 28 September 1936, p. 8. **358.** "Herbert Hoover." *Rochester Times-Union*, 30 September 1936, p. 20. **358.** Platform. *Rochester Democrat and Chronicle*, 30 September 1936, p. 1; *Boston Globe*, 30 September 1936, p. 1; *NY Daily News*, 30 September 1936, p. 4. **358.** ER and Earhart meet. Butler (*Earhart*), p. 280; Cook (*Vol. 2*), p. 95. The luncheon was marred by the unannounced arrival of a relative of some sort. "I always like having the children," Eleanor testily complained, "but don't like having extra vegetables picked just on the chance they may come. They never bother to telephone. . . . But of course they have had no bringing up." **358.** NYA. *Washington Evening Star*, 2 August 1935, p. A-5; Butler (*Earhart*), p. 349. **358–359.** Mechanicville. Rich, p. 229; Butler (*Earhart*), p. 351. **359.** "The one was . . . of the nation." *Ballston Spa Daily Journal*, 28 September 1936, p. 1. **359.** O'Day. *Albany Knickerbocker-Press*, 28 September 1936, p. 8; Butler (*Earhart*), p. 352; Rich, p. 229. **359.** Telegram. Butler (*Earhart*), p. 350. **359.** FDR's reaction. Butler (*Earhart*), p. 350. **359.** Vidal returns. Butler (*Earhart*), pp. 350–51; Cook (*Vol. 2*), p. 346*fn*; Winters, pp. 176–77. **359.** "paid in the . . . only by production." *NY Times*, 20 October 1932, p. 18. **359–360.** "the idea that . . . make to business." *NY Times*, 20 October 1932, p. 18. **360.** "I'm going to . . . ever made it." Rosenman (*Working*), pp. 86–87. FDR's Federal Reserve chief, Marriner Eccles, once remarked of 1932: "Given later developments, the campaign speeches often read like a giant misprint, in which Roosevelt and Hoover speak each other's lines" (Eccles, p. 95). **360.** "The Man Who Saved America." *NY Daily News*, 2 October 1936, p. 4. **360.** WPA band, 50,000 present. *Pittsburgh Post-Gazette*, 2 October 1936, pp. 1–2. **360.** "You could almost . . . as it fell." Davin, p. 228. **360–361.** "[T]he crowd vented . . . with paeans of joy." Stokes, pp. 459–60; Davin, p. 228; Martin, p. 366. **361.** "If the national . . . future of America." *Albany Times-Union*, 2 October 1936, p. 16. In his budget message of 1934, FDR had, however, proclaimed, "We should plan to have a definitely balanced budget for the third year of recovery [1935–36] and from that time on seek a continuing reduction of the national debt" (Hallgren, p. 245). **361.** "florid-faced." *Pittsburgh Sun-Telegraph*, 2 October 1936, p. 25. **361.** "If I find . . . I'll use them." *Buffalo Courier Express*, 2 October 1936, p. 1. **361.** Eleanor. *Pittsburgh Sun-Telegraph*, 2 October 1936, p. 2. **361.** "You're no better than Jimmy Walker!" *NY Daily News*, 2 October 1936, p. 18. **361.** Smith. *Buffalo Courier-Express*, 2 October 1936, p. 1; *Pittsburgh Sun-Telegraph*, 2 October 1936, p. 2. **361–362.** "make his second . . . most to fear." *NY Times*, 1 October 1936, p. 24. **362.** Jersey City visit. *NY Times*, 3 October 1936, pp. 1, 3; *NY Daily News*, 3 October 1936, p. 21; *Pittsburgh Post-Gazette*, 3 October 1936, p. 4; *Rochester Democrat and Chronicle*, 3 October 1936, p. 5; *Elmira Star-Gazette*, 3 October 1936, p. 1. **362.** "through the Bronx . . . displayed great enthusiasm." Ickes (*Diary*), p. 690. **362.** Landon, radio. *Pittsburgh Post-Gazette*,

3 October 1936, p. 4. **362.** Seventh inning. Daniels, p. 281. **363.** His "Mollycoddle Philosophy" . . . and Easy Life." *NY Herald Tribune*, 4 October 1936, p. A3. **363.** "Mother, in a . . . her own name." Roosevelt and Brough (*Hyde Park*), p. 299. **363.** "I realize more . . . be anything else." Lash (*Love*), p. 242. **363.** "I felt entirely detached." Lash (*Love*), p. 240. **363.** "I have a . . . Lord, so indifferent!" Streitmatter, p. 191; Lash (*Love*), p. 240. She also wrote to Lorena: "I wish I could send you some of our cool air or better still that you could get on a magic carpet & come & share my room tonight" (Faber, p. 212). **363–364.** "All your personal . . . have offended you." Streitmatter, p. 190; Lash (*Love*), p. 240. **364.** Strategy session. Faber p. 210. Forbes's first wife was ER's maternal aunt, Edith Livingston "Aunt Puss" Hall. She died in 1920 (*NY Times*, 21 April 1937, p. 23). **364.** "answers in black and white." Weiss (*Vol. 2*), p. 378. **364.** "disgrace . . . await the others." Sheppard, p. 249; Weiss (*Vol. 2*), p. 379. **364.** "No one who . . . of every kind." *Pittsburgh Press*, 5 October 1936, p. 24. Joseph P. Lash wrote that Eleanor was reacting ("a ladylike thrust") to a column by Alice Longworth (Lash [*Eleanor*], p. 448; Peyser and Dwyer, p. 195). This was obviously not so. Alice's thoughts (privately expressed in August 1935) on FDR's infirmities were these: "He has the cripple's psychology . . . he puts his disability out of his mind and makes the most of what is left to him. He treats the American people the same way, distracting them with anything he thinks will keep them happy for the moment, but without any deep thought behind it" (Morris [*Edith*], pp. 482, 558; Peyser & Dwyer, p. 195). **364–365.** FDR Train. Daniels, p. 281. **365.** Landon train. *Des Moines Register*, 6 November 1936, p. 16. **365.** Local politicians. Rosenman (*Working*), pp. 112–13. **365.** "crowds wanted Mrs. . . . husband is about." *Pittsburgh Press*, 10 June 1937, p. 25; Lash (*Eleanor*), pp. 447, 739. **365.** "inconsistent, campaign-devised, half-baked." *NY Daily News*, 11 October 1936, p. 2. **365.** "I have made. . . and party lines." *Brooklyn Times Union*, 11 October 1936, p. 2. **365.** "instead of . . . going to Kansas." Sheppard, pp. 165, 266. **365–366.** William Allen White. *NY Times*, 14 October 1936, p. 1; *Chicago Tribune*, 14, October 1936, p. 6; *Fort Worth Star-Telegraph*, 14 October 1936, p. 5; *Oakland Tribune*, 14 October 1936, p. 18B; Stokes, p. 448; Davis (*FDR*), p. 642. FDR was very much on the mark about being "predestined to be a traveling salesman." Even before reaching the White House, he could figuratively not sit still, constantly in transit between Hyde Park, Albany, East 65th Street, the high seas, and Warm Springs. "[H]e is the most widely traveled president this country has known," wrote a columnist in August 1937. "By last November 15, Mr. Roosevelt had traveled 82,910 miles by railroad, with a total of 33,205 miles in 1936 alone. This is exclusive of five pleasure sea cruises, two long ocean voyages, and many thousands of miles by automobile. Since then [he] has added more thousands to his railroad travel, a 13,000-mile ocean voyage [to South America] and another sea cruise to fish. Because Mr. Roosevelt is so seldom at the White House, the newspaper correspondents assigned to him commenced to refer to Washington as 'a whistle stop'" (*Milford News*, 15 July 1937, p. 8). As president, he traveled a total of over 544,000 miles just by rail (Gallagher, p. 98). **366.** "our old American . . . are a taxpayer." White (*Autobiography*), p. 639. **367.** "Tommy, did you . . . doesn't get it." Lash (*Dealers*), pp. 280–81. **367.** Gallup Poll. *Oakland Tribune*, 14 October 1936, p. 18B. **367.** "Down with the . . . with the *Tribune*!" Schlesinger (*Upheaval*), p. 633. **368.** Balloons, fireworks. Stokes, p. 450. **368.** "Some of these . . . at the doctor." *NY Times*, 15 October 1936, p. 22; Freedman, pp. 360–61. **368.** "HEARD YOUR . . . THE-OFFENSIVE SPEECHES." Freedman, p. 360. **369.** "After careful study . . . nor too happy."

Great Falls Tribune, 13 September 1936, p. 11; McCoy, p. 294. **369.** "changeling candidate . . . the United States." *NY Post*, 21 October 1936, p. 14. **369.** Couzens. Barnard, p. 310. **369.** WPA political reports. Charles, p. 207. **369.** "I thought at . . . to be all-political." Sherwood, p. 68; Kurzman, p. 138. **369.** "Loyalty to the . . . here in Washington," McJimsey, p. 91. **370.** "Mr. Hopkins is . . . wit in Washington." Sherwood, p. 81; Taylor, p. 216. **370.** "The trouble with . . . in a budget." Creel, p. 296. **370.** "injudicious wisecracks." Schlesinger (*Upheaval*), p. 587. **370.** "about 75 percent . . . were about WPA." Davis (*FDR*), p. 628. **370.** Keep silent. Scroop, p. 126. **370–371.** "I am getting . . . that were broke." Sherwood, pp. 83–84. **372.** "This is very . . . the Republican Party." *New York History*, Winter 2014, p. 56. **372.** "I think that . . . be too bad." Sheppard, p. 139. **372.** "[M]y Lord, it's political!" *Pennsylvania Magazine of History and Biography*, April 1971, p. 246. She was not exaggerating. In 1935, a Pittsburgh WPA supervisor vowed that "any WPA worker who is not in sympathy with the WPA program and the Roosevelt administration will be eliminated from WPA payrolls . . . as quickly as I can act" (Sheppard, p. 141). **372.** RCA, Paramount. Beauchamp, pp. 334–43; Beschloss, p. 127. **372.** "if I can be . . . let me know." Koskoff, p. 81. To Missy LeHand, June 15, 1936. **372.** Krock. Krock, pp. 331–32. **372–373.** "an enthusiastic and . . . and Old Dealers." *Saturday Review*, 5 September 1936, pp. 11–12. **373.** "a masterpiece." *NY Daily News*, 6 September 1936, p. 17C; Whalen, p. 185. **373.** "Dear Joe: . . . delighted with it." Whalen, p. 186. Joe was no fool when it came to currying favor with the right people. He bestowed employment in his liquor business for Missy LeHand's older brother Bernard and provided her with vacations to the Grand Canyon and at his Palm Beach estate, as well as with tickets for the 1932 World Series. More significant, of course, was his assistance to James Roosevelt in the insurance trade—and James's subsequent assistance to JPK in lassoing the import liquor trade and the ambassadorship to Britain. Kennedy biographer Ronald Kessler dismissed James as "greedy, dim-witted, and unethical" (Smith [*Gatekeeper*], pp. 111, 160, 193; Koskoff, pp. 51–52; Beschloss, pp. 82–83; Kessler, pp. 104–07, 145–48, 168–69). **373.** "I have no . . . or my children." Kennedy (*Roosevelt*), p. 3; Kessler, p. 135. **373.** "Businessmen for Roosevelt." Koskoff, p. 84; Kessler, p. 135; Beschloss, p. 126. **373.** Radio. Beschloss, p. 127. **373.** "the efforts made . . . program of communism." Koskoff, p. 85. **373.** Oursler. Oursler, pp. 386–87, 405. **373.** Taxes. Trohan, pp. 323–24; Schwarz, pp. 226–27; Kessler, pp. 134–35; Black, pp. 393–96. To one student of such matters, FDR was the "champion abuser" of tax investigations. **374.** Howe, Eleanor. Quirk, pp. 105–06. **374.** "prima donnas . . . hold his hand." Ickes (*Diary*), p. 692. **374.** "You must do this this!" Whalen, p. 186. **374.** Ads. *Chicago Tribune*, 3 September 1936, p. 17; *Chicago Tribune*, 10 September 1936, p. 16. **374.** *Whose Constitution?* Lord, p. 464; Culver & Hyde, p. 162. **374.** "I have not . . . sell 100,000 copies!" Schlesinger (*Upheaval*), p. 575. **374.** Vendors. *St. Louis Globe-Democrat*, 23 June 1936, p. 25; *Tampa Tribune*, 5 July 1936, p. 8. **375.** "the one most . . . given adequate relief." Hopkins, p. 99. Most of Hopkins's written material was ghostwritten (Kurzman, pp. 40–41*fn*). Apparently Hopkins's book was also ghosted by federal employees, for, as a biographer notes, it was compiled "with the help of his staff" (McJimsey, p. 95). **375.** "'Honest Harold's' Sideline. . . on WPA Payroll." *San Francisco Examiner*, 27 August 1936, p. 1; Ickes (*Diary*), p. 668. **375.** "was to be . . . of those services." Ickes (*Diary*), p. 669. **376.** "Fascist Republican." Schlesinger (*Upheaval*), p. 549. **376.** "The defeat of . . . the great masses." Schlesinger (*Upheaval*), p. 595. **376.** "thousands of workers . . . Olson—Governor Landon." *NY Daily Worker*, 26 August 1936, p. 3. **376.** Couzens. Barnard, pp. 313–319. Vandenberg considered Couzens "mentally disturbed." **376.** "I should have . . . true to form." Tully, p. 222. **376.** Waldman. Ross (*Socialist*), p. 374. **376–377.** Check, photo. Black (*Champion*), p. 389. **376.** "No, John, I . . . small need arises." Creel, p. 301; Schlesinger (*Upheaval*), p. 594. **377.** $469,870. Creel, p. 302; Davis (*FDR*), p. 631; Hoover (*Crusade*), p. 97. **377.** "old friend." Fine, p. 246. Aside from his general liberalism, Couzens endorsed FDR because he foresaw war with Japan and viewed Roosevelt as the "one man" to lead it (Barnard, p. 322). **377.** "The evidence speaks for itself." *Chicago Tribune*, 3 November 1936 p. 7. Decades later, Hamilton still protested the veracity of his charges: "We had found—that was true—that they'd ordered these dog-tags that everybody had to wear. . . . We had samples of them [and were] tipped off by a manufacturer in Ohio where they were making them" (Sheppard, p. 184). **377.** "Effective January, 1937 . . . take these chances." *NY Daily News*, 1 November 1936, p. 21. **377.** Farley, Michelson. *NY Times*, 15 November 1936, p. E10; Sheppard, pp. 178, 269. **377–378.** "I want to . . . the worker himself." *Oakland Tribune*, 22 October 1936, p. 12. **378.** "The Republicans are . . . are that dumb." *NY Daily News*, 1 November 1936, p. 21. **378.** "Why didn't the . . . any pay envelopes." Schlesinger (*Upheaval*), p. 636. Industrialist Sterling Morton, tasked with implementing the GOP's pay-envelope scheme, decades later observed to William F. Buckley Jr. that his operation was the only "political committee which got 100 percent results. . . . Every state we worked in went solidly against our candidate" (Lichtman, pp. 89, 475). **378.** "WPA workers are . . . lose their jobs." *Chicago Tribune*, 31 October 1936, pp. 1, 4. **378.** "THE DEPENDABILITY OF . . . with the people." *Syracuse American*, 1 November 1936, p. 9; *Rome Daily Sentinel*, 2 November 1936, p. 13. In June 1933, FDR retreated from cuts on Spanish-American and Great War veterans' pensions inflicted in the Economy Act. **379.** "the most amazing . . . wave of humanity." Burns (*Fox*), p. 282. **379.** Crowd Sizes. Sheppard, p. 175; Burns (*Fox*), p. 282. **379.** "[T]here was a . . . yourself and carefree." Roosevelt (*Remember*), p. 146. **379.** Harvard booing. *Boston Globe*, 22 October 1936, p. 17; *Wisconsin State Journal*, 22 October 1936, p. 1; Sheppard, p. 175. Eleanor said she "was not surprised." **379.** "I could see . . . big for him." Lash (*Eleanor*), p. 448. **380.** Elliott Roosevelt. *Philadelphia Inquirer*, 7 October 1936, pp. 1, 16; *Pittsburgh Post-Gazette*, 7 October 1936, pp. 1, 2; *Chicago Tribune*, 27 October 1936, p. 5; Collier with Horowitz, pp. 374–75; Hansen (Kindle edition). **380.** "Since no sales . . . incident is closed." *NY Times*, 8 October 1936, p. 9; *Boston Globe*, 8 October 1936, p. 15. Also on the committee (and concurring with Nye's inaction) was Arthur Vandenberg. **380.** St. Louis. *Chicago Tribune*, 1 November 1936, p. 1; Sheppard, p. 185. **380.** "halting frequently with . . . much better orator." *Time*, 9 November 1936, p. 14. **381.** "I should like . . . full time pay." *St. Louis Post-Dispatch*, 1 November, 1936, p. 1. **381.** "neither a Communist . . . satisfied with it." *Albany Knickerbocker Press*, 1 November 1936, p. 8. **381.** Knox. *NY Herald Tribune*, 1 November 1936, pp. 1, 19. **381.** Hamilton. *NY Herald Tribune*, 1 November 1936, p. 27. **382.** Coughlin. *NY Herald Tribune*, 1 November 1936, p. 19. **382.** Radio broadcasts. *Brooklyn Times Union*, 31 October 1936, p. 16. **382.** Academy of Music. *Brooklyn Times Union*, 31 October 1936, p. 16; *NY Herald Tribune*, 31 October 1936, p. 8. **382.** "It struck me . . . a Landon button." *Kansas City Star*, 31 October 1936, p. 14. **382.** "this is probably . . . as a candidate." *NY Herald Tribune*, 1 November 1936, p. 30. **383.** Eleanor's schedule. *NY Herald Tribune*, 1 November 1936, p. 30. **383.** FDR Jr. *NY Herald*

Tribune, 1 November 1936, p. 30; Burk, p. 159. **383.** Wagner. Louchheim, p. 202. **383.** "the bearer of our destiny." *Chicago Tribune*, 1 November 1936, p. 1. **384.** "resplendent economic autocracy . . . for the public." *Buffalo Courier-Express*, 4 January 1936, p. 8. **384.** "hatred at home . . . to stave off defeat." *NY Herald Tribune*, 4 January 1936, p. 14. **384.** "[D]esperate men with . . . have more confidence." Rosenman (*1936*), p. 568. **384–385.** "We have not . . . met their master." Rosenman (*1936*), pp. 568–69. **385.** "Many people found . . . a totalitarian technique." Martin, p. 367. **386.** "Of course, they . . . be *too* rich." Martin, p. 367. **386.** "Yes, there it . . . he said it." Stokes, p. 463. **386.** "Thoughtful citizens were . . . that uttered them." Moley (*Seven*), p. 352. **386.** "frankly horrified." Schlesinger (*Upheaval*), p. 640. **386.** "Tommy, is that . . . to say that." Lash (*Dealers*), p. 281.

20 "SEND FOR A PRIEST"

387. Rexall 1916 poll. *Shreveport Times*, 5 November 1916, p. 2. **387.** 2,376,523. *Literary Digest*, 31 October 1936, p. 6. **387.** 1924. *Literary Digest*, 1 November 1924, pp. 5–8. In 1916, the *Digest* concentrated on five significant "doubtful" states (New York, New Jersey, Ohio, Indiana, and Illinois), collecting 80,000 straw votes, and calling all five for Hughes. Hughes carried all but Ohio (*Literary Digest*, 4 November 1916, pp. 1155–56). In 1928, it predicted 63.2%-35.7% for Hoover, the actual percentage being 58.2%-40.8% (*Literary Digest*, 3 November 1928, p. 5). **387.** 1932 *Literary Digest*. *Literary Digest*, 5 November 1932, pp. 8–9, 44. **387.** "[I]t might . . . and in time." *Literary Digest*, 17 September 1932; p. 8. **387–388.** California poll. *Literary Digest*, 5 November 1936, p. 5. **388.** "You do the . . . an election result." *American Magazine*, May 1936, p. 87; *Michigan Historical Review*, Fall 1995, p. 126. Hurja's luck ran out after 1936. He forecast FDR's defeat in both 1940 and 1944. **388.** "scrupulously honest [and] . . . numerous to set forth." *Minneapolis Tribune*, 21 July 1936, p. 8. **388.** January 1936 poll. *Literary Digest*, 11 January 1936, p. 9. **388.** September 1936 poll. *Literary Digest*, 5 September 1936, pp. 7–8. **388–389.** "none of these . . . not feel depressed." *Literary Digest*, 5 September 1936, p. 7. **389.** Early October 1936 poll. *Buffalo Evening News*, 10 October 1936, p. 5. **389.** *Literary Digest* final poll. *Literary Digest*, 31 October 1936, pp. 5–6. **389.** *Literary Digest* return rates. Sheppard, pp. 210, 277. **389.** *Cleveland News* poll. *Philadelphia Inquirer*, 2 November 1936, p. 11. **389.** Collegiate poll. *Philadelphia Inquirer*, 2 November 1936, p. 11. **389.** Yale. *NY Times*, 15 October 1936, p. 18. **389.** *Farm Journal* poll. *NY Herald Tribune*, 2 November 1936, p. 6. **389.** Dunn poll. *NY Post*, 12 September 1936, p. 11. **389.** Starch poll. *Detroit Free Press*, 6 September 1936, p. 4. **389.** July 12 poll. *Philadelphia Inquirer*, 12 July 1936, p. 7. **389.** Michelson. *Minneapolis Tribune*, 21 July 1936, p. 8. **389.** Hurja. Davis (*FDR*), p. 638. **390.** "It will be . . . winning the election." *Boston Globe*, 8 July 1936, p. 2. **390.** August 9 poll. *Philadelphia Inquirer*, 9 August 1936, p. 7. **390.** Leaning/solid. *Philadelphia Inquirer*, 23 August 1936, p. 7. **390.** Final Gallup poll. *Philadelphia Inquirer*, 1 November 1936, p. 11. **390.** *News-Week* survey. *NY Times*, 15 October 1936, p. 23. **390.** 50,000 votes. *Emporia Gazette*, 3 October 1936, p. 4. **390.** Norris. *Arizona Republic*, 19 October 1936, p. 1. **391.** "Americans of future . . . chivalrous and true." *NY Herald Tribune*, 28 October 1936, p. 24. **391.** "You have a . . . you a cent." Daniels, p. 275. **391.** "like a son." McCoy, p. 34. **391.** "I have seen . . . on his train." *Lincoln State Journal*, 29 October 1936 p. 11. **391–392.** "I am sending . . . W. A. WHITE." Freedman, p. 360. **392.** Hamilton public prediction. *NY Herald Tribune*, 31 October 1936, p. 1. **392.** "We are going . . . that on record." *News-Week*, 14 November 1936, p. 16; Sheppard, p. 186. **392.** Hamilton private prediction. Sheppard, p. 186. **393.** Nielsen polling. McCoy, p. 327; Sheppard, p. 179. A September Nielsen poll was similarly dismal (McCoy, p. 291). **393.** "No chance . . . up to you." Terkel, pp. 336–37. **393.** Couch. *NY Herald Tribune*, 1 November 1936, p. 19. **393.** House seat gains. *NY Herald Tribune*, 31 October 1936, p. 5. **393.** "will be put . . . is another thing." Social Security Board, p. 2. **394.** "There is decidedly . . . appointment and approval." His words that April. Lichtman, pp. 86, 475. **394.** "the formidable sect . . . the White House." *El Paso Herald-Post*, 2 November 1936, p. 9. **394.** "Dubinsky, Zaritsky and . . . do you stand?" *Pittsburgh Post-Gazette*, 28 October 1936, p. 8; *Pittsburgh Press*, 28 October 1936, p. 7; *Pittsburgh Sun-Telegraph*, 29 October 1936, p. 25. **394.** "Tell that little . . . where he is." Dubinsky, p. 267. **394.** Landon cabinet. Schlesinger (*Upheaval*), p. 640; Terkel, p. 336. **394.** Methodist service. *NY Herald Tribune*, 2 November 1936, p. 3. **394.** "well and fresh." *NY Herald Tribune*, 2 November 1936, p. 1. **394.** Davies, dachshunds. *NY Daily Worker*, 3 November 1936, p. 2. **394.** "by nature a . . . a political playboy." *SF Examiner*, 2 November 1936, p. 1. **395.** "And now, Dear . . . Devotedly yours, F.F." Freedman, p. 362. **395.** Longworth bet. Brough, p. 297. **396.** "It may comfort . . . named Alexander Woollcott." *Dayton Daily News*, 30 October 1936, p. 29. **396.** Odds. *Atlanta Constitution*, 3 November 1936, p. 17. **396.** GOP betting pool. *NY Daily News*, 4 November 1936, p. 8. Whitney, at roughly this time, was having an affair with Nina Gore Vidal, wife of Gene Vidal (otherwise engaged with Amelia Earhart). Mrs. Whitney was concurrently involved with said Mr. Vidal. If this is not confusing enough, in 1942 Whitney married Betsey Cushing Roosevelt, James Roosevelt's ex-wife. **396.** "put this miserable . . . a perpetual end." *Ballston Spa Daily Journal*, 30 October 1936, p. 2. **396.** "I'm sure the . . . right on praying." *Buffalo Evening News*, 3 November 1936, p. 7. **396.** "Nearly 40 persons . . . of the house." *Buffalo Evening News*, 3 November 1936, p. 7. **396.** Police called. *NY Herald Tribune*, 3 November 1936, p. 19. **396.** LeRoy a Democrat? *Schenectady Gazette*, 3 November 1936, p. 1. **397.** "When this oil . . . a copper kettle." *Buffalo Courier-Express*, 4 November 1936, p. 8. **397.** "I fear Roosevelt . . . like me tomorrow." *NY Herald Tribune*, 2 November 1936 p. 15. **397.** Crossley. *San Francisco Examiner*, 1 November 1936, Sect. 1, p. 14; Sheppard, p. 190. At no time in Crossley's poll was FDR less than eight electoral votes ahead of Landon. **397.** Roper. *NY Times*, 1 May 1971, p. 36; Sheppard, p. 190; Fried (*Polling*), p. 30. **397.** Hurja. *Michigan Historical Review*, Fall 1995, p. 133; Scroop, p. 131; Sheppard, p. 193. **397.** FDR prediction. Schlesinger (*Upheaval*), p. 640; Sheppard, p. 193. **397.** Johnson. *Pittsburgh Press*, 2 November 1936, p. 1. **397–398.** Pearson, Allen. *Pittsburgh Press*, 2 November 1936, p. 1. **398.** Stokes. Stokes, p. 449. **398.** "Polls go wrong . . . is to it." Scroop, p. 130. **398.** "we should carry . . . ahead of Lehman." *New York History*, Winter 2014, p. 61. **398.** "Men and women . . . vote for him." Sheppard, pp. 192, 271. **398.** Times Square. *NY Herald Tribune*, 2 November 1936, pp. 1, 17. **399.** "I have just . . . a dictator absolutely." *NY Herald Tribune*, 2 November 1936, p. 7. In 1942, Jung privately derided Roosevelt as "the limping messenger of the Apocalypse . . . with, like all Americans, a gigantic mother-complex" (McLynn, pp. 387, 452). **399.** Weather. *Manhattan Mercury*, 3 November 1936, p. 1; *Buffalo Courier-Express*, 4 November 1936, p. 2; Schlesinger (*Upheaval*), p. 641. **399.** Grace Gehrke. *Wisconsin State Journal*, 22 February 1936, p. 1. **399.** "I may like . . . The winner." *Poughkeepsie Eagle-News*, 4 November 2, 1936, p. 2. **400.** "continue to vote . . . rheumatism every time." *NY Times*, 4 November 1936, p. 18. **400.** Thrash. *Atlanta Constitution*, 4 November 1936, p. 9; *Chattanooga Times*, 18 December 1943, p. 1. **400.** Edith Roosevelt. *NY Times*, 4 November 1936, p. 5; *Atlanta Constitution*, 4 November 1936, p. 9; Morris [*Edith*], pp. 489, 491. She had fractured her hip in November 1935 and spent five months in the hospital. **400.** "democratic government is at stake." *NY Herald Tribune*, 2 November 1936, p. 6. **400.** Townsend absentee. *Atlanta Constitution*, 4 November 1936, p. 9. **400.** Primary. *NY Times*, 18 September 1936, p. 8; *NY Times*, 1 October 1936, p. 17. **400.** Coughlin votes. *NY Herald Tribune*, 4 November 1936, p. 6. **400.** How Coughlin voted. *Washington Star*, 3 November 1936, p. 4; Fine, p. 248. **400.** Armstrong County. *NY Herald Tribune*, 4 November 1936, p. 15; *Boston Globe*, 4 November 1936, p. 8. **401.** Supreme Court. *Pittsburgh Sun-Telegraph*, 3 November 1936, p. 6. **401.** Kentucky. *Poughkeepsie Eagle-News*, 4 November 2, 1936, p. 2; *Park City Daily News*, 4 November 1936, p. 8; *Park City Daily News*, 7 November 1936, p. 8. **401.** Farley votes. *NY Times*, 4 November 1936, p. 12; *NY Herald Tribune*, 3 November 1936, p. 15. **401.** Thomas votes. *NY Times*, 4 November 1936, p. 12; *NY Herald Tribune*, 3 November 1936, p. 17. **401.** Thomas tours. *NY Herald Tribune*, 3 November 1936, pp. 11, 20. **401.** Lehman votes. *NY Times*, 4 November 1936, p. 12. **401.** Butler. *NY Herald Tribune*, 4 November 1936, p. 20. **401.** 1932 for Hoover. *NY Times*, 4 November 1936, p. 14. **401.** Smith. *Atlanta Constitution*, 4 November 1936, p. 11. **402.** "I wonder if . . . in his favor." *NY Times*, 4 November 1936, p. 6. **402.** Gerard. *Atlanta Constitution*, 4 November 1936, p. 11; *Buffalo Courier-Express*, 4 November 1936, p. 2; *NY Times*, 4 November 1952, p. 24. Thus Eleanor's $1 wager back in Philadelphia with John Nance Garner technically voided her vote. In 1952, the state attorney general's office reported that in sixty years the law had never been enforced. **402.** "Not one of . . . righteous government platform." *NY Daily News*, 4 November 1936, p. 8. **402.** "We must stay . . . give the command," Divine explained. "No doubt it will be 1940." *NY Herald Tribune*, 4 November 1936, p. 17. **403.** Lamb. *NY Daily News*, 4 November 1936, p. 8. **403.** Rabbi Wolf. *Poughkeepsie Eagle-News*, 4 November 2, 1936, p. 2; *NY Daily News*, 4 November 1936, p. 8; *Albany Times-Union*, 8 November 1936, p. 7. **403.** "Last year I . . . would I move." *Atlanta Constitution*, 4 November 1936, p. 11. **403.** Chicago Stadium. *NY Daily Worker*, 30 October 1936, p. 2; *NY Daily Worker*, 4 November 1936, pp. 1, 4. **403.** Browder votes. *NY Daily Worker*, 4 November 1936, p. 1; *NY Herald Tribune*, 4 November 1936, p. 20. **403.** "the most successful . . . by the country." *NY Daily Worker*, 4 November 1936, p. 1. **403.** Union and Communist parties finances. Marshall, p. 170. **403.** "Some of my . . . elect myself President." Blackorby, p. 229. **404.** Landon's vote. *Manhattan Mercury*, 3 November 1936, p. 1; *Washington Star*, 3 November 1936, pp. 1–2; *Baltimore Sun*, 3 November 1936, p. 22; *Geneva Daily Times*, 3 November 1936, p. 1. **404.** October 17. *Buffalo Courier-Express*, 18 October 1936, p. 2. **404.** "I know my . . . whatever I accomplished." Harwood, p. 178. **404.** "That was all . . . and his banks." Michelson, p. 130. **404.** "We got back . . . him some more." Michelson, p. 131. **404–405.** Garner's vote. *Poughkeepsie Eagle-News*, 4 November 2, 1936, p. 2. **405.** "I am glad . . . 'How-di-doo.'" *NY Daily News*, 3 November 1936, p. 6. **405.** "Three times he . . . word of greeting." *NY Herald Tribune*, 3 November 1936, p. 14. **405–406.** Roosevelt entourage votes. *Chicago Tribune*, 4 November 1936, p. 4. **406.** LeHand's fears. Smith (*Gatekeeper*), p. 192. **406.** FDR Jr. *Buffalo Courier-Express*, 4 November 1936, p. 2. **406.** Tom Leonard. *Millbrook Round Table*, 2 July 1985, p. A5.

406. "Reached by phone . . . on the menu." *NY Times*, 4 November 1936, p. 10. **406.** 3:40 vote. *Manhattan Mercury*, 3 November 1936, p. 1. **407.** "*American People: Defeat . . . Party! Vote Communist!*" *NY Daily Worker*, 3 November 1935, p. 1. **407.** "Barnyard debris littered the floor." *Chicago Tribune*, 4 November 1936, p. 3. **407.** Ripon. *Washington Star*, 2 November 1936, p. 1. **407–408.** New Ashford/Millville. *Boston Globe*, 3 November 1936, pp. 1, 15; *Washington Star*, 3 November 1936, p. 1; *NY Herald Tribune*, 2 November 1936, pp. 1–2. **408.** WOR. *NY Times*, 1 November 1936, p. XII; *NY Daily News*, 3 November 1936, p. 48. **408.** *Examiner* returns. *SF Examiner*, 3 November 1936, p. 6. **408.** *Washington Star* efforts. *Washington Star*, 4 November 1936, p. 5. **408.** *Star* reporters. *Washington Star*, 4 November 1936, p. 5. **408.** Washington Monument. *NY Times*, 4 November 1936, p. 7; *Chicago Tribune*, 4 November 1936, p. 10. **408.** *Boston Globe* screen. *Boston Globe*, 2 November 1936, p. 6. **408.** *Tribune* switchboard. *Chicago Tribune*, 4 November 1936, p. 3. **408.** Times Square results. *NY Daily News*, 4 November 1936, p. 3. **408.** St. Regis. Sherwood, p. 87. **408.** Train back to Topeka. *Buffalo Courier-Express*, 4 November 1936, p. 2. **409.** "Theo better have . . . got a chance." *Buffalo Courier-Express*, 4 November 1936, p. 2. **409.** "I'm proud of . . . it may be." *Amsterdam Evening Recorder*, 4 November 2, 1936, p. 9. **409.** "Maybe—just maybe . . . to cut it." *Amsterdam Evening Recorder*, 4 November 2, 1936, p. 9. **409.** "Hughes appeared to . . . yet been reported." *Poughkeepsie Eagle-News*, 4 November 2, 1936, p. 2. **409.** Ziegfeld chorus. *Atlanta Constitution*, 4 November 1936, p. 11. **409.** Pickens. *NY Daily News*, 4 November 1936, p. 8. **409.** Brice/Clark. *Atlanta Constitution*, 4 November 1936, p. 11. **409–410.** Bets. *NY Daily News*, 4 November 1936, p. 8; *NY Daily News*, 5 November 1936, p. 56; *Pasadena Post*, 5 November 1936, p. 3. It was later reported Erickson won "only" $75,000, a revision necessitated, perhaps, from tax concerns (*Buffalo Courier-Express*, 24 November 1936, p. 23). **410.** "Demand a recount . . . for a priest." *NY Herald Tribune*, 4 November 1936, p. 15. **410.** Times Square. *NY Daily News*, 4 November 1936, p. 3; *NY Herald Tribune*, 4 November 1936, p. 9; *Atlanta Constitution*, 4 November 1936, p. 11. **410–411.** "You're not in. . . . Sentence suspended." *NY Times*, 4 November 1936, p. 5. **411.** Richmond. *NY Herald Tribune*, 4 November 1936, p. 17; *Chicago Tribune*, 4 November 1936, p. 6. **411.** *Chicago Tribune*. Stokes, pp. 449–50; Schlesinger (*Upheaval*), p. 641. **411.** "My heartiest congratulations . . . the little man." *NY Times*, 5 November 1936, p. 4. **411.** "How should I . . . the common people." *NY Times*, 5 November 1936, p. 4. **411.** Wigwam Democratic Club. *NY Times*, 4 November 1936, p. 4. **412.** "Roosevelt County." *Pasadena Post*, 4 November 1936, p. 3. **412.** Guests. *Atlanta Constitution*, 4 November 1936, p. 12; *Chicago Tribune*, 4 November 1936, p. 1; *Buffalo Courier-Express*, 4 November 1936, p. 2; Ward (*Companion*), p. 88. **412.** Corcoran parodies. *Chicago Tribune*, 4 November 1936, p. 1; McKean, p. 80. **412.** Reaction to Hamilton. *Chicago Tribune*, 4 November 1936, p. 1. **412.** Eleanor's attire. McKean, p. 80. **412.** "I was expected . . . in the returns." Roosevelt (*Remember*), p. 147; Roosevelt (*Autobiography*), p. 186. **412.** "must be wrong. . . . Wow!" Rosenman (*Working*), pp. 137–38; Schlesinger (*Upheaval*), p. 641. **413.** "Who are the . . . hell with them." Schlesinger (*Upheaval*), p. 642. **413.** "I knew I . . . wouldn't let me." Roosevelt (*Remember*), p. 147. **413.** "beamed." *Chicago Tribune*, 4 November 1936, p. 1. During the campaign, rumors floated that Sara was compensated between $17,000 and $100,000 annually for use of Springwood as presidential offices. They were unfounded (Levin, p. 146; Winfield, p. 82). **413–414.** FDR with crowd. *Atlanta Constitution*, 4 November 1936, p. 12; *Brooklyn Eagle*, 4

November 1936, p. 2. **414.** "Hello, John, this . . . at this end." Ickes (*Diary*), p. 704; Guiles, p. 285. **414.** *Seattle Post-Intelligencer. Wilmington Morning News*, 27 November 1936, p. 13; Asbell, p. 72. FDR later fumed to Eleanor of John and Anna's situation with Hearst, as W. R. continued bashing the administration. Eleanor reminded Franklin of how he had made his own deal with the devil (Hearst) to gain the presidency. FDR angrily alibied, "It was [Howe's] idea. I just went along" (Parks & Leighton, p. 58). **414.** "Cares of a . . . for Colonel Knox!" *St. Louis Post Globe-Democrat*, 30 November 1936, p. 12. **414–415.** Urban GOP wipeout. Trende, p. 14. **415.** Chest cold. *Time*, 16 November 1936, p. 28. **415.** Borah checks. Sheppard, p. 168. **415–416.** "Our ignominious defeat . . . we escape Alcatraz." Manchester, p. 326. **416.** "As Christ had . . . his Father Coughlin." *Boston Globe*, 5 November 1936, p. 1. **416.** Thompson. https://en.wikipedia.org/wiki/1936_United_States_gubernatorial_elections. **416.** NYS Assembly. *Albany Evening News*, 4 November 1936, p. 1; *NY Herald Tribune*, 5 November 1936, p. 12. Not that it mattered that much (save to Jim Farley's place in history), but Lemke's candidacy probably shifted New Hampshire into FDR's column. **416–417.** Will G. West. *Time*, 16 November 1936, p. 28. **417.** "Democrats gained Governors . . . for the country." Ickes (*Diary*), pp. 701–02. Ickes's list likely included Illinois governor Henry Homer and Ohio governor Martin Davies. **417.** Pelley. *California History*, Jun 1986, p. 134; Leuchtenburg (*Legacy*), p. 149. **417.** York. *Time*, 2 November 1936, p. 9. **417.** Teichert. *NY Times*, 27 April 1936, p. 4. **418.** Barred from twelve states. Johnpoll, p. 172. **418.** Thomas reluctant. Johnpoll, pp. 171–72. **418.** "Roosevelt is the . . . will ever have." Leuchtenburg (*Legacy*), p. 156. **418.** Liberty League. Wolfskill, pp. 208–09; Burk, pp. 239–52. **418.** $2.02/$0.11. *Socialist Call*, 25 December 1936, p. 5. **419.** City College. *Brooklyn Eagle*, 2 November 1936, p. 13. FDR won going away, polling 3,238 ballots. **419.** ALP vote. *NY Post*, 3 December 1936, p. 15; *NY Times*, 3 December 1936, p. 10. **419.** $142,000. Michaels, p. 17. **419.** CPUSA in NYS. *NY Times*, 5 November 1936, pp. 1, 5; *NY Herald Tribune*, 5 November 1936, p. 1; *NY Times*, 3 December 1936, p. 10; *Socialist Call*, 12 December 1936, p. 8. Minor ran far behind Israel Amter, the Communist Party's 1932 candidate for governor (now running for president of the City council and polling 62,414 votes) and this year's Socialist gubernatorial candidate Harry Laidler's 86,897. Amter, a slavish imitator of all things Soviet, once opened a party meeting with the words "Workers and Peasants of Brooklyn!" (Lewy, p. 7). **419.** CPUSA infiltration. Casey, pp. 12, 14. **419.** "In 1932 it . . . were for Franklin." Tugwell (*Democratic*), p. 408. **419–420.** "took as their . . . the collateral assaults." *NY Times*, 15 November 1936, p. E10. **420.** Campaign funding. Sheppard, pp. 120–21. **420.** Radio, printed material. *NY Times*, 15 November 1936, p. E10; Winfield, p. 131; Michelson provided the $540,000 figure. **420.** "the support of . . . headed 'editorial suggestion.'" *NY Times*, 15 November 1936, p. E10. **420–421.** Press percentages. White (*Press*), pp. 69–70, 73, 90, 170–71; 189. J. David Stern bettered FDR, placing the percentage at ninety. **421.** Unemployment. Shlaes, pp. 282–83. **421.** "You tell [CWA] . . . first of October!" Schlesinger (*Upheaval*), p. 590. Immediately following the election, Harry Hopkins suddenly stood ready to lay off 150,000 workers (*Collier's*, November 1947, p. 81). **421.** Kansas spending. Sheppard, p. 136. **421.** Kansas votes. Schruben, p. 212. **421.** Relief numbers. Best, p. 124. **421.** "You cannot beat . . . including myself, favored." *Amsterdam Evening Recorder*, 4 November 1936, p. 9. **421.** Buchanan. Trende, p. 14. **421.** Pennsylvania legislature. Sheppard, p. 207. **421.** Pennsylvania registration. *Pittsburgh Sun-Telegraph*, 25 October 1936, p. 13; Savage, p. 116.

421. Pittsburgh. Leuchtenburg (*Legacy*), p. 155. **422.** Catholic vote. *Records of the American Catholic Historical Society of Philadelphia*, Spring 1944, p. 44. **422.** Bishops. Tull, p. 158; Leuchtenburg (*Legacy*), p. 156. **422.** Jewish vote. Savage, p. 127. **422.** Enrollment. Lichtman, p. 92; Savage, pp. 1117, 126–27. Percentages based on two-party totals. **422.** Far West. Leuchtenburg (*Legacy*), p. 146. **422.** Western States spending. *Agricultural History*, October 1970, p. 287; Powell, p. 100. **422.** New England. Leuchtenburg (*Legacy*), p. 146. **422.** Forty-three percent. Trende, p. 14. **422.** Flint. Leuchtenburg (*Legacy*), p. 155. **422.** Michigan. Leuchtenburg (*Legacy*), p. 151. **422.** "Hundreds of thousands . . . as lower-class citizenry." *Literary Digest*, 24 October 1936, p. 1936. p. 20. Frank Murphy received 84.9 percent of Detroit's Polish vote, topping even the 63.5 percent he received from the Black community (Fine, p. 251). **422.** Twelve largest cities. Savage, p. 127. **422.** 106 largest cities. Sheppard, pp. 68, 201. **422–423.** "In . . . 1910 Congress . . . 1930 and 1940." Lubbell, p. 28. Between 1922 and 1938, for example, Bronx Democratic enrollment soared from 90,000 to 500,000 (Trende, p. 15). **423.** Pennsylvania. Sheppard, p. 198. **423.** Northern Protestants. Savage, p. 127. **423.** Income levels. Leuchtenburg (*Legacy*), p. 153. **423–424.** GOP vote flat. Trende, pp. 14–15. **424.** 71%. Rigueur, p. 13. **424.** African-American precincts. Weiss (*Lincoln*), p. 206, Trende, p. 16. **424.** Black legislators. Rigueur, p. 17. **424.** $500,000. Rigueur, p. 17. **424.** "Every Negro I . . . were in distress." Leuchtenburg (*Legacy*), p. 157. **424.** 1920 Southern congressmen. Leuchtenburg (*Legacy*), p. 146. **424.** 1932/1936. Trende, p. 24. **424.** 235/535. Savage, p. 123. **424.** Thirty-five percent. Savage, p. 127. **424–425.** *Fortune* poll. *Brooklyn Eagle*, 3 October 1936, p. 13. **425.** Roper internals. Roper, p. 28. **425–426.** "What frightened you? . . . known conservative tendencies." *Pittsburgh Post-Gazette*, 7 November 1936, p. 2; Schlesinger (*Upheaval*), p. 640. **426.** "I'm simply astounded . . . would be close." *Binghamton Press*, 4 November 1936, p. 10. **426.** "Okay, now do something." *Tampa Tribune* (*American Weekly*), 19 April 1959, p. 19; *Miami Herald*, 25 February 1965, p. 26. **426.** "Ah, here come Maine and Vermont!" Hearst, p. 54; Winkler, 268. Bob Considine tells a slightly different version of this tale, with Jack White himself skewering the Hearsts (Considine, p. 60).

INDEX

Photos included in inserts are indicated by the last page number of text preceding the insert.

Abbott, Florence, 232
Abbott, Horatio J., 232
Acheson, Dean, 21, 55, 75, 315
Administrative Order 129, 351
Aero Digest, 380
African Americans, 6, 19, 25, 34, 41–43, 49, 90, 91, 129–30, 159, 191–92, 204–25, 241, 242, 252, 258–60, 318–35, 337, 340, 342, 400, 424
Agricultural Adjustment Act, 18–19
Agricultural Adjustment Administration (AAA), 5, 19–20, 27–28, 62, 73, 83, 90, 144, 159, 184, 189, 218, 245, 249, 321, 374, 421
Aiken, John, 407, 417
Alabama, 28, 95, 212, 217, 236, 263, 283
Albright, Horace, 25
Aldrich, Winthrop W., 76
Algren, Nelson, 153
All Peoples Party, 338
Allard, Leola, 193–94, 246
Allen, George, 179, 300, *319*
Allen, Gracie, *319*
Allen, Henry, 199, 228
Allen, Oscar "O.K.," 36, 47–48
Allen, Robert S., 25, 304, 398
Alsop, Corinne Robinson, 76, 242, 246, 287
Alsop, Joseph, 76, 287, 405
Alter, Jonathan, 18, 57
American Liberty League, 55–57, 60, 63, 97, 133, 230
American Society of Newspaper Editors, 95
American Workers Party, 150
Annenberg, Moses, 373
Anti-Saloon League, 64, 141, 230
anti-Semitism, 129–33
Arizona, 303, 422
Arkansas, 23, 36, 125
Association Against the Prohibition Amendment (AAPA), 55
Astor, Vincent, 167–68, 352, 412
Avery, Sewell, 57

Bacon, Gaspar Griswold, 242, 246
Bailey, Joseph, W. Jr., 418
Bailey, Josiah, 58
Baker, Josephine, 214
Baker, Newton D., 84, 316
Baker, Ray Standard, 354
Ball, Lucille, 153–54
Barkley, Alben, 57, 80, 255
Barry, John J., 289
Barrymore, Ethel, 186
Barrymore, Lionel, 186
Baruch family, 40
Baruch, Bernard, 2, 16, 136, 258
Baton Rouge, La., 35, 40, 47, 84, 137
Beard, Charles A., 178
Beck, James M., 75
Beecher, Samuel O., 343
Beito, David, 95
Bell Committee, 122, 123, 273, 274
Bell, C. Jasper, 111, 116, 119, 120
Bennett, David, 119
Benson, Elmer, 145
Berkeley, Busby, 119
Berlin, Germany, 171–73, 175, 176, 324–25, 329, 402
Berlin, Irving, 155
Berlin, Richard, 201
Bernard, Sam, 146
Berry, George L., *141,* 376
Bethune, Mary McLeod, 92, *141,* 328–29, 331
Biberman, Herbert, 153
Biddle family, 420
Bingay, Malcolm W., 20–21
Bingham, Hiram, 75, 341
Black Burn, Alan, 287
Black Committee, 97
Black, Hugo, 28, 31, 95–100, 115
Blackburn, Alan, 287, 288
Blackett, Hill, 314
Blacks. *See* African Americans
Bloor, Ella Reeve, 158–59
Blumenfeld, Isadore "Kid Cann," 147
Boettinger, John, 405, 406, 414
Bogue, Clara F., 396
Bolsheviks and Bolshevism, 124, 177, 347, 348
Borah, Paulina, 188, *319*
Borah, William E., 29, 46, 47, 49, 59, 62, 113, 115, 134, 184, 187–92, 196–98, 200, 214, 217, 226–31, 235, 239, 240, 243, 244, 246, 273, 305, 309, *319,* 355, 376, 415
Borden, Gail, 305

Boston, Mass., 56, 67, 98, 113, 126, 157, 161, 162, 164, 189, 193, 242, 264, 276, 286, 289, 290, 296, 327, 329, 379, 381, 388, 408, 415
Bowers, Claude G., 45
Boyd, J. Cookman, 245
Brain Trusters, 1, 14, 78, 129, 198, 296, 338
Brandeis, Louis, 18, 79
Brands, H. W., 13
Brann, Louis, 315
Breckinridge, Henry, 73, 84, 248
Brice, Fanny, 409
Bridges, Harry, 150
Bridges, Styles, 245–46
Brinkley, John R., 200
Brisbane, Arthur, 167–68, 172, 202
Brodsky, Louis B., 411
Bronx, N.Y., 158, 345, 350, 356, 362, 382
Brookline, Mass., 113, 219
Brooklyn, N.Y., 18, 214, 288, 311, 356, 382, 402, 410
Broun, Heywood C., Jr., 79, 155, 178, 238, 239, 261, 314, *319*
Broussard, Edwin, 40
Browder, Earl, 6–7, 146, 148–49, 151–60, 181, 277, 279, 288, *319*, 335, 338, 340–48, 403, 417–19
Brown, James W., 259
Brown, John, 242
Brown, Prentiss, 400
Brown, Walter F., 235
Brownsville Incident, 191
Bruce, William Cabell, 305
Brucker, William M., 376
Bryan, William Jennings, 34, 79, 187
Buchanan, James, 190, 421
Buffalo Courier-Express, 350
Bull Moose Party, 57, 188, 190, 193, 199, 246, 391
Bullitt, William, 58, 168, 181–82, 255, 266, 292, 354–55
Bulow, William, J., 49
Bunche, Ralph, 217
Burdick, Quentin, 59
Burdick, Usher, 278, 282, 415
Burnham, James, 7
Burns, George, *319*
Burns, James MacGregor, 10–11
Butler, Nicholas Murray, 188, 401
Butler, Pierce, 234
Byrd, Harry Flood, 58, 84
Byrnes, Jimmy, 415

Caldwell, Erskine, 153
California, 28, 31, 46, 103, 107, 108, 110, 116, 141, 155, 162–64, 176, 184, 186, 194, 212, 220, 228, 230, 231, 240, 248, 312, 316, 323, 344, 387, 400, 413, 418, 422
Calloway, Cab, 334, 338
Campbell, Alan, 153
Campobello, New Brunswick, 353, 363, 412
Cannon, James, 141
Cantacuzène, Julia Dent, 76
Cantor, Eddie, 153, 325, 330
Capone, Al, 44
Capper, Arthur, 49, 59, 184, 199, 304, 415
Caraway, Hattie, 36
Carlson, Frank, 233
Caro, Robert, 351
Carpenter, R. R. M., 56
Carter, John Franklin, 43, 48
Cartwright, Wilburn, 30
Casey, James, 345–47
Catledge, Turner, 12
CBS, 79–80, 114, 125, 160, 276, 313, 314, 395
Chambers, Whittaker, 159
Chaplin, Charlie, 172
Charles I, 257
Chautauqua Institute, 354
Christenberry, Earle J., 89, 122, 287, 288
Churchill, Winston, 113–14, 169
Civilian Conservation Corps (CCC), 26, 27, 206, 321, 361, 421
Clare, Bonnie, 311
Clark, Bennett Champ, 245, 260–61
Clark, Bobby, 409
Clark, Robert Sterling, 129
Clements, Earl, 107–9, 112, 114–16, 122
Cleveland News, 389
Cleveland Plain Dealer, 202, 245, 258
Cleveland, Grover, 79, 196, 202, 207, 271
Cleveland, Ohio, 136, 140, 158, 235, 238–40, 260, 278, 281–85, 289, 308, 314, 325, 327, 330, 424
Cobb, James A., 75–76
Coblentz, Edmond, 165, 168, 177, 179
Cockran, Bourke, 52, 79
Cogner, E. D., 196
Cohalan, Daniel F., 258
Cohen, Ben, 21, 94, 96, 383–84
Cohn, Alfred A., 316
Colby, Bainbridge, 57, 63, 180, 258, 418
Coleman, M. M., 401
Collier's Weekly, 11, 91, 92, 187, 249, 370
Collins, Amy, 129
Colorado, 210, 295, 296, 298, 299, 300, 302, 308, 324
Columbus, Ohio, 327, 330, 345
Colvin, D. Leigh, 335, 417
Comintern, 151, 181, 182, 345–47
Communist League of America, 150
Communist Party (CPUSA), 146, 148–52, 154–56, 158, 217, 219–24, 277, 328, 339, 343–45, 347, 356, 403, 407, 418, 419
Communists and Communism, 6, 28, 31–32, 37, 57, 59, 91, 92, 109, 124, 125, 129, 130, 138, 144–46, 148–60, 166, 169–70, 177–79, 181–83, 214–25, 247, 272, 277, 280, 281, 283, 285, 287, 289, 290, 299, 307, 308, 316, 317, 336, 338, 340–44, 346, 347, 376, 381, 403, 407, 419–21
Conger, E. D., 196
Connecticut, 54, 75, 76, 390, 396
Connery, William P., Jr., 354
Considine, Bob, 297
Considine, John, Jr., 297
Contemporary Speeches, 80
Cook, Blanche Weisen, 207
Cook, Nancy, 406
Coolidge, Calvin, 13, 55, 129, *141*, 161, 190, 199, 200–203, 236, 272, 306, 359, 365, 387, 398, 423

Coolidge, Grace, 365
Coolidge, T. Jefferson, 55, 79
Cooper, Dexter, 412
Cooper, Jackie, 186
Cooper, John Milton, 190
Copeland, Royal, 202, 258
Copland, Aaron, 341
Corcoran, Tommy "the Cork," 18, 21, 94, 256–58, 269, 270, *319*, 356, 367, 368, 379, 383, 386, 412, 413
Corporate State, The, 17
Costello, Harry J., 291, 292
Costigan, Edward, 210
Couch, Natalie F., 393, 415
Coughlin, Charles E., 2, 6, 32, 108, 122–43, *141*, 162, 167, 168, 183, 184, 247, 252, 271–93, 301, 307–8, *319*, 340, 373, 381, 389, 400, 403, 416, 418
Coutremarsh, Joseph, 248–49
Couzens, James Gould, 184, 232, 369, 376, 377, 392
Cowley, Malcolm, 153
Cox, James M., 52, 261, 378, 402, 423, 424
Creel, George, 11, 187, 249, 370
Crocker, Harry, 171–74
Cuba, 192
Cummings, Homer, 54, 88, 235, 268, 341, 343
Curley, James M., 98, 164, 242, 263–64, 286–87, 329, 415, 416
Curtis, Charles, 228
Cutting, Bronson, 59, 184
Cyr, Paul, 36, 47

Daniels, Josephus, 266, 307, 387
Darrow, Clarence, 108, 127
Dartmouth College, 8, 177
Davenport Democrat and Leader, 398
Davies, Marion, 163, 167, 169, 172, 173, 175, 186, 202, 394, 414
Davis, James P., 111, 218
Davis, John M., 56
Davis, John W., 52–53, 56–58, 63, 74, 75, 77, 79, *141*, 190, 218, 258, 261, 305, 306, 335, 423
Davis, Kenneth S., 143
Davis, Walter D., 283
Day, Donald, 346
Day, Dorothy, 346
Day, Stephen A., 230
Dayton Herald, 245
De Priest, Oscar, 320
Dean, Jerome Herman, 306
Dean, Rodney, 410
Debs, Eugene V., 34, 143, 148, 275, 338, 341, 343
Delano, Daniel Horace, 399–400
Delano, Frederic A., 412
Delaware, 303, 333, 417
DeMille, Cecil B., 235, 298
Democratic National Committee (DNC), 56, 296, 362, 364, 385, 389
Democratic National Convention, 52
Dempsey, Jack, 325, 327–28, 343, 382
Dempsey, John J., 12
Denver, Colo., 127, 341, 365
Desvernine, Raoul E., 61
Detroit, Mich., 20, 22, 32, 123, 124, 125, 127, 130, 162, 197, 288, 314, 327, 346, 377, 393, 394, 422
Dewey, John, 155, 178
Dewson, Molly, 364, 385
Dickenson, John, 269
Dickinson, Lester J. "Dick," 227–29, 231, 244, 415
Dickstein, Samuel, 115
Dilling, Elizabeth, 374
Dimitrov, Georgi, 151, 158, 346
Dingle, Edwin, 109
Divine, Father, 218–25, 336–38
Dixon, Thomas, 308
Dixon, Thomas, Jr., 91, 101, 308
Dobbins, John, 317
Dos Passos, John, 153
Douglas, Lewis, 12, 55, 245, 258, 306
Douglas, Melvyn, 153
Douglass, Frederick, 159, 327
Dow Jones Industrial Average, 9, 14, 247
Dowd, Thomas, 358
Downey, Sheridan, 120–21
Doyle, James, 245
Draper, Theodore, 159
Dreiser, Theodore, 153, 155
du Pont family, 55, 56, 58, 76, 97, 122, 232, 383
du Pont, Alfred, 317
du Pont, Emile F., 76
du Pont, Ethel, 383
du Pont, Eugene E., 76
du Pont, Felix A., 76
du Pont, Henry B., 76
du Pont, Irénée, 58, 65
du Pont, Lammot, 56, 100, 415
du Pont, Octavia, 76
du Pont, Pierre, 56, 61, 74, 76, 79, 100, 383
Dubinsky, David, 289, 292, 338, 339, 394, 419, 420
Dudley, William, 130
Dunn, Betty, 297
Dunn, Rogers C., 297, 389
Durante, Jimmy, 186
Dust Bowl, 302–4
Dyer, Franklin, 116
Dyer, Leonidas, 210, 213
Dziennek Polski, 422

Earhart, Amelia, 358–59
Earle, Howard, III, 360
Early, Jubal A., 209
Early, Steven T., 33, 176, 180, 182, 209, 210, 265, 276, *319*, 329, 346, 354, 356, 364
Edmondson, Robert, 130
Edwards, Willard, 413
Eighteenth Amendment, 15, 55, 64, 77
Einstein, Albert, 108
Electoral College, 248, 272, 309, 354, 389, 390
Ely, Joseph B., 63, 67, 69, 75, 245, 258, 262, 263, 305, 418
Emancipation Proclamation, 333
Emmerz, Joseph, 352
End Poverty in California (EPIC), 31
Engels, Friedrich, 152
Enron, 84
Episcopalianism, 51, 259, 332, 333, 341, 362, 394

Epstein, Abraham, 317
Erickson, Frank, 410
Ethiopia, 7, 153, 156
Evans, Silliman, 75
Export-Import Bank, 380

Fallon, Joseph, 410–11
Farley, Elizabeth Finnegan, 401
Farley, James A., 2, 21–22, 27, 37–38, 44, 46–47, 55, 57, 61, 63, 66, 128, *141,* 147, 161, 191, 206, 209, 231–33, 253, 261, 268, 271, 280–81, 284, 296–97, 301, 308–9, 316, 329, 335, 339, 340, 350, 354, 356, 358, 364–65, 369, 370, 372–74, 376, 377, 388, 397, 398, 401, 406, 413, 419, 420, 426
Farmer-Labor Party, 145–48, 154–56, *319,* 375, 376, 381, 407, 416
Farmers Independence Council, 98
Fawcett, James W., 182
Fechner, Robert, 321
Federal Arts Project, 23
Federal Bureau of Investigation (FBI), 253, 287
Federal Communications Commission, 95
Federal Deposit Insurance Corporation (FDIC), 198
Ferris, Woodbridge, 197
Fifteenth Amendment, 191, 259
Fifth Amendment, 146
Filene, Edward, 56–57
Finan, Christopher, 64
Finkle, Herman H., 325
Finney, Ruth, 365
Fireside Chats, 13, 127
First 100 Days, 18, 24
Fish, Hamilton, 124, 214, 217, 235, 415, 421
Fitzgerald, Frank D., 289
Florida, 212, 248, 262, 340
Fokker, Anthony H. G., 380
Ford, Edsel, 45
Ford, Henry, 45, 103, 124, 306, 393, 394
Ford, James W., 159, 217–18, 221, 328, 341, 344, 418–19
Ford, Michael A., 337
Fore, Marion, 262–63
Forkins, Marty, 326
Fosdick Harry Emerson, 178
Foster, William Z., 149, 155, 158, 181, 343, 418
Fox Studios, 186, 325
France, 129, 151, 193, 214
Frank, Gerold, 284
Frank, Waldo, 341, 343
Frankfeld, Philip, 157
Frankfurter, Felix, 21, 130, 246, 255, 269, 289, 347, 368, 391, 395
Franklin, Jay, 143
Frazier–Lemke Farm Bankruptcy Act, 139–41, 276
Frazier, Lynn, 49, 59, 113, 184, 278, 354
Frelinghuysen, Joseph, 393
Funk, Wilfred J., 426

Gallagher, Hugh Gregory, 267
Gallagher, Michael J., 123, 138, 140, 282
Gallup, George H. and Gallup polls, 8, 227, 229, 249, 271–72, 296–97, 355–65, 367, 388–90, 397, 426
Gannett, Frank, 309
Garbo, Greta, 152
Garner, Ettie, 404, 405
Garner, John Nance "Cactus Jack," 14, 101–2, 164, 185, 198, 205, 263–64, 266, 268, 286, *319,* 354, 404–5, 407
Garvey, Marcus, 218
Garvin, Roy, 204
Gassaway, Percy Lee, 114–15
Gavagan, Joseph, 120
Gaxton, William, 409
Gehrke, Arthur E., 399
Gehrke, Grace, 399
Gellhorn, Martha, 20
Gennerich, Gus, 266, 268
George, Lloyd, 169
Georgia, 37, 46, 80, 81, 82, 89, 200, 205, 207, 209, 218, 248
Gerard, James W., 402
German-American Bund, 6, 306–7
Germany, 86, 129, 130, 150, 169–71, 173–77, 189, 237, 306, 307, 326, 329
Gershwin, George, 155
Gill, Corrington, 421
Gitlow, Benjamin, 146, 148
Glass, Carter, 23, 27, 29, 58, 59, 259
Glavis, Louis Russell, 25–26
Glazer, Nathan, 130
Gleason, John Herbert, 426
Gluck, Alma, 382
Good Neighbor League, 252–53, 282, 327, 332–33
Goodwin, Doris Kearns, 4, 206
Gore, Thomas, 58, 358–59
Göring, Hermann, 131
Gracie, Anna Bulloch, 207–8
Great Depression, 7, 14, 20, 38, 56, 82, 86, 103, 104, 105, 112, 125, 201, 233, 312, 317, 366
Grundy, Joe, 360
Guffey Act, 234
Guggenheim, M. Robert, 76
Guilford, Howard A., 146–47
Guinan, "Texas," 426

Hague, Frank, 329, 330, 362
Hale, Frederick, 29
Hall, Juanita, 334
Halsey, Ed, 268
Hamid, Abdul, 129, 214, 215, 218
Hamilton, John D. M., *141,* 197, 228, 241, 243–45, 295, 297–99, 301–2, 306–8, 312, 349, 356, 377, 381, 392, 409, 412, 415, 420, 423
Hammerstein, Oscar, 153
Hanfstaengl, Ernst "Putzi," 170–73, 175, 288
Harding, Warren G., 142, 199, 230, 236, 387, 392, 423
Hardy, George W., 48
Harriman, W. Averell, 420
Harrison, Benjamin, 207
Harrison, Hugh, 398
Harrison, William Henry, 190
Hart, Moss, 153
Hawaii, 283
Hawley, Ellis, 30

Hayes, Rutherford B., 207
Haywood, Bill, 143
Hearst, George, 162
Hearst, Millicent, 166
Hearst, William Randolph, 5, 45, 63, 91, 134, 160–86, 188, 192–95, 201–4, 230, 237–38, 240, 246, 254, 267, 272, 281, 284, 294, 297, 304, 305, 309, 312, *319*, 345–47, 356, 373, 375, 377, 394, 397, 414, 426
Heflin, Tom, 263
Hellman, Lillian, 153
Hemingway, Ernest, 20, 193
Henie, Sonja, 426
Herald-Examiner, 367
Herdock, Benjamin, 263
Herndon, Angelo, 217, 338
Hickok, Lorena, 5, 17, 19, 200–201, 363, 372
Hicks, Granville, 153, 341
High, Stanley H., 252–57, 269, 270, 332–34, 352, 356, 364, 368, 383, 386, 412, 413
Highley, George, 400
Hiles, Harrison, 120–21
Hill, T. Arnold, 321
Hillman, Sidney, *141*, 339, 376, 394
Hillquit, Morris, 349
Hindenburg, Paul von, 170
Hinshaw, David, 240, 241, 312
Hiss, Alger, 21, 159
Hiss, Donald, 21
Hitler, Adolf, 7, 86, 129, 131, 150, 151, 154, 169–77, 288, 290, 306, 307, 324, 326–27, 419
Hockaday, Frank, 263, 290
Hoffman, Clare, 117–19
Hollywood Anti-Nazi League, 153
Holtzmann, Abraham, 119–20
Hood, W. V., 401
Hoover, Herbert Clark, 10, 13, 14, 20, 27, 30–32, 37, 44, 47, 49, 53–54, 59–60, 80, 101, 103, 111, 125, 126, 134, 149, 161, 164, 185–87, 189–90, 192, 194, 196, 198–200, 202, 205, 208, 224–29, 231, 233–35, 239–41, 243, 244, 248, 252, 253, 263, 297, 306, 310, 312, 313, *319*, 320, 322, 349, 358, 359, 361, 365, 387, 389, 396, 400, 402, 406, 407, 419, 422, 423, 424
Hope, Clifford, 297
Hopkins, Harry, 2, 4, 7, 21, 24–26, 28, 73, 107, 184, 206, 231, 251, 256, *319*, 352, 363, 369–72, 374–75, 408
Howard, Perry W., 242, 245, 246, 258, 260, 323, 324
Howard, Roy, 30, 78
Howe, Louis McHenry, 2–5, 8, 9, 11, 25, 33, 53, 69, 161, 165, 209, 217, 233, 234, 251–54, 297, *319*, 329, 332, 350, 353, 374, 379, 426
Howell, Clark, *319*
Huddleston, George, 95
Huerta, Victoriano, 275
Hughes, Charles Evans, 163, 189, 390, 404, 409
Hughes, Langston, 153, 217, 341
Hull, Cordell, 14, *141*
Hurd, Charles, 353
Hurja, Emil Edward, 272, 296, 309, 386, 388, 389, 398
Hurst, Fannie, 412
Hutchins, Robert Maynard, 178
Hutton, E. F., 57, 60, 65, 97
Hutton, Ina Ray, 43
Huxman, Walter A., 417
Hylan, Mike, 163, 202

Ickes, Harold, 2, 4, 12, 21, 24–26, 28, 38, 44, 58, 71, 79, 80, 101, 136, 139, 148, 167–68, 180, 182, 184, 206, 209, 231, 235, 237, 246, 251, 272, 298, 307, 309, 315, *319*, 341, 351–56, 362, 369, 374–75, 391, 417
Idaho, 28, 46, 113, 184, 187, 189, 191, 214, 240, 305
Illinois, 103, 136, 188, 209, 226, 229, 272, 277, 322, 333, 367, 390, 416
Indiana, 85, 272, 277, 322, 330, 343, 390, 399, 407
Ingram, Rex, 334
Insull, Samuel, 93
Iowa, 6, 24, 135, 227, 231, 302, 303, 309, 365, 390, 415
Irey, Elmer L., 44

Jackson, Andrew, 92
Jackson, Gardner, 307
Jackson, Juanita H., 117
Janeway, Eliot, 4
Japan, 7, 130, 195
Jewish Daily Telegraph, 131–32
Johnson, Hiram, 13, 28, 59, 184, 355
Johnson, Hugh Samuel, 2, 16–18, 21, 135, *141*, 251, 262, 353, 359, 398, 404
Johnson, Magnus, 145
Johnson, Philip, 287–88
Johnson, Walter, 306
Johnston, Jimmy, 141
Jolson, Al, 186, 325
Jones, Jesse, 14, 54, 262
Jones, Sisserietta, 207
Joslin, Ted, 10
Jung, Carl, 399

Kane, Frank L., 416
Kansas, 49, 56, 116, 184, 187, 199–204, 228, 230, 233, 237, 240, 242–44, 263, 272, 273, 278, 290, 295–98, 300, 301, 303, 309, 326, 329, 332, 365, 366, 390, 392, 398, 399, 401, 406, 408, 410, 417, 421, 423
Kaplan, Joseph L., 67
Kaufman, George, 397
Keaton, Buster, 186
Keehn, Roy, 167
Keelon, Francis P., 138
Keeney, Frank, 410
Keller, John, 8
Kellogg, Frank B., 100, 316
Kelly, Ed, 368
Kennedy, David M., 30
Kennedy, Joseph P., 2, 5, 136–37, 372–75
Kent, Frank Richardson, 20, 191
Kent, Rockwell, 341

Kentucky, 57, 80, 333, 387, 401
Keyserling, Leon, 383
Kiefer, John B., 119, 282
Kingsbury, Kenneth R., 176
Kirby, Helen, 115
Kirby, John Henry, 83–84, 89, 90, 92–93, 97–99, 102, 115
Kirstein, Lincoln, 153
Klehr, Harvey, 146, 347
Knox, William Franklin, *141,* 192–96, 199, 200, 226–29, 231, 233, 235, 239, 244–46, 295, 302, 304, 306, 308–10, 315, 326, 361, 381, 390, 407, 414, 415
Knoxville, Tenn., 424
Knudsen, William, 60
Kosta, Hilda, 382
Krock, Arthur, 48, 95, 235, 372, 373
Ku Klux Klan, 86, 91, 99, 100, 116, 124, 126, 141, 199, 228, 260, 345
Kuhn, Fritz, 6, 306–7

La Follette, Robert M., Jr., 28, 29, 178, 190
La Follette, Robert M., Sr., 85, 199, 252, 275
La Follette, Robert, Jr., 355
La Guardia, Fiorello P., 23, 28, 59, 63, 130, 219, *319,* 325, 351, 352, 394, 419
Lamb, John, 219, 221, 403
Landis, James, 21
Landon, Alfred, *141,* 199–204, 227–33, 235–39, 241, 243–46, 253, 264, 266, 270, 272, 273, 277, 279, 283, 285, 290, 293–313, 315–18, *319,* 323–28, 332, 335, 339, 340, 343, 345, 346, 349, 350, 353–55, 357, 361, 362, 365, 369, 372, 375–78, 380–82, 388–400, 402, 404, 406–12, 415, 417–25
Landon, John Cobb, *141*
Landon, Jon Cobb "Jack," 295
Landon, Nancy Jo, 295
Landon, Peggy Ann, 295, 299, 404
Landon, Theo Cobb, *141,* 199, 201, 299, 365, 404, 409
Langer, "Wild Bill," 417
Lardner, John, 244
Lardner, Ring, Jr., 153
Lash, Joseph P., 206
Lasker, Albert, 392
Lawrence, David, 95, 390, 392
Lawson, John Howard, 153
League of American Writers, 153
Lee, Algernon, 148, 156
Lee, Clara, 400
Lee, Robert E., 118
LeHand, Marguerite "Missy," 4, 10, 213, 252, 255, *319,* 352, 364, 372, 374, 406
Lehman, Herbert, 29, *141,* 271, 349–51, 358, 382, 383, 398, 401, 417, 419
Lemke, William F., 6, 59, *141,* 270, 274–79, 281–86, 288, 291, 293, 294, 307, 336, 340, 400, 403, 409, 415, 417, 418
Lenin, Vladimir, 79, 157–59, 217, 219, 280
Leonard, Tom, 406
Leroy, Chauncey N., 396
Leuchtenburg, William, 317
Lewis, John L., *141,* 310–11, 376–77
Lewy, Guenther, 153
Liberty League, 55–62, 65–67
Liggett, Edith, 147
Liggett, Marda, 147
Liggett, Walter W., 147–48
Lilienthal, David, 21
Lincoln, Abraham, 196, 233, 242, 263, 334, 345
Lincoln, Alexander, 98
Lindbergh, Charles, 73
Lindley, Ernest K., 233
Lippincott, J. B., 76
Lippmann, Walter, *141,* 197, 239, 270, 305–6
Literary Digest, 7–8, 66
Little, Arthur W., 245
Litvinov, Maxim, 181
Livingston, Kathleen R., 410
Llosa, Salvador, 342
Lodge, Henry Cabot, Jr., 415–16
Long, Breckinridge, 135, 418
Long, Earl, 44
Long, Huey Pierce, Jr., 2, 6, 12, 29–30, 32–51, 81, 83–89, 101, 103–7, 122, 123, 125, 127, 132, 134–38, *141,* 143, 148, 167, 170, 184, 189, 205, 218, 248, 262, 264, 272, 276, 280, 287, 288, 290, 309, 373, 400, 418
Long, Rose, 35
Longfellow, Henry Wadsworth, 39
Longworth, Alice Roosevelt, 76, 101, 188–89, 230, 235, 238, 262, 300, *319,* 395–96, 404
Longworth, Nicholas, 76, 101, 404
Los Angeles Examiner, 171–72
Louis, Joe, 329
Louisiana, 29, 33–37, 39–41, 43, 44, 46–48, 85, 87–89, 91, 122, 236, 262, 264, 281, 308
Lovejoy, Elijah, 242
Lowden, Frank, 226–27
Lubbell, Samuel, 422
Lubitsch, Ernst, 153
Lucas, Scott, 119
Lundberg, Ferdinand, 178
Lundeen, Ernest, 146, 416
Luther, Hans, 176
Lyons, Eugene, 149, 152
Lyons, Louis M., 264

Madero, Francisco I., 275
Madison, Arthur, 224
Maged, Jacob, 16–17, 411
Main, Verner W., 112
Maine, 29, 125, 192, 283, 315, 352, 353, 388, 390, 392, 413, 416, 422, 426
Mallet-Prevost Murphy, Grayson, 76
Manchester Guardian, 171
Manchester Leader, 193
Mankiewicz, Herman, 153
Mann Act, 213
Manuilsky, D. Z., 151, 158
Mara, Tim, 410
Marcantonio, Vito, 59, 189, 338, 415
March, Fredric, 153
Margett, Edward J., 108, 116, 119
Margold, Nathan, 21

Marinelli, Joe, 264
Mark, David, 427
Markham, Edwin, 267, 269
Martin, George, 385
Martin, Harold, 337
Marx, Karl, 224, 347
Massachusetts, 3, 63, 66, 67, 98, 113, 219, 242, 263, 264, 354, 390, 407, 416, 418
Mathews, J. Maynard, 219
Maurer, James H., 338
Maybank, Burnet, 259
Mayer, Louis B., 174, 186, 297
Maynard, Robert, 178
McAdoo, William Gibbs, 52, 54, 184, 269
McBain, John C., 416
McCarl, John R., 313
McClellan, George B., 163
McConnell, Mary, 187
McCormick, Robert, 98, 304–5, 367, 373
McCormick, Ruth Hanna, 188–89
McCoy, "Kid," 141
McCoy, Donald, 229–30, 312
McDermott, S. Earl, 416
McDuffie, Elizabeth "Lizzie," 208, 330–32
McDuffie, Irwin, 208, *319,* 327, 331
McFadden, James, 285
McFadden, Louis, 125, 129, 417
McGill, George, 49
McGroarty, John S., 107, 110, 115, 248
McHenry, Louis, 4–5
McIntyre, Marvin, 38, 59, 67, 127, 139–40, 209–10, 265, 364
McIntyre, Ross, 364
McKinley, William, 163, 189, 202, 207, 310, 316
McLaughlin, Kathleen, 406
McNary, Charles, 59, 184, 415
McNutt, Paul V., 343, 344
Meany, George, 7, 339
Mellon, Andrew, 360, 373
Mencken, H. L., 103, *141,* 234, 236, 263, 266, 280–81, 299, 305, *319,* 416
Mercer, Lucy, 1
Merriam, Frank, 31, 107, 116, 228, 388
Mexico, 12, 25, 138, 184, 275
Meyer, Eugene, 76
MGM, 152, 174, 186, 297, 410
Michaux, Lightfoot Solomon, 334
Michelson, Charles, 233, 296, 364, 377, 389, 404, 419, 420
Miller, Kelly, 217
Miller, Nathan, 57, 61, 75
Mills, Ogden, 100, 202, 227, 296, 297
Mills, Thelma, 118–19
Minor, Robert, 159, 221, 376, 419
Mitchell, Arthur W., 260, 320, 329, 331
Moffet, James A., 176
Moley, Raymond, 14, 42, 96, 101–2, 161, 168, 251, 253–57, 269–70, 296, *319,* 355–56, 374, 386, 388, 412, 419
Montana, 27, 42, 54, 195, 303, 364, 422
Moran, William, 23, 25
Morehead v. New York ex rel Tipaldo, 234–35, 239
Morgan, Gerald, 412
Morgan, J. P., 40, 97, 128, 160, 300
Morgan, Julia, 169
Morgan, Ted, 152
Morgan, W. Forbes, 364
Morgenthau, Elinor, 66
Morgenthau, Henry, Jr., 11–12, 44, 45, 66, 128, 129, 131, 134, 138, *141,* 148, 167, 350, 412, 421
Morgenthau, Henry, Sr., 128
Moses, Robert, 29, 53, 77, 100, 101, 143, 339, 350–52
Moskowitz, Belle, 53
Mumford, Lewis, 153
Municipal Ownership League, 163
Murdoch, Rupert, 162
Murphy, Frank, 125, 127–28, 136–37, 139, 232, 271, 289, 377, 400, 417
Murphy, Grayson Mallet-Prevost, 76, 129
Murray, Bill "Alfalfa," 305, 412, 418
Muse, Vance, 98–100
Mussolini, Benito, 7, 17, 169, 172, 189, 290, 299

Nadig, Quincy, 407–8
Nation, The, 70
National Association for the Advancement of Colored People (NAACP), 42, *141,* 208–10, 212–14, 324
National Industrial Recovery Act (NIRA), 16, 18, 28, 29, 64, 149
National Party, 287
National Recovery Administration (NRA), 5, 16–18, 20, 28, 45, 80, 91, 135, *141,* 165, 166, 176, 184, 189, 237, 256, 321, 373, 381, 402, 411
National Union for Social Justice (NUSJ), 132–34, 274, 283, 287, 288
National Youth Administration (NYA), 27, 206, 331, 361
Nazis, 6, 129, 145, 170, 171, 174, 177, 287, 288, 307, 324
NBC, 125, 135, 160, 166, 237, 252, 314, 328, 341, 359, 395, 408
Neal, Claude, 212–13
Nebraska, 28, 184, 229, 303, 365, 381, 391, 392, 415
Negro Theatre Project, 23
Neocommunism, 168
Nevada, 29, 162, 364, 422
Nevins, Alan, 349, 350
New Deal, 9–32, 15, 28, 39, 58–60, 65, 76, 83, 88–91, 106, 135, 176, 184, 201, 203, 209–10, 249, 254, 258, 259, 261, 263, 276, 306, 308, 316, 323, 327, 338, 355, 360, 370, 376, 380, 386, 400, 402, 410, 415
New Hampshire, 193, 228, 244, 248, 309, 387, 390, 407
New Jersey, 95, 98, 220, 245, 263, 303, 323, 329, 330, 388, 390, 393
New Leader, 154
New Masses, 341
New Republic, 8, 70
New York Herald Tribune, 72–73, 159, 241, 341
New York Stock Exchange, 10
New York Times, 12, 57, 58, 65, 97, 113, 214–15, 361–62
Newman, David K., 97

Neylan, Francis, 312
Nice, Harry, 245
Niebuhr, Reinhold, 338
Nieves Perez Chaumont de Truffin, Mina, 54
No Deal 1936, 184–204
Norbeck, Peter, 184, 376
Norris, George W., 28, 49, 59, 184, 338, 355, 365, 381, 391, 392, 415
North Carolina, 58, 218, 283, 308
North Dakota, 6, 59, 154, 184, 274–76, 278, 282, 286, 293, 302, 303, 340, 392, 403, 415–18, 422
Nye, Gerald, 49, 59, 115, 184, 355, 380

O'Brien, Thomas, 276, 284–89, 336, 416
O'Connell, Edward J., 335
O'Connell, William, 126
O'Connor, Basil "Doc," 412
O'Connor, James F. T., 297
O'Connor, John J., 140–41
O'Day, Caroline, 333, 359, 393, 415
O'Donnell, John J., 284
O'Mahoney, Joseph C., 364
Oglethorpe University, 13, 15–16
Ohio, 73, 142, 202, 205, 209, 214, 230, 231, 248, 265, 272, 277, 278, 288, 314, 322, 325, 333, 345, 354, 360, 390, 418
Oklahoma, 27, 30, 58, 75, 114, 278, 279, 303, 305, 359, 412
Old-Age Revolving Pension, Ltd. (OARP), 107–8, 111, 112, 113, 115, 116, 118, 120, 132, 273, 274, 277, 278, 282, 283, 285, 400
Olson, Floyd B., 146–48, 154, 375–76, 381
Omnibus Banking Act, 136
Opposition Labor Conference Against Industrial Recovery Bill, 149–50
Oregon, 184, 239, 340, 418, 422
Ornitz, Samuel, 153
Osborn, Chase S., 22, 192
Oswalt, J. Sterling, 344
Oursler, Fulton, 3, 106, 373
Owens, Jesse, 324–30
Owens, Ruth, 325, 327

Pacelli, Eugenio, 290–91
Palestine, 130, 131
Parish, Winn, 34
Parker, Alton B., 243–44, 261
Parker, Dorothy, 153
Parks, Lillian Rogers, 4, 330
Parr, Thomas, 109
Patterson, Eleanor Medill "Cissy," 76, 188, 202, 249–50, 254, 309
Paulen, Ben, 228
Pavy, Benjamin H., 49, 50
Pearson, Drew, 25, 398, 426
Peek, George N., 28, 245, 374
Pegler, Francis J. W., 155, 235–36, 300
Pelley, William Dudley, 6, 86, 130, 417
Pendergast, Tom, 116
Pennsylvania, 10, 29, 75, 125, 136, 191, 248, 264–66, 269, 277, 303, 309, 310, 322, 325, 333, 345, 354, 369, 372, 390, 406, 421, 423
Perelman, S. J., 341
Perkins, Frances, 17, 18, 130, 209, 358, 385–86
Pew, J. Howard, 76, 360
Pew, Joseph, Jr., 326, 415
Phair, George, 348
Philippines, 128, 283
Pickens, Jane, 409
Pittman, Key, 364
Pittsburgh Courier, 206, 325
Pittsburgh, Pa., 97, 162, 206, 284, 306, 312, 320, 325, 327, 341, 359, 360, 394, 422
Pius XI, Pope, 221, 290, 336
Pons, Lily, 266
Poulson, Francis W., 325
Powell, Adam Clayton, Jr., 217
Powell, Adam Clayton, Sr., 332
Progressive National Committee Supporting Franklin D. Roosevelt for President, 373
Prohibition, 15, 32, 52, 55, 64, 96, 125, 141, 201
Proskauer, Joseph, 53, 57
Public Utility Holding Company Act, 94–96
Public Works Administration (PWA), 23, 27, 47, 88, 320, 334, 350–51, 356, 362, 375, 421
Puerto Rico, 215
Purnell, Fred S., 304
Putnam, George P., 358–59

Quarles, James, 214

Rahv, Philip, 154
Rainey, Julian, 329
Randolph, A. Philip, 338
Rankine, Baxter G., 120
Ransdell, Joseph E., 35–36
Raskob, John Jakob, 55–57, 60–61, 65, 67–68, 74, 76, 96, 100–101, *141,* 183, 272–73, 373, 388
Rayburn, Sam, 94, 309
RCA, 372
Reconstruction Finance Corporation, 54, 84, 262
Reed, Clyde, 228, 298
Reed, David A., 75
Reed, James A., 258, 305, 314, 418
Reiber, Torkild, 176
Reid, Mrs. Ogden, 300
Reilly, Michael F., 266–69
Reno, Milo, 6, 27, 31, 135, 154, 252
Reuther, Walter, 338
Richardson, Esco L., 344
Richberg, Donald R., 28, 246, 256, 347, 386
Riefenstahl, Leni, 241
Riggs, John A., 93
Rightor, "Whistle-Britches," 35
Ripley, William Z., 93–94
Ritchie, Albert Cabell, 55, 63, 73, 75, 84, *141,* 245, 305
Rivera, Lino, 215–16
Roach, Hal, 57
Roberts, Roy, 201, 244
Roberts, Warren R., 360
Robinson, Bill "Bojangles," 325
Robinson, Frances "Robby," 18
Robinson, Joe, 23, 29, 36, 37, 80, 197, 211, 255, 266

Roche, Josephine, 92
Rochester, N.Y., 108, 118, 164
Rockefeller, John D., 40, 97, 134
Rodell, Fred, 197
Rodenberg, William A., 75
Rogers, Will, 54–55, 127, 184
Rolph, James, 212
Roman Catholics and Catholicism, 22, 51–53, 55, 63, 68, 126, 128, 131, 138, 140, 141, 169, 183, 205, 224, 263, 275, 276, 285, 324, 346, 373, 422
Roosevelt, Anna, 405, 406, 413, 414
Roosevelt, Edith Kermit, 365, 400
Roosevelt, Eleanor, 1–10, 17, 21, 22, 26, 66–69, 76, 90, 91, 99, 110, 125, 126, *141,* 144, 161, 179, 188, 200, 206–11, 213, 218, 242, 254, 265, 266, 287, 319, *319,* 329, 330, 352–54, 356, 358, 359, 361, 363–65, 374, 379–80, 382, 383, 387–426
Roosevelt, Elliott, 167, 352, 363, 380
Roosevelt, Franklin Delano, 20, *141,* 180, 183
  African Americans shunning, 205–25
  breathing spell, 272
  Coughlin and, 122–41
  Election Day 1936, 387–426
  first term of, 9–32
  following Franklin Field performance, 349–86
  and Hearst, 161–83
  inaugural address, 17
  Left Front of, 273
  and Liberty League, 55–62
  Long–Roosevelt relationship, 33–50
  Long–Talmadge alliance against, 81–102
  maneuvering between poles of public sentiment, 271–93
  mollycoddle slur, 363–64
  New England slog, 379–80
  and No Deal 1936, 184–204
  Norman Thomas and, 142–45
  polio of, 52–55
  potential dictatorship, 296–97
  Public Utility Holding Company Act, 94–95
  pump priming, 106
  radicalism of, 10–14
  reaching out to Hitler, 175–76
  recovery managed by, 247–70
  Roosevelt Bust, 14–15
  Smith–Roosevelt relationship, 51–62, 63–80
  State of the Union Address, 13, 69, 94
  strained loyalties for, 1–8
  Syracuse speech, 356–60
  Talmadge opposition, 81–84
  tax package proposal, 29–32
  Team of Rivals cabinet, 54–55
  Townsend and, 103–21
  two-pronged message, 70–73
  Wilsonian roots, 134
  Worcester counterpunch, 377–78
Roosevelt, Franklin Delano, Jr., 383
Roosevelt, G. Hall, 125
Roosevelt, James, 1
Roosevelt, Nicholas, 111, 190, 363–64
Roosevelt, Sara Delano, 1, *141*
Roosevelt, Ted, 66
Roosevelt, Theodore, 73, 79, 111, *141,* 163, 169, 188–89, 192, 193, 195, 196, 207, 235–36, 238, 246, 391, 400
Roosevelt, Theodore, Jr., 227, 244
Root, Elihu, 57
Roper, Daniel, 45, 54
Roper, Elmo, 397, 425
Rosenberg, Alfred, 171
Rosenman, Dorothy, 364
Rosenman, Sam, 1, 215, 250–57, 269–70, 296, 352, 356, 360, 361, 364, 383–84, 412–13
Ross, C. Ben, 305
Roth, Henry, 401
Rothstein, Arnold, 410
Rovere, Richard, 26
Runyon, Damon, 201–2
Runyon, W. Cleveland, 98
Russell, Richard, 82
Russia. *See* Soviet Union
Ruth, Babe, 124
Ryan, James G., 152, 341
Ryskind, Morrie, 397

St. John, Adela Rogers, 201
Sabin, Pauline, 57, 61, 76
Sanders, Everett, 129
Sapp, Claude Napoleon, 259
Saxon, Paul, 231
Schall, Thomas D., 146, 148
Schechter family, 18, 402, 411
Schenck, Nick, 172, 410
Schenectady, N.Y., 145, 340
Schenk, Nick, 172, 174, 186
Schlesinger, Arthur, Jr., 43, 310, 318
Schlesinger, Isidore, 215
Schmeling, Max, 329
Schneider, Charles, 411
Schneider, Malvina "Tommy," 406
Scholle, Carl, 382
Schreck, Julius, 172–73
Schulberg, Budd, 154
Schwellenbach, Lewis B., 74
Scott, Emmett J., 76
Scottsboro Boys, 153, 217, 332, 342
Scranton, Pa., 262, 344
Scripps-Howard, 30, 63, 78, 155, 206, 262, 365
Seabury, Samuel, 126
Securities and Exchange Commission (SEC), 21, 61, 136, 253, 374
Sedition Act, 34
Seeger, Alan, 270
Seeger, Pete, 220
Select Committee Investigating Old Age Pension Organizations, 115–16
Selwyn, Edgar, 172
Selwyn, Ruth Wilcox, 172
Selznick, Divid O., 330
Sentinels of the Republic, 314
Sewanna, 352–53
Share-Our-Wealth, 38–41, 82, 86, 87, 89, 122, 132, 168, 248, 288, 317
Shepherd, Marshall L., 259
Sheppard, Allen, 99

Sherwood, Robert, 11
Shipstead, Henrik, 145, 147
Shouse, Jouett, 54, 56–59, 61, 74, 77, 96
Sinclair, Upton, 31, 46, 107, 120, 148, 247, 248, 388
Sleeping Car Porters, 217
Sloan, Alfred P., 60, 98, 100
Slomovitz, Philip, 22
Smith, Alfred E., 5–6, 47, 50–80, 84–88, 101, 128, *141,* 155, 157, 163–64, 166, 183, 205, 208, 210, 236, 243–44, 251, 258, 263, 264, 272, 273, 294–95, 305, 306, 308, 320, 338, 349–51, 359, 361, 381, 382, 388, 401–2, 407, 418, 422–23
Smith, Catherine Dunn, 402
Smith, Ellison D., 259–60
Smith, Elna, 85
Smith, George W., 396
Smith, Gerald L. K. "Doc," 6, 43, 84–91, 103, 121–23, 125, 130, *141,* 142, 155, 252, 273–75, 277–85, 291–92, 308, 396–97
Smith, Gomer Griffith, 279, 282, 283
Smith, L. Z., 85
Smith, Mamie, 323
Smith, William Alden, 192, 196
Snell, Bertram, 240
Snipes, Hammie, 215
Social Security Act (SSA), 83, 112, 317–19
Socialists and Socialist Party, 2, 6, 21, 31, 32, 34, 57, 78, 80, 90, 92, 139, 142–45, 148–51, 154–58, 181, 182, 217, 272, 277, 308, 338–40, 347, 349, 376, 381, 401, 407, 417–20
Sokolsky, George, 397
Sousa, John Philip, 196
South Carolina, 56, 259, 415, 424
South Dakota, 49, 103, 184, 302, 340, 363, 376, 390, 392, 399, 400, 416
Southern Committee to Uphold the Constitution (SCUC), 84, 98–100
Southern Tariff Association, 98–99
Soviet Union (USSR, Russia), 25, 79, 109, 124, 134, 150, 152, 154, 156, 159, 160, 173, 177, 179, 181, 182, 189, 220, 237, 292, 317, 348, 379, 380
Spain, 7, 153, 163, 299
Spanish-American War, 193, 214, 378
Spencer, Mason, 48, 49
Spitzer, Marion, 153
Square Deal, 196
Stafford. Earl of, 257
Stalin, Joseph, 149, 151, 157, 158, 166, 180, 307, 380, 399, 419
Stalinists and Stalinism, 154, 160, 216
Standard Oil, 34–35
Starch, Daniel, 228, 389
Steffens, Lincoln, 153
Stegner, Wallace, 124
Stein, Gertrude, 42
Steiwer, Frederick, 239, 240, 244
Stewart, Charles P., 261
Stewart, Donald Ogden, 153
Stiles, Lela, 217
Stimson, Henry, 134, 316
Stix, Thomas, 2
Stokes, Thomas, 63, 262, 360–61, 386, 398
Stolberg, Ben, 39, 92, 135
Stone, Irving, 199, 201, 299, 311
Strawn, Silas Hardy, 96
Suckley, Daisy, 21, 45, 412
Sullivan, Ed, 396
Sullivan, Francis, 68
Sullivan, James R., 116–17
Sullivan, Mark, 20, 21, 68, 73, 291, 390
Sumner, Charles, 242
Supreme Court, 5, 18–20, 33, 45, 73, 78, 165, 215, 217, 234–36, 243, 251, 290, 337, 358, 381, 397, 401
Sushan, Abe, 44
Swanson, Gloria, 374
Sweeney, Martin, 140, 278
Swing, Raymond Gram, 17, 42, 87–88, 194, 203–4, 318
Swope, Herbert Bayard, 410
Syracuse, N.Y., 164, 177, 277, 355, 356, 358, 359, 422

Taft, William Howard, 25, 33, 76, 190, 193, 230, 235, 238, 246, 271
Talmadge, Eugene, 81–84, 89–91, 93, 101, 122, *141,* 200, 248, 308, *319*
Talmadge, Herman, 46, 103
Tammany Hall, 22, 51–53, 63, 65, 142, 163, 210, 258, 280, 281, 356, 382, 383, 402, 411, 412
Tampa, Fla., 341, 342
Teamsters, 150, 339
Teapot Dome scandal, 66, 397
Teichert, Emil, 417
Tennessee, 6, 14, 422
Tennessee Valley Authority (TVA), 21, 23, 27, 28, 94, 189
Terre Haute, Ind., 343
Texaco, 176
Texas, 14, 83, 88, 99, 101, 102, 164, 205, 217, 262, 263, 266, 309, 352, 388, 404, 418, 426
Thälmann, Ernst, 150–51, 158
Thirty Hour Bill, 28
Thomas, Elmer, 27, 31, 49, 75, 278
Thomas, Norman Mattoon, 2, 6, 7, 142–48, 155–57, 203, 252, 275, 279, 313, *319,* 335, 338–41, 343, 347, 401, 417–19
Thompson, Bill, 416
Thompson, Dorothy, 300
Thorp, John S., 335
Thrash, "Uncle Mark," 400
Thurmond, J. Strom, 259
Tilden, Samuel J., 271
Tobin, Dan, 339
Townley, Arthur, 146
Townsend Plan, 221, 279, 281, 288, 317
Townsend, Francis Everett, 6, 31–32, 103–16, 119–23, 136, *141,* 155, 184, 247, 262, 272–74, 277–84, 291–93, 400
Treasury Department, 11, 14, 15, 21, 35, 44, 55, 75, 92, 100, 105, 107, 127–29, 131, 150, 202, 297, 313, 372
Triborough Bridge Authority (TBA), 350–51
Trohan, Walter, 12, 194, 197, 267, 269, 373
True, James, 129–30

Truman, Harry, 116
Tucker, Ray, 134
Tugwell, Rexford Guy, 2, 11, 16, 19, 21, 27, 28, 29, 101, 111, 127, 144, 148, 161, 251–52, 285, 296, 304, 317, *319*, 419, 420
Tully, Grace, 364
Tunney, Gene, 127, 129
Turner, Ted, 162
Tydings, Millard, 58

U.S. Navy, 2, 38, 47, 51–52, 164, 205, 266, 352
Uniontown, Pa., 345
UrbanLeague, 321, 328
USS *Houston,* 26
Uvalde, Tex., 101, 205, 263, 404, 405

Val-Kill Cottage, 356, 406
Vandenberg, Arthur Hendrick, 14, 29, 196–200, 226–29, 231, 238–39, 244, 245, 253, 313–14, *319*
Vanderbilt family, 40
Vanderbilt, Cornelius, Jr., 76
Vanderburg, Arthur Hendrick, 196–98
Vann, Robert Lee, 321, 325, 329, 331
Vatican, 134, 263, 282, 373
Vehanen, Kosti, 207
Vermont, 390, 392, 413, 422, 426
Vidal, Gene, 359
Vidal, Gore, 359
Villard, Oswald Garrison, 264–65
Virginia, 23, 27, 29, 58, 84, 217, 259, 278, 323, 333, 341, 378, 390
Völkischer Beobachter, 170
von Neurath, Konstantin, 176

Wadsworth, James W., Jr., 57, 58, 75, 95, 244
Wagner Act, 136
Wagner-Costigan Anti-Lynching Bill, 91, 100, 333
Wagner, Honus, 306, 338
Wagner, Robert F., *141,* 210, 255, 256, 333, 358, 362, 383
Wakefield, Jessie, 91–92
Waldman, Bella Bernstein, 418
Waldman, Louis, 145, 148, 338, 376, 418
Walker, James J., 126, 142–43, 361, 382
Wall Street Journal, 16
Wallace, Henry, 2, 19, 21, 28, 144, 209, 246, 252–53, 276, *319,* 364, 369, 374
Walmsley, Mayor, 35, 47–48
Walsh, Thomas J., 54
Warburg, James P., 55, 75, 315
Ward, Louis B., 139–40, 400, 416
Ward, Paul, 70, 79, 296, 298
Ware, Harold, 159
Waring, Fred, 80
Warren, Earl, 230, 235, 316
Washington Herald, 76
Washington, Booker T., 76
Washington, George, 159
Watertown, Wis., 399
Watson, Claude A., 417
Watson, Edwin "Pa," 26, 364
Watson, James, 241
Watts, Jill, 331
Weaver, Frederick S., 327
Webber, Abraham, 98
Weber, Max, 341
Weinstone, William, 149, 181
Weir, Ernest T., 76
Weishaupt, Adam, 124
Weiss, Carl Austin, Sr., 50
Weiss, Seymour, 44, 262
Welles, Orson, 23
Welsh, Mary, 193
West, Nathaniel, 153
West, Will G., 417
Wheeler–Rayburn Bill, 94–96
Wheeler, Burton K., 27, 31, 37, 42, 44, 49, 79, 94, 199, 364, 369
Whigs, 416
White, E. B., 119
White, Wallace, 315
White, Walter, 141
White, Walter E., 210
White, Walter F., 210–11, 213–14, 218
White, William Allen, 199, 201, 228, 230, 235, 239–40, 246, 298–99, 316, *319,* 365–66, 390–92
Whitney, Cornelius Vanderbilt, 420
Whitney, John Hay, 396
Whitney, Richard, 373
Wilkerson, Isabel, 212
Wilkins, Roy, 42, 43, 208–9
Williams, Francis, 35
Williams, Marie Selika, 207
Williams, Myrtle, 246
Williams, T. Harry, 38
Willicombe, Joseph, 170, 173, 177
Willkie, Wendell, 94, 96
Wilson, Edith, 365
Wilson, J. Finley, 323
Wilson, Samuel D., 266
Wilson, Woodrow, 27, 79, 134, 144, 164, 169, 189, 190, 246, 261, 271, 275, 308, 338, 365, 390, 409
Winchell, Walter, 155
Winkler, John, 175
Winrod, Gerald, 129
Wolf, Nathan, 403
Wolfskill, George, 97
Wolters, Raymond, 318, 321
Wood, Leonard, 193
Woodin, William, 14, 127
Woodring, Harry, 199–200, 290
Woollcott, Alexander, 395–96
Wormer, Dean, 185
Wright, R. R., 327, 332
Wright, Richard, 153
Wunder, Clinton, 108–9, 115–19, 279–80, 282

Yates, James C., 343
York, Alvin, 417
Young, Gilmour, 283
Young, Marguerite, 238

Zaritsky, Max, 339, 394
Zimbalist, Efrem, Jr., 382

ABOUT THE AUTHOR

Award-winning historian David Pietrusza has been called "the undisputed champion of chronicling American Presidential campaigns" and "one of the great political historians of all time." His books include studies of the 1920, 1932, 1948, and 1960 presidential elections and biographies of gambler Arnold Rothstein (an Edgar Award finalist) and Baseball Commissioner Kenesaw Mountain Landis (a Casey Award winner).

Pietrusza has appeared on NPR, C-SPAN, MSNBC, The Voice of America, The History Channel, AMC, and ESPN. He has spoken at the JFK, FDR, Truman, and Coolidge presidential libraries, and various universities, festivals, and libraries.

Visit davidpietrusza.com.